PETERSON'S DRUG AND ALCOHOL PROGRAMS AND POLICIES AT FOUR-YEAR COLLEGES

Janet Carney Schneider
and Bunny Porter-Shirley,
Editors

With a foreword by Lamar Alexander,
president of the University of Tennessee
and former governor of Tennessee

Peterson's Guides
Princeton, New Jersey

Library of Congress Cataloging-in-Publication Data

Peterson's drug and alcohol programs and policies at four-year colleges / Janet Carney Schneider and Bunny Porter-Shirley, editors; with a foreword by Lamar Alexander.
p. cm.
ISBN 0-87866-731-8
1. College students—United States—Alcohol use. 2. College students—United States—Drug use. 3. Colleges and universities—United States—Directories. I. Schneider, Janet Carney, 1951– . II. Porter-Shirley, Bunny, 1941– . III. Peterson's Guides, Inc.
HV5128.U5P48 1989
362.29'186'088375—dc20 89-8743
CIP

Composition and design by Peterson's Guides

Printed in the United States of America

10 9 8 7 6 5 4 3 2 1

Contents

Foreword

It was "town meeting" time during parents' weekend at our son's midwestern college. Not more than 5 minutes had gone by before someone asked the question. In the back of the hall the vice president for student affairs stood up and began his response: "Not one campus in the United States doesn't have this topic of alcohol and drug abuse as a major concern. . . ."

Times certainly have changed. I had my first beer in Jackson, Mississippi, on Lamar Street, in 1961. The bus had stopped on the way home after the season's last track meet. I tried a Jax, the local brew. About the only thing memorable was that there was not much about that first taste that made me want a second. I was 21 years old, in my junior year at Vanderbilt University. I had never even heard of drugs.

During the nearly thirty years since then I have pretty well lost interest in anything alcoholic and have never even given a thought to trying drugs, but our children live in a world where their friends try beer before high school and where drugs reach out and grab and won't let go. "They tell me you can't quit crack," one bewildered school security officer told me. "They tell me it gives so much pleasure you have to bottom out to get off it."

This Peterson's survey of drug and alcohol programs and policies is a welcome guide for administrators and customers of colleges. It provides information that helps us deal with the real question, which is not *whether* drugs and alcohol exist on campus (although it certainly can make a difference in what degree they exist), but instead, how well do campuses face the issue?

National attitudes have shifted abruptly in the right direction. In the 1970's, drinking was "recreational," marijuana was condoned, and cocaine was fashionable. But in the 1980's, first ladies urged "Just Say No," Congress created a drug czar, and college administrators started speaking out and trying to help. A recent college alcohol survey found "a clear strong trend among colleges adopting tougher alcohol abuse policies and offering more programs." Despite this, there is not much evidence that alcohol-related problems on campus are decreasing. The same survey found that 35 percent of student administrators thought campus problems involving alcohol have increased; 41 percent saw "no change" in the last several years.

But there are signs of lessening drug abuse. "I think the kids are getting educated to drugs," a University of Tennessee campus policeman told me recently. Education *is* most likely the key. Students, parents, and administrators who drag the problem into the open and face it are more likely to deal with it. This book is a must for anyone who cares about this issue that not one campus can ignore.

Lamar Alexander
President, University of Tennessee
May, 1989

Introduction

"What students do in dining halls, on the playing fields and in the rathskeller late at night all combine to influence the outcome of the college education, and the challenge, in the building of community, is to extend the resources for learning on the campus and to see academic and nonacademic life as interlocked.

"48 hours of the week students devote to academics and 50 hours per week to sleep. That leaves approximately 70 hours in the student's life unaccounted for, a block of time greater than either sleep or academics."

Ernest Boyer
College: The Undergraduate Experience in America

College students do have many hours to fill, and most of that time is spent engaged in the social life of their college in some way. So the social atmosphere of a campus is a crucial component of the total college experience. Prospective students and their parents should therefore carefully examine the atmosphere of each campus they're considering in order to make an informed college choice. Examining the "social scene" at colleges not only shows students whether they would fit in and feel comfortable on a particular campus but can also reveal some of the institution's basic philosophies and the overall strength of the educational program. In the end, students, together with their families, have to decide whether their attitudes and values are consonant with those of the college, whether their needs and desires would be met, and ultimately whether they would be happy.

There are some obvious questions that can be asked to elicit information on the social atmosphere of a college: What clubs and organizations are on campus and how active are they? Is there a strong intramural program? Are there common dining halls or do social clubs eat together? If it is a rural campus, what stimulates social life; if it is urban, what draws the school together?

Another important issue, one that has taken on special significance in today's society, is the subject of this book: the stance institutions take concerning alcohol and other drugs on campus, as reflected in the policies they have set and the programs they provide.

Most people would agree that children benefit from a family life based on a strong and systematic set of values, reasonable rules that are clearly communicated, consistent and meaningful consequences for breaking those rules, and concern and support for children should they need special help. Though the college family is larger, the dynamics are similar, and the best college experiences are had where the same fundamentals are present. This is not meant to imply that the college has taken over for the family. Although that may have been the case decades ago when colleges acted *in loco parentis,* that is certainly not so today. College students are given a great deal of independence and the responsibility to make a lot of their own decisions. However, the atmosphere in which they struggle with these choices and the support they receive when they need help go a long way toward helping them make the transition to adulthood a successful one.

Whatever your reason for picking up this guide, it is our hope that it will meet your needs. Prospective students, families, and professionals can learn what particular colleges are doing about drugs and alcohol on campus by reading college profiles and the special alcohol regulations chart. The data cover a broad array of drug and alcohol programs and policies, from regulations and disciplinary actions to support services and education programs.

Students in high-risk or recovering groups will be able to get an idea of institutional commitment by looking at the support services available. Some readers might want to look at the variety of colleges' offerings and will note the many positive and innovative programs being implemented. For students who have had substance abuse problems and for those who have not, this book will help you determine which schools offer an environment in which you can be happy and succeed.

We wish to give very special thanks to a number of people who provided support and assistance on this project: Dr. Tracy Schermer, Director of the College Physical Health and Counseling Center, Kenyon College; Jack Schmid, President of J. Schmid & Associates, Inc.; Bee Robinson, founder of CAN (Chemical Awareness Nashville); Susan Arnold, our stalwart typist; Virginia Rolett, Cork Resource Center; Ron Buckman, FIPSE; Drew Hunter, BACCHUS; Gerardo Gonzales, University of Florida; Vonnie Veltri, U.S. Department of Education; and our families.

Janet Carney Schneider   Bunny Porter-Shirley

Drugs and Alcohol on Campus

THE GRIM STATISTICS

In general, the statistics on the use and abuse of alcohol and other drugs are alarming, and they cause added concern when one focuses on the country's young people. Over the years, many professionals have gathered information specifically from college campuses. The latest findings of a longitudinal study from the University of Michigan's Institute for Social Research ("Illicit Drug Use, Smoking and Drinking by America's High School Students, College Students and Young Adults, 1975–87") reveal that there has been a slight decline in the use of marijuana, stimulants, sedatives, methaqualone, and cocaine but that there has been no decline in the use of alcohol. They found that nearly all high school seniors (92 percent) have had experience with alcohol and two thirds (66 percent) are current users (i.e., have used in the past thirty days). About 5 percent are daily drinkers, and most important, perhaps, is that 37.5 percent reported at least one occasion of heavy drinking (an occasion when they had five or more drinks in a row) in the past two weeks.

Another recent study found that the proportion who drank on college campuses did decline slightly (Engs, Hanson, 1988). Their longitudinal study has shown that the number of student drinkers has decreased slowly since states began raising the legal drinking age. But the proportion of heavy drinkers—those who consumed six or more drinks at one sitting—has remained constant, at about 20 percent. In other words, there was no decline with problem drinkers.

According to Dr. Tracy Schermer, Director of the College Physical Health and Counseling Center at Kenyon College, 10 percent of any given population is chemically dependent; without treatment, 97 percent of those will die prematurely from their disease. With the new freedoms that come with college, the peer pressure, the close living arrangements, and the emphasis on experimentation, the college population is certainly no exception.

In fact, college students may be at an even greater risk than typical populations. One study has found that while 66 percent of the general adult population drink, 80 to 90 percent of college students drink. College students tend to drink more often and more to excess than the general adult population (Engs, 1978; Kodman and Sturmak, 1984; Engs and Hanson, 1985). Also, the proportion of underage students who drink is higher than that of legal-age students who drink (Engs and Hanson, 1987–88). In Dr. Schermer's experience, in 85 percent of all college students' auto accidents, drugs, especially alcohol, are a major contributing factor.

Colleges spend millions of dollars annually repairing destruction caused to classrooms, dormitories, and other facilities by students and others under the influence of alcohol and other drugs. The cost of this destruction can cause tuition rates, which are already high, to soar. Surveys of college administrators have found that alcohol and other drugs are involved in a variety of disruptive and dangerous incidents on campus, including property damage, violent behavior, rape and other crimes, accidental injuries, and suicide attempts (Anderson and Gadaleto, 1984). Statistics are not available on how many classes are missed or how many students are unable to apply themselves fully to their academic work due to alcohol or drug use, but one can project from other statistics that the numbers would be staggering.

WHAT'S BEING DONE

Because of an ever-increasing awareness of the tragedies related to substance abuse, many college administrators have joined forces with parent groups, student groups, community organizations, national professional organizations, and state and federal officials in a nationwide campaign to tackle the problems of abuse. Colleges are formulating new programs and policies or updating existing ones to better address these issues. Awareness of the problem and steps being taken to solve it have never been greater.

Studies have shown that colleges are substantially expanding their alcohol education and prevention activities (Anderson and Gadaleto). Community organizations such as AA, NA, Al-Anon, and ACOA have opened chapters on college campuses, and new campus organizations, such as BACCHUS (Boost Alcohol Consciousness Concerning the Health of University Students), have emerged to help students act responsibly regarding alcohol and drug use. Fraternities and sororities, often the subject of media attention about alcohol on campus, sponsor awareness and education programs. Colleges nationwide are participating in National Alcohol Awareness Week and National Drug Awareness Week. College and university administrators, government officials, and other professionals have set up networks, such as the Inter-Association Task Force on Alcohol and Other Substance Abuse Issues and the Network of Colleges and Universities Committed to the Elimination of Drug and Alcohol Abuse, for research and development of meaningful programs and policies. (For a list of organizations involved in alcohol and other drug issues on campus, see Appendix 3.)

In addition, the U.S. Government has responded by setting up new agencies and by pumping government money into both new and existing agencies and organizations. New laws have been passed. The legal drinking age is now 21 throughout the fifty states. In 1986 Congress passed the "Anti Drug Abuse Act," which included the "Drug Free Schools and Communities Act" to establish, implement, and expand programs of drug abuse education and prevention (including rehabilitation referral) for students enrolled in college. As a result, the U.S. Department of Education became responsible for awarding grants to colleges developing drug and alcohol programs. (See Appendix 2 for the over 130 four-year colleges that have received FIPSE grants in the past two years.) Still other laws actually require colleges to set up programs or risk losing federal funds.

Through all these avenues, colleges nationwide are striving to balance legal, economic, and personal ramifications in order to provide programs that minimize the risk of property damage and personal tragedy.

WHAT TO LOOK FOR IN A CAMPUS PROGRAM

There is no one right set of policies and no one right set of services to look for at a college. Instead, readers should be looking for what's right *for them.* For students who are recovering addicts, it will be very important to look specifically at particular support services. For other students, the focus will be different. College programs and policies vary in order to address the needs of specific populations. Some are just being set up while others are more established. Professional organizations and private consultants are assisting colleges in setting up programs, and some, such as the Network, have set forth guidelines for colleges to follow as they set up programs (see Appendix 1).

The National Clearinghouse for Alcohol and Drug Information (NCADI) compiled a list of program components that have been implemented in various college programs across the country. These include: an explicit statement of college policies, a new-student orientation, student assistance programs, peer counselors, wellness centers, workshops for friends and relatives, substance abuse classes for preprofessionals, informational displays, alcohol-free and tobacco-free residence halls, prevention messages, alcohol- and drug-use testing, promotional policies for student activities, policies on marketing alcohol on campus, cooperation with local pub owners and bartenders, and spotlights on nonalcoholic beverages. Gerardo Gonzales, head of counselor education at the University of Florida, cofounder of BACCHUS, and a leader in alcohol education on college campuses, has set forth his own components for model alcohol programs: alcohol awareness activities, an alcohol information and resource center, alcohol and health promotion workshops, BACCHUS, courses for academic credit, an advisory committee, counseling and referral, training and supervision, and research and evaluation.

Many of these items can be found in the college profiles or the special alcohol regulation table. For other information, students, parents, and counselors should contact the colleges themselves. Some questions not covered in this book that students and their parents might want to ask include:

- Are alcohol-free and tobacco-free dorms or floors available?
- Is there a freshman orientation program on alcohol and other drugs? Is it mandatory? How long does it run, and what is included?
- To whom is a student referred for a substance abuse assessment?
- Is anyone specifically charged with identifying students who develop a problem? If so, who?
- How are resident advisers selected? For how many students is a resident adviser responsible?
- What are your policies concerning parties?

For those students who are recovering from chemical dependency, there may be additional questions:

- Does the campus have an after-care program? Who runs it? How often does it meet? How many students are in the after-care group?
- If AA or NA is available on campus, how often are meetings?
- How do students learn about meetings of AA, NA, Al-Anon, ACOA, or privately run groups?
- If a student relapses, is there a specific procedure that is followed?

If the admissions office does not have answers to your specific questions on drug and alcohol issues, student health offices or deans of students should be able to provide you with the information you need.

As mentioned previously, there currently are no definitive standards for successful prevention or support programs. Many concerned professionals are continuing to conduct research to determine program effectiveness, but in the meantime, readers should judge for themselves the policies and programs colleges have established—how they affect the college community and contribute to the overall educational climate. Certainly, never have colleges and universities offered so much. One cannot forget, however, that no matter what college programs are made available to students, it is students themselves who make choices concerning alcohol and other drug use and who are responsible for the choices they make.

A User's Guide to the College Profiles and Comparative Table

Peterson's Drug and Alcohol Programs and Policies at Four-Year Colleges contains a wealth of information for anyone interested in drug and alcohol issues on campus. This section gives readers an overview of the data-based components of the book and presents explanatory material to help them interpret the data it contains. The data on drug and alcohol issues included in the profiles and table that follow were collected through a special survey that was sent to all accredited U.S. four-year colleges during the fall and winter of 1988–89. Over 900 institutions responded, and the surveys were edited and responses verified with the colleges if questions arose. The information reported in this guide was provided by prominent university officials, mainly directors of student affairs and deans of students. Additional general information about the colleges was collected through Peterson's Annual Survey of Undergraduate Institutions. Because the material came directly from the colleges and because of Peterson's comprehensive editorial review, we have every reason to believe that the information is accurate as of publication. However, readers are encouraged to check with colleges, since changes in program offerings do occur.

COLLEGE PROFILES

The college profiles present data for each college in a standard format for easy comparison. The material that follows will help clarify terms and abbreviations that may be unfamiliar to students and will help readers understand the variety of programs offered.

General Information

This section presents basic information about an institution so the reader can assess drug and alcohol programs and policies in a broader context. Some abbreviations are included:

Degrees awarded: A—associate degree, B—bachelor's degree, M—master's degree, D—doctoral degree.

Accreditation: AABC—American Association of Bible Colleges, AICS—Association of Independent Colleges and Schools, NASAD—National Association of Schools of Art and Design, NATTS—National Association of Trade and Technical Schools.

Drug and Alcohol Information

Education

Whether or not drug and alcohol prevention/education programs are available to or required for students is listed. If programs are available and they are directed toward specific groups, such as freshmen, social organization members, athletes/coaches, faculty, administrators, resident advisers, or student leaders, that too is shown.

Programs at different campuses address different topics, but most focus on rules and regulations surrounding the use of alcohol and other drugs, prevention of alcohol and other drug abuse, identification of students who are in trouble with alcohol and/or other drugs, proper reactions to drug and alcohol abusers, and promotion of responsible drinking. Programs vary in depth and duration. Some consist of short classes offered during freshman orientation, while others include longer ongoing classes. Some institutions even offer drug and alcohol education courses as part of the curriculum, giving credit towards graduation.

At some colleges, students have a great deal of responsibility in developing programs; at others, education programs are developed by professionals involved in student health services or the dean of students' office. Whoever the originator, there is no doubt that there has been a rapid growth in alcohol and drug awareness education on campuses.

National organizations and agencies are also developing programs in conjunction with and in support of colleges' actions. BACCHUS, one such organization, has chapters on many campuses for the purpose of educating and helping students to talk honestly about and develop responsible habits and attitudes toward the use or nonuse of alcohol. Colleges with BACCHUS chapters on campus are listed, as are those with other campus groups concerned about responsible drinking.

Colleges may also offer alcohol or drug awareness weeks as part of their education efforts.

As one reads the information in this book, it is wrong to simply draw conclusions from numbers. Colleges with a great number of programs or a great number of organizations involved with programs do not necessarily create a better (or worse) environment than those with fewer offerings, students, or organizations involved. (Some colleges, such as those with largely commuting populations, may not address education issues at all, so be sure to examine offerings in the context of the general college information.)

As with any educational program, the effectiveness of the drug and alcohol education program depends on a number of factors, such as the strength of commitment of the administration, the quality of the curriculum, the quality of teaching, and the quality of students. Timing is also critical. So as you read about education programs, try to get a general idea of what a college is doing. If you have specific questions or concerns about this or any issue, contact the person listed at the end of each profile. Usually colleges are willing to send information on educational programs or organizations' specific materials.

Identification of Problems

Today, with heightened public awareness, it has become much more acceptable for students to admit a problem they have had with alcohol or other drugs. In fact, some colleges view a student's admission of chemical dependency and recovery as positive and make some allowances for poor high school performance during a period of substance abuse. However, few colleges have a question on their admission application about alcohol/drug dependency, and most questions are asked in the context of a student's health history.

Colleges were also asked how they respond to the currently enrolled student who is identified as chemically dependent—whether the student is allowed to remain at the institution and whether he or she must receive treatment. When viewed with other factors, this can help a student identify an institution's approach to chemical dependency. Some colleges have specific training programs for college community members on identifying students with potential substance abuse problems, so that these students can be referred to appropriate resources. If training programs are for targeted groups, such as resident advisers, coaches, Greek officers, faculty, or administrators, they will be listed. Also listed is whether colleges have written procedures for students or staff to refer to when substance abuse problems are suspected. Training programs and written procedures are often vital means of communication on college policies and support.

Support Services

Colleges can have many or few support services for students who are recovering from chemical dependency or are children or family members of substance abusers. Support services can include such national organizations as AA (Alcoholics Anonymous), NA (Narcotics Anonymous), Al-Anon, and ACOA (Adult Children of Alcoholics) or local organizations unique to a campus or an area. Private or individual counseling and employee assistance programs may be available. Colleges may also have many or few staff members, full-time or part-time, who deal with alcohol and other drug-related problems and issues.

Disciplinary Actions

Colleges were surveyed as to their regulations concerning alcohol use, and the results can be found in the Comparative Table that follows the profile section. Results of infractions of these regulations are shown in the profiles themselves, as are actions taken when students are found to be using, possessing, or selling drugs. Results of infractions can include a chemical dependency assessment, counseling, a warning, probation, suspension, and expulsion, or the profile may state that the action varies depending on the situation. Colleges were also asked to differentiate, where appropriate, between actions taken for first-time and subsequent drug offenses. By looking at the standard group of actions a college takes, we hope the reader will be able to get an idea of a college's approach—whether it is primarily educational (corrective) or punitive, for example.

Additional Information from the College

If there is additional information about the treatment of alcohol- and drug-related issues that a college felt was not covered elsewhere in the profile, that information will appear here.

For More Information

If you still have questions about a college's programs and policies, contact the person or office identified at the end of each profile for more information.

COMPARATIVE TABLE OF ALCOHOL REGULATIONS

The Comparative Table shows the reader at a glance the basic regulations a college has regarding the use and consumption of alcohol on campus. It will also reveal basic similarities and differences among colleges' policies.

For example, some colleges do not permit alcohol on campus, and those colleges will have a mark in the first column to indicate that. Other campuses have many rules and regulations surrounding alcohol use. Keep in mind, however, that the fact that a college forbids alcohol does not mean that alcohol does not exist on campus. Similarly, when a college allows alcohol but states that there are many rules and regulations, it does not necessarily mean that there is more control and less of a problem. As with all rules and regulations, successful policies result from having meaningful rules, good communication about and understanding of those rules, and consistent enforcement and action when rules are broken.

One final note: Regulations that would be redundant, such as not permitting alcohol at social events at a college where alcohol is already not permitted on campus, have been omitted for ease of reading.

Profiles of the Colleges

ACADEMY OF ART COLLEGE
San Francisco, California

General Information
Proprietary 5-year coed college. Founded 1929. Awards B, M. Primary accreditation: regional (candidate) and NATTS. Metropolitan setting. Total enrollment: 2,140. Faculty: 140 (16 full-time, 124 part-time).

Drug and Alcohol Information
Education

On campus Drug and alcohol education/prevention programs offered for: all students. College holds an annual alcohol awareness week and drug awareness week.

Identification of Problems

Admissions College application does not ask about prior substance abuse problems.

On campus Current students identified as chemically dependent may remain enrolled, but treatment is required. Training program on identifying students with potential substance abuse problems for: resident advisers, faculty, administration. Written procedures for students and staff if substance abuse is suspected.

Support Services

On campus Support groups, private counseling, referral service.

Employee assistance Program for chemically dependent employees available. Staff working with drug/alcohol-related issues: 1 part-time.

Disciplinary Actions

Alcohol Results of infractions of alcohol regulations (see Comparative Table of Alcohol Regulations) vary by situation. Comments: Disciplinary action is taken.

Drugs For any use or possession: varies by situation. For any sale: expulsion.

For More Information

Contact: Jan M. Schroeder, Vice President, Academy of Art College, 540 Powell St., San Francisco, CA 94108. Telephone: 415-765-4200.

ADAMS STATE COLLEGE
Alamosa, Colorado

General Information
State-supported 5-year coed college. Founded 1921. Awards A (college transfer and terminal), B, M. Primary accreditation: regional. Small-town setting; 90-acre campus. Total enrollment: 2,476. Faculty: 115 (89 full-time, 26 part-time). Social organization: 1 national fraternity; 1% of eligible undergraduate men are members.

Drug and Alcohol Information
Education

On campus Drug and alcohol education/prevention programs required for: all students. Authorized group concerned with responsible drinking. College holds an annual alcohol awareness week and drug awareness week.

Identification of Problems

Admissions College application does not ask about prior substance abuse problems.

On campus Current students identified as chemically dependent may remain enrolled, but treatment is required. Training program on identifying students with potential substance abuse problems for: resident advisers, coaches. Written procedures for students and staff if substance abuse is suspected.

Support Services

On campus Support groups, private counseling.

Employee assistance Program for chemically dependent employees not available.

Disciplinary Actions

Alcohol Results of infractions of alcohol regulations (see Comparative Table of Alcohol Regulations) vary by situation but can include chemical dependency assessment, counseling, warning, probation, suspension, expulsion.

Drugs For first-time use or possession: counseling, warning, probation. For subsequent use or possession: expulsion. For first-time sale: suspension, expulsion. For subsequent sale: expulsion.

For More Information

Contact: L. Gomez, Dean of Students, Adams State College, Alamosa, CO 81102. Telephone: 719-589-7221.

ADELPHI UNIVERSITY
Garden City, New York

General Information
Independent comprehensive coed institution. Founded 1896. Awards B, M, D. Primary accreditation: regional. Small-town setting; 75-acre campus. Total enrollment: 9,062. Faculty: 770 (320 full-time, 450 part-time). Social organizations: 7 national fraternities, 5 national sororities, 1 local fraternity, 2 local sororities; 10% of eligible undergraduate men and 10% of eligible undergraduate women are members.

Drug and Alcohol Information
Education

On campus Drug and alcohol education/prevention programs offered for: all students, athletes/coaches, faculty, administration; required for: freshmen, resident advisers. Authorized group concerned with responsible drinking. College holds an annual alcohol awareness week and drug awareness week.

Identification of Problems

Admissions College application does not ask about prior substance abuse problems.

On campus Current students identified as chemically dependent may remain enrolled. Treatment is encouraged but not required unless student is already on probation. Training program on identifying students with potential substance abuse problems for: resident advisers, coaches, Greek officers, faculty, administration. Written procedures for students and staff if substance abuse is suspected.

Support Services

On campus AA, NA, ACOA, support groups (SADD, peer

Adelphi University (continued)

crisis intervention), private counseling, psycho-educational counseling, assessment, referrals, follow-up.

Employee assistance Program for chemically dependent employees available informally if requested. Staff working with drug/alcohol-related issues: 1 full-time and several part-time.

Disciplinary Actions

Alcohol Results of infractions of alcohol regulations (see Comparative Table of Alcohol Regulations) vary by situation but can include chemical dependency assessment, counseling, warning, probation, suspension.

Drugs For any use or possession: varies by situation. For any sale: expulsion.

For More Information

Contact: Nancy Geygan Schreier, Counselor/Coordinator of Alcohol and Drug Education and Prevention, Adelphi University, South Ave., Garden City, NY 11530. Telephone: 516-294-8700 Ext. 7441.

AGNES SCOTT COLLEGE

Decatur, Georgia

General Information

Independent 4-year women's college, affiliated with Presbyterian Church. Founded 1889. Awards B. Primary accreditation: regional. Small-town setting; 100-acre campus. Total enrollment: 526. Faculty: 79 (62 full-time, 17 part-time).

Drug and Alcohol Information

Education

On campus Drug and alcohol education/prevention programs offered for: all students. College holds an annual alcohol awareness week.

Identification of Problems

Admissions College application does not ask about prior substance abuse problems.

On campus Current students identified as chemically dependent may remain enrolled, but treatment is required. Training program on identifying students with potential substance abuse problems for: resident advisers. No written procedures for students and staff if substance abuse is suspected.

Support Services

On campus Private counseling, counseling and/or referral through Student Health Services.

Employee assistance Program for chemically dependent employees not available. Staff working with drug/alcohol-related issues: 1 part-time.

Disciplinary Actions

Alcohol Results of infractions of alcohol regulations (see Comparative Table of Alcohol Regulations) vary by situation but can include counseling, warning. Comments: Decisions on disciplinary action made by Interdormitory Council or Honor Court.

Drugs For first-time use: varies by situation. For first-time possession or sale: varies by situation—probation, suspension, expulsion. For subsequent use, possession, or sale: suspension, expulsion.

For More Information

Contact: Karen Green, Director of Student Activities, Agnes Scott College, Decatur, GA 30030. Telephone: 404-371-6438.

ALASKA PACIFIC UNIVERSITY

Anchorage, Alaska

General Information

Independent United Methodist 5-year coed college. Founded 1959. Awards A (college transfer and terminal), B, M, D. Primary accreditation: regional. City setting; 270-acre campus. Total enrollment: 851. Faculty: 58 (50 full-time, 8 part-time).

Drug and Alcohol Information

Education

On campus Drug and alcohol education/prevention programs offered for: all students. Bacchus chapter: 5 members. College holds an annual alcohol awareness week.

Identification of Problems

Admissions College application does not ask about prior substance abuse problems.

On campus Current students identified as chemically dependent may remain enrolled. No training program on identifying students with potential substance abuse problems. No written procedures for students and staff if substance abuse is suspected.

Support Services

On campus No support services on campus.

Employee assistance Program for chemically dependent employees not available. Staff working with drug/alcohol-related issues: 2–3 part-time.

Disciplinary Actions

Alcohol Results of infractions of alcohol regulations (see Comparative Table of Alcohol Regulations) include counseling, warning, probation, suspension.

Drugs For first-time use or possession: probation. For subsequent use or possession: suspension. For any sale: expulsion.

For More Information

Contact: Chipp Leibach, Dean of Students, Alaska Pacific University, 4101 University Dr., Anchorage, AK 99508. Telephone: 907-564-8287.

ALBANY COLLEGE OF PHARMACY OF UNION UNIVERSITY

Albany, New York

General Information

Independent upper-level specialized coed institution. Part of Union University (Albany Law School, Albany Medical College, Union College, NY). Founded 1881. Awards B. Primary accreditation: regional. City setting; 1-acre campus. Total enrollment: 652. Faculty: 129 (29 full-time, 100 part-time). Social organizations: 4 national fraternities, 4 national sororities; 30% of eligible undergraduate men and 30% of eligible undergraduate women are members.

Drug and Alcohol Information

Education

On campus Drug and alcohol education/prevention programs offered for: students who appear to have problems in these areas. Authorized group concerned with responsible drinking.

Identification of Problems

Admissions College application does not ask about prior substance abuse problems.

On campus Current students identified as chemically dependent may remain enrolled, but treatment is required. No training program on identifying students with potential substance abuse problems. Written procedures for students and staff if substance abuse is suspected.

Support Services

On campus Private counseling, impaired pharmacists' AA.

Employee assistance Program for chemically dependent employees not available. Staff working with drug/alcohol-related issues: 2 part-time.

Disciplinary Actions

Alcohol Results of infractions of alcohol regulations (see Comparative Table of Alcohol Regulations) vary by situation but can include chemical dependency assessment, counseling, warning, probation, suspension.

Drugs For any use or possession: varies by situation. For first-time sale: chemical dependency assessment, expulsion. For subsequent sale: expulsion.

For More Information

Contact: Mary Anne Chylinski, Director of Student Services, Albany College of Pharmacy of Union University, 106 New Scotland Ave., Albany, NY 12208. Telephone: 518-445-7257.

ALBANY STATE COLLEGE

Albany, Georgia

General Information

State-supported 5-year coed college. Part of University System of Georgia. Founded 1903. Awards A (college transfer), B, M. Primary accreditation: regional. City setting; 131-acre campus. Total enrollment: 2,105. Faculty: 151 (132 full-time, 19 part-time). Social organizations: 4 national fraternities, 4 national sororities; 3% of eligible undergraduate men and 2% of eligible undergraduate women are members.

Drug and Alcohol Information

Education

On campus Drug and alcohol education/prevention programs offered for: all students; required for: freshmen. Authorized group concerned with responsible drinking. College holds an annual alcohol awareness week and drug awareness week.

Identification of Problems

Admissions College application does not ask about prior substance abuse problems.

On campus Current students identified as chemically dependent may remain enrolled, but treatment is required. Training program on identifying students with potential substance abuse problems for: resident advisers, student leaders. No written procedures for students and staff if substance abuse is suspected.

Support Services

On campus Private counseling.

Employee assistance Program for chemically dependent employees available. Staff working with drug/alcohol-related issues: 2 part-time.

Disciplinary Actions

Alcohol Results of infractions of alcohol regulations (see Comparative Table of Alcohol Regulations) include counseling, warning, probation, suspension, expulsion.

Drugs For first-time use or possession: varies by situation. For subsequent use or possession: counseling, suspension, expulsion. For first-time sale: suspension, expulsion. For subsequent sale: counseling, expulsion.

For More Information

Contact: Terry L. Willis, Director of Student Activities, P.O. Box 8996, Albany State College, 504 College Dr., Albany, GA 31705. Telephone: 912-430-4739.

ALDERSON-BROADDUS COLLEGE

Philippi, West Virginia

General Information

Independent 4-year coed college, affiliated with Baptist Church. Founded 1871. Awards B. Primary accreditation: regional. Rural setting; 170-acre campus. Total enrollment: 759. Faculty: 74 (55 full-time, 19 part-time). Social organizations: 4 local fraternities, 4 local sororities; 25% of eligible undergraduate men and 25% of eligible undergraduate women are members.

Drug and Alcohol Information

Education

On campus Drug and alcohol education/prevention programs offered for: all students. College holds an annual alcohol awareness week.

Identification of Problems

Admissions College application does not ask about prior substance abuse problems.

On campus Current students identified as chemically dependent may remain enrolled. No training program on identifying students with potential substance abuse problems. No written procedures for students and staff if substance abuse is suspected.

Support Services

On campus Private counseling.

Employee assistance Program for chemically dependent employees not available.

Disciplinary Actions

Alcohol Results of infractions of alcohol regulations (see Comparative Table of Alcohol Regulations) include counseling, probation, suspension, expulsion.

Drugs For first-time use or possession: suspension. For subsequent use or possession: expulsion. For any sale: expulsion.

For More Information

Contact: Kathy Short, Director of Student Development,

Alderson-Broaddus College (continued)

Box 1368, Alderson-Broaddus College, Philippi, WV 26416. Telephone: 304-457-1700.

ALFRED UNIVERSITY

Alfred, New York

General Information

Independent comprehensive coed institution. Founded 1836. Awards B, M, D. Primary accreditation: regional. Rural setting; 232-acre campus. Total enrollment: 2,593. Faculty: 175. Social organizations: 4 national fraternities, 3 local fraternities, 3 local sororities; 26% of eligible undergraduate men and 12% of eligible undergraduate women are members.

Drug and Alcohol Information

Education

On campus Drug and alcohol education/prevention programs not offered. Authorized group concerned with responsible drinking.

Identification of Problems

Admissions College application does not ask about prior substance abuse problems.

On campus Current students identified as chemically dependent may remain enrolled. No training program on identifying students with potential substance abuse problems. No written procedures for students and staff if substance abuse is suspected.

Support Services

On campus AA, private counseling.

Employee assistance Program for chemically dependent employees not available. Staff working with drug/alcohol-related issues: 2 part-time.

Disciplinary Actions

Alcohol Results of infractions of alcohol regulations (see Comparative Table of Alcohol Regulations) vary by situation.

Drugs For first-time use, possession, or sale: varies by situation. For subsequent use: varies by situation—counseling, warning. For subsequent possession: varies by situation—counseling, warning, probation. For subsequent sale: varies by situation.

Additional Information from the College

A University-wide committee is currently investigating attitudes and beliefs about substance abuse on campus, reviewing the current discipline system, and exploring chemical-abuse assistance and educational programs.

For More Information

Contact: Matthew M. Dubai Jr., Associate Dean for Student Affairs, Alfred University, P.O. Box 781, Alfred, NY 14802. Telephone: 607-871-2134.

ALICE LLOYD COLLEGE

Pippa Passes, Kentucky

General Information

Independent 4-year coed college. Founded 1923. Awards A (college transfer), B. Primary accreditation: regional. Rural setting; 175-acre campus. Total enrollment: 507. Faculty: 30 (25 full-time, 5 part-time).

Drug and Alcohol Information

Education

On campus Drug and alcohol education/prevention programs offered for: all students, athletes/coaches. Authorized group concerned with responsible drinking. College holds an annual alcohol awareness week and drug awareness week.

Identification of Problems

Admissions College application does not ask about prior substance abuse problems.

On campus Current students identified as chemically dependent may not remain enrolled. Comments: They may not return until they have had treatment. No training program on identifying students with potential substance abuse problems.

Support Services

On campus Private counseling.

Employee assistance Program for chemically dependent employees not available. Staff working with drug/alcohol-related issues: 3 part-time.

Disciplinary Actions

Alcohol Results of infractions of alcohol regulations (see Comparative Table of Alcohol Regulations) include suspension for one semester.

Drugs For any use, possession, or sale: suspension.

Additional Information from the College

Because Alice Lloyd College is a small community, the staff becomes aware of emotional or substance abuse problems quickly. Students with particular problems are referred for counseling, and their continued enrollment may depend on their participation in counseling.

For More Information

Contact: Christine Stumbo, Dean of Women, Purpose Road, Alice Lloyd College, Pippa Passes, KY 41844. Telephone: 606-368-2101.

ALLEGHENY COLLEGE

Meadville, Pennsylvania

General Information

Independent 5-year coed college, affiliated with United Methodist Church. Founded 1815. Awards B, M (M offered only in education). Primary accreditation: regional. Small-town setting; 254-acre campus. Total enrollment: 1,981. Faculty: 186 (155 full-time, 31 part-time). Social organizations: 6 national fraternities, 5 national sororities, 1 eating club; 45% of eligible undergraduate men and 45% of eligible undergraduate women are members.

Drug and Alcohol Information

Education

On campus Drug and alcohol education/prevention programs offered for: all students. Bacchus chapter: 6 members. College holds an annual alcohol awareness week and drug awareness week.

Identification of Problems

Admissions College application does not ask about prior substance abuse problems.

On campus Current students identified as chemically dependent may remain enrolled, but treatment is required. Training program on identifying students with potential substance abuse problems for: resident advisers. No written procedures for students and staff if substance abuse is suspected, but policy and procedures are clearly communicated and practical.

Support Services

On campus AA, Al-Anon, ACOA, support groups, private counseling.

Employee assistance Program for chemically dependent employees available. Staff working with drug/alcohol-related issues: 5 part-time.

Disciplinary Actions

Alcohol Results of infractions of alcohol regulations (see Comparative Table of Alcohol Regulations) vary by situation but can include chemical dependency assessment, counseling, warning, probation, suspension, expulsion. Comments: Violators of the College's alcohol policy are required to attend the Alcohol Education Program (an assessment and 3 class sessions).

Drugs For first-time use, possession, or sale: varies by situation—chemical dependency assessment, warning, Alcohol Education Program. For subsequent use, possession, or sale: varies by situation—chemical dependency assessment, probation, Alcohol Education Program.

Additional Information from the College

The Alcohol Education Program has significantly reduced alcohol-related violations on campus, and the local magistrate refers students arrested for alcohol-related offenses to the program.

For More Information

Contact: Ron Cantor, Director of Residence Life, Box R, Allegheny College, Meadville, PA 16335. Telephone: 814-724-3865.

ALLENTOWN COLLEGE OF ST. FRANCIS DE SALES

Center Valley, Pennsylvania

General Information

Independent Roman Catholic 5-year coed college. Founded 1962. Awards B, M. Primary accreditation: regional. Rural setting; 300-acre campus. Total enrollment: 1,700. Faculty: 90 (60 full-time, 30 part-time). Social organizations: local fraternities, local sororities; 45% of eligible undergraduate men and 45% of eligible undergraduate women are members.

Drug and Alcohol Information

Education

On campus Drug and alcohol education/prevention programs offered for: all students, athletes/coaches, faculty, administration; required for: freshmen, resident advisers. College holds an annual alcohol awareness week.

Identification of Problems

Admissions College application does not ask about prior substance abuse problems.

On campus Current students identified as chemically dependent may remain enrolled, but treatment is required. Training program on identifying students with potential substance abuse problems for: resident advisers.

Support Services

On campus Private counseling.

Employee assistance Program for chemically dependent employees not available. Staff working with drug/alcohol-related issues: 4 part-time.

Disciplinary Actions

Alcohol Results of infractions of alcohol regulations (see Comparative Table of Alcohol Regulations) include chemical dependency assessment, mandatory counseling, probation, suspension, fines, community service.

Drugs For first-time use or possession: counseling, probation, automatic residential suspension. For subsequent use or possession: varies by situation.

For More Information

Contact: Dr. Gregg Amore, Director, Counseling Center, Allentown College of St. Francis de Sales, Center Valley, PA 18034. Telephone: 215-282-1100.

ALMA COLLEGE

Alma, Michigan

General Information

Independent Presbyterian 4-year coed college. Founded 1886. Awards B. Primary accreditation: regional. Small-town setting; 80-acre campus. Total enrollment: 1,198. Faculty: 99 (66 full-time, 33 part-time). Social organizations: 4 national fraternities, 3 national sororities, 1 local fraternity, 1 local sorority; 50% of eligible undergraduate men and 50% of eligible undergraduate women are members.

Drug and Alcohol Information

Education

On campus Drug and alcohol education/prevention programs offered for: all students. Authorized group concerned with responsible drinking. College holds an annual alcohol awareness week and drug awareness week.

Identification of Problems

Admissions College application does not ask about prior substance abuse problems.

On campus Current students identified as chemically dependent may remain enrolled, but treatment is required. Training program on identifying students with potential substance abuse problems for: residence hall staff. Written procedures for students and staff if substance abuse is suspected.

Support Services

On campus Private counseling. Staff working with drug/alcohol-related issues: 9 part-time.

Disciplinary Actions

Alcohol Results of infractions of alcohol regulations (see Comparative Table of Alcohol Regulations) vary by situation but can include counseling, warning, probation, suspension.

Drugs For first-time use or possession: varies by situation—counseling, warning, probation. For subsequent use or possession: varies by situation—probation, suspension. For first-time sale: suspension. For subsequent sale: expulsion.

For More Information

Contact: James W. Kridler, Dean of Students, Alma College, Alma, MI 48801. Telephone: 517-463-7333.

ALVERNO COLLEGE
Milwaukee, Wisconsin

General Information
Independent 4-year women's college. Founded 1887. Awards A (college transfer), B. Primary accreditation: regional. Metropolitan setting; 50-acre campus. Total enrollment: 2,191. Faculty: 161 (89 full-time, 72 part-time).

Drug and Alcohol Information
Education
On campus Drug and alcohol education/prevention programs offered for: all students, faculty, administration.

Identification of Problems
Admissions College application does not ask about prior substance abuse problems.

On campus Current students identified as chemically dependent may remain enrolled. No training program on identifying students with potential substance abuse problems. No written procedures for students and staff if substance abuse is suspected.

Support Services
On campus AA, ACOA, private counseling, campus ministry.

Employee assistance Program for chemically dependent employees not available.

Disciplinary Actions
Alcohol Results of infractions of alcohol regulations (see Comparative Table of Alcohol Regulations) include counseling, warning.

Drugs For first-time use or possession: counseling, warning. For first-time sale: counseling, warning. For subsequent sale: expulsion.

Additional Information from the College
Over 80 percent of Alverno College's students are nontraditional. The average age is 33, and most students commute. It is therefore difficult for College personnel to identify drug and alcohol problems.

For More Information
Contact: Jennie Ragland, Coordinator of Student Life, Alverno College, 3401 S. 39th St., Milwaukee, WI 53215. Telephone: 414-382-6116.

AMBER UNIVERSITY
Garland, Texas

General Information
Independent coed college. Founded 1971. Awards B, M. Primary accreditation: regional. City setting; 5-acre campus. Total enrollment: 926. Faculty: 50 (30 full-time, 20 part-time).

Drug and Alcohol Information
Education
On campus Drug and alcohol education/prevention programs not offered.

Identification of Problems
Admissions College application does not ask about prior substance abuse problems.

On campus Current students identified as chemically dependent may remain enrolled. Comments: On-campus use is prohibited. No training program on identifying students with potential substance abuse problems. No written procedures for students and staff if substance abuse is suspected.

Support Services
On campus No support services on campus.

Employee assistance Program for chemically dependent employees not available.

Disciplinary Actions
Alcohol Results of infractions of alcohol regulations (see Comparative Table of Alcohol Regulations) vary by situation.

Drugs Comments: Drug abuse problems have not been identified.

For More Information
Contact: Dr. John J. Cosher, Dean, University Services, Amber University, 1700 Eastgate Dr., Garland, TX 75041. Telephone: 214-279-6511.

ANDERSON UNIVERSITY
Anderson, Indiana

General Information
Independent 5-year coed college, affiliated with Church of God. Founded 1917. Awards A (college transfer and terminal), B, M. Primary accreditation: regional. City setting; 77-acre campus. Total enrollment: 2,050. Faculty: 167 (93 full-time, 74 part-time). Social organizations: 11 social clubs.

Drug and Alcohol Information
Education
On campus Drug and alcohol education/prevention programs offered for: all students, athletes/coaches. College holds an annual alcohol awareness week.

Identification of Problems
Admissions College application does not ask about prior substance abuse problems.

On campus Current students identified as chemically dependent may remain enrolled, but treatment is required. Training program on identifying students with potential substance abuse problems for: resident advisers, coaches, administration. No written procedures for students and staff if substance abuse is suspected.

Support Services
On campus Al-Anon, ACOA.

Employee assistance Program for chemically dependent employees not available. Staff working with drug/alcohol-related issues: 3 part-time.

Disciplinary Actions
Alcohol Results of infractions of alcohol regulations (see Comparative Table of Alcohol Regulations) vary by situation but can include chemical dependency assessment, counseling, warning, probation, expulsion.

Drugs For first-time use or possession: varies by situation—chemical dependency assessment, counseling, probation. For subsequent use or possession: varies by situation—chemical dependency assessment, counseling, expulsion. For any sale: expulsion.

For More Information

Contact: H. L. Baker, Dean of Student Services, Anderson University, Anderson, IN 46012-3462. Telephone: 317-641-4192.

ANDREWS UNIVERSITY
Berrien Springs, Michigan

General Information
Independent Seventh-day Adventist comprehensive coed institution. Founded 1874. Awards A (college transfer and terminal), B, M, D. Primary accreditation: regional. Small-town setting; 1,650-acre campus. Total enrollment: 2,469. Faculty: 282 (232 full-time, 50 part-time).

Drug and Alcohol Information
Education

On campus Drug and alcohol education/prevention programs offered for: all students. College holds an annual alcohol awareness week and drug awareness week.

Identification of Problems

Admissions College application question about prior substance abuse problems is used for counseling and referral, if student is admitted; in the admissions decision.

On campus Current students identified as chemically dependent may remain enrolled, but treatment is required. Training program on identifying students with potential substance abuse problems for: resident advisers, faculty, administration. Written procedures for students and staff if substance abuse is suspected.

Support Services

On campus Support groups, private counseling.

Employee assistance Program for chemically dependent employees not available. Staff working with drug/alcohol-related issues: 1 part-time.

Disciplinary Actions

Alcohol Results of infractions of alcohol regulations (see Comparative Table of Alcohol Regulations) include chemical dependency assessment, suspension.

Drugs For any use or possession: varies by situation. For any sale: expulsion.

Additional Information from the College

Andrews University employs a substance abuse screening/evaluation process. Students identified as casual users undergo an 8–10 hour educational program. A program of classes for students identified as abusers is planned.

For More Information

Contact: Herdley Paolini, Substance Abuse Counselor, Counseling Center, Andrews University, Berrien Springs, MI 49103. Telephone: 616-471-3470.

ANTIOCH UNIVERSITY SANTA BARBARA
Santa Barbara, California

General Information
Independent coed college. Part of Antioch University. Founded 1977. Awards B, M. Primary accreditation: regional. City setting. Total enrollment: 139. Faculty: 10 (2 full-time, 8 part-time).

Drug and Alcohol Information
Education

On campus Drug and alcohol education/prevention programs offered for: all students.

Identification of Problems

Admissions College application does not ask about prior substance abuse problems.

On campus Current students identified as chemically dependent may remain enrolled, but treatment is required. Training program on identifying students with potential substance abuse problems for: faculty, administration. Written procedures for students and staff if substance abuse is suspected.

Support Services

On campus Chemical dependency curriculum in psychology department.

Employee assistance Program for chemically dependent employees available. Staff working with drug/alcohol-related issues: 3 full-time.

Disciplinary Actions

Alcohol Results of infractions of alcohol regulations (see Comparative Table of Alcohol Regulations) include counseling.

Drugs For any use, possession, or sale: varies by situation.

Additional Information from the College

Students range in age from 24 to 65. The University has no athletic teams or social organizations and does not attempt to regulate students' behavior outside of classes.

For More Information

Contact: Donna Starr, Assistant Dean, Antioch University Santa Barbara, 801 Garden St., Santa Barbara, CA 93101. Telephone: 805-962-8179.

ANTIOCH UNIVERSITY SEATTLE
Seattle, Washington

General Information
Independent 5-year coed college. Part of Antioch University. Founded 1975. Awards B, M. Primary accreditation: regional. Metropolitan setting. Total enrollment: 382. Faculty: 14 (5 full-time, 9 part-time).

Drug and Alcohol Information
Education

On campus Drug and alcohol education/prevention programs offered on a general basis. Printed material available to anyone on request. Authorized groups concerned with responsible drinking. College holds an annual alcohol awareness week and drug awareness week.

Identification of Problems

Admissions College application does not ask about prior substance abuse problems.

On campus Current students identified as chemically dependent may remain enrolled. Comments: Treatment may or may not be required. No training program on identifying students with potential substance abuse problems. Written procedures for students and staff if substance abuse is suspected.

Antioch University Seattle (continued)

Support Services

On campus No support services on campus.

Employee assistance Program for chemically dependent employees available.

Disciplinary Actions

Alcohol Results of infractions of alcohol regulations (see Comparative Table of Alcohol Regulations) vary by situation. Comments: No such problem has arisen.

Drugs For any use: varies by situation. For any possession or sale: varies by situation—expulsion.

For More Information

Contact: Karen Gottlieb, Personnel Director, or Gary Zimmerman, Provost, Antioch University Seattle, 2607 2nd Ave., Seattle, WA 98121. Telephone: 206-441-5352.

APPALACHIAN BIBLE COLLEGE

Bradley, West Virginia

General Information

Independent Baptist 4-year specialized coed college. Founded 1950. Awards B. Primary accreditation: AABC. Small-town setting; 110-acre campus. Total enrollment: 182. Faculty: 21 (15 full-time, 6 part-time).

Drug and Alcohol Information

Education

On campus Drug and alcohol education/prevention programs offered for: all students.

Identification of Problems

Admissions College application question about prior substance abuse problems is used in the admissions decision.

On campus Current students identified as chemically dependent may not remain enrolled. No training program on identifying students with potential substance abuse problems. No written procedures for students and staff if substance abuse is suspected.

Support Services

On campus Private counseling.

Employee assistance Program for chemically dependent employees not available. Staff working with drug/alcohol-related issues: 3 part-time.

Disciplinary Actions

Alcohol Results of infractions of alcohol regulations (see Comparative Table of Alcohol Regulations) vary by situation but can include counseling, probation, suspension, expulsion.

Drugs For first-time use: varies by situation. For first-time possession: legal action. For subsequent use or possession: expulsion. For any sale: expulsion and legal action.

For More Information

Contact: Dwight Lehman, Dean of Students, Appalachian Bible College, Box ABC, Bradley, WV 25818. Telephone: 304-877-6428.

AQUINAS COLLEGE

Grand Rapids, Michigan

General Information

Independent Roman Catholic 5-year coed college. Founded 1886. Awards A (college transfer), B, M. Primary accreditation: regional. City setting; 98-acre campus. Total enrollment: 2,535. Faculty: 169 (87 full-time, 82 part-time).

Drug and Alcohol Information

Education

On campus Drug and alcohol education/prevention programs offered for: all students. Bacchus chapter: 60 members. College holds an annual alcohol awareness week.

Identification of Problems

Admissions College application does not ask about prior substance abuse problems.

On campus Current students identified as chemically dependent may not remain enrolled, but treatment is required. Training program on identifying students with potential substance abuse problems for: resident advisers, student development personnel. Written procedures for students and staff if substance abuse is suspected.

Support Services

On campus ACOA, support groups, private counseling.

Employee assistance Program for chemically dependent employees available. Staff working with drug/alcohol-related issues: 4 part-time.

Disciplinary Actions

Alcohol Results of infractions of alcohol regulations (see Comparative Table of Alcohol Regulations) vary by situation but can include chemical dependency assessment, counseling, warning, probation, suspension.

Drugs For first-time use or possession: varies by situation—counseling, warning, probation. For subsequent use or possession: suspension, expulsion. For first-time sale: suspension, expulsion. For subsequent sale: expulsion.

For More Information

Contact: R. Paul Nelson, Dean for Student Development, Aquinas College, Grand Rapids, MI 49506. Telephone: 616-459-8281 Ext. 3677.

ARIZONA STATE UNIVERSITY

Tempe, Arizona

General Information

State-supported comprehensive coed institution. Founded 1885. Awards B, M, D. Primary accreditation: regional. City setting; 566-acre campus. Total enrollment: 43,426. Faculty: 2,713 (1,843 full-time, 870 part-time). Social organizations: 22 national fraternities, 13 national sororities; 15% of eligible undergraduate men and 10% of eligible undergraduate women are members.

Drug and Alcohol Information

Education

On campus Drug and alcohol education/prevention programs offered for: all students, athletes/coaches. Bacchus chapter: 5 members. College holds an annual alcohol awareness week.

Identification of Problems

Admissions College application does not ask about prior substance abuse problems.

On campus Current students identified as chemically dependent may remain enrolled, but treatment is required. Training program on identifying students with potential substance abuse problems for: resident advisers, coaches, Greek officers. No written procedures for students and staff if substance abuse is suspected.

Support Services

On campus AA, Al-Anon, ACOA.

Employee assistance Program for chemically dependent employees available. Staff working with drug/alcohol-related issues: 1 full-time and 1 part-time.

Disciplinary Actions

Alcohol Results of infractions of alcohol regulations (see Comparative Table of Alcohol Regulations) include chemical dependency assessment, counseling, warning, probation, suspension, expulsion, substantial fines.

Drugs For first-time use: varies by situation—counseling, warning, probation. For first-time possession: varies by situation—probation. For subsequent use or possession: suspension. For any sale: suspension. Comments: Criminal charges are filed by campus police for second sale.

For More Information

Contact: Carla Fortunato, Counselor, Alcohol and Substance Abuse, Student Health, Arizona State University, Tempe, AZ 85287. Telephone: 602-965-4726.

ARKANSAS BAPTIST COLLEGE

Little Rock, Arkansas

General Information

Independent Baptist 4-year coed college. Founded 1884. Awards B. Primary accreditation: regional. City setting. Total enrollment: 268. Faculty: 23 (10 full-time, 13 part-time).

Drug and Alcohol Information

Education

On campus Drug and alcohol education/prevention programs offered for: all students, athletes/coaches. Authorized group concerned with responsible drinking.

Identification of Problems

Admissions College application does not ask about prior substance abuse problems.

On campus Current students identified as chemically dependent may remain enrolled, but treatment is required. No training program on identifying students with potential substance abuse problems. Written procedures for students and staff if substance abuse is suspected.

Support Services

On campus Support groups, private counseling.

Employee assistance Program for chemically dependent employees not available.

Disciplinary Actions

Alcohol Results of infractions of alcohol regulations (see Comparative Table of Alcohol Regulations) vary by situation but can include chemical dependency assessment, counseling, warning, probation, suspension, expulsion.

Drugs For first-time use: varies by situation—counseling, warning, probation. For first-time possession: varies by situation. For subsequent use or possession: expulsion. For any sale: expulsion.

For More Information

Contact: Mary R. Jarrett, Dean for Academic Affairs, Arkansas Baptist College, 1600 Bishop St., Little Rock, AR 72202. Telephone: 501-374-7856.

ARKANSAS STATE UNIVERSITY

State University, Arkansas

General Information

State-supported 5-year coed college. Founded 1909. Awards A (terminal), B, M. Primary accreditation: regional. Small-town setting; 800-acre campus. Total enrollment: 9,026. Faculty: 360. Social organizations: 11 national fraternities, 7 national sororities, 1 local fraternity; 5% of eligible undergraduate men and 5% of eligible undergraduate women are members.

Drug and Alcohol Information

Education

On campus Drug and alcohol education/prevention programs offered for: all students, athletes/coaches. Authorized group concerned with responsible drinking. College holds an annual alcohol awareness week and drug awareness week.

Identification of Problems

Admissions College application does not ask about prior substance abuse problems.

On campus Current students identified as chemically dependent may remain enrolled. No training program on identifying students with potential substance abuse problems. No written procedures for students and staff if substance abuse is suspected.

Support Services

On campus Private counseling.

Employee assistance Program for chemically dependent employees not available.

Disciplinary Actions

Alcohol Results of infractions of alcohol regulations (see Comparative Table of Alcohol Regulations) vary by situation but can include counseling, warning, probation, suspension.

Drugs For any use, possession, or sale: varies by situation.

For More Information

Contact: Cynthia Bryant, Student Life Counselor, Arkansas State University, P.O. Box 1210, State University, AR 72467. Telephone: 501-972-2038.

ARKANSAS TECH UNIVERSITY

Russellville, Arkansas

General Information

State-supported 5-year coed college. Founded 1909. Awards A (college transfer and terminal), B, M. Primary

Arkansas Tech University (continued)

accreditation: regional. Small-town setting; 475-acre campus. Total enrollment: 3,588. Faculty: 196 (157 full-time, 39 part-time). Social organizations: 6 national fraternities, 3 national sororities; 19% of eligible undergraduate men and 12% of eligible undergraduate women are members.

Drug and Alcohol Information

Education

On campus Drug and alcohol education/prevention programs offered for: all students. Bacchus chapter: 35 members. College holds an annual alcohol awareness week.

Identification of Problems

Admissions College application does not ask about prior substance abuse problems.

On campus Training program on identifying students with potential substance abuse problems for: resident advisers. No written procedures for students and staff if substance abuse is suspected.

Support Services

On campus Student Assistance Alcohol Education Program.

Employee assistance Program for chemically dependent employees not available.

Disciplinary Actions

Alcohol Results of infractions of alcohol regulations (see Comparative Table of Alcohol Regulations) include counseling, probation, fines.

Drugs For first-time use, possession, or sale: varies by situation—suspension. For subsequent use, possession, or sale: suspension, expulsion.

For More Information

Contact: Jimmy L. Ferguson, Assistant Vice President for Student Affairs, Arkansas Tech University, Russellville, AR 72801. Telephone: 501-968-0239.

ARMSTRONG STATE COLLEGE

Savannah, Georgia

General Information

State-supported 5-year coed college. Part of University System of Georgia. Founded 1935. Awards A (college transfer and terminal), B, M. Primary accreditation: regional. City setting; 250-acre campus. Total enrollment: 3,232. Faculty: 166 (125 full-time, 41 part-time). Social organizations: 2 national fraternities, 3 national sororities; 1% of eligible undergraduate men and 1% of eligible undergraduate women are members.

Drug and Alcohol Information

Education

On campus Drug and alcohol education/prevention programs offered for: all students. College holds an annual alcohol awareness week and drug awareness week.

Identification of Problems

Admissions College application does not ask about prior substance abuse problems.

On campus Current students identified as chemically dependent may remain enrolled. No training program on identifying students with potential substance abuse problems. No written procedures for students and staff if substance abuse is suspected.

Support Services

On campus No support services on campus.

Disciplinary Actions

Alcohol Results of infractions of alcohol regulations (see Comparative Table of Alcohol Regulations) include warning, probation, suspension, expulsion.

Drugs For any use or possession: varies by situation. For any sale: suspension.

For More Information

Contact: Joe Buck, Vice President for Student Affairs, Armstrong State College, 11935 Abercorn St., Savannah, GA 31419. Telephone: 912-927-5271.

ART INSTITUTE OF SOUTHERN CALIFORNIA

Laguna Beach, California

General Information

Independent 4-year specialized coed college. Founded 1962. Awards B. Primary accreditation: NASAD. Small-town setting. Total enrollment: 92. Faculty: 22 (7 full-time, 15 part-time).

Drug and Alcohol Information

Education

On campus Drug and alcohol education/prevention programs not offered. College holds an annual drug awareness week.

Identification of Problems

Admissions College application does not ask about prior substance abuse problems.

On campus Current students identified as chemically dependent may remain enrolled, but treatment is required. No training program on identifying students with potential substance abuse problems. Written procedures for students and staff if substance abuse is suspected.

Support Services

On campus No support services on campus.

Off campus Referral to National Council on Alcoholism.

Employee assistance Program for chemically dependent employees not available.

Disciplinary Actions

Alcohol Results of infractions of alcohol regulations (see Comparative Table of Alcohol Regulations) vary by situation but can include chemical dependency assessment, counseling, warning, probation.

Drugs For any use, possession, or sale: varies by situation.

For More Information

Contact: Molly McGuire, Director, Student Services, Art Institute of Southern California, 2222 Laguna Canyon Rd., Laguna Beach, CA 92651. Telephone: 714-497-3309.

ATLANTA COLLEGE OF ART

Atlanta, Georgia

General Information

Independent 4-year specialized coed college. Founded 1928. Awards B. Primary accreditation: regional. Metropolitan setting; 6-acre campus. Total enrollment: 340. Faculty: 40 (25 full-time, 15 part-time).

Drug and Alcohol Information

Education

On campus Drug and alcohol education/prevention programs offered for: all students. College holds an annual alcohol awareness week and drug awareness week.

Identification of Problems

Admissions College application does not ask about prior substance abuse problems.

On campus Current students identified as chemically dependent may remain enrolled. Training program on identifying students with potential substance abuse problems for: resident advisers. Written procedures now being formulated for students and staff if substance abuse is suspected.

Support Services

On campus Private counseling.

Employee assistance Program for chemically dependent employees available. Staff working with drug/alcohol-related issues: 2 part-time.

Disciplinary Actions

Alcohol Results of infractions of alcohol regulations (see Comparative Table of Alcohol Regulations) vary by situation but can include counseling, warning, probation.

Drugs For first-time use or possession: counseling, warning. For subsequent use or possession: probation. For first-time sale: probation. For subsequent sale: varies by situation.

For More Information

Contact: R. Thomas Fitch, Dean of Students, Atlanta College of Art, 1280 Peachtree St., NE, Atlanta, GA 30309. Telephone: 404-898-1161.

ATLANTIC UNION COLLEGE

South Lancaster, Massachusetts

General Information

Independent Seventh-day Adventist 4-year coed college. Founded 1882. Awards A (college transfer and terminal), B. Primary accreditation: regional. Small-town setting; 314-acre campus. Total enrollment: 752. Faculty: 76 (45 full-time, 31 part-time).

Drug and Alcohol Information

Education

On campus Drug and alcohol education/prevention programs offered for: all students. College holds an annual alcohol awareness week and drug awareness week.

Identification of Problems

Admissions College application does not ask about prior substance abuse problems.

On campus Current students identified as chemically dependent may remain enrolled, but treatment is required. No training program on identifying students with potential substance abuse problems. No written procedures for students and staff if substance abuse is suspected.

Support Services

On campus Private counseling. Off campus AA, NA, Al-Anon, ACOA.

Employee assistance Program for chemically dependent employees not available. Staff working with drug/alcohol-related issues: 2 part-time.

Disciplinary Actions

Alcohol Results of infractions of alcohol regulations (see Comparative Table of Alcohol Regulations) vary by situation.

Drugs For any use, possession, or sale: varies by situation.

For More Information

Contact: Sandra J. Nelson, Health Service Director, Atlantic Union College, South Lancaster, MA 01561. Telephone: 508-365-4561.

AUBURN UNIVERSITY

Auburn University, Alabama

General Information

State-supported comprehensive coed institution. Founded 1856. Awards B, M, D. Primary accreditation: regional. Small-town setting; 1,871-acre campus. Total enrollment: 20,553. Faculty: 1,144 (1,061 full-time, 83 part-time). Social organizations: 30 national fraternities, 17 national sororities; 18% of eligible undergraduate men and 26% of eligible undergraduate women are members.

Drug and Alcohol Information

Education

On campus Drug and alcohol education/prevention programs offered for: all students. Authorized group concerned with responsible drinking. College holds an annual alcohol awareness week and drug awareness week.

Identification of Problems

Admissions College application does not ask about prior substance abuse problems.

On campus Current students identified as chemically dependent may remain enrolled. Training program on identifying students with potential substance abuse problems for: resident advisers. No written procedures for students and staff if substance abuse is suspected.

Support Services

On campus AA, NA, Al-Anon, ACOA, private counseling, resource center.

Employee assistance Program for chemically dependent employees not available.

Disciplinary Actions

Alcohol Results of infractions of alcohol regulations (see Comparative Table of Alcohol Regulations) vary by situation but can include warning. Comments: Depends on where student resides.

Drugs For first-time use: chemical dependency assessment. For subsequent use: varies by situation. For first-time possession or sale: chemical dependency assessment, suspension. For subsequent possession or sale: varies by situation.

Auburn University (continued)

Additional Information from the College

An alcohol and drug information center, primarily run by students, is available in the Student Union.

For More Information

Contact: Ann Gleason, Student Affairs Assistant, Cater Hall, Auburn University, Auburn University, AL 36849. Telephone: 205-826-4710.

AUGSBURG COLLEGE

Minneapolis, Minnesota

General Information

Independent Lutheran 5-year coed college. Founded 1869. Awards B, M. Primary accreditation: regional. Metropolitan setting; 28-acre campus. Total enrollment: 2,532. Faculty: 123 (77 full-time, 46 part-time).

Drug and Alcohol Information

Education

On campus Drug and alcohol education/prevention programs offered for: all students, faculty, administration. Authorized group concerned with responsible drinking. College holds an annual alcohol awareness week.

Identification of Problems

Admissions College application does not ask about prior substance abuse problems.

On campus Current students identified as chemically dependent may remain enrolled, but treatment is required. No training program on identifying students with potential substance abuse problems. Written procedures for students and staff if substance abuse is suspected.

Support Services

On campus AA, private counseling, SADD.

Off campus Community services in Minneapolis.

Employee assistance Program for chemically dependent employees available. Staff working with drug/alcohol-related issues: 6 part-time.

Disciplinary Actions

Alcohol Results of infractions of alcohol regulations (see Comparative Table of Alcohol Regulations) vary by situation but can include chemical dependency assessment, counseling, warning, probation, suspension, expulsion, fine, eviction.

Drugs For any use or possession: varies by situation. For any sale: expulsion.

For More Information

Contact: William R. Rosser, Dean of Students, Augsburg College, 731 21st Ave. S., Minneapolis, MN 55454. Telephone: 612-330-1160.

AUGUSTANA COLLEGE

Rock Island, Illinois

General Information

Independent 4-year coed college, affiliated with Lutheran Church. Founded 1860. Awards B. Primary accreditation: regional. City setting; 100-acre campus. Total enrollment: 2,241. Faculty: 158 (120 full-time, 38 part-time). Social organizations: 7 local fraternities, 7 local sororities; 15% of eligible undergraduate men and 15% of eligible undergraduate women are members.

Drug and Alcohol Information

Education

On campus Drug and alcohol education/prevention programs offered for: all students. Bacchus chapter: 20 members. College holds an annual alcohol awareness week.

Identification of Problems

Admissions College application does not ask about prior substance abuse problems.

On campus Current students identified as chemically dependent may remain enrolled, but treatment is required. Training program on identifying students with potential substance abuse problems for: resident advisers, Greek officers, faculty, administration.

Support Services

On campus Private counseling. Off campus AA, NA, Al-Anon, ACOA, other support groups.

Employee assistance Program for chemically dependent employees not available. Staff working with drug/alcohol-related issues: 3 part-time.

Disciplinary Actions

Alcohol Results of infractions of alcohol regulations (see Comparative Table of Alcohol Regulations) vary by situation but can include chemical dependency assessment, counseling, warning, probation. Comments: The College tries to deal with students in a counseling context.

Drugs For first-time use: varies by situation—chemical dependency assessment, counseling. For first-time possession: chemical dependency assessment, counseling. For subsequent use or possession: varies by situation. For any sale: suspension.

For More Information

Contact: John W. Hullett, Dean of Student Services, Augustana College, 639 38th St., Rock Island, IL 61201. Telephone: 309-794-7314.

AUGUSTANA COLLEGE

Sioux Falls, South Dakota

General Information

Independent 5-year coed college, affiliated with Evangelical Lutheran Church in America. Founded 1860. Awards A (terminal), B, M. Primary accreditation: regional. City setting; 100-acre campus. Total enrollment: 2,048. Faculty: 176 (125 full-time, 51 part-time). Social organizations: 7 local fraternities, 7 local sororities; 10% of eligible undergraduate men and 10% of eligible undergraduate women are members.

Drug and Alcohol Information

Education

On campus Drug and alcohol education/prevention programs offered for: all students, faculty, administration. Authorized group concerned with responsible drinking. College holds an annual alcohol awareness week and drug awareness week.

Identification of Problems

Admissions College application does not ask about prior substance abuse problems.

On campus Current students identified as chemically

dependent may remain enrolled. Training program on identifying students with potential substance abuse problems for: resident advisers. No written procedures for students and staff if substance abuse is suspected.

Support Services

On campus AA, Al-Anon, ACOA, support groups, private counseling.

Employee assistance Program for chemically dependent employees not available. Staff working with drug/alcohol-related issues: 5 part-time.

Disciplinary Actions

Alcohol Results of infractions of alcohol regulations (see Comparative Table of Alcohol Regulations) vary by situation but can include chemical dependency assessment, counseling, warning, probation, suspension, expulsion.

Drugs For first-time use or possession: varies by situation—chemical dependency assessment, counseling, probation. For subsequent use or possession: varies by situation. For any sale: suspension, expulsion.

For More Information

Contact: William Hauck, Wellness Center Director, Augustana College, Sioux Falls, SD 57197. Telephone: 605-336-5552.

AURORA UNIVERSITY

Aurora, Illinois

General Information

Independent 5-year coed college. Founded 1893. Awards B, M. Primary accreditation: regional. City setting; 26-acre campus. Total enrollment: 2,079. Faculty: 193 (89 full-time, 104 part-time). Social organizations: 3 national fraternities, 2 national sororities, local fraternities, local sororities.

Drug and Alcohol Information

Education

On campus Drug and alcohol education/prevention programs offered for: freshmen, resident advisers. Authorized group concerned with responsible drinking. College holds an annual alcohol awareness week.

Identification of Problems

Admissions College application does not ask about prior substance abuse problems.

On campus Current students identified as chemically dependent may remain enrolled, but treatment is required. Training program on identifying students with potential substance abuse problems for: resident advisers, administration.

Support Services

On campus AA, private counseling, assessment services.

Employee assistance Program for chemically dependent employees not available. Staff working with drug/alcohol-related issues: 6 part-time.

Disciplinary Actions

Alcohol Results of infractions of alcohol regulations (see Comparative Table of Alcohol Regulations) vary by situation but can include counseling, probation, suspension.

Drugs For first-time use: varies by situation—probation. For subsequent use: chemical dependency assessment, suspension. For first-time possession: chemical dependency assessment, suspension. For subsequent possession: suspension, expulsion. For any sale: expulsion.

For More Information

Contact: James H. Schmid, Dean of Student Development, Aurora University, Aurora, IL 60506. Telephone: 312-844-5449.

AUSTIN COLLEGE

Sherman, Texas

General Information

Independent Presbyterian 5-year coed college. Founded 1849. Awards B, M. Primary accreditation: regional. Small-town setting; 60-acre campus. Total enrollment: 1,269. Faculty: 89 (84 full-time, 5 part-time). Social organizations: 7 local fraternities, 7 local sororities; 35% of eligible undergraduate men and 35% of eligible undergraduate women are members.

Drug and Alcohol Information

Education

On campus Drug and alcohol education/prevention programs offered for: all students; required for: freshmen, social organization members, resident advisers. Bacchus chapter: 5 members. Authorized group concerned with responsible drinking. College holds an annual alcohol awareness week and drug awareness week.

Identification of Problems

Admissions College application does not ask about prior substance abuse problems.

On campus Current students identified as chemically dependent may remain enrolled, but treatment is required. Training program on identifying students with potential substance abuse problems for: resident advisers, Greek officers, peer substance abuse counselors. No written procedures for students and staff if substance abuse is suspected.

Support Services

On campus AA, support groups (peer substance abuse counseling).

Employee assistance Program for chemically dependent employees not available. Staff working with drug/alcohol-related issues: 2 part-time.

Disciplinary Actions

Alcohol Results of infractions of alcohol regulations (see Comparative Table of Alcohol Regulations) vary by situation but can include chemical dependency assessment, counseling, warning, probation, attendance of workshops.

Drugs For first-time use or possession: varies by situation—probation. For subsequent use or possession: chemical dependency assessment, suspension. For first-time sale: suspension. For subsequent sale: expulsion.

For More Information

Contact: Janet A. Heeter, Director of the Student Union/Activities, Box J, Austin College, Sherman, TX 75091. Telephone: 214-892-9101 Ext. 306.

AUSTIN PEAY STATE UNIVERSITY

Clarksville, Tennessee

General Information

State-supported 5-year coed college. Part of State University

Austin Peay State University (continued)

and Community College System of Tennessee. Founded 1927. Awards A (terminal), B, M. Primary accreditation: regional. City setting; 200-acre campus. Total enrollment: 5,013. Faculty: 251 (198 full-time, 53 part-time). Social organizations: 7 national fraternities, 5 national sororities; 15% of eligible undergraduate men and 15% of eligible undergraduate women are members.

Drug and Alcohol Information

Education

On campus Drug and alcohol education/prevention programs offered for: all students; required for: athletes/coaches. Bacchus chapter: 10 members. College holds an annual alcohol awareness week and drug awareness week.

Identification of Problems

Admissions College application does not ask about prior substance abuse problems.

On campus Current students identified as chemically dependent may remain enrolled, but treatment is required. Training program on identifying students with potential substance abuse problems for: resident advisers. No written procedures for students and staff if substance abuse is suspected.

Support Services

On campus AA.

Employee assistance Program for chemically dependent employees available. Staff working with drug/alcohol-related issues: 4 part-time.

Disciplinary Actions

Alcohol Results of infractions of alcohol regulations (see Comparative Table of Alcohol Regulations) include counseling, probation, suspension.

Drugs For first-time use or possession: chemical dependency assessment, counseling, probation. For subsequent use or possession: varies by situation. For first-time sale: counseling, suspension. For subsequent sale: expulsion.

For More Information

Contact: Diane Berty, Director of Student Health Services, Austin Peay State University, P.O. Box 4655, Clarksville, TN 37044. Telephone: 615-648-7107.

AVERETT COLLEGE

Danville, Virginia

General Information

Independent Baptist 5-year coed college. Founded 1859. Awards A (terminal), B, M. Primary accreditation: regional. City setting; 25-acre campus. Total enrollment: 982. Faculty: 65 (60 full-time, 5 part-time). Social organizations: 1 national fraternity, 2 local fraternities, 1 local sorority; 15% of eligible undergraduate men and 12% of eligible undergraduate women are members.

Drug and Alcohol Information

Education

On campus Drug and alcohol education/prevention programs offered for: all students. Authorized group concerned with responsible drinking. College holds an annual alcohol awareness week and drug awareness week.

Identification of Problems

Admissions College application does not ask about prior substance abuse problems.

On campus Current students identified as chemically dependent may remain enrolled. Training program on identifying students with potential substance abuse problems for: resident advisers. No written procedures for students and staff if substance abuse is suspected.

Support Services

On campus Private counseling.

Off campus AA, Al-Anon next door.

Employee assistance Program for chemically dependent employees not available. Staff working with drug/alcohol-related issues: 4 part-time.

Disciplinary Actions

Alcohol Results of infractions of alcohol regulations (see Comparative Table of Alcohol Regulations) vary by situation but can include chemical dependency assessment, counseling, warning, probation, suspension, expulsion, attendance at alcohol education class.

Drugs For first-time use or possession: suspension. For subsequent use or possession: expulsion. For any sale: expulsion.

For More Information

Contact: William L. Trimyer, Director of Counseling, Averett College, 420 W. Main St., Danville, VA 24541. Telephone: 804-790-5624.

AZUSA PACIFIC UNIVERSITY

Azusa, California

General Information

Independent interdenominational 5-year coed college. Founded 1899. Awards A (college transfer), B, M (offers associate only through external degree home study program). Primary accreditation: regional. Small-town setting; 52-acre campus. Total enrollment: 2,833. Faculty: 180 (120 full-time, 60 part-time).

Drug and Alcohol Information

Education

On campus Drug and alcohol education/prevention programs offered for: all students, athletes/coaches. Bacchus chapter. College holds an annual alcohol awareness week.

Identification of Problems

Admissions College application does not ask about prior substance abuse problems.

On campus Current students identified as chemically dependent may remain enrolled, but treatment is required. Training program on identifying students with potential substance abuse problems for: resident advisers, coaches, faculty. Written procedures for students and staff if substance abuse is suspected.

Support Services

On campus No support services on campus. Off campus AA, NA, Al-Anon, ACOA, support groups, private counseling available by referral.

Employee assistance Program for chemically dependent employees not available. Staff working with drug/alcohol-related issues: 10 part-time.

Disciplinary Actions

Alcohol Results of infractions of alcohol regulations (see Comparative Table of Alcohol Regulations) vary by situation but can include chemical dependency assessment, counseling, warning, probation, suspension, expulsion.

Drugs For first-time use or possession: varies by situation. For subsequent use or possession: expulsion. For any sale: expulsion.

For More Information

Contact: Linda Miller, Associate Dean of Students, Azusa Pacific University, P.O. Box APU, Azusa, CA 91702-7000. Telephone: 818-969-3434 Ext. 3056.

BAKER COLLEGE

Flint, Michigan

General Information

Independent 4-year coed college. Part of Baker College System. Founded 1911. Awards A (terminal), B. Primary accreditation: regional and AICS. City setting; 30-acre campus. Total enrollment: 2,675. Faculty: 98 (24 full-time, 74 part-time).

Drug and Alcohol Information

Education

On campus Drug and alcohol education/prevention programs offered for: all students.

Identification of Problems

Admissions College application does not ask about prior substance abuse problems.

On campus Current students identified as chemically dependent may remain enrolled, but treatment is required. Training program on identifying students with potential substance abuse problems for: resident advisers, counselors. Written procedures for students and staff if substance abuse is suspected.

Support Services

On campus No support services on campus. Off campus AA, NA, other community agencies.

Employee assistance Program for chemically dependent employees available. Staff working with drug/alcohol-related issues: 2 part-time.

Disciplinary Actions

Alcohol Results of infractions of alcohol regulations (see Comparative Table of Alcohol Regulations) include counseling, expulsion, referral to an agency in the community.

Drugs For first-time use, possession, or sale: referral to an agency in the community, counseling, expulsion. For subsequent use, possession, or sale: expulsion.

For More Information

Contact: Georgia G. Geiger, Counselor, Baker College, G-1050 W. Bristol Rd., Flint, MI 48507. Telephone: 313-767-7600.

BAKER COLLEGE OF OWOSSO

Owosso, Michigan

General Information

Independent 4-year coed college. Part of Baker College System. Founded 1984. Awards A (college transfer and terminal), B. Primary accreditation: regional. Small-town setting; 32-acre campus. Total enrollment: 900. Faculty: 37 (7 full-time, 30 part-time).

Drug and Alcohol Information

Education

On campus Drug and alcohol education/prevention programs not offered. College holds an annual alcohol awareness week and drug awareness week.

Identification of Problems

Admissions College application does not ask about prior substance abuse problems.

On campus Current students identified as chemically dependent may remain enrolled, but treatment is required. No training program on identifying students with potential substance abuse problems. Written procedures for students and staff if substance abuse is suspected.

Support Services

On campus No support services on campus.

Employee assistance Program for chemically dependent employees available.

Disciplinary Actions

Alcohol Results of infractions of alcohol regulations (see Comparative Table of Alcohol Regulations) include expulsion.

Drugs For first-time use or possession: counseling. For subsequent use or possession: expulsion. For any sale: expulsion.

For More Information

Contact: Thomas J. Perkin, Vice President for Academics, Baker College of Owosso, 1020 S. Washington, Owosso, MI 48867. Telephone: 517-723-5251.

BALDWIN-WALLACE COLLEGE

Berea, Ohio

General Information

Independent Methodist 5-year coed college. Founded 1845. Awards B, M. Primary accreditation: regional. Small-town setting; 56-acre campus. Total enrollment: 4,564. Faculty: 263 (138 full-time, 125 part-time). Social organizations: 9 national fraternities, 9 national sororities, 3 local fraternities, 3 local sororities; 40% of eligible undergraduate men and 40% of eligible undergraduate women are members.

Drug and Alcohol Information

Education

On campus Drug and alcohol education/prevention programs offered for: freshmen, resident advisers, students living in residence halls. Authorized group concerned with responsible drinking.

Baldwin-Wallace College (continued)

Identification of Problems

Admissions College application does not ask about prior substance abuse problems.

On campus Current students identified as chemically dependent may remain enrolled, but treatment is required. Training program on identifying students with potential substance abuse problems for: resident advisers. Written procedures for students and staff if substance abuse is suspected.

Support Services

On campus Private counseling. Off campus AA. Staff working with drug/alcohol-related issues: 3 part-time.

Disciplinary Actions

Alcohol Results of infractions of alcohol regulations (see Comparative Table of Alcohol Regulations) vary by situation but can include counseling, warning, probation, expulsion, participation in educational programs.

Drugs For first-time use: varies by situation—educational sanctions, probation. For subsequent use: varies by situation—removal from residence hall. For first-time possession: varies by situation—educational sanctions, removal from residence hall, probation. For subsequent possession: suspension. For first-time sale: suspension, removal from residence hall. For subsequent sale: dismissal.

For More Information

Contact: Denise Reading, Assistant to the Vice President of Student Affairs, Bond Administration Bldg., Baldwin-Wallace College, Berea, OH 44017. Telephone: 216-826-2157.

BALL STATE UNIVERSITY

Muncie, Indiana

General Information

State-supported comprehensive coed institution. Founded 1918. Awards A (college transfer and terminal), B, M, D. Primary accreditation: regional. City setting; 956-acre campus. Total enrollment: 18,156. Faculty: 973 (934 full-time, 39 part-time). Social organizations: 20 national fraternities, 14 national sororities; 11% of eligible undergraduate men and 10% of eligible undergraduate women are members.

Drug and Alcohol Information

Education

On campus Drug and alcohol education/prevention programs offered for: all students; resident advisers. Bacchus chapter: 8 members. College holds an annual alcohol awareness week and drug awareness week.

Identification of Problems

Admissions College application does not ask about prior substance abuse problems.

On campus Current students identified as chemically dependent may remain enrolled. Training program on identifying students with potential substance abuse problems for: resident advisers. Written procedures for students and staff if substance abuse is suspected.

Support Services

On campus ACOA, private counseling. Off campus AA near campus.

Employee assistance Program for chemically dependent employees available. Staff working with drug/alcohol-related issues: 1 full-time and 2 part-time.

Disciplinary Actions

Alcohol Results of infractions of alcohol regulations (see Comparative Table of Alcohol Regulations) vary by situation but can include warning, probation, suspension, expulsion.

Drugs For any use or possession: varies by situation. For any sale: expulsion.

For More Information

Contact: Anna Lamb, Alcohol Education Coordinator, Health Center, Ball State University, Neely Ave., Muncie, IN 47306. Telephone: 317-285-8431.

BAPTIST BIBLE COLLEGE OF PENNSYLVANIA

Clarks Summit, Pennsylvania

General Information

Independent Baptist 5-year coed college. Founded 1932. Awards A (college transfer), B, M. Primary accreditation: regional and AABC. Small-town setting; 143-acre campus. Total enrollment: 620. Faculty: 36 (30 full-time, 6 part-time).

Drug and Alcohol Information

Education

On campus Drug and alcohol education/prevention programs not offered.

Identification of Problems

Admissions College application question about prior substance abuse problems is used in the admissions decision.

On campus Current students identified as chemically dependent may not remain enrolled. No training program on identifying students with potential substance abuse problems. No written procedures for students and staff if substance abuse is suspected.

Support Services

On campus No support services on campus.

Employee assistance Program for chemically dependent employees not available.

Disciplinary Actions

Alcohol Results of infractions of alcohol regulations (see Comparative Table of Alcohol Regulations) vary by situation but can include suspension.

Drugs For any use, possession, or sale: expulsion.

For More Information

Contact: F. Loescher, Vice President–Student Development, Baptist Bible College of Pennsylvania, 538 Venard Rd., Clarks Summit, PA 18411. Telephone: 717-587-1172.

BAPTIST COLLEGE AT CHARLESTON

Charleston, South Carolina

General Information

Independent Baptist 5-year coed college. Founded 1964. Awards A (college transfer and terminal), B, M. Primary accreditation: regional. City setting; 350-acre campus. Total enrollment: 1,926. Faculty: 85 (65 full-time, 20 part-time). Social organizations: national fraternities, national sororities, local fraternities, local sororities.

Drug and Alcohol Information

Education

On campus Drug and alcohol education/prevention programs offered for: all students; required for: athletes/coaches. College holds an annual alcohol awareness week and drug awareness week.

Identification of Problems

Admissions College application does not ask about prior substance abuse problems.

On campus Current students identified as chemically dependent may remain enrolled, but treatment is required. Comments: Possession of drugs on campus mandates suspension. No training program on identifying students with potential substance abuse problems. Written procedures for students and staff if substance abuse is suspected.

Support Services

On campus Private counseling.

Employee assistance Program for chemically dependent employees not available. Staff working with drug/alcohol-related issues: 3 part-time.

Disciplinary Actions

Alcohol Results of infractions of alcohol regulations (see Comparative Table of Alcohol Regulations) vary by situation but can include probation.

Drugs For first-time use, possession, or sale: suspension. For subsequent use, possession, or sale: possible expulsion.

For More Information

Contact: Dr. Bruce Harshbarger, Dean of Students, Baptist College at Charleston, P.O. Box 10087, Charleston, SC 29411. Telephone: 803-797-4122.

BARD COLLEGE

Annandale-on-Hudson, New York

General Information

Independent 5-year coed college. Founded 1860. Awards B, M. Primary accreditation: regional. Rural setting; 600-acre campus. Total enrollment: 996. Faculty: 109 (90 full-time, 19 part-time).

Drug and Alcohol Information

Education

On campus Drug and alcohol education/prevention programs offered for: all students, athletes/coaches. Authorized group concerned with responsible drinking.

Identification of Problems

Admissions College application does not ask about prior substance abuse problems.

On campus Current students identified as chemically dependent may remain enrolled. Comments: Treatment is not required, but is strongly urged. Training program on identifying students with potential substance abuse problems for: resident advisers, coaches, student affairs staff. Written procedures for students and staff if substance abuse is suspected.

Support Services

On campus AA, NA, Al-Anon, ACOA, support groups, private counseling.

Employee assistance Program for chemically dependent employees not available. Staff working with drug/alcohol-related issues: 6 part-time.

Disciplinary Actions

Alcohol Results of infractions of alcohol regulations (see Comparative Table of Alcohol Regulations) vary by situation but can include chemical dependency assessment, counseling, warning, probation, campus social service, inability to host or register events.

Drugs For first-time use: varies by situation—chemical dependency assessment, counseling. For subsequent use: varies by situation—chemical dependency assessment, counseling, warning. For first-time possession: varies by situation—chemical dependency assessment, counseling, warning. For subsequent possession: probation, suspension. For any sale: suspension, expulsion.

Additional Information from the College

Bard College views the issue of substance abuse as a college-wide concern (not strictly one of student life) and attempts to address it educationally, through prevention, counseling, and referral. The College is prepared to advise newly admitted students about support services on campus and aids to recovery.

For More Information

Contact: Stephen J. Nelson, Dean of Students, Bard College, Annandale-on-Hudson, NY 12504. Telephone: 914-758-7454.

BARNARD COLLEGE

New York, New York

General Information

Independent 4-year women's college. Part of Columbia University. Founded 1889. Awards B. Primary accreditation: regional. Metropolitan setting; 4-acre campus. Total university enrollment: 18,254. Faculty: 260 (160 full-time, 100 part-time). Social organization: 1 local sorority; 1% of eligible undergraduates are members.

Drug and Alcohol Information

Education

On campus Drug and alcohol education/prevention programs offered for: all students, athletes/coaches. Authorized group concerned with responsible drinking. College holds an annual health awareness week.

Identification of Problems

Admissions College application does not ask about prior substance abuse problems.

On campus Current students identified as chemically dependent may remain enrolled, but treatment is required.

Barnard College (continued)

No training program on identifying students with potential substance abuse problems. Written procedures for students and staff if substance abuse is suspected.

Support Services

On campus Support groups, private counseling. Off campus AA, Al-Anon.

Employee assistance Program for chemically dependent employees available. Staff working with drug/alcohol-related issues: 8 part-time.

Disciplinary Actions

Alcohol Results of infractions of alcohol regulations (see Comparative Table of Alcohol Regulations) vary by situation but can include chemical dependency assessment, counseling, warning, probation, suspension, expulsion.

Drugs For any use, possession, or sale: varies by situation.

Additional Information from the College

Barnard is affiliated with Columbia University; their policies and procedures are coordinated, and their resources are often combined. The urban setting means that a multitude of resources are available in the community.

For More Information

Contact: Harriette Mogul, M.D., Director, Health Services, Barnard College, New York, NY 10027-6598. Telephone: 212-854-2091.

BARTLESVILLE WESLEYAN COLLEGE

Bartlesville, Oklahoma

General Information

Independent 4-year coed college, affiliated with Wesleyan Church. Founded 1909. Awards A (college transfer), B. Primary accreditation: regional. Small-town setting; 127-acre campus. Total enrollment: 430. Faculty: 64 (34 full-time, 30 part-time).

Drug and Alcohol Information

Education

On campus Drug and alcohol education/prevention programs offered for: all students; required for: athletes/coaches.

Identification of Problems

Admissions College application does not ask about prior substance abuse problems.

On campus Current students identified as chemically dependent may remain enrolled, but treatment is required. No training program on identifying students with potential substance abuse problems. No written procedures for students and staff if substance abuse is suspected.

Support Services

On campus Support groups, private counseling.

Employee assistance Program for chemically dependent employees not available.

Disciplinary Actions

Alcohol Results of infractions of alcohol regulations (see Comparative Table of Alcohol Regulations) include probation, suspension. Comments: Continued infractions result in expulsion.

Drugs For first-time use or possession: probation. For first-time sale: suspension. For subsequent use, possession, or sale: expulsion.

Additional Information from the College

Upon enrollment, students are required to sign a statement that they will not use drugs or alcohol either on or off campus. Therefore, there are very few problems in this area (one or two a year), which explains the apparent lack of attention to these issues.

For More Information

Contact: Claudia M. Flye, Director of Student Development, Bartlesville Wesleyan College, 2201 Silver Lake Rd., Bartlesville, OK 74006. Telephone: 918-333-6151.

BARUCH COLLEGE OF THE CITY UNIVERSITY OF NEW YORK

New York, New York

General Information

State and locally supported 5-year coed college. Part of City University of New York System. Founded 1968. Awards B, M. Primary accreditation: regional. Metropolitan setting. Total enrollment: 18,100. Faculty: 850 (550 full-time, 300 part-time). Social organizations: local fraternities.

Drug and Alcohol Information

Education

On campus Drug and alcohol education/prevention programs offered for: all students. College holds an annual alcohol awareness week and drug awareness week.

Identification of Problems

Admissions College application does not ask about prior substance abuse problems.

On campus Current students identified as chemically dependent may remain enrolled. Comments: Whether or not treatment is required depends on individual circumstances. Training program on identifying students with potential substance abuse problems for: faculty, administration, counselors. Written procedures for students and staff if substance abuse is suspected.

Support Services

On campus ACOA, support groups (group counseling), private counseling, literature and referral services.

Employee assistance Program for chemically dependent employees available. Staff working with drug/alcohol-related issues: 2 part-time.

Disciplinary Actions

Alcohol Results of infractions of alcohol regulations (see Comparative Table of Alcohol Regulations) vary by situation but can include chemical dependency assessment, counseling, warning, probation, suspension, expulsion.

Drugs For any use, possession, or sale: varies by situation.

Additional Information from the College

1. There is a Task Force for Substance Abuse Issues; it is composed of faculty, staff, and students. A "wellness" model is utilized, incorporating a wide range of health-related issues, including alcohol/drug use and abuse issues.

For More Information

Contact: Pierre Tribaudi, Coordinator, Student Assistance Program, Baruch College of the City University of New

York, Box 304, 17 Lexington Ave., New York, NY 10010. Telephone: 212-725-3347 or 4458.

BASSIST COLLEGE
Portland, Oregon

General Information
Proprietary 4-year coed college. Founded 1963. Awards A (terminal), B (distribution requirements for baccalaureate must be earned at another institution). Primary accreditation: regional. Metropolitan setting. Total enrollment: 208. Faculty: 16 (11 full-time, 5 part-time).

Drug and Alcohol Information
Education

On campus Drug and alcohol education/prevention programs not offered.

Identification of Problems

Admissions College application does not ask about prior substance abuse problems.

On campus Current students identified as chemically dependent may remain enrolled, but treatment is required. No training program on identifying students with potential substance abuse problems. Written procedures for students and staff if substance abuse is suspected.

Support Services

On campus Private counseling.

Employee assistance Program for chemically dependent employees not available.

Disciplinary Actions

Alcohol Results of infractions of alcohol regulations (see Comparative Table of Alcohol Regulations) include expulsion.

Drugs For any use, possession, or sale: expulsion.

For More Information

Contact: Donald Bassist, President, Bassist College, 2000 SW Fifth Ave., Portland, OR 97201. Telephone: 503-228-6528.

BAYAMÓN CENTRAL UNIVERSITY
Bayamón, Puerto Rico

General Information
Independent Roman Catholic 5-year coed college. Founded 1970. Awards A (college transfer), B, M. Primary accreditation: regional. City setting; 55-acre campus. Total enrollment: 2,796. Faculty: 132 (68 full-time, 64 part-time).

Drug and Alcohol Information
Education

On campus Drug and alcohol education/prevention programs offered for: all students, athletes/coaches.

Identification of Problems

Admissions College application does not ask about prior substance abuse problems.

On campus Current students identified as chemically dependent may not remain enrolled. Training program on identifying students with potential substance abuse problems for: faculty, administration.

Support Services

On campus Counseling Center.

Employee assistance Program for chemically dependent employees not available. Staff working with drug/alcohol-related issues: 3 full-time.

Disciplinary Actions

Alcohol Results of infractions of alcohol regulations (see Comparative Table of Alcohol Regulations) include suspension, expulsion.

Drugs For any use, possession, or sale: expulsion.

For More Information

Contact: José Arnaldo Torres, Dean of Students, Bayamón Central University, Box 1725, Bayamón, PR 00619. Telephone: 809-786-3030 Ext. 223.

BAYLOR UNIVERSITY
Waco, Texas

General Information
Independent Baptist comprehensive coed institution. Founded 1845. Awards B, M, D. Primary accreditation: regional. City setting; 428-acre campus. Total enrollment: 11,772. Faculty: 563 (485 full-time, 78 part-time). Social organizations: 14 national fraternities, 10 national sororities, 4 local fraternities; 21% of eligible undergraduate men and 32% of eligible undergraduate women are members.

Drug and Alcohol Information
Education

On campus Drug and alcohol education/prevention programs offered for: all students, athletes/coaches, faculty, administration. Authorized group concerned with responsible drinking. College holds an annual alcohol awareness week and drug awareness week.

Identification of Problems

Admissions College application question about prior substance abuse problems is part of student's health record and is considered privileged information.

On campus Current students identified as chemically dependent may remain enrolled, but treatment is required. Training program on identifying students with potential substance abuse problems for: resident advisers, coaches, Greek officers, faculty, administration. Written procedures for students and staff if substance abuse is suspected.

Support Services

On campus Support groups, private counseling.

Employee assistance Program for chemically dependent employees not available. Staff working with drug/alcohol-related issues: 1 full-time and all staff part-time.

Disciplinary Actions

Alcohol Results of infractions of alcohol regulations (see Comparative Table of Alcohol Regulations) vary by situation.

Drugs For first-time use or possession: varies by situation. For subsequent use or possession: expulsion. For any sale: expulsion.

Additional Information from the College

At Baylor, emphasis is placed on providing good

Baylor University (continued)

information that facilitates students' making responsible decisions about alcohol and substance use.

For More Information

Contact: Dr. Jesse C. Sawyer, Assistant Vice President and Dean of Students, Baylor University, Waco, TX 76798. Telephone: 817-755-1761.

BELHAVEN COLLEGE

Jackson, Mississippi

General Information

Independent Presbyterian 4-year coed college. Founded 1883. Awards B. Primary accreditation: regional. City setting; 42-acre campus. Total enrollment: 700. Faculty: 76 (34 full-time, 42 part-time).

Drug and Alcohol Information

Education

On campus Drug and alcohol education/prevention programs offered for: all students. College holds an annual alcohol awareness week and drug awareness week.

Identification of Problems

Admissions College application does not ask about prior substance abuse problems.

On campus Current students identified as chemically dependent may remain enrolled, but treatment is required. Comments: Identification of students as chemically dependent is difficult. Training program on identifying students with potential substance abuse problems for: resident advisers. No written procedures for students and staff if substance abuse is suspected.

Support Services

On campus Private counseling.

Employee assistance Program for chemically dependent employees not available. Staff working with drug/alcohol-related issues: 2 part-time.

Disciplinary Actions

Alcohol Results of infractions of alcohol regulations (see Comparative Table of Alcohol Regulations) include probation, suspension. Comments: First offense: $100 fine and social probation; second offense: suspension for at least one semester.

Drugs For first-time use or possession: suspension. For subsequent use or possession: expulsion. For any sale: expulsion.

Additional Information from the College

Each student is dealt with individually, but on-campus violations result in mandatory penalties. The College attempts to intervene in off-campus situations by giving counseling and information.

For More Information

Contact: Dr. Pamela K. Jones, Dean of Students, Belhaven College, Jackson, MS 39202. Telephone: 601-968-5932.

BELLARMINE COLLEGE

Louisville, Kentucky

General Information

Independent Roman Catholic 5-year coed college. Founded 1950. Awards A (college transfer), B, M. Primary accreditation: regional. Metropolitan setting; 115-acre campus. Total enrollment: 2,584. Faculty: 196 (92 full-time, 104 part-time).

Drug and Alcohol Information

Education

On campus Drug and alcohol education/prevention programs offered for: all students, athletes/coaches. College holds an annual alcohol awareness week.

Identification of Problems

Admissions College application does not ask about prior substance abuse problems.

On campus Current students identified as chemically dependent may remain enrolled. No training program on identifying students with potential substance abuse problems. Written procedures for students and staff if substance abuse is suspected.

Support Services

On campus Support groups, private counseling, referral agency.

Employee assistance Program for chemically dependent employees not available.

Disciplinary Actions

Alcohol Results of infractions of alcohol regulations (see Comparative Table of Alcohol Regulations) vary by situation but can include chemical dependency assessment, counseling, warning, probation, suspension, fines. Comments: Penalties become more severe if infraction is repeated during the same academic year.

Drugs For first-time use: varies by situation—warning, probation. For subsequent use: varies by situation—counseling, suspension, probation. For first-time possession: varies by situation—suspension. For subsequent possession: expulsion. For first-time sale: varies by situation—expulsion. For subsequent sale: expulsion.

Additional Information from the College

The College is in the process of reviewing its policies and procedures with regard to drug and alcohol use and abuse.

For More Information

Contact: Marilyn Staples, Acting Dean of Students, Bellarmine College, 2001 Newburg Rd., Louisville, KY 40205. Telephone: 502-452-8150.

BELLEVUE COLLEGE

Bellevue, Nebraska

General Information

Independent 4-year coed college. Founded 1965. Awards B. Primary accreditation: regional. Metropolitan setting; 19-acre campus. Total enrollment: 1,862. Faculty: 58 (35 full-time, 23 part-time).

Drug and Alcohol Information

Education

On campus Drug and alcohol education/prevention

programs offered for: all students, faculty, administration; required for: athletes/coaches. Authorized group concerned with responsible drinking. College holds an annual alcohol awareness week and drug awareness week.

Identification of Problems

Admissions College application does not ask about prior substance abuse problems.

On campus Current students identified as chemically dependent may remain enrolled, but treatment is required. No training program on identifying students with potential substance abuse problems. Written procedures for students and staff if substance abuse is suspected are currently being developed.

Support Services

On campus Support groups.

Employee assistance Program for chemically dependent employees not available.

Disciplinary Actions

Alcohol Results of infractions of alcohol regulations (see Comparative Table of Alcohol Regulations) include counseling, warning, probation, suspension, expulsion, referral services.

Drugs For any use: varies by situation. For first-time possession: counseling, warning, probation. For subsequent possession: varies by situation. For any sale: probation, suspension, expulsion.

For More Information

Contact: Dr. Harold F. Carpenter, Vice President, Bellevue College, Galvin Rd., Bellevue, NE 68005. Telephone: 402-293-3761.

BELLIN COLLEGE OF NURSING

Green Bay, Wisconsin

General Information

Independent 4-year specialized coed college. Founded 1909. Awards B. Primary accreditation: regional. City setting. Total enrollment: 161. Faculty: 21 (17 full-time, 4 part-time).

Drug and Alcohol Information

Education

On campus Drug and alcohol education/prevention programs required for: freshmen. Authorized group concerned with responsible drinking.

Identification of Problems

Admissions College application does not ask about prior substance abuse problems.

On campus Current students identified as chemically dependent may not remain enrolled. No training program on identifying students with potential substance abuse problems. No written procedures for students and staff if substance abuse is suspected.

Support Services

On campus Private counseling.

Employee assistance Program for chemically dependent employees available.

Disciplinary Actions

Alcohol Results of infractions of alcohol regulations (see Comparative Table of Alcohol Regulations) vary by situation but can include probation, suspension, expulsion.

Drugs For any use, possession, or sale: varies by situation.

Additional Information from the College

Information about alcohol and drug abuse is included in the first-year nursing curriculum, and students work with patients being treated for substance abuse.

For More Information

Contact: Teresa Westphal, Assistant Dean of Support Services, Bellin College of Nursing, P.O. Box 1700, Green Bay, WI 54305. Telephone: 414-433-3673.

BELMONT ABBEY COLLEGE

Belmont, North Carolina

General Information

Independent Roman Catholic 4-year coed college. Founded 1876. Awards B. Primary accreditation: regional. Small-town setting; 650-acre campus. Total enrollment: 1,055. Faculty: 84 (54 full-time, 30 part-time). Social organizations: 5 national fraternities, 4 local sororities; 35% of eligible undergraduate men and 35% of eligible undergraduate women are members.

Drug and Alcohol Information

Education

On campus Drug and alcohol education/prevention programs offered for: all students, athletes/coaches, administration. Bacchus chapter: 13 members. College holds an annual alcohol awareness week and drug awareness week.

Identification of Problems

Admissions College application does not ask about prior substance abuse problems.

On campus Current students identified as chemically dependent may remain enrolled, but treatment is required. Training program on identifying students with potential substance abuse problems for: resident advisers, administration. No written procedures for students and staff if substance abuse is suspected.

Support Services

On campus AA, ACOA, private counseling.

Employee assistance Program for chemically dependent employees not available. Staff working with drug/alcohol-related issues: 4 part-time.

Disciplinary Actions

Alcohol Results of infractions of alcohol regulations (see Comparative Table of Alcohol Regulations) vary by situation but can include chemical dependency assessment, counseling, warning, probation, suspension, fines, community service.

Drugs For first-time use: varies by situation—chemical dependency assessment, counseling, probation. For subsequent use: varies by situation. For any possession: varies by situation—notification of parents and police. For any sale: expulsion, notification of parents and police.

For More Information

Contact: Angie Wheeler, Director, Counseling Center, Belmont Abbey College, Belmont, NC 28012. Telephone: 704-825-6250.

BEMIDJI STATE UNIVERSITY
Bemidji, Minnesota

General Information
State-supported 5-year coed college. Part of Minnesota State University System. Founded 1919. Awards A (terminal), B, M. Primary accreditation: regional. Small-town setting; 83-acre campus. Total enrollment: 5,021. Faculty: 250 (220 full-time, 30 part-time). Social organizations: 3 national fraternities, 2 national sororities, 1 local fraternity; 2% of eligible undergraduate men and 1% of eligible undergraduate women are members.

Drug and Alcohol Information
Education
On campus Drug and alcohol education/prevention programs offered for: all students, athletes/coaches, faculty, administration. Authorized group concerned with responsible drinking. College holds an annual alcohol awareness week and drug awareness week.

Identification of Problems
Admissions College application question about prior substance abuse problems is used for counseling and referral, if student is admitted.

On campus Current students identified as chemically dependent may remain enrolled. Training program on identifying students with potential substance abuse problems for: resident advisers, coaches, Greek officers, faculty, administration. Written procedures for students and staff if substance abuse is suspected.

Support Services
On campus AA, NA, Al-Anon, ACOA, private counseling, SADD.

Employee assistance Program for chemically dependent employees available. Staff working with drug/alcohol-related issues: 1 full-time.

Disciplinary Actions
Alcohol Results of infractions of alcohol regulations (see Comparative Table of Alcohol Regulations) vary by situation but can include chemical dependency assessment, counseling, warning, probation, suspension, expulsion.

Drugs For any use, possession, or sale: varies by situation.

For More Information
Contact: Lynn Kistler, Coordinator, Drug/Alcohol Program, Bemidji State University, 1500 Birchmont Dr., NE, Bemidji, MN 56601. Telephone: 218-755-4020.

BENEDICT COLLEGE
Columbia, South Carolina

General Information
Independent Baptist 4-year coed college. Founded 1870. Awards B. Primary accreditation: regional. City setting; 22-acre campus. Total enrollment: 1,448. Faculty: 116 (101 full-time, 15 part-time). Social organizations: 4 national fraternities, 4 national sororities.

Drug and Alcohol Information
Education
On campus Drug and alcohol education/prevention programs offered for: all students, athletes/coaches, faculty, administration; required for: freshmen. Bacchus chapter: 20 members. College holds an annual alcohol awareness week and drug awareness week.

Identification of Problems
Admissions College application does not ask about prior substance abuse problems.

On campus Current students identified as chemically dependent may remain enrolled, but treatment is required. Training program on identifying students with potential substance abuse problems for: resident advisers, coaches, Greek officers, faculty, administration, peer leaders. Written procedures for students and staff if substance abuse is suspected.

Support Services
On campus Referral.

Employee assistance Program for chemically dependent employees available. Staff working with drug/alcohol-related issues: 6 part-time.

Disciplinary Actions
Alcohol Results of infractions of alcohol regulations (see Comparative Table of Alcohol Regulations) include counseling, warning, probation, suspension, expulsion.

Drugs For first-time use, possession, or sale: varies by situation. For subsequent use: varies by situation. For subsequent possession or sale: counseling, probation, suspension.

For More Information
Contact: Gloria S. Simmons, Counselor/Coordinator of Drug and Alcohol Programs, Benedict College, Harden and Blanding Sts., Columbia, SC 29204. Telephone: 803-253-5214.

BENEDICTINE COLLEGE
Atchison, Kansas

General Information
Independent Roman Catholic 4-year coed college. Founded 1859. Awards A (college transfer), B. Primary accreditation: regional. Small-town setting; 225-acre campus. Total enrollment: 803. Faculty: 88 (57 full-time, 31 part-time).

Drug and Alcohol Information
Education
On campus Drug and alcohol education/prevention programs offered for: all students, athletes/coaches. College holds an annual alcohol awareness week and drug awareness week.

Identification of Problems
Admissions College application does not ask about prior substance abuse problems.

On campus Current students identified as chemically dependent may or may not remain enrolled, depending on circumstances. No training program on identifying students with potential substance abuse problems.

Support Services
On campus AA, support groups (student group), private counseling.

Employee assistance Program for chemically dependent employees not available.

Disciplinary Actions

Alcohol Results of infractions of alcohol regulations (see Comparative Table of Alcohol Regulations) vary by situation but can include chemical dependency assessment, counseling, warning, probation, participation in education program.

Drugs For any use or possession: varies by situation. For any sale: expulsion.

For More Information

Contact: Sr. Jeannine Neavitt, O.S.B., Assistant Dean of Students, Benedictine College, Atchison, KS 66002. Telephone: 913-367-5340 Ext. 500.

BENNINGTON COLLEGE

Bennington, Vermont

General Information

Independent 5-year coed college. Founded 1932. Awards B, M. Primary accreditation: regional. Rural setting; 550-acre campus. Total enrollment: 613. Faculty: 78 (57 full-time, 21 part-time).

Drug and Alcohol Information

Education

On campus Drug and alcohol education/prevention programs offered for: all students, faculty, administration. Authorized group concerned with responsible drinking.

Identification of Problems

Admissions College application does not ask about prior substance abuse problems.

On campus Continued enrollment and treatment for current students identified as chemically dependent vary by situation. Training program on identifying students with potential substance abuse problems for: resident advisers, faculty, administration, interested students. No written procedures for students and staff if substance abuse is suspected, but policies currently under review.

Support Services

On campus AA, NA, Al-Anon, support groups, private counseling.

Employee assistance Program for chemically dependent employees not available. Staff working with drug/alcohol-related issues: 3 part-time.

Disciplinary Actions

Alcohol Results of infractions of alcohol regulations (see Comparative Table of Alcohol Regulations) vary by situation. Comments: Disciplinary actions are based on severity and number of infractions.

Drugs For any use, possession, or sale: varies by situation.

Additional Information from the College

Bennington College is evaluating and modifying its approach to address early identification and treatment of chemically dependent persons. Efforts are being made to establish a community assistance program, and a college-wide advisory board is in place to establish, evaluate, and implement programming.

For More Information

Contact: Mary Ellen Gilroy, Director of Student Services, Bennington College, Bennington, VT 05201. Telephone: 802-442-5401 Ext. 100.

BENTLEY COLLEGE

Waltham, Massachusetts

General Information

Independent 5-year coed college. Founded 1917. Awards A (college transfer), B, M. Primary accreditation: regional. City setting; 110-acre campus. Total enrollment: 7,150. Faculty: 363 (210 full-time, 153 part-time). Social organizations: 3 national fraternities, 1 national sorority, 3 local fraternities, 3 local sororities; 15% of eligible undergraduate men and 10% of eligible undergraduate women are members.

Drug and Alcohol Information

Education

On campus Drug and alcohol education/prevention programs offered for: freshmen, social organization members; required for: resident advisers. Bacchus chapter: 20 members. College holds an annual alcohol awareness week and drug awareness week.

Identification of Problems

Admissions College application does not ask about prior substance abuse problems.

On campus Current students identified as chemically dependent may remain enrolled. Training program on identifying students with potential substance abuse problems for: resident advisers. No written procedures for students and staff if substance abuse is suspected.

Support Services

On campus ACOA, private counseling.

Employee assistance Program for chemically dependent employees available. Staff working with drug/alcohol-related issues: 5 part-time.

Disciplinary Actions

Alcohol Results of infractions of alcohol regulations (see Comparative Table of Alcohol Regulations) vary by situation but can include counseling, warning, probation, suspension, expulsion, fines, written or service projects.

Drugs For any use, possession, or sale: varies by situation.

For More Information

Contact: Roger Danchise, Ph.D., Director, Office of Counseling and Student Development, Bentley College, Waltham, MA 02254. Telephone: 617-891-2274.

BERKLEE COLLEGE OF MUSIC

Boston, Massachusetts

General Information

Independent 4-year specialized coed college. Founded 1945. Awards B. Primary accreditation: regional. Metropolitan setting. Total enrollment: 2,829.

Drug and Alcohol Information

Education

On campus Drug and alcohol education/prevention programs offered for: all students. Authorized group concerned with responsible drinking. College holds an annual alcohol awareness week and drug awareness week.

Berklee College of Music (continued)

Identification of Problems

Admissions College application does not ask about prior substance abuse problems.

On campus Current students identified as chemically dependent may remain enrolled, but treatment is required. Training program on identifying students with potential substance abuse problems for: resident advisers. No written procedures for students and staff if substance abuse is suspected.

Support Services

On campus AA, Al-Anon, support groups, private counseling.

Employee assistance Program for chemically dependent employees available.

Disciplinary Actions

Alcohol Results of infractions of alcohol regulations (see Comparative Table of Alcohol Regulations) include chemical dependency assessment, counseling, warning, probation, suspension, expulsion.

Drugs For first-time use: chemical dependency assessment, counseling, warning. For subsequent use: probation, suspension. For first-time possession: varies by situation. For subsequent possession: probation, suspension, expulsion. For first-time sale: suspension, expulsion. For subsequent sale: expulsion.

For More Information

Contact: Lawrence E. Bethone, Dean of Students, Berklee College of Music, 1140 Boylston St., Boston, MA 02215. Telephone: 617-266-1400 Ext. 231.

BERRY COLLEGE

Rome, Georgia

General Information

Independent 5-year coed college. Founded 1902. Awards A (college transfer), B, M. Primary accreditation: regional. Small-town setting; 28,000-acre campus. Total enrollment: 1,734.

Drug and Alcohol Information

Education

On campus Drug and alcohol education/prevention programs offered for: all students; required for: athletes/ coaches. Bacchus chapter: 30 members. College holds an annual alcohol awareness week and drug awareness week.

Identification of Problems

Admissions College application does not ask about prior substance abuse problems.

On campus Current students identified as chemically dependent may remain enrolled, but treatment is required. Training program on identifying students with potential substance abuse problems for: resident advisers, coaches. Written procedures for students and staff if substance abuse is suspected.

Support Services

On campus Private counseling, referrals.

Employee assistance Program for chemically dependent employees not available. Staff working with drug/alcohol-related issues: 2 full-time.

Disciplinary Actions

Alcohol Results of infractions of alcohol regulations (see Comparative Table of Alcohol Regulations) vary by situation but can include counseling, warning, probation.

Drugs For any use or possession: varies by situation. For first-time sale: suspension, expulsion. For subsequent sale: expulsion.

For More Information

Contact: Thomas W. Carver, Vice President/Student Affairs, Berry College, Mount Berry Station, Rome, GA 30149. Telephone: 404-236-2204.

BETHANY COLLEGE

Lindsborg, Kansas

General Information

Independent Lutheran 4-year coed college. Founded 1881. Awards B. Primary accreditation: regional. Small-town setting; 48-acre campus. Total enrollment: 722. Faculty: 84 (55 full-time, 29 part-time). Social organizations: 3 local fraternities, 3 local sororities; 10% of eligible undergraduate men and 15% of eligible undergraduate women are members.

Drug and Alcohol Information

Education

On campus Drug and alcohol education/prevention programs offered for: all students, athletes/coaches, faculty, administration. Authorized group concerned with responsible drinking. College holds an annual alcohol awareness week and drug awareness week.

Identification of Problems

Admissions College application does not ask about prior substance abuse problems.

On campus Current students identified as chemically dependent are dealt with on a case-by-case basis. Training program on identifying students with potential substance abuse problems for: resident advisers, coaches, faculty, administration. Written procedures for students and staff if substance abuse is suspected.

Support Services

On campus AA, ACOA, support groups, private counseling.

Employee assistance Program for chemically dependent employees not available. Staff working with drug/alcohol-related issues: 3 full-time and 9 part-time.

Disciplinary Actions

Alcohol Results of infractions of alcohol regulations (see Comparative Table of Alcohol Regulations) vary by situation but can include chemical dependency assessment, counseling, warning, probation, suspension, dismissal, fines.

Drugs For any use or possession: varies by situation. For first-time sale: suspension, dismissal. For subsequent sale: dismissal.

Additional Information from the College

Chemically dependent employees may participate in an area assistance program through the College's health insurance. Bethany College is engaged in the ongoing production and delivery of educational programs about alcohol and drugs; provides information and assistance so that individuals with chemical abuse problems can obtain proper advice and treatment; and is committed to supporting individuals and groups interested in controlling and reducing chemical abuse problems in society.

For More Information

Contact: Donna Bliss, College Counselor, Bethany College, Lindsborg, KS 67456. Telephone: 913-227-3311.

BETHANY COLLEGE

Bethany, West Virginia

General Information

Independent 4-year coed college, affiliated with Christian Church (Disciples of Christ). Founded 1840. Awards B. Primary accreditation: regional. Rural setting; 1,600-acre campus. Total enrollment: 844. Faculty: 71 (56 full-time, 15 part-time). Social organizations: 6 national fraternities, 4 national sororities; 60% of eligible undergraduate men and 60% of eligible undergraduate women are members.

Drug and Alcohol Information

Education

On campus Drug and alcohol education/prevention programs offered for: all students, athletes/coaches, faculty, administration. Authorized group concerned with responsible drinking. College holds an annual alcohol awareness week and drug awareness week.

Identification of Problems

Admissions College application does not ask about prior substance abuse problems.

On campus Current students identified as chemically dependent may remain enrolled, but treatment is required. Training program on identifying students with potential substance abuse problems for: resident advisers, coaches, Greek officers, faculty, administration. Written procedures for students and staff if substance abuse is suspected.

Support Services

On campus ACOA, support groups (recovery), private counseling.

Off campus AA (transportation provided).

Employee assistance Program for chemically dependent employees available. Staff working with drug/alcohol-related issues: 4 full-time and 1 part-time.

Disciplinary Actions

Alcohol Results of infractions of alcohol regulations (see Comparative Table of Alcohol Regulations) vary by situation but can include chemical dependency assessment, warning.

Drugs For first-time use: varies by situation—counseling, warning, fine. For first-time possession or sale: varies by situation—fine. For subsequent use: varies by situation. For subsequent possession or sale: expulsion.

Additional Information from the College

The College has had a drug and alcohol program for eight years, which includes campus education and support group programs. AA participation is encouraged for recovering students and faculty. A course is offered in substance abuse.

For More Information

Contact: Dr. Lynn Adkins, Head, Sociology and Social Work, Bethany College, Bethany, WV 26032. Telephone: 304-829-7551.

BETHEL COLLEGE

North Newton, Kansas

General Information

Independent 4-year coed college, affiliated with General Conference Mennonite Church. Founded 1887. Awards A (terminal), B. Primary accreditation: regional. Small-town setting; 47-acre campus. Total enrollment: 621. Faculty: 77 (41 full-time, 36 part-time).

Drug and Alcohol Information

Education

On campus Drug and alcohol education/prevention programs offered for: all students, faculty, administration. Authorized group concerned with responsible drinking. College holds an annual alcohol awareness week.

Identification of Problems

Admissions College application does not ask about prior substance abuse problems.

On campus Current students identified as chemically dependent may remain enrolled, but treatment is required. Training program on identifying students with potential substance abuse problems for: resident advisers. Written procedures for students and staff if substance abuse is suspected.

Support Services

On campus Private counseling, education sessions.

Employee assistance Program for chemically dependent employees available. Staff working with drug/alcohol-related issues: 2 part-time.

Disciplinary Actions

Alcohol Results of infractions of alcohol regulations (see Comparative Table of Alcohol Regulations) vary by situation but can include chemical dependency assessment, counseling, warning, probation, suspension, expulsion.

Drugs For any use, possession, or sale: varies by situation.

For More Information

Contact: Ron Flaming, Dean of Students, Bethel College, 300 E. 27th, North Newton, KS 67117. Telephone: 316-283-2500.

BETHEL COLLEGE

St. Paul, Minnesota

General Information

Independent 4-year coed college, affiliated with Baptist General Conference. Founded 1871. Awards A (college transfer), B. Primary accreditation: regional. Metropolitan setting; 231-acre campus. Total enrollment: 1,800. Faculty: 149 (102 full-time, 47 part-time).

Drug and Alcohol Information

Education

On campus Drug and alcohol education/prevention programs offered for: all students. Authorized group concerned with responsible drinking. College holds an annual alcohol awareness week.

Identification of Problems

Admissions College application does not ask about prior substance abuse problems.

Bethel College (continued)

On campus Current students identified as chemically dependent may remain enrolled, but treatment is required. No training program on identifying students with potential substance abuse problems. No written procedures for students and staff if substance abuse is suspected.

Support Services

On campus AA, ACOA, support groups, private counseling.

Employee assistance Program for chemically dependent employees not available.

Disciplinary Actions

Alcohol Results of infractions of alcohol regulations (see Comparative Table of Alcohol Regulations) vary by situation but can include chemical dependency assessment, counseling, warning, probation, suspension, expulsion. Comments: The individual's need and attitude and the circumstances of the infraction are all taken into consideration.

Drugs For any use or possession: varies by situation. For any sale: expulsion.

Additional Information from the College

Bethel College's goal is to have students practice total abstinence.

For More Information

Contact: Judith A. Moseman, Vice President for Student Life, Bethel College, 3900 Bethel Dr., St. Paul, MN 55112. Telephone: 612-638-6300.

BETH-EL COLLEGE OF NURSING

Colorado Springs, Colorado

General Information

City-supported 4-year specialized primarily women's college. Founded 1904. Awards B. Primary accreditation: regional. City setting; 1-acre campus. Total enrollment: 185. Faculty: 16 (7 full-time, 9 part-time).

Drug and Alcohol Information

Education

On campus Drug and alcohol education/prevention programs offered for: all students. College holds an annual alcohol awareness week and drug awareness week.

Identification of Problems

Admissions College application question about prior substance abuse problems is used to inform admitted students of State Board of Nursing regulations for licensing.

On campus Current students identified as chemically dependent may remain enrolled, but treatment is required. No training program on identifying students with potential substance abuse problems. Written procedures for students and staff if substance abuse is suspected.

Support Services

On campus Private counseling.

Employee assistance Program for chemically dependent employees available.

Disciplinary Actions

Alcohol Results of infractions of alcohol regulations (see Comparative Table of Alcohol Regulations) include counseling, warning.

Drugs For first-time use: varies by situation—counseling, warning. For subsequent use: varies by situation. For any possession or sale: expulsion.

Additional Information from the College

Teaching faculty are all RNs trained to spot potential problems. Students are informed that state licenses may be revoked, suspended, or withheld from substance abusers.

For More Information

Contact: Marilyn J. Atwood, Director, Student Affairs, Beth-El College of Nursing, 10 N. Farragut Ave., Colorado Springs, CO 80909. Telephone: 719-475-5170.

BETHUNE-COOKMAN COLLEGE

Daytona Beach, Florida

General Information

Independent Methodist 4-year coed college. Founded 1904. Awards B. Primary accreditation: regional. City setting; 52-acre campus. Total enrollment: 1,860. Faculty: 173 (107 full-time, 66 part-time). Social organizations: 4 national fraternities, 4 national sororities, local fraternities, local sororities; 2% of eligible undergraduate men and 5% of eligible undergraduate women are members.

Drug and Alcohol Information

Education

On campus Drug and alcohol education/prevention programs offered for: all students. College holds an annual alcohol awareness week and drug awareness week.

Identification of Problems

Admissions College application does not ask about prior substance abuse problems.

On campus Current students identified as chemically dependent may remain enrolled, but treatment is required. Training program on identifying students with potential substance abuse problems for: resident advisers. Written procedures for students and staff if substance abuse is suspected.

Support Services

On campus Private counseling.

Employee assistance Program for chemically dependent employees not available.

Disciplinary Actions

Alcohol Results of infractions of alcohol regulations (see Comparative Table of Alcohol Regulations) include suspension.

Drugs For first-time use or possession: suspension. For subsequent use or possession: expulsion. For any sale: expulsion.

For More Information

Contact: Clarence N. Childs, Vice President for Student Affairs, Bethune-Cookman College, Daytona Beach, FL 32015. Telephone: 904-255-1401.

BIOLA UNIVERSITY

La Mirada, California

General Information

Independent nondenominational comprehensive coed institution. Founded 1908. Awards B, M, D. Primary accreditation: regional. Small-town setting; 100-acre campus. Total enrollment: 2,552. Faculty: 224 (138 full-time, 86 part-time).

Drug and Alcohol Information

Education

On campus Drug and alcohol education/prevention programs offered for: all students.

Identification of Problems

Admissions College application does not ask about prior substance abuse problems.

On campus Current students identified as chemically dependent may remain enrolled, but treatment is required. Training program on identifying students with potential substance abuse problems for: resident advisers, administration. No written procedures for students and staff if substance abuse is suspected.

Support Services

On campus Private counseling.

Employee assistance Program for chemically dependent employees not available.

Disciplinary Actions

Alcohol Results of infractions of alcohol regulations (see Comparative Table of Alcohol Regulations) vary by situation.

Drugs For any use or possession: varies by situation. For any sale: expulsion.

For More Information

Contact: Sharon Roysten, Associate Dean, Residence Life, Biola University, 13800 Biola Ave., La Mirada, CA 90639. Telephone: 213-944-0351.

BIRMINGHAM-SOUTHERN COLLEGE

Birmingham, Alabama

General Information

Independent Methodist 5-year coed college. Founded 1856. Awards B, M. Primary accreditation: regional. Metropolitan setting; 185-acre campus. Total enrollment: 1,836. Faculty: 146 (98 full-time, 48 part-time). Social organizations: 6 national fraternities, 6 national sororities; 50% of eligible undergraduate men and 50% of eligible undergraduate women are members.

Drug and Alcohol Information

Education

On campus Drug and alcohol education/prevention programs offered for: all students, faculty, administration; required for: athletes/coaches. Authorized group concerned with responsible drinking. College holds an annual alcohol awareness week and drug awareness week.

Identification of Problems

Admissions College application does not ask about prior substance abuse problems.

On campus Current students identified as chemically dependent may remain enrolled, but treatment is required. Training program on identifying students with potential substance abuse problems for: resident advisers, coaches, Greek officers, faculty, administration. Written procedures for students and staff if substance abuse is suspected.

Support Services

On campus ACOA, support groups, private counseling.

Employee assistance Program for chemically dependent employees available. Staff working with drug/alcohol-related issues: 8 part-time.

Disciplinary Actions

Alcohol Results of infractions of alcohol regulations (see Comparative Table of Alcohol Regulations) vary by situation but can include chemical dependency assessment, counseling, warning, probation, suspension, expulsion.

Drugs For first-time use or possession: varies by situation. For subsequent use or possession: varies by situation—suspension, expulsion. For first-time sale: varies by situation—counseling, expulsion. For subsequent sale: varies by situation—expulsion.

Additional Information from the College

Birmingham-Southern College approaches abuse and liability from an educational standpoint. College policies are in line with the applicable laws.

For More Information

Contact: Dudley Long, Vice President for Student Affairs, Birmingham-Southern College, Box A-14, 900 Arkadelphia Road, Birmingham, AL 35212. Telephone: 205-226-4731.

BLACKBURN COLLEGE

Carlinville, Illinois

General Information

Independent Presbyterian 4-year coed college. Founded 1837. Awards B. Primary accreditation: regional. Small-town setting; 80-acre campus. Total enrollment: 521. Faculty: 53 (39 full-time, 14 part-time).

Drug and Alcohol Information

Education

On campus Drug and alcohol education/prevention programs offered for: all students, athletes/coaches, faculty, administration. Bacchus chapter: 10 members.

Identification of Problems

Admissions College application does not ask about prior substance abuse problems.

On campus Current students identified as chemically dependent may remain enrolled, but treatment is required. Training program on identifying students with potential substance abuse problems for: resident advisers, faculty, administration. Written procedures for students and staff if substance abuse is suspected.

Support Services

On campus AA, Al-Anon, private counseling.

Employee assistance Program for chemically dependent employees available. Staff working with drug/alcohol-related issues: 1 full-time and 2 part-time.

Blackburn College (continued)

Disciplinary Actions

Alcohol Results of infractions of alcohol regulations (see Comparative Table of Alcohol Regulations) vary by situation but can include counseling, warning, probation, suspension.

Drugs For first-time use or possession: varies by situation. For subsequent use or possession: varies by situation—probation, suspension. For any sale: suspension.

For More Information

Contact: Lee Boblitt, College Counselor, Blackburn College, 700 College Ave., Carlinville, IL 62626. Telephone: 217-854-3231.

BLACK HILLS STATE COLLEGE

Spearfish, South Dakota

General Information

State-supported 5-year coed college. Founded 1883. Awards A (college transfer and terminal), B, M (M in summer session only). Primary accreditation: regional. Small-town setting; 123-acre campus. Total enrollment: 2,282. Faculty: 106 (72 full-time, 34 part-time). Social organizations: 2 national fraternities, 2 national sororities.

Drug and Alcohol Information

Education

On campus Drug and alcohol education/prevention programs offered for: all students, athletes/coaches, faculty, administration. Bacchus chapter: 24 members. College holds an annual alcohol awareness week and drug awareness week.

Identification of Problems

Admissions College application does not ask about prior substance abuse problems.

On campus Current students identified as chemically dependent may remain enrolled. No training program on identifying students with potential substance abuse problems. Written procedures for students and staff if substance abuse is suspected.

Support Services

On campus AA, NA, Al-Anon, private counseling.

Employee assistance Program for chemically dependent employees not available.

Disciplinary Actions

Alcohol Results of infractions of alcohol regulations (see Comparative Table of Alcohol Regulations) vary by situation but can include chemical dependency assessment, counseling, probation.

Drugs For first-time use, possession, or sale: varies by situation—chemical dependency assessment, counseling, probation. For subsequent use, possession, or sale: varies by situation.

For More Information

Contact: Michael Corfin, Alcohol and Drug Awareness Coordinator, Black Hills State College, Box 9022, Spearfish, SD 57783. Telephone: 605-642-6113 or 6291.

BLOOMFIELD COLLEGE

Bloomfield, New Jersey

General Information

Independent 4-year coed college, affiliated with Presbyterian Church. Founded 1868. Awards B. Primary accreditation: regional. City setting; 10-acre campus. Total enrollment: 1,484. Faculty: 124 (41 full-time, 83 part-time). Social organizations: 2 national fraternities, 2 national sororities, 2 local fraternities, 1 local sorority, 10 coed social clubs; 9% of eligible undergraduate men and 12% of eligible undergraduate women are members.

Drug and Alcohol Information

Education

On campus Drug and alcohol education/prevention programs offered for: all students, athletes/coaches, faculty, administration. College holds an annual alcohol awareness week and drug awareness week.

Identification of Problems

Admissions College application does not ask about prior substance abuse problems.

On campus Current students identified as chemically dependent may remain enrolled, but treatment is required. No training program on identifying students with potential substance abuse problems. Written procedures for students and staff if substance abuse is suspected.

Support Services

On campus Private counseling.

Employee assistance Program for chemically dependent employees available. Staff working with drug/alcohol-related issues: 5 part-time.

Disciplinary Actions

Alcohol Results of infractions of alcohol regulations (see Comparative Table of Alcohol Regulations) vary by situation. Comments: Each case is reviewed by the appropriate judiciary board.

Drugs For first-time use or possession: counseling, suspension. For subsequent use or possession: expulsion. For any sale: expulsion.

Additional Information from the College

Bloomfield College is sharpening its focus on, and increasing its efforts in, the area of drug and alcohol awareness programming.

For More Information

Contact: Dr. Pargellan A. McCall, Vice President for Student Affairs, Bloomfield College, 467 Franklin St., Bloomfield, NJ 07003. Telephone: 201-748-9000 Ext. 245.

BLOOMSBURG UNIVERSITY OF PENNSYLVANIA

Bloomsburg, Pennsylvania

General Information

State-supported 5-year coed college. Part of State System of Higher Education. Founded 1839. Awards A (terminal), B, M. Primary accreditation: regional. Small-town setting; 177-acre campus. Total enrollment: 6,804. Faculty: 389 (345 full-time, 44 part-time). Social organizations: 4 national fraternities, 4 national sororities, 5 local fraternities, 6 local sororities; 25% of eligible undergraduate men and 25% of eligible undergraduate women are members.

Drug and Alcohol Information

Education

On campus Drug and alcohol education/prevention programs offered for: all students, administration. College holds an annual alcohol awareness week and drug awareness week.

Identification of Problems

Admissions College application does not ask about prior substance abuse problems.

On campus Current students identified as chemically dependent may remain enrolled. Comments: Treatment may or may not be required. Training program on identifying students with potential substance abuse problems for: resident advisers, hall directors. Written procedures for students and staff if substance abuse is suspected.

Support Services

On campus Private counseling.

Employee assistance Program for chemically dependent employees available.

Disciplinary Actions

Alcohol Results of infractions of alcohol regulations (see Comparative Table of Alcohol Regulations) include chemical dependency assessment, counseling, warning, probation, suspension.

Drugs For any use: varies by situation. For first-time possession: warning, probation. For first-time sale: warning, probation, suspension. For subsequent possession or sale: varies by situation.

For More Information

Contact: Jennie H. Carpenter, Director of Residence Life, Bloomsburg University of Pennsylvania, Bloomsburg, PA 17815. Telephone: 717-389-4089.

BLUEFIELD STATE COLLEGE

Bluefield, West Virginia

General Information

State-supported 4-year coed college. Founded 1895. Awards A (college transfer and terminal), B. Primary accreditation: regional. Small-town setting; 40-acre campus. Total enrollment: 2,558. Faculty: 125 (72 full-time, 53 part-time). Social organizations: national fraternities, national sororities, local fraternities, local sororities; 80% of eligible undergraduate men and 80% of eligible undergraduate women are members.

Drug and Alcohol Information

Education

On campus Drug and alcohol education/prevention programs offered for: all students, athletes/coaches. Authorized group concerned with responsible drinking. College holds an annual alcohol awareness week and drug awareness week.

Identification of Problems

Admissions College application does not ask about prior substance abuse problems.

On campus Current students identified as chemically dependent may remain enrolled. Training program on identifying students with potential substance abuse problems. No written procedures for students and staff if substance abuse is suspected.

Support Services

On campus Private counseling.

Employee assistance Program for chemically dependent employees not available. Staff working with drug/alcohol-related issues: 1 part-time.

Disciplinary Actions

Alcohol Results of infractions of alcohol regulations (see Comparative Table of Alcohol Regulations) include chemical dependency assessment, counseling, warning, probation, suspension, expulsion.

Drugs For first-time use: varies by situation—chemical dependency assessment, warning, suspension. For subsequent use: varies by situation—suspension, expulsion. For first-time possession: varies by situation—expulsion. For subsequent possession: expulsion. For any sale: expulsion.

For More Information

Contact: John Cardwell, Assistant Dean of Students, Bluefield State College, 219 Rock St., Bluefield, WV 24701. Telephone: 304-327-4186.

BLUE MOUNTAIN COLLEGE

Blue Mountain, Mississippi

General Information

Independent Southern Baptist 4-year primarily women's college. Founded 1873. Awards B. Primary accreditation: regional. Rural setting; 44-acre campus. Total enrollment: 374. Faculty: 33 (24 full-time, 9 part-time). Social organizations: 3 societies for women; 50% of eligible undergraduate women are members.

Drug and Alcohol Information

Education

On campus Drug and alcohol education/prevention programs offered for: all students.

Identification of Problems

Admissions College application does not ask about prior substance abuse problems.

On campus Current students identified as chemically dependent may remain enrolled, but treatment is required. No training program on identifying students with potential substance abuse problems.

Support Services

On campus Private counseling.

Employee assistance Program for chemically dependent employees not available.

Disciplinary Actions

Alcohol Results of infractions of alcohol regulations (see Comparative Table of Alcohol Regulations) include counseling, warning, probation, suspension.

Drugs For any use, possession, or sale: varies by situation.

For More Information

Contact: Rebecca B. Bennett, Dean of Students, Blue Mountain College, Box 308, Blue Mountain, MS 38610. Telephone: 601-685-4771.

BLUFFTON COLLEGE
Bluffton, Ohio

General Information
Independent Mennonite 4-year coed college. Founded 1899. Awards B. Primary accreditation: regional. Small-town setting; 60-acre campus. Total enrollment: 608. Faculty: 55 (46 full-time, 9 part-time).

Drug and Alcohol Information
Education
On campus Drug and alcohol education/prevention programs offered for: all students, athletes/coaches. Authorized group concerned with responsible drinking. College holds an annual alcohol awareness week.

Identification of Problems
Admissions College application does not ask about prior substance abuse problems.

On campus Current students identified as chemically dependent may remain enrolled, but treatment is required. Training program on identifying students with potential substance abuse problems for: resident advisers. Written procedures for students and staff if substance abuse is suspected.

Support Services
On campus No support services on campus.

Off campus Many support services.

Employee assistance Program for chemically dependent employees not available.

Disciplinary Actions
Alcohol Results of infractions of alcohol regulations (see Comparative Table of Alcohol Regulations) vary by situation by can include chemical dependency assessment, counseling, probation, suspension. Comments: Assessment and counseling are required for repeated offenses.

Drugs For first-time use, possession, or sale: counseling, suspension. For subsequent use, possession, or sale: counseling, expulsion.

For More Information
Contact: Kevin D. Cluts, Director of Student Activities, Box 1026, Bluffton College, Bluffton, OH 45817. Telephone: 419-358-8015 Ext. 218.

BOISE BIBLE COLLEGE
Boise, Idaho

General Information
Independent nondenominational 4-year specialized coed college. Founded 1945. Awards A (college transfer), B. Primary accreditation: AABC. City setting; 17-acre campus. Total enrollment: 80. Faculty: 16 (5 full-time, 11 part-time).

Drug and Alcohol Information
Education
On campus Drug and alcohol education/prevention programs offered for: all students. Authorized group concerned with responsible drinking. College holds an annual alcohol awareness week and drug awareness week.

Identification of Problems
Admissions College application question about prior substance abuse problems is used in the admissions decision.

On campus Current students identified as chemically dependent may remain enrolled, but treatment is required. Comments: This is possible, but not invariable. No training program on identifying students with potential substance abuse problems. Written procedures for students and staff if substance abuse is suspected.

Support Services
On campus No support services on campus.

Employee assistance Program for chemically dependent employees not available. Staff working with drug/alcohol-related issues: 2 part-time.

Disciplinary Actions
Alcohol Results of infractions of alcohol regulations (see Comparative Table of Alcohol Regulations) vary by situation but can include counseling, probation. Comments: Students are helped to find an off-campus treatment program, and their treatment is monitored and assisted by the College.

Drugs For first-time use or possession: varies by situation—counseling, probation. For first-time sale: varies by situation—probation. For subsequent use, possession, or sale: suspension.

For More Information
Contact: Ted Baimbridge, Student Dean, Boise Bible College, 8695 Marigold St., Boise, ID 83714. Telephone: 208-376-7731.

BOISE STATE UNIVERSITY
Boise, Idaho

General Information
State-supported 5-year coed college. Founded 1932. Awards A (terminal), B, M. Primary accreditation: regional. City setting; 130-acre campus. Total enrollment: 11,429. Faculty: 449 (335 full-time, 114 part-time). Social organizations: 4 national fraternities, 3 national sororities, 4 local fraternities, 4 local sororities; 1% of eligible undergraduate men and 1% of eligible undergraduate women are members.

Drug and Alcohol Information
Education
On campus Drug and alcohol education/prevention programs offered for: all students, athletes/coaches, faculty, administration. College holds an annual alcohol awareness week and drug awareness week.

Identification of Problems
Admissions College application does not ask about prior substance abuse problems.

On campus Current students identified as chemically dependent may remain enrolled. No training program on identifying students with potential substance abuse problems. Written procedures for students and staff if substance abuse is suspected.

Support Services
On campus AA, NA, ACOA, private counseling.

Employee assistance Program for chemically dependent employees available.

Disciplinary Actions
Alcohol Results of infractions of alcohol regulations (see

Comparative Table of Alcohol Regulations) vary by situation.

Drugs For any use, possession, or sale: referral to local authorities.

For More Information

Contact: Phyllis Sawyer, Health Promotion Director, College of Education, Boise State University, 1910 University Dr., Boise, ID 83725. Telephone: 208-385-3364.

BOSTON COLLEGE

Chestnut Hill, Massachusetts

General Information

Independent Roman Catholic comprehensive coed institution. Founded 1863. Awards B, M, D. Primary accreditation: regional. City setting; 240-acre campus. Total enrollment: 14,561. Faculty: 914 (572 full-time, 342 part-time).

Drug and Alcohol Information

Education

On campus Drug and alcohol education/prevention programs offered for: freshmen, athletes/coaches. Authorized group concerned with responsible drinking. College holds an annual alcohol awareness week.

Identification of Problems

Admissions College application does not ask about prior substance abuse problems.

On campus Current students identified as chemically dependent may remain enrolled, but treatment is required. Training program on identifying students with potential substance abuse problems for: resident advisers, coaches. Written procedures for students and staff if substance abuse is suspected.

Support Services

On campus AA, Al-Anon, ACOA, alcohol/drug education program.

Employee assistance Program for chemically dependent employees available.

Disciplinary Actions

Alcohol Results of infractions of alcohol regulations (see Comparative Table of Alcohol Regulations) vary by situation but can include probation, suspension, alcohol education program.

Drugs For first-time use or possession: varies by situation—counseling, probation. For subsequent use: varies by situation. For subsequent possession: suspension, expulsion. For first-time sale: varies by situation—suspension, expulsion. For subsequent sale: suspension, expulsion.

For More Information

Contact: Paul J. Chebator, Associate Dean for Student Development, McElroy 233, Boston College, Chestnut Hill, MA 02167. Telephone: 617-552-3470.

BOWDOIN COLLEGE

Brunswick, Maine

General Information

Independent 4-year coed college. Founded 1794. Awards B. Primary accreditation: regional. Small-town setting; 110-acre campus. Total enrollment: 1,350. Faculty: 130 (125 full-time, 5 part-time). Social organizations: 6 national fraternities, 3 local fraternities, 9 coed fraternities; 28% of eligible undergraduate men and 9% of eligible undergraduate women are members.

Drug and Alcohol Information

Education

On campus Drug and alcohol education/prevention programs required for: freshmen. Authorized group concerned with responsible drinking. College holds an annual alcohol awareness week and drug awareness week.

Identification of Problems

Admissions College application does not ask about prior substance abuse problems.

On campus Current students identified as chemically dependent may remain enrolled. Training program on identifying students with potential substance abuse problems for: resident advisers, administration, counseling service. Written procedures for students and staff if substance abuse is suspected.

Support Services

On campus ACOA, support groups (peer advisers), private counseling.

Off campus AA, Al-Anon.

Employee assistance Program for chemically dependent employees available. Staff working with drug/alcohol-related issues: 3 part-time.

Disciplinary Actions

Alcohol Results of infractions of alcohol regulations (see Comparative Table of Alcohol Regulations) vary by situation.

Drugs For any use or possession: varies by situation. For any sale: expulsion.

For More Information

Contact: Beverly Gelwick, Director of the Counseling Service, Bowdoin College, Brunswick, ME 04011. Telephone: 207-725-3145.

BOWIE STATE UNIVERSITY

Bowie, Maryland

General Information

State-supported 5-year coed college. Part of Maryland State Colleges and Universities System. Founded 1865. Awards B, M. Primary accreditation: regional. Small-town setting; 287-acre campus. Total enrollment: 3,327. Faculty: 167 (102 full-time, 65 part-time). Social organizations: 4 national fraternities, 4 national sororities; 2% of eligible undergraduate men and 2% of eligible undergraduate women are members.

Drug and Alcohol Information

Education

On campus Drug and alcohol education/prevention programs offered for: athletes/coaches, administration; required for: freshmen. College holds an annual alcohol awareness week and drug awareness week.

Identification of Problems

Admissions College application does not ask about prior substance abuse problems.

Bowie State University (continued)

On campus Current students identified as chemically dependent may remain enrolled, but treatment is required. No training program on identifying students with potential substance abuse problems. Written procedures for students and staff if substance abuse is suspected.

Support Services

On campus Private counseling.

Employee assistance Program for chemically dependent employees available. Staff working with drug/alcohol-related issues: 1 full-time.

Disciplinary Actions

Alcohol Results of infractions of alcohol regulations (see Comparative Table of Alcohol Regulations) vary by situation but can include counseling, warning, probation, suspension.

Drugs For any use: varies by situation. For first-time possession or sale: varies by situation—expulsion. For subsequent possession or sale: varies by situation.

For More Information

Contact: Patricia Wheeler, Dean of Students, Bowie State University, Jericho Park Road, Bowie, Maryland 20715. Telephone: 301-464-6526.

BOWLING GREEN STATE UNIVERSITY

Bowling Green, Ohio

General Information

State-supported comprehensive coed institution. Founded 1910. Awards A (terminal), B, M, D. Primary accreditation: regional. Small-town setting; 1,247-acre campus. Total enrollment: 17,882. Faculty: 845 (728 full-time, 117 part-time). Social organizations: 23 national fraternities, 18 national sororities; 22% of eligible undergraduate men and 16% of eligible undergraduate women are members.

Drug and Alcohol Information

Education

On campus Drug and alcohol education/prevention programs offered for: all students, athletes/coaches. Authorized group concerned with responsible drinking. College holds an annual alcohol awareness week and drug awareness week.

Identification of Problems

Admissions College application does not ask about prior substance abuse problems.

On campus Current students identified as chemically dependent may remain enrolled, but treatment is required. No training program on identifying students with potential substance abuse problems. Written procedures for students and staff if substance abuse is suspected.

Support Services

On campus Private counseling.

Employee assistance Program for chemically dependent employees available. Staff working with drug/alcohol-related issues: 1 full-time.

Disciplinary Actions

Alcohol Results of infractions of alcohol regulations (see Comparative Table of Alcohol Regulations) include counseling, warning, probation, suspension.

Drugs For first-time use, possession, or sale: probation. For subsequent use, possession, or sale: suspension.

For More Information

Contact: Jacqueline Daley, Director, Center for Alcohol and Substance Abuse Prevention, Bowling Green State University, Bowling Green, OH 43403. Telephone: 419-372-2130.

BRADFORD COLLEGE

Bradford, Massachusetts

General Information

Independent 4-year coed college. Founded 1803. Awards B. Primary accreditation: regional. Small-town setting; 70-acre campus. Total enrollment: 450. Faculty: 45 (34 full-time, 11 part-time).

Drug and Alcohol Information

Education

On campus Drug and alcohol education/prevention programs offered for: all students, faculty, administration. Authorized group concerned with responsible drinking. College holds an annual alcohol awareness week.

Identification of Problems

Admissions College application does not ask about prior substance abuse problems.

On campus Current students identified as chemically dependent may remain enrolled, but treatment is required. Training program on identifying students with potential substance abuse problems for: resident advisers. Written procedures for students and staff if substance abuse is suspected.

Support Services

On campus Private counseling, resident advisers.

Employee assistance Program for chemically dependent employees not available.

Disciplinary Actions

Alcohol Results of infractions of alcohol regulations (see Comparative Table of Alcohol Regulations) include counseling, warning, possible Judicial Council action.

Drugs For first-time use: varies by situation—chemical dependency assessment, counseling. For subsequent use: varies by situation—chemical dependency assessment, probation. For first-time possession: varies by situation. For subsequent possession: suspension. For any sale: expulsion.

For More Information

Contact: John Schneider, Assistant Dean of Students, Bradford College, Main St., Bradford, MA 01830. Telephone: 508-372-7161.

BRADLEY UNIVERSITY

Peoria, Illinois

General Information

Independent 5-year coed college. Founded 1897. Awards B, M. Primary accreditation: regional. City setting; 65-acre campus. Total enrollment: 5,174. Faculty: 369 (283 full-time, 86 part-time). Social organizations: 18 national fraternities, 9 national sororities, 1 local sorority; 41% of eligible undergraduate men and 34% of eligible undergraduate women are members.

Drug and Alcohol Information

Education

On campus Drug and alcohol education/prevention programs offered for: freshmen, social organization members; required for: resident advisers. Bacchus chapter being reactivated. College holds an annual alcohol awareness week.

Identification of Problems

Admissions College application does not ask about prior substance abuse problems.

On campus Current students identified as chemically dependent may remain enrolled, but treatment is required. Training program on identifying students with potential substance abuse problems for: resident advisers. Written procedures for students and staff if substance abuse is suspected.

Support Services

On campus AA, ACOA, private counseling.

Employee assistance Program for chemically dependent employees not available. Staff working with drug/alcohol-related issues: 1 part-time.

Disciplinary Actions

Alcohol Results of infractions of alcohol regulations (see Comparative Table of Alcohol Regulations) include chemical dependency assessment, counseling, warning, probation.

Drugs For first-time use and possession: varies by situation—chemical dependency assessment, counseling, probation. For subsequent use or possession: varies by situation—suspension. For any sale: suspension.

For More Information

Contact: Dr. Marlene Kuskie, Acting Director, Center for Counseling and Wellness, Bradley University, 1501 W. Bradley Ave., Peoria, IL 61625. Telephone: 309-677-2409.

BRESCIA COLLEGE

Owensboro, Kentucky

General Information

Independent Roman Catholic 4-year coed college. Founded 1950. Awards A (terminal), B. Primary accreditation: regional. City setting; 6-acre campus. Total enrollment: 646. Faculty: 61 (40 full-time, 21 part-time).

Drug and Alcohol Information

Education

On campus Drug and alcohol education/prevention programs offered for: all students; required for: athletes/coaches. College holds an annual alcohol awareness week.

Identification of Problems

Admissions College application does not ask about prior substance abuse problems.

On campus Current students identified as chemically dependent may remain enrolled, but treatment is required.No training program on identifying students with potential substance abuse problems. No written procedures for students and staff if substance abuse is suspected.

Support Services

On campus Private counseling.

Employee assistance Program for chemically dependent employees not available.

Disciplinary Actions

Alcohol Results of infractions of alcohol regulations (see Comparative Table of Alcohol Regulations) include counseling, probation, suspension.

Drugs For any use, possession, or sale: expulsion.

For More Information

Contact: Barry McArdle, Dean of Students, Brescia College, 717 Frederica, Owensboro, KY 42301. Telephone: 502-685-3131.

BRIAR CLIFF COLLEGE

Sioux City, Iowa

General Information

Independent Roman Catholic 4-year coed college. Founded 1930. Awards A (college transfer and terminal), B. Primary accreditation: regional. City setting; 70-acre campus. Total enrollment: 1,103. Faculty: 82 (67 full-time, 15 part-time).

Drug and Alcohol Information

Education

On campus Drug and alcohol education/prevention programs offered for: all students, athletes/coaches, faculty, administration, security personnel, food service staff. Bacchus chapter: 40 members. College holds an annual alcohol awareness week.

Identification of Problems

Admissions College application does not ask about prior substance abuse problems.

On campus Current students identified as chemically dependent may remain enrolled, but treatment is required if student lives on campus. Training program on identifying students with potential substance abuse problems for: resident advisers, coaches, faculty, administration. No written procedures for students and staff if substance abuse is suspected.

Support Services

On campus AA, private counseling.

Employee assistance Program for chemically dependent employees not available. Staff working with drug/alcohol-related issues: 2 part-time.

Disciplinary Actions

Alcohol Results of infractions of alcohol regulations (see Comparative Table of Alcohol Regulations) include fines. Other measures may also be taken.

Drugs For any use: varies by situation—counseling, warning. For first-time possession: varies by situation—counseling, warning. For subsequent possession: varies by situation—warning. For first-time sale: varies by situation—counseling, suspension. For subsequent sale: varies by situation.

Additional Information from the College

The College has been awarded an FIPSE Alcohol and Drug Prevention grant. Briar Cliff's approach to prevention and treatment is broadly based on concepts of addiction and the family. Programs have featured speakers on addiction, treatment, ACOA, and nonalcoholic programming. Very active Bacchus chapter.

For More Information

Contact: Donna L. Gilligan McMillan, Director of Residence Life, 3303 Rebecca St., Briar Cliff College, Sioux City, IA 51104. Telephone: 712-279-5494.

BRIDGEWATER STATE COLLEGE

Bridgewater, Massachusetts

General Information

State-supported 5-year coed college. Founded 1840. Awards B, M. Primary accreditation: regional. Small-town setting; 170-acre campus. Total enrollment: 5,339. Faculty: 324 (266 full-time, 58 part-time). Social organizations: 3 national fraternities, 2 national sororities, 3 local fraternities, 1 local sorority, 2 coed fraternities; 8% of eligible undergraduate men and 3% of eligible undergraduate women are members.

Drug and Alcohol Information

Education

On campus Drug and alcohol education/prevention programs offered for: all students, faculty, administration. Authorized group concerned with responsible drinking. College holds an annual alcohol awareness week.

Identification of Problems

Admissions College application does not ask about prior substance abuse problems.

On campus Current students identified as chemically dependent may remain enrolled. Comments: Subject to College due process procedures. No training program on identifying students with potential substance abuse problems. No written procedures for students and staff if substance abuse is suspected.

Support Services

On campus AA, ACOA, private counseling, referral to off-campus agencies.

Employee assistance Program for chemically dependent employees available. Staff working with drug/alcohol-related issues: 6 part-time.

Disciplinary Actions

Alcohol Results of infractions of alcohol regulations (see Comparative Table of Alcohol Regulations) vary by situation but can include counseling, warning, probation, suspension, expulsion. Comments: Subject to College due process procedures.

Drugs For any use, possession, or sale: suspension, expulsion. Comments: Students who violate College policies regarding drugs and/or alcohol may also be subject to criminal prosecution under state and federal laws.

Additional Information from the College

To fulfill its responsibilities to keep students informed on the issues, Bridgewater State College has formed the Drug and Alcohol Awareness Task Force program, a comprehensive program with four components: policy development, educational programming, intervention, and enforcement. Students, faculty, and professional staff all participate.

For More Information

Contact: Pam K. Arrighi, Associate for Student Services and Activities, Rondileau Campus Center, Bridgewater State College, Bridgewater, MA 02324. Telephone: 617-697-1273.

BRIGHAM YOUNG UNIVERSITY–HAWAII CAMPUS

Laie, Oahu, Hawaii

General Information

Independent 4-year coed college, affiliated with Church of Jesus Christ of Latter-day Saints. Administratively affiliated with Brigham Young University. Founded 1955. Awards A (college transfer and terminal), B. Primary accreditation: regional. Small-town setting; 60-acre campus. Total enrollment: 2,142. Faculty: 138 (98 full-time, 40 part-time).

Drug and Alcohol Information

Education

On campus Drug and alcohol education/prevention programs offered for: all students.

Identification of Problems

Admissions College application does not ask about prior substance abuse problems.

On campus Current students identified as chemically dependent may not remain enrolled. No training program on identifying students with potential substance abuse problems. Written procedures for students and staff if substance abuse is suspected.

Support Services

On campus Private counseling.

Off campus Ecclesiastical counseling.

Employee assistance Program for chemically dependent employees not available. Staff working with drug/alcohol-related issues: 1 part-time.

Disciplinary Actions

Alcohol Results of infractions of alcohol regulations (see Comparative Table of Alcohol Regulations) include counseling, probation, suspension.

Drugs For first-time use, possession, or sale: suspension. For subsequent use, possession, or sale: expulsion.

Additional Information from the College

Students are required, before admission, to sign a commitment to refrain from all alcohol use, on or off campus. A student who has had past problems but is no longer using drugs and is working with a counselor and an ecclesiastical leader may remain enrolled at the University.

For More Information

Contact: Calley Haneberg, Coordinator of Placement, Cooperative Education, P.O. Box 1978, Brigham Young University–Hawaii, Laie, HI 96762-1294. Telephone: 808-293-3526.

BROWN UNIVERSITY

Providence, Rhode Island

General Information

Independent comprehensive coed institution. Founded 1764. Awards B, M, D. Primary accreditation: regional. City setting; 146-acre campus. Total enrollment: 7,612. Faculty: 548 (538 full-time, 10 part-time). Social organizations: 10 national fraternities, 1 national sorority, 4 coed fraternities;

11% of eligible undergraduate men and 1% of eligible undergraduate women are members.

Drug and Alcohol Information

Education

On campus Drug and alcohol education/prevention programs offered for: all students, athletes/coaches, faculty, administration, children of alcoholics; required for: freshmen. Authorized group concerned with responsible drinking. College holds an annual alcohol awareness week and drug awareness week.

Identification of Problems

Admissions College application question about prior substance abuse problems is part of the health history form.

On campus Current students identified as chemically dependent may remain enrolled, but treatment is required. Training program on identifying students with potential substance abuse problems for: resident advisers, coaches, Greek officers, faculty, administration. Written procedures for students and staff if substance abuse is suspected.

Support Services

On campus AA, NA, Al-Anon, ACOA, support groups (abstinence support), private counseling.

Employee assistance Program for chemically dependent employees available. Staff working with drug/alcohol-related issues: 1 full-time and 4 part-time.

Disciplinary Actions

Alcohol Results of infractions of alcohol regulations (see Comparative Table of Alcohol Regulations) vary by situation but can include chemical dependency assessment, counseling, warning, probation, suspension, expulsion.

Drugs For any use: varies by situation. For first-time possession: varies by situation—chemical dependency assessment, counseling, warning. For subsequent possession: varies by situation. For first-time sale: probation, suspension, expulsion. For subsequent sale: suspension, expulsion.

For More Information

Contact: Roger Pyle, Health Educator, Office of Health Education, Box 1928, Brown University, Providence, RI 02912. Telephone: 401-863-2794.

BRYN MAWR COLLEGE

Bryn Mawr, Pennsylvania

General Information

Independent comprehensive primarily women's institution. Founded 1885. Awards B, M, D. Primary accreditation: regional. Small-town setting; 135-acre campus. Total enrollment: 1,847. Faculty: 196 (124 full-time, 72 part-time).

Drug and Alcohol Information

Education

On campus Drug and alcohol education/prevention programs offered for: all students, faculty, administration; required for freshmen, athletes/coaches, resident advisers. Authorized group concerned with responsible drinking. College holds an annual alcohol awareness week and drug awareness week.

Identification of Problems

Admissions College application question about prior substance abuse problems is used to explain past academic performance; for counseling and referral, if student is admitted; in the admissions decision. The College requires extensive medical information from those admitted, but does not discriminate against applicants who are recovering from chemical dependency.

On campus Current students identified as chemically dependent may remain enrolled, but treatment is required. Training program on identifying students with potential substance abuse problems for: resident advisers, coaches, administration. Written procedures for students and staff if substance abuse is suspected.

Support Services

On campus AA, NA, Al-Anon, private counseling.

Employee assistance Program for chemically dependent employees available. Staff working with drug/alcohol-related issues: 1 full-time and 6 part-time.

Disciplinary Actions

Alcohol Results of infractions of alcohol regulations (see Comparative Table of Alcohol Regulations) vary by situation but can include chemical dependency assessment, counseling, warning, probation, suspension, expulsion. Comments: Decision is made by Honor Board.

Drugs For any use, possession, or sale: varies by situation—decision is made by Honor Board. Comments: In its work, the Honor Board makes use of consultants with expertise in chemical dependency and its assessment.

Additional Information from the College

At Bryn Mawr and Haverford colleges, professional staff and volunteer student peer educators provide a comprehensive program of education, referral, and support. Rehabilitation services are available off campus. Freshmen participate in a thirteen-week wellness program that includes sessions on alcohol and drug abuse prevention.

For More Information

Contact: Charles Heyduk, Director of Student Services, Campus Center Building, Bryn Mawr College, Bryn Mawr, PA 19010. Telephone: 215-526-7331.

BUENA VISTA COLLEGE

Storm Lake, Iowa

General Information

Independent Presbyterian 4-year coed college. Founded 1891. Awards B. Primary accreditation: regional. Small-town setting; 40-acre campus. Total enrollment: 1,086. Faculty: 87 (70 full-time, 17 part-time). Social organization: 1 national fraternity; 3% of eligible undergraduate men and 2% of eligible undergraduate women are members.

Drug and Alcohol Information

Education

On campus Drug and alcohol education/prevention programs offered for: all students. Authorized group concerned with responsible drinking. College holds an annual alcohol awareness week and drug awareness week.

Identification of Problems

Admissions College application does not ask about prior substance abuse problems.

On campus Current students identified as chemically dependent may remain enrolled, but treatment is required.

Buena Vista College (continued)

No training program on identifying students with potential substance abuse problems. Written procedures for students and staff if substance abuse is suspected.

Support Services

On campus ACOA.

Employee assistance Program for chemically dependent employees available. Staff working with drug/alcohol-related issues: 7 part-time.

Disciplinary Actions

Alcohol Results of infractions of alcohol regulations (see Comparative Table of Alcohol Regulations) vary by situation but can include chemical dependency assessment, counseling, warning, probation, suspension, expulsion, fines.

Drugs For any use or possession: varies by situation. For first-time sale: probation, suspension, expulsion. For subsequent sale: expulsion.

Additional Information from the College

Although there is no formal assistance program for chemically dependent employees, the part-time substance abuse counselor has helped employees as well as students.

For More Information

Contact: Ivan Harlan, Vice President for Student Services, Buena Vista College, College and W. 4th Sts., Storm Lake, IA 50588. Telephone: 712-749-2123.

BURLINGTON COLLEGE

Burlington, Vermont

General Information

Independent 4-year coed college. Founded 1972. Awards A (college transfer), B. Primary accreditation: regional. Small-town setting; 1-acre campus. Total enrollment: 183.

Drug and Alcohol Information

Education

On campus Drug and alcohol education/prevention programs offered for: all students.

Identification of Problems

Admissions College application does not ask about prior substance abuse problems.

On campus Current students identified as chemically dependent may remain enrolled. No training program on identifying students with potential substance abuse problems.

Support Services

On campus No support services on campus.

Off campus AA, NA, Al-Anon, ACOA, other support groups.

Employee assistance Program for chemically dependent employees not available.

Disciplinary Actions

Alcohol Results of infractions of alcohol regulations (see Comparative Table of Alcohol Regulations) vary by situation.

Drugs For any use, possession, or sale: varies by situation.

Additional Information from the College

Burlington College serves a number of "at risk" adults, many in various stages of recovery, and is becoming more sensitive to their special needs. Increased support services and staff training options are being explored. The College feels it inappropriate to become involved in the personal lives of its adult, nonresident students. A student whose academic progress is endangered by substance abuse and who refuses treatment would be asked to leave. However, Burlington College is sensitive to the problem and tries to steer students toward treatments.

For More Information

Contact: Dennis McBee, Director of Admissions, Burlington College, 95 North Ave., Burlington, VT 05401. Telephone: 802-862-9616.

BUTLER UNIVERSITY

Indianapolis, Indiana

General Information

Independent 5-year coed college. Founded 1855. Awards A (college transfer), B, M. Primary accreditation: regional. Metropolitan setting; 290-acre campus. Total enrollment: 3,912. Faculty: 392 (191 full-time, 201 part-time). Social organizations: 7 national fraternities, 7 national sororities, minority chapters community-wide; 43% of eligible undergraduate men and 38% of eligible undergraduate women are members.

Drug and Alcohol Information

Education

On campus Drug and alcohol education/prevention programs offered for: all students, athletes/coaches, faculty, administration; required for: resident advisers, peer educators, Bacchus members. Bacchus chapter: 27 members. College holds an annual alcohol awareness week and drug awareness week.

Identification of Problems

Admissions College application does not ask about prior substance abuse problems, but this policy is being reevaluated.

On campus Current students identified as chemically dependent may remain enrolled, but treatment is required. Comments: Decisions concerning intervention are made on a case-by-case basis. Training program on identifying students with potential substance abuse problems for: resident advisers, Greek officers; for coaches, faculty, administration, peer educators, Bacchus members on request. Written procedures for students and staff if substance abuse is suspected.

Support Services

On campus AA, ACOA, support groups, private counseling, psychiatric consultations.

Off campus NA, Al-Anon.

Employee assistance Program for chemically dependent employees available. Staff working with drug/alcohol-related issues: 1 full-time.

Disciplinary Actions

Alcohol Results of infractions of alcohol regulations (see Comparative Table of Alcohol Regulations) vary by situation but can include chemical dependency assessment, counseling, warning, probation, suspension, expulsion, mandatory Alcohol Education Program.

Drugs For any use, possession, or sale: varies by situation.

Additional Information from the College

Butler University's utilization of peer educators has

resulted in a national model. The Bacchus chapter has been named as outstanding in the nation for three years in the private college category, its adviser similarly acknowledged for the two years such an honor has been bestowed. Both the adviser and the group have consulted with colleges and universities nationwide.

For More Information

Contact: Robert P. Kirsch, Director, Alcohol and Drug Center, Butler University, 4600 Sunset Ave., Indianapolis, IN 46208. Telephone: 317-283-9385.

CABRINI COLLEGE

Radnor, Pennsylvania

General Information

Independent Roman Catholic 5-year coed college. Founded 1957. Awards B, M. Primary accreditation: regional. Small-town setting; 110-acre campus. Total enrollment: 1,264. Faculty: 97 (31 full-time, 66 part-time). Social organization: 1 national fraternity.

Drug and Alcohol Information

Education

On campus Drug and alcohol education/prevention programs offered for: all students, faculty, administration; required for: resident advisers. Authorized group concerned with responsible drinking. College holds an annual alcohol awareness week and drug awareness week.

Identification of Problems

Admissions College application does not ask about prior substance abuse problems.

On campus Current students identified as chemically dependent may remain enrolled, but treatment is required. No training program on identifying students with potential substance abuse problems. No written procedures for students and staff if substance abuse is suspected.

Support Services

On campus AA, support groups (peer support), private counseling.

Employee assistance Program for chemically dependent employees not available. Staff working with drug/alcohol-related issues: 2 part-time.

Disciplinary Actions

Alcohol Results of infractions of alcohol regulations (see Comparative Table of Alcohol Regulations) include counseling, fines. Comments: Depends on severity of infraction.

Drugs For first-time use or possession: chemical dependency assessment, counseling, probation. For subsequent use or possession: varies by situation. For any sale: expulsion.

For More Information

Contact: Cynthia Galan, Health Educator, Cabrini College, Eagle and King of Prussia Rds., Radnor, PA 19087. Telephone: 215-971-8400.

CALDWELL COLLEGE

Caldwell, New Jersey

General Information

Independent Roman Catholic 4-year coed college. Founded 1939. Awards B. Primary accreditation: regional. Small-town setting; 100-acre campus. Total enrollment: 950. Faculty: 79 (38 full-time, 41 part-time). Social organizations: 1 national sorority, 1 local sorority.

Drug and Alcohol Information

Education

On campus Drug and alcohol education/prevention programs offered for: all students, faculty, administration; required for freshmen, athletes/coaches, student leaders. Authorized group concerned with responsible drinking. College holds an annual alcohol awareness week and drug awareness week.

Identification of Problems

Admissions College application does not ask about prior substance abuse problems.

On campus Current students identified as chemically dependent may remain enrolled, but treatment is required. No training program on identifying students with potential substance abuse problems. No written procedures for students and staff if substance abuse is suspected.

Support Services

On campus Support groups (group counseling workshops), private counseling.

Employee assistance Program for chemically dependent employees not available. Staff working with drug/alcohol-related issues: 3 part-time.

Disciplinary Actions

Alcohol Results of infractions of alcohol regulations (see Comparative Table of Alcohol Regulations) include counseling, probation, suspension. Comments: Repeated infractions by an individual may lead to expulsion.

Drugs For any use: varies by situation—counseling, suspension. For any possession: varies by situation—counseling, warning, probation. For any sale: expulsion.

For More Information

Contact: Bernadette Manno, Director of Counseling Center, Caldwell College, Caldwell, NJ 07006. Telephone: 201-228-4424.

CALIFORNIA BAPTIST COLLEGE

Riverside, California

General Information

Independent Southern Baptist 5-year coed college. Founded 1950. Awards B, M. Primary accreditation: regional. City setting; 75-acre campus. Total enrollment: 666. Faculty: 64 (42 full-time, 22 part-time).

Drug and Alcohol Information

Education

On campus Drug and alcohol education/prevention programs offered for: all students, athletes/coaches; required for freshmen, resident advisers, student leaders.

Identification of Problems

Admissions College application question about prior substance abuse prroblems is used for counseling and referral, if student is admitted; in the admissions decision.

On campus Current students identified as chemically dependent may remain enrolled, but treatment is required. Training program on identifying students with potential

California Baptist College (continued)

substance abuse problems for: resident advisers. Written procedures for students and staff if substance abuse is suspected.

Support Services

On campus Support groups, private counseling.

Employee assistance Program for chemically dependent employees not available. Staff working with drug/alcohol-related issues: 8 part-time.

Disciplinary Actions

Alcohol Results of infractions of alcohol regulations (see Comparative Table of Alcohol Regulations) include chemical dependency assessment, counseling, warning, probation, suspension, expulsion.

Drugs For any use, possession, or sale: expulsion.

For More Information

Contact: Dr. Dennis Sheriden, Vice President for Student Life, California Baptist College, 8432 Magnolia Ave., Riverside, CA 92504. Telephone: 714-689-5771.

CALIFORNIA INSTITUTE OF TECHNOLOGY

Pasadena, California

General Information

Independent comprehensive coed institution. Founded 1891. Awards B, M, D. Primary accreditation: regional. City setting; 124-acre campus. Total enrollment: 1,841. Faculty: 270.

Drug and Alcohol Information

Education

On campus Drug and alcohol education/prevention programs offered for: all students, athletes/coaches, faculty, administration; required for: freshmen, resident advisers, student affairs staff, student peer counselors.

Identification of Problems

Admissions College application does not ask about prior substance abuse problems.

On campus Current students identified as chemically dependent may remain enrolled. Comments: Whether or not treatment is required varies by situation. Training program on identifying students with potential substance abuse problems for: resident advisers, administration, student affairs staff, student peer counselors. Written procedures for students and staff if substance abuse is suspected.

Support Services

On campus AA, private counseling, assessment and referrals by Human Relations Advisor.

Employee assistance Program for chemically dependent employees available. Staff working with drug/alcohol-related issues: 1 full-time and 7 part-time.

Disciplinary Actions

Alcohol Results of infractions of alcohol regulations (see Comparative Table of Alcohol Regulations) vary by situation. Comments: The student Honor System Board reviews each infraction on a case-by-case basis.

Drugs For any use, possession, or sale: varies by situation.

Additional Information from the College

For the past two years, Caltech has engaged the counseling services of a prominent expert in the field of substance abuse prevention and treatment. She has helped in the formulation of the Institute's student and staff education, training programs, and policy. Caltech believes that they have been quite successful with their student substance abuse prevention program, especially in making students aware that they should act responsibly and refrain from actions that are damaging to others.

For More Information

Contact: Jeanne Noda, Associate Dean of Students, Office of the Dean 102-31, California Institute of Technology, 1201 E. California Blvd., Pasadena, CA 91125. Telephone: 818-356-6351.

CALIFORNIA INSTITUTE OF THE ARTS

Valencia, California

General Information

Independent 5-year coed college. Founded 1961. Awards B, M. Primary accreditation: regional. Small-town setting; 60-acre campus. Total enrollment: 850. Faculty: 175 (91 full-time, 84 part-time).

Drug and Alcohol Information

Education

On campus Drug and alcohol education/prevention programs not offered. Authorized group concerned with responsible drinking.

Identification of Problems

Admissions College application does not ask about prior substance abuse problems.

On campus Current students identified as chemically dependent may remain enrolled. No training program on identifying students with potential substance abuse problems. Written procedures for students and staff if substance abuse is suspected.

Support Services

On campus Private counseling.

Employee assistance Program for chemically dependent employees available.

Disciplinary Actions

Alcohol Results of infractions of alcohol regulations (see Comparative Table of Alcohol Regulations) include counseling, warning.

Drugs For first-time use or possession: varies by situation. For subsequent use: counseling. For subsequent possession: warning. For any sale: expulsion.

For More Information

Contact: Yvonne Guy, Counselor, California Institute of the Arts, 24700 McBean Pkwy., Valencia, CA 91355. Telephone: 805-255-1050 Ext. 2522.

CALIFORNIA MARITIME ACADEMY
Vallejo, California

General Information
State-supported 4-year specialized primarily men's college. Founded 1929. Awards B. Primary accreditation: regional. City setting; 67-acre campus. Total enrollment: 295. Faculty: 30 (26 full-time, 4 part-time).

Drug and Alcohol Information
Education
On campus Drug and alcohol education/prevention programs offered for: all students, athletes/coaches, faculty, administration; required for: freshmen. College holds an annual alcohol awareness week and drug awareness week.

Identification of Problems
Admissions College application question about prior substance abuse problems is used because a student must be drug-free to be eligible for necessary maritime documents issued by the U.S. Coast Guard.

On campus Current students identified as chemically dependent may remain enrolled, but treatment is required. No training program on identifying students with potential substance abuse problems. Written procedures for students and staff if substance abuse is suspected.

Support Services
On campus Private counseling, referral.

Employee assistance Program for chemically dependent employees available. Staff working with drug/alcohol-related issues: 10 part-time.

Disciplinary Actions
Alcohol Results of infractions of alcohol regulations (see Comparative Table of Alcohol Regulations) can include chemical dependency assessment, counseling, warning, probation, suspension, expulsion.

Drugs For first-time use or possession: suspension. For subsequent use or possession: expulsion. For any sale: expulsion.

Additional Information from the College
The Academy's goal is an environment that does not tolerate alcohol abuse or drug use on the campus.

For More Information
Contact: Dr. Louis M. McDermott, Vice President for Student Affairs, California Maritime Academy, P.O. Box 1392, Vallejo, CA 94590. Telephone: 707-648-4213.

CALIFORNIA POLYTECHNIC STATE UNIVERSITY, SAN LUIS OBISPO
San Luis Obispo, California

General Information
State-supported 5-year coed college. Part of California State University System. Founded 1901. Awards A (terminal), B, M. Primary accreditation: regional. Small-town setting; 5,000-acre campus. Total enrollment: 16,553. Faculty: 1,167 (788 full-time, 379 part-time). Social organizations: 19 national fraternities, 8 national sororities, 3 local fraternities; 10% of eligible undergraduate men and 10% of eligible undergraduate women are members.

Drug and Alcohol Information
Education
On campus Drug and alcohol education/prevention programs offered for: all students, athletes/coaches, faculty, administration. Authorized group concerned with responsible drinking. College holds an annual alcohol awareness week and drug awareness week.

Identification of Problems
Admissions College application does not ask about prior substance abuse problems.

On campus Current students identified as chemically dependent may remain enrolled. No training program on identifying students with potential substance abuse problems. No written procedures for students and staff if substance abuse is suspected.

Support Services
On campus AA, NA, Al-Anon, ACOA, private counseling.

Employee assistance Program for chemically dependent employees not available. Staff working with drug/alcohol-related issues: 5 part-time.

Disciplinary Actions
Alcohol Results of infractions of alcohol regulations (see Comparative Table of Alcohol Regulations) include chemical dependency assessment, counseling, warning, suspension. Comments: Expulsion is possible, but most unlikely.

Drugs For first-time use, possession, or sale: varies by situation—counseling, warning. For subsequent use, possession, or sale: varies by situation.

For More Information
Contact: Carolyn Hurwitz, Health Educator, Health Center, California Polytechnic State University, San Luis Obispo, San Luis Obispo, CA 93407. Telephone: 805-756-1211.

CALIFORNIA STATE POLYTECHNIC UNIVERSITY, POMONA
Pomona, California

General Information
State-supported 5-year coed college. Part of California State University System. Founded 1938. Awards B, M. Primary accreditation: regional. City setting; 1,500-acre campus. Total enrollment: 18,930. Faculty: 1,082 (667 full-time, 415 part-time). Social organizations: 11 national fraternities, 6 national sororities, local fraternities, local sororities, 1 coed fraternity.

Drug and Alcohol Information
Education
On campus Drug and alcohol education/prevention programs offered for: all students, athletes/coaches. Authorized group concerned with responsible drinking. College holds an annual alcohol awareness week.

Identification of Problems
Admissions College application does not ask about prior substance abuse problems.

California State Polytechnic University, Pomona (continued)

On campus Current students identified as chemically dependent may remain enrolled. Training program on identifying students with potential substance abuse problems for: resident advisers, coaches, counselors, health personnel. No written procedures for students and staff if substance abuse is suspected.

Support Services

On campus AA, private counseling.

Employee assistance Program for chemically dependent employees available.

Disciplinary Actions

Alcohol Results of infractions of alcohol regulations (see Comparative Table of Alcohol Regulations) vary by situation.

Drugs For first-time use or possession: counseling, probation, suspension. For subsequent use: suspension. For subsequent possession: suspension, expulsion. For any sale: expulsion.

For More Information

Contact: Dr. Sara Arroyo, Director, Health and Psychological Sciences, California State Polytechnic University, Pomona, 3801 W. Temple Ave., Pomona, CA 91768. Telephone: 714-869-2760.

CALIFORNIA STATE UNIVERSITY, BAKERSFIELD

Bakersfield, California

General Information

State-supported 5-year coed college. Part of California State University System. Founded 1970. Awards B, M. Primary accreditation: regional. City setting; 375-acre campus. Total enrollment: 4,930. Faculty: 257 (194 full-time, 63 part-time). Social organizations: 3 national fraternities, 2 national sororities; 1% of eligible undergraduate men and 1% of eligible undergraduate women are members.

Drug and Alcohol Information

Education

On campus Drug and alcohol education/prevention programs offered for: all students, athletes/coaches, faculty, administration. Authorized group concerned with responsible drinking. College holds an annual alcohol awareness week and drug awareness week.

Identification of Problems

Admissions College application does not ask about prior substance abuse problems.

On campus Current students identified as chemically dependent may remain enrolled. Training program on identifying students with potential substance abuse problems for: resident advisers, coaches, Greek officers, faculty, administration. Written procedures for students and staff if substance abuse is suspected.

Support Services

On campus AA.

Employee assistance Program for chemically dependent employees not available. Staff working with drug/alcohol-related issues: 10 part-time.

Disciplinary Actions

Alcohol Results of infractions of alcohol regulations (see Comparative Table of Alcohol Regulations) vary by situation but can include chemical dependency assessment.

Drugs For any use, possession, or sale: varies by situation.

For More Information

Contact: Willis Hill, Counselor, California State University, Bakersfield, 9001 Stockdale Hwy., Bakersfield, CA 93311-1099. Telephone: 805-664-2131.

CALIFORNIA STATE UNIVERSITY, DOMINGUEZ HILLS

Carson, California

General Information

State-supported 5-year coed college. Part of California State University System. Founded 1960. Awards B, M. Primary accreditation: regional. City setting; 350-acre campus. Total enrollment: 7,869. Social organizations: 1 national fraternity, 1 national sorority.

Drug and Alcohol Information

Education

On campus Drug and alcohol education/prevention programs offered for: all students, athletes/coaches, faculty, administration. College holds an annual alcohol awareness week and drug awareness week.

Identification of Problems

Admissions College application does not ask about prior substance abuse problems.

On campus Current students identified as chemically dependent may remain enrolled. No training program on identifying students with potential substance abuse problems. No written procedures for students and staff if substance abuse is suspected.

Support Services

On campus AA, NA, Al-Anon, private counseling, ACA therapy group.

Employee assistance Program for chemically dependent employees available. Staff working with drug/alcohol-related issues: 1 full-time and 4 part-time.

Disciplinary Actions

Alcohol Results of infractions of alcohol regulations (see Comparative Table of Alcohol Regulations) include counseling, warning, probation, suspension, expulsion. Comments: Campus organization can lose recognition and registration.

Drugs For any use, possession, or sale: varies by situation.

Additional Information from the College

The Serenity Center, a drug and alcohol information center, was established under a FIPSE grant in January 1988. An alcohol and drug free policy is being written that will address not only allowable uses but also enforcement and disciplinary procedures for abuse and violations of the law.

For More Information

Contact: Bob Hargrave, Coordinator, Serenity Center, California State University, Dominguez Hills, 1000 E. Victoria St., Carson, CA 90747. Telephone: 213-516-3656.

CALIFORNIA STATE UNIVERSITY, FRESNO

Fresno, California

General Information

State-supported 5-year coed college. Part of California State University System. Founded 1911. Awards B, M. Primary accreditation: regional. City setting; 1,410-acre campus. Total enrollment: 19,124. Faculty: 1,143 (792 full-time, 351 part-time). Social organizations: 11 national fraternities, 6 national sororities; 4% of eligible undergraduate men and 3% of eligible undergraduate women are members.

Drug and Alcohol Information

Education

On campus Drug and alcohol education/prevention programs offered for: all students, faculty. Authorized group concerned with responsible drinking. College holds an annual alcohol awareness week.

Identification of Problems

Admissions College application does not ask about prior substance abuse problems.

On campus Current students identified as chemically dependent may remain enrolled. No training program on identifying students with potential substance abuse problems. No written procedures for students and staff if substance abuse is suspected.

Support Services

On campus AA, NA, Al-Anon, private counseling.

Employee assistance Program for chemically dependent employees available.

Disciplinary Actions

Alcohol Results of infractions of alcohol regulations (see Comparative Table of Alcohol Regulations) vary by situation but can include chemical dependency assessment, counseling, warning, probation, suspension, expulsion, involvement of police.

Drugs For first-time use or possession: varies by situation. For subsequent use: counseling, probation, suspension. For subsequent possession: probation, suspension. For first-time sale: suspension, expulsion, referral to police. For subsequent sale: expulsion, referral to police.

For More Information

Contact: Sam Gitchell, Health Educator, Student Health Center, California State University, Fresno, Shaw and Cedar Aves., Fresno, CA 93740. Telephone: 209-294-2734.

CALIFORNIA STATE UNIVERSITY, FULLERTON

Fullerton, California

General Information

State-supported 5-year coed college. Part of California State University System. Founded 1957. Awards B, M. Primary accreditation: regional. City setting; 225-acre campus. Total enrollment: 24,700. Faculty: 1,398 (732 full-time, 666 part-time). Social organizations: 12 national fraternities, 8 national sororities, local fraternities, local sororities; 9% of eligible undergraduate men and 8% of eligible undergraduate women are members.

Drug and Alcohol Information

Education

On campus Drug and alcohol education/prevention programs offered for: all students. College holds an annual alcohol awareness week.

Identification of Problems

Admissions College application does not ask about prior substance abuse problems.

On campus Current students identified as chemically dependent may remain enrolled. No training program on identifying students with potential substance abuse problems. No written procedures for students and staff if substance abuse is suspected.

Support Services

On campus AA, Al-Anon, ACOA, private counseling.

Employee assistance Program for chemically dependent employees available.

Disciplinary Actions

Alcohol Results of infractions of alcohol regulations (see Comparative Table of Alcohol Regulations) vary by situation.

Drugs For any use or possession: varies by situation. For first-time sale: suspension. For subsequent sale: expulsion.

For More Information

Contact: Roger Nudd, Substance Abuse Education Officer, Career Development Center, California State University, Fullerton, Fullerton, CA 92634. Telephone: 714-773-3121.

CALIFORNIA STATE UNIVERSITY, SACRAMENTO

Sacramento, California

General Information

State-supported 5-year coed college. Part of California State University System. Founded 1947. Awards B, M. Primary accreditation: regional. Metropolitan setting; 288-acre campus. Total enrollment: 25,153. Faculty: 1,378 (870 full-time, 508 part-time). Social organizations: 15 national fraternities, 8 national sororities, 1 local sorority; 7% of eligible undergraduate men and 4% of eligible undergraduate women are members.

Drug and Alcohol Information

Education

On campus Drug and alcohol education/prevention programs offered for: social organization members. Authorized group concerned with responsible drinking.

Identification of Problems

On campus Current students identified as chemically dependent may remain enrolled.

Support Services

On campus NA, Al-Anon, ACOA.

Disciplinary Actions

Alcohol Results of infractions of alcohol regulations (see Comparative Table of Alcohol Regulations) include probation, suspension, expulsion.

Drugs For any use, possession, or sale: varies by situation.

California State University, Sacramento (continued)

For More Information

Contact: Laurie Bisset-Grady, Health Educator, California State University, Sacramento, 6000 J Street, Sacramento, CA 95819. Telephone: 916-278-6665.

CALIFORNIA STATE UNIVERSITY, SAN BERNARDINO

San Bernardino, California

General Information

State-supported 5-year coed college. Part of California State University System. Founded 1962. Awards B, M. Primary accreditation: regional. City setting; 430-acre campus. Total enrollment: 8,300. Social organizations: national fraternities, national sororities, local fraternities, local sororities.

Drug and Alcohol Information

Education

On campus Drug and alcohol education/prevention programs offered for: all students. Bacchus chapter: 44 members. College holds an annual alcohol awareness week and drug awareness week.

Identification of Problems

Admissions College application does not ask about prior substance abuse problems.

On campus Current students identified as chemically dependent may remain enrolled. Training program on identifying students with potential substance abuse problems for: resident advisers, coaches, Greek officers, faculty, administration. Written procedures for students and staff if substance abuse is suspected.

Support Services

On campus Al-Anon, private counseling.

Employee assistance Program for chemically dependent employees available. Staff working with drug/alcohol-related issues: 2 full-time.

Disciplinary Actions

Alcohol Results of infractions of alcohol regulations (see Comparative Table of Alcohol Regulations) include warning, probation, suspension.

Drugs For any use: varies by situation—counseling, warning, probation. For any possession: varies by situation—counseling, probation. For any sale: varies by situation—suspension, expulsion.

For More Information

Contact: Bridget Tucker, Counselor, California State University, San Bernardino, 5500 University Parkway, San Bernardino, CA 92407. Telephone: 714-887-7437.

CALIFORNIA STATE UNIVERSITY, STANISLAUS

Turlock, California

General Information

State-supported 5-year coed college. Part of California State University System. Founded 1957. Awards B, M. Primary accreditation: regional. Small-town setting; 230-acre campus. Total enrollment: 5,282. Faculty: 300 (214 full-time, 86 part-time).

Drug and Alcohol Information

Education

On campus Drug and alcohol education/prevention programs offered for: all students, athletes/coaches. Authorized group concerned with responsible drinking. College holds an annual alcohol awareness week.

Identification of Problems

Admissions College application does not ask about prior substance abuse problems.

On campus Current students identified as chemically dependent may remain enrolled. No training program on identifying students with potential substance abuse problems. No written procedures for students and staff if substance abuse is suspected.

Support Services

On campus Private counseling.

Employee assistance Program for chemically dependent employees not available.

Disciplinary Actions

Alcohol Results of infractions of alcohol regulations (see Comparative Table of Alcohol Regulations) include warning.

Drugs For any use, possession, or sale: varies by situation.

For More Information

Contact: Terry Peyton, Director of Student Life, California State University, Stanislaus, 801 West Monte Vista Ave., Turlock, CA 95380. Telephone: 209-667-3177.

CALIFORNIA UNIVERSITY OF PENNSYLVANIA

California, Pennsylvania

General Information

State-supported 5-year coed college. Part of State System of Higher Education. Founded 1852. Awards A (college transfer and terminal), B, M. Primary accreditation: regional. Small-town setting; 148-acre campus. Total enrollment: 6,313. Faculty: 354 (303 full-time, 51 part-time). Social organizations: 9 national fraternities, 7 national sororities; 10% of eligible undergraduate men and 10% of eligible undergraduate women are members.

Drug and Alcohol Information

Education

On campus Drug and alcohol education/prevention programs offered for: all students, athletes/coaches. College holds an annual alcohol awareness week and drug awareness week.

Identification of Problems

Admissions College application does not ask about prior substance abuse problems.

On campus Current students identified as chemically dependent may remain enrolled. Training program on identifying students with potential substance abuse problems for: resident advisers, anyone who requests it. Written procedures for students and staff if substance abuse is suspected.

Support Services

On campus AA, NA, ACOA, support groups, private counseling.

Employee assistance Program for chemically dependent employees available. Staff working with drug/alcohol-related issues: 1 full-time.

Disciplinary Actions

Alcohol Results of infractions of alcohol regulations (see Comparative Table of Alcohol Regulations) vary by situation but can include chemical dependency assessment.

Drugs For first-time use: varies by situation—chemical dependency assessment, warning. For first-time possession: chemical dependency assessment, warning. For subsequent use or possession: chemical dependency assessment, probation. For first-time sale: chemical dependency assessment, probation. For subsequent sale: chemical dependency assessment, suspension.

For More Information

Contact: Elizabeth Gruber, Drug and Alcohol Specialist, LRC 202, California University of Pennsylvania, California, PA 15419. Telephone: 412-938-4056.

CAMERON UNIVERSITY

Lawton, Oklahoma

General Information

State-supported 5-year coed college. Founded 1908. Awards A (terminal), B, M. Primary accreditation: regional. City setting; 160-acre campus. Total enrollment: 5,574. Faculty: 234 (185 full-time, 49 part-time). Social organizations: 3 national fraternities, 2 national sororities; 2% of eligible undergraduate men and 1% of eligible undergraduate women are members.

Drug and Alcohol Information

Education

On campus Drug and alcohol education/prevention programs offered for: social organization members; required for: resident advisers. College holds an annual alcohol awareness week.

Identification of Problems

Admissions College application does not ask about prior substance abuse problems.

On campus Current students identified as chemically dependent may not remain enrolled. Training program on identifying students with potential substance abuse problems for: resident advisers.

Support Services

On campus Private counseling.

Employee assistance Program for chemically dependent employees not available.

Disciplinary Actions

Alcohol Results of infractions of alcohol regulations (see Comparative Table of Alcohol Regulations) include counseling, warning, probation, suspension.

Drugs For first-time use: suspension. For first-time possession: probation, suspension. For first-time sale: suspension, expulsion. For subsequent use, possession, or sale: suspension, expulsion.

Additional Information from the College

Additional services and resources are planned, beginning in fall 1990. Free presentations on alcohol and drug abuse are available on request to all members of the academic community.

For More Information

Contact: Steve Rook, Director of Student Organizations and Activities, Cameron University, 2800 W. Gore, Lawton, OK 73505. Telephone: 405-581-2217.

CAMPBELLSVILLE COLLEGE

Campbellsville, Kentucky

General Information

Independent Baptist 4-year coed college. Founded 1906. Awards A (college transfer and terminal), B. Primary accreditation: regional. Small-town setting; 35-acre campus. Total enrollment: 734. Faculty: 56 (43 full-time, 13 part-time).

Drug and Alcohol Information

Education

On campus Drug and alcohol education/prevention programs offered for: all students, athletes/coaches. College holds an annual alcohol awareness week and drug awareness week (athletes required to attend).

Identification of Problems

Admissions College application does not ask about prior substance abuse problems.

On campus Current students identified as chemically dependent may remain enrolled, but treatment is required. Training program on identifying students with potential substance abuse problems for: resident advisers, faculty. Written procedures for students and staff if substance abuse is suspected.

Support Services

On campus Support groups, private counseling.

Off campus AA, substance abuse seminars.

Employee assistance Program for chemically dependent employees not available. Staff working with drug/alcohol-related issues: 2–3 part-time.

Disciplinary Actions

Alcohol Results of infractions of alcohol regulations (see Comparative Table of Alcohol Regulations) vary by situation but can include chemical dependency assessment, counseling, probation, suspension. Comments: More than 3 offenses merits suspension.

Drugs For first-time use: chemical dependency assessment, counseling, probation. For subsequent use: referral to counseling, suspension. For any possession: suspension. For any sale: suspension.

Additional Information from the College

Students who come for help voluntarily or are referred by faculty or staff members are not treated as discipline problems but are given counseling or referred to an off-campus agency. They are allowed to remain in classes, and the matter is kept confidential.

For More Information

Contact: Jeanette Hampton, RN, Campus Nurse, Campbellsville College, Box 575, 200 College St., Campbellsville, KY 42718. Telephone: 502-465-8158 Ext. 6223.

CAMPBELL UNIVERSITY

Buies Creek, North Carolina

General Information

Independent Baptist comprehensive coed institution. Founded 1887. Awards A (college transfer), B, M, D. Primary accreditation: regional. Rural setting; 1,200-acre campus. Total enrollment: 4,195. Faculty: 154 (120 full-time, 34 part-time).

Drug and Alcohol Information

Education

On campus Drug and alcohol education/prevention programs required for: freshmen.

Identification of Problems

Admissions College application question about prior substance abuse problems is used in the admissions decision.

On campus Current students identified as chemically dependent may not remain enrolled. Training program on identifying students with potential substance abuse problems for: resident advisers, coaches. Written procedures for students and staff if substance abuse is suspected.

Support Services

On campus Private counseling.

Employee assistance Program for chemically dependent employees not available. Staff working with drug/alcohol-related issues: 6 part-time.

Disciplinary Actions

Alcohol Results of infractions of alcohol regulations (see Comparative Table of Alcohol Regulations) include counseling, warning, probation, suspension.

Drugs For any use or possession: suspension. For any sale: expulsion.

Additional Information from the College

Campbell University is a member of the Christian Coalition. The use of alcohol or any drugs is strictly prohibited for faculty, staff, and students.

For More Information

Contact: Phillip L. Melvin, Dean of Student Life, Campbell University, P.O. Box 95, Buies Creek, NC 27506. Telephone: 919-893-4111 Ext. 2500.

CANISIUS COLLEGE

Buffalo, New York

General Information

Independent 5-year coed college. Founded 1870. Awards B, M. Primary accreditation: regional. Metropolitan setting; 22-acre campus. Total enrollment: 4,515. Faculty: 309 (184 full-time, 125 part-time). Social organizations: 1 national fraternity, 1 national sorority, 2 professional fraternities; 9% of eligible undergraduate men and 5% of eligible undergraduate women are members.

Drug and Alcohol Information

Education

On campus Drug and alcohol education/prevention programs offered for: all students; required for: social organization members, resident advisers. Bacchus chapter: 25 members. College holds an annual alcohol awareness week and drug awareness week.

Identification of Problems

Admissions College application does not ask about prior substance abuse problems.

On campus Current students identified as chemically dependent may remain enrolled. No training program on identifying students with potential substance abuse problems. No written procedures for students and staff if substance abuse is suspected.

Support Services

On campus Support groups, private counseling.

Employee assistance Program for chemically dependent employees available.

Disciplinary Actions

Alcohol Results of infractions of alcohol regulations (see Comparative Table of Alcohol Regulations) include counseling, warning, probation, suspension.

Drugs For any use, possession, or sale: varies by situation.

For More Information

Contact: Patricia Rissmeyer, Dean of Students, Canisius College, 2001 Main Street, Buffalo, NY 14208. Telephone: 716-888-2132.

CAPITAL UNIVERSITY

Columbus, Ohio

General Information

Independent 5-year coed college, affiliated with Evangelical Lutheran Church in America. Founded 1830. Awards B, M, D. Primary accreditation: regional. Metropolitan setting; 48-acre campus. Total enrollment: 3,016. Faculty: 163. Social organizations: 4 local fraternities, 4 local sororities; 20% of eligible undergraduate men and 25% of eligible undergraduate women are members.

Drug and Alcohol Information

Education

On campus Drug and alcohol education/prevention programs offered for: all students. Authorized group concerned with responsible drinking. College holds an annual alcohol awareness week and drug awareness week.

Identification of Problems

Admissions College application does not ask about prior substance abuse problems.

On campus Current students identified as chemically dependent may remain enrolled. Comments: Whether they are required to have treatment varies by situation. Training program on identifying students with potential substance abuse problems for: resident advisers. Written procedures for students and staff if substance abuse is suspected.

Support Services

On campus ACOA, support groups, private counseling.

Employee assistance Program for chemically dependent employees not available. Staff working with drug/alcohol-related issues: 15 part-time.

Disciplinary Actions

Alcohol Results of infractions of alcohol regulations (see Comparative Table of Alcohol Regulations) vary by situation.

Drugs For first-time use: varies by situation—chemical dependency assessment, counseling, probation. For first-time possession: varies by situation—probation. For subsequent use or possession: varies by situation. For any sale: expulsion.

For More Information

Contact: Ron Bell, Director of Residence Life, Capital University, 2199 E. Main St., Columbus, OH 43209. Telephone: 614-236-6811.

CAPITOL COLLEGE

Laurel, Maryland

General Information

Independent 4-year specialized coed college. Founded 1964. Awards A (college transfer and terminal), B. Primary accreditation: regional. Small-town setting; 52-acre campus. Total enrollment: 777. Faculty: 59 (19 full-time, 40 part-time).

Drug and Alcohol Information

Education

On campus Drug and alcohol education/prevention programs offered for: all students. Authorized group concerned with responsible drinking. College holds an annual alcohol awareness week and drug awareness week.

Identification of Problems

Admissions College application does not ask about prior substance abuse problems.

On campus Current students identified as chemically dependent may remain enrolled. Training program on identifying students with potential substance abuse problems for: resident advisers. No written procedures for students and staff if substance abuse is suspected.

Support Services

On campus Private counseling.

Employee assistance Program for chemically dependent employees not available.

Disciplinary Actions

Alcohol Results of infractions of alcohol regulations (see Comparative Table of Alcohol Regulations) vary by situation.

Drugs For any use or possession: varies by situation. For any sale: expulsion.

For More Information

Contact: Don Dresner, Coordinator of Student Development, Capitol College, 11301 Springfield Rd., Laurel, MD 20708.Telephone: 301-953-0060 Ext. 120.

CARDINAL STRITCH COLLEGE

Milwaukee, Wisconsin

General Information

Independent Roman Catholic 5-year coed college. Founded 1937. Awards A (college transfer and terminal), B, M. Primary accreditation: regional. Metropolitan setting; 40-acre campus. Total enrollment: 3,050. Faculty: 167 (43 full-time, 124 part-time).

Drug and Alcohol Information

Education

On campus Drug and alcohol education/prevention programs offered for: all students, athletes/coaches, faculty, administration. Authorized group concerned with responsible drinking. College holds an annual alcohol awareness week and drug awareness week.

Identification of Problems

Admissions College application question about prior substance abuse problems is used for counseling and referral, if student is admitted.

On campus Current students identified as chemically dependent may remain enrolled, but treatment is required. Training program on identifying students with potential substance abuse problems for: resident advisers, coaches, faculty, administration. Written procedures for students and staff if substance abuse is suspected.

Support Services

On campus ACOA, private counseling.

Off campus AA, NA, Al-Anon, and other support groups.

Employee assistance Program for chemically dependent employees available.

Disciplinary Actions

Alcohol Results of infractions of alcohol regulations (see Comparative Table of Alcohol Regulations) vary by situation but can include chemical dependency assessment, counseling, probation, suspension.

Drugs For first-time use or possession: varies by situation. For subsequent use or possession: expulsion. For any sale: expulsion.

Additional Information from the College

A detailed statement of Cardinal Stritch College's policies and procedures is available on request.

For More Information

Contact: Jean Masty, RN, Director, Health Service, Cardinal Stritch College, 6801 N. Yates Rd., Milwaukee, WI 53217. Telephone: 414-352-5400 Ext. 238.

CARLETON COLLEGE

Northfield, Minnesota

General Information

Independent 4-year coed college. Founded 1866. Awards B. Primary accreditation: regional. Small-town setting; 955-acre campus. Total enrollment: 1,885. Faculty: 151 (141 full-time, 10 part-time).

Drug and Alcohol Information

Education

On campus Drug and alcohol education/prevention programs offered for: all students, faculty, administration. Authorized group concerned with responsible drinking. College holds an annual alcohol awareness week and drug awareness week.

Identification of Problems

Admissions College application does not ask about prior substance abuse problems; however, housing application form does.

On campus Current students identified as chemically dependent may remain enrolled. Training program on identifying students with potential substance abuse

Carleton College (continued)

problems for: resident advisers. Written procedures for students and staff if substance abuse is suspected.

Support Services

On campus AA, Al-Anon, support groups, private counseling.

Employee assistance Program for chemically dependent employees available.

Disciplinary Actions

Alcohol Results of infractions of alcohol regulations (see Comparative Table of Alcohol Regulations) vary by situation but can include chemical dependency assessment, counseling, warning, probation, suspension, expulsion.

Drugs For any use or possession: varies by situation. For first-time sale: probation, suspension, expulsion. For subsequent sale: suspension, expulsion.

For More Information

Contact: Cris T. Roosenraad, Dean of Students, Carleton College, Northfield, MN 55057. Telephone: 507-663-4074.

CARLOW COLLEGE

Pittsburgh, Pennsylvania

General Information

Independent Roman Catholic 5-year primarily women's college. Founded 1929. Awards B, M. Primary accreditation: regional. Metropolitan setting; 13-acre campus. Total enrollment: 962. Faculty: 122 (52 full-time, 70 part-time).

Drug and Alcohol Information

Education

On campus Drug and alcohol education/prevention programs offered for: all students.

Identification of Problems

Admissions College application does not ask about prior substance abuse problems.

On campus Current students identified as chemically dependent may remain enrolled, but treatment is required. No training program on identifying students with potential substance abuse problems. Written procedures for students and staff if substance abuse is suspected.

Support Services

On campus AA, ACOA, private counseling.

Employee assistance Program for chemically dependent employees not available.

Disciplinary Actions

Alcohol Results of infractions of alcohol regulations (see Comparative Table of Alcohol Regulations) vary by situation.

Drugs For first-time use or possession: chemical dependency assessment, counseling, warning. For subsequent use: probation. For subsequent possession: probation, suspension. For any sale: expulsion.

For More Information

Contact: Suzanne Mobberley, Assistant Dean of Students, Carlow College, 3333 Fifth Ave., Pittsburgh, PA 15213. Telephone: 412-578-6000.

CARNEGIE MELLON UNIVERSITY

Pittsburgh, Pennsylvania

General Information

Independent comprehensive coed institution. Founded 1900. Awards B, M, D. Primary accreditation: regional. Metropolitan setting; 103-acre campus. Total enrollment: 6,993. Faculty: 737 (517 full-time, 220 part-time). Social organizations: 14 national fraternities, 5 national sororities; 30% of eligible undergraduate men and 30% of eligible undergraduate women are members.

Drug and Alcohol Information

Education

On campus Drug and alcohol education/prevention programs offered for: all students, athletes/coaches, faculty, administration. Bacchus chapter being established. College holds an annual alcohol awareness week and drug awareness week.

Identification of Problems

Admissions College application does not ask about prior substance abuse problems.

On campus Current students identified as chemically dependent may remain enrolled. Training program on identifying students with potential substance abuse problems for: resident advisers, coaches, Greek officers, faculty, administration. Written procedures for students and staff if substance abuse is suspected.

Support Services

On campus Support groups, private counseling.

Employee assistance Program for chemically dependent employees available. Staff working with drug/alcohol-related issues: 5 part-time.

Disciplinary Actions

Alcohol Results of infractions of alcohol regulations (see Comparative Table of Alcohol Regulations) include chemical dependency assessment, counseling, warning, probation, suspension.

Drugs For first-time use: varies by situation—chemical dependency assessment, counseling, probation. For subsequent use: varies by situation—counseling, suspension. For first-time possession: probation. For subsequent possession: suspension. For any sale: expulsion.

For More Information

Contact: Donna M. Morosky, Director of Health Education, Carnegie Mellon University, Pittsburgh, PA 15213. Telephone: 412-268-2075.

CARROLL COLLEGE

Waukesha, Wisconsin

General Information

Independent Presbyterian 4-year coed college. Founded 1846. Awards B. Primary accreditation: regional. City setting; 36-acre campus. Total enrollment: 1,393. Faculty: 133 (82 full-time, 51 part-time). Social organizations: 4 national fraternities, 4 national sororities; 30% of eligible undergraduate men and 25% of eligible undergraduate women are members.

Drug and Alcohol Information

Education

On campus Drug and alcohol education/prevention programs offered for: all students, athletes/coaches, faculty, administration. College holds an annual alcohol awareness week and drug awareness week.

Identification of Problems

Admissions College application does not ask about prior substance abuse problems.

On campus Current students identified as chemically dependent may remain enrolled, but treatment is required. Training program on identifying students with potential substance abuse problems for: resident advisers, coaches, Greek officers, faculty, administration. Written procedures for students and staff if substance abuse is suspected.

Support Services

On campus ACOA, private counseling.

Employee assistance Program for chemically dependent employees not available. Staff working with drug/alcohol-related issues: 1 full-time.

Disciplinary Actions

Alcohol Results of infractions of alcohol regulations (see Comparative Table of Alcohol Regulations) vary by situation but can include chemical dependency assessment, counseling, probation, suspension, expulsion. Comments: For the first offense, enrollment in an Alcohol Education class (fee $20).

Drugs For first-time use or possession: chemical dependency assessment, probation. For subsequent use or possession: suspension. For first-time sale: suspension. For subsequent sale: varies by situation.

For More Information

Contact: Mary Jo Fay, Director, Student Assistance Program, Carroll College, 100 N. East Ave., Waukesha, WI 53186. Telephone: 414-524-7335.

CARSON-NEWMAN COLLEGE

Jefferson City, Tennessee

General Information

Independent Southern Baptist 5-year coed college. Founded 1851. Awards B, M. Primary accreditation: regional. Small-town setting; 100-acre campus. Total enrollment: 2,003. Faculty: 122 (107 full-time, 15 part-time). Social organizations: 2 local fraternities, 2 local sororities; 50% of eligible undergraduate men and 50% of eligible undergraduate women are members.

Drug and Alcohol Information

Education

On campus Drug and alcohol education/prevention programs not offered. Authorized group concerned with responsible drinking.

Identification of Problems

Admissions College application does not ask about prior substance abuse problems.

On campus Current students identified as chemically dependent may remain enrolled, but treatment is required. No training program on identifying students with potential substance abuse problems. No written procedures for students and staff if substance abuse is suspected.

Support Services

On campus Private counseling.

Employee assistance Program for chemically dependent employees not available. Staff working with drug/alcohol-related issues: 2 part-time.

Disciplinary Actions

Alcohol Results of infractions of alcohol regulations (see Comparative Table of Alcohol Regulations) include counseling, probation, suspension.

Drugs For first-time use, possession, or sale: suspension. For subsequent use, possession, or sale: expulsion.

For More Information

Contact: T. Clark Bryan, Vice President for Student Development, Carson-Newman College, Russell Ave., Jefferson City, TN 37760. Telephone: 615-475-9061.

CARTHAGE COLLEGE

Kenosha, Wisconsin

General Information

Independent 5-year coed college, affiliated with Lutheran Church in America. Founded 1847. Awards B, M. Primary accreditation: regional. City setting; 85-acre campus. Total enrollment: 1,842. Faculty: 113 (88 full-time, 25 part-time). Social organizations: 1 national fraternity, 5 local fraternities, 4 local sororities; 20% of eligible undergraduate men and 35% of eligible undergraduate women are members.

Drug and Alcohol Information

Education

On campus Drug and alcohol education/prevention programs offered for: all students, athletes/coaches, parents. Authorized group concerned with responsible drinking. College holds an annual alcohol awareness week.

Identification of Problems

Admissions College application does not ask about prior substance abuse problems.

On campus Current students identified as chemically dependent may remain enrolled, but treatment is required. Training program on identifying students with potential substance abuse problems for: resident advisers. Written procedures for students and staff if substance abuse is suspected.

Support Services

On campus Private counseling.

Employee assistance Program for chemically dependent employees not available. Staff working with drug/alcohol-related issues: 2–3 part-time.

Disciplinary Actions

Alcohol Results of infractions of alcohol regulations (see Comparative Table of Alcohol Regulations) varies by situation but can include chemical dependency assessment, counseling, warning (first offense), suspension (second offense).

Drugs For first-time use, possession or sale: varies by situation—chemical dependency assessment, counseling, warning. For subsequent use, possession, or sale: varies by situation—chemical dependency assessment, counseling, suspension.

Additional Information from the College

Off-campus offenses are dealt with by the local authorities.

Carthage College (continued)

For More Information

Contact: Lori Berkiel, Counselor, Carthage College, 2001 Alford Dr., Kenosha, WI 53141. Telephone: 414-551-8500.

CASE WESTERN RESERVE UNIVERSITY

Cleveland, Ohio

General Information

Independent comprehensive coed institution. Founded 1826. Awards B, M, D. Primary accreditation: regional. Metropolitan setting; 150-acre campus. Total enrollment: 8,333. Faculty: 1,674 (1,534 full-time, 140 part-time). Social organizations: 16 national fraternities, 3 national sororities, 1 local sorority; 36% of eligible undergraduate men and 26% of eligible undergraduate women are members.

Drug and Alcohol Information

Education

On campus Drug and alcohol education/prevention programs offered for: freshmen, social organization members, resident advisers, student leaders. Authorized group concerned with responsible drinking. College holds an annual alcohol awareness week.

Identification of Problems

Admissions College application does not ask about prior substance abuse problems.

On campus Current students identified as chemically dependent may remain enrolled, but treatment is required. No training program on identifying students with potential substance abuse problems. Written procedures for students and staff if substance abuse is suspected.

Support Services

On campus Private counseling.

Employee assistance Program for chemically dependent employees not available.

Disciplinary Actions

Alcohol Results of infractions of alcohol regulations (see Comparative Table of Alcohol Regulations) include counseling, warning, probation.

Drugs For first-time use or possession: varies by situation. For first-time sale: suspension. For subsequent use, possession, or sale: suspension.

Additional Information from the College

Case Western Reserve University is located adjacent to University Hospital and the Cleveland Clinic, both of which have numerous treatment programs for alcohol and drug dependency. The University makes referrals to these programs, rather than developing its own program.

For More Information

Contact: Marilyn Caldwell, Manager, Employee Relations, Case Western Reserve University, 10900 Euclid Ave., Cleveland, OH 44106. Telephone: 216-368-4504.

CATAWBA COLLEGE

Salisbury, North Carolina

General Information

Independent 5-year coed college, affiliated with United Church of Christ. Founded 1851. Awards B, M. Primary accreditation: regional. Small-town setting; 210-acre campus. Total enrollment: 1,030. Faculty: 74 (62 full-time, 12 part-time).

Drug and Alcohol Information

Education

On campus Drug and alcohol education/prevention programs offered for: all students, athletes/coaches; required for: resident advisers. Authorized group concerned with responsible drinking. College holds an annual alcohol awareness week and drug awareness week.

Identification of Problems

Admissions College application does not ask about prior substance abuse problems.

On campus Training program on identifying students with potential substance abuse problems for: resident advisers. No written procedures for students and staff if substance abuse is suspected.

Support Services

On campus AA, Al-Anon, support groups, private counseling.

Employee assistance Program for chemically dependent employees available. Staff working with drug/alcohol-related issues: 8 part-time.

Disciplinary Actions

Alcohol Results of infractions of alcohol regulations (see Comparative Table of Alcohol Regulations) varies by situation but can include chemical dependency assessment, counseling, warning, probation, suspension.

Drugs For first-time use or possession: probation, suspension. For subsequent use or possession: expulsion. For any sale: expulsion.

For More Information

Contact: Dr. Bob Welch, Dean of Students, Catawba College, Salisbury, NC 28144. Telephone: 704-637-4410.

CEDAR CREST COLLEGE

Allentown, Pennsylvania

General Information

Independent 4-year primarily women's college, affiliated with United Church of Christ. Founded 1867. Awards B. Primary accreditation: regional. City setting; 84-acre campus. Total enrollment: 1,039. Faculty: 123 (55 full-time, 68 part-time).

Drug and Alcohol Information

Education

On campus Drug and alcohol education/prevention programs offered for: all students; required for: athletes/coaches. College holds an annual alcohol awareness week.

Identification of Problems

Admissions College application does not ask about prior substance abuse problems.

On campus Current students identified as chemically dependent may remain enrolled, but treatment is required. Comments: Judgment is based on degree of chemical dependence. Training program on identifying students with potential substance abuse problems for: resident advisers. No written procedures for students and staff if substance abuse is suspected.

Support Services

On campus AA, support groups.

Employee assistance Program for chemically dependent employees available. Staff working with drug/alcohol-related issues: 1 part-time.

Disciplinary Actions

Alcohol Results of infractions of alcohol regulations (see Comparative Table of Alcohol Regulations) varies by situation but can include chemical dependency assessment, counseling, warning, probation.

Drugs For first-time use: varies by situation—chemical dependency assessment, warning, probation. For subsequent use: varies by situation—suspension, expulsion. For first-time possession: chemical dependency assessment, probation. For subsequent possession: suspension, expulsion. For first-time sale: chemical dependency assessment, probation, suspension. For subsequent sale: expulsion. Comments: Penalties for possession depend on intent to use or to sell, quantity, kind, etc.

Additional Information from the College

The faculty; academic advisers; student affairs, residence hall, and health service staffs; part-time college counselor (a clinical psychologist who works with a consulting psychiatrist); and the Student Council, Judicial Board, and College Center Board all maintain close communications through which they handle student problems on an individual basis.

For More Information

Contact: Richard Begbie, Director of College Center, Cedar Crest College, Allentown, PA 18104. Telephone: 215-437-4471.

CEDARVILLE COLLEGE

Cedarville, Ohio

General Information

Independent Baptist 4-year coed college. Founded 1887. Awards A (terminal), B. Primary accreditation: regional. Rural setting; 105-acre campus. Total enrollment: 1,879. Faculty: 143 (87 full-time, 56 part-time).

Drug and Alcohol Information

Education

On campus Drug and alcohol education/prevention programs not offered.

Identification of Problems

Admissions College application question about prior substance abuse problems is used in the admissions decision.

On campus Current students identified as chemically dependent may not remain enrolled. No training program on identifying students with potential substance abuse problems. No written procedures for students and staff if substance abuse is suspected.

Support Services

On campus Support groups, private counseling.

Employee assistance Program for chemically dependent employees not available.

Disciplinary Actions

Alcohol Results of infractions of alcohol regulations (see Comparative Table of Alcohol Regulations) varies by situation but can include counseling, suspension, expulsion.

Drugs For any use, possession, or sale: expulsion.

For More Information

Contact: Pat Bates, Dean of Women, Cedarville College, Box 601, Cedarville, OH 45314. Telephone: 513-766-2211.

CENTENARY COLLEGE

Hackettstown, New Jersey

General Information

Independent Methodist 4-year primarily women's college. Founded 1867. Awards A (college transfer and terminal), B. Primary accreditation: regional. Small-town setting; 42-acre campus. Total enrollment: 820. Faculty: 88 (31 full-time, 57 part-time). Social organizations: 3 local sororities; 25% of eligible undergraduate women are members.

Drug and Alcohol Information

Education

On campus Drug and alcohol education/prevention programs offered for: all students, faculty, administration. Authorized group concerned with responsible drinking. College holds an annual alcohol awareness week and drug awareness week.

Identification of Problems

Admissions College application does not ask about prior substance abuse problems.

On campus Current students identified as chemically dependent may remain enrolled, but treatment is required. Training program on identifying students with potential substance abuse problems for: resident advisers, Greek officers, faculty, administration. Written procedures for students and staff if substance abuse is suspected.

Support Services

On campus Private counseling, referrals.

Employee assistance Program for chemically dependent employees not available. Staff working with drug/alcohol-related issues: 3 part-time.

Disciplinary Actions

Alcohol Results of infractions of alcohol regulations (see Comparative Table of Alcohol Regulations) include chemical dependency assessment, counseling, warning, probation, suspension, expulsion.

Drugs For first-time use or possession: suspension. For subsequent use or possession: expulsion. For any sale: expulsion.

For More Information

Contact: Debra Smith, Director of Counseling Services, Centenary College, 400 Jefferson St., Hackettstown, NJ 07840. Telephone: 201-852-1400.

CENTRAL CONNECTICUT STATE UNIVERSITY

New Britain, Connecticut

General Information

State-supported 5-year coed college. Part of Connecticut State University System. Founded 1849. Awards B, M. Primary accreditation: regional. City setting; 142-acre campus. Total enrollment: 14,198. Faculty: 732 (482 full-time, 250 part-time). Social organizations: 2 national fraternities, 2 national sororities; 1% of eligible undergraduate men and 1% of eligible undergraduate women are members.

Drug and Alcohol Information

Education

On campus Drug and alcohol education/prevention programs offered for: all students, athletes/coaches, faculty, administration. Authorized group concerned with responsible drinking. College holds an annual alcohol awareness week and drug awareness week.

Identification of Problems

Admissions College application does not ask about prior substance abuse problems.

On campus Current students identified as chemically dependent may remain enrolled, but treatment is required. Training program on identifying students with potential substance abuse problems for: resident advisers, coaches, faculty, administration, Health Center staff. Written procedures for students and staff if substance abuse is suspected.

Support Services

On campus AA, Al-Anon, ACOA, private counseling, Student Assistance Program.

Employee assistance Program for chemically dependent employees available. Staff working with drug/alcohol-related issues: 1 full-time and 1 part-time.

Disciplinary Actions

Alcohol Results of infractions of alcohol regulations (see Comparative Table of Alcohol Regulations) vary by situation but can include chemical dependency assessment, counseling, warning, probation, suspension, expulsion.

Drugs For first-time use: counseling, probation. For first-time possession: varies by situation. For subsequent use or possession: suspension. For any sale: expulsion.

For More Information

Contact: Connie Boston, Coordinator, Substance Abuse Prevention Program, Central Connecticut State University, New Britain, CT 06050. Telephone: 203-827-7883.

CENTRAL METHODIST COLLEGE

Fayette, Missouri

General Information

Independent Methodist 4-year coed college. Founded 1854. Awards A (college transfer), B. Primary accreditation: regional. Rural setting; 65-acre campus. Total enrollment: 714. Faculty: 70 (53 full-time, 17 part-time). Social organizations: 6 local fraternities, 5 local sororities; 70% of eligible undergraduate men and 80% of eligible undergraduate women are members.

Drug and Alcohol Information

Education

On campus Drug and alcohol education/prevention programs offered for: all students. Bacchus chapter: 7 members. College holds an annual alcohol awareness week.

Identification of Problems

Admissions College application does not ask about prior substance abuse problems.

On campus Current students identified as chemically dependent may remain enrolled, but treatment is required. Training program on identifying students with potential substance abuse problems for: resident advisers, administration. Written procedures for students and staff if substance abuse is suspected.

Support Services

On campus Private counseling.

Off campus AA, NA.

Employee assistance Program for chemically dependent employees available. Staff working with drug/alcohol-related issues: 1 full-time and 6 part-time.

Disciplinary Actions

Alcohol Results of infractions of alcohol regulations (see Comparative Table of Alcohol Regulations) varies by situation depending on quantity, attitude, and previous infractions.

Drugs For any use, possession, or sale: varies by situation.

For More Information

Contact: William Sheehan Jr., Director of Residence Life, 411 CMC Square, Central Methodist College, Fayette, MO 65248. Telephone: 816-248-3391 Ext. 223.

CENTRAL MICHIGAN UNIVERSITY

Mount Pleasant, Michigan

General Information

State-supported comprehensive coed institution. Founded 1892. Awards B, M, D. Primary accreditation: regional. Small-town setting; 854-acre campus. Total enrollment: 17,032. Faculty: 789 (699 full-time, 90 part-time). Social organizations: 13 national fraternities, 10 national sororities, 1 local sorority; 11% of eligible undergraduate men and 8% of eligible undergraduate women are members.

Drug and Alcohol Information

Education

On campus Drug and alcohol education/prevention programs offered for: all students, athletes/coaches. Authorized group concerned with responsible drinking. College holds an annual alcohol awareness week and drug awareness week.

Identification of Problems

Admissions College application question about prior substance abuse problems is used for medical history.

On campus Current students identified as chemically dependent may remain enrolled. Training program on identifying students with potential substance abuse

problems for: resident advisers. Written procedures for staff if substance abuse is suspected.

Support Services

On campus AA, NA, ACOA, support groups, private counseling.

Off campus Al-Anon.

Employee assistance Program for chemically dependent employees available. Staff working with drug/alcohol-related issues: about 75 part-time.

Disciplinary Actions

Alcohol Results of infractions of alcohol regulations (see Comparative Table of Alcohol Regulations) vary by situation. Comments: Students may be required to attend an Alcohol Education Discipline Program of five 1-hour sessions.

Drugs For any use, possession, or sale: varies by situation.

Additional Information from the College

Central Michigan University has received an FIPSE grant for the next two years to expand its alcohol/drug abuse educational efforts. Its Alcohol Awareness Week programs have been recognized three times by the Inter-Association Task Force on Alcohol and Other Substance Abuse Issues. Housing staff will, upon request, try to arrange for drug-free roommates for students who have or have had alcohol or drug problems. Throughout the housing system there is a "carefrontation" program to help identify students with problems and refer them for assistance. The orientation program addresses alcohol/drug abuse issues, provides parents with information, and suggests constructive activities. The University's student group, PRIDE, is nationally recognized for its outreach work with high school students and for its self-esteem-enhancing message.

For More Information

Contact: Dr. Ross J. Rapaport, Coordinator, Alcohol and Drug Abuse Intervention and Prevention Program, Counseling Center, 102 Forest Hall, Central Michigan University, Mount Pleasant, MI 48859. Telephone: 517-774-3381.

CENTRAL MISSOURI STATE UNIVERSITY

Warrensburg, Missouri

General Information

State-supported 5-year coed college. Founded 1871. Awards A (college transfer and terminal), B, M. Primary accreditation: regional. Small-town setting; 1,000-acre campus. Total enrollment: 10,104. Faculty: 461 (418 full-time, 43 part-time). Social organizations: 15 national fraternities, 11 national sororities; 12% of eligible undergraduate men and 9% of eligible undergraduate women are members.

Drug and Alcohol Information

Information from the College

Central Missouri State University is in the process of formulating an all-inclusive, University-wide policy to deal with drug and alcohol issues.

For More Information

Contact: Merle H. Charnay, Director, Student Health Center, Central Missouri State University, Warrensburg, MO 64093. Telephone: 816-429-4772.

CENTRAL STATE UNIVERSITY

Edmond, Oklahoma

General Information

State-supported 5-year coed college. Founded 1890. Awards B, M. Primary accreditation: regional. Small-town setting; 200-acre campus. Total enrollment: 13,866. Social organizations: 3 national fraternities, 3 national sororities; 1% of eligible undergraduate men and 1% of eligible undergraduate women are members.

Drug and Alcohol Information

Education

On campus Drug and alcohol education/prevention programs offered for: all students. Bacchus chapter: 12 members. College holds an annual alcohol awareness week.

Identification of Problems

Admissions College application does not ask about prior substance abuse problems.

On campus Current students identified as chemically dependent may remain enrolled. No training program on identifying students with potential substance abuse problems. No written procedures for students and staff if substance abuse is suspected.

Support Services

On campus Private counseling.

Employee assistance Program for chemically dependent employees available.

Disciplinary Actions

Alcohol Results of infractions of alcohol regulations (see Comparative Table of Alcohol Regulations) vary by situation but can include chemical dependency assessment, counseling, probation.

Drugs For first-time use: varies by situation—counseling, probation, police action. For subsequent use: varies by situation—probation, suspension, police action. For first-time possession: varies by situation—probation, suspension, police action. For subsequent possession: varies by situation—suspension, police action. For any sale: varies by situation—suspension, expulsion, police action.

For More Information

Contact: Peggy Foster, Counseling and Testing Services, Central State University, 100 N. University Dr. AD210–G, Edmond, OK 73034. Telephone: 405-341-2980 Ext. 2215.

CENTRAL UNIVERSITY OF IOWA

Pella, Iowa

General Information

Independent 4-year coed college, affiliated with Reformed Church in America. Founded 1853. Awards B. Primary accreditation: regional. Small-town setting; 111-acre campus. Total enrollment: 1,680. Faculty: 110 (79 full-time, 31 part-time). Social organizations: 3 local fraternities, 2 local sororities; 7% of eligible undergraduate men and 4% of eligible undergraduate women are members.

Central University of Iowa (continued)

Drug and Alcohol Information

Education

On campus Drug and alcohol education/prevention programs offered for: all students; required for: freshmen, resident advisers. Authorized group concerned with responsible drinking. College holds an annual alcohol awareness week and drug awareness week.

Identification of Problems

Admissions College application does not ask about prior substance abuse problems.

On campus Current students identified as chemically dependent may remain enrolled, but treatment is required. No training program on identifying students with potential substance abuse problems. Written procedures for students and staff if substance abuse is suspected.

Support Services

On campus Support groups (run by Counseling Service), private counseling.

Employee assistance Program for chemically dependent employees not available. Staff working with drug/alcohol-related issues: 3 part-time.

Disciplinary Actions

Alcohol Results of infractions of alcohol regulations (see Comparative Table of Alcohol Regulations) are determined after a hearing before the Judicial Board.

Drugs For first-time use or possession: hearing before the Judicial Board—probation. For first-time sale: hearing before the Judicial Board—suspension. For subsequent use, possession, or sale: hearing before the Judicial Board—suspension, expulsion.

Additional Information from the College

A statement of the College's alcohol policy is sent to all new students and their parents for review and discussion before enrollment. Orientation for new students includes a video presentation and discussion about drinking and driving and an explanation of the campus "buddy system."

For More Information

Contact: Bill Hinga, Vice President for Student Affairs, Central University of Iowa, Pella, IA 50219. Telephone: 515-628-5249.

CENTRAL WASHINGTON UNIVERSITY

Ellensburg, Washington

General Information

State-supported 5-year coed college. Founded 1891. Awards B, M. Primary accreditation: regional. Small-town setting; 350-acre campus. Total enrollment: 7,109. Faculty: 312 (242 full-time, 70 part-time).

Drug and Alcohol Information

Education

On campus Drug and alcohol education/prevention programs offered for: all students, athletes/coaches, faculty, administration. Bacchus chapter: 30 members. College holds an annual alcohol awareness.

Identification of Problems

Admissions College application does not ask about prior substance abuse problems.

On campus Current students identified as chemically dependent may remain enrolled, but treatment is required. Training program on identifying students with potential substance abuse problems for: resident advisers, faculty. Written procedures for students and staff if substance abuse is suspected.

Support Services

On campus AA, support groups, private counseling.

Employee assistance Program for chemically dependent employees not available. Staff working with drug/alcohol-related issues: 1 full-time and 4 part-time.

Disciplinary Actions

Alcohol Results of infractions of alcohol regulations (see Comparative Table of Alcohol Regulations) vary by situation but can include warning.

Drugs For first-time use or possession: varies by situation—probation. For subsequent use or possession: chemical dependency assessment, suspension. For first-time sale: varies by situation—suspension. For subsequent sale: chemical dependency assessment, expulsion. Comments: The University has a deferred suspension sanction, which may be applied.

For More Information

Contact: Deacon Meier, Assistant Vice President of Student Affairs, Central Washington University, Ellensburg, WA 98926. Telephone: 509-963-1515.

CENTRE COLLEGE

Danville, Kentucky

General Information

Independent 4-year coed college, affiliated with Presbyterian Church. Founded 1819. Awards B. Primary accreditation: regional. Small-town setting; 75-acre campus. Total enrollment: 860. Faculty: 81 (69 full-time, 12 part-time). Social organizations: 6 national fraternities, 4 national sororities; 80% of eligible undergraduate men and 65% of eligible undergraduate women are members.

Drug and Alcohol Information

Education

On campus Drug and alcohol education/prevention programs offered for: all students, athletes/coaches, faculty, administration. College holds an annual alcohol awareness week and drug awareness week.

Identification of Problems

Admissions College application does not ask about prior substance abuse problems.

On campus Current students identified as chemically dependent may remain enrolled, but treatment is required. Training program on identifying students with potential substance abuse problems for: resident advisers. Written procedures for students and staff if substance abuse is suspected.

Support Services

On campus Private counseling, counseling from mental health agency contracted by the College.

Employee assistance Program for chemically dependent employees not available. Staff working with drug/alcohol-related issues: 3 part-time.

Disciplinary Actions

Alcohol Results of infractions of alcohol regulations (see Comparative Table of Alcohol Regulations) vary by situation.

Drugs For first-time use, possession, or sale: suspension. For subsequent use, possession, or sale: expulsion.

For More Information

Contact: Nancy S. Lackey, Associate Dean of Students, Centre College, Box 822, Danville, KY 40422. Telephone: 606-236-5211 Ext. 387.

CENTRO DE ESTUDIOS AVANZADOS DE PUERTO RICO Y EL CARIBE

Old San Juan, Puerto Rico

General Information

Independent 5-year coed college. Founded 1976. Awards B, M. Primary accreditation: regional. Metropolitan setting. Total enrollment: 196.

Drug and Alcohol Information

Comments from the College

The Center is a small institution with a student population (mostly graduate) of adult professionals. Classes are held in the evening. There have been no drugs or alcohol problems; if any arise, they will be dealt with on an individual basis.

For More Information

Contact: Dr. J. I. Soto, Academic Assistant, Centro de Estudios Avanzados de Puerto Rico y el Caribe, Casa Blanca, San Juan, PR 00904. Telephone: 809-723-4481.

CHAMINADE UNIVERSITY OF HONOLULU

Honolulu, Hawaii

General Information

Independent Roman Catholic 5-year coed college. Founded 1955. Awards A (college transfer), B, M. Primary accreditation: regional. Metropolitan setting; 62-acre campus. Total enrollment: 2,556. Faculty: 195 (56 full-time, 139 part-time). Social organization: 1 local fraternity; 4% of eligible undergraduate men are members.

Drug and Alcohol Information

Education

On campus Drug and alcohol education/prevention programs offered for: all students, faculty, administration; required for: athletes/coaches, resident advisers. Authorized group concerned with responsible drinking. College holds an annual alcohol awareness week.

Identification of Problems

Admissions College application does not ask about prior substance abuse problems.

On campus Current students identified as chemically dependent may remain enrolled, but treatment is required. Training program on identifying students with potential substance abuse problems for: resident advisers. Written procedures for students and staff if substance abuse is suspected.

Support Services

On campus Support groups, private counseling, referrals.

Employee assistance Program for chemically dependent employees not available. Staff working with drug/alcohol-related issues: 6 part-time.

Disciplinary Actions

Alcohol Results of infractions of alcohol regulations (see Comparative Table of Alcohol Regulations) vary by situation but can include chemical dependency assessment, counseling, warning, probation, suspension.

Drugs For first-time use or possession: varies by situation—counseling, warning. For subsequent use or possession: varies by situation—counseling, probation, suspension. For first-time sale: varies by situation. For subsequent sale: suspension, expulsion.

For More Information

Contact: Sharon Goo, Dean of Students, Chaminade University of Honolulu, 3140 Waialae Ave., Honolulu, HI 96816. Telephone: 808-735-4772.

CHAPMAN COLLEGE

Orange, California

General Information

Independent 5-year coed college, affiliated with Christian Church (Disciples of Christ). Founded 1861. Awards B, M. Primary accreditation: regional. City setting; 35-acre campus. Total enrollment: 2,185. Faculty: 138 (101 full-time, 37 part-time). Social organizations: 1 national fraternity, 4 local fraternities, 5 local sororities; 30% of eligible undergraduate men and 30% of eligible undergraduate women are members.

Drug and Alcohol Information

Education

On campus Drug and alcohol education/prevention programs offered for: all students, athletes/coaches, faculty, administration. College holds an annual alcohol awareness week and drug awareness week.

Identification of Problems

Admissions College application does not ask about prior substance abuse problems.

On campus Current students identified as chemically dependent may remain enrolled, but treatment is required. Training program on identifying students with potential substance abuse problems for: resident advisers, administration, counselors. Written procedures for students and staff if substance abuse is suspected.

Support Services

On campus AA, private counseling.

Employee assistance Program for chemically dependent employees available. Staff working with drug/alcohol-related issues: 6–8 part-time.

Disciplinary Actions

Alcohol Results of infractions of alcohol regulations (see Comparative Table of Alcohol Regulations) include chemical dependency assessment, counseling, warning, probation, suspension, expulsion. Infractions may also result in loss of the privilege of having alcohol at future events.

Drugs For first-time use or possession: chemical

Chapman College (continued)

dependency assessment, counseling, probation. For subsequent use or possession: chemical dependency assessment, counseling, suspension. For first-time sale: suspension. For subsequent sale: expulsion.

For More Information

Contact: Susan Hunter Hancock, Vice President for Student Life, Chapman College, 333 N. Glassell St., Orange, CA 92666. Telephone: 714-997-6721.

CHATHAM COLLEGE

Pittsburgh, Pennsylvania

General Information

Independent 4-year women's college. Founded 1869. Awards B. Primary accreditation: regional. Metropolitan setting; 55-acre campus. Total enrollment: 684. Faculty: 61 (46 full-time, 15 part-time).

Drug and Alcohol Information

Education

On campus Drug and alcohol education/prevention programs offered for: all students.

Identification of Problems

Admissions College application does not ask about prior substance abuse problems.

On campus Current students identified as chemically dependent may remain enrolled. No training program on identifying students with potential substance abuse problems. Written procedures for students and staff if substance abuse is suspected.

Support Services

On campus ACOA, private counseling, referrals.

Employee assistance Program for chemically dependent employees not available. Staff working with drug/alcohol-related issues: 1 part-time.

Disciplinary Actions

Alcohol Results of infractions of alcohol regulations (see Comparative Table of Alcohol Regulations) vary by situation. Comments: A new policy is being defined.

Drugs For any use, possession, or sale: varies by situation.

For More Information

Contact: Marjorie R. Harrison, Dean of Student Affairs, Chatham College, Woodland Rd., Pittsburgh, PA 15232. Telephone: 412-365-1286.

CHEYNEY UNIVERSITY OF PENNSYLVANIA

Cheyney, Pennsylvania

General Information

State-supported 5-year coed college. Part of State System of Higher Education. Founded 1837. Awards A (college transfer and terminal), B, M. Primary accreditation: regional. Rural setting; 275-acre campus. Total enrollment: 1,666. Social organizations: 4 national fraternities, 4 national sororities, 2 local fraternities, 1 local sorority, 2 coed fraternities; 50% of eligible undergraduate men and 50% of eligible undergraduate women are members.

Drug and Alcohol Information

Education

On campus Drug and alcohol education/prevention programs offered for: all students, athletes/coaches; required for: freshmen. Authorized group concerned with responsible drinking. College holds an annual alcohol awareness week and drug awareness week.

Identification of Problems

Admissions College application question about prior substance abuse problems is used for counseling and referral, if student is admitted.

On campus Current students identified as chemically dependent may remain enrolled, but treatment is required. Training program on identifying students with potential substance abuse problems for: resident advisers, coaches, faculty. Written procedures for students and staff if substance abuse is suspected.

Support Services

On campus Private counseling, newly formed student group.

Employee assistance Program for chemically dependent employees available. Staff working with drug/alcohol-related issues: 4 part-time.

Disciplinary Actions

Alcohol Results of infractions of alcohol regulations (see Comparative Table of Alcohol Regulations) include chemical dependency assessment, counseling, warning, probation, suspension, expulsion.

Drugs For any use, possession, or sale: varies by situation.

For More Information

Contact: J. Byrne, Director, Health Services, Cheyney University of Pennsylvania, Cheyney, PA 19319. Telephone: 215-399-2260.

CHRIST COLLEGE IRVINE

Irvine, California

General Information

Independent 5-year coed college, affiliated with Lutheran Church–Missouri Synod. Founded 1972. Awards B, M (M in education only). Primary accreditation: regional. City setting; 113-acre campus. Total enrollment: 572. Faculty: 80 (38 full-time, 42 part-time).

Drug and Alcohol Information

Education

On campus Drug and alcohol education/prevention programs offered for: all students; required for: athletes/coaches, resident advisers. Authorized group concerned with responsible drinking. College holds an annual alcohol awareness week and drug awareness week.

Identification of Problems

Admissions College application does not ask about prior substance abuse problems.

On campus Current students identified as chemically dependent may remain enrolled, but treatment is required. Training program on identifying students with potential substance abuse problems for: resident advisers, coaches. Written procedures for students and staff if substance abuse is suspected.

Support Services

On campus Private counseling.

Employee assistance Program for chemically dependent employees available. Staff working with drug/alcohol-related issues: 2 full-time.

Disciplinary Actions

Alcohol Results of infractions of alcohol regulations (see Comparative Table of Alcohol Regulations) include chemical dependency assessment, counseling, probation, writing a 5-page research paper on alcohol abuse.

Drugs For first-time use or possession: varies by situation—chemical dependency assessment, counseling, suspension. For subsequent use or possession: suspension. For any sale: expulsion.

For More Information

Contact: Charles Connor, Director of Resident Life, Christ College Irvine, 1530 Concordia, Irvine, CA 92715. Telephone: 714-854-8002 Ext. 417.

CHRISTIAN BROTHERS COLLEGE

Memphis, Tennessee

General Information

Independent Roman Catholic 5-year coed college. Founded 1871. Awards A (terminal), B, M. Primary accreditation: regional. Metropolitan setting; 60-acre campus. Total enrollment: 1,740. Faculty: 120 (108 full-time, 12 part-time). Social organizations: 2 national fraternities, 2 national sororities, 2 local fraternities, 23 social clubs; 70% of eligible undergraduate men and 70% of eligible undergraduate women are members.

Drug and Alcohol Information

Education

On campus Drug and alcohol education/prevention programs not offered. College holds an annual alcohol awareness week and drug awareness week.

Identification of Problems

Admissions College application does not ask about prior substance abuse problems.

On campus Current students identified as chemically dependent may remain enrolled, but treatment is required. Training program on identifying students with potential substance abuse problems for: resident advisers. No written procedures for students and staff if substance abuse is suspected.

Support Services

On campus Private counseling.

Employee assistance Program for chemically dependent employees not available.

Disciplinary Actions

Alcohol Results of infractions of alcohol regulations (see Comparative Table of Alcohol Regulations) vary by situation but can include counseling, warning.

Drugs For first-time use or possession: warning. For subsequent use or possession: probation. For any sale: suspension, expulsion.

For More Information

Contact: Kevin Keegan, Director of Student Life, Christian Brothers College, 650 E. Parkway S., Memphis, TN 38104. Telephone: 901-722-0200.

THE CITADEL, THE MILITARY COLLEGE OF SOUTH CAROLINA

Charleston, South Carolina

General Information

State-supported 5-year men's college. Founded 1842. Awards B, M. Primary accreditation: regional. City setting; 130-acre campus. Total enrollment: 3,488. Faculty: 152 (144 full-time, 8 part-time).

Drug and Alcohol Information

Education

On campus Drug and alcohol education/prevention programs offered for: all students, faculty, administration; required for: freshmen, sophomores. Authorized group concerned with responsible drinking. College holds an annual alcohol awareness week and drug awareness week.

Identification of Problems

On campus Current students identified as chemically dependent may not remain enrolled. Training program on identifying students with potential substance abuse problems for: medical and counseling personnel. Written procedures for students and staff if substance abuse is suspected.

Support Services

On campus AA, support groups, private counseling.

Employee assistance Program for chemically dependent employees available. Staff working with drug/alcohol-related issues: 6 part-time.

Disciplinary Actions

Alcohol Results of infractions of alcohol regulations (see Comparative Table of Alcohol Regulations) vary by situation but can include probation, suspension, expulsion.

Drugs For any use, possession, or sale: expulsion.

For More Information

Contact: Lee Martin, Director, Personnel and Administration, The Citadel, The Military College of South Carolina, Charleston, SC 29409. Telephone: 803-792-5115.

CITY COLLEGE OF THE CITY UNIVERSITY OF NEW YORK

New York, New York

General Information

State and locally supported comprehensive coed institution. Part of City University of New York System. Founded 1847. Awards B, M, D. Primary accreditation: regional. Metropolitan setting; 35-acre campus. Total enrollment: 12,780. Faculty: 1,352 (699 full-time, 653 part-time). Social organizations: 6 national fraternities.

Drug and Alcohol Information

Education

On campus Drug and alcohol education/prevention programs offered for: all students, athletes/coaches.

City College of the City University of New York (continued)

Authorized group concerned with responsible drinking. College holds an annual alcohol awareness week and drug awareness week.

Identification of Problems

Admissions College application does not ask about prior substance abuse problems.

On campus Current students identified as chemically dependent may remain enrolled, but treatment is required. Training program on identifying students with potential substance abuse problems for: administration. Written procedures for students and staff if substance abuse is suspected.

Support Services

On campus Abuse Center.

Employee assistance Program for chemically dependent employees not available. Staff working with drug/alcohol-related issues: 2 full-time and 3 part-time.

Disciplinary Actions

Alcohol Results of infractions of alcohol regulations (see Comparative Table of Alcohol Regulations) include counseling, warning, probation.

Drugs For first-time use: counseling, warning, probation. For subsequent use: suspension, expulsion. For any possession or sale: expulsion.

For More Information

Contact: Fred Kogut, Director of Support Services, City College of the City University of New York, Convent Ave. at 138th St., New York, NY 10031. Telephone: 212-690-5345.

CLAFLIN COLLEGE

Orangeburg, South Carolina

General Information

Independent United Methodist 4-year coed college. Founded 1869. Awards B. Primary accreditation: regional. Small-town setting; 50-acre campus. Total enrollment: 742. Faculty: 59 (all full-time). Social organizations: 4 national fraternities, 4 national sororities; 10% of eligible undergraduate men and 10% of eligible undergraduate women are members.

Drug and Alcohol Information

Education

On campus Drug and alcohol education/prevention programs offered for: all students, athletes/coaches, faculty, administration. College holds an annual alcohol awareness week and drug awareness week.

Identification of Problems

Admissions College application does not ask about prior substance abuse problems.

On campus Current students identified as chemically dependent may remain enrolled, but treatment is required. Training program on identifying students with potential substance abuse problems for: resident advisers. Written procedures for students and staff if substance abuse is suspected.

Support Services

On campus Private counseling.

Employee assistance Program for chemically dependent employees available. Staff working with drug/alcohol-related issues: 1 full-time.

Disciplinary Actions

Alcohol Results of infractions of alcohol regulations (see Comparative Table of Alcohol Regulations) include probation, suspension.

Drugs For first-time use, possession, or sale: counseling. For subsequent use, possession, or sale: suspension.

For More Information

Contact: Hampton Jordan, Director of Student Activities, Box 58, Claflin College, Orangeburg, SC 29115. Telephone: 803-534-2710.

CLARION UNIVERSITY OF PENNSYLVANIA

Clarion, Pennsylvania

General Information

State-supported 5-year coed college. Part of State System of Higher Education. Founded 1867. Awards A (college transfer and terminal), B, M. Primary accreditation: regional. Small-town setting; 100-acre campus. Total enrollment: 6,601. Faculty: 383 (356 full-time, 27 part-time). Social organizations: 11 national fraternities, 6 national sororities, 2 local fraternities, 2 local sororities; 15% of eligible undergraduate men and 12% of eligible undergraduate women are members.

Drug and Alcohol Information

Education

On campus Drug and alcohol education/prevention programs offered for: all students. Bacchus chapter: 25 members. College holds an annual alcohol awareness week.

Identification of Problems

Admissions College application does not ask about prior substance abuse problems.

On campus Current students identified as chemically dependent may remain enrolled. No training program on identifying students with potential substance abuse problems. No written procedures for students and staff if substance abuse is suspected.

Support Services

On campus Support groups, private counseling.

Employee assistance Program for chemically dependent employees available. Staff working with drug/alcohol-related issues: 7 part-time.

Disciplinary Actions

Alcohol Results of infractions of alcohol regulations (see Comparative Table of Alcohol Regulations) vary by situation.

Drugs For any use, possession, or sale: varies by situation.

For More Information

Contact: Diana Anderson, Director of Greek Life & Special Activity Programs, Clarion University of Pennsylvania, Clarion, PA 16214. Telephone: 814-226-2351.

CLEARY COLLEGE

Ypsilanti, Michigan

General Information

Independent 4-year specialized coed college. Founded 1883. Awards A (terminal), B. Primary accreditation: regional and AICS. Small-town setting; 22-acre campus. Total enrollment: 1,200. Faculty: 67 (22 full-time, 45 part-time).

Drug and Alcohol Information

Education

On campus Drug and alcohol education/prevention programs offered for: all students. College holds an annual alcohol awareness week and drug awareness week.

Identification of Problems

Admissions College application does not ask about prior substance abuse problems.

On campus Current students identified as chemically dependent may remain enrolled. No training program on identifying students with potential substance abuse problems. Written procedures for students and staff if substance abuse is suspected.

Support Services

On campus Private counseling, referral.

Employee assistance Program for chemically dependent employees not available. Staff working with drug/alcohol-related issues: 4 part-time.

Disciplinary Actions

Alcohol Results of infractions of alcohol regulations (see Comparative Table of Alcohol Regulations) vary by situation but can include counseling.

Drugs For first-time use, possession, or sale: varies by situation—counseling. For subsequent use, possession, or sale: varies by situation.

For More Information

Contact: Diane C. Lawshe, Director of Student Services, Cleary College, 2170 Washtenaw Ave., Ypsilanti, MI 48197. Telephone: 313-483-4400 Ext. 318.

COGSWELL POLYTECHNICAL COLLEGE

Cupertino, California

General Information

Independent 4-year coed college. Founded 1887. Awards A (college transfer), B. Primary accreditation: regional. Small-town setting; 2-acre campus. Total enrollment: 247. Faculty: 33 (8 full-time, 25 part-time).

Drug and Alcohol Information

Education

On campus Drug and alcohol education/prevention programs not offered.

Identification of Problems

Admissions College application does not ask about prior substance abuse problems.

On campus Current students identified as chemically dependent may remain enrolled. No training program on identifying students with potential substance abuse problems. Written procedures for students and staff if substance abuse is suspected.

Support Services

On campus No support services on campus.

Employee assistance Program for chemically dependent employees not available. Staff working with drug/alcohol-related issues: 1 part-time.

Disciplinary Actions

Alcohol Results of infractions of alcohol regulations (see Comparative Table of Alcohol Regulations) include counseling, warning, probation, suspension, expulsion.

Drugs For any use, possession, or sale: varies by situation.

Additional Information from the College

Cogswell Polytechnical College is a nonresidential college, most of whose students come for evening classes. The average student age is over 30. There are no sports programs or social organizations. So far, the College has had no problems with alcohol or drug abuse. Any that arise would be treated on a case-by-case basis.

For More Information

Contact: JoAnn Vandenberg, Dean, Student Affairs, Cogswell Polytechnical College, 10420 Bubb Rd., Cupertino, CA 95014. Telephone: 408-252-5550.

COKER COLLEGE

Hartsville, South Carolina

General Information

Independent 4-year coed college. Founded 1908. Awards B. Primary accreditation: regional. Small-town setting; 15-acre campus. Total enrollment: 540. Faculty: 47 (43 full-time, 4 part-time).

Drug and Alcohol Information

Education

On campus Drug and alcohol education/prevention programs offered for: all students. College holds an annual alcohol awareness week and drug awareness week.

Identification of Problems

Admissions College application does not ask about prior substance abuse problems.

On campus Current students identified as chemically dependent may remain enrolled, but treatment is required. Training program on identifying students with potential substance abuse problems for: resident advisers. Written procedures for students and staff if substance abuse is suspected.

Support Services

On campus No support services on campus.

Off campus Counseling at an alcohol/drug treatment center.

Employee assistance Program for chemically dependent employees not available. Staff working with drug/alcohol-related issues: 3 part-time.

Disciplinary Actions

Alcohol Results of infractions of alcohol regulations (see Comparative Table of Alcohol Regulations) vary by situation but can include counseling, warning, probation.

Drugs For first-time use: warning. For subsequent use: counseling, probation. For first-time possession or sale:

Coker College (continued)

probation. For subsequent possession or sale: counseling, suspension.

Additional Information from the College

A campus organization that is concerned about responsible drinking is being formed.

For More Information

Contact: Ken Waldrop, Director, Student Life, Coker College, Hartsville, SC 29550. Telephone: 803-332-1381.

COLBY COLLEGE

Waterville, Maine

General Information

Independent 4-year coed college. Founded 1813. Awards B. Primary accreditation: regional. Small-town setting; 900-acre campus. Total enrollment: 1,736. Faculty: 164 (133 full-time, 31 part-time).

Drug and Alcohol Information

Education

On campus Drug and alcohol education/prevention programs offered for: all students, athletes/coaches, faculty, administration. Authorized group concerned with responsible drinking.

Identification of Problems

Admissions College application question about prior substance abuse problems is part of health history.

On campus Current students identified as chemically dependent may remain enrolled, but treatment is required. Training program on identifying students with potential substance abuse problems for: resident advisers, coaches, administration. Written procedures for students and staff if substance abuse is suspected.

Support Services

On campus AA, private counseling.

Off campus Treatment at local hospital facility.

Employee assistance Program for chemically dependent employees available. Staff working with drug/alcohol-related issues: 3 part-time.

Disciplinary Actions

Alcohol Results of infractions of alcohol regulations (see Comparative Table of Alcohol Regulations) include chemical dependency assessment, counseling, warning, probation, suspension, outpatient or inpatient treatment at a local hospital.

Drugs For first-time use or possession: chemical dependency assessment, counseling, probation. For subsequent use or possession: medical treatment, suspension. For any sale: suspension. Comments: Colby College does not have significant problems with drug abuse; alcohol is the most serious concern.

Additional Information from the College

There is an excellent ongoing student committee, BAR (Better Alcohol Responsibility), which suggests what campus rules should be and conducts educational programs. Colby College is constantly reviewing and strengthening its social rules to minimize alcohol abuse.

For More Information

Contact: Dr. William Bennett, College Physician, Colby College, Waterville, ME 04901. Telephone: 207-872-3394.

COLGATE UNIVERSITY

Hamilton, New York

General Information

Independent 5-year coed college. Founded 1819. Awards B, M. Primary accreditation: regional. Rural setting; 1,400-acre campus. Total enrollment: 2,766. Faculty: 246 (189 full-time, 57 part-time). Social organizations: 8 national fraternities, 5 national sororities, 1 local fraternity, 1 coed fraternity; 44% of eligible undergraduate men and 31% of eligible undergraduate women are members.

Drug and Alcohol Information

Education

On campus Drug and alcohol education/prevention programs offered for: all students; required for: freshmen, social organization members and pledges, resident advisers. Authorized group concerned with responsible drinking. College holds an annual alcohol week and drug awareness week.

Identification of Problems

Admissions College application does not ask about prior substance abuse problems.

On campus Current students identified as chemically dependent may remain enrolled, but treatment is required. Training program on identifying students with potential substance abuse problems for: resident advisers. Written procedures for students and staff if substance abuse is suspected.

Support Services

On campus ACOA, private counseling.

Employee assistance Program for chemically dependent employees not available. Staff working with drug/alcohol-related issues: 2 part-time.

Disciplinary Actions

Alcohol Results of infractions of alcohol regulations (see Comparative Table of Alcohol Regulations) include chemical dependency assessment, counseling, warning, probation.

Drugs For first-time use: chemical dependency assessment, counseling, warning. For first-time possession: warning. For subsequent use or possession: varies by situation. For first-time sale: suspension, legal action. For subsequent sale: expulsion.

For More Information

Contact: Susan E. Allen, Acting Dean of Students, Colgate University, Hamilton, NY 13346. Telephone: 315-824-1000 Ext. 372.

COLLEGE MISERICORDIA

Dallas, Pennsylvania

General Information

Independent Roman Catholic 5-year coed college. Founded 1924. Awards B, M. Primary accreditation: regional. Small-town setting; 100-acre campus. Total enrollment: 1,114. Faculty: 120 (62 full-time, 58 part-time). Social organizations: 1 national fraternity, local sororities; 3% of eligible undergraduate men and 3% of eligible undergraduate women are members.

Drug and Alcohol Information

Education

On campus Drug and alcohol education/prevention programs offered for: all students; required for: freshmen, resident advisers. Bacchus chapter: 7 members. College holds an annual alcohol awareness week.

Identification of Problems

Admissions College application does not ask about prior substance abuse problems.

On campus Current students identified as chemically dependent may remain enrolled, but treatment is required. Training program on identifying students with potential substance abuse problems for: resident advisers, administration. Written procedures for students and staff if substance abuse is suspected.

Support Services

On campus Support groups, private counseling.

Employee assistance Program for chemically dependent employees not available. Staff working with drug/alcohol-related issues: 2 part-time.

Disciplinary Actions

Alcohol Results of infractions of alcohol regulations (see Comparative Table of Alcohol Regulations) include counseling, warning, probation, suspension, expulsion.

Drugs For first-time use: counseling. For subsequent use: chemical dependency assessment, expulsion. For first-time possession: counseling, probation, suspension. For subsequent possession: expulsion. For any sale: expulsion.

For More Information

Contact: Geraldine Wall, College Counselor, College Misericordia, Lake St., Dallas, PA 18612. Telephone: 717-675-2181 Ext. 318.

COLLEGE OF AERONAUTICS

Flushing, New York

General Information

Independent 4-year specialized primarily men's college. Founded 1932. Awards A (college transfer and terminal), B. Primary accreditation: regional. Metropolitan setting; 6-acre campus. Total enrollment: 1,300. Faculty: 70 (61 full-time, 9 part-time).

Drug and Alcohol Information

Education

On campus Drug and alcohol education/prevention programs offered for: all students, faculty. College holds an annual alcohol awareness week and drug awareness week.

Identification of Problems

Admissions College application does not ask about prior substance abuse problems.

On campus Current students identified as chemically dependent may remain enrolled, but treatment is required. Training program on identifying students with potential substance abuse problems for: administration. Written procedures for students and staff if substance abuse is suspected.

Support Services

On campus Private counseling.

Employee assistance Program for chemically dependent employees not available.

Disciplinary Actions

Alcohol Results of infractions of alcohol regulations (see Comparative Table of Alcohol Regulations) include suspension.

Drugs For any use or possession: counseling. For any sale: counseling, expulsion.

Additional Information from the College

The College of Aeronautics holds a Substance Abuse Prevention Week every spring. Posters, pamphlets, lectures, and films are used to promote awareness of substance abuse.

For More Information

Contact: John Rossillo, Director of Student Services, College of Aeronautics, LaGuardia Airport, Flushing, NY 11371. Telephone: 718-429-6600.

COLLEGE OF BOCA RATON

Boca Raton, Florida

General Information

Independent 5-year coed college. Founded 1963. Awards A (college transfer and terminal), B, M. Primary accreditation: regional. City setting; 123-acre campus. Total enrollment: 1,150. Faculty: 75.

Drug and Alcohol Information

Education

On campus Drug and alcohol education/prevention programs offered for: all students; required for: freshmen. College holds an annual alcohol awareness week and drug awareness week.

Identification of Problems

Admissions College application does not ask about prior substance abuse problems.

On campus Current students identified as chemically dependent may not remain enrolled. No training program on identifying students with potential substance abuse problems. Written procedures for students and staff if substance abuse is suspected.

Support Services

On campus Private counseling.

Employee assistance Program for chemically dependent employees not available. Staff working with drug/alcohol-related issues: 4 part-time.

Disciplinary Actions

Alcohol Results of infractions of alcohol regulations (see Comparative Table of Alcohol Regulations) include counseling, warning, probation, suspension, expulsion.

Drugs For any use, possession, or sale: varies by situation. Comments: Legal authorities may be notified.

For More Information

Contact: Melinda Shoemaker, Director of Counseling, College of Boca Raton, 3601 N. Military Tr., Boca Raton, FL 33431. Telephone: 407-994-0770.

COLLEGE OF CHARLESTON

Charleston, South Carolina

General Information

State-supported 5-year coed college. Founded 1770. Awards B, M. Primary accreditation: regional. City setting; 8-acre campus. Total enrollment: 6,205. Faculty: 348 (248 full-time, 100 part-time). Social organizations: 8 national fraternities, 9 national sororities.

Drug and Alcohol Information

Education

On campus Drug and alcohol education/prevention programs offered for: all students. Authorized group concerned with responsible drinking. College holds an annual alcohol awareness week and drug awareness week.

Identification of Problems

Admissions College application does not ask about prior substance abuse problems.

On campus Current students identified as chemically dependent may remain enrolled. Training program on identifying students with potential substance abuse problems for: resident advisers, coaches, Greek officers. Written procedures for students and staff if substance abuse is suspected.

Support Services

On campus AA, NA, ACOA, support groups, private counseling.

Employee assistance Program for chemically dependent employees available. Staff working with drug/alcohol-related issues: 1 full-time and 4 part-time.

Disciplinary Actions

Alcohol Results of infractions of alcohol regulations (see Comparative Table of Alcohol Regulations) vary by situation but can include chemical dependency assessment, counseling, warning, probation, suspension, fines.

Drugs For first-time use: varies by situation—chemical dependency assessment, counseling, warning. For subsequent use: varies by situation. For first-time possession: varies by situation. For subsequent possession: suspension. For first-time sale: varies by situation—suspension, expulsion. For subsequent sale: expulsion.

Additional Information from the College

The College of Charleston has a peer-based program called Leadership Education for Alcohol/Drugs and Driving Safety (LEADS), funded by the U.S. Department of Transportation. Peer leaders are trained in summer and weekend workshops and make presentations to classes, social groups, and student organizations. Response from faculty, students, and staff has been excellent.

For More Information

Contact: George E. Haborak, Senior Vice President for Student Affairs, College of Charleston, 66 George St., Charleston, SC 29424. Telephone: 803-792-5522.

COLLEGE OF GREAT FALLS

Great Falls, Montana

General Information

Independent Roman Catholic 5-year coed college. Founded 1932. Awards A (college transfer and terminal), B, M. Primary accreditation: regional. City setting; 40-acre campus. Total enrollment: 1,200. Faculty: 80 (39 full-time, 41 part-time).

Drug and Alcohol Information

Education

On campus Drug and alcohol education/prevention programs offered for: all students. College holds an annual alcohol awareness week.

Identification of Problems

Admissions College application does not ask about prior substance abuse problems.

On campus Current students identified as chemically dependent may remain enrolled. No training program on identifying students with potential substance abuse problems. No written procedures for students and staff if substance abuse is suspected.

Support Services

On campus AA, NA, Al-Anon, ACOA, private counseling, Alateen.

Employee assistance Program for chemically dependent employees available. Staff working with drug/alcohol-related issues: 4 part-time.

Disciplinary Actions

Alcohol Results of infractions of alcohol regulations (see Comparative Table of Alcohol Regulations) include counseling, warning, probation.

Drugs For first-time use, possession, or sale: counseling, warning. For subsequent use or possession: counseling, probation. For subsequent sale: counseling, suspension.

For More Information

Contact: Rev. James M. Sikora, Dean of Student Services, College of Great Falls, 1301 20th St. S., Great Falls, MT 59405. Telephone: 406-761-8210 Ext. 210.

COLLEGE OF IDAHO

Caldwell, Idaho

General Information

Independent Presbyterian 5-year coed college. Founded 1891. Awards B, M. Primary accreditation: regional. Small-town setting; 50-acre campus. Total enrollment: 969. Faculty: 101 (50 full-time, 51 part-time). Social organizations: 1 national fraternity, 2 local fraternities, 4 local sororities.

Drug and Alcohol Information

Education

On campus Drug and alcohol education/prevention programs offered for: all students. Authorized group concerned with responsible drinking. College holds an annual alcohol awareness week.

Identification of Problems

Admissions College application does not ask about prior substance abuse problems.

On campus Current students identified as chemically dependent may remain enrolled, but treatment is required. Training program on identifying students with potential substance abuse problems for: resident advisers. Written procedures for students and staff if substance abuse is suspected.

Support Services

On campus AA, ACOA, support groups, private counseling.

Employee assistance Program for chemically dependent employees not available.

Disciplinary Actions

Alcohol Results of infractions of alcohol regulations (see Comparative Table of Alcohol Regulations) vary by situation but can include chemical dependency assessment, probation, suspension.

Drugs For first-time use, possession, or sale: varies by situation. For subsequent use, possession, or sale: suspension.

For More Information

Contact: Dennis Freeburn, Dean of Students, College of Idaho, Caldwell, ID 83605. Telephone: 208-459-5527.

COLLEGE OF INSURANCE

New York, New York

General Information

Independent 5-year coed college. Founded 1962. Awards A (terminal), B, M. Primary accreditation: regional. Metropolitan setting. Total enrollment: 1,064. Faculty: 82 (17 full-time, 65 part-time).

Drug and Alcohol Information

Education

On campus Drug and alcohol education/prevention programs offered for: all students. College holds an annual alcohol awareness week and drug awareness week.

Identification of Problems

Admissions College application does not ask about prior substance abuse problems.

On campus Current students identified as chemically dependent may remain enrolled, but treatment is required. No training program on identifying students with potential substance abuse problems. No written procedures for students and staff if substance abuse is suspected.

Support Services

On campus Referral.

Employee assistance Program for chemically dependent employees not available.

Disciplinary Actions

Alcohol Results of infractions of alcohol regulations (see Comparative Table of Alcohol Regulations) include counseling, warning, probation.

Drugs For first-time use or possession: counseling, warning, probation. For subsequent use or possession: varies by situation. For any sale: varies by situation.

For More Information

Contact: Maureen Furlong-Weber, Director of Student Life, College of Insurance, 1 Insurance Plaza, 101 Murray St., New York, NY 10007. Telephone: 212-962-4111 Ext. 392.

COLLEGE OF MOUNT SAINT VINCENT

Riverdale, New York

General Information

Independent 5-year primarily women's college. Founded 1847. Awards A (college transfer), B, M. Primary accreditation: regional. Metropolitan setting; 70-acre campus. Total enrollment: 1,120. Faculty: 83 (59 full-time, 24 part-time).

Drug and Alcohol Information

Education

On campus Drug and alcohol education/prevention programs offered for: all students, athletes/coaches, faculty, administration, alumni. Authorized group concerned with responsible drinking. College holds an annual alcohol awareness week.

Identification of Problems

Admissions College application does not ask about prior substance abuse problems.

On campus Current students identified as chemically dependent may remain enrolled, but treatment is required. Training program on identifying students with potential substance abuse problems for: resident advisers. No written procedures for students and staff if substance abuse is suspected.

Support Services

On campus Support groups, private counseling, the College's own programs dealing with alcohol abuse and the problems of adult children of alcoholics.

Employee assistance Program for chemically dependent employees not available.

Disciplinary Actions

Alcohol Results of infractions of alcohol regulations (see Comparative Table of Alcohol Regulations) vary by situation but can include chemical dependency assessment, counseling, warning, probation, suspension, fines.

Drugs For first-time use or possession: counseling, probation, fine. For subsequent use or possession: varies by situation. For first-time sale: suspension, expulsion. For subsequent sale: expulsion.

Additional Information from the College

Because the College of Mount Saint Vincent has a small student population, faculty and staff can readily identify potential drug and/or alcohol problems and make the necessary referrals. Each student is treated as an individual in a unique set of circumstances.

For More Information

Contact: Debbie Pincus, Director of the Counseling Center, College of Mount Saint Vincent, Riverdale Avenue at 263rd St., Riverdale, NY 10471. Telephone: 212-549-8000.

COLLEGE OF NEW ROCHELLE

New Rochelle, New York

General Information

Independent 5-year primarily women's college. Founded 1904. Awards B, M. Primary accreditation: regional. City

College of New Rochelle (continued)

setting; 20-acre campus. Total enrollment: 2,240. Faculty: 173 (93 full-time, 80 part-time).

Drug and Alcohol Information

Education

On campus Drug and alcohol education/prevention programs offered for: all students. Authorized group concerned with responsible drinking. College holds an annual alcohol awareness week and drug awareness week.

Identification of Problems

Admissions College application does not ask about prior substance abuse problems.

On campus Current students identified as chemically dependent may remain enrolled, but treatment is required. Training program on identifying students with potential substance abuse problems for: resident advisers, administration. Written procedures for students and staff if substance abuse is suspected.

Support Services

On campus Private counseling.

Employee assistance Program for chemically dependent employees available.

Disciplinary Actions

Alcohol Results of infractions of alcohol regulations (see Comparative Table of Alcohol Regulations) vary by situation.

Drugs For first-time use: chemical dependency assessment, counseling, probation, suspension. For subsequent use: suspension. For first-time possession: counseling, probation, suspension. For subsequent possession: expulsion. For any sale: expulsion.

For More Information

Contact: Student Life Office, College of New Rochelle, Castle Place, New Rochelle, NY 10805. Telephone: 914-654-5364.

COLLEGE OF NOTRE DAME

Belmont, California

General Information

Independent Roman Catholic 5-year coed college. Founded 1851. Awards A (college transfer), B, M. Primary accreditation: regional. Small-town setting; 100-acre campus. Total enrollment: 1,052. Faculty: 94 (46 full-time, 48 part-time).

Drug and Alcohol Information

Education

On campus Drug and alcohol education/prevention programs offered for: all students; required for: resident advisers. College holds an annual alcohol awareness week.

Identification of Problems

Admissions College application does not ask about prior substance abuse problems.

On campus Current students identified as chemically dependent may remain enrolled. Training program on identifying students with potential substance abuse problems for: resident advisers. Written procedures for students and staff if substance abuse is suspected.

Support Services

On campus Private counseling.

Employee assistance Program for chemically dependent employees not available.

Disciplinary Actions

Alcohol Results of infractions of alcohol regulations (see Comparative Table of Alcohol Regulations) vary by situation.

Drugs For any use, possession, or sale: Offenders are subject to the College's disciplinary process.

For More Information

Contact: Lee Cauble, Director, Campus Activities, College of Notre Dame, Belmont, CA 94015. Telephone: 415-593-1601.

COLLEGE OF SAINT BENEDICT

Saint Joseph, Minnesota

General Information

Independent Roman Catholic 4-year women's college, coordinate with Saint John's University (MN). Founded 1887. Awards B. Primary accreditation: regional. Small-town setting; 700-acre campus. Total enrollment: 2,196. Faculty: 130 (111 full-time, 19 part-time). Social organization: 1 national sorority; 2% of eligible undergraduates are members.

Drug and Alcohol Information

Education

On campus Drug and alcohol education/prevention programs offered for: all students, athletes/coaches, faculty, administration. Bacchus chapter: 20 members. College holds an annual alcohol awareness week.

Identification of Problems

Admissions College application does not ask about prior substance abuse problems.

On campus Current students identified as chemically dependent may remain enrolled. Comments: Whether treatment is required is decided on a case-by-case basis. Training program on identifying students with potential substance abuse problems for: resident advisers, coaches, counselors. Written procedures for students and staff if substance abuse is suspected.

Support Services

On campus AA, Al-Anon, ACOA, support groups, private counseling.

Employee assistance Program for chemically dependent employees available. Staff working with drug/alcohol-related issues: 14 part-time.

Disciplinary Actions

Alcohol Results of infractions of alcohol regulations (see Comparative Table of Alcohol Regulations) vary by situation but can include chemical dependency assessment, counseling, warning, probation, suspension, fines.

Drugs For any use or possession: varies by situation. For any sale: suspension, expulsion; law enforcement authorities notified.

For More Information

Contact: Janine Thull, Joint Director of Student

Activities, Mary Commons, College of Saint Benedict, Saint Joseph, MN 56374. Telephone: 612-363-5035.

COLLEGE OF ST. CATHERINE

St. Paul, Minnesota

General Information

Independent Roman Catholic 5-year women's college. Founded 1905. Awards B, M. Primary accreditation: regional. Metropolitan setting; 110-acre campus. Total enrollment: 2,729. Faculty: 153. Social organizations: Little Sisters of TKE.

Drug and Alcohol Information

Education

On campus Drug and alcohol education/prevention programs offered for: all students. Authorized group concerned with responsible drinking. College holds an annual alcohol awareness week.

Identification of Problems

Admissions College application does not ask about prior substance abuse problems.

On campus Current students identified as chemically dependent may remain enrolled, but treatment is required. Training program on identifying students with potential substance abuse problems for: resident advisers. Written procedures for students and staff if substance abuse is suspected.

Support Services

On campus Private counseling, referrals.

Employee assistance Program for chemically dependent employees available. Staff working with drug/alcohol-related issues: 10 part-time.

Disciplinary Actions

Alcohol Results of infractions of alcohol regulations (see Comparative Table of Alcohol Regulations) vary by situation but can include chemical dependency assessment, counseling, warning, probation, suspension, expulsion. Comments: Alcohol-related infractions are dealt with primarily by referral, rather than being considered discipline problems.

Drugs For first-time use or possession: judicial assessment of chemical dependency, warning. For subsequent use: chemical dependency assessment, counseling, suspension. For subsequent possession: suspension. For first-time sale: varies by situation, but penalty is more severe than for use or possession. For subsequent sale: suspension, expulsion.

For More Information

Contact: Cindy McVenes, Assistant Director of Student Life, P.O. Box 4261, College of St. Catherine, 2004 Randolph Ave., St. Paul, MN 55105. Telephone: 612-690-6514.

COLLEGE OF SAINT ELIZABETH

Convent Station, New Jersey

General Information

Independent Roman Catholic 4-year primarily women's college. Founded 1899. Awards B. Primary accreditation: regional. Small-town setting; 200-acre campus. Total enrollment: 1,040. Faculty: 103 (46 full-time, 57 part-time).

Drug and Alcohol Information

Education

On campus Drug and alcohol education/prevention programs required for: all students. Authorized group concerned with responsible drinking. College holds an annual alcohol awareness week and drug awareness week.

Identification of Problems

Admissions College application does not ask about prior substance abuse problems.

On campus Current students identified as chemically dependent may remain enrolled, but treatment is required. No training program on identifying students with potential substance abuse problems. Written procedures for students and staff if substance abuse is suspected.

Support Services

On campus Private counseling.

Employee assistance Program for chemically dependent employees not available. Staff working with drug/alcohol-related issues: 4 part-time.

Disciplinary Actions

Alcohol Results of infractions of alcohol regulations (see Comparative Table of Alcohol Regulations) include counseling, warning, probation.

Drugs For first-time use, possession, or sale: varies by situation—counseling, warning, probation. For subsequent use, possession, or sale: varies by situation—probation, suspension.

For More Information

Contact: Diane Giachetti, Director of Counseling, College of Saint Elizabeth, Convent Station, NJ 07961. Telephone: 201-292-6444.

COLLEGE OF SAINT MARY

Omaha, Nebraska

General Information

Independent Roman Catholic 4-year primarily women's college. Founded 1923. Awards A (college transfer and terminal), B. Primary accreditation: regional. Metropolitan setting; 45-acre campus. Total enrollment: 1,133. Faculty: 139 (51 full-time, 88 part-time).

Drug and Alcohol Information

Education

On campus Drug and alcohol education/prevention programs offered for: all students, faculty, administration. Authorized group concerned with responsible drinking. College holds an annual alcohol awareness week.

Identification of Problems

Admissions College application does not ask about prior substance abuse problems.

On campus Current students identified as chemically dependent may remain enrolled, but treatment is required. No written procedures for students and staff if substance abuse is suspected.

Support Services

On campus AA, private counseling, referral.

Employee assistance Program for chemically dependent

College of Saint Mary (continued)

employees not available. Staff working with drug/alcohol-related issues: 3 part-time.

Disciplinary Actions

Alcohol Results of infractions of alcohol regulations (see Comparative Table of Alcohol Regulations) vary by situation but can include counseling, warning, probation.

Drugs For first-time use or possession: suspension. For subsequent use or possession: expulsion. For any sale: expulsion.

For More Information

Contact: Diane Proulx, Dean of Students, College of Saint Mary, 1901 S. 72nd St., Omaha, NE 68124. Telephone: 402-399-2458.

COLLEGE OF ST. SCHOLASTICA

Duluth, Minnesota

General Information

Independent 5-year coed college, affiliated with Roman Catholic Church. Founded 1906. Awards B, M. Primary accreditation: regional. City setting; 160-acre campus. Total enrollment: 1,835. Faculty: 142 (100 full-time, 42 part-time).

Drug and Alcohol Information

Education

On campus Drug and alcohol education/prevention programs offered for: all students, faculty. Bacchus chapter: 15 members. College holds an annual alcohol awareness week and drug awareness week.

Identification of Problems

Admissions College application does not ask about prior substance abuse problems.

On campus Current students identified as chemically dependent may remain enrolled, but treatment is required. Training program on identifying students with potential substance abuse problems for: resident advisers. No written procedures for students and staff if substance abuse is suspected.

Support Services

On campus AA, Al-Anon, ACOA, private counseling.

Employee assistance Program for chemically dependent employees not available.

Disciplinary Actions

Alcohol Results of infractions of alcohol regulations (see Comparative Table of Alcohol Regulations) include chemical dependency assessment, counseling, warning, fines.

Drugs For first-time use: varies by situation—chemical dependency assessment, warning. For first-time possession: varies by situation—warning. For subsequent use or possession: varies by situation—suspension. For first-time sale: varies by situation—probation. For subsequent sale: varies by situation—expulsion.

For More Information

Contact: Betsy Kneepkens, Director of Student Activities, College of St. Scholastica, 1200 Kenwood Ave., Duluth, MN 55811. Telephone: 218-723-6147.

COLLEGE OF ST. THOMAS

St. Paul, Minnesota

General Information

Independent Roman Catholic 5-year coed college. Founded 1885. Awards B, M, D. Primary accreditation: regional. Metropolitan setting; 78-acre campus. Total enrollment: 8,790. Faculty: 495 (231 full-time, 264 part-time). Social organizations: 2 national fraternities, 2 national sororities, 1 local fraternity, 2 local sororities.

Drug and Alcohol Information

Education

On campus Drug and alcohol education/prevention programs offered for: all students. Bacchus chapter: 40 members.

Identification of Problems

Admissions College application does not ask about prior substance abuse problems.

On campus Current students identified as chemically dependent may remain enrolled, but treatment is required. Training program on identifying students with potential substance abuse problems for: resident advisers, administration, student leaders. Written procedures for students and staff if substance abuse is suspected.

Support Services

On campus AA, ACOA, private counseling.

Employee assistance Program for chemically dependent employees available. Staff working with drug/alcohol-related issues: 1 full-time and 2 part-time.

Disciplinary Actions

Alcohol Results of infractions of alcohol regulations (see Comparative Table of Alcohol Regulations) vary by situation but can include chemical dependency assessment, warning, probation, suspension.

Drugs For first-time use or possession: varies by situation—chemical dependency assessment, probation. For subsequent use or possession: varies by situation—suspension. For first-time sale: suspension. For subsequent sale: expulsion.

For More Information

Contact: John Fennig, Alcohol and Drug Counselor, P.O. Box 5052, College of St. Thomas, St. Paul, MN 55105. Telephone: 612-647-5625.

COLLEGE OF SANTA FE

Santa Fe, New Mexico

General Information

Independent Roman Catholic 5-year coed college. Founded 1947. Awards A (college transfer and terminal), B, M. Primary accreditation: regional. City setting; 118-acre campus. Total enrollment: 1,602. Faculty: 63 (38 full-time, 25 part-time). Social organizations: 1 local fraternity, 1 local sorority, 6 social clubs; 35% of eligible undergraduate men and 48% of eligible undergraduate women are members.

Drug and Alcohol Information

Education

On campus Drug and alcohol education/prevention programs offered for: all students. Authorized group concerned with responsible drinking. College holds an annual alcohol awareness week.

Identification of Problems

Admissions College application does not ask about prior substance abuse problems.

On campus Current students identified as chemically dependent may remain enrolled, but treatment is required. Training program on identifying students with potential substance abuse problems for: resident advisers, faculty, administration. Written procedures for students and staff if substance abuse is suspected.

Support Services

On campus Al-Anon, private counseling.

Employee assistance Program for chemically dependent employees not available. Staff working with drug/alcohol-related issues: 4 part-time.

Disciplinary Actions

Alcohol Results of infractions of alcohol regulations (see Comparative Table of Alcohol Regulations) vary by situation but can include chemical dependency assessment, counseling, warning, probation.

Drugs For any use or possession: varies by situation. For first-time sale: suspension, expulsion. For subsequent sale: varies by situation.

For More Information

Contact: Yvonne Russell, Dean of Students, College of Santa Fe, Saint Michael's Dr., Santa Fe, NM 87501. Telephone: 505-473-6221.

COLLEGE OF STATEN ISLAND OF THE CITY UNIVERSITY OF NEW YORK

Staten Island, New York

General Information

State and locally supported 5-year coed college. Part of City University of New York System. Founded 1955. Awards A (college transfer and terminal), B, M. Primary accreditation: regional. Metropolitan setting; 40-acre campus. Total enrollment: 10,673. Faculty: 634 (335 full-time, 299 part-time). Social organizations: 5 social clubs.

Drug and Alcohol Information

Education

On campus Drug and alcohol education/prevention programs offered for: all students, faculty, administration. College holds an annual alcohol awareness week and drug awareness week.

Identification of Problems

Admissions College application does not ask about prior substance abuse problems.

On campus Current students identified as chemically dependent may remain enrolled. No training program on identifying students with potential substance abuse problems. No written procedures for students and staff if substance abuse is suspected.

Support Services

On campus Private counseling.

Employee assistance Program for chemically dependent employees available. Staff working with drug/alcohol-related issues: 4 part-time.

Disciplinary Actions

Alcohol Results of infractions of alcohol regulations (see Comparative Table of Alcohol Regulations) vary by situation.

Drugs For any use, possession, or sale: varies by situation.

For More Information

Contact: Mary Ruth Culbert, Assistant Professor and Counselor, College of Staten Island of the City University of New York, 715 Ocean Terrace, Staten Island, NY 10301. Telephone: 718-390-7630.

COLLEGE OF THE SOUTHWEST

Hobbs, New Mexico

General Information

Independent 4-year coed college. Founded 1962. Awards B. Primary accreditation: regional. Small-town setting; 162-acre campus. Total enrollment: 215. Faculty: 32 (9 full-time, 23 part-time).

Drug and Alcohol Information

Education

On campus Drug and alcohol education/prevention programs offered for: all students.

Identification of Problems

On Campus Current students identified as chemically dependent may remain enrolled, but treatment is required. No training program on identifying students with potential substance abuse problems. Written procedures for students and staff if substance abuse is suspected.

Support Services

On campus No support services on campus.

Employee assistance Program for chemically dependent employees not available.

Disciplinary Actions

Alcohol Results of infractions of alcohol regulations (see Comparative Table of Alcohol Regulations) include suspension. Comments: For a first infraction, a student is placed on social suspension; for the second, he or she is suspended from the College.

Drugs For first-time use, possession, or sale: varies by situation. For subsequent use, possession, or sale: suspension.

For More Information

Contact: Glenna M. Ohaver, Registrar, College of the Southwest, 6610 Lovington Highway, Hobbs, NM 88240. Telephone: 505-392-6561.

COLLEGE OF WILLIAM AND MARY

Williamsburg, Virginia

General Information

State-supported comprehensive coed institution. Founded 1693. Awards B, M, D. Primary accreditation: regional. Small-town setting; 1,200-acre campus. Total enrollment: 7,372. Faculty: 716 (574 full-time, 142 part-time). Social organizations: 13 national fraternities, 12 national

College of William and Mary (continued)

sororities; 35% of eligible undergraduate men and 35% of eligible undergraduate women are members.

Drug and Alcohol Information

Education

On campus Drug and alcohol education/prevention programs offered for: all students, athletes/coaches; required for: freshmen. Bacchus chapter. College holds an annual alcohol awareness week and drug awareness week.

Identification of Problems

Admissions College application does not ask about prior substance abuse problems.

On campus Current students identified as chemically dependent may remain enrolled, but treatment is required. Training program on identifying students with potential substance abuse problems for: resident advisers, coaches. Written procedures for students and staff if substance abuse is suspected.

Support Services

On campus AA, ACOA, support groups, private counseling.

Employee assistance Program for chemically dependent employees available. Staff working with drug/alcohol-related issues: 1 full-time and 8 part-time.

Disciplinary Actions

Alcohol Results of infractions of alcohol regulations (see Comparative Table of Alcohol Regulations) vary by situation.

Drugs For any use or possession: varies by situation. For first-time sale: suspension. For subsequent sale: varies by situation—expulsion.

For More Information

Contact: Cynthia Burwell, Health Educator, Student Health Service, College of William and Mary, Williamsburg, VA 23185. Telephone: 804-253-4386.

COLLEGE OF WOOSTER

Wooster, Ohio

General Information

Independent 4-year coed college, affiliated with Presbyterian Church. Founded 1866. Awards B. Primary accreditation: regional. Small-town setting; 320-acre campus. Total enrollment: 1,904. Faculty: 159 (147 full-time, 12 part-time). Social organizations: 7 local fraternities, 5 local sororities, eating clubs, coed fraternity; 24% of eligible undergraduate men and 17% of eligible undergraduate women are members.

Drug and Alcohol Information

Education

On campus Drug and alcohol education/prevention programs offered for: all students, athletes/coaches. Bacchus chapter: 4 members. Authorized group concerned with responsible drinking. College holds an annual alcohol awareness week.

Identification of Problems

Admissions College application does not ask about prior substance abuse problems.

On campus Current students identified as chemically dependent may remain enrolled, but treatment is required. Training program on identifying students with potential substance abuse problems for: resident advisers, coaches, Greek officers, administration. Written procedures for students and staff if substance abuse is suspected.

Support Services

On campus Private counseling.

Employee assistance Program for chemically dependent employees not available. Staff working with drug/alcohol-related issues: 2 part-time.

Disciplinary Actions

Alcohol Results of infractions of alcohol regulations (see Comparative Table of Alcohol Regulations) vary by situation but can include chemical dependency assessment, counseling.

Drugs For any use or possession: varies by situation. For any sale: expulsion.

Additional Information from the College

In its expectations of students' behavior, the College believes that its goals are best served in an atmosphere of personal self-discipline, guided by respect for the rights of others. Students are expected to know the Ohio state laws regarding sale and consumption of alcohol. The College makes it plain to students that it in no way condones drug abuse. At the same time, it is committed to helping individuals achieve a realistic understanding of the consequences of drug use for themselves and society. Literature concerning drugs is made available, as is therapeutic and counseling assistance on a confidential basis for any member of the community.

For More Information

Contact: Kenneth R. Plusquellec, Dean of Students, Galpin Hall, College of Wooster, Wooster, OH 44691. Telephone: 216-263-2545.

COLORADO TECHNICAL COLLEGE

Colorado Springs, Colorado

General Information

Proprietary 4-year coed college. Founded 1965. Awards A (college transfer and terminal), B. Primary accreditation: regional. City setting; 13-acre campus. Total enrollment: 1,147. Faculty: 50 (21 full-time, 29 part-time).

Drug and Alcohol Information

Education

On campus Drug and alcohol education/prevention programs offered for: all students, faculty, administration.

Identification of Problems

On campus Current students identified as chemically dependent may remain enrolled. No training program on identifying students with potential substance abuse problems.

Support Services

On campus No support services on campus.

Employee assistance Program for chemically dependent employees not available.

Disciplinary Actions

Alcohol Results of infractions of alcohol regulations (see Comparative Table of Alcohol Regulations) vary by situation but can include suspension, expulsion.

Drugs For first-time use, possession, or sale: suspension, expulsion. For subsequent use, possession, or sale: expulsion.

For More Information

Contact: Karen Nauman, Registrar, Colorado Technical College, 4435 N. Chestnut St., Colorado Springs, CO 80907. Telephone: 719-598-0200.

COLUMBIA CHRISTIAN COLLEGE

Portland, Oregon

General Information

Independent 4-year coed college, affiliated with Church of Christ. Founded 1956. Awards B. Primary accreditation: regional. Metropolitan setting; 15-acre campus. Total enrollment: 275. Faculty: 47 (28 full-time, 19 part-time). Social organizations: 2 local fraternities, 2 local sororities; 37% of eligible undergraduate men and 37% of eligible undergraduate women are members.

Drug and Alcohol Information

Education

On campus Drug and alcohol education/prevention programs offered for: all students.

Identification of Problems

Admissions College application question about prior substance abuse problems is used for counseling and referral, if student is admitted; in the admissions decision.

On campus Current students identified as chemically dependent may remain enrolled, but treatment is required. Training program on identifying students with potential substance abuse problems for: resident advisers. No written procedures for students and staff if substance abuse is suspected.

Support Services

On campus Support groups, private counseling.

Employee assistance Program for chemically dependent employees available. Staff working with drug/alcohol-related issues: 1 part-time.

Disciplinary Actions

Alcohol Results of infractions of alcohol regulations (see Comparative Table of Alcohol Regulations) vary by situation but can include chemical dependency assessment, counseling, warning, probation, suspension, expulsion.

Drugs For any use or possession: varies by situation—probation. For any sale: expulsion.

Additional Information from the College

Columbia Christian College has formed a committee to define and communicate a comprehensive drug and alcohol policy.

For More Information

Contact: Donald J. Boderman, Dean of Student Affairs, Columbia Christian College, 9101 E. Burnside St., Portland, OR 97216. Telephone: 503-255-7060.

COLUMBIA COLLEGE

Hollywood, California

General Information

Independent 4-year coed college. Founded 1952. Awards A (college transfer), B. Primary accreditation: NATTS. Metropolitan setting; 1-acre campus. Total enrollment: 200. Faculty: 28 (all part-time).

Drug and Alcohol Information

Education

On campus Drug and alcohol education/prevention programs not offered.

Identification of Problems

Admissions College application does not ask about prior substance abuse problems.

On campus Current students identified as chemically dependent may remain enrolled, but treatment is required. No training program on identifying students with potential substance abuse problems. No written procedures for students and staff if substance abuse is suspected.

Support Services

On campus No support services on campus.

Employee assistance Program for chemically dependent employees not available.

Disciplinary Actions

Alcohol Results of infractions of alcohol regulations (see Comparative Table of Alcohol Regulations) include expulsion.

Drugs For any use, possession, or sale: expulsion.

For More Information

Contact: Jamie Sullivan, Operations Manager, Columbia College, 925 N. LaBrea Ave., Hollywood, CA 90038. Telephone: 213-851-0550.

COLUMBIA COLLEGE

Chicago, Illinois

General Information

Independent 5-year coed college. Founded 1890. Awards B, M. Primary accreditation: regional. Metropolitan setting. Total enrollment: 6,045. Faculty: 575 (125 full-time, 450 part-time).

Drug and Alcohol Information

Education

On campus Drug and alcohol education/prevention programs offered for: all students, administration. Authorized group concerned with responsible drinking. College holds an annual alcohol awareness week.

Identification of Problems

Admissions College application does not ask about prior substance abuse problems.

On campus Current students identified as chemically dependent may remain enrolled, but treatment is required. Training program on identifying students with potential substance abuse problems for: administration. Written procedures for students and staff if substance abuse is suspected.

Columbia College (continued)

Support Services

On campus Private counseling.

Employee assistance Program for chemically dependent employees available. Staff working with drug/alcohol-related issues: 4 part-time.

Disciplinary Actions

Alcohol Results of infractions of alcohol regulations (see Comparative Table of Alcohol Regulations) include counseling, warning, probation, suspension, expulsion.

Drugs For any use or possession: varies by situation. For any sale: expulsion.

For More Information

Contact: Hermann Conaway, Dean of Students, Columbia College, 600 S. Michigan Ave., Chicago, IL 60605. Telephone: 312-663-1600.

COLUMBIA COLLEGE

Columbia, Missouri

General Information

Independent 4-year coed college, affiliated with Christian Church (Disciples of Christ). Founded 1851. Awards A (college transfer and terminal), B. Primary accreditation: regional. City setting; 20-acre campus. Total enrollment: 714. Faculty: 56 (41 full-time, 15 part-time).

Drug and Alcohol Information

Education

On campus Drug and alcohol education/prevention programs offered for: all students, athletes/coaches; required for: resident advisers. Authorized group concerned with responsible drinking. College holds an annual alcohol awareness week.

Identification of Problems

Admissions College application question about prior substance abuse problems is used for counseling and referral, if student is admitted.

On campus Current students identified as chemically dependent may remain enrolled. Training program on identifying students with potential substance abuse problems for: resident advisers, faculty, administration. Written procedures for students and staff if substance abuse is suspected.

Support Services

On campus Support groups, private counseling.

Off campus AA, NA, Al-Anon, ACOA.

Employee assistance Program for chemically dependent employees available. Staff working with drug/alcohol-related issues: 1 full-time and 2 part-time.

Disciplinary Actions

Alcohol Results of infractions of alcohol regulations (see Comparative Table of Alcohol Regulations) vary by situation but can include chemical dependency assessment, counseling, warning, community service.

Drugs For first-time use or possession: varies by situation—chemical dependency assessment, probation. For subsequent use: varies by situation—chemical dependency assessment, counseling, probation. For subsequent possession: expulsion. For any sale: expulsion.

Additional Information from the College

Columbia College's WellWay Program offers the most up-to-date information about wellness-centered life-styles as well as assessment, counseling, support and discussion groups, and referrals.

For More Information

Contact: Deborah Beste, Director, WellWay, Columbia College, 10th and Rogers, Columbia, MO 65216. Telephone: 314-875-7435.

COLUMBIA COLLEGE

New York, New York

General Information

Independent 4-year coed college. Part of Columbia University. Founded 1754. Awards B. Primary accreditation: regional. Metropolitan setting; 35-acre campus. Total university enrollment: 18,940. Faculty: 420. Social organizations: 17 national fraternities, 5 national sororities; 15% of eligible undergraduate men and 15% of eligible undergraduate women are members.

Drug and Alcohol Information

Education

On campus Drug and alcohol education/prevention programs offered for: all students, athletes/coaches.

Identification of Problems

Admissions College application does not ask about prior substance abuse problems.

On campus Current students identified as chemically dependent may remain enrolled. Comments: Treatment may or may not be required. Training program on identifying students with potential substance abuse problems for: resident advisers, administration, student/peer educators. No written procedures for students and staff if substance abuse is suspected.

Support Services

On campus AA, NA, Al-Anon, ACOA, private counseling, full-time alcohol educator/therapist.

Employee assistance Program for chemically dependent employees not available. Staff working with drug/alcohol-related issues: 1 full-time and 2 part-time.

Disciplinary Actions

Alcohol Results of infractions of alcohol regulations (see Comparative Table of Alcohol Regulations) vary by situation but can include chemical dependency assessment, counseling, warning, probation, suspension, expulsion.

Drugs For any use, possession, or sale: varies by situation.

For More Information

Contact: Ann Williams, Health Educator, Health Services, John Jay Hall, Columbia University, Broadway and 116th St., New York, NY 10027. Telephone: 212-280-5453.

COLUMBUS COLLEGE

Columbus, Georgia

General Information

State-supported 5-year coed college. Part of University System of Georgia. Founded 1958. Awards A (college transfer and terminal), B, M. Primary accreditation: regional. City setting; 157-acre campus. Total enrollment: 3,803. Social organizations: 7 national fraternities, 4 national sororities; 10% of eligible undergraduate men and 10% of eligible undergraduate women are members.

Drug and Alcohol Information

Education

On campus Drug and alcohol education/prevention programs offered for: all students; required for: athletes/coaches. Authorized group concerned with responsible drinking. College holds an annual alcohol awareness week and drug awareness week.

Identification of Problems

Admissions College application does not ask about prior substance abuse problems.

On campus Current students identified as chemically dependent may remain enrolled, but treatment is required. Training program on identifying students with potential substance abuse problems for: administration, students who have taken drug prevention seminar. Written procedures for students and staff if substance abuse is suspected.

Support Services

On campus Counseling center.

Employee assistance Program for chemically dependent employees not available. Staff working with drug/alcohol-related issues: 1 part-time.

Disciplinary Actions

Alcohol Results of infractions of alcohol regulations (see Comparative Table of Alcohol Regulations) include counseling, warning, probation.

Drugs For first-time use, possession, or sale: counseling, warning, probation. For subsequent use, possession, or sale: suspension.

For More Information

Contact: James H. Patrick, Assistant Vice President for Student Affairs, Room 274, Davidson Ctr., Columbus College, Columbus, GA 31993. Telephone: 404-568-2026.

COLUMBUS COLLEGE OF ART AND DESIGN

Columbus, Ohio

General Information

Independent 4-year specialized coed college. Founded 1879. Awards B. Primary accreditation: regional. Metropolitan setting; 13-acre campus. Total enrollment: 1,293. Faculty: 92 (53 full-time, 39 part-time).

Drug and Alcohol Information

Education

On campus Drug and alcohol education/prevention programs offered for: all students. College holds an annual alcohol awareness week.

Identification of Problems

Admissions College application does not ask about prior substance abuse problems.

On campus Current students identified as chemically dependent may remain enrolled, but treatment is required. No training program on identifying students with potential substance abuse problems. Written procedures for students and staff if substance abuse is suspected.

Support Services

On campus Private counseling.

Employee assistance Program for chemically dependent employees not available. Staff working with drug/alcohol-related issues: 3 part-time.

Disciplinary Actions

Alcohol Results of infractions of alcohol regulations (see Comparative Table of Alcohol Regulations) vary by situation but can include warning, probation, suspension, expulsion.

Drugs For first-time use: counseling, probation. For subsequent use: counseling, suspension. For first-time possession: counseling, warning. For subsequent possession: counseling, probation. For any sale: expulsion.

For More Information

Contact: Michael A. Young, Director of Student Affairs, Columbus College of Art and Design, 47 N. Washington Ave., Columbus, OH 43215. Telephone: 614-224-9101.

COMBS COLLEGE OF MUSIC

Philadelphia, Pennsylvania

General Information

Independent 5-year specialized coed college. Founded 1885. Awards B, M. Primary accreditation: regional. Metropolitan setting; 38-acre campus. Total enrollment: 67. Faculty: 15 (6 full-time, 9 part-time). Social organizations: 1 national fraternity, 1 national sorority; 15% of eligible undergraduate men and 15% of eligible undergraduate women are members.

Drug and Alcohol Information

Education

On campus Drug and alcohol education/prevention programs offered for: all students.

Identification of Problems

Admissions College application does not ask about prior substance abuse problems.

On campus Current students identified as chemically dependent may remain enrolled, but treatment is required. No training program on identifying students with potential substance abuse problems. No written procedures for students and staff if substance abuse is suspected.

Support Services

On campus Private counseling.

Employee assistance Program for chemically dependent employees not available.

Disciplinary Actions

Alcohol Results of infractions of alcohol regulations (see Comparative Table of Alcohol Regulations) vary by situation but can include chemical dependency assessment, counseling, warning, probation, suspension, expulsion, referral to law-enforcement authorities.

Drugs For any use or possession: varies by situation—counseling, warning. For first-time sale: varies by situation—counseling, warning, referral to law-enforcement officials. For subsequent sale: expulsion, referral to law-enforcement officials.

Additional Information from the College

Combs College of Music is located on the campus of Spring Garden College, which administers all substance abuse education and regulations for both colleges. Combs College

Combs College of Music (continued)

itself is a small, closely knit community where any problem can be discussed and addressed with compassion, concern, and fairness to all.

For More Information

Contact: Peter Rondinaro, Director, Student Development, Spring Garden College, 7500 Germantown Ave., Philadelphia, PA 19119. Telephone: 215-248-7910.

CONCORDIA COLLEGE

Ann Arbor, Michigan

General Information

Independent 4-year coed college, affiliated with Lutheran Church–Missouri Synod. Founded 1963. Awards A (college transfer), B. Primary accreditation: regional. City setting; 234-acre campus. Total enrollment: 422. Faculty: 77.

Drug and Alcohol Information

Education

On campus Drug and alcohol education/prevention programs offered for: all students, athletes/coaches, faculty, administration; required for: freshmen, resident advisers, student leaders. Authorized group concerned with responsible drinking. College holds an annual alcohol awareness week.

Identification of Problems

Admissions College application does not ask about prior substance abuse problems.

On campus Current students identified as chemically dependent may remain enrolled, but treatment is required. Training program on identifying students with potential substance abuse problems for: resident advisers, coaches, faculty, administration. Written procedures for students and staff if substance abuse is suspected.

Support Services

On campus Support groups, private counseling.

Employee assistance Program for chemically dependent employees not available.

Disciplinary Actions

Alcohol Results of infractions of alcohol regulations (see Comparative Table of Alcohol Regulations) vary by situation but can include chemical dependency assessment, counseling, warning, probation.

Drugs For first-time use or possession: varies by situation. For subsequent use or possession: expulsion. For any sale: expulsion.

For More Information

Contact: E. David Dolak, Dean of Student Services, Concordia College, 4090 Geddes Rd., Ann Arbor, MI 48105. Telephone: 313-995-7300.

CONCORDIA COLLEGE

Moorhead, Minnesota

General Information

Independent 4-year coed college, affiliated with Lutheran Church. Founded 1891. Awards B. Primary accreditation: regional. City setting; 120-acre campus. Total enrollment: 2,880. Faculty: 234 (185 full-time, 49 part-time).

Drug and Alcohol Information

Education

On campus Drug and alcohol education/prevention programs offered for: all students; required for resident advisers. Authorized group concerned with responsible drinking. College holds an annual alcohol awareness week.

Identification of Problems

Admissions College application does not ask about prior substance abuse problems.

On campus Current students identified as chemically dependent may remain enrolled. Comments: Treatment may or may not be required. Training program on identifying students with potential substance abuse problems for: resident advisers, administration.

Support Services

On campus AA, support groups, private counseling.

Employee assistance Program for chemically dependent employees available. Staff working with drug/alcohol-related issues: 18 part-time.

Disciplinary Actions

Alcohol Results of infractions of alcohol regulations (see Comparative Table of Alcohol Regulations) vary by situation but can include chemical dependency assessment, counseling, probation, suspension, expulsion, fines.

Drugs For first-time use: varies by situation—counseling, probation, suspension. For subsequent use: varies by situation—chemical dependency assessment, suspension, expulsion. For first-time possession: varies by situation. For subsequent possession: varies by situation—suspension, expulsion. For first-time sale: probation, suspension, expulsion. For subsequent sale: expulsion.

For More Information

Contact: Barbara Eiden-Molinaro, Associate Dean of Students, Concordia College, Moorhead, MN 56560. Telephone: 218-299-3455.

CONCORDIA COLLEGE

St. Paul, Minnesota

General Information

Independent 4-year coed college, affiliated with Lutheran Church–Missouri Synod. Founded 1893. Awards A (college transfer and terminal), B. Primary accreditation: regional. Metropolitan setting; 26-acre campus. Total enrollment: 1,133. Faculty: 85 (47 full-time, 38 part-time).

Drug and Alcohol Information

Education

On campus Drug and alcohol education/prevention programs offered for: all students, athletes/coaches. Authorized group concerned with responsible drinking. College holds an annual alcohol awareness week and drug awareness week.

Identification of Problems

Admissions College application does not ask about prior substance abuse problems.

On campus Current students identified as chemically dependent may remain enrolled. No training program on identifying students with potential substance abuse problems. Written procedures for students and staff if substance abuse is suspected.

Support Services

On campus Private counseling.

Employee assistance Program for chemically dependent employees not available.

Disciplinary Actions

Alcohol Results of infractions of alcohol regulations (see Comparative Table of Alcohol Regulations) vary by situation but can include chemical dependency assessment, counseling, warning, probation, suspension, expulsion.

Drugs For first-time use, possession, or sale: warning, fine. For subsequent use, possession, or sale: varies by situation—chemical dependency assessment, fine.

For More Information

Contact: Philip Tesch, Vice President for Student Services, Concordia College, 275 N. Syndicate, St. Paul, MN 55104. Telephone: 612-641-8216.

CONCORDIA COLLEGE

Bronxville, New York

General Information

Independent Lutheran 4-year coed college. Founded 1881. Awards A (college transfer and terminal), B. Primary accreditation: regional. Small-town setting; 33-acre campus. Total enrollment: 408. Faculty: 44 full-time.

Drug and Alcohol Information

Education

On campus Drug and alcohol education/prevention programs offered for: all students, faculty, administration; required for: athletes/coaches, resident advisers. Authorized group concerned with responsible drinking. College holds an annual alcohol awareness week and drug awareness week.

Identification of Problems

Admissions College application does not ask about prior substance abuse problems.

On campus Current students identified as chemically dependent may remain enrolled, but treatment is required. Training program on identifying students with potential substance abuse problems for: resident advisers, coaches. Written procedures for students and staff if substance abuse is suspected.

Support Services

On campus Support groups, private counseling.

Employee assistance Program for chemically dependent employees available. Staff working with drug/alcohol-related issues: 8 part-time.

Disciplinary Actions

Alcohol Results of infractions of alcohol regulations (see Comparative Table of Alcohol Regulations) vary by situation but can include counseling, probation, suspension, expulsion. For providing alcohol to underage students: suspension (first offense), expulsion (second offense).

Drugs For first-time use or possession: counseling, probation, suspension. For subsequent possession: expulsion. For any sale: expulsion.

For More Information

Contact: Linda Seeger, Director, Student Activities, Concordia College, 171 White Plains Rd., Bronxville, NY 10708. Telephone: 914-337-9300.

CONCORDIA LUTHERAN COLLEGE

Austin, Texas

General Information

Independent 4-year coed college, affiliated with Lutheran Church–Missouri Synod. Founded 1926. Awards A (college transfer), B. Primary accreditation: regional. City setting; 20-acre campus. Total enrollment: 507. Faculty: 43 (31 full-time, 12 part-time).

Drug and Alcohol Information

Education

On campus Drug and alcohol education/prevention programs offered for: all students, athletes/coaches, faculty, administration; required for: freshmen. Authorized group concerned with responsible drinking. College holds an annual alcohol awareness week and drug awareness week.

Identification of Problems

Admissions College application does not ask about prior substance abuse problems.

On campus Current students identified as chemically dependent may remain enrolled, but treatment is required. Training program on identifying students with potential substance abuse problems for: resident advisers, coaches, faculty. Written procedures for students and staff if substance abuse is suspected.

Support Services

On campus Private counseling.

Employee assistance Program for chemically dependent employees available.

Disciplinary Actions

Alcohol Results of infractions of alcohol regulations (see Comparative Table of Alcohol Regulations) include chemical dependency assessment, counseling, warning, probation, suspension.

Drugs For first-time use or possession: chemical dependency assessment, counseling, probation. For subsequent use or possession: suspension. For any sale: expulsion.

Additional Information from the College

Concordia Lutheran College's primary goal in its policy and program is to help any student or employee who is identified as having a problem. Suspension and/or expulsion are used only in cases where students refuse help. The College has established a formal relationship with a local treatment center. This center also helps with the College's education and prevention programming.

For More Information

Contact: Dr. Jim Koerscher, Dean of Student Services, Concordia Lutheran College, 3400 I-35 North, Austin, TX 78705. Telephone: 512-452-7661 Ext. 224.

CONCORDIA TEACHERS COLLEGE

Seward, Nebraska

General Information

Independent 5-year coed college, affiliated with Lutheran Church–Missouri Synod. Founded 1894. Awards B, M.

Concordia Teachers College (continued)

Primary accreditation: regional. Small-town setting; 120-acre campus. Total enrollment: 780. Faculty: 75 (66 full-time, 9 part-time).

Drug and Alcohol Information

Education

On campus Drug and alcohol education/prevention programs offered for: all students, faculty, administration; required for: freshmen, athletes/coaches, resident advisers. Authorized group concerned with responsible drinking. College holds an annual alcohol awareness week and drug awareness week.

Identification of Problems

Admissions College application does not ask about prior substance abuse problems.

On campus Current students identified as chemically dependent may remain enrolled, but treatment is required. Training program on identifying students with potential substance abuse problems for: resident advisers, administration. Written procedures for students and staff if substance abuse is suspected.

Support Services

On campus Private counseling.

Employee assistance Program for chemically dependent employees available.

Disciplinary Actions

Alcohol Results of infractions of alcohol regulations (see Comparative Table of Alcohol Regulations) include chemical dependency assessment, counseling, warning, probation, suspension, expulsion.

Drugs For first-time use: varies by situation—chemical dependency assessment, counseling, probation. For first-time possession: varies by situation—counseling, probation. For subsequent use or possession: suspension. For any sale: expulsion.

For More Information

Contact: Tom Baack, Director of Developmental Programming, Concordia Teachers College, Seward, NE 68434. Telephone: 402-643-7373.

CONSERVATORY OF MUSIC OF PUERTO RICO

Santurce, Puerto Rico

General Information

Commonwealth-supported 4-year specialized coed college. Founded 1959. Awards B. Primary accreditation: regional. Metropolitan setting; 6-acre campus. Total enrollment: 264. Faculty: 54 (23 full-time, 31 part-time).

Drug and Alcohol Information

Education

On campus Drug and alcohol education/prevention programs not offered.

Identification of Problems

Admissions College application does not ask about prior substance abuse problems.

On campus Current students identified as chemically dependent may remain enrolled. Comments: This situation has not arisen. No training program on identifying students with potential substance abuse problems. No written procedures for students and staff if substance abuse is suspected.

Support Services

On campus Private counseling.

Employee assistance Program for chemically dependent employees not available. Staff working with drug/alcohol-related issues: 1 part-time.

Disciplinary Actions

Alcohol Results of infractions of alcohol regulations (see Comparative Table of Alcohol Regulations) vary by situation.

Drugs For any use, possession, or sale: varies by situation.

Additional Information from the College

The Conservatory of Music of Puerto Rico is a small institution that has not experienced major problems of substance abuse. Individuals with difficulties are referred to the counselor.

For More Information

Contact: Mari Rosa Bruno, Counselor, Conservatory of Music of Puerto Rico, P.O. Box 41227, Minillas Station, Santurce, PR 00940. Telephone: 809-751-0160.

CONVERSE COLLEGE

Spartanburg, South Carolina

General Information

Independent 5-year women's college. Founded 1889. Awards B, M. Primary accreditation: regional. City setting; 70-acre campus. Total enrollment: 1,254. Faculty: 90.

Drug and Alcohol Information

Education

On campus Drug and alcohol education/prevention programs offered for: all students; required for: freshmen, athletes/coaches, resident advisers. Authorized group concerned with responsible drinking. College holds an annual alcohol awareness week and drug awareness week.

Identification of Problems

Admissions College application does not ask about prior substance abuse problems.

On campus Current students identified as chemically dependent may remain enrolled, but treatment is required. Training program on identifying students with potential substance abuse problems for: resident advisers, administration. No written procedures for students and staff if substance abuse is suspected.

Support Services

On campus ACOA, private counseling.

Employee assistance Program for chemically dependent employees available. Staff working with drug/alcohol-related issues: 1 full-time and 5 part-time.

Disciplinary Actions

Alcohol Results of infractions of alcohol regulations (see Comparative Table of Alcohol Regulations) include chemical dependency assessment, counseling, 4 days of campus restriction.

Drugs For first-time use or possession: varies by situation. For subsequent use or possession: suspension. For any sale: expulsion.

For More Information

Contact: Mary Helen Smith, Alcohol/Drug Educator, Converse College, 580 East Main, Spartansburg, SC 29301. Telephone: 803-596-9117.

COOPER UNION FOR THE ADVANCEMENT OF SCIENCE AND ART

New York, New York

General Information

Independent 5-year coed college. Founded 1859. Awards B, M. Primary accreditation: regional. Metropolitan setting. Total enrollment: 1,001. Faculty: 167 (59 full-time, 108 part-time). Social organizations: 3 national fraternities, 2 national sororities; 30% of eligible undergraduate men and 20% of eligible undergraduate women are members.

Drug and Alcohol Information

Education

On campus Drug and alcohol education/prevention programs not offered.

Identification of Problems

Admissions College application does not ask about prior substance abuse problems.

On campus Comments: Cooper Union has no experience with students who have been identified as chemically dependent. No training program on identifying students with potential substance abuse problems. No written procedures for students and staff if substance abuse is suspected.

Support Services

On campus Support groups (peers), private counseling.

Employee assistance Program for chemically dependent employees not available.

Disciplinary Actions

Alcohol Results of infractions of alcohol regulations (see Comparative Table of Alcohol Regulations) vary by situation. Comments: Results of infractions are assessed by the student judiciary.

Drugs For any use, possession, or sale: offenses are weighed by the student judiciary.

For More Information

Contact: Marylyn B. Gore, Dean of Students, Cooper Union for the Advancement of Science and Art, 41 Cooper Sq., New York, NY 10003. Telephone: 212-353-4115.

CORNELL COLLEGE

Mount Vernon, Iowa

General Information

Independent Methodist 4-year coed college. Founded 1853. Awards B. Primary accreditation: regional. Small-town setting; 110-acre campus. Total enrollment: 1,129. Faculty: 84 (73 full-time, 11 part-time). Social organizations: 5 local fraternities, 5 local sororities, 1 coed fraternity; 30% of eligible undergraduate men and 29% of eligible undergraduate women are members.

Drug and Alcohol Information

Education

On campus Drug and alcohol education/prevention programs offered for: all students. Bacchus chapter: 15 members. College holds an annual alcohol awareness week and drug awareness week.

Identification of Problems

Admissions College application does not ask about prior substance abuse problems.

On campus Current students identified as chemically dependent may remain enrolled, but treatment is required. No training program on identifying students with potential substance abuse problems. No written procedures for students and staff if substance abuse is suspected.

Support Services

On campus ACOA, private counseling, referral.

Employee assistance Program for chemically dependent employees not available. Staff working with drug/alcohol-related issues: 9 part-time.

Disciplinary Actions

Alcohol Results of infractions of alcohol regulations (see Comparative Table of Alcohol Regulations) vary by situation.

Drugs For any use, possession, or sale: varies by situation.

For More Information

Contact: Sharon Dendurent, Dean of Students, Cornell College, Mount Vernon, IA 52314. Telephone: 319-895-4000.

CORNELL UNIVERSITY

Ithaca, New York

General Information

Independent comprehensive coed institution. Founded 1865. Awards B, M, D. Primary accreditation: regional. Small-town setting; 740-acre campus. Total enrollment: 18,088. Faculty: 1,597 (1,551 full-time, 46 part-time). Social organizations: 43 national fraternities, 14 national sororities, 3 local fraternities, 1 local sorority; 36% of eligible undergraduate men and 32% of eligible undergraduate women are members.

Drug and Alcohol Information

Education

On campus Drug and alcohol education/prevention programs offered for: all students, faculty, administration, staff members; required for: athletes/coaches. Authorized group concerned with responsible drinking. College holds an annual alcohol awareness week and drug awareness week.

Identification of Problems

Admissions College application does not ask about prior substance abuse problems.

On campus Current students identified as chemically dependent may remain enrolled. Training program on identifying students with potential substance abuse problems for: resident advisers, ALERT peer educators. Written procedures for students and staff if substance abuse is suspected.

Support Services

On campus AA, Al-Anon, ACOA, private counseling.

Employee assistance Program for chemically dependent

Cornell University (continued)

employees available. Staff working with drug/alcohol-related issues: 1 full-time and 7 part-time.

Disciplinary Actions

Alcohol Results of infractions of alcohol regulations (see Comparative Table of Alcohol Regulations) vary by situation but can include chemical dependency assessment, counseling, warning, probation, suspension, expulsion, community service. Comments: Infractions are weighed by the Judicial Administrator and/or the University Hearing Board.

Drugs For first-time use or possession: varies by situation—warning. For subsequent use or possession: varies by situation. For any sale: varies by situation—suspension, expulsion.

Additional Information from the College

The Alcohol IQ Network is an interactive educational computer program much used by students. The University is using FIPSE funds to extend this program to include other potentially dangerous substances. The health education department conducts surveys, and its members give consultation and training programs as well as offer written resource materials on drug and alcohol topics. ALERT (Alcohol Education, Resource and Training) Peer Education Workshops are conducted by students who have had 13 weeks of training and cover a wide spectrum of issues related to drug and alcohol use and abuse.

For More Information

Contact: Kelly Enright, Health Educator, Gannett Health Center, Cornell University, 10 Central Ave., Ithaca, NY 14853. Telephone: 607-255-4782.

CORNISH COLLEGE OF THE ARTS

Seattle, Washington

General Information

Independent 4-year coed college. Founded 1914. Awards B. Primary accreditation: regional. Metropolitan setting; 4-acre campus. Total enrollment: 549. Faculty: 118 (28 full-time, 90 part-time).

Drug and Alcohol Information

Education

On campus Drug and alcohol education/prevention programs offered for: all students. College holds an annual alcohol awareness week and drug awareness week.

Identification of Problems

Admissions College application does not ask about prior substance abuse problems.

On campus Current students identified as chemically dependent may not remain enrolled. Comments: Occasionally, students may remain enrolled if they are in a treatment program. Informal training program on identifying students with potential substance abuse problems for: administration. Written procedures for students and staff if substance abuse is suspected.

Support Services

On campus Private counseling, referral.

Off campus AA, NA.

Employee assistance Program for chemically dependent employees not available. Staff working with drug/alcohol-related issues: 1 part-time.

Disciplinary Actions

Alcohol Results of infractions of alcohol regulations (see Comparative Table of Alcohol Regulations) include probation, suspension.

Drugs For any use, possession, or sale: varies by situation.

Additional Information from the College

Students with substance abuse problems are usually given an immediate medical leave of absence to seek appropriate treatment. When they return, the counselor sees them on a regular basis to aid in adjustment.

For More Information

Contact: William N. Oye, Ombudsman/Counselor, Cornish College of the Arts, 710 E. Roy St., Seattle, WA 98102. Telephone: 206-323-1400.

COVENANT COLLEGE

Lookout Mountain, Georgia

General Information

Independent 4-year coed college, affiliated with Presbyterian Church in America. Founded 1955. Awards A (college transfer and terminal), B. Primary accreditation: regional. Small-town setting; 70-acre campus. Total enrollment: 540. Faculty: 49 (42 full-time, 7 part-time).

Drug and Alcohol Information

Education

On campus Drug and alcohol education/prevention programs offered for: all students. Authorized group concerned with responsible drinking. College holds an annual alcohol awareness week and drug awareness week.

Identification of Problems

Admissions College application does not ask about prior substance abuse problems.

On campus Current students identified as chemically dependent may remain enrolled, but treatment is required. Training program on identifying students with potential substance abuse problems for: resident advisers, coaches. No written procedures for students and staff if substance abuse is suspected.

Support Services

On campus Support groups, private counseling.

Employee assistance Program for chemically dependent employees not available.

Disciplinary Actions

Alcohol Results of infractions of alcohol regulations (see Comparative Table of Alcohol Regulations) vary by situation but can include counseling, warning, probation, suspension, expulsion.

Drugs For first-time use: varies by situation—counseling, warning, probation. For first-time possession or sale: varies by situation—warning, probation. For subsequent use or possession: varies by situation—suspension. For subsequent sale: varies by situation—expulsion.

For More Information

Contact: Scott Raymond, Dean of Students, Covenant College, Lookout Mountain, GA 30750. Telephone: 404-820-1560.

CULVER-STOCKTON COLLEGE

Canton, Missouri

General Information

Independent 4-year coed college, affiliated with Christian Church (Disciples of Christ). Founded 1853. Awards A (terminal), B. Primary accreditation: regional. Small-town setting; 112-acre campus. Total enrollment: 1,032. Faculty: 60 (48 full-time, 12 part-time). Social organizations: 5 national fraternities, 3 national sororities, 1 local fraternity; 38% of eligible undergraduate men and 46% of eligible undergraduate women are members.

Drug and Alcohol Information

Education

On campus Drug and alcohol education/prevention programs offered for: all students; required for: athletes/coaches, resident advisers. Authorized group concerns with responsible drinking. College holds an annual alcohol awareness week and drug awareness week.

Identification of Problems

Admissions College application does not ask about prior substance abuse problems.

On campus Current students identified as chemically dependent may remain enrolled, but treatment is required. Training program on identifying students with potential substance abuse problems for: resident advisers, coaches. No written procedures for students and staff if substance abuse is suspected.

Support Services

On campus No support services on campus. Off-campus AA, Al-Anon.

Employee assistance Program for chemically dependent employees not available.

Disciplinary Actions

Alcohol Results of infractions of alcohol regulations (see Comparative Table of Alcohol Regulations) vary by situation but can include suspension.

Drugs For first-time use or possession: varies by situation. For subsequent use or possession: expulsion. For any sale: expulsion.

For More Information

Contact: Dr. Ken Hansmeier, Vice President of Student Services, Culver-Stockton College, Canton, MO 63435. Telephone: 314-288-3912.

DAKOTA WESLEYAN UNIVERSITY

Mitchell, South Dakota

General Information

Independent United Methodist 4-year coed college. Founded 1885. Awards A (college transfer), B. Primary accreditation: regional. Small-town setting; 40-acre campus. Total enrollment: 668. Faculty: 56 (37 full-time, 19 part-time).

Drug and Alcohol Information

Education

On campus Drug and alcohol education/prevention programs offered for: all students; required for: athletes/coaches. Authorized group concerned with responsible drinking. College holds an annual alcohol awareness week.

Identification of Problems

Admissions College application does not ask about prior substance abuse problems.

On campus Current students identified as chemically dependent may remain enrolled, but treatment is required. Training program on identifying students with potential substance abuse problems for: resident advisers. Written procedures for students and staff if substance abuse is suspected.

Support Services

On campus Private counseling.

Employee assistance Program for chemically dependent employees not available. Staff working with drug/alcohol-related issues: 6 part-time.

Disciplinary Actions

Alcohol Results of infractions of alcohol regulations (see Comparative Table of Alcohol Regulations) vary by situation.

Drugs For first-time use or possession: varies by situation—chemical dependency assessment, counseling, probation. For subsequent use or possession: varies by situation. For any sale: expulsion.

For More Information

Contact: David Mathieu, Dean of Student Development, Dakota Wesleyan University, 1200 W. University Ave., Mitchell, SD 57301. Telephone: 605-995-2950.

DANA COLLEGE

Blair, Nebraska

General Information

Independent Evangelical Lutheran Church in America 4-year coed college. Founded 1884. Awards B. Primary accreditation: regional. Small-town setting; 150-acre campus. Total enrollment: 500. Faculty: 60 (34 full-time, 26 part-time).

Drug and Alcohol Information

Education

On campus Drug and alcohol education/prevention programs offered for: all students, athletes/coaches. Bacchus chapter: 10 members. College holds an annual alcohol awareness week.

Identification of Problems

Admissions College application does not ask about prior substance abuse problems.

On campus Current students identified as chemically dependent may remain enrolled, but treatment is required. Training program on identifying students with potential substance abuse problems for: resident advisers, Student Services staff. No written procedures for students and staff if substance abuse is suspected.

Support Services

On campus Private counseling.

Employee assistance Program for chemically dependent employees available.

Disciplinary Actions

Alcohol Results of infractions of alcohol regulations (see

Dana College (continued)

Comparative Table of Alcohol Regulations) vary by situation but can include chemical dependency assessment, counseling, probation, suspension, expulsion, fines.

Drugs For first-time use, possession, or sale: varies by situation. For subsequent use, possession, or sale: expulsion.

For More Information

Contact: Dan Travaille, Dean of Student Services, Dana College, Blair, NE 68008. Telephone: 402-426-7252.

DANIEL WEBSTER COLLEGE

Nashua, New Hampshire

General Information

Independent 4-year coed college. Founded 1965. Awards A (college transfer and terminal), B. Primary accreditation: regional. City setting; 60-acre campus. Total enrollment: 544. Faculty: 35 (23 full-time, 12 part-time).

Drug and Alcohol Information

Education

On campus Drug and alcohol education/prevention programs offered for: all students; required for: resident advisers. College holds an annual alcohol awareness week and drug awareness week.

Identification of Problems

Admissions College application does not ask about prior substance abuse problems.

On campus Current students identified as chemically dependent may remain enrolled. No training program on identifying students with potential substance abuse problems. No written procedures for students and staff if substance abuse is suspected.

Support Services

On campus Private counseling.

Employee assistance Program for chemically dependent employees not available. Staff working with drug/alcohol-related issues: 1 part-time.

Disciplinary Actions

Alcohol Results of infractions of alcohol regulations (see Comparative Table of Alcohol Regulations) vary by situation.

Drugs For first-time use or possession: probation. For subsequent use or possession: suspension. For first-time sale: suspension. For subsequent sale: expulsion.

For More Information

Contact: Debra Roberge, Director, Student Health Services, Daniel Webster College, 20 University Dr., Nashua, NH 03063. Telephone: 603-883-6772.

DARTMOUTH COLLEGE

Hanover, New Hampshire

General Information

Independent comprehensive coed institution. Founded 1769. Awards B, M, D. Primary accreditation: regional. Rural setting; 265-acre campus. Total enrollment: 5,400. Faculty: 304 (291 full-time, 13 part-time). Social organizations: 9 national fraternities, 8 national sororities, 8 local fraternities, 1 local sorority, 5 coed fraternities.

Drug and Alcohol Information

Education

On campus Drug and alcohol education/prevention programs offered for: all students, athletes/coaches, administration; required for: freshmen. Authorized group concerned with responsible drinking. College holds an annual alcohol awareness week and drug awareness week.

Identification of Problems

Admissions College application does not ask about prior substance abuse problems.

On campus Current students identified as chemically dependent may remain enrolled. Comments: Treatment may or may not be required. Training program on identifying students with potential substance abuse problems for: resident advisers, coaches, Greek officers, administration. Written procedures for students and staff if substance abuse is suspected.

Support Services

On campus AA, Al-Anon, ACOA, support groups, private counseling.

Employee assistance Program for chemically dependent employees available. Staff working with drug/alcohol-related issues: 2 full-time and 5 part-time.

Disciplinary Actions

Alcohol Results of infractions of alcohol regulations (see Comparative Table of Alcohol Regulations) vary by situation.

Drugs For any use or possession: varies by situation. For first-time sale: suspension, expulsion. For subsequent sale: expulsion.

Additional Information from the College

Dartmouth College offers a wide array of services and opportunities for addressing the issues of alcohol and drug abuse, including counseling and medical services; educational programming; films, brochures, and posters; protocols for handling emergencies; liaisons with community and national resources; survey research; and the College Committee on Alcohol and Other Drugs.

For More Information

Contact: Dr. Philip W. Meilman, Coordinator of Alcohol and Drug Programs, Health Service, Dartmouth College, Hanover, NH 03755. Telephone: 603-646-5442.

DAVIDSON COLLEGE

Davidson, North Carolina

General Information

Independent Presbyterian 4-year coed college. Founded 1837. Awards B. Primary accreditation: regional. Small-town setting; 464-acre campus. Total enrollment: 1,376. Faculty: 116 full-time. Social organizations: 7 national fraternities, 3 local sororities, 1 eating club; 60% of eligible undergraduate men and 60% of eligible undergraduate women are members.

Drug and Alcohol Information

Education

On campus Drug and alcohol education/prevention programs offered for: all students.

Identification of Problems

Admissions College application does not ask about prior substance abuse problems.

On campus Current students identified as chemically dependent may remain enrolled, but treatment is required. Training program on identifying students with potential substance abuse problems for: resident advisers, administration.

Support Services

On campus AA, NA, ACOA. Staff working with drug/alcohol-related issues: 1 part-time.

Disciplinary Actions

Alcohol Results of infractions of alcohol regulations (see Comparative Table of Alcohol Regulations) include chemical dependency assessment, counseling, warning, probation.

Drugs For first-time use or possession: chemical dependency assessment, counseling, warning, probation. For subsequent use: counseling, probation, suspension. For any sale: suspension.

For More Information

Contact: Harriette Fulton, Assistant Dean of Students, Davidson College, P.O. Box 1719, Davidson, NC 28036. Telephone: 704-892-2225.

DAVIS & ELKINS COLLEGE

Elkins, West Virginia

General Information

Independent Presbyterian 4-year coed college. Founded 1904. Awards A (terminal), B. Primary accreditation: regional. Small-town setting; 170-acre campus. Total enrollment: 811. Faculty: 77 (52 full-time, 25 part-time). Social organizations: 4 national fraternities, 3 national sororities; 15% of eligible undergraduate men and 15% of eligible undergraduate women are members.

Drug and Alcohol Information

Education

On campus Drug and alcohol education/prevention programs offered for: all students, athletes/coaches. College holds an annual alcohol awareness week and drug awareness week.

Identification of Problems

Admissions College application does not ask about prior substance abuse problems.

On campus Current students identified as chemically dependent may remain enrolled, but treatment is required. Training program on identifying students with potential substance abuse problems for: resident advisers. No written procedures for students and staff if substance abuse is suspected.

Support Services

On campus AA, support groups, private counseling.

Employee assistance Program for chemically dependent employees not available. Staff working with drug/alcohol-related issues: 7 part-time.

Disciplinary Actions

Alcohol Results of infractions of alcohol regulations (see Comparative Table of Alcohol Regulations) include warning, probation, suspension.

Drugs For first-time use: counseling, warning. For subsequent use: warning, probation. For first-time possession: counseling, suspension. For subsequent possession: probation, suspension. For first-time sale: counseling, expulsion. For subsequent sale: suspension, expulsion.

For More Information

Contact: David H. Wilkey, Vice President, Student Administration, Davis & Elkins College, 100 Sycamore St., Elkins, WV 26241. Telephone: 304-636-1900.

DEACONESS COLLEGE OF NURSING

St. Louis, Missouri

General Information

Independent 4-year specialized primarily women's college, affiliated with United Church of Christ. Founded 1889. Awards B. Primary accreditation: regional. Metropolitan setting. Total enrollment: 183. Faculty: 13 (all full-time). Social organizations: Christian Fellowship and Student Nurse Association; 11% of eligible undergraduate men and 15% of eligible undergraduate women are members.

Drug and Alcohol Information

Education

On campus Drug and alcohol education/prevention programs offered for: all students.

Identification of Problems

Admissions College application does not ask about prior substance abuse problems.

On campus Current students identified as chemically dependent may remain enrolled, but treatment is required. Training program on identifying students with potential substance abuse problems for: resident advisers, administration. Written procedures for students and staff if substance abuse is suspected.

Support Services

On campus AA, support groups (Employee Assistance Program), private counseling.

Employee assistance Program for chemically dependent employees available.

Disciplinary Actions

Alcohol Results of infractions of alcohol regulations (see Comparative Table of Alcohol Regulations) include warning.

Drugs For first-time use or possession: chemical dependency assessment, counseling. For subsequent use or possession: counseling, probation. For any sale: expulsion.

Additional Information from the College

The College is fortunate in having the Deaconess Hospital Drug Abuse Department at its disposal.

For More Information

Contact: Kelly Avant, Director, Employee Assistance Program, Deaconess Hospital, 6150 Oakland Ave., St. Louis, MO 63139. Telephone: 314-768-3830.

DEFIANCE COLLEGE

Defiance, Ohio

General Information

Independent 4-year coed college, affiliated with United Church of Christ. Founded 1850. Awards A (college transfer and terminal), B. Primary accreditation: regional. Small-town setting; 150-acre campus. Total enrollment: 1,033. Faculty: 77 (55 full-time, 22 part-time). Social organizations: 3 national fraternities, 2 national sororities, 1 local sorority; 30% of eligible undergraduate men and 30% of eligible undergraduate women are members.

Drug and Alcohol Information

Education

On campus Drug and alcohol education/prevention programs offered for: all students; required for: freshmen. College holds an annual alcohol awareness week.

Identification of Problems

Admissions College application does not ask about prior substance abuse problems.

On campus Current students identified as chemically dependent may remain enrolled, but treatment is required. No training program on identifying students with potential substance abuse problems. Written procedures for students and staff if substance abuse is suspected.

Support Services

On campus Private counseling.

Employee assistance Program for chemically dependent employees not available.

Disciplinary Actions

Alcohol Results of infractions of alcohol regulations (see Comparative Table of Alcohol Regulations) vary by situation but can include counseling, warning, probation.

Drugs For first-time use or possession: probation. For subsequent use or possession: suspension. For first-time sale: suspension. For subsequent sale: expulsion.

For More Information

Contact: Joel Daniels, Dean of Students, Defiance College, 701 N. Clinton St., Defiance, OH 43512. Telephone: 419-784-4010.

DELAWARE VALLEY COLLEGE

Doylestown, Pennsylvania

General Information

Independent 4-year coed college. Founded 1896. Awards A (terminal), B. Primary accreditation: regional. Rural setting; 710-acre campus. Total enrollment: 1,165. Faculty: 80 (70 full-time, 10 part-time).

Drug and Alcohol Information

Education

On campus Drug and alcohol education/prevention programs offered for: all students, athletes/coaches, faculty, administration, peer counselors, community coordinators; required for: freshmen, resident advisers. Authorized group concerned with responsible drinking. College holds an annual alcohol awareness week and drug awareness week.

Identification of Problems

Admissions College application does not ask about prior substance abuse problems.

On campus Current students identified as chemically dependent may remain enrolled. Comments: Treatment is not required, but is highly recommended. Training program on identifying students with potential substance abuse problems for: resident advisers, coaches, faculty, administration. Written procedures for students and staff if substance abuse is suspected.

Support Services

On campus Private counseling, referral.

Disciplinary Actions

Alcohol Results of infractions of alcohol regulations (see Comparative Table of Alcohol Regulations) include counseling, warning, probation, suspension, expulsion.

Drugs For first-time use, possession, or sale: varies by situation. For subsequent use, possession, or sale: counseling, expulsion.

For More Information

Contact: H. William Craver, Dean of Students, Delaware Valley College, Doylestown, PA 18901. Telephone: 215-345-1500 Ext. 2216.

DENISON UNIVERSITY

Granville, Ohio

General Information

Independent 4-year coed college. Founded 1831. Awards B. Primary accreditation: regional. Small-town setting; 1,100-acre campus. Total enrollment: 2,108. Faculty: 176 (161 full-time, 15 part-time). Social organizations: 9 national fraternities, 7 national sororities; 57% of eligible undergraduate men and 66% of eligible undergraduate women are members.

Drug and Alcohol Information

Education

On campus Drug and alcohol education/prevention programs offered for: all students, faculty. Bacchus chapter: 15 members. College holds an annual alcohol awareness week and drug awareness week.

Identification of Problems

Admissions College application does not ask about prior substance abuse problems.

On campus Current students identified as chemically dependent may remain enrolled, but treatment is required. Training program on identifying students with potential substance abuse problems for: resident advisers, Greek officers, faculty, administration. Written procedures for students and staff if substance abuse is suspected.

Support Services

On campus AA, ACOA, private counseling, Peer Advisory Network (PAN).

Employee assistance Program for chemically dependent employees available. Staff working with drug/alcohol-related issues: 4 part-time.

Disciplinary Actions

Alcohol Results of infractions of alcohol regulations (see Comparative Table of Alcohol Regulations) include chemical dependency assessment, counseling, probation, suspension.

Drugs For first-time use or possession: varies by

situation—chemical dependency assessment, probation, suspension. For subsequent use or possession: varies by situation—chemical dependency assessment, suspension. For first-time sale: varies by situation—chemical dependency assessment, suspension. For subsequent sale: varies by situation—chemical dependency assessment, suspension, expulsion.

Additional Information from the College

Denison College has a very specific intervention and training model. When a behavioral infraction occurs, an investigation is made to determine whether alcohol was involved, and, if so, action is taken on both counts. Severe cases of intoxication are referred off campus for assessment and, if necessary, treatment.

For More Information

Contact: Dr. Jeff Pollard, Director, Office of Counseling Services, Denison University, Box H, Granville, OH 43023. Telephone: 614-587-6697.

DETROIT COLLEGE OF BUSINESS–FLINT

Flint, Michigan

General Information

Independent 4-year coed college. Part of Detroit College of Business. Founded 1974. Awards A (terminal), B. Primary accreditation: regional. City setting; 1-acre campus. Total enrollment: 728. Faculty: 45 (5 full-time, 40 part-time).

Drug and Alcohol Information

Education

On campus Drug and alcohol education/prevention programs offered for: all students, faculty, administration.

Identification of Problems

Admissions College application does not ask about prior substance abuse problems.

On campus Current students identified as chemically dependent may remain enrolled. Training program on identifying students with potential substance abuse problems for: faculty, administration. Written procedures for students and staff if substance abuse is suspected.

Support Services

On campus Private counseling.

Employee assistance Program for chemically dependent employees available. Staff working with drug/alcohol-related issues: 1 part-time.

Disciplinary Actions

Alcohol Results of infractions of alcohol regulations (see Comparative Table of Alcohol Regulations) vary by situation but can include chemical dependency assessment, counseling, warning, suspension, expulsion.

Drugs For any use, possession, or sale: varies by situation.

For More Information

Contact: Cari Skirlo, Director, Student Development Center, Detroit College of Business–Flint, 3115 Lawndale Ave., Flint, MI 48504. Telephone: 313-239-1443.

DEVRY INSTITUTE OF TECHNOLOGY

City of Industry, California

General Information

Proprietary 4-year coed college. Part of DeVry Inc/Keller Graduate School of Management. Founded 1983. Awards A (terminal), B. Primary accreditation: regional and NATTS. Metropolitan setting; 12-acre campus. Total enrollment: 2,251. Faculty: 56 (42 full-time, 14 part-time). Social organization: 1 local sorority.

Drug and Alcohol Information

Education

On campus Drug and alcohol education/prevention programs offered for: social organization members, resident advisers, students leaders; required for: freshmen. College holds an annual alcohol awareness week and drug awareness week.

Identification of Problems

Admissions College application does not ask about prior substance abuse problems.

On campus Current students identified as chemically dependent may remain enrolled. Comments: Treatment is recommended but not required. No training program on identifying students with potential substance abuse problems. No written procedures for students and staff if substance abuse is suspected.

Support Services

On campus Private counseling.

Employee assistance Program for chemically dependent employees available.

Disciplinary Actions

Alcohol Results of infractions of alcohol regulations (see Comparative Table of Alcohol Regulations) include counseling, warning, probation, suspension.

Drugs For first-time use or possession: counseling, probation. For subsequent use or possession: suspension. For first-time sale: suspension, expulsion. For subsequent sale: expulsion.

For More Information

Contact: Cary A. Whitcup, Dean of Students, DeVry Institute of Technology, 12801 Crossroad Pkwy. S., City of Industry, CA 91746-3495. Telephone: 213-699-9927 Ext. 556.

DEVRY INSTITUTE OF TECHNOLOGY

Decatur, Georgia

General Information

Proprietary 4-year coed college. Part of DeVry Inc. Founded 1969. Awards A (terminal), B. Primary accreditation: regional and NATTS. Small-town setting; 21-acre campus. Total enrollment: 3,085.

Drug and Alcohol Information

Education

On campus Drug and alcohol education/prevention programs offered for: resident advisers, student leaders;

DeVry Institute of Technology (continued)

required for: freshmen. College holds an annual alcohol awareness week and drug awareness week.

Identification of Problems

Admissions College application does not ask about prior substance abuse problems.

On campus No training program on identifying students with potential substance abuse problems. Written procedures for students and staff if substance abuse is suspected.

Support Services

On campus Referral.

Employee assistance Program for chemically dependent employees available.

Disciplinary Actions

Alcohol Results of infractions of alcohol regulations (see Comparative Table of Alcohol Regulations) vary by situation but can include probation, suspension.

Drugs For first-time use or possession: varies by situation—counseling. For subsequent use or possession: varies by situation. For any sale: varies by situation.

For More Information

Contact: Penny Morse, Associate Dean of Students, DeVry Institute of Technology, 250 N. Arcadia Ave., Decatur, GA 30030. Telephone: 404-292-7900.

DEVRY INSTITUTE OF TECHNOLOGY

Chicago, Illinois

General Information

Proprietary 5-year coed college. Part of DeVry Inc. Founded 1931. Awards A (terminal), B, M. Primary accreditation: regional and NATTS. Metropolitan setting; 17-acre campus. Total enrollment: 3,417.

Drug and Alcohol Information

Education

On campus Drug and alcohol education/prevention programs offered for: all students. Authorized group concerned with responsible drinking. College holds an annual alcohol awareness week and drug awareness week.

Identification of Problems

Admissions College application does not ask about prior substance abuse problems.

On campus Current students identified as chemically dependent may remain enrolled, but treatment is required. No training program on identifying students with potential substance abuse problems. Written procedures for students and staff if substance abuse is suspected.

Support Services

On campus NA, private counseling.

Employee assistance Program for chemically dependent employees available.

Disciplinary Actions

Alcohol Results of infractions of alcohol regulations (see Comparative Table of Alcohol Regulations) include chemical dependency assessment, counseling, warning, probation, suspension, expulsion.

Drugs For first-time use or possession: varies by situation. For first-time sale: chemical dependency assessment, counseling, expulsion. For subsequent use, possession, or sale: expulsion.

For More Information

Contact: Chris A. Murphy, Dean of Students, DeVry Institute of Technology, 3300 N. Campbell Ave., Chicago, IL 60618. Telephone: 312-929-8500.

DEVRY INSTITUTE OF TECHNOLOGY

Kansas City, Missouri

General Information

Proprietary 4-year coed college. Part of DeVry Inc/Keller Graduate School of Management. Founded 1931. Awards A (terminal), B. Primary accreditation: regional and NATTS. Metropolitan setting; 12-acre campus. Total enrollment: 1,607. Faculty: 48 (42 full-time, 6 part-time).

Drug and Alcohol Information

Education

On campus Drug and alcohol education/prevention programs offered for: all students; required for: freshmen. Authorized group concerned with responsible drinking. College holds an annual alcohol awareness week.

Identification of Problems

Admissions College application does not ask about prior substance abuse problems.

On campus Current students identified as chemically dependent may remain enrolled, but treatment is required. No training program on identifying students with potential substance abuse problems.

Support Services

On campus Referral.

Employee assistance Program for chemically dependent employees available. Staff working with drug/alcohol-related issues: 3 part-time.

Disciplinary Actions

Alcohol Results of infractions of alcohol regulations (see Comparative Table of Alcohol Regulations) vary by situation.

Drugs For first-time use, possession, or sale: varies by situation. For subsequent use, possession, or sale: suspension.

For More Information

Contact: Phil Kimmi, Director of Retention, DeVry Institute of Technology, 11224 Holmes Rd., Kansas City, MO 64131. Telephone: 816-941-0430.

DICKINSON COLLEGE

Carlisle, Pennsylvania

General Information

Independent 4-year coed college. Founded 1773. Awards B. Primary accreditation: regional. Small-town setting; 140-acre campus. Total enrollment: 1,991. Faculty: 146. Social organizations: 9 national fraternities, 4 national sororities, 1 local fraternity, 1 local sorority; 48% of eligible undergraduate men and 45% of eligible undergraduate women are members.

Drug and Alcohol Information

Education

On campus Drug and alcohol education/prevention programs offered for: all students, athletes/coaches, faculty, administration. Bacchus chapter: 34 members. College holds an annual alcohol awareness week.

Identification of Problems

Admissions College application does not ask about prior substance abuse problems.

On campus Current students identified as chemically dependent may remain enrolled. Training program on identifying students with potential substance abuse problems for: resident advisers, coaches, faculty, administration. Written procedures for students and staff if substance abuse is suspected.

Support Services

On campus AA, ACOA, support groups, private counseling.

Employee assistance Program for chemically dependent employees not available. Staff working with drug/alcohol-related issues: 1 full-time and 5 part-time.

Disciplinary Actions

Alcohol Results of infractions of alcohol regulations (see Comparative Table of Alcohol Regulations) can include chemical dependency assessment, counseling, warning, probation, suspension, expulsion, educational seminars.

Drugs For any use or possession: varies by situation. For any sale: suspension, expulsion.

Additional Information from the College

Dickinson College has received a FIPSE-funded grant to promote educational programs dealing with drugs and alcohol. A comprehensive substance abuse policy has been developed, and the positions of Alcohol and Drug Education Coordinator and Health Educator have been created and filled. A nonalcoholic coffeehouse for students is being built on campus. All these efforts on the part of the College have been met with a positive response.

For More Information

Contact: George Obermeier, Alcohol and Drug Education Coordinator, Dickinson College, Carlisle, PA 17013. Telephone: 717-245-1485.

DIVINE WORD COLLEGE

Epworth, Iowa

General Information

Independent Roman Catholic 4-year men's college. Founded 1912. Awards A (college transfer), B. Primary accreditation: regional. Rural setting; 28-acre campus. Total enrollment: 61. Faculty: 25 (23 full-time, 2 part-time).

Drug and Alcohol Information

Education

On campus Drug and alcohol education/prevention programs offered for: all students. Authorized group concerned with responsible drinking.

Identification of Problems

Admissions College application question about prior substance abuse problems is used to explain past academic performance; for counseling and referral, if student is admitted; in the admissions decision.

On campus Current students identified as chemically dependent may remain enrolled, but treatment is required. No training program on identifying students with potential substance abuse problems. Written procedures for students and staff if substance abuse is suspected.

Support Services

On campus Private counseling.

Off campus AA, NA, Al-Anon, ACOA.

Employee assistance Program for chemically dependent employees not available.

Disciplinary Actions

Alcohol Results of infractions of alcohol regulations (see Comparative Table of Alcohol Regulations) include counseling, warning, probation.

Drugs For any use, possession, or sale: expulsion.

For More Information

Contact: Bernard P. Spitzley, Dean of Students, Divine Word College, Epworth, IA 52045. Telephone: 319-876-3353.

DOANE COLLEGE

Crete, Nebraska

General Information

Independent 4-year coed college, affiliated with United Church of Christ. Founded 1872. Awards B. Primary accreditation: regional. Small-town setting; 360-acre campus. Total enrollment: 625. Faculty: 66 (46 full-time, 20 part-time). Social organizations: 5 local fraternities, 3 local sororities; 50% of eligible undergraduate men and 50% of eligible undergraduate women are members.

Drug and Alcohol Information

Education

On campus Drug and alcohol education/prevention programs offered for: all students, athletes/coaches. College holds an annual alcohol awareness week.

Identification of Problems

Admissions College application does not ask about prior substance abuse problems.

On campus Current students identified as chemically dependent may remain enrolled, but treatment is required. Training program on identifying students with potential substance abuse problems for: resident advisers, administration (Student Life). Written procedures for students and staff if substance abuse is suspected.

Support Services

On campus Private counseling, referral.

Employee assistance Program for chemically dependent employees not available. Staff working with drug/alcohol-related issues: 1 part-time.

Disciplinary Actions

Alcohol Results of infractions of alcohol regulations (see Comparative Table of Alcohol Regulations) vary by situation but can include chemical dependency assessment, counseling, warning, probation, attendance at educational programs, fines, writing a paper on the impact of alcohol use.

Drugs For first-time use: varies by situation. For first-time possession: suspension. For subsequent use or possession: chemical dependency assessment, counseling, suspension. For any sale: expulsion.

Doane College (continued)

For More Information

Contact: Dana Miller, Dean for Student Life, Doane College, 1014 Boswell Ave., Crete, NE 68333. Telephone: 402-826-8278.

DOMINICAN COLLEGE OF SAN RAFAEL

San Rafael, California

General Information

Independent Roman Catholic 5-year coed college. Founded 1890. Awards B, M. Primary accreditation: regional. Small-town setting; 80-acre campus. Total enrollment: 714. Faculty: 95 (45 full-time, 50 part-time).

Drug and Alcohol Information

Education

On campus Drug and alcohol education/prevention programs offered for: all students, athletes/coaches, faculty, staff. College holds an annual alcohol awareness week and drug awareness week.

Identification of Problems

Admissions College application does not ask about prior substance abuse problems.

On campus Current students identified as chemically dependent may remain enrolled, but treatment is required. Training program on identifying students with potential substance abuse problems for: resident advisers. Written procedures for students and staff if substance abuse is suspected.

Support Services

On campus No support services on campus.

Employee assistance Program for chemically dependent employees not available.

Disciplinary Actions

Alcohol Results of infractions of alcohol regulations (see Comparative Table of Alcohol Regulations) include chemical dependency assessment, counseling, warning, probation, suspension.

Drugs For first-time use or possession: varies by situation. For subsequent use: varies by situation—suspension. For subsequent possession: varies by situation—probation, suspension. For first-time sale: varies by situation—counseling, expulsion. For subsequent sale: varies by situation—expulsion.

For More Information

Contact: John Kennedy, Dean of Students, Dominican College of San Rafael, 1520 Grand Ave., San Rafael, CA 94901. Telephone: 415-485-3282.

DON BOSCO COLLEGE

Newton, New Jersey

General Information

Independent Roman Catholic 4-year specialized coed college. Founded 1928. Awards B. Primary accreditation: regional. Small-town setting; 180-acre campus. Total enrollment: 42. Faculty: 19 (6 full-time, 13 part-time).

Drug and Alcohol Information

Identification of Problems

Admissions College application question about prior substance abuse problems is used in the admissions decision.

Additional Information from the College

Don Bosco College is dedicated to the academic preparation of young men and women who feel called to the priesthood, brotherhood, or sisterhood in the Catholic Church. Students are well aware of the problems of substance abuse, but they would not be accepted as candidates for the priesthood or other ministries if they had these problems themselves. Therefore, no drug or alcohol programs are needed at Don Bosco College.

For More Information

Contact: Rev. David G. Moreno, Academic Dean – Registrar, Don Bosco College, Swartswood Rd., Newton, NJ 07860. Telephone: 201-383-3900.

DORDT COLLEGE

Sioux Center, Iowa

General Information

Independent Christian Reformed 4-year coed college. Founded 1955. Awards A (terminal), B. Primary accreditation: regional. Rural setting; 45-acre campus. Total enrollment: 987. Faculty: 70 (61 full-time, 9 part-time).

Drug and Alcohol Information

Education

On campus Drug and alcohol education/prevention programs offered for: all students; required for: freshmen. Authorized group concerned with responsible drinking. College holds an annual alcohol awareness week.

Identification of Problems

Admissions College application does not ask about prior substance abuse problems.

On campus Current students identified as chemically dependent may remain enrolled, but treatment is required. Training program on identifying students with potential substance abuse problems for: resident advisers. Written procedures for students and staff if substance abuse is suspected.

Support Services

On campus Private counseling.

Off campus Alcohol and Drug Rehabilitation Center in town.

Employee assistance Program for chemically dependent employees not available. Staff working with drug/alcohol-related issues: 2 part-time.

Disciplinary Actions

Alcohol Results of infractions of alcohol regulations (see Comparative Table of Alcohol Regulations) include chemical dependency assessment, counseling, probation, suspension, expulsion.

Drugs For first-time use: chemical dependency assessment, counseling, probation. For first-time possession or sale: suspension. For subsequent use, possession, or sale: expulsion.

For More Information

Contact: Glenda Droogsma, Director of Personal

Counseling, Dordt College, Sioux Center, IA 51250. Telephone: 712-722-6070.

DRAKE UNIVERSITY

Des Moines, Iowa

General Information

Independent comprehensive coed institution. Founded 1881. Awards B, M, D. Primary accreditation: regional. City setting; 120-acre campus. Total enrollment: 6,618. Faculty: 256 (242 full-time, 14 part-time). Social organizations: 12 national fraternities, 8 national sororities; 27% of eligible undergraduate men and 31% of eligible undergraduate women are members.

Drug and Alcohol Information

Education

On campus Drug and alcohol education/prevention programs offered for: all students, athletes/coaches. College holds an annual alcohol awareness week.

Identification of Problems

Admissions College application does not ask about prior substance abuse problems.

On campus Current students identified as chemically dependent may remain enrolled, but treatment is required. Training program on identifying students with potential substance abuse problems for: resident advisers, coaches, administration, Health and Counseling Center staff. Written procedures for students and staff if substance abuse is suspected.

Support Services

On campus AA, support groups (peer counseling), private counseling.

Employee assistance Program for chemically dependent employees available.

Disciplinary Actions

Alcohol Results of infractions of alcohol regulations (see Comparative Table of Alcohol Regulations) vary by situation but can include chemical dependency assessment, counseling, warning, probation, suspension, expulsion.

Drugs For first-time use, possession, or sale: varies by situation. For subsequent use or possession: varies by situation. For subsequent sale: suspension, expulsion.

For More Information

Contact: Robert Brodie, Director of Student Life, Drake University, Des Moines, IA 50311. Telephone: 515-271-3713.

D'YOUVILLE COLLEGE

Buffalo, New York

General Information

Independent 5-year coed college. Founded 1908. Awards B, M. Primary accreditation: regional. Metropolitan setting; 5-acre campus. Total enrollment: 1,100. Faculty: 97 (75 full-time, 22 part-time).

Drug and Alcohol Information

Education

On campus Drug and alcohol education/prevention programs offered for: all students. College holds an annual alcohol awareness week.

Identification of Problems

Admissions College application does not ask about prior substance abuse problems.

On campus Current students identified as chemically dependent may remain enrolled, but treatment is required. No training program on identifying students with potential substance abuse problems. No written procedures for students and staff if substance abuse is suspected.

Support Services

On campus Support groups, private counseling.

Employee assistance Program for chemically dependent employees not available.

Disciplinary Actions

Alcohol Results of infractions of alcohol regulations (see Comparative Table of Alcohol Regulations) can include counseling, warning, probation, suspension, expulsion.

Drugs For first-time use or possession: varies by situation—counseling, probation. For subsequent use or possession: varies by situation. For first-time sale: suspension. For subsequent sale: expulsion.

For More Information

Contact: Robert Murphy, Vice President, Student Affairs, D'Youville College, 320 Porter Ave., Buffalo, NY 14201. Telephone: 716-881-7685.

EARLHAM COLLEGE

Richmond, Indiana

General Information

Independent 5-year coed college, affiliated with Society of Friends. Founded 1847. Awards B, M. Primary accreditation: regional. Small-town setting; 800-acre campus. Total enrollment: 1,232. Faculty: 122 (82 full-time, 40 part-time).

Drug and Alcohol Information

Education

On campus Drug and alcohol education/prevention programs offered for: all students, athletes/coaches, faculty, administration, support staff. Authorized group concerned with responsible drinking. College holds an annual alcohol awareness week and drug awareness week.

Identification of Problems

Admissions College application does not ask about prior substance abuse problems.

On campus Current students identified as chemically dependent may remain enrolled, but treatment is required. Training program on identifying students with potential substance abuse problems for: resident advisers, coaches, faculty, administration, any interested students. Written procedures for students and staff if substance abuse is suspected.

Support Services

On campus Al-Anon, ACOA, support groups, private counseling.

Employee assistance Program for chemically dependent employees not available.

Disciplinary Actions

Alcohol Results of infractions of alcohol regulations (see Comparative Table of Alcohol Regulations) vary by situation.

Earlham College (continued)

Drugs For any use, possession, or sale: varies by situation.

For More Information

Contact: Anne Wright, Dean of Student Development, Earlham College, Richmond, IN 47374. Telephone: 317-983-1311.

EAST CAROLINA UNIVERSITY

Greenville, North Carolina

General Information

State-supported comprehensive coed institution. Part of University of North Carolina System. Founded 1907. Awards B, M, D. Primary accreditation: regional. Small-town setting; 411-acre campus. Total enrollment: 15,579. Faculty: 1,041 (1,026 full-time, 15 part-time). Social organizations: 19 national fraternities, 12 national sororities; 8% of eligible undergraduate men and 8% of eligible undergraduate women are members.

Drug and Alcohol Information

Education

On campus Drug and alcohol education/prevention programs offered for: all students; required for: athletes/coaches, resident advisers. Bacchus chapter: 20 members. College holds an annual alcohol awareness week and drug awareness week.

Identification of Problems

Admissions College application does not ask about prior substance abuse problems.

On campus Current students identified as chemically dependent may remain enrolled, but treatment is required. Training program on identifying students with potential substance abuse problems for: resident advisers, coaches, administration. Written procedures for students and staff if substance abuse is suspected.

Support Services

On campus No support services on campus.

Employee assistance Program for chemically dependent employees available. Staff working with drug/alcohol-related issues: 2 full-time.

Disciplinary Actions

Alcohol Results of infractions of alcohol regulations (see Comparative Table of Alcohol Regulations) vary by situation but can include warning, probation.

Drugs For first-time use or possession: chemical dependency assessment, counseling, probation (marijuana); suspension (cocaine). For first-time sale: suspension (marijuana), expulsion (cocaine). For subsequent use, possession, or sale: expulsion.

For More Information

Contact: Ron Speier, Assistant Vice Chancellor for Student Life, 209 Whichard, East Carolina University, Greenville, NC 27834. Telephone: 919-757-6824.

EAST COAST BIBLE COLLEGE

Charlotte, North Carolina

General Information

Independent 4-year coed college, affiliated with Church of God. Founded 1976. Awards A (college transfer), B. Primary accreditation: regional (candidate) and AABC. City setting; 100-acre campus. Total enrollment: 252. Faculty: 15 (8 full-time, 7 part-time). Social organizations: local fraternities, local sororities.

Drug and Alcohol Information

Education

On campus Drug and alcohol education/prevention programs not offered.

Identification of Problems

Admissions

On campus Current students identified as chemically dependent may not remain enrolled. No training program on identifying students with potential substance abuse problems. Written procedures for students and staff if substance abuse is suspected.

Support Services

On campus Private counseling.

Employee assistance Program for chemically dependent employees not available.

Disciplinary Actions

Alcohol Results of infractions of alcohol regulations (see Comparative Table of Alcohol Regulations): expulsion.

Drugs For any use, possession, or sale: expulsion.

For More Information

Contact: Bobby Gilley, Dean of Students, East Coast Bible College, 6900 Wilkinson Blvd., Charlotte, NC 28214. Telephone: 704-394-2307 Ext. 22.

EASTERN CHRISTIAN COLLEGE

Bel Air, Maryland

General Information

Independent 4-year coed college, affiliated with Church of Christ. Founded 1946. Awards A (college transfer and terminal), B. Primary accreditation: U.S. Department of Education (3IC). Rural setting; 44-acre campus. Total enrollment: 45. Faculty: 13 (4 full-time, 9 part-time).

Drug and Alcohol Information

Education

On campus Drug and alcohol education/prevention programs offered as needed.

Identification of Problems

Admissions College application question about prior substance abuse problems is used in the admissions decision.

On campus Current students identified as chemically dependent may remain enrolled, but treatment is required. No training program on identifying students with potential substance abuse problems. Written procedures for students and staff if substance abuse is suspected.

Support Services

On campus Private counseling.

Employee assistance Program for chemically dependent employees not available.

Disciplinary Actions

Alcohol Results of infractions of alcohol regulations (see Comparative Table of Alcohol Regulations) include counseling, probation, suspension.

Drugs For first-time use, possession, or sale: counseling, probation, suspension. For subsequent use, possession, or sale: suspension.

For More Information

Contact: Terry Silence, Dean of Students, Eastern Christian College, P.O. Box 629, Bel Air, MD 21014. Telephone: 301-734-7727.

EASTERN COLLEGE

Saint Davids, Pennsylvania

General Information

Independent American Baptist 5-year coed college. Founded 1932. Awards B, M. Primary accreditation: regional. Small-town setting; 100-acre campus. Total enrollment: 1,178. Faculty: 100 (60 full-time, 40 part-time).

Drug and Alcohol Information

Education

On campus Drug and alcohol education/prevention programs offered for: all students. Authorized group concerned with responsible drinking. College holds an annual alcohol awareness week.

Identification of Problems

Admissions College application does not ask about prior substance abuse problems.

On campus Current students identified as chemically dependent may remain enrolled, but treatment is required. Training program on identifying students with potential substance abuse problems for: resident advisers, residence hall staff. No written procedures for students and staff if substance abuse is suspected.

Support Services

On campus ACOA, support groups, private counseling.

Employee assistance Program for chemically dependent employees not available. Staff working with drug/alcohol-related issues: 3 part-time.

Disciplinary Actions

Alcohol Results of infractions of alcohol regulations (see Comparative Table of Alcohol Regulations) vary by situation but can include chemical dependency assessment, counseling, warning, probation, suspension, expulsion.

Drugs For any use: varies by situation. For first-time possession: varies by situation—probation, suspension. For subsequent possession: suspension. For any sale: expulsion.

Additional Information from the College

Eastern College makes use of off-campus, community-based services for a host of dependency-related problems. The College community is small, and much outreach work with students is done by the Residence Life and Dean of Students' office staffs.

For More Information

Contact: B. A. Brigham, Associate Dean of Students, Eastern College, Fairview Dr., Saint Davids, PA 19087. Telephone: 215-341-5822.

EASTERN ILLINOIS UNIVERSITY

Charleston, Illinois

General Information

State-supported 5-year coed college. Part of Board of Governors of State Colleges and Universities. Founded 1895. Awards B, M. Primary accreditation: regional. Small-town setting; 316-acre campus. Total enrollment: 10,510. Faculty: 570 (450 full-time, 120 part-time). Social organizations: 12 national fraternities, 13 national sororities; 8% of eligible undergraduate men and 9% of eligible undergraduate women are members.

Drug and Alcohol Information

Education

On campus Drug and alcohol education/prevention programs offered for: all students. Bacchus chapter: 57 members. College holds an annual alcohol awareness week and drug awareness week.

Identification of Problems

Admissions College application does not ask about prior substance abuse problems.

On campus Current students identified as chemically dependent may remain enrolled, but treatment is required. No training program on identifying students with potential substance abuse problems. No written procedures for students and staff if substance abuse is suspected.

Support Services

On campus ACOA, support groups, private counseling.

Employee assistance Program for chemically dependent employees available. Staff working with drug/alcohol-related issues: 1 full-time.

Disciplinary Actions

Alcohol Results of infractions of alcohol regulations (see Comparative Table of Alcohol Regulations) vary by situation but can include warning, fines, community service.

Drugs For first-time use: varies by situation—warning. For subsequent use: varies by situation—probation. For first-time possession: varies by situation. For subsequent possession: varies by situation—suspension. For any sale: varies by situation-expulsion.

For More Information

Contact: Sandy Gallion, Drug, Alcohol, and AIDS Information Coordinator, Pemberton Hall, Eastern Illinois University, Charleston, IL 61920. Telephone: 217-581-2478.

EASTERN MENNONITE COLLEGE

Harrisonburg, Virginia

General Information

Independent Mennonite 4-year coed college. Administratively affiliated with Eastern Mennonite

Eastern Mennonite College (continued)

Seminary. Founded 1917. Awards A (college transfer and terminal), B. Primary accreditation: regional. Small-town setting; 88-acre campus. Total enrollment: 967. Faculty: 80 (56 full-time, 24 part-time).

Drug and Alcohol Information

Education

On campus Drug and alcohol education/prevention programs offered for: all students.

Identification of Problems

Admissions College application does not ask about prior substance abuse problems.

On campus Current students identified as chemically dependent may remain enrolled, but treatment is required. No training program on identifying students with potential substance abuse problems. No written procedures for students and staff if substance abuse is suspected.

Support Services

On campus Private counseling.

Employee assistance Program for chemically dependent employees not available. Staff working with drug/alcohol-related issues: 6 part-time.

Disciplinary Actions

Alcohol Results of infractions of alcohol regulations (see Comparative Table of Alcohol Regulations) include chemical dependency assessment, counseling, warning, probation, suspension.

Drugs For any use, possession, or sale: varies by situation.

For More Information

Contact: Peggy H. Landis, Director of Student Life, Eastern Mennonite College, 1200 Park Rd., Harrisonburg, VA 22801. Telephone: 703-433-2771 Ext. 128.

EASTERN MICHIGAN UNIVERSITY

Ypsilanti, Michigan

General Information

State-supported 5-year coed college. Founded 1849. Awards B, M. Primary accreditation: regional. Small-town setting; 460-acre campus. Total enrollment: 23,641. Faculty: 1,049 (677 full-time, 372 part-time). Social organizations: 12 national fraternities, 9 national sororities, 1 local fraternity, 1 local sorority; 5% of eligible undergraduate men and 2% of eligible undergraduate women are members.

Drug and Alcohol Information

Education

On campus Drug and alcohol education/prevention programs offered for: all students. Authorized group concerned with responsible drinking. College holds an annual alcohol awareness week and drug awareness week.

Identification of Problems

Admissions College application does not ask about prior substance abuse problems.

On campus Current students identified as chemically dependent may remain enrolled. Training program on identifying students with potential substance abuse problems for: resident advisers, coaches, faculty. No written procedures for students and staff if substance abuse is suspected.

Support Services

On campus AA, Al-Anon, ACOA.

Employee assistance Program for chemically dependent employees not available. Staff working with drug/alcohol-related issues: 1 full-time and 3 part-time.

Disciplinary Actions

Alcohol Results of infractions of alcohol regulations (see Comparative Table of Alcohol Regulations) vary by situation.

Drugs For first-time use or possession: probation. For subsequent use or possession: suspension. For any sale: expulsion.

Additional Information from the College

Eastern Michigan University has received an FIPSE grant to expand its staffing and its training programs in the area of substance abuse.

For More Information

Contact: Dr. Rosalyn Barclay, Associate Director of Counseling Services, Snow Health Center, Eastern Michigan University, Ypsilanti, MI 48197. Telephone: 313-487-1118.

EASTERN MONTANA COLLEGE

Billings, Montana

General Information

State-supported 5-year coed college. Part of Montana University System. Founded 1927. Awards A (college transfer and terminal), B, M. Primary accreditation: regional. City setting; 92-acre campus. Total enrollment: 3,994. Faculty: 156 (150 full-time, 6 part-time). Social organizations: 1 local fraternity, 1 local sorority.

Drug and Alcohol Information

Education

On campus Drug and alcohol education/prevention programs offered for: all students. Authorized group concerned with responsible drinking. College holds an annual alcohol awareness week and drug awareness week.

Identification of Problems

Admissions College application does not ask about prior substance abuse problems.

On campus Current students identified as chemically dependent may remain enrolled, but treatment is required. No training program on identifying students with potential substance abuse problems. No written procedures for students and staff if substance abuse is suspected.

Support Services

On campus AA, support groups, private counseling.

Employee assistance Program for chemically dependent employees not available.

Disciplinary Actions

Alcohol Results of infractions of alcohol regulations (see Comparative Table of Alcohol Regulations) vary by situation but can include chemical dependency assessment, counseling, warning, probation, suspension, expulsion.

Drugs For first-time use or possession: varies by situation.

For subsequent use or possession: suspension, expulsion. For any sale: suspension, expulsion.

For More Information

Contact: Lowell Dunlop, Dean of Students, Eastern Montana College, 1500 N. 27th St., Billings, MT 59101. Telephone: 406-657-2308.

EASTERN NEW MEXICO UNIVERSITY

Portales, New Mexico

General Information

State-supported 5-year coed college. Part of Eastern New Mexico University System. Founded 1934. Awards A (college transfer and terminal), B, M. Primary accreditation: regional. Small-town setting; 240-acre campus. Total enrollment: 3,418. Faculty: 200 (141 full-time, 59 part-time). Social organizations: 6 national fraternities, 3 national sororities; 15% of eligible undergraduate men and 5% of eligible undergraduate women are members.

Drug and Alcohol Information

Education

On campus Drug and alcohol education/prevention programs offered for: social organization members, resident advisers. Authorized group concerned with responsible drinking. College holds an annual alcohol awareness week.

Identification of Problems

Admissions College application does not ask about prior substance abuse problems.

On campus Current students identified as chemically dependent may remain enrolled. No training program on identifying students with potential substance abuse problems. No written procedures for students and staff if substance abuse is suspected.

Support Services

On campus AA, ACOA.

Employee assistance Program for chemically dependent employees not available.

Disciplinary Actions

Alcohol Results of infractions of alcohol regulations (see Comparative Table of Alcohol Regulations) include counseling.

For More Information

Contact: Betty Johnson, ENMU Sta. 34, Eastern New Mexico State University, Portales, NM 88130. Telephone: 505-562-2760.

EASTERN WASHINGTON UNIVERSITY

Cheney, Washington

General Information

State-supported 5-year coed college. Founded 1882. Awards B, M. Primary accreditation: regional. Small-town setting; 335-acre campus. Total enrollment: 8,198. Faculty: 469 (349 full-time, 120 part-time). Social organizations: 3 national fraternities, 4 national sororities, local fraternities, local sororities; 3% of eligible undergraduate men and 4% of eligible undergraduate women are members.

Drug and Alcohol Information

Education

On campus Drug and alcohol education/prevention programs offered for: all students. Authorized group concerned with responsible drinking. College holds an annual alcohol awareness week and drug awareness week.

Identification of Problems

Admissions College application does not ask about prior substance abuse problems.

On campus Current students identified as chemically dependent may remain enrolled, but treatment is usually required. Training program on identifying students with potential substance abuse problems for: resident advisers.

Support Services

On campus AA, ACOA, private counseling.

Employee assistance Program for chemically dependent employees available. Staff working with drug/alcohol-related issues: 1 full-time and 3 part-time.

Disciplinary Actions

Alcohol Results of infractions of alcohol regulations (see Comparative Table of Alcohol Regulations) vary by situation. Comments: Some disciplinary action is taken.

Drugs For first-time use, possession, or sale: varies by situation—referral to Discipline Officer. For subsequent use, possession, or sale: varies by situation.

For More Information

Contact: Bernard Taylor, Director, Counseling Center, Eastern Washington University, 117 Showilter Hill, Cheney, WA 99004. Telephone: 509-359-2366.

EAST STROUDSBURG UNIVERSITY OF PENNSYLVANIA

East Stroudsburg, Pennsylvania

General Information

State-supported 5-year coed college. Part of State System of Higher Education. Founded 1893. Awards A (terminal), B, M. Primary accreditation: regional. Small-town setting; 140-acre campus. Total enrollment: 4,909. Faculty: 289 (279 full-time, 10 part-time). Social organizations: 11 national fraternities, 6 national sororities.

Drug and Alcohol Information

Education

On campus Drug and alcohol education/prevention programs offered for: all students, athletes/coaches. Authorized group concerned with responsible drinking. College holds an annual alcohol awareness week.

Identification of Problems

Admissions College application does not ask about prior substance abuse problems.

On campus Current students identified as chemically dependent may remain enrolled. No training program on identifying students with potential substance abuse problems. Written procedures for students and staff if substance abuse is suspected.

Support Services

On campus Private counseling, University counseling.

East Stroudsburg University of Pennsylvania (continued)

Employee assistance Program for chemically dependent employees available.

Disciplinary Actions

Alcohol Results of infractions of alcohol regulations (see Comparative Table of Alcohol Regulations) vary by situation but can include chemical dependency assessment, counseling, warning, probation, suspension, expulsion.

Drugs For any use, possession, or sale: varies by situation.

For More Information

Contact: Dean Valerie Hodge, Assistant Vice President for Special Programs, East Stroudsburg University of Pennsylvania, East Stroudsburg, PA 18301. Telephone: 717-424-3730.

EAST TEXAS BAPTIST UNIVERSITY

Marshall, Texas

General Information

Independent Baptist 4-year coed college. Founded 1912. Awards A (college transfer), B. Primary accreditation: regional. Small-town setting; 180-acre campus. Total enrollment: 716. Faculty: 64 (46 full-time, 18 part-time).

Drug and Alcohol Information

Education

On campus Drug and alcohol education/prevention programs offered for: freshmen.

Identification of Problems

Admissions College application does not ask about prior substance abuse problems.

On campus Current students identified as chemically dependent may not remain enrolled. No training program on identifying students with potential substance abuse problems. Written procedures for students and staff if substance abuse is suspected.

Support Services

On campus Private counseling.

Employee assistance Program for chemically dependent employees not available. Staff working with drug/alcohol-related issues: 4 part-time.

Disciplinary Actions

Alcohol Results of infractions of alcohol regulations (see Comparative Table of Alcohol Regulations) include warning, probation, suspension, expulsion.

Drugs For first-time use, possession, or sale: varies by situation. For subsequent use, possession, or sale: varies by situation—counseling, expulsion.

For More Information

Contact: Dr. Don Rominger, Vice President/Student Affairs, East Texas Baptist University, 1209 N. Grove, Marshall, TX 75670. Telephone: 214-935-7963.

EAST TEXAS STATE UNIVERSITY AT TEXARKANA

Texarkana, Texas

General Information

State-supported coed college. Part of East Texas State University Complex. Founded 1971. Awards B, M. Primary accreditation: regional. Small-town setting. Total enrollment: 1,144.

Drug and Alcohol Information

Education

On campus Drug and alcohol education/prevention programs not offered.

Identification of Problems

Admissions College application does not ask about prior substance abuse problems.

On campus Current students identified as chemically dependent may remain enrolled, but treatment may be required. No training program on identifying students with potential substance abuse problems. Written procedures for students and staff if substance abuse is suspected.

Support Services

On campus No support services on campus.

Off campus Referrals.

Employee assistance Program for chemically dependent employees not available.

Disciplinary Actions

Alcohol Results of infractions of alcohol regulations (see Comparative Table of Alcohol Regulations) vary by situation but can include counseling, probation, suspension, expulsion.

Drugs For any use, possession, or sale: varies by situation.

Additional Information from the College

The University is a single-building, totally commuter campus. The average age of students is 32.8, and most are employed full-time, own homes, and have families. Students or staff with drug and/or alcohol problems are referred for help in a manner that ensures their privacy.

For More Information

Contact: Harry Muir, Director of Academic and Student Services, East Texas State University at Texarkana, P.O. Box 5518, Texarkana, TX 75505. Telephone: 214-838-6514.

ECKERD COLLEGE

St. Petersburg, Florida

General Information

Independent Presbyterian 4-year coed college. Founded 1958. Awards B. Primary accreditation: regional. Metropolitan setting; 280-acre campus. Total enrollment: 1,325. Faculty: 109 (79 full-time, 30 part-time).

Drug and Alcohol Information

Education

On campus Drug and alcohol education/prevention programs offered for: all students. Authorized group concerned with responsible drinking.

Identification of Problems

Admissions College application does not ask about prior substance abuse problems.

On campus Current students identified as chemically dependent may remain enrolled, but treatment is required. Training program on identifying students with potential substance abuse problems for: resident advisers. Written procedures for students and staff if substance abuse is suspected.

Support Services

On campus Al-Anon, ACOA, support groups, private counseling.

Employee assistance Program for chemically dependent employees not available.

Disciplinary Actions

Alcohol Results of infractions of alcohol regulations (see Comparative Table of Alcohol Regulations) include chemical dependency assessment, counseling, warning, probation, suspension.

Drugs For first-time use or possession: varies by situation. For subsequent use or possession: suspension. For any sale: expulsion.

For More Information

Contact: Mark W. Smith, Dean of Students, Eckerd College, Box 12560, St. Petersburg, FL 33733. Telephone: 813-864-8421.

EDGEWOOD COLLEGE

Madison, Wisconsin

General Information

Independent Roman Catholic 5-year coed college. Founded 1927. Awards A (college transfer), B, M. Primary accreditation: regional. City setting; 55-acre campus. Total enrollment: 1,110. Faculty: 90 (53 full-time, 37 part-time).

Drug and Alcohol Information

Education

On campus Drug and alcohol education/prevention programs offered for: all students, athletes/coaches, faculty, administration. College holds an annual alcohol awareness week.

Identification of Problems

Admissions College application does not ask about prior substance abuse problems.

On campus Current students identified as chemically dependent may remain enrolled, but treatment is required. No training program on identifying students with potential substance abuse problems. No written procedures for students and staff if substance abuse is suspected.

Support Services

On campus Private counseling.

Employee assistance Program for chemically dependent employees not available.

Disciplinary Actions

Alcohol Results of infractions of alcohol regulations (see Comparative Table of Alcohol Regulations) vary by situation but can include chemical dependency assessment, counseling, warning, probation, suspension, expulsion.

Drugs For any use, possession, or sale: varies by situation.

For More Information

Contact: James DiTulio, Counselor, Edgewood College, 855 Woodrow St., Madison, WI 53711. Telephone: 608-257-4861 Ext. 2287.

EDINBORO UNIVERSITY OF PENNSYLVANIA

Edinboro, Pennsylvania

General Information

State-supported 5-year coed college. Part of State System of Higher Education. Founded 1857. Awards A (college transfer and terminal), B, M. Primary accreditation: regional. Small-town setting; 600-acre campus. Total enrollment: 7,001. Faculty: 343 (322 full-time, 21 part-time). Social organizations: 9 national fraternities, 6 national sororities.

Drug and Alcohol Information

Education

On campus Drug and alcohol education/prevention programs offered for: all students; required for: violators of alcohol regulations. College holds an annual alcohol awareness week.

Identification of Problems

Admissions College application does not ask about prior substance abuse problems.

On campus Current students identified as chemically dependent may remain enrolled, but treatment is required. Training program on identifying students with potential substance abuse problems for: resident advisers. No written procedures for students and staff if substance abuse is suspected.

Support Services

On campus AA, NA, Al-Anon, private counseling.

Employee assistance Program for chemically dependent employees not available. Staff working with drug/alcohol-related issues: 1 part-time.

Disciplinary Actions

Alcohol Results of infractions of alcohol regulations (see Comparative Table of Alcohol Regulations) vary by situation but can include chemical dependency assessment, counseling, warning, probation, suspension, attendance at alcohol awareness program.

Drugs For first-time use or possession: varies by situation. For subsequent use or possession: suspension. For any sale: suspension.

For More Information

Contact: Dr. Glenda M. Lawhorn, Vice President for Student Affairs, Reeder Hall, Edinboro University of Pennsylvania, Edinboro, PA 16444. Telephone: 814-732-2852.

ELIZABETHTOWN COLLEGE

Elizabethtown, Pennsylvania

General Information

Independent 4-year coed college, affiliated with Church of the Brethren. Founded 1899. Awards B. Primary accreditation: regional. Small-town setting; 110-acre

Elizabethtown College (continued)

campus. Total enrollment: 1,773. Faculty: 144 (105 full-time, 39 part-time).

Drug and Alcohol Information

Education

On campus Drug and alcohol education/prevention programs offered for: all students, athletes/coaches, administration. Authorized group concerned with responsible drinking. College holds an annual alcohol awareness week.

Identification of Problems

Admissions College application does not ask about prior substance abuse problems.

On campus Current students identified as chemically dependent may remain enrolled, but treatment is required. Training program on identifying students with potential substance abuse problems for: resident advisers, coaches, administration. Written procedures for students and staff if substance abuse is suspected.

Support Services

On campus No support services on campus.

Employee assistance Program for chemically dependent employees not available. Staff working with drug/alcohol-related issues: 1 part-time.

Disciplinary Actions

Alcohol Results of infractions of alcohol regulations (see Comparative Table of Alcohol Regulations) include chemical dependency assessment, counseling, warning, probation, suspension, fines.

Drugs For first-time use or possession: chemical dependency assessment, suspension from College housing. For subsequent use or possession: suspension. For first-time sale: suspension. For subsequent sale: expulsion.

For More Information

Contact: Walter Shaw, Dean of the College, Elizabethtown College, 1 Alpha Drive, Elizabethtown, PA 17022. Telephone: 717-367-1151.

ELMHURST COLLEGE

Elmhurst, Illinois

General Information

Independent 4-year coed college, affiliated with United Church of Christ. Founded 1871. Awards B. Primary accreditation: regional. City setting; 38-acre campus. Total enrollment: 3,135. Faculty: 142 (101 full-time, 41 part-time). Social organizations: 4 national fraternities, 3 national sororities, 1 local fraternity, local sororities, 1 coed fraternity; 13% of eligible undergraduate men and 14% of eligible undergraduate women are members.

Drug and Alcohol Information

Education

On campus Drug and alcohol education/prevention programs offered for: all students, athletes/coaches.

Identification of Problems

Admissions College application question about prior substance abuse problems is used for counseling and referral, if student is admitted; in the admissions decision.

On campus Current students identified as chemically dependent may remain enrolled, but treatment is required. Training program on identifying students with potential substance abuse problems for: resident advisers, coaches. No written procedures for students and staff if substance abuse is suspected.

Support Services

On campus AA, ACOA, private counseling.

Employee assistance Program for chemically dependent employees not available. Staff working with drug/alcohol-related issues: 10 part-time.

Disciplinary Actions

Alcohol Results of infractions of alcohol regulations (see Comparative Table of Alcohol Regulations) vary by situation.

Drugs For first-time use: chemical dependency assessment. For first-time possession: varies by situation. For subsequent use or possession: suspension. For any sale: suspension.

For More Information

Contact: Jim Cunningham, Dean of Students, Elmhurst College, 190 Prospect, Elmhurst, IL 60126. Telephone: 312-617-3187.

ELMIRA COLLEGE

Elmira, New York

General Information

Independent 5-year coed college. Founded 1855. Awards A (college transfer and terminal), B, M. Primary accreditation: regional. Small-town setting; 40-acre campus. Total enrollment: 1,998. Faculty: 91 (61 full-time, 30 part-time).

Drug and Alcohol Information

Education

On campus Drug and alcohol education/prevention programs offered for: all students, administration; required for: freshmen, resident advisers. Authorized group concerned with responsible drinking.

Identification of Problems

Admissions College application does not ask about prior substance abuse problems.

On campus Current students identified as chemically dependent may not remain enrolled. Training program on identifying students with potential substance abuse problems for: administration. No written procedures for students and staff if substance abuse is suspected.

Support Services

On campus Support groups, private counseling.

Employee assistance Program for chemically dependent employees available.

Disciplinary Actions

Alcohol Results of infractions of alcohol regulations (see Comparative Table of Alcohol Regulations) include chemical dependency assessment, counseling, warning, probation.

Drugs For first-time use, possession, or sale: suspension, expulsion. For subsequent use, possession, or sale: expulsion.

For More Information

Contact: Dr. W. Douglas Couchon, Director of Counseling Services, Elmira College, Park Place, Elmira, NY 14901. Telephone: 607-734-3911 Ext. 217.

ELMS COLLEGE
Chicopee, Massachusetts

General Information
Independent Roman Catholic 5-year women's college. Founded 1928. Awards A (college transfer and terminal), B, M. Primary accreditation: regional. City setting; 32-acre campus. Total enrollment: 650. Faculty: 79 (50 full-time, 29 part-time).

Drug and Alcohol Information
Education

On campus Drug and alcohol education/prevention programs offered for: all students, administration; required for: resident advisers. College holds an annual alcohol awareness week and drug awareness week.

Identification of Problems

Admissions College application does not ask about prior substance abuse problems.

On campus Current students identified as chemically dependent may remain enrolled, but treatment is required. Training program on identifying students with potential substance abuse problems for: resident advisers, coaches, faculty, administration. Written procedures for students and staff if substance abuse is suspected.

Support Services

On campus ACOA, support groups, private counseling.

Employee assistance Program for chemically dependent employees not available.

Disciplinary Actions

Alcohol Results of infractions of alcohol regulations (see Comparative Table of Alcohol Regulations) include counseling, warning, probation.

Drugs For first-time use or possession: warning. For subsequent use or possession: counseling, probation. For any sale: varies by situation.

For More Information

Contact: Elizabeth Woods, Assistant Dean of Students, Elms College, 291 Springfield St., Chicopee, MA 01013. Telephone: 413-594-2761.

ELON COLLEGE
Elon College, North Carolina

General Information
Independent 5-year coed college, affiliated with United Church of Christ. Founded 1889. Awards B, M. Primary accreditation: regional. Small-town setting; 150-acre campus. Total enrollment: 3,314. Faculty: 175 (119 full-time, 56 part-time). Social organizations: 9 national fraternities, 6 national sororities; 25% of eligible undergraduate men and 25% of eligible undergraduate women are members.

Drug and Alcohol Information
Education

On campus Drug and alcohol education/prevention programs offered for: all students, athletes/coaches, faculty, administration; required for: freshmen, resident advisers. Bacchus chapter: 40 members. College holds an annual alcohol awareness week and drug awareness week.

Identification of Problems

Admissions College application does not ask about prior substance abuse problems.

On campus Current students identified as chemically dependent may remain enrolled, but treatment is required. Training program on identifying students with potential substance abuse problems for: resident advisers, peer facilitators. No written procedures for students and staff if substance abuse is suspected.

Support Services

On campus AA, ACOA, support groups, private counseling, peer counselors.

Employee assistance Program for chemically dependent employees not available.

Disciplinary Actions

Alcohol Results of infractions of alcohol regulations (see Comparative Table of Alcohol Regulations) include chemical dependency assessment, counseling, warning, probation, suspension, expulsion.

Drugs For first-time use or possession: suspension. For subsequent use or possession: expulsion. For any sale: expulsion.

Additional Information from the College

The alcohol and drug program at Elon College has a strong commitment to peer education. The campus community supports the promotion of a drug-free campus. The focus of the program is on wellness.

For More Information

Contact: Jana Lynn Fields Patterson, Assistant Dean of Students, Campus Box 2203, Elon College, Elon College, NC 27244. Telephone: 919-584-2218.

EMBRY-RIDDLE AERONAUTICAL UNIVERSITY
Daytona Beach, Florida

General Information
Independent 5-year specialized coed college. Part of Embry-Riddle Aeronautical University. Founded 1926. Awards A (terminal), B, M. Primary accreditation: regional. City setting; 86-acre campus. Total enrollment: 5,317. Faculty: 213 (all full-time). Social organizations: 9 national fraternities, 2 national sororities; 6% of eligible undergraduate men are members.

Drug and Alcohol Information
Education

On campus Drug and alcohol education/prevention programs offered for: all students, faculty, administration. Authorized group concerned with responsible drinking. College holds an annual alcohol awareness week and drug awareness week.

Identification of Problems

Admissions College application does not ask about prior substance abuse problems.

On campus Current students identified as chemically dependent may not remain enrolled. No training program on identifying students with potential substance abuse problems. Written procedures for students and staff if substance abuse is suspected.

Embry-Riddle Aeronautical University (continued)

Support Services

On campus Private counseling, referrals.

Employee assistance Program for chemically dependent employees not available. Staff working with drug/alcohol-related issues: 1 part-time.

Disciplinary Actions

Alcohol Results of infractions of alcohol regulations (see Comparative Table of Alcohol Regulations) vary by situation.

Drugs For any use, possession, or sale: suspension.

Additional Information from the College

The Substance Awareness Committee at Embry-Riddle Aeronautical University is made up of faculty, staff, and students and coordinates awareness programs throughout the year. The University's educational program will continue and expand in the future.

For More Information

Contact: Laurie Ranfos, Student Activities Coordinator, Embry-Riddle Aeronautical University, Daytona Beach, FL 32014. Telephone: 904-239-6039.

EMBRY-RIDDLE AERONAUTICAL UNIVERSITY, COLLEGE OF CONTINUING EDUCATION

Daytona Beach, Florida

General Information

Independent 5-year specialized coed college. Part of Embry-Riddle Aeronautical University. Programs offered at 95 military bases worldwide. Founded 1926. Awards A (terminal), B, M. Primary accreditation: regional. City setting. Total enrollment: 3,808.

Drug and Alcohol Information

Education

On campus Drug and alcohol education/prevention programs offered for: all students. Authorized group concerned with responsible drinking. College holds an annual alcohol awareness week and drug awareness week.

Identification of Problems

Admissions College application does not ask about prior substance abuse problems.

On campus Whether current students identified as chemically dependent may remain enrolled depends on the circumstances. Training program on identifying students with potential substance abuse problems being prepared for: resident advisers, Greek officers, faculty, administration, club officers. No written procedures for students and staff if substance abuse is suspected, but this project is being worked on by the Substance Awareness Committee.

Support Services

On campus Private counseling, Substance Awareness Committee.

Employee assistance Program for chemically dependent employees not available. Staff working with drug/alcohol-related issues: 10 part-time.

Disciplinary Actions

Alcohol Results of infractions of alcohol regulations (see Comparative Table of Alcohol Regulations) vary by situation but can include counseling, warning, probation.

Drugs For any use, possession, or sale: expulsion.

For More Information

Contact: Laurie Ranfos, Student Activities Coordinator, Embry-Riddle Aeronautical University, College of Continuing Education, 950 Williamson Blvd., Daytona Beach, FL 32014. Telephone: 904-239-6039.

EMMANUEL COLLEGE

Boston, Massachusetts

General Information

Independent Roman Catholic 5-year primarily women's college. Founded 1919. Awards B, M. Primary accreditation: regional. Metropolitan setting; 16-acre campus. Total enrollment: 973. Faculty: 87 (62 full-time, 25 part-time).

Drug and Alcohol Information

Education

On campus Drug and alcohol education/prevention programs offered for: all students. College holds an annual alcohol awareness week and drug awareness week.

Identification of Problems

Admissions College application does not ask about prior substance abuse problems.

On campus Current students identified as chemically dependent may remain enrolled, but treatment is required.

Support Services

On campus Support groups (through Counseling and Health Services), private counseling.

Employee assistance Program for chemically dependent employees not available.

Disciplinary Actions

Alcohol Results of infractions of alcohol regulations (see Comparative Table of Alcohol Regulations) vary by situation.

Drugs For any use or possession: varies by situation. For first-time sale: suspension, expulsion. For subsequent sale: expulsion.

For More Information

Contact: Sr. Ann Rachel Sharry, S.N.D., Associate Dean for Counseling and Health Services, Emmanuel College, 300 The Fenway, Boston, MA 02115. Telephone: 617-735-9920.

EMMANUEL COLLEGE SCHOOL OF CHRISTIAN MINISTRIES

Franklin Springs, Georgia

General Information

Independent specialized coed college, affiliated with Pentecostal Holiness Church. Founded 1973. Awards B. Primary accreditation: AABC. Rural setting; 90-acre campus. Total enrollment: 30. Faculty: 6 (all part-time).

Drug and Alcohol Information

Education

On campus Drug and alcohol education/prevention programs offered for: all students. Authorized group concerned with responsible drinking.

Identification of Problems

Admissions College application does not ask about prior substance abuse problems.

On campus Current students identified as chemically dependent may not remain enrolled. Training program on identifying students with potential substance abuse problems for: resident advisers. Written procedures for students and staff if substance abuse is suspected.

Support Services

On campus No support services on campus.

Employee assistance Program for chemically dependent employees not available.

Disciplinary Actions

Alcohol Results of infractions of alcohol regulations (see Comparative Table of Alcohol Regulations) vary by situation but can include counseling, probation, suspension, expulsion.

Drugs For first-time use: counseling, probation. For subsequent use: expulsion. For any possession or sale: expulsion.

Additional Information from the College

Emmanuel College is a Bible college, and drug/alcohol offenders are not permitted to enroll or, when detected, remain enrolled. The College has experienced very little difficulty in maintaining abstinence from drugs and alcohol.

For More Information

Contact: Ron White, Student Dean, Emmanuel College School of Christian Ministries, P.O. Box 129, Franklin Springs, GA 30639. Telephone: 404-245-7226.

EMMAUS BIBLE COLLEGE

Dubuque, Iowa

General Information

Independent nondenominational 4-year coed college. Founded 1942. Awards B. Primary accreditation: AABC (candidate). City setting. Total enrollment: 204. Faculty: 15 (all full-time).

Drug and Alcohol Information

Education

On campus Drug and alcohol education/prevention programs not offered.

Identification of Problems

Admissions College application does not ask about prior substance abuse problems.

On campus Current students identified as chemically dependent may sometimes remain enrolled, but treatment is required. Training program on identifying students with potential substance abuse problems for: resident advisers. No written procedures for students and staff if substance abuse is suspected.

Support Services

On campus Private counseling.

Employee assistance Program for chemically dependent employees not available. Staff working with drug/alcohol-related issues: 1 part-time.

Disciplinary Actions

Alcohol Results of infractions of alcohol regulations (see Comparative Table of Alcohol Regulations) vary by situation but can include warning, probation, suspension.

Drugs For first-time use: varies by situation—counseling, probation. For first-time possession or sale: varies by situation—counseling, suspension. For subsequent use, possession, or sale: varies by situation—suspension.

For More Information

Contact: Ron Serpliss, Dean of Students, Emmaus Bible College, 2570 Asbury Rd., Dubuque, IA 52001. Telephone: 319-588-8000.

EMORY & HENRY COLLEGE

Emory, Virginia

General Information

Independent United Methodist 4-year coed college. Founded 1836. Awards B. Primary accreditation: regional. Rural setting; 150-acre campus. Total enrollment: 788. Faculty: 61 (54 full-time, 7 part-time). Social organizations: 5 local fraternities, 6 local sororities; 20% of eligible undergraduate men and 20% of eligible undergraduate women are members.

Drug and Alcohol Information

Education

On campus Drug and alcohol education/prevention programs offered for: all students; required for: resident advisers. Authorized group concerned with responsible drinking. College holds an annual alcohol awareness week and drug awareness week.

Identification of Problems

Admissions College application does not ask about prior substance abuse problems.

On campus Current students identified as chemically dependent may remain enrolled, but treatment is required. No training program on identifying students with potential substance abuse problems. Written procedures for students and staff if substance abuse is suspected.

Support Services

On campus AA, private counseling.

Employee assistance Program for chemically dependent employees not available. Staff working with drug/alcohol-related issues: 2 part-time.

Disciplinary Actions

Alcohol Results of infractions of alcohol regulations (see Comparative Table of Alcohol Regulations) vary by situation but can include counseling, warning, probation, suspension.

Drugs For first-time use or possession: varies by situation—counseling, probation. For subsequent use: suspension. For first-time sale: suspension, expulsion. For subsequent possession or sale: expulsion.

For More Information

Contact: William M. Malloy, Dean of Students, Emory & Henry College, Emory, VA 24327. Telephone: 703-944-3121.

EMPORIA STATE UNIVERSITY

Emporia, Kansas

General Information

State-supported 5-year coed college. Founded 1863. Awards A (college transfer and terminal), B, M. Primary accreditation: regional. Small-town setting; 207-acre campus. Total enrollment: 5,763. Faculty: 294 (234 full-time, 60 part-time). Social organizations: 10 national fraternities, 7 national sororities; 18% of eligible undergraduate men and 12% of eligible undergraduate women are members.

Drug and Alcohol Information

Education

On campus Drug and alcohol education/prevention programs offered for: all students, athletes/coaches, faculty, administration, staff. Authorized group concerned with responsible drinking. College holds an annual alcohol awareness week and drug awareness week.

Identification of Problems

Admissions College application does not ask about prior substance abuse problems.

On campus Current students identified as chemically dependent may remain enrolled. Training program on identifying students with potential substance abuse problems for: resident advisers, classified employees and supervisors. No written procedures for students and staff if substance abuse is suspected.

Support Services

On campus AA, Al-Anon, private counseling, NAR-Anon.

Employee assistance Program for chemically dependent employees available. Staff working with drug/alcohol-related issues: 1 full-time and 2 part-time.

Disciplinary Actions

Alcohol Results of infractions of alcohol regulations (see Comparative Table of Alcohol Regulations) include chemical dependency assessment, counseling, warning.

Drugs For any use, possession, or sale: varies by situation.

For More Information

Contact: Dr. Pat Wade, Associate Dean of Students, Emporia State University, 1200 Commercial St., Emporia, KS 66801. Telephone: 316-343-5221.

EVERGREEN STATE COLLEGE

Olympia, Washington

General Information

State-supported 5-year coed college. Founded 1967. Awards B, M. Primary accreditation: regional. Small-town setting; 1,000-acre campus. Total enrollment: 3,250. Faculty: 330 (150 full-time, 180 part-time).

Drug and Alcohol Information

Education

On campus Drug and alcohol education/prevention programs offered for: all students, athletes/coaches. Authorized group concerned with responsible drinking. College holds an annual alcohol awareness.

Identification of Problems

Admissions College application does not ask about prior substance abuse problems.

On campus Current students identified as chemically dependent may remain enrolled, but treatment is required for severe cases. Training program on identifying students with potential substance abuse problems for: anyone interested. Written procedures for students and staff if substance abuse is suspected.

Support Services

On campus AA, NA, ACOA, support groups, private counseling.

Employee assistance Program for chemically dependent employees available. Staff working with drug/alcohol-related issues: 8 part-time.

Disciplinary Actions

Alcohol Results of infractions of alcohol regulations (see Comparative Table of Alcohol Regulations) include chemical dependency assessment, counseling, warning, probation, suspension, police citation.

Drugs For first-time use, possession, or sale: varies by situation. For subsequent use: probation, suspension. For subsequent possession or sale: suspension, expulsion.

Additional Information from the College

Evergreen State College hopes to add a full-time substance abuse counselor to its counseling staff.

For More Information

Contact: Shary Smith, Director of Counseling, Evergreen State College, Olympia, WA 98505. Telephone: 206-866-6000 Ext. 6800.

FAIRFIELD UNIVERSITY

Fairfield, Connecticut

General Information

Independent Roman Catholic 5-year coed college. Founded 1942. Awards B, M. Primary accreditation: regional. City setting; 200-acre campus. Total enrollment: 4,878. Faculty: 330 (188 full-time, 142 part-time).

Drug and Alcohol Information

Education

On campus Drug and alcohol education/prevention programs offered for: all students; required for: freshmen, athletes/coaches, resident advisers, peer counselors. Authorized group concerned with responsible drinking. College holds an annual alcohol awareness week and drug awareness week.

Identification of Problems

Admissions College application does not ask about prior substance abuse problems.

On campus Current students identified as chemically dependent may remain enrolled, but treatment is required. Training program on identifying students with potential substance abuse problems for: resident advisers, peer counselors. Written procedures for students and staff if substance abuse is suspected.

Support Services

On campus AA, Al-Anon, ACOA, private counseling.

Employee assistance Program for chemically dependent employees available. Staff working with drug/alcohol-related issues: 1 full-time.

Disciplinary Actions

Alcohol Results of infractions of alcohol regulations (see Comparative Table of Alcohol Regulations) vary by situation but can include counseling, warning, probation.

Drugs For first-time use: varies by situation—counseling, probation. For subsequent use: varies by situation—counseling, probation, suspension. For first-time possession: varies by situation—counseling, probation, suspension. For first-time sale: varies by situation. For subsequent possession or sale: varies by situation.

For More Information

Contact: Barry M. Vesciglio, Substance Abuse Counselor, Fairfield University, Fairfield, CT 06430. Telephone: 203-254-4000 Ext. 2443.

FASHION INSTITUTE OF TECHNOLOGY

New York, New York

General Information

State and locally supported 5-year coed college. Part of State University of New York System. Founded 1944. Awards A (terminal), B, M. Primary accreditation: regional. Metropolitan setting. Total enrollment: 11,944. Faculty: 789 (221 full-time, 568 part-time).

Drug and Alcohol Information

Education

On campus Drug and alcohol education/prevention programs offered for: all students, faculty; required for: resident advisers, dorm residents. Authorized group concerned with responsible drinking. College holds an annual alcohol awareness week and drug awareness week.

Identification of Problems

Admissions College application does not ask about prior substance abuse problems.

On campus Current students identified as chemically dependent may remain enrolled. Training program on identifying students with potential substance abuse problems for: resident advisers. Written procedures for students and staff if substance abuse is suspected.

Support Services

On campus Support groups, private counseling, networking group.

Employee assistance Program for chemically dependent employees not yet available. Staff working with drug/alcohol-related issues: 6 part-time.

Disciplinary Actions

Alcohol Results of infractions of alcohol regulations (see Comparative Table of Alcohol Regulations) vary by situation but can include counseling, warning, probation, suspension, expulsion.

Drugs For first-time use or possession: varies by situation—counseling, warning. For first-time sale: varies by situation. For subsequent use, possession, or sale: varies by situation.

For More Information

Contact: Dr. Martha Cottrell, Director of Medical Services, Fashion Institute of Technology, 4th Floor, 227 W. 27th St., New York, NY 10001. Telephone: 212-760-7625.

FERRIS STATE UNIVERSITY

Big Rapids, Michigan

General Information

State-supported 5-year coed college. Founded 1884. Awards A (college transfer and terminal), B, M, D. Primary accreditation: regional. Small-town setting; 650-acre campus. Total enrollment: 11,762. Faculty: 638 (482 full-time, 156 part-time). Social organizations: national fraternities, national sororities, local fraternities, local sororities; 5% of eligible undergraduate men and 4% of eligible undergraduate women are members.

Drug and Alcohol Information

Education

On campus Drug and alcohol education/prevention programs offered for: all students, athletes/coaches, faculty, administration, parents; required for: resident advisers. Authorized group concerned with responsible drinking. College holds an annual alcohol awareness week and drug awareness week.

Identification of Problems

Admissions College application does not ask about prior substance abuse problems.

On campus Current students identified as chemically dependent may remain enrolled. Training program on identifying students with potential substance abuse problems for: resident advisers, coaches/athletes, faculty, administration, students. No written procedures for students and staff if substance abuse is suspected.

Support Services

On campus AA, ACOA, private counseling, group counseling.

Employee assistance Program for chemically dependent employees not available. Staff working with drug/alcohol-related issues: 1 full-time and 2–3 part-time.

Disciplinary Actions

Alcohol Results of infractions of alcohol regulations (see Comparative Table of Alcohol Regulations) vary by situation but can include chemical dependency assessment, counseling, warning, probation, suspension, alcohol and other drug education class.

Drugs For any use, possession, or sale: varies by situation.

Additional Information from the College

Date-rape education program has been instituted because of high incidence of alcohol/drug abuse in these cases. In addition, limited pilot program available for chemically dependent students in the process of recovery. Program provides support and access to after-care opportunities.

For More Information

Contact: Lenny Shible, Substance Abuse Educator/Counselor, 221 Rankin Center, Ferris State University, Big Rapids, MI 49307. Telephone: 616-592-5968.

FISK UNIVERSITY

Nashville, Tennessee

General Information

Independent 5-year coed college, affiliated with United Church of Christ. Founded 1866. Awards B, M. Primary accreditation: regional. Metropolitan setting; 40-acre campus. Total enrollment: 774. Faculty: 81 (71 full-time, 10

Fisk University (continued)

part-time). Social organizations: 4 national fraternities, 4 national sororities; 25% of eligible undergraduate men and 35% of eligible undergraduate women are members.

Drug and Alcohol Information

Education

On campus Drug and alcohol education/prevention programs offered for: all students. College holds an annual alcohol awareness week and drug awareness week.

Identification of Problems

Admissions College application does not ask about prior substance abuse problems.

On campus Current students identified as chemically dependent may remain enrolled, but treatment is required. No training program on identifying students with potential substance abuse problems. No written procedures for students and staff if substance abuse is suspected.

Support Services

On campus No support services on campus. Off campus city support services.

Employee assistance Program for chemically dependent employees not available.

Disciplinary Actions

Alcohol Results of infractions of alcohol regulations (see Comparative Table of Alcohol Regulations) include counseling, warning, probation.

Drugs For first-time use: counseling, warning, probation. For subsequent use: varies by situation. For first-time possession: varies by situation—probation, suspension. For subsequent possession: varies by situation—suspension. For first-time sale: varies by situation—suspension. For subsequent sale: varies by situation—suspension, expulsion.

For More Information

Contact: Ronald F. Myles, Director for Student Affairs, Fisk University, 1000 17th Ave. N., Nashville, TN 37208-3051. Telephone: 615-329-8597 or 8714.

FITCHBURG STATE COLLEGE

Fitchburg, Massachusetts

General Information

State-supported 5-year coed college. Founded 1894. Awards B, M. Primary accreditation: regional. Small-town setting; 92-acre campus. Total enrollment: 6,224. Faculty: 274 (234 full-time, 40 part-time). Social organizations: 4 local fraternities, 6 local sororities; 20% of eligible undergraduate men and 30% of eligible undergraduate women are members.

Drug and Alcohol Information

Education

On campus Drug and alcohol education/prevention programs offered for: all students, athletes/coaches, faculty, administration. Authorized group concerned with responsible drinking. College holds an annual alcohol awareness week and drug awareness week.

Identification of Problems

Admissions College application does not ask about prior substance abuse problems.

On campus Current students identified as chemically dependent may remain enrolled. Training program on identifying students with potential substance abuse problems for: resident advisers, coaches. Written procedures for students and staff if substance abuse is suspected.

Support Services

On campus ACOA, private counseling, referrals.

Employee assistance Program for chemically dependent employees available. Staff working with drug/alcohol-related issues: 2 part-time.

Disciplinary Actions

Alcohol Results of infractions of alcohol regulations (see Comparative Table of Alcohol Regulations) vary by situation but can include chemical dependency assessment, counseling, warning, probation, suspension, expulsion, community service, or other educational sanctions.

Drugs For any use, possession, or sale: varies by situation.

For More Information

Contact: Sherri Nickel-Milstone, Coordinator, Student Life Programs, Fitchburg State College, 160 Pearl St., Fitchburg, MA 01420. Telephone: 508-345-2151 Ext. 3130.

FLAGLER COLLEGE

St. Augustine, Florida

General Information

Independent 4-year coed college. Founded 1968. Awards B. Primary accreditation: regional. Small-town setting; 36-acre campus. Total enrollment: 1,166. Faculty: 92 (43 full-time, 49 part-time).

Drug and Alcohol Information

Education

On campus Drug and alcohol education/prevention programs offered for: all students. Authorized group concerned with responsible drinking. College holds an annual alcohol awareness week.

Identification of Problems

Admissions College application does not ask about prior substance abuse problems.

On campus Current students identified as chemically dependent may not remain enrolled. No training program on identifying students with potential substance abuse problems. No written procedures for students and staff if substance abuse is suspected.

Support Services

On campus Private counseling.

Employee assistance Program for chemically dependent employees not available. Staff working with drug/alcohol-related issues: 3 part-time.

Disciplinary Actions

Alcohol Results of infractions of alcohol regulations (see Comparative Table of Alcohol Regulations) vary by situation but can include probation.

Drugs For any use, possession, or sale: expulsion.

For More Information

Contact: Patricia Blair, College Counselor, Flagler College, P.O. Box 1027, St. Augustine, FL 32085. Telephone: 904-829-6481.

FLAMING RAINBOW UNIVERSITY
Stilwell, Oklahoma

General Information
Independent 4-year coed college. Founded 1971. Awards B. Primary accreditation: regional. Rural setting; 2-acre campus. Total enrollment: 227.

Drug and Alcohol Information
Education
On campus Drug and alcohol education/prevention programs not offered.

Identification of Problems
Admissions College application does not ask about prior substance abuse problems.

On campus Current students identified as chemically dependent may remain enrolled. No training program on identifying students with potential substance abuse problems. No written procedures for students and staff if substance abuse is suspected.

Support Services
On campus No support services on campus.

Employee assistance Program for chemically dependent employees not available.

Disciplinary Actions
Alcohol Results of infractions of alcohol regulations (see Comparative Table of Alcohol Regulations) include counseling, warning.

For More Information
Contact: George Poolaw, President, Flaming Rainbow University, 419 N. Second St., Stilwell, OK 74960. Telephone: 918-696-3644.

FLORIDA ATLANTIC UNIVERSITY
Boca Raton, Florida

General Information
State-supported comprehensive coed institution. Part of State University System of Florida. Founded 1961. Awards B, M, D. Primary accreditation: regional. City setting; 1,000-acre campus. Total enrollment: 8,387. Faculty: 456. Social organizations: 2 national fraternities, 2 national sororities; 1% of eligible undergraduate men and 1% of eligible undergraduate women are members.

Drug and Alcohol Information
Education
On campus Drug and alcohol education/prevention programs offered for: all students, athletes/coaches, faculty, administration. Bacchus chapter: 32 members. College holds an annual alcohol awareness week and drug awareness week.

Identification of Problems
Admissions College application does not ask about prior substance abuse problems.

On campus Current students identified as chemically dependent may remain enrolled. Training program on identifying students with potential substance abuse problems for: resident advisers, Greek officers, faculty, administration. Written procedures for students and staff if substance abuse is suspected.

Support Services
On campus Support groups, private counseling.

Employee assistance Program for chemically dependent employees available.

Disciplinary Actions
Alcohol Results of infractions of alcohol regulations (see Comparative Table of Alcohol Regulations) vary by situation but can include chemical dependency assessment, counseling, warning, probation, suspension, expulsion.

Drugs For first-time use, possession, or sale: expulsion.

For More Information
Contact: Diane Moorman, Director, Drug and Alcohol Resource Center, Florida Atlantic University, Boca Raton, FL 33431. Telephone: 407-367-3542.

FLORIDA INSTITUTE OF TECHNOLOGY
Melbourne, Florida

General Information
Independent comprehensive coed institution. Founded 1958. Awards A (terminal), B, M, D. Primary accreditation: regional. Small-town setting; 146-acre campus. Total enrollment: 4,117. Faculty: 683 (320 full-time, 363 part-time). Social organizations: 7 national fraternities, 2 national sororities, 1 local fraternity; 8% of eligible undergraduate men and 10% of eligible undergraduate women are members.

Drug and Alcohol Information
Education
On campus Drug and alcohol education/prevention programs not offered. Bacchus chapter: 20 members. College holds an annual alcohol awareness week and drug awareness week.

Identification of Problems
Admissions College application question about prior substance abuse problems is used for counseling and referral, if student is admitted; in the admissions decision.

On campus Current students identified as chemically dependent may remain enrolled, but treatment is required. Training program on identifying students with potential substance abuse problems for: resident advisers, Greek officers. Written procedures for students and staff if substance abuse is suspected.

Support Services
On campus Private counseling, Counseling Center.

Employee assistance Program for chemically dependent employees available.

Disciplinary Actions
Alcohol Results of infractions of alcohol regulations (see Comparative Table of Alcohol Regulations) vary by situation but can include chemical dependency assessment, counseling, warning, probation, suspension, expulsion.

Drugs For any use, possession, or sale: varies by situation.

Florida Institute of Technology (continued)

For More Information

Contact: Dr. Richard A. Hudson, Dean of Students, Florida Institute of Technology, 150 W. University Blvd., Melbourne, FL 32901. Telephone: 407-768-8000 Ext. 8134.

FLORIDA INTERNATIONAL UNIVERSITY

Miami, Florida

General Information

State-supported comprehensive coed institution. Part of State University System of Florida. Founded 1965. Awards B, M, D. Primary accreditation: regional. Metropolitan setting; 537-acre campus. Total enrollment: 17,482. Faculty: 862 (571 full-time, 291 part-time). Social organizations: 4 national fraternities, 2 national sororities, 2 local fraternities, 2 local sororities; 4% of eligible undergraduate men and 4% of eligible undergraduate women are members.

Drug and Alcohol Information

Education

On campus Drug and alcohol education/prevention programs offered for: all students, athletes/coaches. Bacchus chapter. College holds an annual alcohol awareness week and drug awareness week.

Identification of Problems

Admissions College application does not ask about prior substance abuse problems.

On campus Current students identified as chemically dependent may remain enrolled. Training program on identifying students with potential substance abuse problems for: resident advisers, Greek officers, administration. No written procedures for students and staff if substance abuse is suspected.

Support Services

On campus AA, NA, support groups, private counseling.

Employee assistance Program for chemically dependent employees not available. Staff working with drug/alcohol-related issues: 2 part-time.

Disciplinary Actions

Alcohol Results of infractions of alcohol regulations (see Comparative Table of Alcohol Regulations) vary by situation.

Drugs For any use, possession, or sale: varies by situation.

Additional Information from the College

Florida International University is currently revising its alcohol policy.

For More Information

Contact: Jennifer King, Coordinator, Student Affairs, U.H. 340, Florida International University, Tamiami Trail, Miami, FL 33199. Telephone: 305-554-3532.

FLORIDA STATE UNIVERSITY

Tallahassee, Florida

General Information

State-supported comprehensive coed institution. Part of State University System of Florida. Founded 1857. Awards A (college transfer), B, M, D. Primary accreditation: regional. City setting; 343-acre campus. Total enrollment: 23,883. Faculty: 1,434 (1,247 full-time, 187 part-time). Social organizations: national fraternities, national sororities, local fraternities, local sororities; 25% of eligible undergraduate men and 25% of eligible undergraduate women are members.

Drug and Alcohol Information

Education

On campus Drug and alcohol education/prevention programs offered for: all students, athletes/coaches. Bacchus chapter: 28 members. College holds an annual alcohol awareness week and drug awareness week.

Identification of Problems

Admissions College application does not ask about prior substance abuse problems.

On campus Current students identified as chemically dependent may remain enrolled. No training program on identifying students with potential substance abuse problems. No written procedures for students and staff if substance abuse is suspected.

Support Services

On campus AA, ACOA.

Employee assistance Program for chemically dependent employees available. Staff working with drug/alcohol-related issues: 1 full-time and 1 part-time.

Disciplinary Actions

Alcohol Results of infractions of alcohol regulations (see Comparative Table of Alcohol Regulations) vary by situation but can include warning, probation, suspension, expulsion, Student Assistance Program, attendance at workshop. Comments: Residence halls handle infractions that take place in them.

Drugs For first-time use: varies by situation. For subsequent use: varies by situation—chemical dependency assessment, counseling. For any possession: varies by situation. For first-time sale: suspension. For subsequent sale: dismissal (indefinite termination with readmission possible only by petition).

For More Information

Contact: Carolyn Cornelison, Director, Campus Alcohol and Drug Information Center, 305 Bryan Hall, Florida State University, Tallahassee, FL 32306. Telephone: 904-644-1741.

FONTBONNE COLLEGE

St. Louis, Missouri

General Information

Independent Roman Catholic 5-year coed college. Founded 1917. Awards B, M. Primary accreditation: regional. Metropolitan setting; 13-acre campus. Total enrollment: 1,036. Faculty: 99 (58 full-time, 41 part-time).

Drug and Alcohol Information

Education

On campus Drug and alcohol education/prevention programs offered for: all students, athletes/coaches. Authorized group concerned with responsible drinking. College holds an annual alcohol awareness week and drug awareness week.

Identification of Problems

Admissions College application does not ask about prior substance abuse problems.

On campus Current students identified as chemically dependent may remain enrolled. No training program on identifying students with potential substance abuse problems. Written procedures for students and staff if substance abuse is suspected.

Support Services

On campus Private counseling, campus ministry.

Employee assistance Program for chemically dependent employees not available.

Disciplinary Actions

Alcohol Results of infractions of alcohol regulations (see Comparative Table of Alcohol Regulations) vary by situation but can include counseling, warning, probation, suspension, expulsion.

Drugs For first-time use or possession: varies by situation—counseling, warning. For subsequent use or possession: varies by situation. For any sale: expulsion.

For More Information

Contact: Gary Zack, Vice President, Enrollment/Student Services, Fontbonne College, 6800 Wydown Blvd., St. Louis, MO 63105. Telephone: 314-889-1411.

FORDHAM UNIVERSITY

New York, New York

General Information

Independent Roman Catholic comprehensive coed institution. 86-acre campus at Rose Hill and 8-acre campus at Lincoln Center. Founded 1841. Awards B, M, D. Primary accreditation: regional. Metropolitan setting; 86-acre campus. Total enrollment: 13,036. Faculty: 933 (489 full-time, 444 part-time).

Drug and Alcohol Information

Education

On campus Drug and alcohol education/prevention programs offered for: all students. College holds an annual alcohol awareness week and drug awareness week.

Identification of Problems

Admissions College application does not ask about prior substance abuse problems.

On campus Current students identified as chemically dependent may remain enrolled, but treatment is required. Training program on identifying students with potential substance abuse problems for: resident advisers. Written procedures for students and staff if substance abuse is suspected.

Support Services

On campus AA, ACOA, private counseling.

Employee assistance Program for chemically dependent employees not available.

Disciplinary Actions

Alcohol Results of infractions of alcohol regulations (see Comparative Table of Alcohol Regulations) may include counseling, warning, probation.

Drugs For first-time use: varies by situation. For subsequent use: varies by situation—probation. For first-time possession: probation. For subsequent possession: varies by situation—suspension. For first-time sale: suspension. For subsequent sale: expulsion.

For More Information

Contact: Henry P. Toutain, Dean of Students, Fordham University, E. Fordham Rd., Bronx, NY 10458. Telephone: 212-579-2514.

FORT HAYS STATE UNIVERSITY

Hays, Kansas

General Information

State-supported 5-year coed college. Founded 1902. Awards A (college transfer and terminal), B, M. Primary accreditation: regional. Small-town setting; 200-acre campus. Total enrollment: 5,005. Social organizations: 5 national fraternities, 3 national sororities; 3% of eligible undergraduate men and 2% of eligible undergraduate women are members.

Drug and Alcohol Information

Education

On campus Drug and alcohol education/prevention programs offered for: all students, athletes/coaches, faculty, administration; required for: freshmen. Bacchus chapter: 25 members. College holds an annual alcohol awareness week and drug awareness week.

Identification of Problems

Admissions College application does not ask about prior substance abuse problems.

On campus Current students identified as chemically dependent may remain enrolled, but treatment is required. Training program on identifying students with potential substance abuse problems for: resident advisers, Greek officers, administration. Written procedures for students and staff if substance abuse is suspected.

Support Services

On campus AA, NA, ACOA, private counseling.

Employee assistance Program for chemically dependent employees not available. Staff working with drug/alcohol-related issues: 1 full-time and 7 part-time.

Disciplinary Actions

Alcohol Results of infractions of alcohol regulations (see Comparative Table of Alcohol Regulations) vary by situation but can include chemical dependency assessment, counseling, warning, probation, suspension, expulsion.

Drugs For first-time use: varies by situation—counseling, suspension. For subsequent use: expulsion. For first-time possession: chemical dependency assessment, counseling, probation, suspension. For subsequent possession: suspension. For any sale: expulsion.

For More Information

Contact: Jim Dawson, Vice President for Student Affairs, Fort Hays State University, 600 Park St., Hays, KS 67601. Telephone: 913-628-4277.

FORT VALLEY STATE COLLEGE

Fort Valley, Georgia

General Information

State-supported 5-year coed college. Part of University System of Georgia. Founded 1895. Awards A (terminal), B, M. Primary accreditation: regional. Small-town setting; 660-acre campus. Total enrollment: 1,915. Faculty: 148 (all full-time). Social organizations: 4 national fraternities, 4 national sororities.

Drug and Alcohol Information

Education

On campus Drug and alcohol education/prevention programs offered for: all students, athletes/coaches. Authorized group concerned with responsible drinking. College holds an annual alcohol awareness week and drug awareness week.

Identification of Problems

Admissions College application does not ask about prior substance abuse problems.

On campus Current students identified as chemically dependent may remain enrolled, but treatment is required. No training program on identifying students with potential substance abuse problems. No written procedures for students and staff if substance abuse is suspected.

Support Services

On campus Private counseling.

Employee assistance Program for chemically dependent employees not available.

Disciplinary Actions

Alcohol Results of infractions of alcohol regulations (see Comparative Table of Alcohol Regulations) vary by situation but can include warning, probation, suspension.

Drugs For first-time use or possession: probation. For subsequent use or possession: suspension. For first-time sale: suspension. For subsequent sale: expulsion.

For More Information

Contact: Thomas J. Palmer, Vice President for Student Affairs, Fort Valley State College, P.O. Box 5050, State College Dr., Fort Valley, GA 31030. Telephone: 912-825-6290.

FRAMINGHAM STATE COLLEGE

Framingham, Massachusetts

General Information

State-supported 5-year coed college. Founded 1839. Awards B, M. Primary accreditation: regional. City setting; 73-acre campus. Total enrollment: 3,368.

Drug and Alcohol Information

Education

On campus Drug and alcohol education/prevention programs offered for: all students, athletes/coaches. Authorized group concerned with responsible drinking. College holds an annual alcohol awareness week and drug awareness week.

Identification of Problems

Admissions College application does not ask about prior substance abuse problems.

On campus Current students identified as chemically dependent may remain enrolled, but treatment is required. Training program on identifying students with potential substance abuse problems for: resident advisers, coaches, faculty, administration. Written procedures for students and staff if substance abuse is suspected.

Support Services

On campus AA, ACOA, support groups (Self-Esteem), private counseling, alcohol education.

Employee assistance Program for chemically dependent employees available. Staff working with drug/alcohol-related issues: 1 full-time and 10 part-time.

Disciplinary Actions

Alcohol Results of infractions of alcohol regulations (see Comparative Table of Alcohol Regulations) include chemical dependency assessment, probation, removal from residence hall.

Drugs For first-time use: varies by situation—chemical dependency assessment, probation. For subsequent use: varies by situation—probation, suspension. For first-time possession: varies by situation. For subsequent possession: suspension. For first-time sale: varies by situation—suspension, expulsion. For subsequent sale: expulsion.

For More Information

Contact: Cynthia S. Forrest, Dean of Students, Framingham State College, 100 State St., Framingham, MA 01701. Telephone: 508-626-4636.

FRANKLIN AND MARSHALL COLLEGE

Lancaster, Pennsylvania

General Information

Independent 4-year coed college. Founded 1787. Awards B. Primary accreditation: regional. City setting; 125-acre campus. Total enrollment: 1,850. Faculty: 160 (135 full-time, 25 part-time).

Drug and Alcohol Information

Education

On campus Drug and alcohol education/prevention programs offered for: all students. Bacchus chapter. College holds an annual alcohol awareness week.

Identification of Problems

Admissions College application does not ask about prior substance abuse problems.

On campus Current students identified as chemically dependent may remain enrolled. Comments: Treatment may or may not be required. No training program on identifying students with potential substance abuse problems. No written procedures for students and staff if substance abuse is suspected.

Support Services

On campus Private counseling, referrals.

Employee assistance Program for chemically dependent employees available. Staff working with drug/alcohol-related issues: 4 part-time.

Disciplinary Actions

Alcohol Results of infractions of alcohol regulations (see Comparative Table of Alcohol Regulations) vary by situation but can include confiscation of liquor, referral to Committee on Student Conduct.

Drugs For any use, possession, or sale: varies by situation.

For More Information

Contact: Dr. Mark Hemlick, Co-Chairman, Alcohol Awareness Committee, Counseling Service, Franklin and Marshall College, P.O. Box 3003, Lancaster, PA 17604. Telephone: 717-291-4083.

FRANKLIN COLLEGE OF INDIANA

Franklin, Indiana

General Information

Independent 4-year coed college, affiliated with American Baptist Churches in the U.S.A. Founded 1834. Awards A (college transfer), B. Primary accreditation: regional. Small-town setting; 76-acre campus. Total enrollment: 780. Faculty: 73 (51 full-time, 22 part-time). Social organizations: 5 national fraternities, 4 national sororities; 41% of eligible undergraduate men and 48% of eligible undergraduate women are members.

Drug and Alcohol Information

Education

On campus Drug and alcohol education/prevention programs offered for: all students, faculty, administration; required for: freshmen. Authorized group concerned with responsible drinking. College holds an annual alcohol awareness week.

Identification of Problems

Admissions College application does not ask about prior substance abuse problems.

On campus Current students identified as chemically dependent may remain enrolled, but treatment is required. Training program on identifying students with potential substance abuse problems for: resident advisers, Greek officers. Written procedures for students and staff if substance abuse is suspected.

Support Services

On campus Support groups, private counseling.

Employee assistance Program for chemically dependent employees available. Staff working with drug/alcohol-related issues: 2 part-time.

Disciplinary Actions

Alcohol Results of infractions of alcohol regulations (see Comparative Table of Alcohol Regulations) vary by situation.

Drugs For first-time use or possession: probation. For subsequent use or possession: suspension. For any sale: expulsion.

For More Information

Contact: D. Thomas Ramey, Vice President for Student Services, Franklin College of Indiana, 501 E. Monroe St., Franklin, IN 46131. Telephone: 317-736-8441.

FRANKLIN PIERCE COLLEGE

Rindge, New Hampshire

General Information

Independent 4-year coed college. Founded 1962. Awards B. Primary accreditation: regional. Rural setting; 1,000-acre campus. Total enrollment: 1,183. Faculty: 94 (63 full-time, 31 part-time).

Drug and Alcohol Information

Education

On campus Drug and alcohol education/prevention programs offered for: all students, athletes/coaches, faculty, administration. Bacchus chapter: 15 members. College holds an annual alcohol awareness week and drug awareness week.

Identification of Problems

Admissions College application does not ask about prior substance abuse problems.

On campus Current students identified as chemically dependent may remain enrolled, but treatment is required. Training program on identifying students with potential substance abuse problems for: resident advisers, coaches, faculty. Written procedures for students and staff if substance abuse is suspected.

Support Services

On campus AA, Al-Anon, ACOA, private counseling.

Employee assistance Program for chemically dependent employees available. Staff working with drug/alcohol-related issues: 3 part-time.

Disciplinary Actions

Alcohol Results of infractions of alcohol regulations (see Comparative Table of Alcohol Regulations) vary by situation but can include chemical dependency assessment, counseling, warning, probation, suspension, suspension from residence.

Drugs For first-time use or possession: varies by situation. For subsequent use: varies by situation—chemical dependency assessment, counseling, fines. For subsequent possession: varies by situation. For first-time sale: suspension, expulsion. For subsequent sale: expulsion.

Additional Information from the College

An Alcohol and Other Drugs Committee, representing all members of the campus community, monitors laws and liability and recommends appropriate campus policies and programs. The West Campus residence area is totally alcohol free.

For More Information

Contact: Paula Phillips, Acting Director, Counseling Center, The Manor, Franklin Pierce College, Rindge, NH 03461. Telephone: 603-899-5111 Ext. 272.

FRANKLIN UNIVERSITY

Columbus, Ohio

General Information

Independent 4-year coed college. Founded 1902. Awards A (college transfer and terminal), B. Primary accreditation: regional. Metropolitan setting; 13-acre campus. Total enrollment: 4,160. Faculty: 206 (56 full-time, 150 part-time).

Franklin University (continued)

Drug and Alcohol Information

Education

On campus Drug and alcohol education/prevention programs offered for: all students. Authorized group concerned with responsible drinking. College holds an annual alcohol awareness week.

Identification of Problems

Admissions College application does not ask about prior substance abuse problems.

On campus No training program on identifying students with potential substance abuse problems. Written procedures for students and staff if substance abuse is suspected.

Support Services

On campus Private counseling, referrals.

Employee assistance Program for chemically dependent employees not available. Staff working with drug/alcohol-related issues: 1 full-time.

Disciplinary Actions

Alcohol Results of infractions of alcohol regulations (see Comparative Table of Alcohol Regulations) vary by situation.

Drugs For any use, possession, or sale: varies by situation.

Additional Information from the College

Franklin University provides education for personal and career development; this can be impeded by substance abuse. The needs of individuals in the University community are met in a confidential and caring manner through education and referral to appropriate community resources.

For More Information

Contact: J. Beresford, Assistant Director of Counseling, Franklin University, 201 S. Grant Ave., Columbus, OH 43215. Telephone: 614-224-6237 Ext. 259.

FRESNO PACIFIC COLLEGE

Fresno, California

General Information

Independent 5-year coed college, affiliated with Mennonite Brethren Church. Founded 1944. Awards A (college transfer), B, M. Primary accreditation: regional. City setting; 40-acre campus. Total enrollment: 1,223. Faculty: 43 (35 full-time, 8 part-time).

Drug and Alcohol Information

Education

On campus Drug and alcohol education/prevention programs offered for: all students, athletes/coaches, faculty.

Identification of Problems

Admissions College application does not ask about prior substance abuse problems.

On campus Current students identified as chemically dependent may remain enrolled, but treatment is required. No training program on identifying students with potential substance abuse problems. Written procedures for students and staff if substance abuse is suspected.

Support Services

On campus Private counseling. ACOA group is beginning.

Employee assistance Program for chemically dependent employees available.

Disciplinary Actions

Alcohol Results of infractions of alcohol regulations (see Comparative Table of Alcohol Regulations) vary by situation but can include counseling, warning, suspension, expulsion, behavior contract.

Drugs For first-time use: chemical dependency assessment, counseling, warning. For first-time possession: counseling, warning. For subsequent use or possession: varies by situation. For first-time sale: suspension. For subsequent sale: expulsion.

For More Information

Contact: Gary Nachtigall, Dean of Students, Fresno Pacific College, 1717 S. Chestnut Ave., Fresno, CA 93702. Telephone: 209-453-2032.

FRIENDS UNIVERSITY

Wichita, Kansas

General Information

Independent 5-year coed college, affiliated with Society of Friends. Founded 1898. Awards A (terminal), B, M. Primary accreditation: regional. City setting; 54-acre campus. Total enrollment: 1,185. Faculty: 93 (53 full-time, 40 part-time). Social organizations: 2 local fraternities, 2 local sororities; 13% of eligible undergraduate men and 11% of eligible undergraduate women are members.

Drug and Alcohol Information

Education

On campus Drug and alcohol education/prevention programs offered for: all students, athletes/coaches, faculty, administration. Authorized group concerned with responsible drinking. College holds an annual alcohol awareness week and drug awareness week.

Identification of Problems

Admissions College application does not ask about prior substance abuse problems.

On campus Current students identified as chemically dependent may remain enrolled. No training program on identifying students with potential substance abuse problems. No written procedures for students and staff if substance abuse is suspected.

Support Services

On campus Support groups.

Employee assistance Program for chemically dependent employees not available. Staff working with drug/alcohol-related issues: 2 part-time.

Disciplinary Actions

Alcohol Results of infractions of alcohol regulations (see Comparative Table of Alcohol Regulations) vary by situation.

Drugs For first-time use, possession, or sale: varies by situation. For subsequent use, possession, or sale: suspension.

For More Information

Contact: Bill Allen, Family Life Professor, Friends

University, 2100 University, Wichita, KS 67213. Telephone: 316-261-5800.

FURMAN UNIVERSITY

Greenville, South Carolina

General Information

Independent Baptist 5-year coed college. Founded 1826. Awards B, M. Primary accreditation: regional. City setting; 750-acre campus. Total enrollment: 2,794. Faculty: 206 (201 full-time, 5 part-time). Social organizations: 5 local fraternities, 3 local sororities; 16% of eligible undergraduate men and 9% of eligible undergraduate women are members.

Drug and Alcohol Information

Education

On campus Drug and alcohol education/prevention programs offered for: all students, athletes/coaches. Authorized group concerned with responsible drinking. College holds an annual alcohol awareness week and drug awareness week.

Identification of Problems

Admissions College application does not ask about prior substance abuse problems.

On campus Current students identified as chemically dependent may remain enrolled, but treatment is required. Training program on identifying students with potential substance abuse problems for: resident assistants, coaches. Written procedures for students and staff if substance abuse is suspected.

Support Services

On campus Al-Anon, support groups, private counseling.

Employee assistance Program for chemically dependent employees available. Staff working with drug/alcohol-related issues: 7 part-time.

Disciplinary Actions

Alcohol Results of infractions of alcohol regulations (see Comparative Table of Alcohol Regulations) vary by situation.

Drugs For first-time use or possession: suspension. For subsequent use or possession: expulsion. For any sale: expulsion.

For More Information

Contact: Dr. Harry B. Shucker, Vice President for Student Services, Furman University, Poinsett Hwy., Greenville, SC 29613. Telephone: 803-294-2202.

GALLAUDET UNIVERSITY

Washington, District of Columbia

General Information

Independent 5-year coed college. Founded 1856. Awards A (terminal), B, M, D (all undergraduate programs open primarily to hearing impaired). Primary accreditation: regional. Metropolitan setting; 100-acre campus. Total enrollment: 2,391. Faculty: 330 (300 full-time, 30 part-time). Social organizations: 1 national fraternity, 1 national sorority, 2 local fraternities, 2 local sororities, coed social clubs; 40% of eligible undergraduate men and 45% of eligible undergraduate women are members.

Drug and Alcohol Information

Education

On campus Drug and alcohol education/prevention programs offered for: all students; required for: social organization members, resident advisers.

Identification of Problems

Admissions College application does not ask about prior substance abuse problems.

On campus Current students identified as chemically dependent may remain enrolled. No training program on identifying students with potential substance abuse problems. No written procedures for students and staff if substance abuse is suspected.

Support Services

On campus Private counseling.

Employee assistance Program for chemically dependent employees not available.

Disciplinary Actions

Alcohol Results of infractions of alcohol regulations (see Comparative Table of Alcohol Regulations) include warning, probation, suspension.

Drugs For first-time use: warning, probation, suspension. For subsequent use: counseling, suspension. For first-time possession: probation, suspension. For subsequent possession: suspension, expulsion. For any sale: expulsion.

For More Information

Contact: Hillel Goldberg, Director, University Center, Gallaudet University, 800 Florida Ave., NE, Washington, D.C., 20002. Telephone: 202-651-5144.

GANNON UNIVERSITY

Erie, Pennsylvania

General Information

Independent Roman Catholic 5-year coed college. Founded 1944. Awards A (college transfer and terminal), B, M. Primary accreditation: regional. City setting; 18-acre campus. Total enrollment: 3,592. Faculty: 156 (148 full-time, 8 part-time). Social organizations: 10 national fraternities, 4 national sororities; 20% of eligible undergraduate men and 5% of eligible undergraduate women are members.

Drug and Alcohol Information

Education

On campus Drug and alcohol education/prevention programs offered for: all students; required for: athletes/coaches. College holds an annual alcohol awareness week.

Identification of Problems

Admissions College application does not ask about prior substance abuse problems.

On campus Current students identified as chemically dependent may remain enrolled. Comments: Whether treatment is required depends on the circumstances. Training program on identifying students with potential substance abuse problems for: resident advisers.

Support Services

On campus Private counseling.

Employee assistance Program for chemically dependent employees being developed. Staff working with drug/alcohol-related issues: 10 part-time.

Gannon University (continued)

Disciplinary Actions

Alcohol Results of infractions of alcohol regulations (see Comparative Table of Alcohol Regulations) include probation.

Drugs For any use or possession: suspension. For any sale: expulsion.

For More Information

Contact: Jim Fitzpatrick, Director, Student Development, Gannon University, University Square, Erie, PA 16541. Telephone: 814-871-7662.

GENEVA COLLEGE

Beaver Falls, Pennsylvania

General Information

Independent 5-year coed college, affiliated with Reformed Presbyterian Church. Founded 1848. Awards A (college transfer and terminal), B, M. Primary accreditation: regional. Small-town setting; 55-acre campus. Total enrollment: 1,445. Faculty: 105 (56 full-time, 49 part-time).

Drug and Alcohol Information

Education

On campus Drug and alcohol education/prevention programs offered for: freshmen, athletes/coaches, resident advisers.

Identification of Problems

Admissions College application does not ask about prior substance abuse problems.

On campus Current students identified as chemically dependent may not remain enrolled. No training program on identifying students with potential substance abuse problems. Written procedures for students and staff if substance abuse is suspected.

Support Services

On campus AA.

Employee assistance Program for chemically dependent employees not available.

Disciplinary Actions

Alcohol Results of infractions of alcohol regulations (see Comparative Table of Alcohol Regulations) vary by situation but can include chemical dependency assessment, counseling, warning, probation, suspension, expulsion, fines, prevention-intervention sessions or rehab.

Drugs For any use, possession, or sale: counseling, probation, suspension, fines. Comments: Dismissal is recommended for a third offense.

Additional Information from the College

An all-college prevention/education program is being developed. However, Geneva College's problems have been minimal because of its strict regulations regarding drug and alcohol use by students, faculty, and staff.

For More Information

Contact: Karl Cunningham, Dean of Students, Geneva College, College Avenue, Beaver Falls, PA 15010. Telephone: 412-846-5100.

GEORGE MASON UNIVERSITY

Fairfax, Virginia

General Information

State-supported comprehensive coed institution. Founded 1957. Awards B, M, D. Primary accreditation: regional. Small-town setting; 567-acre campus. Total enrollment: 18,965. Faculty: 879 (519 full-time, 360 part-time). Social organizations: 5 national fraternities, 6 national sororities; 1% of eligible undergraduate men and 1% of eligible undergraduate women are members.

Drug and Alcohol Information

Education

On campus Drug and alcohol education/prevention programs offered for: all students, athletes/coaches. Authorized group concerned with responsible drinking. College holds an annual alcohol awareness week and drug awareness week.

Identification of Problems

Admissions College application does not ask about prior substance abuse problems.

On campus Current students identified as chemically dependent may remain enrolled, but treatment may be required, depending on the situation. Training program on identifying students with potential substance abuse problems for: resident advisers, coaches. Written procedures for students and staff if substance abuse is suspected.

Support Services

On campus AA, ACOA, support groups, private counseling.

Employee assistance Program for chemically dependent employees available. Staff working with drug/alcohol-related issues: 2 full-time and 4 part-time.

Disciplinary Actions

Alcohol Results of infractions of alcohol regulations (see Comparative Table of Alcohol Regulations) include chemical dependency assessment, counseling, warning, probation, suspension.

Drugs For first-time use or possession: varies by situation. For subsequent use or possession: probation, suspension, expulsion. For first-time sale: probation, suspension, expulsion. For subsequent sale: suspension, expulsion.

For More Information

Contact: Substance Abuse Coordinator, George Mason University, 4400 University Dr.–SUB1, Room 302, Fairfax, VA 22030. Telephone: 703-323-2522.

GEORGETOWN COLLEGE

Georgetown, Kentucky

General Information

Independent 5-year coed college, affiliated with Baptist Church. Founded 1829. Awards B, M. Primary accreditation: regional. Small-town setting; 52-acre campus. Total enrollment: 1,471. Faculty: 93 (64 full-time, 29 part-time). Social organizations: 4 national fraternities, 3 national sororities, 1 local fraternity; 35% of eligible undergraduate men and 32% of eligible undergraduate women are members.

Drug and Alcohol Information

Education

On campus Drug and alcohol education/prevention programs offered for: all students, athletes/coaches, faculty, administration. Authorized group concerned with responsible drinking. College holds an annual alcohol awareness week.

Identification of Problems

Admissions College application question about prior substance abuse problems is used for counseling and referral, if student is admitted.

On campus Current students identified as chemically dependent may remain enrolled, but treatment is required. No training program on identifying students with potential substance abuse problems. Written procedures for students and staff if substance abuse is suspected.

Support Services

On campus Private counseling.

Employee assistance Program for chemically dependent employees available.

Disciplinary Actions

Alcohol Results of infractions of alcohol regulations (see Comparative Table of Alcohol Regulations) vary by situation but can include counseling, probation, suspension.

Drugs For first-time use, possession, or sale: suspension. For subsequent use, possession, or sale: expulsion.

For More Information

Contact: Dr. Macy Wyatt, Counseling Psychologist, Georgetown College, 400 E. College St., Georgetown, KY 40324. Telephone: 502-863-8165.

GEORGIA INSTITUTE OF TECHNOLOGY

Atlanta, Georgia

General Information

State-supported comprehensive coed institution. Part of University System of Georgia. Founded 1885. Awards B, M, D. Primary accreditation: regional. Metropolitan setting; 330-acre campus. Total enrollment: 11,887. Faculty: 547 (537 full-time, 10 part-time). Social organizations: 31 national fraternities, 7 national sororities; 27% of eligible undergraduate men and 24% of eligible undergraduate women are members.

Drug and Alcohol Information

Education

On campus Drug and alcohol education/prevention programs offered for: all students, athletes/coaches, faculty, administration. Authorized group concerned with responsible drinking. College holds an annual alcohol awareness week and drug awareness week.

Identification of Problems

Admissions College application does not ask about prior substance abuse problems.

On campus Current students identified as chemically dependent may remain enrolled, but treatment is required. No training program on identifying students with potential substance abuse problems. No written procedures for students and staff if substance abuse is suspected.

Support Services

On campus AA, NA, Al-Anon, support groups, private counseling.

Employee assistance Program for chemically dependent employees available. Staff working with drug/alcohol-related issues: 10 part-time.

Disciplinary Actions

Alcohol Results of infractions of alcohol regulations (see Comparative Table of Alcohol Regulations) vary by situation but can include counseling, warning, probation, suspension.

Drugs For any use, possession, or sale: varies by situation.

For More Information

Contact: Director of Counseling, Dean of Students Bldg., Georgia Institute of Technology, Atlanta, GA 30332. Telephone: 404-894-2575.

GEORGIAN COURT COLLEGE

Lakewood, New Jersey

General Information

Independent Roman Catholic 5-year primarily women's college. Founded 1908. Awards B, M. Primary accreditation: regional. Small-town setting; 152-acre campus. Total enrollment: 2,054. Faculty: 131 (66 full-time, 65 part-time).

Drug and Alcohol Information

Education

On campus Drug and alcohol education/prevention programs offered for: all students, athletes/coaches. Authorized group concerned with responsible drinking. College holds an annual alcohol awareness week and drug awareness week.

Identification of Problems

Admissions College application does not ask about prior substance abuse problems.

On campus Current students identified as chemically dependent may remain enrolled, but treatment is required. No training program on identifying students with potential substance abuse problems. No written procedures for students and staff if substance abuse is suspected.

Support Services

On campus ACOA, private counseling.

Employee assistance Program for chemically dependent employees not available. Staff working with drug/alcohol-related issues: 2 part-time.

Disciplinary Actions

Alcohol Results of infractions of alcohol regulations (see Comparative Table of Alcohol Regulations) vary by situation but can include chemical dependency assessment, counseling, warning, probation.

Drugs For first-time use, possession, or sale: varies by situation. For subsequent use: varies by situation—chemical dependency assessment, suspension, expulsion. For subsequent possession: varies by situation—chemical dependency assessment, expulsion. For subsequent sale: chemical dependency assessment, expulsion.

For More Information

Contact: Kathleen Rieth, Director of Counseling, Georgian Court College, Lakewood, NJ 08701. Telephone: 201-364-2200 Ext. 680.

GEORGIA SOUTHERN COLLEGE

Statesboro, Georgia

General Information

State-supported 5-year coed college. Part of University System of Georgia. Founded 1906. Awards A (college transfer), B, M. Primary accreditation: regional. Small-town setting; 457-acre campus. Total enrollment: 9,841. Faculty: 492 (449 full-time, 43 part-time). Social organizations: 13 national fraternities, 9 national sororities; 25% of eligible undergraduate men and 21% of eligible undergraduate women are members.

Drug and Alcohol Information

Education

On campus Drug and alcohol education/prevention programs offered for: all students; required for: social organization members, athletes/coaches, resident advisers. College holds an annual alcohol awareness week.

Identification of Problems

Admissions College application does not ask about prior substance abuse problems.

On campus Current students identified as chemically dependent may remain enrolled, but treatment is required. Training program on identifying students with potential substance abuse problems for: resident advisers. Written procedures for students and staff if substance abuse is suspected.

Support Services

On campus AA, private counseling.

Employee assistance Program for chemically dependent employees not available.

Disciplinary Actions

Alcohol Results of infractions of alcohol regulations (see Comparative Table of Alcohol Regulations) include probation, required educational program.

Drugs For first-time use or possession: probation. For subsequent use or possession: suspension. For first-time sale: suspension. For subsequent sale: expulsion.

For More Information

Contact: Dr. Jane Thompson, Assistant Dean of Students, Georgia Southern College, Landrum Box 8063, Statesboro, GA 30460. Telephone: 912-681-5409.

GEORGIA STATE UNIVERSITY

Atlanta, Georgia

General Information

State-supported comprehensive coed institution. Part of University System of Georgia. Founded 1913. Awards A (college transfer and terminal), B, M, D. Primary accreditation: regional. Metropolitan setting; 24-acre campus. Total enrollment: 22,245. Social organizations: 10 national fraternities, 9 national sororities; 10% of eligible undergraduate men and 11% of eligible undergraduate women are members.

Drug and Alcohol Information

Education

On campus Drug and alcohol education/prevention programs offered for: all students, athletes/coaches. Bacchus chapter: 160 members. College holds an annual alcohol awareness week and drug awareness week.

Identification of Problems

Admissions College application does not ask about prior substance abuse problems.

On campus Current students identified as chemically dependent may remain enrolled. Comments: The Dean of Students decides whether treatment is required on a case-by-case basis. No training program on identifying students with potential substance abuse problems. No written procedures for students and staff if substance abuse is suspected.

Support Services

On campus AA, ACOA.

Employee assistance Program for chemically dependent employees available. Staff working with drug/alcohol-related issues: 3 part-time.

Disciplinary Actions

Alcohol Results of infractions of alcohol regulations (see Comparative Table of Alcohol Regulations) vary by situation but can include counseling, warning, probation, suspension, expulsion.

Drugs Comments: All drug offenses are referred to the police.

For More Information

Contact: Dr. Carole Pearson, Assistant Dean, 402 Student Center, Georgia State University, Atlanta, GA 30303. Telephone: 404-651-2206.

GETTYSBURG COLLEGE

Gettysburg, Pennsylvania

General Information

Independent 4-year coed college, affiliated with Evangelical Lutheran Church in America. Founded 1832. Awards B. Primary accreditation: regional. Small-town setting; 200-acre campus. Total enrollment: 1,900. Faculty: 150 (140 full-time, 10 part-time). Social organizations: 11 national fraternities, 7 national sororities; 55% of eligible undergraduate men and 45% of eligible undergraduate women are members.

Drug and Alcohol Information

Education

On campus Drug and alcohol education/prevention programs offered for: all students, faculty, judicial referrals; required for: freshmen, athletes/coaches, resident advisers. Bacchus chapter: 25 members. College holds an annual alcohol awareness week and drug awareness week.

Identification of Problems

Admissions College application does not ask about prior substance abuse problems.

On campus Current students identified as chemically dependent may remain enrolled, but treatment may be required. Comments: Depends on behavioral/academic issues. Training program on identifying students with potential substance abuse problems for: resident advisers, coaches, faculty, health care providers. Written procedures for students and staff if substance abuse is suspected.

Support Services

On campus AA, ACOA, support groups, private counseling.

Employee assistance Program for chemically dependent employees available. Staff working with drug/alcohol-related issues: 1 full-time.

Disciplinary Actions

Alcohol Results of infractions of alcohol regulations (see Comparative Table of Alcohol Regulations) vary by situation but can include chemical dependency assessment, counseling, probation, suspension, fine.

Drugs For any use or possession: varies by situation. For first-time sale: suspension, expulsion. For subsequent sale: expulsion.

Additional Information from the College

The alcohol policy is currently under revision and will be substantially altered for the next academic year.

For More Information

Contact: Jill A. Schumann, Drug and Alcohol Education Coordinator, Gettysburg College, Box 424, Gettysburg, PA 17325. Telephone: 717-337-6960.

GLASSBORO STATE COLLEGE

Glassboro, New Jersey

General Information

State-supported 5-year coed college. Part of New Jersey State College System. Founded 1923. Awards B, M. Primary accreditation: regional. Small-town setting; 180-acre campus. Total enrollment: 9,500. Faculty: 445 (345 full-time, 100 part-time). Social organizations: 5 national fraternities, 5 national sororities, 2 local fraternities, 2 local sororities; 18% of eligible undergraduate men and 12% of eligible undergraduate women are members.

Drug and Alcohol Information

Education

On campus Drug and alcohol education/prevention programs offered for: all students. Authorized group concerned with responsible drinking. College holds an annual alcohol awareness week and drug awareness week.

Identification of Problems

Admissions College application does not ask about prior substance abuse problems.

On campus Current students identified as chemically dependent may or may not remain enrolled. Comments: Decisions are made on a case-by-case basis. Training program on identifying students with potential substance abuse problems for: resident advisers, administration. Written procedures for students and staff if substance abuse is suspected.

Support Services

On campus ACOA, private counseling.

Employee assistance Program for chemically dependent employees available. Staff working with drug/alcohol-related issues: 4 part-time.

Disciplinary Actions

Alcohol Results of infractions of alcohol regulations (see Comparative Table of Alcohol Regulations) vary by situation but can include probation, suspension.

Drugs For first-time use or possession: varies by situation—probation. For subsequent use or possession: suspension. For first-time sale: suspension. For subsequent sale: expulsion.

For More Information

Contact: Wayne Hoffner, Dean of Students, Glassboro State College, Glassboro, NJ 08028. Telephone: 609-863-6359.

GLENVILLE STATE COLLEGE

Glenville, West Virginia

General Information

State-supported 4-year coed college. Founded 1872. Awards A (terminal), B. Primary accreditation: regional. Small-town setting. Total enrollment: 2,204. Faculty: 88 (72 full-time, 16 part-time). Social organizations: 3 national fraternities, 2 national sororities; 15% of eligible undergraduate men and 20% of eligible undergraduate women are members.

Drug and Alcohol Information

Education

On campus Drug and alcohol education/prevention programs offered for: all students. Authorized group concerned with responsible drinking. College holds an annual alcohol awareness week and drug awareness week.

Identification of Problems

Admissions College application does not ask about prior substance abuse problems.

On campus Current students identified as chemically dependent may remain enrolled, but treatment is required. Training program on identifying students with potential substance abuse problems for: resident advisers. No written procedures for students and staff if substance abuse is suspected.

Support Services

On campus Referrals.

Off campus AA in the community.

Employee assistance Program for chemically dependent employees not available. Staff working with drug/alcohol-related issues: 7 part-time.

Disciplinary Actions

Alcohol Results of infractions of alcohol regulations (see Comparative Table of Alcohol Regulations) include counseling, warning, probation, suspension.

Drugs For first-time use: counseling, probation. For first-time possession: probation. For subsequent use or possession: suspension. For first-time sale: suspension. For subsequent sale: expulsion.

For More Information

Contact: Richard Bowers, Director of Pioneer Center Activities, Glenville State College, 200 High Street, Glenville, WV 26351. Telephone: 304-462-7361 Ext. 112.

GMI ENGINEERING & MANAGEMENT INSTITUTE
Flint, Michigan

General Information
Independent 5-year coed college. Founded 1919. Awards B, M. Primary accreditation: regional. City setting; 49-acre campus. Total enrollment: 3,068. Faculty: 125 full-time. Social organizations: 14 national fraternities, 6 national sororities; 45% of eligible undergraduate men and 45% of eligible undergraduate women are members.

Drug and Alcohol Information
Education
On campus Drug and alcohol education/prevention programs offered for: all students. Bacchus chapter: 5 members. College holds an annual alcohol awareness week.

Identification of Problems
On campus No training program on identifying students with potential substance abuse problems. No written procedures for students and staff if substance abuse is suspected.

Support Services
On campus Private counseling.

Employee assistance Staff working with drug/alcohol-related issues: 2 part-time.

Disciplinary Actions
Alcohol Results of infractions of alcohol regulations (see Comparative Table of Alcohol Regulations) include counseling, warning, probation, administrative or board hearing.

For More Information
Contact: Lisa E. McGill, Counselor, GMI Engineering and Management Institute, 1700 W. Third Ave., Flint, MI 48504. Telephone: 313-762-9873.

GODDARD COLLEGE
Plainfield, Vermont

General Information
Independent 5-year coed college. Founded 1938. Awards B, M. Primary accreditation: regional. Rural setting; 450-acre campus. Total enrollment: 400. Faculty: 31 (21 full-time, 10 part-time).

Drug and Alcohol Information
Education
On campus Drug and alcohol education/prevention programs not offered. Authorized group concerned with responsible drinking.

Identification of Problems
Admissions College application does not ask about prior substance abuse problems.

On campus Current students identified as chemically dependent may remain enrolled, but treatment is required. No training program on identifying students with potential substance abuse problems. Written procedures for students and staff if substance abuse is suspected.

Support Services
On campus ACOA, support groups.

Employee assistance Program for chemically dependent employees not available. Staff working with drug/alcohol-related issues: 3 part-time.

Disciplinary Actions
Alcohol Results of infractions of alcohol regulations (see Comparative Table of Alcohol Regulations) vary by situation.

Drugs For any use, possession, or sale: varies by situation.

For More Information
Contact: Martin Johnson, Coordinator of Community Life, Goddard College, Plainfield, VT 05667. Telephone: 802-454-8311.

GOLDEN GATE UNIVERSITY
San Francisco, California

General Information
Independent comprehensive coed institution. Founded 1901. Awards A (college transfer), B, M, D. Primary accreditation: regional. Metropolitan setting. Total enrollment: 9,338. Faculty: 760 (60 full-time, 700 part-time).

Drug and Alcohol Information
Education
On campus Drug and alcohol education/prevention programs offered for: all students, faculty, administration. College holds an annual alcohol awareness week.

Identification of Problems
Admissions College application does not ask about prior substance abuse problems.

On campus Current students identified as chemically dependent may remain enrolled, but treatment is required. No training program on identifying students with potential substance abuse problems.

Support Services
On campus Private counseling, referrals.

Employee assistance Program for chemically dependent employees available.

Disciplinary Actions
Alcohol Results of infractions of alcohol regulations (see Comparative Table of Alcohol Regulations) vary by situation.

Drugs For first-time use or possession: counseling, warning. For subsequent use or possession: expulsion. For any sale: expulsion.

For More Information
Contact: Patrick F. O'Brien, Dean, Student Services, Golden Gate University, 536 Mission St., San Francisco, CA 94105. Telephone: 415-442-7245.

GOLDEY-BEACOM COLLEGE
Wilmington, Delaware

General Information
Independent 4-year coed college. Founded 1886. Awards A (college transfer), B. Primary accreditation: regional. City setting; 27-acre campus. Total enrollment: 2,500. Faculty:

66 (36 full-time, 30 part-time). Social organizations: 2 local fraternities, 2 local sororities; 10% of eligible undergraduate men and 10% of eligible undergraduate women are members.

Drug and Alcohol Information

Education

On campus Drug and alcohol education/prevention programs offered for: all students. College holds an annual alcohol awareness week and drug awareness week.

Identification of Problems

Admissions College application does not ask about prior substance abuse problems.

On campus Current students identified as chemically dependent may remain enrolled, but treatment is required. No training program on identifying students with potential substance abuse problems.

Support Services

On campus Referrals.

Employee assistance Program for chemically dependent employees available. Staff working with drug/alcohol-related issues: 3 part-time.

Disciplinary Actions

Alcohol Results of infractions of alcohol regulations (see Comparative Table of Alcohol Regulations) vary by situation but can include counseling, warning, probation, suspension, expulsion.

Drugs For first-time use or possession: varies by situation—probation. For subsequent use or possession: varies by situation. For any sale: varies by situation.

For More Information

Contact: Gary L. Wirt, Dean of Students, Goldey-Beacom College, 4701 Limestone Rd., Wilmington, DE 19808. Telephone: 302-998-8814.

GONZAGA UNIVERSITY

Spokane, Washington

General Information

Independent Roman Catholic comprehensive coed institution. Founded 1887. Awards B, M, D. Primary accreditation: regional. City setting; 85-acre campus. Total enrollment: 3,895. Faculty: 288 (208 full-time, 80 part-time). Social organizations: Knights, Spurs; 1% of eligible undergraduate men and 1% of eligible undergraduate women are members.

Drug and Alcohol Information

Education

On campus Drug and alcohol education/prevention programs offered for: freshmen, athletes/coaches, resident advisers. Authorized group concerned with responsible drinking. College holds an annual alcohol awareness week and drug awareness week.

Identification of Problems

Admissions College application does not ask about prior substance abuse problems.

On campus Current students identified as chemically dependent may remain enrolled, but treatment is required. Training program on identifying students with potential substance abuse problems for: resident advisers. Written procedures for students and staff if substance abuse is suspected.

Support Services

On campus AA, ACOA, private counseling.

Employee assistance Program for chemically dependent employees not available. Staff working with drug/alcohol-related issues: 1 full-time and 2 part-time.

Disciplinary Actions

Alcohol Results of infractions of alcohol regulations (see Comparative Table of Alcohol Regulations) include chemical dependency assessment, counseling, warning, probation, suspension, expulsion.

Drugs For any use, possession, or sale: varies by situation.

For More Information

Contact: Len Sitter, S.J., Alcohol and Substance Abuse Coordinator, Gonzaga University, Spokane, WA 99258. Telephone: 509-328-4220.

GORDON COLLEGE

Wenham, Massachusetts

General Information

Independent interdenominational 4-year coed college. Founded 1889. Awards B. Primary accreditation: regional. Small-town setting; 800-acre campus. Total enrollment: 1,183. Faculty: 89 (65 full-time, 24 part-time).

Drug and Alcohol Information

Education

On campus Drug and alcohol education/prevention programs not offered. Bacchus chapter: 8 members. College holds an annual alcohol awareness week.

Identification of Problems

Admissions College application does not ask about prior substance abuse problems.

On campus Current students identified as chemically dependent may often remain enrolled, but treatment is usually required. Decisions on this depend on the situation. Training program on identifying students with potential substance abuse problems for: Bacchus peer counselors. No written procedures for students and staff if substance abuse is suspected.

Support Services

On campus AA, ACOA, private counseling.

Employee assistance Program for chemically dependent employees not available.

Disciplinary Actions

Alcohol Results of infractions of alcohol regulations (see Comparative Table of Alcohol Regulations) vary by situation but can include chemical dependency assessment, counseling, warning, probation, suspension, expulsion.

Drugs For first-time use, possession, or sale: varies by situation—suspension. For subsequent use, possession, or sale: suspension.

For More Information

Contact: Kelly Higgins, Director of Leadership Development, Gordon College, 255 Grapevine Rd., Wenham, MA 01984. Telephone: 508-927-2300 Ext. 4263.

GOSHEN COLLEGE

Goshen, Indiana

General Information

Independent Mennonite 4-year coed college. Founded 1894. Awards B. Primary accreditation: regional. Small-town setting; 135-acre campus. Total enrollment: 1,085. Faculty: 112 (79 full-time, 33 part-time).

Drug and Alcohol Information

Education

On campus Drug and alcohol education/prevention programs offered for: all students; required for: resident advisers. Authorized group concerned with responsible drinking. College holds an annual alcohol awareness week and drug awareness week.

Identification of Problems

Admissions College application question about prior substance abuse problems is used in the admissions decision.

On campus Current students identified as chemically dependent may remain enrolled, but treatment is required. Training program on identifying students with potential substance abuse problems for: resident advisers, coaches. Written procedures for students and staff if substance abuse is suspected.

Support Services

On campus AA, support groups, private counseling.

Employee assistance Program for chemically dependent employees not available. Staff working with drug/alcohol-related issues: 4 part-time.

Disciplinary Actions

Alcohol Results of infractions of alcohol regulations (see Comparative Table of Alcohol Regulations) vary by situation but can include chemical dependency assessment, counseling, warning, probation, suspension.

Drugs For any use, possession, or sale: varies by situation.

For More Information

Contact: Norman Kauffmann, Dean of Students, Goshen College, Goshen, IN 46526. Telephone: 219-535-7539.

GOVERNORS STATE UNIVERSITY

University Park, Illinois

General Information

State-supported coed college. Part of State Colleges and Universities of Illinois System. Founded 1969. Awards B, M. Primary accreditation: regional. Small-town setting; 750-acre campus. Total enrollment: 5,092. Faculty: 276 (146 full-time, 130 part-time).

Drug and Alcohol Information

Education

On campus Drug and alcohol education/prevention programs offered for: all students. College holds an annual alcohol awareness week and drug awareness week.

Identification of Problems

Admissions College application does not ask about prior substance abuse problems.

On campus Current students identified as chemically dependent may remain enrolled. Comments: Sanctions would be imposed based on the situation. No training program on identifying students with potential substance abuse problems. Written procedures for students and staff if substance abuse is suspected.

Support Services

On campus Support groups (Employee Assistance Program), private counseling.

Employee assistance Program for chemically dependent employees available. Staff working with drug/alcohol-related issues: 10 part-time.

Disciplinary Actions

Alcohol Results of infractions of alcohol regulations (see Comparative Table of Alcohol Regulations) vary by situation. Comments: Student conduct code regulations cover these infractions.

Drugs For any use, possession, or sale: varies by situation.

Additional Information from the College

The student body of Governors State University is predominantly adult (average age 34) and part-time (85 percent). All students commute. There are no fraternities or sororities. Permission to serve alcohol at any campus event must be obtained from the President.

For More Information

Contact: M. Catherine Taylor, Dean, Student Affairs, Governors State University, University Parkway, University Park, IL 60466. Telephone: 312-534-5000 Ext. 2553.

GRAMBLING STATE UNIVERSITY

Grambling, Louisiana

General Information

State-supported 5-year coed college. Founded 1901. Awards A (college transfer and terminal), B, M. Primary accreditation: regional. Small-town setting; 340-acre campus. Total enrollment: 5,224.

Drug and Alcohol Information

Education

On campus Drug and alcohol education/prevention programs offered for: all students, administration. College holds an annual alcohol awareness week.

Identification of Problems

Admissions College application does not ask about prior substance abuse problems.

On campus Current students identified as chemically dependent may remain enrolled. Comments: Such students are encouraged, but not required, to seek treatment. No training program on identifying students with potential substance abuse problems. No written procedures for students and staff if substance abuse is suspected.

Support Services

On campus Support groups.

Employee assistance Program for chemically dependent employees not available. Staff working with drug/alcohol-related issues: 1 full-time and 3 part-time.

Disciplinary Actions

Alcohol Results of infractions of alcohol regulations (see

Comparative Table of Alcohol Regulations) include counseling, probation, suspension, appearance before judicial bodies for disciplinary action.

Drugs For any use, possession, or sale: varies by situation, but is generally the same as in the case of infractions of the alcohol regulations.

For More Information

Contact: Joyce Guy, Counselor, Grambling State University, P.O. Drawer 566, Grambling, LA 71245. Telephone: 318-274-4763.

GRAND VIEW COLLEGE

Des Moines, Iowa

General Information

Independent 4-year coed college, affiliated with Evangelical Lutheran Church in America. Founded 1896. Awards A (college transfer), B. Primary accreditation: regional. City setting; 25-acre campus. Total enrollment: 1,359. Faculty: 110 (67 full-time, 43 part-time).

Drug and Alcohol Information

Education

On campus Drug and alcohol education/prevention programs offered for: all students, faculty, administration; required for: athletes/coaches. Authorized group concerned with responsible drinking. College holds an annual alcohol awareness week.

Identification of Problems

Admissions College application does not ask about prior substance abuse problems.

On campus Current students identified as chemically dependent may remain enrolled. Training program on identifying students with potential substance abuse problems for: resident advisers, coaches, faculty, administration, student resident assistants. Written procedures for students and staff if substance abuse is suspected.

Support Services

On campus AA, ACOA, support groups, private counseling.

Employee assistance Program for chemically dependent employees available. Staff working with drug/alcohol-related issues: 5 part-time.

Disciplinary Actions

Alcohol Results of infractions of alcohol regulations (see Comparative Table of Alcohol Regulations) include chemical dependency assessment, counseling, warning, probation, suspension.

Drugs For first-time use: varies by situation—chemical dependency assessment, counseling, probation. For subsequent use: varies by situation. For first-time possession: chemical dependency assessment, counseling, probation. For subsequent possession: varies by situation. For first-time sale: suspension, expulsion. For subsequent sale: expulsion.

For More Information

Contact: Dr. Edwin D. Heusinkveld, Dean of Students, Grand View College, 1200 Grand View Avenue, Des Moines, IA 50316. Telephone: 515-263-2890.

GREEN MOUNTAIN COLLEGE

Poultney, Vermont

General Information

Independent 4-year coed college. Founded 1834. Awards A (college transfer), B. Primary accreditation: regional. Small-town setting; 155-acre campus. Total enrollment: 550. Faculty: 47 (35 full-time, 12 part-time).

Drug and Alcohol Information

Education

On campus Drug and alcohol education/prevention programs offered for: all students, faculty, administration, all members of the college community; required for: freshmen, athletes/coaches. Authorized group concerned with responsible drinking. College holds an annual alcohol awareness week and drug awareness week.

Identification of Problems

Admissions College application question about prior substance abuse problems is used for counseling and referral, if student is admitted. The question is part of the Health Assessment.

On campus Current students identified as chemically dependent may remain enrolled, but treatment is required. Training program on identifying students with potential substance abuse problems for: resident advisers, coaches, administration. Written procedures for students and staff if substance abuse is suspected.

Support Services

On campus AA, Al-Anon, private counseling, counseling center.

Employee assistance Program for chemically dependent employees available. Staff working with drug/alcohol-related issues: 4 part-time.

Disciplinary Actions

Alcohol Results of infractions of alcohol regulations (see Comparative Table of Alcohol Regulations) vary by situation but can include counseling, probation, suspension, expulsion.

Drugs For first-time use or possession: varies by situation. For subsequent use or possession: counseling, suspension. For first-time sale: suspension, expulsion. For subsequent sale: expulsion.

Additional Information from the College

Green Mountain College focuses on education and assistance as well as observance of state laws.

For More Information

Contact: F. Bozen, Dean of Student Affairs, Green Mountain College, College St., Poultney, VT 05764. Telephone: 802-287-9313.

GRINNELL COLLEGE

Grinnell, Iowa

General Information

Independent 4-year coed college. Founded 1846. Awards B. Primary accreditation: regional. Small-town setting; 90-acre campus. Total enrollment: 1,276. Faculty: 122 (108 full-time, 14 part-time).

Grinnell College (continued)

Drug and Alcohol Information

Education

On campus Drug and alcohol education/prevention programs offered for: all students, administration. Authorized group concerned with responsible drinking. College holds an annual alcohol awareness week.

Identification of Problems

Admissions College application does not ask about prior substance abuse problems.

On campus Current students identified as chemically dependent may remain enrolled. Training program on identifying students with potential substance abuse problems for: resident advisers, hall directors. No written procedures for students and staff if substance abuse is suspected.

Support Services

On campus ACOA, referrals.

Employee assistance Program for chemically dependent employees available. Staff working with drug/alcohol-related issues: 3 part-time.

Disciplinary Actions

Alcohol Results of infractions of alcohol regulations (see Comparative Table of Alcohol Regulations) vary by situation. Comments: Incidents are handled on a case-by-case basis, possibly involving the judicial hearing board or the Dean's Office.

Drugs For first-time use: varies by situation—counseling. For subsequent use: counseling. For any possession: varies by situation. For first-time sale: varies by situation—warning. For subsequent sale: varies by situation. Comments: Grinnell College does not act as police but does try to make repeated offenders aware of state laws and penalties and of their responsibility to the campus community.

Additional Information from the College

Grinnell College imposes as few rules as possible upon its students, but expects them to act responsibly and comply with the law.

For More Information

Contact: Steven E. Jones, Associate Dean of Students, Grinnell College, P.O. Box 805, Grinnell, IA 50112. Telephone: 515-269-3700.

GROVE CITY COLLEGE

Grove City, Pennsylvania

General Information

Independent Presbyterian 4-year coed college. Founded 1876. Awards B. Primary accreditation: regional. Small-town setting; 150-acre campus. Total enrollment: 2,148. Faculty: 124 (103 full-time, 21 part-time). Social organizations: 10 local fraternities, 9 local sororities; 30% of eligible undergraduate men and 45% of eligible undergraduate women are members.

Drug and Alcohol Information

Education

On campus Drug and alcohol education/prevention programs offered for: freshmen. College holds an annual alcohol awareness week.

Identification of Problems

Admissions College application does not ask about prior substance abuse problems.

On campus Current students identified as chemically dependent may remain enrolled, but treatment is required. Training program on identifying students with potential substance abuse problems for: resident advisers. Written procedures for students and staff if substance abuse is suspected.

Support Services

On campus Private counseling.

Employee assistance Program for chemically dependent employees not available.

Disciplinary Actions

Alcohol Results of infractions of alcohol regulations (see Comparative Table of Alcohol Regulations) include suspension.

Drugs For first-time use, possession, or sale: suspension, expulsion. For subsequent use, possession, or sale: expulsion.

Additional Information from the College

Although related to the Presbyterian Church (U.S.A.), Grove City College does not forbid the use of alcohol and drugs on campus for religious reasons. The College believes that alcohol and drugs are not compatible with an academic environment.

For More Information

Contact: Dr. Ross A. Foster, Vice President, Student Affairs, Crawford Hall, Grove City College, Grove City, PA 16127. Telephone: 412-458-2169.

GUILFORD COLLEGE

Greensboro, North Carolina

General Information

Independent 4-year coed college, affiliated with Society of Friends. Founded 1837. Awards B. Primary accreditation: regional. City setting; 300-acre campus. Total enrollment: 1,250. Faculty: 114 (90 full-time, 24 part-time).

Drug and Alcohol Information

Education

On campus Drug and alcohol education/prevention programs offered for: all students, athletes/coaches, faculty, administration. College holds an annual alcohol awareness week and drug awareness week.

Identification of Problems

Admissions College application does not ask about prior substance abuse problems.

On campus Current students identified as chemically dependent may remain enrolled, but treatment is required. Training program on identifying students with potential substance abuse problems for: resident advisers, coaches, faculty, administration. Written procedures for students and staff if substance abuse is suspected.

Support Services

On campus AA, Al-Anon, ACOA, support groups, private counseling.

Employee assistance Program for chemically dependent employees not available. Staff working with drug/alcohol-related issues: 1 full-time and 2 part-time.

Disciplinary Actions

Alcohol Results of infractions of alcohol regulations (see Comparative Table of Alcohol Regulations) include chemical dependency assessment, counseling, probation, suspension, expulsion.

Drugs For first-time use: varies by situation. For subsequent use: chemical dependency assessment, counseling, suspension. For first-time possession: counseling, probation. For subsequent possession: chemical dependency assessment, counseling, expulsion. For any sale: expulsion.

For More Information

Contact: Ernest A. McCoy, Assistant Dean of Students, Guilford College, 5800 W. Friendly Ave., Greensboro, NC 27410. Telephone: 919-292-5511 Ext. 143.

HAMILTON COLLEGE

Clinton, New York

General Information

Independent 4-year coed college. Founded 1812. Awards B. Primary accreditation: regional. Rural setting; 1,200-acre campus. Total enrollment: 1,654. Faculty: 159 (139 full-time, 20 part-time). Social organizations: 8 national fraternities, 2 local sororities, 1 private society; 45% of eligible undergraduate men and 12% of eligible undergraduate women are members.

Drug and Alcohol Information

Education

On campus Drug and alcohol education/prevention programs offered for: freshmen, athletes/coaches, resident advisers. College holds an annual alcohol awareness week and drug awareness week.

Identification of Problems

Admissions College application does not ask about prior substance abuse problems.

On campus Current students identified as chemically dependent may remain enrolled. Training program on identifying students with potential substance abuse problems for: resident advisers. Written procedures for students and staff if substance abuse is suspected.

Support Services

On campus AA, ACOA, private counseling.

Employee assistance Program for chemically dependent employees not available. Staff working with drug/alcohol-related issues: 9 part-time.

Disciplinary Actions

Alcohol Results of infractions of alcohol regulations (see Comparative Table of Alcohol Regulations) vary by situation.

Drugs For any use, possession, or sale: varies by situation.

For More Information

Contact: Nancy Thompson, Dean of Student Life, Hamilton College, Clinton, NY 13323. Telephone: 315-859-4022.

HAMPDEN-SYDNEY COLLEGE

Hampden-Sydney, Virginia

General Information

Independent Presbyterian 4-year men's college. Founded 1776. Awards B. Primary accreditation: regional. Rural setting; 566-acre campus. Total enrollment: 937. Faculty: 88 (72 full-time, 16 part-time). Social organizations: 12 national fraternities; 57% of eligible undergraduates are members.

Drug and Alcohol Information

Education

On campus Drug and alcohol education/prevention programs offered for: all students, athletes/coaches, faculty, administration.

Identification of Problems

Admissions College application does not ask about prior substance abuse problems.

On campus Current students identified as chemically dependent may remain enrolled. Training program on identifying students with potential substance abuse problems for: resident advisers. No written procedures for students and staff if substance abuse is suspected.

Support Services

On campus Support groups, private counseling.

Employee assistance Program for chemically dependent employees not available.

Disciplinary Actions

Alcohol Results of infractions of alcohol regulations (see Comparative Table of Alcohol Regulations) include chemical dependency assessment, counseling, warning, probation, suspension, expulsion.

Drugs For first-time use or possession: probation. For subsequent use or possession: suspension. For any sale: expulsion. Comments: Penalties are subject to review by the Student Court.

Additional Information from the College

While there is not a specific student group that is concerned about responsible drinking, there is general concern about this issue, and broad efforts are being made.

For More Information

Contact: Linda Martin, Director, Health Services, Box 336, Hampden-Sydney College, Hampden-Sydney, VA 23943. Telephone: 804-223-4381 Ext. 167.

HANNIBAL-LAGRANGE COLLEGE

Hannibal, Missouri

General Information

Independent Southern Baptist 4-year coed college. Founded 1858. Awards A (college transfer and terminal), B. Primary accreditation: regional. Small-town setting; 110-acre campus. Total enrollment: 853. Faculty: 73 (35 full-time, 38 part-time).

Hannibal-LaGrange College (continued)

Drug and Alcohol Information

Education

On campus Drug and alcohol education/prevention programs offered for: all students. Authorized group concerned with responsible drinking.

Identification of Problems

Admissions College application does not ask about prior substance abuse problems.

On campus Current students identified as chemically dependent may not remain enrolled. Training program on identifying students with potential substance abuse problems for: resident advisers. No written procedures for students and staff if substance abuse is suspected.

Support Services

On campus No support services on campus.

Employee assistance Program for chemically dependent employees not available.

Disciplinary Actions

Alcohol Results of infractions of alcohol regulations (see Comparative Table of Alcohol Regulations) vary by situation but can include probation, suspension.

Drugs For first-time use or possession: suspension. For subsequent use or possession: expulsion. For any sale: expulsion.

For More Information

Contact: Tom Dugger, Dean of Student Affairs, Hannibal–LaGrange College, 2800 Palmyra Rd., Hannibal, MO 63401. Telephone: 314-221-3675.

HARDIN-SIMMONS UNIVERSITY

Abilene, Texas

General Information

Independent Baptist 5-year coed college. Founded 1891. Awards A (terminal), B, M. Primary accreditation: regional. City setting; 40-acre campus. Total enrollment: 1,747. Faculty: 138 (95 full-time, 43 part-time). Social organizations: 4 local fraternities, 4 local sororities; 13% of eligible undergraduate men and 13% of eligible undergraduate women are members.

Drug and Alcohol Information

Education

On campus Drug and alcohol education/prevention programs offered for: all students, athletes/coaches.

Identification of Problems

Admissions College application question about prior substance abuse problems is used for counseling and referral, if student is admitted.

On campus Current students identified as chemically dependent may remain enrolled, but treatment is required. Training program on identifying students with potential substance abuse problems for: resident advisers, coaches. No written procedures for students and staff if substance abuse is suspected.

Support Services

On campus Support groups, private counseling.

Employee assistance Program for chemically dependent employees not available. Staff working with drug/alcohol-related issues: 3 part-time.

Disciplinary Actions

Alcohol Results of infractions of alcohol regulations (see Comparative Table of Alcohol Regulations) vary by situation but can include chemical dependency assessment, counseling, warning.

Drugs For first-time use: varies by situation—chemical dependency assessment, counseling, warning. For first-time possession: varies by situation—chemical dependency assessment, probation. For subsequent use or possession: varies by situation. For first-time sale: varies by situation—chemical dependency assessment, suspension. For subsequent sale: suspension, expulsion.

Additional Information from the College

Hardin-Simmons University is a private, Baptist-affiliated institution with a philosophy of discipline that is redemptive in nature. The University attempts to bring students to the point of recognizing a problem, and then the University supports them as they seek help. Hardin-Simmons University is now engaged in updating its written policy and improving the way its contents are communicated to members of the campus community.

For More Information

Contact: Linda Carleton, Associate Dean of Students, Box 801, Hardin-Simmons University, 2200 Hickory St., Abilene, TX 79698. Telephone: 915-670-1250.

HARTWICK COLLEGE

Oneonta, New York

General Information

Independent 4-year coed college. Founded 1797. Awards B. Primary accreditation: regional. Small-town setting; 375-acre campus. Total enrollment: 1,515. Faculty: 145 (109 full-time, 36 part-time). Social organizations: 2 national fraternities, 1 national sorority, 1 local fraternity, 2 local sororities; 30% of eligible undergraduate men and 25% of eligible undergraduate women are members.

Drug and Alcohol Information

Education

On campus Drug and alcohol education/prevention programs offered for: all students, athletes/coaches. Authorized group concerned with responsible drinking. College holds an annual alcohol awareness week.

Identification of Problems

Admissions College application does not ask about prior substance abuse problems.

On campus Current students identified as chemically dependent may remain enrolled, but treatment is required. Training program on identifying students with potential substance abuse problems for: resident advisers, coaches, Greek officers, faculty, administration, roommates. Written procedures for students and staff if substance abuse is suspected.

Support Services

On campus ACOA, support groups, (Education and Abstinence Group), private counseling.

Employee assistance Program for chemically dependent employees not available.

Disciplinary Actions

Alcohol Results of infractions of alcohol regulations (see Comparative Table of Alcohol Regulations) vary by situation but can include chemical dependency assessment, counseling, probation. Comments: Based on the assessment, attendance at one of several support groups may be required.

Drugs For first-time use: varies by situation—chemical dependency assessment, probation. For first-time possession: chemical dependency assessment, probation. For subsequent use or possession: suspension. For any sale: suspension.

For More Information

Contact: Mark Britten, Director of Counseling, Hartwick College, Oneonta, NY 13820. Telephone: 607-432-4200.

HENDERSON STATE UNIVERSITY

Arkadelphia, Arkansas

General Information

State-supported 5-year coed college. Founded 1890. Awards A (terminal), B, M. Primary accreditation: regional. Small-town setting; 132-acre campus. Total enrollment: 3,209. Faculty: 163 (140 full-time, 23 part-time). Social organizations: 6 national fraternities, 6 national sororities.

Drug and Alcohol Information

Education

On campus Drug and alcohol education/prevention programs offered for: all students. College holds an annual alcohol awareness week and drug awareness week.

Identification of Problems

Admissions College application does not ask about prior substance abuse problems.

On campus Current students identified as chemically dependent may remain enrolled, but treatment is required. Training program on identifying students with potential substance abuse problems for: resident advisers. Written procedures for students and staff if substance abuse is suspected.

Support Services

On campus No support services on campus.

Employee assistance Program for chemically dependent employees not available.

Disciplinary Actions

Alcohol Results of infractions of alcohol regulations (see Comparative Table of Alcohol Regulations) include probation.

Drugs For first-time use or possession: counseling, probation. For subsequent use or possession: suspension. For first-time sale: suspension. For subsequent sale: expulsion.

For More Information

Contact: Dr. Gary D. Anderson, Vice President for Student Affairs, Box 7533, Henderson State University, Arkadelphia, AR 71923. Telephone: 501-246-5511 Ext. 3235.

HENDRIX COLLEGE

Conway, Arkansas

General Information

Independent United Methodist 4-year coed college. Founded 1876. Awards B. Primary accreditation: regional. Small-town setting; 160-acre campus. Total enrollment: 1,029. Faculty: 73 (62 full-time, 11 part-time).

Drug and Alcohol Information

Education

On campus Drug and alcohol education/prevention programs offered for: all students; required for: freshmen. Authorized group concerned with responsible drinking.

Identification of Problems

Admissions College application question about prior substance abuse problems is used for counseling and referral, if student is admitted; in the admissions decision.

On campus Current students identified as chemically dependent may remain enrolled, but treatment is required. Training program on identifying students with potential substance abuse problems for: resident advisers, administration. Written procedures for students and staff if substance abuse is suspected.

Support Services

On campus AA, private counseling.

Employee assistance Program for chemically dependent employees not available. Staff working with drug/alcohol-related issues: 4 part-time.

Disciplinary Actions

Alcohol Results of infractions of alcohol regulations (see Comparative Table of Alcohol Regulations) vary by situation but can include counseling, warning, probation, suspension.

Drugs For first-time use or possession: counseling, probation. For subsequent use or possession: suspension. For first-time sale: suspension. For subsequent sale: expulsion.

For More Information

Contact: Gary L. Valen, Dean of Students, Hendrix College, Conway, AR 72032. Telephone: 501-450-1372.

HERITAGE COLLEGE

Toppenish, Washington

General Information

Independent 5-year coed college. Founded 1907. Awards A (college transfer), B, M. Primary accreditation: regional. Rural setting; 10-acre campus. Total enrollment: 379. Faculty: 59 (16 full-time, 43 part-time).

Drug and Alcohol Information

Education

On campus Drug and alcohol education/prevention programs offered for: all students, faculty, administration. Authorized group concerned with responsible drinking. College holds an annual alcohol awareness week and drug awareness week.

Identification of Problems

Admissions College application does not ask about prior substance abuse problems.

Heritage College (continued)

On campus Current students identified as chemically dependent may remain enrolled. Training program on identifying students with potential substance abuse problems for: administration. Written procedures for students and staff if substance abuse is suspected.

Support Services

On campus Counseling.

Employee assistance Program for chemically dependent employees not available. Staff working with drug/alcohol-related issues: 1 part-time.

Disciplinary Actions

Alcohol Results of infractions of alcohol regulations (see Comparative Table of Alcohol Regulations) include counseling, probation, expulsion.

Drugs For first-time use: counseling, warning. For first-time possession: probation. For first-time sale: expulsion. For subsequent use, possession, or sale: counseling, expulsion.

For More Information

Contact: Barbara Wasserman, Counselor/Chaplain, Heritage College, Rte. 3, Box 3540, Toppenish, WA 98948. Telephone: 509-865-2244.

HILLSDALE FREE WILL BAPTIST COLLEGE

Moore, Oklahoma

General Information

Independent Free Will Baptist 4-year coed college. Founded 1959. Awards A (college transfer), B. Primary accreditation: U.S. Department of Education (3IC). Small-town setting; 40-acre campus. Total enrollment: 116. Faculty: 19 (7 full-time, 12 part-time). Social organizations: 3 local fraternities, 3 local sororities; 95% of eligible undergraduate men and 98% of eligible undergraduate women are members.

Drug and Alcohol Information

Education

On campus Drug and alcohol education/prevention programs offered for: all students.

Identification of Problems

Admissions College application does not ask about prior substance abuse problems.

On campus Current students identified as chemically dependent may not remain enrolled. No training program on identifying students with potential substance abuse problems. Written procedures for students and staff if substance abuse is suspected.

Support Services

On campus No support services on campus.

Employee assistance Program for chemically dependent employees not available.

Disciplinary Actions

Alcohol Results of infractions of alcohol regulations (see Comparative Table of Alcohol Regulations) include expulsion.

Drugs For any use, possession, or sale: expulsion.

For More Information

Contact: Dr. Thomas Marberry, Vice President, Academic Affairs, Hillsdale Free Will Baptist College, P.O. Box 7208, Moore, OK 73153. Telephone: 405-794-6661.

HOFSTRA UNIVERSITY

Hempstead, New York

General Information

Independent comprehensive coed institution. Founded 1935. Awards B, M, D. Primary accreditation: regional. City setting; 238-acre campus. Total enrollment: 12,210. Faculty: 822 (435 full-time, 387 part-time). Social organizations: 9 national fraternities, 5 national sororities, 5 local fraternities, 4 local sororities; 6% of eligible undergraduate men and 6% of eligible undergraduate women are members.

Drug and Alcohol Information

Education

On campus Drug and alcohol education/prevention programs offered for: all students, athletes/coaches, faculty, administration. Authorized group concerned with responsible drinking. College holds an annual alcohol awareness week.

Identification of Problems

Admissions College application does not ask about prior substance abuse problems.

On campus Current students identified as chemically dependent may remain enrolled, but treatment is required. Training program on identifying students with potential substance abuse problems for: resident advisers, coaches, administration, Infirmary and Counseling Center staff. Written procedures for students and staff if substance abuse is suspected.

Support Services

On campus Private counseling.

Employee assistance Program for chemically dependent employees available. Staff working with drug/alcohol-related issues: 5 part-time.

Disciplinary Actions

Alcohol Results of infractions of alcohol regulations (see Comparative Table of Alcohol Regulations) vary by situation but can include counseling, warning, probation, suspension, community service.

Drugs For first-time use or possession: varies by situation—counseling. For subsequent use or possession: suspension. For any sale: expulsion.

For More Information

Contact: Dr. Maureen Murphy, Dean of Students, 213 Student Center, Hofstra University, Hempstead, NY 11550. Telephone: 516-560-6913.

HOLY FAMILY COLLEGE

Philadelphia, Pennsylvania

General Information

Independent Roman Catholic 4-year coed college. Founded 1954. Awards B. Primary accreditation: regional. Metropolitan setting; 47-acre campus. Total enrollment: 1,685. Faculty: 162 (62 full-time, 100 part-time).

Drug and Alcohol Information

Education

On campus Drug and alcohol education/prevention programs offered for: all students, athletes/coaches. College holds an annual alcohol awareness week and drug awareness week.

Identification of Problems

Admissions College application does not ask about prior substance abuse problems.

On campus Current students identified as chemically dependent may remain enrolled, but treatment is required. Comments: The severity of the problem affects this decision. No training program on identifying students with potential substance abuse problems.

Support Services

On campus AA, Al-Anon, private counseling.

Employee assistance Program for chemically dependent employees not available. Staff working with drug/alcohol-related issues: 1 full-time and 2 part-time.

Disciplinary Actions

Alcohol Results of infractions of alcohol regulations (see Comparative Table of Alcohol Regulations) include counseling, suspension, expulsion.

Drugs For first-time use: varies by situation—counseling. For subsequent use: varies by situation. For any possession: expulsion. For any sale: expulsion.

Additional Information from the College

Holy Family College's students are all commuters, and most are employed, so the College does not have drug or alcohol problems on the scale that a residential college might. When problems do arise, they are handled individually.

For More Information

Contact: Sister Patrice Feher, Dean of Students, Holy Family College, Grant and Frankford Aves., Philadelphia, PA 19114. Telephone: 215-637-7700.

HOLY NAMES COLLEGE

Oakland, California

General Information

Independent Roman Catholic 5-year coed college. Founded 1868. Awards B, M. Primary accreditation: regional. City setting; 60-acre campus. Total enrollment: 720. Faculty: 79 (50 full-time, 29 part-time).

Drug and Alcohol Information

Education

On campus Drug and alcohol education/prevention programs offered for: all students. Authorized group concerned with responsible drinking. College holds an annual alcohol awareness week.

Identification of Problems

Admissions College application does not ask about prior substance abuse problems.

On campus Current students identified as chemically dependent may remain enrolled. Training program on identifying students with potential substance abuse problems for: resident advisers, administration. No written procedures for students and staff if substance abuse is suspected.

Support Services

On campus AA, ACOA.

Employee assistance Program for chemically dependent employees not available. Staff working with drug/alcohol-related issues: 4 part-time.

Disciplinary Actions

Alcohol Results of infractions of alcohol regulations (see Comparative Table of Alcohol Regulations) vary by situation but can include chemical dependency assessment, counseling, warning, probation, suspension, expulsion.

Drugs For first-time use or possession: varies by situation—counseling, warning. For subsequent use: varies by situation—warning, probation. For subsequent possession: warning, probation. For first-time sale: varies by situation—counseling, warning, expulsion. For subsequent sale: warning, probation, expulsion.

For More Information

Contact: Ron Rettig-Zucchi, Dean of Students, Holy Names College, 3500 Mountain Blvd., Oakland, CA 94619. Telephone: 415-436-1360.

HOOD COLLEGE

Frederick, Maryland

General Information

Independent 5-year primarily women's college, affiliated with United Church of Christ. Founded 1893. Awards B, M. Primary accreditation: regional. Small-town setting; 50-acre campus. Total enrollment: 1,874. Faculty: 115 (78 full-time, 37 part-time).

Drug and Alcohol Information

Education

On campus Drug and alcohol education/prevention programs offered for: all students, faculty; required for: student leaders. Authorized group concerned with responsible drinking. College holds an annual alcohol awareness week.

Identification of Problems

Admissions College application does not ask about prior substance abuse problems.

On campus Current students identified as chemically dependent may remain enrolled. Comments: Treatment may or may not be required. Training program on identifying students with potential substance abuse problems for: faculty, administration, student leaders, counselors. No written procedures for students and staff if substance abuse is suspected.

Support Services

On campus AA, NA, Al-Anon, ACOA, private counseling, referrals.

Employee assistance Program for chemically dependent employees not available. Staff working with drug/alcohol-related issues: 6 part-time.

Disciplinary Actions

Alcohol Results of infractions of alcohol regulations (see Comparative Table of Alcohol Regulations) vary by situation. Comments: Violation of state laws results in fines. Violation of College policy results in discipline imposed by administrator or student-run judicial board.

Drugs For first-time use, possesion, or sale: varies by situation. For subsequent use, possession, or sale: varies by situation—usually suspension or dismissal.

Hood College (continued)

Additional Information from the College

Many students and faculty and staff members have volunteered to work on ADAPT (Alcohol and Drug Abuse Prevention Team), a college committee that provides educational and prevention programs. A consortium of Maryland colleges is working with the Maryland State Police in a cooperative effort to provide drug and alcohol education programs to local communities. In 1988, Hood established the first SADD chapter in the state of Maryland.

For More Information

Contact: Angela L. Sievers, Director of Residence Life, Hood College, Rosemont Ave., Frederick, MD 21701. Telephone: 301-663-3131 Ext. 213.

HOUGHTON COLLEGE

Houghton, New York

General Information

Independent Wesleyan 4-year coed college. Founded 1883. Awards A (college transfer), B. Primary accreditation: regional. Rural setting; 1,200-acre campus. Total enrollment: 1,126. Faculty: 89 (74 full-time, 15 part-time).

Drug and Alcohol Information

Education

On campus Drug and alcohol education/prevention programs offered for: all students, faculty, administration.

Identification of Problems

Admissions College application question about prior substance abuse problems is used to explain past academic performance; for counseling and referral, if student is admitted; in the admissions decision.

On campus Current students identified as chemically dependent may remain enrolled, but treatment is required. No training program on identifying students with potential substance abuse problems. Written procedures for students and staff if substance abuse is suspected.

Support Services

On campus ACOA, support groups (Counseling Center), private counseling.

Employee assistance Program for chemically dependent employees not available.

Disciplinary Actions

Alcohol Results of infractions of alcohol regulations (see Comparative Table of Alcohol Regulations) vary by situation but can include chemical dependency assessment, counseling, warning, probation, suspension, expulsion.

Drugs For any use, possession, or sale: varies by situation.

Additional Information from the College

Houghton College is church-related and requires abstinence from use of alcohol and drugs from all members of the college community: administration, faculty, staff, and students.

For More Information

Contact: Robert F. Danner, Vice President for Student Development, Houghton College, Houghton, NY 14744. Telephone: 716-567-2211 Ext. 220.

HOWARD PAYNE UNIVERSITY

Brownwood, Texas

General Information

Independent Southern Baptist 4-year coed college. Founded 1889. Awards B. Primary accreditation: regional. Small-town setting; 30-acre campus. Total enrollment: 1,247. Faculty: 92 (68 full-time, 24 part-time).

Drug and Alcohol Information

Education

On campus Drug and alcohol education/prevention programs offered for: all students. Authorized group concerned with responsible drinking. College holds an annual alcohol awareness week and drug awareness week.

Identification of Problems

Admissions College application does not ask about prior substance abuse problems.

On campus Current students identified as chemically dependent may remain enrolled, but treatment is required. Training program on identifying students with potential substance abuse problems for: resident advisers, all residential staff. Written procedures for students and staff if substance abuse is suspected.

Support Services

On campus Private counseling, Student Ministries Program.

Employee assistance Program for chemically dependent employees not available. Staff working with drug/alcohol-related issues: 2 part-time.

Disciplinary Actions

Alcohol Results of infractions of alcohol regulations (see Comparative Table of Alcohol Regulations) include suspension.

Drugs For first-time use or possession: suspension. For subsequent use or possession: expulsion. For any sale: expulsion.

For More Information

Contact: Ann Harris, Director, Student Life, Howard Payne University, Brownwood, TX 76801. Telephone: 915-646-2502.

HOWARD UNIVERSITY

Washington, District of Columbia

General Information

Independent comprehensive coed institution. Founded 1867. Awards B, M, D. Primary accreditation: regional. Metropolitan setting; 242-acre campus. Total enrollment: 11,742. Faculty: 1,877 (1,539 full-time, 338 part-time). Social organizations: 4 national fraternities, 4 national sororities, 3 local fraternities; 1% of eligible undergraduate men and 1% of eligible undergraduate women are members.

Drug and Alcohol Information

Education

On campus Drug and alcohol education/prevention programs offered for: all students. College holds an annual alcohol awareness week and drug awareness week.

Identification of Problems

Admissions College application does not ask about prior substance abuse problems.

On campus Current students identified as chemically dependent may remain enrolled. Comments: Treatment may or may not be required, depending on circumstances. Training program on identifying students with potential substance abuse problems for: resident advisers, Student Affairs staff. Written procedures for students and staff if substance abuse is suspected.

Support Services

On campus AA, NA, Al-Anon, ACOA, support groups, private counseling.

Employee assistance Program for chemically dependent employees available. Staff working with drug/alcohol-related issues: 10–12 full-time and 5 part-time.

Disciplinary Actions

Alcohol Results of infractions of alcohol regulations (see Comparative Table of Alcohol Regulations) vary by situation.

Drugs For any use, possession, or sale: varies by situation.

For More Information

Contact: Dr. Russell Miller, Vice President for Health Affairs, Howard University, 2400 Sixth St., NW, Washington, DC 20059. Telephone: 202-636-7470.

HUMBOLDT STATE UNIVERSITY

Arcata, California

General Information

State-supported 5-year coed college. Part of California State University System. Founded 1913. Awards B, M. Primary accreditation: regional. Rural setting; 142-acre campus. Total enrollment: 6,245. Social organizations: 2 national fraternities, 1 local sorority; 1% of eligible undergraduate men and 1% of eligible undergraduate women are members.

Drug and Alcohol Information

Education

On campus Drug and alcohol education/prevention programs required for: resident advisers, residence hall residents, students whose behavior is cause for concern. College holds an annual alcohol awareness week and is planning a drug awareness week.

Identification of Problems

Admissions College application does not ask about prior substance abuse problems.

On campus Current students identified as chemically dependent may remain enrolled, but treatment is required for those who live in residence halls. Training program on identifying students with potential substance abuse problems for: resident advisers. Written procedures for students and staff if substance abuse is suspected.

Support Services

On campus AA, NA, Al-Anon, ACOA, support groups, private counseling, residence hall educational consultants.

Employee assistance Program for chemically dependent employees not available. Staff working with drug/alcohol-related issues: 1 part-time.

Disciplinary Actions

Alcohol Results of infractions of alcohol regulations (see Comparative Table of Alcohol Regulations) include chemical dependency assessment, counseling, warning, probation, suspension, expulsion.

Drugs For any use or possession: varies by situation. For any sale: varies by situation—suspension, expulsion.

Additional Information from the College

Humboldt State University has only recently begun to tackle the problems and issues of drug and alcohol abuse and to frame campuswide programs for faculty, staff, students, and spouses.

For More Information

Contact: John Capaccio, Assistant Director, Residence Life, Jolly Giant Commons, Humboldt State University, Arcata, CA 95521. Telephone: 707-826-3451.

HUNTINGDON COLLEGE

Montgomery, Alabama

General Information

Independent United Methodist 4-year coed college. Founded 1854. Awards A (terminal), B (terminal associate degree programs in evening only). Primary accreditation: regional. City setting; 58-acre campus. Total enrollment: 866. Faculty: 71 (46 full-time, 25 part-time). Social organizations: 2 national fraternities, 2 national sororities; 26% of eligible undergraduate men and 11% of eligible undergraduate women are members.

Drug and Alcohol Information

Education

On campus Drug and alcohol education/prevention programs offered for: all students. College holds an annual alcohol awareness week and drug awareness week.

Identification of Problems

Admissions College application does not ask about prior substance abuse problems.

On campus Current students identified as chemically dependent may remain enrolled, but treatment is required. No training program on identifying students with potential substance abuse problems. No written procedures for students and staff if substance abuse is suspected.

Support Services

On campus Private counseling.

Employee assistance Program for chemically dependent employees not available.

Disciplinary Actions

Alcohol Results of infractions of alcohol regulations (see Comparative Table of Alcohol Regulations) vary by situation.

Drugs For first-time use, possession, or sale: suspension. For subsequent use, possession, or sale: expulsion.

For More Information

Contact: Catherine Ingalls, Director of Human Resources Center, Huntingdon College, 1500 E. Fairview Ave., Montgomery, AL 36194-6201. Telephone: 205-265-0511.

HUNTINGTON COLLEGE

Huntington, Indiana

General Information

Independent 5-year coed college, affiliated with Church of the United Brethren in Christ. Founded 1897. Awards A (college transfer and terminal), B, M. Primary accreditation: regional. Small-town setting; 100-acre campus. Total enrollment: 587. Faculty: 42 (35 full-time, 7 part-time). Social organizations: 1 national fraternity, 1 national sorority; 7% of eligible undergraduate men and 10% of eligible undergraduate women are members.

Drug and Alcohol Information

Education

On campus Drug and alcohol education/prevention programs offered for: all students, athletes/coaches. Authorized group concerned with responsible drinking. College holds an annual alcohol awareness week and drug awareness week.

Identification of Problems

Admissions College application question about prior substance abuse problems is used in the admissions decision.

On campus Current students identified as chemically dependent may not remain enrolled. Training program on identifying students with potential substance abuse problems for: resident advisers, coaches. No written procedures for students and staff if substance abuse is suspected.

Support Services

On campus No support services on campus.

Employee assistance Program for chemically dependent employees not available.

Disciplinary Actions

Alcohol Results of infractions of alcohol regulations (see Comparative Table of Alcohol Regulations) include chemical dependency assessment, counseling, probation, suspension.

Drugs For any use, possession, or sale: varies by situation.

Additional Information from the College

Huntington College is a Christian college and, as such, expects behavior that is consistent with the beliefs of its supporting denomination. The College does not permit the use of alcohol and/or drugs while the student is enrolled or the employee employed.

For More Information

Contact: Jerry Davis, Associate Dean of Students, Huntington College, 2303 College Ave., Huntington, IN 46750. Telephone: 219-356-6000.

HUSSON COLLEGE

Bangor, Maine

General Information

Independent 5-year coed college. Founded 1898. Awards A (college transfer and terminal), B, M. Primary accreditation: regional. Small-town setting; 250-acre campus. Total enrollment: 1,792. Faculty: 49 (39 full-time, 10 part-time). Social organizations: 2 national fraternities, 3 national sororities; 17% of eligible undergraduate men and 16% of eligible undergraduate women are members.

Drug and Alcohol Information

Education

On campus Drug and alcohol education/prevention programs offered for: all students, athletes/coaches, faculty, administration. Authorized group concerned with responsible drinking. College holds an annual alcohol awareness week and drug awareness week.

Identification of Problems

Admissions College application does not ask about prior substance abuse problems.

On campus Current students identified as chemically dependent may remain enrolled. Training program on identifying students with potential substance abuse problems for: resident advisers. Written procedures for students and staff if substance abuse is suspected.

Support Services

On campus Al-Anon, support groups, private counseling.

Employee assistance Program for chemically dependent employees not available. Staff working with drug/alcohol-related issues: 7 part-time.

Disciplinary Actions

Alcohol Results of infractions of alcohol regulations (see Comparative Table of Alcohol Regulations) vary by situation but can include chemical dependency assessment, counseling, warning, probation, suspension, expulsion.

Drugs For any use: varies by situation. For first-time possession: varies by situation. For subsequent possession: suspension, expulsion. For any sale: suspension, expulsion.

For More Information

Contact: John Rubino, Dean for Student Affairs, Husson College, 1 College Circle, Bangor, ME 04401. Telephone: 207-947-1121.

IDAHO STATE UNIVERSITY

Pocatello, Idaho

General Information

State-supported comprehensive coed institution. Founded 1901. Awards A (college transfer and terminal), B, M, D. Primary accreditation: regional. Small-town setting; 274-acre campus. Total enrollment: 7,616. Faculty: 459 (374 full-time, 85 part-time). Social organizations: 2 national fraternities.

Drug and Alcohol Information

Education

On campus Drug and alcohol education/prevention programs offered for: all students, athletes/coaches, faculty, administration; required for: resident advisers. Authorized group concerned with responsible drinking. College holds an annual alcohol awareness week.

Identification of Problems

Admissions College application does not ask about prior substance abuse problems.

On campus Current students identified as chemically dependent may remain enrolled. No training program on identifying students with potential substance abuse problems. Written procedures for students and staff if substance abuse is suspected.

Support Services

On campus AA, NA, Al-Anon, ACOA, private counseling.

Employee assistance Program for chemically dependent employees not available.

Disciplinary Actions

Alcohol Results of infractions of alcohol regulations (see Comparative Table of Alcohol Regulations) vary by situation.

Drugs For any use, possession, or sale: varies by situation.

Additional Information from the College

A Substance Abuse Policy has been adopted, an Education Committee on substance abuse is being established, a budget has been committed, and a full-time specialist in substance abuse has been requested as a new member of the Counseling Center staff.

For More Information

Contact: Ernest C. Naftzger, Associate Dean of Students, P.O. Box 8123, Idaho State University, Pocatello, ID 83209. Telephone: 208-236-2794.

ILLINOIS BENEDICTINE COLLEGE

Lisle, Illinois

General Information

Independent Roman Catholic 5-year coed college. Founded 1887. Awards B, M. Primary accreditation: regional. Small-town setting; 108-acre campus. Total enrollment: 2,514. Faculty: 195 (88 full-time, 107 part-time).

Drug and Alcohol Information

Education

On campus Drug and alcohol education/prevention programs offered for: all students, faculty, administration. Authorized group concerned with responsible drinking. College holds an annual alcohol awareness week.

Identification of Problems

Admissions College application question about prior substance abuse problems is used for counseling and referral, if student is admitted.

On campus Current students identified as chemically dependent may remain enrolled, but treatment is required. Training program on identifying students with potential substance abuse problems for: administration.

Support Services

On campus AA, ACOA, private counseling.

Employee assistance Program for chemically dependent employees not available.

Disciplinary Actions

Alcohol Results of infractions of alcohol regulations (see Comparative Table of Alcohol Regulations) include counseling, warning, probation, suspension.

Drugs For first-time use: warning. For first-time possession: warning, probation. For subsequent use or possession: probation. For any sale: expulsion.

For More Information

Contact: James W. Bell, Dean of Students, Illinois Benedictine College, 5700 College Road, Lisle, IL 60532. Telephone: 312-960-1500 Ext. 4440.

ILLINOIS INSTITUTE OF TECHNOLOGY

Chicago, Illinois

General Information

Independent comprehensive coed institution. Founded 1892. Awards B, M, D. Primary accreditation: regional. Metropolitan setting; 120-acre campus. Total enrollment: 6,208. Faculty: 492 (288 full-time, 204 part-time). Social organizations: 9 national fraternities, 2 national sororities.

Drug and Alcohol Information

Education

On campus Drug and alcohol education/prevention programs offered for: all students, athletes/coaches. Authorized group concerned with responsible drinking. College holds an annual alcohol awareness week.

Identification of Problems

Admissions College application does not ask about prior substance abuse problems.

On campus Current students identified as chemically dependent may remain enrolled. Comments: Treatment may or may not be required, depending on the circumstances. Training program on identifying students with potential substance abuse problems for: resident advisers, Greek officers. Written procedures for students and staff if substance abuse is suspected.

Support Services

On campus Support groups, private counseling.

Employee assistance Program for chemically dependent employees not available. Staff working with drug/alcohol-related issues: 6 part-time.

Disciplinary Actions

Alcohol Results of infractions of alcohol regulations (see Comparative Table of Alcohol Regulations) include counseling, warning, probation.

Drugs For any use or possession: varies by situation. For first-time sale: suspension. For subsequent sale: expulsion.

For More Information

Contact: William D. Schafer, Dean of Student Life, Illinois Institute of Technology, 40 W. 33rd St., Chicago, IL 60616. Telephone: 312-567-3080.

ILLINOIS STATE UNIVERSITY

Normal, Illinois

General Information

State-supported comprehensive coed institution. Founded 1857. Awards B, M, D. Primary accreditation: regional. City setting; 850-acre campus. Total enrollment: 21,394. Faculty: 1,048 (826 full-time, 222 part-time). Social organizations: 18 national fraternities, 14 national sororities; 20% of eligible undergraduate men and 20% of eligible undergraduate women are members.

Drug and Alcohol Information

Education

On campus Drug and alcohol education/prevention programs offered for: social organization members, judicial

Illinois State University (continued)

offenders; required for: freshmen, athletes/coaches, resident advisers. Authorized group concerned with responsible drinking. College holds an annual alcohol awareness week and drug awareness week.

Identification of Problems

Admissions College application does not ask about prior substance abuse problems.

On campus Current students identified as chemically dependent may remain enrolled. Training program on identifying students with potential substance abuse problems for: resident advisers. No written procedures for students and staff if substance abuse is suspected.

Support Services

On campus AA, NA, ACOA.

Employee assistance Program for chemically dependent employees available. Staff working with drug/alcohol-related issues: 2 full-time and 3 part-time.

Disciplinary Actions

Alcohol Results of infractions of alcohol regulations (see Comparative Table of Alcohol Regulations) vary by situation but can include chemical dependency assessment, counseling, warning, probation, suspension, expulsion.

Drugs For first-time use or possession: varies by situation. For subsequent use or possession: varies by situation—probation, suspension, expulsion. For first-time sale: suspension. For subsequent sale: expulsion.

For More Information

Contact: Dana Farley, Health Educator, Illinois State University, Normal, IL 61761-6901. Telephone: 309-438-5948.

IMMACULATA COLLEGE

Immaculata, Pennsylvania

General Information

Independent Roman Catholic 5-year primarily women's college. Founded 1920. Awards A (college transfer and terminal), B, M. Primary accreditation: regional. Small-town setting; 390-acre campus. Total enrollment: 2,100. Faculty: 152 (70 full-time, 82 part-time).

Drug and Alcohol Information

Education

On campus Drug and alcohol education/prevention programs offered for: freshmen, resident advisers, student leaders. College holds an annual alcohol awareness week and drug awareness week.

Identification of Problems

Admissions College application does not ask about prior substance abuse problems.

On campus Current students identified as chemically dependent may remain enrolled, but treatment is required. Training program on identifying students with potential substance abuse problems for: resident advisers. Written procedures for students and staff if substance abuse is suspected.

Support Services

On campus Private counseling. Staff working with drug/alcohol-related issues: 9 part-time.

Disciplinary Actions

Alcohol Results of infractions of alcohol regulations (see Comparative Table of Alcohol Regulations) include counseling, fines (beginning at $50), and expulsion from college housing.

Drugs For first-time use: counseling, probation. For first-time possession: probation. For first-time sale: expulsion. For subsequent use, possession, or sale: varies by situation—counseling, probation, expulsion.

For More Information

Contact: Denise Travis, Coordinator, Student Life Programs, Immaculata College, Immaculata, PA 19345. Telephone: 215-647-4400 Ext. 394.

INCARNATE WORD COLLEGE

San Antonio, Texas

General Information

Independent Roman Catholic 5-year coed college. Founded 1881. Awards B, M. Primary accreditation: regional. Metropolitan setting; 52-acre campus. Total enrollment: 2,240. Faculty: 142 (85 full-time, 57 part-time). Social organization: 1 local sorority; 4% of eligible undergraduate women are members.

Drug and Alcohol Information

Education

On campus Drug and alcohol education/prevention programs offered for: all students. College holds an annual alcohol awareness week and drug awareness week.

Identification of Problems

Admissions College application does not ask about prior substance abuse problems.

On campus Current students identified as chemically dependent may remain enrolled, but treatment is required. Training program on identifying students with potential substance abuse problems for: resident advisers, administration. Written procedures for students and staff if substance abuse is suspected.

Support Services

On campus Private counseling.

Employee assistance Program for chemically dependent employees not available. Staff working with drug/alcohol-related issues: 1 full-time and 2 part-time.

Disciplinary Actions

Alcohol Results of infractions of alcohol regulations (see Comparative Table of Alcohol Regulations) include probation, suspension, expulsion.

Drugs For first-time use, possession, or sale: warning. For subsequent use, possession, or sale: probation, suspension, expulsion.

For More Information

Contact: Marlon Anderson, Coordinator of Residential Life, Incarnate Word College, 4301 Broadway, San Antonio, TX 78209. Telephone: 512-828-1261.

INDIANA INSTITUTE OF TECHNOLOGY

Fort Wayne, Indiana

General Information

Independent 4-year coed college. Founded 1930. Awards A (college transfer), B. Primary accreditation: regional. City setting; 25-acre campus. Total enrollment: 623. Faculty: 42 (20 full-time, 22 part-time). Social organizations: 3 national fraternities; 25% of eligible undergraduate men are members.

Drug and Alcohol Information

Education

On campus Drug and alcohol education/prevention programs offered for: all students, faculty; required for: freshmen, athletes/coaches. Authorized group concerned with responsible drinking.

Identification of Problems

Admissions College application does not ask about prior substance abuse problems.

On campus Current students identified as chemically dependent may remain enrolled, but treatment is required. Training program on identifying students with potential substance abuse problems for: resident advisers, coaches. No written procedures for students and staff if substance abuse is suspected.

Support Services

On campus Private counseling.

Employee assistance Program for chemically dependent employees not available.

Disciplinary Actions

Alcohol Results of infractions of alcohol regulations (see Comparative Table of Alcohol Regulations) include counseling, warning, probation, suspension, expulsion.

Drugs For first-time use, possession, or sale: varies by situation. For subsequent use or possession: suspension. For subsequent sale: expulsion.

For More Information

Contact: Dan J. Kline, Director of Student Life, Indiana Institute of Technology, 1600 E. Washington Blvd., Fort Wayne, IN 46803. Telephone: 219-422-5561.

INDIANA STATE UNIVERSITY

Terre Haute, Indiana

General Information

State-supported comprehensive coed institution. Founded 1865. Awards A (college transfer and terminal), B, M, D. Primary accreditation: regional. City setting; 91-acre campus. Total enrollment: 11,677. Social organizations: 18 national fraternities, 13 national sororities; 11% of eligible undergraduate men and 11% of eligible undergraduate women are members.

Drug and Alcohol Information

Education

On campus Drug and alcohol education/prevention programs offered for: all students, athletes/coaches, faculty, administration; required for: resident advisers. Bacchus chapter: 15 members. College holds an annual alcohol awareness week and drug awareness week.

Identification of Problems

Admissions College application does not ask about prior substance abuse problems.

On campus Current students identified as chemically dependent may remain enrolled. Training program on identifying students with potential substance abuse problems for: resident advisers. Written procedures for students and staff if substance abuse is suspected.

Support Services

On campus ACOA, support groups (Bacchus), private counseling.

Employee assistance Program for chemically dependent employees available. Staff working with drug/alcohol-related issues: 2 full-time and 10 part-time.

Disciplinary Actions

Alcohol Results of infractions of alcohol regulations (see Comparative Table of Alcohol Regulations) vary by situation but can include warning, probation, suspension, expulsion.

Drugs For first-time use or possession: probation. For subsequent use or possession: varies by situation. For any sale: suspension.

For More Information

Contact: Jan Miltenberger, Associate Director, Health Promotion, Student Health Center, Indiana State University, Terre Haute, IN 47809. Telephone: 812-237-3883.

INDIANA UNIVERSITY BLOOMINGTON

Bloomington, Indiana

General Information

State-supported comprehensive coed institution. Part of Indiana University System. Founded 1820. Awards A (college transfer and terminal), B, M, D. Primary accreditation: regional. City setting; 1,800-acre campus. Total enrollment: 33,776. Faculty: 1,595 (1,375 full-time, 220 part-time). Social organizations: 32 national fraternities, 24 national sororities; 20% of eligible undergraduate men and 15% of eligible undergraduate women are members.

Drug and Alcohol Information

Education

On campus Drug and alcohol education/prevention programs offered for: all students, athletes/coaches, faculty, administration. Bacchus chapter: 45 members. College holds an annual alcohol awareness week and drug awareness week.

Identification of Problems

Admissions College application does not ask about prior substance abuse problems.

On campus Current students identified as chemically dependent may remain enrolled. Comments: Treatment is not required unless disciplinary problems ensue. Training program on identifying students with potential substance abuse problems for: resident advisers, coaches, Greek officers, faculty, administration, anyone who is interested. Written procedures for students and staff if substance abuse is suspected.

Indiana University Bloomington (continued)

Support Services

On campus AA, NA, Al-Anon, ACOA, support groups (Women For Sobriety), private counseling.

Employee assistance Program for chemically dependent employees available. Staff working with drug/alcohol-related issues: 1 full-time and 4 part-time.

Disciplinary Actions

Alcohol Results of infractions of alcohol regulations (see Comparative Table of Alcohol Regulations) vary by situation but can include chemical dependency assessment, counseling, warning, probation, suspension, expulsion, required education program. Comments: Suspension and expulsion are rare.

Drugs For any use or possession: varies by situation. For any sale: suspension, expulsion.

For More Information

Contact: William J. Bailey, Director, Alcohol-Drug Information Center, Student Bldg. 011, Indiana University Bloomington, Bloomington, IN 47405. Telephone: 812-855-5414.

INDIANA UNIVERSITY EAST

Richmond, Indiana

General Information

State-supported 4-year coed college. Part of Indiana University System. Founded 1971. Awards A (college transfer and terminal), B (also offers some graduate courses). Primary accreditation: regional. Small-town setting; 194-acre campus. Total enrollment: 1,570.

Drug and Alcohol Information

Education

On campus Drug and alcohol education/prevention programs offered for: all students, faculty, administration. Authorized group concerned with responsible drinking. College holds an annual alcohol awareness week and drug awareness week.

Identification of Problems

Admissions College application does not ask about prior substance abuse problems.

On campus Current students identified as chemically dependent may remain enrolled. Training program on identifying students with potential substance abuse problems for: faculty, administration, peer advisers. No written procedures for students and staff if substance abuse is suspected.

Support Services

On campus Student Assistance and EA programs.

Employee assistance Program for chemically dependent employees available. Staff working with drug/alcohol-related issues: 1 full-time and 3 part-time.

Disciplinary Actions

Alcohol Results of infractions of alcohol regulations (see Comparative Table of Alcohol Regulations) include chemical dependency assessment, counseling, warning, probation, suspension, expulsion.

Drugs For any use or possession: varies by situation. For first-time sale: suspension, expulsion. For subsequent sale: expulsion.

For More Information

Contact: Cory Rosenkranz, Director, Prevention Education Resource Center, Indiana University East, 2230 Chester Blvd., Richmond, IN 47374. Telephone: 317-973-8200.

INDIANA UNIVERSITY OF PENNSYLVANIA

Indiana, Pennsylvania

General Information

State-supported comprehensive coed institution. Part of State System of Higher Education. Founded 1875. Awards A (college transfer and terminal), B, M, D. Primary accreditation: regional. Small-town setting; 162-acre campus. Total enrollment: 13,650. Faculty: 818 (729 full-time, 89 part-time). Social organizations: 18 national fraternities, 17 national sororities, 1 local fraternity; 15% of eligible undergraduate men and 10% of eligible undergraduate women are members.

Drug and Alcohol Information

Education

On campus Drug and alcohol education/prevention programs offered for: all students, athletes/coaches, faculty, administration. Bacchus chapter: 20 members. College holds an annual alcohol awareness week and drug awareness week.

Identification of Problems

Admissions College application does not ask about prior substance abuse problems.

On campus Current students identified as chemically dependent may remain enrolled. Training program on identifying students with potential substance abuse problems for: resident advisers, coaches, Greek officers, administration.

Support Services

On campus AA, NA, Al-Anon, ACOA, private counseling.

Employee assistance Program for chemically dependent employees not available. Staff working with drug/alcohol-related issues: 1 full-time.

Disciplinary Actions

Alcohol Results of infractions of alcohol regulations (see Comparative Table of Alcohol Regulations) include chemical dependency assessment, counseling, warning, probation, suspension, expulsion.

Drugs For any use, possession, or sale: varies by situation.

For More Information

Contact: Kelly Heryla, Chemical Health Coordinator, Pechan Health Center, Indiana University of Pennsylvania, Indiana, PA 15705. Telephone: 412-357-2550.

INDIANA UNIVERSITY SOUTHEAST

New Albany, Indiana

General Information

State-supported 5-year coed college. Part of Indiana University System. Founded 1941. Awards A (college transfer), B, M. Primary accreditation: regional. Small-town setting; 180-acre campus. Total enrollment: 5,267. Faculty: 289 (123 full-time, 166 part-time). Social organizations: 2 national fraternities, 3 national sororities, 1 local fraternity, 1 local sorority; 12% of eligible undergraduate men and 12% of eligible undergraduate women are members.

Drug and Alcohol Information

Education

On campus Drug and alcohol education/prevention programs offered for: all students, faculty, administration. Authorized group concerned with responsible drinking. College holds an annual alcohol awareness week.

Identification of Problems

Admissions College application does not ask about prior substance abuse problems.

On campus Current students identified as chemically dependent may remain enrolled. Training program on identifying students with potential substance abuse problems for: faculty, administration. No written procedures for students and staff if substance abuse is suspected.

Support Services

On campus Private counseling.

Employee assistance Program for chemically dependent employees not available. Staff working with drug/alcohol-related issues: 2 part-time.

Disciplinary Actions

Alcohol Results of infractions of alcohol regulations (see Comparative Table of Alcohol Regulations) vary by situation but can include warning.

Drugs For any use: varies by situation—counseling, suspension. For first-time possession: varies by situation—counseling, probation. For subsequent possession: varies by situation—counseling, probation, suspension. For first-time sale: varies by situation—counseling, expulsion. For subsequent sale: expulsion.

For More Information

Contact: Herbert (Butch) Griffin, Coordinator, Student Activities, Indiana University Southeast, 4201 Grant Line Rd., New Albany, IN 47150. Telephone: 812-945-2731 Ext. 316.

INDIANA WESLEYAN UNIVERSITY

Marion, Indiana

General Information

Independent Wesleyan 5-year coed college. Founded 1920. Awards A (college transfer and terminal), B, M. Primary accreditation: regional. Small-town setting; 75-acre campus. Total enrollment: 1,002. Faculty: 100 (65 full-time, 35 part-time).

Drug and Alcohol Information

Education

On campus Drug and alcohol education/prevention programs offered for: freshmen, athletes/coaches, resident advisers, student leaders.

Identification of Problems

Admissions College application question about prior substance abuse problems is used for counseling and referral, if student is admitted; in the admissions decision.

On campus Current students identified as chemically dependent may remain enrolled depending on the situation. Training program on identifying students with potential substance abuse problems for: resident advisers. No written procedures for students and staff if substance abuse is suspected.

Support Services

On campus Support groups, private counseling.

Employee assistance Program for chemically dependent employees not available. Staff working with drug/alcohol-related issues: 6 part-time.

Disciplinary Actions

Alcohol Results of infractions of alcohol regulations (see Comparative Table of Alcohol Regulations) include chemical dependency assessment, counseling, probation, suspension.

Drugs For first-time use: varies by situation. For first-time possession or sale: varies by situation—counseling, probation, suspension. For subsequent use, possession, or sale: varies by situation.

For More Information

Contact: Dr. Barry R. May, Dean of Student Development, Indiana Wesleyan University, 4201 S. Washington St., Marion, IN 46953. Telephone: 317-674-6901.

INTER AMERICAN UNIVERSITY OF PUERTO RICO, ARECIBO REGIONAL COLLEGE

Arecibo, Puerto Rico

General Information

Independent 4-year coed college. Part of Inter American University of Puerto Rico. Founded 1957. Awards A (terminal), B. Primary accreditation: regional. City setting. Total enrollment: 3,389.

Drug and Alcohol Information

Education

On campus Drug and alcohol education/prevention programs offered for: freshmen, social organization members, faculty, administration. Authorized group concerned with responsible drinking. College holds an annual alcohol awareness week and drug awareness week.

Identification of Problems

Admissions College application does not ask about prior substance abuse problems.

On campus Current students identified as chemically dependent may remain enrolled. Training program on identifying students with potential substance abuse problems for: faculty, administration. No written procedures for students and staff if substance abuse is suspected.

Support Services

On campus Drug prevention committee.

Employee assistance Program for chemically dependent employees available. Staff working with drug/alcohol-related issues: 1 part-time.

Inter American University of Puerto Rico, Arecibo Regional College (continued)

Disciplinary Actions

Alcohol Results of infractions of alcohol regulations (see Comparative Table of Alcohol Regulations) include counseling, warning, probation, suspension.

Drugs For first-time use: counseling, warning. For subsequent use, possession, or sale: suspension. For first-time possession: varies by situation—warning. For first-time sale: varies by situation—probation.

For More Information

Contact: Leticia Garcia, Counselor, Inter American University of Puerto Rico, Arecibo Regional College, Call Box UI, Arecibo, PR 00613. Telephone: 809-878-5475.

INTER AMERICAN UNIVERSITY OF PUERTO RICO, METROPOLITAN CAMPUS

Hato Rey, Puerto Rico

General Information

Independent 5-year coed college. Part of Inter American University of Puerto Rico. Founded 1960. Awards A (college transfer and terminal), B, M, D. Primary accreditation: regional. Metropolitan setting. Total enrollment: 13,910.

Drug and Alcohol Information

Education

On campus Drug and alcohol education/prevention programs offered for: all students. College holds an annual alcohol awareness week and drug awareness week.

Identification of Problems

Admissions College application does not ask about prior substance abuse problems.

On campus Current students identified as chemically dependent may not remain enrolled. No training program on identifying students with potential substance abuse problems. No written procedures for students and staff if substance abuse is suspected.

Support Services

On campus Counseling program.

Employee assistance Program for chemically dependent employees not available.

Disciplinary Actions

Alcohol Results of infractions of alcohol regulations (see Comparative Table of Alcohol Regulations) include counseling, warning, probation.

Drugs For first-time use or possession: varies by situation. For subsequent use or possession: expulsion. For any sale: expulsion.

For More Information

Contact: Helen Sosa, Dean of Student Affairs, Inter American University of Puerto Rico, Metropolitan Campus, P.O. Box 1293, Hato Ray, PR 00919. Telephone: 809-764-0887.

INTERNATIONAL ACADEMY OF MERCHANDISING & DESIGN, LTD.

Chicago, Illinois

General Information

Proprietary 4-year coed college. Founded 1977. Awards A (terminal), B. Primary accreditation: AICS. Metropolitan setting. Total enrollment: 753. Faculty: 75 (all part-time).

Drug and Alcohol Information

Education

On campus Drug and alcohol education/prevention programs offered for: all students.

Identification of Problems

Admissions College application does not ask about prior substance abuse problems.

On campus Current students identified as chemically dependent may remain enrolled, but treatment is required. No training program on identifying students with potential substance abuse problems. No written procedures for students and staff if substance abuse is suspected.

Support Services

Employee assistance Program for chemically dependent employees not available.

Disciplinary Actions

Alcohol Results of infractions of alcohol regulations (see Comparative Table of Alcohol Regulations) include expulsion.

Drugs For any use, possession, or sale: expulsion.

For More Information

Contact: Pat Giovacchini, Executive Director, International Academy of Merchandising & Design, Ltd., 350 N. Orleans #134, Chicago, IL 60654. Telephone: 312-828-0202.

INTERNATIONAL BIBLE COLLEGE

Florence, Alabama

General Information

Independent 4-year specialized coed college, affiliated with Church of Christ. Founded 1971. Awards A (college transfer), B. Primary accreditation: AABC. Small-town setting; 46-acre campus. Total enrollment: 131. Faculty: 18 (9 full-time, 9 part-time).

Drug and Alcohol Information

Education

On campus Drug and alcohol education/prevention programs not offered.

Identification of Problems

Admissions College application question about prior substance abuse problems is used in the admissions decision.

On campus Current students identified as chemically dependent may not remain enrolled. No training program on identifying students with potential substance abuse problems. Written procedures for students and staff if substance abuse is suspected.

Support Services

On campus Private counseling.

Employee assistance Program for chemically dependent employees not available. Staff working with drug/alcohol-related issues: 2 part-time.

Disciplinary Actions

Alcohol Results of infractions of alcohol regulations (see Comparative Table of Alcohol Regulations) include expulsion.

Drugs For any use, possession, or sale: expulsion.

For More Information

Contact: George E. Goldman, Dean of Students, International Bible College, P.O. Box IBC, Florence, AL 35630. Telephone: 800-982-4807.

IOWA STATE UNIVERSITY OF SCIENCE AND TECHNOLOGY

Ames, Iowa

General Information

State-supported comprehensive coed institution. Founded 1858. Awards B, M, D. Primary accreditation: regional. City setting; 1,000-acre campus. Total enrollment: 25,448. Faculty: 2,076 (1,890 full-time, 186 part-time). Social organizations: 32 national fraternities, 16 national sororities, 1 local fraternity; 9% of eligible undergraduate men and 7% of eligible undergraduate women are members.

Drug and Alcohol Information

Education

On campus Drug and alcohol education/prevention programs offered for: all students. Authorized group concerned with responsible drinking. College holds an annual alcohol awareness week.

Identification of Problems

Admissions College application does not ask about prior substance abuse problems.

On campus Current students identified as chemically dependent may remain enrolled. Training program on identifying students with potential substance abuse problems for: resident advisers, Greek officers, faculty. Written procedures for students and staff if substance abuse is suspected.

Support Services

On campus Support groups, private counseling.

Off campus AA, NA, Al-Anon, ACOA, support groups.

Employee assistance Program for chemically dependent employees available. Staff working with drug/alcohol-related issues: 3 part-time.

Disciplinary Actions

Alcohol Results of infractions of alcohol regulations (see Comparative Table of Alcohol Regulations) vary by situation but can include chemical dependency assessment, counseling, warning, probation, suspension, expulsion.

Drugs For any use, possession, or sale: varies by situation.

For More Information

Contact: Dr. Augustine W. Pounds, Dean of Students, 2nd Floor, Student Services Bldg., Iowa State University of Science and Technology, Ames, IA 50011. Telephone: 515-294-1020.

IOWA WESLEYAN COLLEGE

Mount Pleasant, Iowa

General Information

Independent United Methodist 4-year coed college. Founded 1842. Awards B. Primary accreditation: regional. Small-town setting; 60-acre campus. Total enrollment: 679. Faculty: 52 (39 full-time, 13 part-time). Social organizations: 2 national fraternities, 3 national sororities; 12% of eligible undergraduate men and 38% of eligible undergraduate women are members.

Drug and Alcohol Information

Education

On campus Drug and alcohol education/prevention programs offered for: all students, faculty; required for: athletes/coaches. College holds an annual alcohol awareness week.

Identification of Problems

Admissions College application does not ask about prior substance abuse problems.

On campus Current students identified as chemically dependent may sometimes remain enrolled. Training program on identifying students with potential substance abuse problems for: resident advisers, coaches. No written procedures for students and staff if substance abuse is suspected.

Support Services

On campus Private counseling.

Employee assistance Program for chemically dependent employees not available.

Disciplinary Actions

Alcohol Results of infractions of alcohol regulations (see Comparative Table of Alcohol Regulations) include chemical dependency assessment, counseling, warning, probation, suspension, expulsion.

Drugs For any use: varies by situation. For any possession or sale: expulsion.

For More Information

Contact: Tom L. Dean, Associate Dean of Students, Iowa Wesleyan College, North Main, Mount Pleasant, IA 52641. Telephone: 319-385-6258.

JACKSONVILLE STATE UNIVERSITY

Jacksonville, Alabama

General Information

State-supported 5-year coed college. Founded 1883. Awards B, M. Primary accreditation: regional. Small-town setting; 345-acre campus. Total enrollment: 7,511. Faculty: 367 (267 full-time, 100 part-time). Social organizations: 10 national fraternities, 6 national sororities; 10% of eligible undergraduate men and 5% of eligible undergraduate women are members.

Jacksonville State University (continued)

Drug and Alcohol Information

Education

On campus Drug and alcohol education/prevention programs not offered. College holds an annual alcohol awareness week.

Identification of Problems

Admissions College application does not ask about prior substance abuse problems.

On campus Current students identified as chemically dependent may remain enrolled. No training program on identifying students with potential substance abuse problems. No written procedures for students and staff if substance abuse is suspected.

Support Services

On campus Private counseling.

Employee assistance Program for chemically dependent employees not available.

Disciplinary Actions

Alcohol Results of infractions of alcohol regulations (see Comparative Table of Alcohol Regulations) vary by situation.

Drugs For any use, possession, or sale: varies by situation.

Additional Information from the College

The Career Development and Counseling Services office is interested in developing services directed toward drug abuse.

For More Information

Contact: Dr. Don Schmitz, Dean of Student Affairs, Jacksonville State University, North Pelham Rd., Jacksonville, AL 36265. Telephone: 205-231-5472.

JACKSONVILLE UNIVERSITY

Jacksonville, Florida

General Information

Independent 5-year coed college. Founded 1934. Awards B, M. Primary accreditation: regional. Metropolitan setting; 214-acre campus. Total enrollment: 2,257. Social organizations: 6 national fraternities, 5 national sororities; 25% of eligible undergraduate men and 22% of eligible undergraduate women are members.

Drug and Alcohol Information

Education

On campus Drug and alcohol education/prevention programs offered for: all students. Authorized group concerned with responsible drinking. College holds an annual alcohol awareness week and drug awareness week.

Identification of Problems

Admissions College application does not ask about prior substance abuse problems.

On campus Current students identified as chemically dependent may or may not remain enrolled. Comments: Decisions are made on a case-by-case basis. Training program on identifying students with potential substance abuse problems for: resident advisers. No written procedures for students and staff if substance abuse is suspected.

Support Services

On campus AA, ACOA, private counseling.

Employee assistance Program for chemically dependent employees not available. Staff working with drug/alcohol-related issues: 1 part-time.

Disciplinary Actions

Alcohol Results of infractions of alcohol regulations (see Comparative Table of Alcohol Regulations) vary by situation.

Drugs For any use, possession, or sale: varies by situation.

For More Information

Contact: Sara J. Myers, Assistant Dean of Students, Jacksonville University, 2800 University Blvd. N., Jacksonville, FL 32211. Telephone: 904-744-3950.

JAMESTOWN COLLEGE

Jamestown, North Dakota

General Information

Independent Presbyterian 4-year coed college. Founded 1883. Awards B. Primary accreditation: regional. Small-town setting; 107-acre campus. Total enrollment: 796. Faculty: 58 (43 full-time, 15 part-time). Social organization: 1 local sorority; 5% of eligible undergraduate women are members.

Drug and Alcohol Information

Education

On campus Drug and alcohol education/prevention programs offered for: all students, athletes/coaches.

Identification of Problems

Admissions College application does not ask about prior substance abuse problems.

On campus Current students identified as chemically dependent may remain enrolled, but treatment is required. Training program on identifying students with potential substance abuse problems for: resident advisers.

Support Services

On campus Private Counseling.

Employee assistance Program for chemically dependent employees not available.

Disciplinary Actions

Alcohol Results of infractions of alcohol regulations (see Comparative Table of Alcohol Regulations) include chemical dependency assessment, counseling, probation, $50 fine.

Drugs For any use or possession: varies by situation. For first-time sale: expulsion.

For More Information

Contact: Carol Schmeichel, Dean of Students, Box 6081, Jamestown College, Jamestown, ND 58401. Telephone: 701-252-3467.

JERSEY CITY STATE COLLEGE

Jersey City, New Jersey

General Information

State-supported 5-year coed college. Founded 1927. Awards

B, M. Primary accreditation: regional. City setting; 17-acre campus. Total enrollment: 6,717. Faculty: 420 (267 full-time, 153 part-time). Social organizations: 3 national fraternities, local fraternities, local sororities; 1% of eligible undergraduate men and 1% of eligible undergraduate women are members.

Drug and Alcohol Information

Education

On campus Drug and alcohol education/prevention programs offered for: all students. Authorized group concerned with responsible drinking. College holds an annual alcohol awareness week and drug awareness week.

Identification of Problems

Admissions College application does not ask about prior substance abuse problems.

On campus Current students identified as chemically dependent may remain enrolled, but treatment is required. Training program on identifying students with potential substance abuse problems for: resident advisers, Greek officers, administration. Written procedures for students and staff if substance abuse is suspected.

Support Services

On campus Support groups, private counseling.

Employee assistance Program for chemically dependent employees available. Staff working with drug/alcohol-related issues: 3 part-time.

Disciplinary Actions

Alcohol Results of infractions of alcohol regulations (see Comparative Table of Alcohol Regulations) vary by situation.

Drugs For any use, possession, or sale: varies by situation.

For More Information

Contact: Dr. Marco Cirincion, Dean of Students, Jersey City State College, 2039 Kennedy Blvd., Jersey City, NJ 07305. Telephhone: 201-547-3526.

JEWISH THEOLOGICAL SEMINARY OF AMERICA

New York, New York

General Information

Independent Jewish comprehensive specialized coed institution. Founded 1886. Awards B, M, D (double B with Barnard College or Columbia College). Primary accreditation: regional. Metropolitan setting; 1-acre campus. Total enrollment: 512. Faculty: 105 (55 full-time, 50 part-time).

Drug and Alcohol Information

Education

On campus Drug and alcohol education/prevention programs offered for: freshmen, resident advisers. Student government concerned with responsible drinking.

Identification of Problems

Admissions College application does not ask about prior substance abuse problems.

On campus Current students identified as chemically dependent may remain enrolled, but treatment is required. Training program on identifying students with potential substance abuse problems for: resident advisers. Written procedures for students and staff if substance abuse is suspected.

Support Services

Off campus AA, Al-Anon, ACOA.

Employee assistance Program for chemically dependent employees not available. Staff working with drug/alcohol-related issues: 3 part-time.

Disciplinary Actions

Alcohol Results of infractions of alcohol regulations (see Comparative Table of Alcohol Regulations) include counseling, warning, suspension from housing.

Drugs For any use or possession: varies by situation. For first-time sale: suspension. For subsequent sale: expulsion.

For More Information

Contact: Bonnie J. Zaben, Assistant Dean for Student Life, Jewish Theological Seminary of America, 3080 Broadway, New York, NY 10027-4649. Telephone: 212-678-8838.

JOHN BASTYR COLLEGE

Seattle, Washington

General Information

Independent specialized coed college. Founded 1978. Awards B, M, D. Primary accreditation: regional (candidate). Metropolitan setting; 3-acre campus. Total enrollment: 166. Faculty: 64 (8 full-time, 56 part-time).

Drug and Alcohol Information

Education

On campus Drug and alcohol education/prevention programs offered for: all students.

Identification of Problems

Admissions College application does not ask about prior substance abuse problems.

On campus Current students identified as chemically dependent may remain enrolled, but treatment is required. Training program on identifying students with potential substance abuse problems for: faculty, administration. Written procedures for students and staff if substance abuse is suspected.

Support Services

On campus Support groups, private counseling. Staff working with drug/alcohol-related issues: 2 part-time.

Disciplinary Actions

Alcohol Results of infractions of alcohol regulations (see Comparative Table of Alcohol Regulations) vary by situation but can include counseling, suspension.

Drugs For first-time use or possession: varies by situation—counseling, suspension. For subsequent use or possession: varies by situation—chemical dependency assessment, expulsion. For first-time sale: expulsion.

For More Information

Contact: Sandy Veit, Dean of Students, John Bastyr College, 144 Northeast 54th St., Seattle, WA 98105. Telephone: 206-523-9585.

JOHN BROWN UNIVERSITY

Siloam Springs, Arkansas

General Information

Independent nondenominational 4-year coed college. Founded 1919. Awards A (college transfer and terminal), B. Primary accreditation: regional. Rural setting; 200-acre campus. Total enrollment: 874. Faculty: 70 (59 full-time, 11 part-time).

Drug and Alcohol Information

Education

On campus Drug and alcohol education/prevention programs offered for: all students. College holds an annual alcohol awareness week.

Identification of Problems

Admissions College application does not ask about prior substance abuse problems.

On campus Current students identified as chemically dependent may remain enrolled, but they must abstain from use of the substance. No training program on identifying students with potential substance abuse problems. No written procedures for students and staff if substance abuse is suspected.

Support Services

On campus ACOA, private counseling.

Employee assistance Program for chemically dependent employees not available.

Disciplinary Actions

Alcohol Results of infractions of alcohol regulations (see Comparative Table of Alcohol Regulations) include counseling, probation, suspension, expulsion.

Drugs For first-time use or possession: varies by situation. For subsequent use or possession: expulsion. For first-time sale: expulsion.

For More Information

Contact: Tim Aycock, Counselor, John Brown University, Siloam Springs, AR 72761. Telephone: 501-524-3131.

JOHN CARROLL UNIVERSITY

University Heights, Ohio

General Information

Independent Roman Catholic 5-year coed college. Founded 1886. Awards B, M. Primary accreditation: regional. Small-town setting; 66-acre campus. Total enrollment: 4,082. Faculty: 268 (198 full-time, 70 part-time). Social organizations: 2 national fraternities, 10 local fraternities, 6 local sororities; 18% of eligible undergraduate men and 10% of eligible undergraduate women are members.

Drug and Alcohol Information

Education

On campus Drug and alcohol education/prevention programs offered for: all students. College holds an annual alcohol awareness week.

Identification of Problems

Admissions College application does not ask about prior substance abuse problems.

On campus Current students identified as chemically dependent may remain enrolled, but treatment is required. Training program on identifying students with potential substance abuse problems for: resident advisers, administration.

Support Services

On campus AA, Al-Anon.

Employee assistance Program for chemically dependent employees available.

Disciplinary Actions

Alcohol Results of infractions of alcohol regulations (see Comparative Table of Alcohol Regulations) vary by situation but can include chemical dependency assessment, counseling, warning, probation, suspension, expulsion.

Drugs For first-time use or possession: varies by situation. For subsequent use or possession: suspension, expulsion. For any sale: suspension, expulsion.

For More Information

Contact: Larry Hauserman, Assistant to the Dean of Students, John Carroll University, 20700 North Park Blvd., University Heights, OH 44118. Telephone: 216-397-4401.

JOHNSON & WALES UNIVERSITY

Providence, Rhode Island

General Information

Independent 5-year coed college. Founded 1914. Awards A (college transfer and terminal), B, M. Primary accreditation: AICS. City setting; 100-acre campus. Total enrollment: 7,210. Faculty: 240 (180 full-time, 60 part-time). Social organizations: 2 local fraternities, 1 local sorority; 1% of eligible undergraduate men and 1% of eligible undergraduate women are members.

Drug and Alcohol Information

Education

On campus Drug and alcohol education/prevention programs offered for: all students, faculty, administration; required for: freshmen, resident advisers. Bacchus chapter: 30 members. College holds an annual alcohol awareness week and drug awareness week.

Identification of Problems

Admissions College application does not ask about prior substance abuse problems.

On campus Current students identified as chemically dependent may remain enrolled. Comments: Whether treatment is required depends on circumstances. Training program on identifying students with potential substance abuse problems for: resident advisers, faculty, administration, counselors. No written procedures for students and staff if substance abuse is suspected.

Support Services

On campus Private counseling.

Employee assistance Program for chemically dependent employees not available. Staff working with drug/alcohol-related issues: 5 part-time.

Disciplinary Actions

Alcohol Results of infractions of alcohol regulations (see Comparative Table of Alcohol Regulations) vary by situation but can include chemical dependency assessment, counseling, warning.

Drugs For first-time use: counseling, warning, fines. For subsequent use: chemical dependency assessment, counseling, warning. For any possession: warning, fines. For first-time sale: varies by situation. For subsequent sale: suspension.

For More Information

Contact: Janice Pothier Pac, Director, Counseling and Student Development, Johnson & Wales University, 274 Weybosset St., Providence, RI 02903. Telephone: 401-456-1846.

JOHNSON C. SMITH UNIVERSITY

Charlotte, North Carolina

General Information

Independent 4-year coed college. Founded 1867. Awards B. Primary accreditation: regional. City setting; 97-acre campus. Total enrollment: 1,197. Faculty: 91 (73 full-time, 18 part-time). Social organizations: 4 national fraternities, 5 national sororities, 2 local fraternities; 10% of eligible undergraduate men and 8% of eligible undergraduate women are members.

Drug and Alcohol Information

Education

On campus Drug and alcohol education/prevention programs offered for: all students, athletes/coaches, faculty, administration. College holds an annual alcohol awareness week and drug awareness week.

Identification of Problems

Admissions College application does not ask about prior substance abuse problems.

On campus Current students identified as chemically dependent may not remain enrolled. Training program on identifying students with potential substance abuse problems for: resident advisers, faculty. No written procedures for students and staff if substance abuse is suspected.

Support Services

On campus Private counseling.

Employee assistance Program for chemically dependent employees not available. Staff working with drug/alcohol-related issues: 6 part-time.

Disciplinary Actions

Alcohol Results of infractions of alcohol regulations (see Comparative Table of Alcohol Regulations) vary by situation but can include counseling, probation, suspension.

Drugs For first-time use or possession: counseling, suspension. For subsequent use or possession: suspension. For first-time sale: expulsion.

For More Information

Contact: Dr. Art Flagg, Director, Counseling, Johnson C. Smith University, 100–300 Beatties Ford Rd., Charlotte, NC 28216. Telephone: 704-378-1043.

JONES COLLEGE

Jacksonville, Florida

General Information

Independent 4-year coed college. Founded 1918. Awards A (college transfer and terminal), B. Primary accreditation: AICS. Metropolitan setting; 5-acre campus. Total enrollment: 1,500. Faculty: 57 (23 full-time, 34 part-time). Social organizations: 1 national fraternity, 1 national sorority; 2% of eligible undergraduate men and 2% of eligible undergraduate women are members.

Drug and Alcohol Information

Education

On campus Drug and alcohol education/prevention programs offered for: all students.

Identification of Problems

Admissions College application does not ask about prior substance abuse problems.

On campus Current students identified as chemically dependent may remain enrolled. No training program on identifying students with potential substance abuse problems. No written procedures for students and staff if substance abuse is suspected.

Support Services

On campus Private counseling.

Employee assistance Program for chemically dependent employees not available.

Disciplinary Actions

Alcohol Results of infractions of alcohol regulations (see Comparative Table of Alcohol Regulations) vary by situation. Comments: Decisions are made by the Dean.

Drugs For any use: varies by situation. For first-time possession or sale: varies by situation. For subsequent possession: suspension. For subsequent sale: expulsion.

For More Information

Contact: Raymond Gross, Dean, Jones College, 5353 Arlington Expressway, Jacksonville, FL 32211. Telephone: 904-743-1122.

JUDSON COLLEGE

Elgin, Illinois

General Information

Independent Baptist 4-year coed college. Founded 1963. Awards B. Primary accreditation: regional. City setting; 75-acre campus. Total enrollment: 534. Faculty: 65 (27 full-time, 38 part-time).

Drug and Alcohol Information

Education

On campus Drug and alcohol education/prevention programs offered for: all students.

Identification of Problems

Admissions College application does not ask about prior substance abuse problems.

On campus Current students identified as chemically dependent may remain enrolled, but treatment is required. Training program on identifying students with potential substance abuse problems for: resident advisers. No written

Judson College (continued)

procedures for students and staff if substance abuse is suspected.

Support Services

On campus Private counseling.

Employee assistance Program for chemically dependent employees not available.

Disciplinary Actions

Alcohol Results of infractions of alcohol regulations (see Comparative Table of Alcohol Regulations) include suspension.

Drugs For any use, possession, or sale: counseling, suspension.

Additional Information from the College

Judson College is small, and infractions of the drug and alcohol regulations occur only rarely. The College feels that its strict rules, clearly communicated and strictly but fairly enforced, are the best answer to drug problems.

For More Information

Contact: Joan Didier, Director of the Health Center, Judson College, 1151 N. State St., Elgin, IL 60123. Telephone: 312-695-2500.

KALAMAZOO COLLEGE

Kalamazoo, Michigan

General Information

Independent 4-year coed college. Founded 1833. Awards B. Primary accreditation: regional. City setting; 60-acre campus. Total enrollment: 1,255. Faculty: 99 (78 full-time, 21 part-time).

Drug and Alcohol Information

Education

On campus Drug and alcohol education/prevention programs offered for: all students; required for: resident advisers.

Identification of Problems

Admissions College application does not ask about prior substance abuse problems.

On campus Current students identified as chemically dependent may remain enrolled. Training program on identifying students with potential substance abuse problems for: resident advisers. Written procedures for students and staff if substance abuse is suspected.

Support Services

On campus ACOA, private counseling.

Employee assistance Program for chemically dependent employees available.

Disciplinary Actions

Alcohol Results of infractions of alcohol regulations (see Comparative Table of Alcohol Regulations) vary by situation but can include chemical dependency assessment, counseling, warning, probation, suspension, expulsion.

Drugs For first-time use: counseling. For subsequent use: varies by situation. For any possession or sale: varies by situation.

Additional Information from the College

The college is small and therefore able to deal with substance abuse on an individualized basis. A strong network of faculty and staff helps to identify substance abusers and refer them to appropriate professionals.

For More Information

Contact: Shirley Barron, Director of Health Services, Kalamazoo College, 1200 Academy St., Kalamazoo, MI 49007. Telephone: 616-383-8441.

KANSAS STATE UNIVERSITY

Manhattan, Kansas

General Information

State-supported comprehensive coed institution. Founded 1863. Awards A (college transfer), B, M, D. Primary accreditation: regional. Small-town setting; 668-acre campus. Total enrollment: 19,301. Faculty: 1,250 (1,100 full-time, 150 part-time). Social organizations: 25 national fraternities, 12 national sororities; 17% of eligible undergraduate men and 16% of eligible undergraduate women are members.

Drug and Alcohol Information

Education

On campus Drug and alcohol education/prevention programs offered for: all students. Bacchus chapter. College holds an annual alcohol awareness week and drug awareness week.

Identification of Problems

Admissions College application does not ask about prior substance abuse problems.

On campus Current students identified as chemically dependent may remain enrolled. No training program on identifying students with potential substance abuse problems. Written procedures for students and staff if substance abuse is suspected.

Support Services

On campus Support groups, private counseling.

Employee assistance Program for chemically dependent employees available. Staff working with drug/alcohol-related issues: 2 full-time.

Disciplinary Actions

Alcohol Results of infractions of alcohol regulations (see Comparative Table of Alcohol Regulations) vary by situation. Comments: Results depend on a judicial hearing.

Drugs For any use, possession, or sale: varies by situation.

For More Information

Contact: Bill Arck, Director, Alcohol, Drug, and Other Substances Programs, Kansas State University, Manhattan, KS 66506. Telephone: 913-532-6544.

KEAN COLLEGE OF NEW JERSEY

Union, New Jersey

General Information

State-supported 5-year coed college. Part of New Jersey State College System. Founded 1855. Awards B, M. Primary accreditation: regional. City setting; 148-acre campus. Total enrollment: 12,372. Faculty: 771 (336 full-time, 435 part-time). Social organizations: national fraternities, national sororities, local fraternities, local sororities, eating clubs.

Drug and Alcohol Information

Education

On campus Drug and alcohol education/prevention programs offered for: all students, athletes/coaches, faculty, administration, clerical and maintenance staff. Authorized group concerned with responsible drinking. College holds an annual alcohol awareness week.

Identification of Problems

Admissions College application does not ask about prior substance abuse problems.

On campus Current students identified as chemically dependent may remain enrolled. Training program on identifying students with potential substance abuse problems for: resident advisers, coaches, Greek officers, faculty, administration. Written procedures for students and staff if substance abuse is suspected.

Support Services

On campus AA, ACOA, private counseling, group counseling.

Employee assistance Program for chemically dependent employees available. Staff working with drug/alcohol-related issues: 2 full-time and 10 part-time.

Disciplinary Actions

Alcohol Results of infractions of alcohol regulations (see Comparative Table of Alcohol Regulations) vary by situation but can include chemical dependency assessment, counseling, warning, probation, suspension, expulsion.

Drugs For first-time use: chemical dependency assessment, counseling, probation. For subsequent use: suspension. For first-time possession: counseling, suspension. For first-time sale: counseling, expulsion. For subsequent possession or sale: expulsion.

Additional Information from the College

Kean College of New Jersey has a Presidential Task Force on Alcohol and Substance Abuse, which deals with educational and current research issues related to policies and programs for students, faculty members, and other college personnel.

For More Information

Contact: Patrick J. Ippolito, Vice President, Student Services, Kean College of New Jersey, T-122 Morris Avenue, Union, NJ 07083. Telephone: 201-527-2190.

KEARNEY STATE COLLEGE

Kearney, Nebraska

General Information

State-supported 5-year coed college. Part of Nebraska State College System. Founded 1903. Awards B, M. Primary accreditation: regional. Small-town setting; 200-acre campus. Total enrollment: 9,381. Faculty: 379 (309 full-time, 70 part-time). Social organizations: 7 national fraternities, 4 national sororities.

Drug and Alcohol Information

Education

On campus Drug and alcohol education/prevention programs offered for: all students. Authorized group concerned with responsible drinking. College holds an annual alcohol awareness week.

Identification of Problems

Admissions College application does not ask about prior substance abuse problems.

On campus Current students identified as chemically dependent may remain enrolled. Training program on identifying students with potential substance abuse problems for: resident advisers. No written procedures for students and staff if substance abuse is suspected.

Support Services

On campus AA, ACOA.

Employee assistance Program for chemically dependent employees not available. Staff working with drug/alcohol-related issues: 3 part-time.

Disciplinary Actions

Alcohol Results of infractions of alcohol regulations (see Comparative Table of Alcohol Regulations) include counseling. Comments: The Greek system is in the process of developing an alcohol policy.

Drugs For first-time use or possession: counseling, warning. For subsequent use or possession: probation, suspension. For any sale: expulsion.

For More Information

Contact: Leslie Boughton, Academic Advisor, Counseling and Advising Center, Kearney State College, Kearney, NE 68849. Telephone: 308-234-8248.

KEENE STATE COLLEGE

Keene, New Hampshire

General Information

State-supported 5-year coed college. Part of University System of New Hampshire. Founded 1909. Awards A (college transfer and terminal), B, M. Primary accreditation: regional. Small-town setting; 150-acre campus. Total enrollment: 2,893. Faculty: 250 (170 full-time, 80 part-time). Social organizations: 1 national fraternity, 1 national sorority, 5 local fraternities, 5 local sororities; 15% of eligible undergraduate men and 15% of eligible undergraduate women are members.

Drug and Alcohol Information

Education

On campus Drug and alcohol education/prevention programs offered for: all students, faculty, administration; required for: resident advisers. Authorized group concerned with responsible drinking. College holds an annual alcohol awareness week and drug awareness week.

Identification of Problems

Admissions College application does not ask about prior substance abuse problems.

On campus Current students identified as chemically dependent may remain enrolled, but treatment is required. Training program on identifying students with potential substance abuse problems for: resident advisers. No written procedures for students and staff if substance abuse is suspected.

Support Services

On campus AA, ACOA, support groups, private counseling.

Employee assistance Program for chemically dependent employees available. Staff working with drug/alcohol-related issues: 1 full-time and 6 part-time.

Keene State College (continued)

Disciplinary Actions

Alcohol Results of infractions of alcohol regulations (see Comparative Table of Alcohol Regulations) vary by situation.

Drugs For first-time use, possession, or sale: varies by situation. For subsequent use, possession, or sale: varies by situation—chemical dependency assessment, suspension, expulsion.

For More Information

Contact: Ernest O. Gendron, Associate Dean of Student Affairs/Student Development, Keene State College, 229 Maine, Keene, NH 03431. Telephone: 603-352-1909 Ext. 355.

KENDALL COLLEGE

Evanston, Illinois

General Information

Independent United Methodist 4-year coed college. Founded 1934. Awards A (college transfer), B. Primary accreditation: regional. City setting; 1-acre campus. Total enrollment: 400. Faculty: 34 (25 full-time, 9 part-time).

Drug and Alcohol Information

Education

On campus Drug and alcohol education/prevention programs required for: all students. Student Governing Board concerned with responsible drinking. College holds an annual alcohol awareness week and drug awareness week.

Identification of Problems

Admissions College application does not ask about prior substance abuse problems.

On campus Current students identified as chemically dependent may remain enrolled, but treatment is required. No training program on identifying students with potential substance abuse problems.

Support Services

On campus AA, NA.

Employee assistance Program for chemically dependent employees available.

Disciplinary Actions

Alcohol Results of infractions of alcohol regulations (see Comparative Table of Alcohol Regulations) vary by situation.

Drugs For first-time use or possession: chemical dependency assessment, probation. For subsequent use or possession: expulsion. For first-time sale: expulsion.

For More Information

Contact: John Kelley, Dean of Students, Kendall College, 2408 Orrington Ave., Evanston, IL 60201. Telephone: 312-866-1272.

KENNESAW STATE COLLEGE

Marietta, Georgia

General Information

State-supported 5-year coed college. Part of University System of Georgia. Founded 1966. Awards A (college transfer), B, M. Primary accreditation: regional. Small-town setting; 152-acre campus. Total enrollment: 8,614. Faculty: 417 (230 full-time, 187 part-time). Social organizations: 2 national fraternities, 2 national sororities; 10% of eligible undergraduate men and 11% of eligible undergraduate women are members.

Drug and Alcohol Information

Education

On campus Drug and alcohol education/prevention programs offered for: all students; required for: social organization members, athletes/coaches. Authorized group concerned with responsible drinking. College holds an annual alcohol awareness week and drug awareness week.

Identification of Problems

Admissions College application does not ask about prior substance abuse problems.

On campus Current students identified as chemically dependent may remain enrolled. No training program on identifying students with potential substance abuse problems. No written procedures for students and staff if substance abuse is suspected.

Support Services

On campus Private counseling, referral.

Off campus AA, NA, Al-Anon, ACOA.

Employee assistance Program for chemically dependent employees not available.

Disciplinary Actions

Alcohol Results of infractions of alcohol regulations (see Comparative Table of Alcohol Regulations) vary by situation but can include chemical dependency assessment, counseling, warning, probation, suspension, expulsion.

Drugs For any use, possession, or sale: varies by situation.

For More Information

Contact: Brian Glankler, Counselor, Kennesaw State College, P.O. Box 444, Marietta, GA 30061. Telephone: 404-423-6600.

KENT STATE UNIVERSITY

Kent, Ohio

General Information

State-supported comprehensive coed institution. Part of Kent State University System. Founded 1910. Awards B, M, D. Primary accreditation: regional. Small-town setting; 1,200-acre campus. Total enrollment: 22,753. Faculty: 1,118 (730 full-time, 388 part-time). Social organizations: 17 national fraternities, 10 national sororities, 1 local sorority; 6% of eligible undergraduate men and 4% of eligible undergraduate women are members.

Drug and Alcohol Information

Education

On campus Drug and alcohol education/prevention programs offered for: all students, athletes/coaches, Student Affairs staff. College holds an annual alcohol awareness week.

Identification of Problems

Admissions College application does not ask about prior substance abuse problems.

On campus Current students identified as chemically dependent may remain enrolled. Training program on identifying students with potential substance abuse

problems for: resident advisers, coaches. Written procedures for students and staff if substance abuse is suspected.

Support Services

On campus AA, University Health Services.

Employee assistance Program for chemically dependent employees not available. Staff working with drug/alcohol-related issues: 1 full-time and 2 part-time.

Disciplinary Actions

Alcohol Results of infractions of alcohol regulations (see Comparative Table of Alcohol Regulations) include chemical dependency assessment, counseling, warning, probation, suspension, expulsion.

Drugs For first-time use: varies by situation—chemical dependency assessment, counseling, warning. For subsequent use: varies by situation. For first-time possession or sale: varies by situation. For subsequent possession: probation, suspension, expulsion. For subsequent sale: suspension, expulsion.

For More Information

Contact: Dr. Richard Rynearson, Director–University Health Services, DeWeese Health Center, Kent State University, Kent, OH 44242. Telephone: 216-672-2443.

KENTUCKY CHRISTIAN COLLEGE

Grayson, Kentucky

General Information

Independent 4-year coed college, affiliated with Christian Churches and Churches of Christ. Founded 1919. Awards A (college transfer), B. Primary accreditation: regional and AABC. Rural setting; 65-acre campus. Total enrollment: 491. Faculty: 35 (24 full-time, 11 part-time).

Drug and Alcohol Information

Education

On campus Drug and alcohol education/prevention programs not offered.

Identification of Problems

Admissions College application question about prior substance abuse problems is used to explain past academic performance; for counseling and referral, if student is admitted; in the admissions decision.

On campus Current students identified as chemically dependent may remain enrolled, but treatment is required. Training program on identifying students with potential substance abuse problems for: resident advisers. Written procedures for students and staff if substance abuse is suspected.

Support Services

On campus Support groups, private counseling.

Employee assistance Program for chemically dependent employees not available. Staff working with drug/alcohol-related issues: 5 part-time.

Disciplinary Actions

Alcohol Results of infractions of alcohol regulations (see Comparative Table of Alcohol Regulations) vary by situation but can include counseling, suspension, expulsion.

Drugs For first-time use, possession, or sale: varies by situation—counseling, suspension, expulsion. For subsequent use, possession, or sale: expulsion.

For More Information

Contact: Randy Kirk, Dean of Student Affairs, Kentucky Christian College, Box 538, Grayson, Kentucky 41143. Telephone: 606-474-6613.

KENTUCKY STATE UNIVERSITY

Frankfort, Kentucky

General Information

State-related 5-year coed college. Founded 1886. Awards A (college transfer and terminal), B, M. Primary accreditation: regional. Small-town setting; 485-acre campus. Total enrollment: 2,222. Faculty: 128 (120 full-time, 8 part-time). Social organizations: 3 national fraternities, 3 national sororities, 2 local fraternities, 3 local sororities; 6% of eligible undergraduate men and 4% of eligible undergraduate women are members.

Drug and Alcohol Information

Education

On campus Drug and alcohol education/prevention programs offered for: all students, faculty, administration, staff; required for: athletes/coaches, resident advisers. College holds an annual alcohol awareness week and drug awareness week.

Identification of Problems

Admissions College application does not ask about prior substance abuse problems.

On campus Current students identified as chemically dependent may remain enrolled, but treatment is required. Training program on identifying students with potential substance abuse problems for: resident advisers, coaches, faculty, administration. Written procedures for students and staff if substance abuse is suspected.

Support Services

On campus Support groups, private counseling, referral.

Off campus AA, NA, Al-Anon, ACOA.

Employee assistance Program for chemically dependent employees not available. Staff working with drug/alcohol-related issues: 1 part-time.

Disciplinary Actions

Alcohol Results of infractions of alcohol regulations (see Comparative Table of Alcohol Regulations) vary by situation but can include chemical dependency assessment, counseling, warning, probation, suspension, expulsion.

Drugs For any use or possession: varies by situation. For first-time sale: suspension. For subsequent sale: expulsion.

Additional Information from the College

Kentucky State University regards substance abuse issues as critical to the success of its educational program. Prevention is stressed, but treatment is provided when needed. A University psychodrama group presentation, designed to stimulate discussion on substance abuse, has been well received, and its repetition has been requested by local elementary and secondary schools.

For More Information

Contact: Dr. Susan M. Turner, Comprehensive Counselor, Betty White Health Center, Kentucky State University, East Main St., Frankfort, KY 40601. Telephone: 502-223-5629.

KENTUCKY WESLEYAN COLLEGE

Owensboro, Kentucky

General Information

Independent Methodist 4-year coed college. Founded 1858. Awards A (college transfer and terminal), B. Primary accreditation: regional. City setting; 72-acre campus. Total enrollment: 765. Faculty: 80 (54 full-time, 26 part-time). Social organizations: 3 national fraternities, 3 national sororities, 1 local sorority; 28% of eligible undergraduate men and 31% of eligible undergraduate women are members.

Drug and Alcohol Information

Education

On campus Drug and alcohol education/prevention programs offered for: all students. College holds an annual alcohol awareness week.

Identification of Problems

Admissions College application does not ask about prior substance abuse problems.

On campus Current students identified as chemically dependent may remain enrolled, but treatment is required. Training program on identifying students with potential substance abuse problems for: resident advisers. Written procedures for students and staff if substance abuse is suspected.

Support Services

On campus Referrals to community resources.

Employee assistance Program for chemically dependent employees not available.

Disciplinary Actions

Alcohol Results of infractions of alcohol regulations (see Comparative Table of Alcohol Regulations) vary by situation but can include probation, fines.

Drugs For first-time use or possession: varies by situation—counseling, probation, fine. For subsequent use or possession: varies by situation—probation, larger fine. For first-time sale: expulsion.

For More Information

Contact: Paul R. Rittof, Dean of Students, Kentucky Wesleyan College, 3000 Frederica, Owensboro, KY 42301. Telephone: 502-926-3111 Ext. 151.

KEUKA COLLEGE

Keuka Park, New York

General Information

Independent 4-year coed college. Founded 1890. Awards B. Primary accreditation: regional. Rural setting; 173-acre campus. Total enrollment: 604. Faculty: 67 (40 full-time, 27 part-time).

Drug and Alcohol Information

Education

On campus Drug and alcohol education/prevention programs offered for: all students. College holds an annual alcohol awareness week and drug awareness week.

Identification of Problems

Admissions College application does not ask about prior substance abuse problems.

On campus Current students identified as chemically dependent may remain enrolled, but treatment is required. Training program on identifying students with potential substance abuse problems for: resident advisers, Residence Life and Student Life staff. Written procedures for students and staff if substance abuse is suspected are being formulated.

Support Services

On campus ACOA.

Disciplinary Actions

Alcohol Results of infractions of alcohol regulations (see Comparative Table of Alcohol Regulations) vary by situation but can include chemical dependency assessment, counseling, warning, probation, suspension, expulsion.

Drugs For first-time use: warning. For subsequent use: varies by situation. For first-time possession: confiscation of drug; warning. For subsequent possession: varies by situation. For any sale: varies by situation.

Additional Information from the College

Keuka College is interested in forming a Bacchus group.

For More Information

Contact: W. Averell H. Bauder, Director of Student Life, Keuka College, Keuka Park, NY 14478. Telephone: 315-536-4411 Ext. 215.

KING COLLEGE

Bristol, Tennessee

General Information

Independent 4-year coed college, affiliated with Presbyterian Church (U.S.A.). Founded 1867. Awards B. Primary accreditation: regional. City setting; 135-acre campus. Total enrollment: 588. Faculty: 63 (33 full-time, 30 part-time).

Drug and Alcohol Information

Education

On campus Drug and alcohol education/prevention programs offered for: all students.

Identification of Problems

Admissions College application does not ask about prior substance abuse problems.

On campus Current students identified as chemically dependent may possibly remain enrolled, but treatment is required. No training program on identifying students with potential substance abuse problems. Written procedures for students and staff if substance abuse is suspected.

Support Services

On campus Private counseling.

Employee assistance Program for chemically dependent employees available. Staff working with drug/alcohol-related issues: 1 part-time.

Disciplinary Actions

Alcohol Results of infractions of alcohol regulations (see Comparative Table of Alcohol Regulations) vary by situation.

Drugs For any use, possession, or sale: expulsion.

Additional Information from the College

King College considers the individual's needs and circumstances when assessing alcohol/drug abuse problems. Many of the community's resources are used in helping students and employees with problems.

For More Information

Contact: Dr. Joe Martin, Director of Counseling, King College, Bristol, TN 37620. Telephone: 615-968-1187.

KNOX COLLEGE

Galesburg, Illinois

General Information

Independent 4-year coed college. Founded 1837. Awards B. Primary accreditation: regional. Small-town setting; 65-acre campus. Total enrollment: 1,024. Faculty: 80 (76 full-time, 4 part-time). Social organizations: 5 national fraternities, 3 national sororities; 35% of eligible undergraduate men and 20% of eligible undergraduate women are members.

Drug and Alcohol Information

Education

On campus Drug and alcohol education/prevention programs offered for: all students. Authorized group concerned with responsible drinking. College holds an annual alcohol awareness week.

Identification of Problems

Admissions College application does not ask about prior substance abuse problems.

On campus Current students identified as chemically dependent may remain enrolled, but treatment is required. Training program on identifying students with potential substance abuse problems for: resident advisers. Written procedures for students and staff if substance abuse is suspected.

Support Services

On campus Private counseling.

Off campus AA, NA, Al-Anon, ACOA, support groups.

Employee assistance Program for chemically dependent employees not available. Staff working with drug/alcohol-related issues: 5 part-time.

Disciplinary Actions

Alcohol Results of infractions of alcohol regulations (see Comparative Table of Alcohol Regulations) vary by situation.

Drugs For any use, possession, or sale: varies by situation.

For More Information

Contact: Anand Dyal-Chand, Dean of Students, Knox College, Galesburg, IL 61401. Telephone: 309-343-0112 Ext. 221.

KOL YAAKOV TORAH CENTER

Monsey, New York

General Information

Independent Jewish 5-year specialized men's college. Founded 1980. Awards degrees equivalent to B, M. Primary accreditation: AARTS (candidate). Small-town setting; 3-acre campus. Total enrollment: 41. Faculty: 13 (10 full-time, 3 part-time).

Drug and Alcohol Information

Comments from the College

Kol Yaakov Torah Center is a religious institution and screens its candidates very carefully. A candidate who proved, on close investigation, to be chemically dependent would be referred to a special substance abuse rehabilitation facility in the area. The school has virtually no problem with student substance abuse.

For More Information

Contact: Rabbi A. Parry, Student Counselor, Kol Yaakov Torah Center, 29 West Maple Ave., Monsey, NY 10952. Telephone: 914-425-3863.

KUTZTOWN UNIVERSITY OF PENNSYLVANIA

Kutztown, Pennsylvania

General Information

State-supported 5-year coed college. Part of State System of Higher Education. Founded 1866. Awards B, M. Primary accreditation: regional. Rural setting; 325-acre campus. Total enrollment: 7,168. Faculty: 355 (341 full-time, 14 part-time). Social organizations: 4 national fraternities, 2 national sororities, 1 local fraternity, 1 local sorority; 3% of eligible undergraduate men and 3% of eligible undergraduate women are members.

Drug and Alcohol Information

Education

On campus Drug and alcohol education/prevention programs offered for: all students. Authorized group concerned with responsible drinking.

Identification of Problems

Admissions College application does not ask about prior substance abuse problems.

On campus Current students identified as chemically dependent may remain enrolled. Training program on identifying students with potential substance abuse problems for: resident advisers, faculty. Written procedures for students and staff if substance abuse is suspected.

Support Services

On campus Private counseling.

Employee assistance Program for chemically dependent employees available.

Disciplinary Actions

Alcohol Results of infractions of alcohol regulations (see Comparative Table of Alcohol Regulations) include chemical dependency assessment, counseling, warning, probation, suspension.

Drugs For first-time use, possession, or sale: varies by situation. For subsequent use, possession, or sale: varies by situation—chemical dependency assessment, counseling, suspension.

For More Information

Contact: Dr. Russ Bumba, Dean for Student Services, 104 North Student Center, Kutztown University of Pennsylvania, Kutztown, PA 19530. Telephone: 215-683-4087.

LAFAYETTE COLLEGE

Easton, Pennsylvania

General Information

Independent 4-year coed college, affiliated with Presbyterian Church (U.S.A.). Founded 1826. Awards B. Primary accreditation: regional. Small-town setting; 110-acre campus. Total enrollment: 2,039. Faculty: 195 (161 full-time, 34 part-time). Social organizations: 12 national fraternities, 5 national sororities, 2 social dorms; 65% of eligible undergraduate men and 50% of eligible undergraduate women are members.

Drug and Alcohol Information

Education

On campus Drug and alcohol education/prevention programs offered for: all students, athletes/coaches. Authorized group concerned with responsible drinking. College holds an annual alcohol awareness week and drug awareness week.

Identification of Problems

Admissions College application does not ask about prior substance abuse problems.

On campus Current students identified as chemically dependent might be allowed to remain enrolled, but treatment may be required. Training program on identifying students with potential substance abuse problems for: resident advisers, coaches. No written procedures for students and staff if substance abuse is suspected.

Support Services

On campus Support groups, private counseling.

Off campus AA, NA, Al-Anon.

Employee assistance Program for chemically dependent employees available. Staff working with drug/alcohol-related issues: 6 part-time.

Disciplinary Actions

Alcohol Results of infractions of alcohol regulations (see Comparative Table of Alcohol Regulations) vary by situation but can include chemical dependency assessment, counseling, warning, probation, suspension, expulsion.

Drugs For any use, possession, or sale: varies by situation.

For More Information

Contact: H. C. Kissiah, Dean of Students, Lafayette College, Easton, PA 18042. Telephone: 215-250-5082.

LAGRANGE COLLEGE

LaGrange, Georgia

General Information

Independent United Methodist 5-year coed college. Founded 1831. Awards A (college transfer and terminal), B, M. Primary accreditation: regional. Small-town setting; 35-acre campus. Total enrollment: 956. Faculty: 74 (all full-time). Social organizations: 4 national fraternities, 4 national sororities; 30% of eligible undergraduate men and 30% of eligible undergraduate women are members.

Drug and Alcohol Information

Education

On campus Drug and alcohol education/prevention programs offered for: all students, athletes/coaches.

Identification of Problems

Admissions College application does not ask about prior substance abuse problems.

On campus Current students identified as chemically dependent may remain enrolled, but treatment is required. Training program on identifying students with potential substance abuse problems for: resident advisers, coaches, faculty. No written procedures for students and staff if substance abuse is suspected.

Support Services

On campus Private counseling.

Employee assistance Program for chemically dependent employees not available. Staff working with drug/alcohol-related issues: 1 part-time.

Disciplinary Actions

Alcohol Results of infractions of alcohol regulations (see Comparative Table of Alcohol Regulations) include counseling, warning, probation, suspension, expulsion.

Drugs For first-time use: counseling, warning, probation. For subsequent use: suspension. For first-time possession: suspension. For subsequent possession: expulsion. For any sale: expulsion.

For More Information

Contact: Charlie Lincoln, Associate Dean of Student Development, LaGrange College, 601 Broad St., LaGrange, GA 30240. Telephone: 404-882-2911.

LAKE FOREST COLLEGE

Lake Forest, Illinois

General Information

Independent 5-year coed college. Founded 1857. Awards B, M. Primary accreditation: regional. Small-town setting; 110-acre campus. Total enrollment: 1,132. Faculty: 105 (82 full-time, 23 part-time). Social organizations: 3 local fraternities, 2 local sororities; 9% of eligible undergraduate men and 7% of eligible undergraduate women are members.

Drug and Alcohol Information

Education

On campus Drug and alcohol education/prevention programs offered for: all students, athletes/coaches. Authorized group concerned with responsible drinking. College holds an annual alcohol awareness week and drug awareness week.

Identification of Problems

Admissions College application does not ask about prior substance abuse problems.

On campus Current students identified as chemically dependent may remain enrolled, but treatment is required. Training program on identifying students with potential substance abuse problems for: resident advisers. Written procedures for students and staff if substance abuse is suspected.

Support Services

On campus AA, ACOA, support groups, private counseling.

Employee assistance Program for chemically dependent employees available. Staff working with drug/alcohol-related issues: 6 part-time.

Disciplinary Actions

Alcohol Results of infractions of alcohol regulations (see Comparative Table of Alcohol Regulations) include chemical dependency assessment, counseling, warning, probation.

Drugs For any use or possession: varies by situation. For any sale: expulsion.

For More Information

Contact: Ron Miller, Dean of Students, Lake Forest College, Lake Forest, IL 60045. Telephone: 312-234-3100 Ext. 285.

LAKE SUPERIOR STATE UNIVERSITY

Sault Sainte Marie, Michigan

General Information

State-supported 5-year coed college. Founded 1946. Awards A (college transfer and terminal), B, M. Primary accreditation: regional. Small-town setting; 115-acre campus. Total enrollment: 3,155. Faculty: 155 (115 full-time, 40 part-time). Social organizations: 3 national fraternities, 2 national sororities, 1 local fraternity, 2 local sororities.

Drug and Alcohol Information

Education

On campus Drug and alcohol education/prevention programs offered for: all students, athletes/coaches. Bacchus chapter: 30 members. College holds an annual alcohol awareness week and drug awareness week.

Identification of Problems

Admissions College application does not ask about prior substance abuse problems.

On campus Current students identified as chemically dependent may remain enrolled, but treatment is required. Training program on identifying students with potential substance abuse problems for: resident advisers, coaches, faculty. Written procedures for students and staff if substance abuse is suspected.

Support Services

On campus AA, Al-Anon, support groups, private counseling.

Employee assistance Program for chemically dependent employees available. Staff working with drug/alcohol-related issues: 6 part-time.

Disciplinary Actions

Alcohol Results of infractions of alcohol regulations (see Comparative Table of Alcohol Regulations) include chemical dependency assessment, counseling, warning, probation, suspension, expulsion.

Drugs For first-time use or possession: probation. For subsequent use or possession: chemical dependency assessment, suspension. For first-time sale: expulsion.

For More Information

Contact: Harry Pike, Executive Vice President, Lake Superior State University, Sault Sainte Marie, MI 49783. Telephone: 906-635-2684.

LANDER COLLEGE

Greenwood, South Carolina

General Information

State-supported 5-year coed college. Founded 1872. Awards B, M. Primary accreditation: regional. Small-town setting; 75-acre campus. Total enrollment: 2,479. Faculty: 156 (118 full-time, 38 part-time). Social organizations: 6 national fraternities, 6 national sororities, 1 local fraternity, 1 local sorority; 5% of eligible undergraduate men and 5% of eligible undergraduate women are members.

Drug and Alcohol Information

Education

On campus Drug and alcohol education/prevention programs offered for: all students, athletes/coaches. Authorized group concerned with responsible drinking. College holds an annual alcohol awareness week and drug awareness week.

Identification of Problems

Admissions College application does not ask about prior substance abuse problems.

On campus Current students identified as chemically dependent may remain enrolled, but treatment is required. Training program on identifying students with potential substance abuse problems for: resident advisers, coaches, student leaders.

Support Services

On campus AA, support groups, private counseling, Mental Health Center Health Service.

Employee assistance Program for chemically dependent employees available.

Disciplinary Actions

Alcohol Results of infractions of alcohol regulations (see Comparative Table of Alcohol Regulations) vary by situation.

Drugs For first-time use: varies by situation—counseling, warning, probation. For first-time possession: varies by situation—arrest. For first-time sale: varies by situation—arrest, suspension. For subsequent use, possession, or sale: varies by situation—suspension.

For More Information

Contact: H. Randall Bouknight, Vice President for Student Affairs, Lander College, Stanley Ave., Greenwood, SC 29646. Telephone: 803-229-8240.

LANE COLLEGE

Jackson, Tennessee

General Information

Independent 4-year coed college, affiliated with Christian Methodist Episcopal Church. Founded 1882. Awards B. Primary accreditation: regional. City setting; 15-acre campus. Total enrollment: 501. Social organizations: 4 national fraternities, 4 national sororities; 65% of eligible undergraduate men and 70% of eligible undergraduate women are members.

Drug and Alcohol Information

Education

On campus Drug and alcohol education/prevention programs offered for: all students, faculty, administration.

Lane College (continued)

College holds an annual alcohol awareness week and drug awareness week.

Identification of Problems

On campus Current students identified as chemically dependent may remain enrolled, but treatment is required. Training program on identifying students with potential substance abuse problems for: peer counselors. Written procedures for students and staff if substance abuse is suspected.

Support Services

On campus Private counseling, referral.

Employee assistance Program for chemically dependent employees not available. Staff working with drug/alcohol-related issues: 1 part-time.

Disciplinary Actions

Alcohol Results of infractions of alcohol regulations (see Comparative Table of Alcohol Regulations) include counseling, warning, probation, suspension.

Drugs For first-time use or possession: varies by situation—suspension. For first-time sale: expulsion. For subsequent use, possession, or sale: expulsion.

For More Information

Contact: Darlene Thomas, Director, Counseling Center, Lane College, 545 Lane Ave., Jackson, TN 38301. Telephone: 901-424-4600 Ext. 220.

LANGSTON UNIVERSITY

Langston, Oklahoma

General Information

State-supported 5-year coed college. Founded 1897. Awards B, M. Primary accreditation: regional. Rural setting; 40-acre campus. Total enrollment: 2,514. Faculty: 128 (51 full-time, 77 part-time). Social organizations: 4 national fraternities, 4 national sororities.

Drug and Alcohol Information

Education

On campus Drug and alcohol education/prevention programs offered for: all students. College holds an annual alcohol awareness week and drug awareness week.

Identification of Problems

Admissions College application does not ask about prior substance abuse problems.

On campus No training program on identifying students with potential substance abuse problems.

Support Services

On campus Support groups, private counseling. Staff working with drug/alcohol-related issues: 2 full-time.

Disciplinary Actions

Alcohol Results of infractions of alcohol regulations (see Comparative Table of Alcohol Regulations) include probation.

Drugs For first-time use or possession: varies by situation. For subsequent use: referral to community substance abuse center, suspension. For subsequent possession: suspension, expulsion. For first-time sale: expulsion.

For More Information

Contact: Larecia Tillman, Counselor, Chemical Dependency, Langston University, P.O. Box 658, Langston, OK 73050. Telephone: 405-466-2231 Ext. 401.

LAREDO STATE UNIVERSITY

Laredo, Texas

General Information

State-supported coed college. Part of University System of South Texas. Founded 1969. Awards B, M. Primary accreditation: regional. City setting; 196-acre campus. Total enrollment: 1,077. Faculty: 54 (26 full-time, 28 part-time).

Drug and Alcohol Information

Education

On campus Drug and alcohol education/prevention programs offered for: all students, faculty, administration. College holds an annual alcohol awareness week and drug awareness week.

Identification of Problems

Admissions College application does not ask about prior substance abuse problems.

On campus Current students identified as chemically dependent may remain enrolled, but treatment is required. Training program on identifying students with potential substance abuse problems for: faculty, administration. Written procedures for students and staff if substance abuse is suspected.

Support Services

On campus Private counseling.

Employee assistance Program for chemically dependent employees not available. Staff working with drug/alcohol-related issues: 16 part-time.

Disciplinary Actions

Alcohol Results of infractions of alcohol regulations (see Comparative Table of Alcohol Regulations) vary by situation but can include counseling, possibly arrest.

Drugs For any use: chemical dependency assessment, counseling, warning. For any possession: counseling, warning. For any sale: probation, suspension, expulsion.

For More Information

Contact: David E. VerMilyea, Director of Student Affairs, Laredo State University, 1 Washington St., Laredo, TX 78040. Telephone: 512-722-8001 Ext. 340.

LA SALLE UNIVERSITY

Philadelphia, Pennsylvania

General Information

Independent Roman Catholic 5-year coed college. Founded 1863. Awards B, M. Primary accreditation: regional. Metropolitan setting; 85-acre campus. Total enrollment: 6,464. Faculty: 269 (215 full-time, 54 part-time). Social organizations: 7 national fraternities, 4 national sororities, 1 local fraternity, 1 local sorority; 12% of eligible undergraduate men and 12% of eligible undergraduate women are members.

Drug and Alcohol Information

Education

On campus Drug and alcohol education/prevention programs offered for: all students, faculty, administration;

required for: athletes/coaches, resident advisers. Bacchus chapter: 12 members. College holds an annual alcohol awareness week and drug awareness week.

Identification of Problems

Admissions College application does not ask about prior substance abuse problems.

On campus Current students identified as chemically dependent may remain enrolled, but treatment is required. Training program on identifying students with potential substance abuse problems for: resident advisers, coaches, Greek officers, faculty, administration, peer counselors. Written procedures for students and staff if substance abuse is suspected is being prepared.

Support Services

On campus AA, Al-Anon, ACOA, private counseling, referral services.

Employee assistance Program for chemically dependent employees not available. Staff working with drug/alcohol-related issues: 1 full-time and 10 part-time.

Disciplinary Actions

Alcohol Results of infractions of alcohol regulations (see Comparative Table of Alcohol Regulations) vary by situation but can include chemical dependency assessment, counseling, warning, probation.

Drugs For first-time use, possession, or sale: varies by situation. For subsequent use or possession: chemical dependency assessment, counseling, suspension. For subsequent sale: expulsion.

Additional Information from the College

La Salle University has a very popular and successful alcohol-free night club and restaurant. Recently, receipt of a FIPSE grant has enabled the University to appoint a full-time coordinator who will expand current programs and services and create new ones.

For More Information

Contact: Robert Chapman, Coordinator, Alcohol and Other Drug Education and Prevention Programs, Counseling Center, La Salle University, 20th St. at Olney Ave., Philadelphia, PA 19141. Telephone: 215-951-1355.

LAWRENCE UNIVERSITY

Appleton, Wisconsin

General Information

Independent 4-year coed college. Founded 1847. Awards B. Primary accreditation: regional. City setting; 88-acre campus. Total enrollment: 1,224. Faculty: 115. Social organizations: 5 national fraternities, 3 national sororities; 45% of eligible undergraduate men and 35% of eligible undergraduate women are members.

Drug and Alcohol Information

Education

On campus Drug and alcohol education/prevention programs offered for: all students. College holds an annual alcohol awareness week.

Identification of Problems

Admissions College application does not ask about prior substance abuse problems.

On campus Current students identified as chemically dependent may remain enrolled, but treatment may be required, depending on the situation. Training program on identifying students with potential substance abuse problems for: resident advisers, Greek officers, administration. Written procedures for students and staff if substance abuse is suspected.

Support Services

On campus Al-Anon, private counseling.

Employee assistance Program for chemically dependent employees available. Staff working with drug/alcohol-related issues: 14 part-time.

Disciplinary Actions

Alcohol Results of infractions of alcohol regulations (see Comparative Table of Alcohol Regulations) vary by situation but can include chemical dependency assessment, counseling, warning, probation, suspension, expulsion. Comments: Decisions are made by the Judicial Board.

Drugs For any use or possession: varies by situation. For first-time sale: varies by situation. For subsequent sale: varies by situation—counseling, suspension.

For More Information

Contact: Abbas Yaghmaian, Alcohol and Drug Education Committee Member, Lawrence University, P.O. Box 597, Appleton, WI 54912. Telephone: 414-735-6595.

LEES-MCRAE COLLEGE

Banner Elk, North Carolina

General Information

Independent 4-year coed college, affiliated with Presbyterian Church (U.S.A.). Founded 1900. Awards A (college transfer), B. Primary accreditation: regional. Rural setting; 300-acre campus. Total enrollment: 787. Faculty: 58 (48 full-time, 10 part-time).

Drug and Alcohol Information

Education

On campus Drug and alcohol education/prevention programs offered for: all students; required for: freshmen. Authorized group concerned with responsible drinking. College holds an annual alcohol awareness week.

Identification of Problems

Admissions College application question about prior substance abuse problems is used for counseling and referral, if student is admitted.

On campus Current students identified as chemically dependent may remain enrolled. No training program on identifying students with potential substance abuse problems. No written procedures for students and staff if substance abuse is suspected.

Support Services

On campus Referrals.

Off campus AA, NA.

Employee assistance Program for chemically dependent employees not available. Staff working with drug/alcohol-related issues: 1 part-time.

Disciplinary Actions

Alcohol Results of infractions of alcohol regulations (see Comparative Table of Alcohol Regulations) include counseling, warning, probation, suspension, expulsion.

Drugs For first-time use: counseling, probation, suspension. For subsequent use: suspension. For first-time possession: varies by situation—counseling, probation, suspension. For subsequent possession: varies by situation—

Lees-McRae College (continued)

suspension. For first-time sale: suspension, expulsion. For subsequent sale: expulsion.

Additional Information from the College

Residence hall programs on alcohol education are given.

For More Information

Contact: Helen Tester, Director of Counseling, Lees-McRae College, P.O. Box 128, Banner Elk, NC 28604. Telephone: 704-898-5241.

LEHIGH UNIVERSITY

Bethlehem, Pennsylvania

General Information

Independent comprehensive coed institution. Founded 1865. Awards B, M, D. Primary accreditation: regional. City setting; 1,600-acre campus. Total enrollment: 6,569. Faculty: 487 (392 full-time, 95 part-time). Social organizations: 32 national fraternities, 8 national sororities; 54% of eligible undergraduate men and 46% of eligible undergraduate women are members.

Drug and Alcohol Information

Education

On campus Drug and alcohol education/prevention programs offered for: all students, athletes/coaches, faculty, administration; required for: freshmen, resident advisers, social hosts. Authorized group concerned with responsible drinking. College holds an annual alcohol awareness week.

Identification of Problems

Admissions College application does not ask about prior substance abuse problems.

On campus Current students identified as chemically dependent may remain enrolled. Training program on identifying students with potential substance abuse problems for: resident advisers, Greek officers. Written procedures for students and staff if substance abuse is suspected.

Support Services

On campus AA, private counseling. Staff working with drug/alcohol-related issues: 1 full-time.

Disciplinary Actions

Alcohol Results of infractions of alcohol regulations (see Comparative Table of Alcohol Regulations) vary by situation but can include chemical dependency assessment, counseling, warning, probation, suspension, community service.

Drugs For any use or possession: varies by situation. For first-time sale: varies by situation. For subsequent sale: varies by situation—chemical dependency assessment, counseling, suspension.

For More Information

Contact: Kevin Siddons, Drug and Alcohol Counselor, Rm. 10 Johnson Hall #36, Lehigh University, Bethlehem, PA 18015. Telephone: 215-758-5359.

LEHMAN COLLEGE OF THE CITY UNIVERSITY OF NEW YORK

Bronx, New York

General Information

State and locally supported 5-year coed college. Part of City University of New York System. Founded 1931. Awards B, M. Primary accreditation: regional. Metropolitan setting; 37-acre campus. Total enrollment: 9,598. Faculty: 603 (381 full-time, 222 part-time). Social organization: 1 national sorority.

Drug and Alcohol Information

Education

On campus Drug and alcohol education/prevention programs offered for: all students. Authorized group concerned with responsible drinking. College holds an annual alcohol awareness week.

Identification of Problems

Admissions College application does not ask about prior substance abuse problems.

On campus Current students identified as chemically dependent may remain enrolled. Training program on identifying students with potential substance abuse problems for: peer counselors. Written procedures for students and staff if substance abuse is suspected.

Support Services

On campus AA, ACOA, peer counseling.

Employee assistance Program for chemically dependent employees available. Staff working with drug/alcohol-related issues: 2 part-time.

Disciplinary Actions

Alcohol Results of infractions of alcohol regulations (see Comparative Table of Alcohol Regulations) include counseling, warning.

Drugs For first-time use or possession: varies by situation—counseling. For first-time sale: varies by situation. Comments: Lehman College has not experienced repeated drug offenses.

For More Information

Contact: Dr. Peter C. Schaehrer, Coordinator of Student Affairs, Lehman College of the City University of New York, Bedford Park Blvd. W., Bronx, NY 10468. Telephone: 212-960-8551.

LENOIR-RHYNE COLLEGE

Hickory, North Carolina

General Information

Independent Lutheran 5-year coed college. Founded 1891. Awards B, M. Primary accreditation: regional. Small-town setting; 100-acre campus. Total enrollment: 1,616. Faculty: 135 (95 full-time, 40 part-time). Social organizations: 4 national fraternities, 3 national sororities; 25% of eligible undergraduate men and 25% of eligible undergraduate women are members.

Drug and Alcohol Information

Education

On campus Drug and alcohol education/prevention programs offered for: all students. College holds an annual alcohol awareness week.

Identification of Problems

Admissions College application does not ask about prior substance abuse problems.

On campus Current students identified as chemically dependent may remain enrolled, but treatment is required. Training program on identifying students with potential substance abuse problems for: resident advisers. No written procedures for students and staff if substance abuse is suspected.

Support Services

On campus Private counseling.

Off campus AA, NA, Al-Anon, in close proximity to campus.

Employee assistance Program for chemically dependent employees not available. Staff working with drug/alcohol-related issues: 1 part-time.

Disciplinary Actions

Alcohol Results of infractions of alcohol regulations (see Comparative Table of Alcohol Regulations) vary by situation but can include counseling, warning, probation, suspension. Comments: Individual sanction may differ from organizational sanction.

Drugs For first-time use: varies by situation—counseling, probation. For subsequent use: suspension. For any possession or sale: suspension.

For More Information

Contact: Mike Riley, Director, Counseling and Student Development, Box 7547, Lenoir-Rhyne College, Hickory, NC 28603. Telephone: 704-328-7252.

LEWIS-CLARK STATE COLLEGE

Lewiston, Idaho

General Information

State-supported 4-year coed college. Founded 1894. Awards A (college transfer and terminal), B. Primary accreditation: regional. Small-town setting; 44-acre campus. Total enrollment: 2,164. Faculty: 107 (92 full-time, 15 part-time).

Drug and Alcohol Information

Education

On campus Drug and alcohol education/prevention programs offered for: all students. College holds an annual alcohol awareness week and drug awareness week.

Identification of Problems

Admissions College application does not ask about prior substance abuse problems.

On campus Current students identified as chemically dependent may remain enrolled. No training program on identifying students with potential substance abuse problems. No written procedures for students and staff if substance abuse is suspected.

Support Services

On campus AA, ACOA, private counseling.

Employee assistance Program for chemically dependent employees not available. Staff working with drug/alcohol-related issues: 2 part-time.

Disciplinary Actions

Alcohol Results of infractions of alcohol regulations (see Comparative Table of Alcohol Regulations) include counseling, warning.

Drugs For any use, possession, or sale: varies by situation.

Additional Information from the College

Lewis-Clark State College has formed a committee that is in the process of establishing a drug/alcohol policy for students and employees.

For More Information

Contact: Vicki L. Johnson, Director of Counseling, SGC 42, Lewis-Clark State College, 8th Ave. and 6th St., Lewiston, ID 83501. Telephone: 208-799-2210.

LIBERTY UNIVERSITY

Lynchburg, Virginia

General Information

Independent Baptist 5-year coed college. Founded 1971. Awards A (college transfer), B, M. Primary accreditation: regional. City setting; 5,700-acre campus. Total enrollment: 10,902. Faculty: 255 (210 full-time, 45 part-time).

Drug and Alcohol Information

Education

On campus Drug and alcohol education/prevention programs offered for: all students, athletes/coaches. College holds an annual alcohol awareness week.

Identification of Problems

Admissions College application question about prior substance abuse problems is used to explain past academic performance; for counseling and referral, if student is admitted; in the admissions decision.

On campus Current students identified as chemically dependent may not remain enrolled. Training program on identifying students with potential substance abuse problems for: resident advisers. Written procedures for students and staff if substance abuse is suspected.

Support Services

On campus Private counseling.

Employee assistance Program for chemically dependent employees not available. Staff working with drug/alcohol-related issues: 1 part-time.

Disciplinary Actions

Alcohol Results of infractions of alcohol regulations (see Comparative Table of Alcohol Regulations) include expulsion.

Drugs For any use, possession, or sale: expulsion.

For More Information

Contact: Jonathan M. Purple, Dean of Students, Liberty University, 3765 Candlers Mountain Rd., Box 20000, Lynchburg, VA 24506. Telephone: 804-582-2828.

LIMESTONE COLLEGE

Gaffney, South Carolina

General Information

Independent 4-year coed college. Founded 1845. Awards B. Primary accreditation: regional. Small-town setting; 115-acre campus. Total enrollment: 952. Faculty: 63. Social organizations: 2 local fraternities, 2 local sororities; 60% of eligible undergraduate men and 50% of eligible undergraduate women are members.

Drug and Alcohol Information

Education

On campus Drug and alcohol education/prevention programs offered for: all students; required for: athletes.

Identification of Problems

Admissions College application does not ask about prior substance abuse problems.

On campus Current students identified as chemically dependent may remain enrolled, but treatment is required. No training program on identifying students with potential substance abuse problems. No written procedures for students and staff if substance abuse is suspected.

Support Services

On campus Private counseling.

Employee assistance Program for chemically dependent employees not available.

Disciplinary Actions

Alcohol Results of infractions of alcohol regulations (see Comparative Table of Alcohol Regulations) vary by situation but can include counseling, warning, probation.

Drugs For any use, possession, or sale: counseling, expulsion.

For More Information

Contact: Les Gregory, Assistant Dean of Men, Limestone College, 1115 College Dr., Gaffney, SC 29340. Telephone: 803-489-7151.

LINCOLN MEMORIAL UNIVERSITY

Harrogate, Tennessee

General Information

Independent 5-year coed college. Founded 1897. Awards A (college transfer and terminal), B, M. Primary accreditation: regional. Rural setting; 990-acre campus. Total enrollment: 1,582. Faculty: 101 (49 full-time, 52 part-time). Social organizations: 3 local fraternities, 3 local sororities; 5% of eligible undergraduate men and 5% of eligible undergraduate women are members.

Drug and Alcohol Information

Education

On campus Drug and alcohol education/prevention programs offered for: all students, athletes/coaches. College holds an annual alcohol awareness week.

Identification of Problems

Admissions College application does not ask about prior substance abuse problems.

On campus Current students identified as chemically dependent may remain enrolled. No training program on identifying students with potential substance abuse problems. No written procedures for students and staff if substance abuse is suspected.

Support Services

On campus Private counseling.

Employee assistance Program for chemically dependent employees not available.

Disciplinary Actions

Alcohol Results of infractions of alcohol regulations (see Comparative Table of Alcohol Regulations) vary by situation.

Drugs For first-time use or possession: varies by situation—warning, probation, suspension. For subsequent use or possession: suspension. For any sale: suspension.

For More Information

Contact: Judy Hill, Dean of Students, Lincoln Memorial University, Highway 25E, Harrogate, TN 37752. Telephone: 615-869-3611 Ext. 505.

LINDENWOOD COLLEGE

St. Charles, Missouri

General Information

Independent 5-year coed college. Founded 1827. Awards B, M. Primary accreditation: regional. City setting; 100-acre campus. Total enrollment: 1,766. Faculty: 108 (48 full-time, 60 part-time).

Drug and Alcohol Information

Education

On campus Drug and alcohol education/prevention programs offered for: all students, faculty, administration; required for: athletes/coaches. Authorized group concerned with responsible drinking. College holds an annual alcohol awareness week and drug awareness week.

Identification of Problems

Admissions College application does not ask about prior substance abuse problems.

On campus Current students identified as chemically dependent may remain enrolled, and treatment may be required, depending on the circumstances. Training program on identifying students with potential substance abuse problems for: resident advisers, coaches. Written procedures for students and staff if substance abuse is suspected.

Support Services

On campus Support groups (peer counseling).

Employee assistance Program for chemically dependent employees not available. Staff working with drug/alcohol-related issues: 6 part-time.

Disciplinary Actions

Alcohol Results of infractions of alcohol regulations (see Comparative Table of Alcohol Regulations) vary by situation.

Drugs For any use, possession, or sale: varies by situation.

For More Information

Contact: Allen Schwab, Dean of the Undergraduate College, Lindenwood College, St. Charles, MO 63301. Telephone: 314-949-2000 Ext. 230.

LINFIELD COLLEGE

McMinnville, Oregon

General Information

Independent American Baptist 5-year coed college. Founded 1849. Awards B, M. Primary accreditation: regional. Small-town setting; 100-acre campus. Total enrollment: 1,283. Faculty: 150 (112 full-time, 38 part-time). Social organizations: 3 national fraternities, 1 national sorority, 1 local fraternity, 3 local sororities; 20% of eligible undergraduate men and 25% of eligible undergraduate women are members.

Drug and Alcohol Information

Education

On campus Drug and alcohol education/prevention programs offered for: all students, athletes/coaches, faculty, administration; required for: freshmen, social organization members, resident advisers. Authorized group concerned with responsible drinking. College holds an annual alcohol awareness week.

Identification of Problems

Admissions College application does not ask about prior substance abuse problems.

On campus Current students identified as chemically dependent may remain enrolled, but treatment is required. No training program on identifying students with potential substance abuse problems. Written procedures for students and staff if substance abuse is suspected.

Support Services

On campus Private counseling.

Employee assistance Program for chemically dependent employees not available.

Disciplinary Actions

Alcohol Results of infractions of alcohol regulations (see Comparative Table of Alcohol Regulations) vary by situation but can include chemical dependency assessment, counseling, warning, probation, suspension, expulsion.

Drugs For first-time use or possession: varies by situation—chemical dependency assessment, counseling, probation. For subsequent use or possession: varies by situation. For first-time sale: varies by situation—suspension, expulsion. For subsequent sale: suspension, expulsion.

For More Information

Contact: Dave Hansen, Dean of Students, Linfield College, McMinnville, OR 97128. Telephone: 503-472-3673.

LOCK HAVEN UNIVERSITY OF PENNSYLVANIA

Lock Haven, Pennsylvania

General Information

State-supported 5-year coed college. Part of State System of Higher Education. Founded 1870. Awards B, M. Primary accreditation: regional. Small-town setting; 135-acre campus. Total enrollment: 3,012. Faculty: 188 (177 full-time, 11 part-time). Social organizations: 7 national fraternities, 4 national sororities; 8% of eligible undergraduate men and 8% of eligible undergraduate women are members.

Drug and Alcohol Information

Education

On campus Drug and alcohol education/prevention programs offered for: all students, athletes/coaches, faculty, administration. Authorized group concerned with responsible drinking. College holds an annual alcohol awareness week and drug awareness week.

Identification of Problems

Admissions College application does not ask about prior substance abuse problems.

On campus Current students identified as chemically dependent may remain enrolled, but treatment is required. No training program on identifying students with potential substance abuse problems. No written procedures for students and staff if substance abuse is suspected.

Support Services

On campus Support groups (Campus Alcohol Misuse Program Service—CAMPS).

Employee assistance Program for chemically dependent employees available. Staff working with drug/alcohol-related issues: 3 part-time.

Disciplinary Actions

Alcohol Results of infractions of alcohol regulations (see Comparative Table of Alcohol Regulations) vary by situation but can include warning, probation, suspension.

Drugs For any use, possession, or sale: varies by situation.

For More Information

Contact: Timothy Susick, Associate Dean of Students, Lock Haven University of Pennsylvania, Lock Haven, PA 17745. Telephone: 717-893-2317.

LONG ISLAND UNIVERSITY, C. W. POST CAMPUS

Brookville, New York

General Information

Independent 5-year coed college. Part of Long Island University. Founded 1954. Awards A (college transfer), B, M. Primary accreditation: regional. Small-town setting; 410-acre campus. Total enrollment: 8,771. Faculty: 685 (319 full-time, 366 part-time). Social organizations: national fraternities, national sororities, local fraternities, local sororities; 10% of eligible undergraduate men and 10% of eligible undergraduate women are members.

Drug and Alcohol Information

Education

On campus Drug and alcohol education/prevention programs offered for: freshmen, resident advisers. Authorized group concerned with responsible drinking. College holds an annual alcohol awareness week.

Identification of Problems

Admissions College application does not ask about prior substance abuse problems.

On campus Current students identified as chemically dependent may remain enrolled, but treatment is required. Training program on identifying students with potential substance abuse problems for: resident advisers, administration.

Long Island University, C. W. Post Campus (continued)

Support Services

On campus Support groups, private counseling.

Employee assistance Program for chemically dependent employees not available. Staff working with drug/alcohol-related issues: 6 part-time.

Disciplinary Actions

Alcohol Results of infractions of alcohol regulations (see Comparative Table of Alcohol Regulations) include chemical dependency assessment, counseling, warning, probation, suspension.

Drugs For first-time use or possession: varies by situation. For first-time sale: chemical dependency assessment, counseling, suspension. For subsequent use, possession, or sale: chemical dependency assessment, counseling, suspension.

For More Information

Contact: W. E. Milford, Director of Student Health and Counseling, Long Island University, C. W. Post Campus, Brookville, NY 11548. Telephone: 516-299-2345.

LONG ISLAND UNIVERSITY, SOUTHAMPTON CAMPUS

Southampton, New York

General Information

Independent 5-year coed college. Part of Long Island University. Founded 1963. Awards B, M. Primary accreditation: regional. Rural setting; 110-acre campus. Total enrollment: 1,224. Faculty: 131 (77 full-time, 54 part-time).

Drug and Alcohol Information

Education

On campus Drug and alcohol education/prevention programs offered for: all students, athletes/coaches, faculty, administration; required for: freshmen, resident advisers, student leaders. Authorized group concerned with responsible drinking. College holds an annual alcohol awareness week and drug awareness week.

Identification of Problems

Admissions College application does not ask about prior substance abuse problems.

On campus Current students identified as chemically dependent may remain enrolled. Training program on identifying students with potential substance abuse problems for: resident advisers, faculty. Written procedures for students and staff if substance abuse is suspected.

Support Services

On campus AA, ACOA, private counseling, substance abuse counselor.

Employee assistance Program for chemically dependent employees available. Staff working with drug/alcohol-related issues: 1 part-time.

Disciplinary Actions

Alcohol Results of infractions of alcohol regulations (see Comparative Table of Alcohol Regulations) include chemical dependency assessment, counseling, warning, probation, suspension, expulsion.

Drugs For any use: varies by situation—chemical dependency assessment, counseling, suspension. For first-time possession: suspension. For subsequent possession: varies by situation—counseling, suspension. For any sale: expulsion.

Additional Information from the College

Long Island University, Southampton Campus is aware of a continuous need for education for faculty, staff, and students. Substance abuse is attacked at many different levels through many approaches. Denial is a problem, as is ignorance of alcohol as a drug.

For More Information

Contact: Patricia A. Medio, RN, CAC, Director of Student Health, Long Island University, Southampton Campus, Southampton, NY 11968. Telephone: 516-283-0570.

LONGWOOD COLLEGE

Farmville, Virginia

General Information

State-supported 5-year coed college. Founded 1839. Awards B, M. Primary accreditation: regional. Small-town setting; 158-acre campus. Total enrollment: 2,955. Faculty: 184 (139 full-time, 45 part-time). Social organizations: 10 national fraternities, 11 national sororities; 30% of eligible undergraduate men and 30% of eligible undergraduate women are members.

Drug and Alcohol Information

Education

On campus Drug and alcohol education/prevention programs offered for: all students, required for: freshmen, resident advisers, alcohol-related disciplinary cases. Bacchus chapter: 12 members. College holds an annual alcohol awareness week and drug awareness week.

Identification of Problems

Admissions College application does not ask about prior substance abuse problems.

On campus Current students identified as chemically dependent may remain enrolled, but treatment is required. Training program on identifying students with potential substance abuse problems for: resident advisers, Judicial Board members. Written procedures for students and staff if substance abuse is suspected.

Support Services

On campus AA, NA, Al-Anon, ACOA, support groups, private counseling, Counseling Center.

Employee assistance Program for chemically dependent employees available. Staff working with drug/alcohol-related issues: 8 part-time.

Disciplinary Actions

Alcohol Results of infractions of alcohol regulations (see Comparative Table of Alcohol Regulations) vary by situation but can include probation, suspension.

Drugs For first-time use, possession, or sale: suspension. For subsequent use, possession, or sale: suspension, expulsion.

Additional Information from the College

Longwood is committed to education and prevention programs on substance abuse. Longwood is also committed to providing counseling and referral services to students who desire to discuss substance abuse problems without fear of reprisal.

For More Information

Contact: Joseph C. McGill, Director of Student Services, Longwood College, Farmville, VA 23901. Telephone: 804-392-9201.

LORAS COLLEGE

Dubuque, Iowa

General Information

Independent Roman Catholic 5-year coed college. Founded 1839. Awards A (college transfer), B, M. Primary accreditation: regional. City setting; 70-acre campus. Total enrollment: 2,004. Faculty: 156 (121 full-time, 35 part-time). Social organizations: 2 national fraternities, 4 local fraternities, 2 local sororities; 15% of eligible undergraduate men and 5% of eligible undergraduate women are members.

Drug and Alcohol Information

Education

On campus Drug and alcohol education/prevention programs offered for: all students; required for: athletes/coaches. College holds an annual alcohol awareness week and drug awareness week.

Identification of Problems

Admissions College application does not ask about prior substance abuse problems.

On campus Current students identified as chemically dependent may remain enrolled. Whether treatment is required varies from one case to another. Training program on identifying students with potential substance abuse problems for: resident advisers, coaches. Written procedures for students and staff if substance abuse is suspected.

Support Services

On campus AA, Al-Anon, ACOA, private counseling.

Employee assistance Program for chemically dependent employees not available. Staff working with drug/alcohol-related issues: 1 full-time and 8 part-time.

Disciplinary Actions

Alcohol Results of infractions of alcohol regulations (see Comparative Table of Alcohol Regulations) vary by situation but can include chemical dependency assessment, counseling, warning, probation, suspension, expulsion.

Drugs For first-time use: varies by situation—chemical dependency assessment, counseling, warning. For subsequent use: chemical dependency assessment, counseling, probation. For first-time possession: varies by situation—chemical dependency assessment. For subsequent possession: varies by situation—probation. For any sale: expulsion.

For More Information

Contact: Michael Hager, Coordinator, Alcohol and Drug Education, Loras College, Dubuque, IA 52004-0178. Telephone: 319-588-7203.

LOUISIANA COLLEGE

Pineville, Louisiana

General Information

Independent Southern Baptist 4-year coed college. Founded 1906. Awards A (college transfer and terminal), B. Primary accreditation: regional. Small-town setting; 80-acre campus. Total enrollment: 1,017. Faculty: 81 (59 full-time, 22 part-time). Social organizations: 2 local fraternities, 3 local sororities; 10% of eligible undergraduate men and 20% of eligible undergraduate women are members.

Drug and Alcohol Information

Education

On campus Drug and alcohol education/prevention programs offered for: all students; required for: athletes/coaches. College holds an annual alcohol awareness week and drug awareness week.

Identification of Problems

Admissions College application does not ask about prior substance abuse problems.

On campus Current students identified as chemically dependent may or may not remain enrolled, depending on the situation. No training program on identifying students with potential substance abuse problems. No written procedures for students and staff if substance abuse is suspected.

Support Services

On campus Private counseling, referrals.

Employee assistance Program for chemically dependent employees not available. Staff working with drug/alcohol-related issues: 4 part-time.

Disciplinary Actions

Alcohol Results of infractions of alcohol regulations (see Comparative Table of Alcohol Regulations) vary by situation but can include chemical dependency assessment, counseling, warning, probation, suspension, expulsion.

Drugs For first-time use or possession: varies by situation. For subsequent use or possession: expulsion. For any sale: expulsion.

For More Information

Contact: Wade M. Tyler, Director of Counseling and Orientation, Louisiana College, 1140 College Dr., Pineville, LA 71359. Telephone: 318-487-7140.

LOUISIANA STATE UNIVERSITY IN SHREVEPORT

Shreveport, Louisiana

General Information

State-supported 5-year coed college. Part of Louisiana State University System. Founded 1965. Awards B, M. Primary accreditation: regional. City setting; 200-acre campus. Total enrollment: 4,499. Faculty: 218 (170 full-time, 48 part-time). Social organizations: 4 national fraternities, 4 national sororities; 5% of eligible undergraduate men and 5% of eligible undergraduate women are members.

Drug and Alcohol Information

Education

On campus Drug and alcohol education/prevention programs offered for: all students, faculty, administration, staff.

Support Services

On campus Private counseling, referral.

Louisiana State University in Shreveport (continued)

Employee assistance Program for chemically dependent employees available.

Additional Information from the College

The School of Medicine at Louisiana State University in Shreveport offers diagnosis and treatment for substance abuse problems, as well as referral to off-campus facilities.

For More Information

Contact: Dr. Robert F. Dyer, Vice Chancellor for Academic Affairs and Dean, Louisiana State University Medical Center, Suite 1510, 1440 Canal St., New Orleans, LA 70112-2784. Telephone: 504-568-4800.

LOUISIANA STATE UNIVERSITY MEDICAL CENTER

New Orleans, Louisiana

General Information

State-supported comprehensive coed institution. Part of Louisiana State University System. Founded 1931. Awards A (terminal), B, M, D. Primary accreditation: regional. Metropolitan setting. Total enrollment: 2,600.

Drug and Alcohol Information

Education

On campus Drug and alcohol education/prevention programs offered for: all students, faculty, administration, staff.

Support Services

On campus Private counseling, referral.

Employee assistance Program for chemically dependent employees available.

Additional Information from the College

An extensive amount of educational material that deals with substance abuse is incorporated into the curricula of the Louisiana State University Medical Center's schools. There are also workshops, task forces, and committees that address these problems.

For More Information

Contact: Dr. Robert F. Dyer, Vice Chancellor for Academic Affairs and Dean, Louisiana State University Medical Center, Suite 1510, 1440 Canal St., New Orleans, LA 70112-2784. Telephone: 504-568-4800.

LOYOLA COLLEGE

Baltimore, Maryland

General Information

Independent Roman Catholic 5-year coed college. Founded 1852. Awards B, M. Primary accreditation: regional. Metropolitan setting; 65-acre campus. Total enrollment: 5,650. Faculty: 376 (198 full-time, 178 part-time).

Drug and Alcohol Information

Education

On campus Drug and alcohol education/prevention programs offered for: all students, athletes/coaches. Authorized group concerned with responsible drinking. College holds an annual alcohol awareness week.

Identification of Problems

Admissions College application does not ask about prior substance abuse problems.

On campus Current students identified as chemically dependent may remain enrolled. No training program on identifying students with potential substance abuse problems. No written procedures for students and staff if substance abuse is suspected.

Support Services

On campus Support groups.

Employee assistance Program for chemically dependent employees not available. Staff working with drug/alcohol-related issues: 1 part-time.

Disciplinary Actions

Alcohol Results of infractions of alcohol regulations (see Comparative Table of Alcohol Regulations) include counseling, warning, probation, suspension, expulsion.

Drugs For first-time use or possession: counseling, fine. For subsequent use or possession: expulsion. For any sale: expulsion.

For More Information

Contact: Jim Henschen, Substance Abuse Counselor, Loyola College, 4501 N. Charles St., Baltimore, MD 21210. Telephone: 301-532-5109.

LOYOLA MARYMOUNT UNIVERSITY

Los Angeles, California

General Information

Independent Roman Catholic 5-year coed college. Founded 1911. Awards B, M, D. Primary accreditation: regional. Metropolitan setting; 130-acre campus. Total enrollment: 4,869. Faculty: 386 (241 full-time, 145 part-time). Social organizations: 7 national fraternities, 3 national sororities, 1 local fraternity, 1 local sorority; 5% of eligible undergraduate men and 5% of eligible undergraduate women are members.

Drug and Alcohol Information

Education

On campus Drug and alcohol education/prevention programs offered for: all students, athletes/coaches. Authorized group concerned with responsible drinking. College holds an annual alcohol awareness week.

Identification of Problems

Admissions College application does not ask about prior substance abuse problems.

On campus Current students identified as chemically dependent may remain enrolled, but treatment is required. Training program on identifying students with potential substance abuse problems for: resident advisers, administration. No written procedures for students and staff if substance abuse is suspected.

Support Services

On campus AA, ACOA, private counseling.

Employee assistance Program for chemically dependent employees available. Staff working with drug/alcohol-related issues: 1 full-time and 9 part-time.

Disciplinary Actions

Alcohol Results of infractions of alcohol regulations (see Comparative Table of Alcohol Regulations) vary by situation but can include chemical dependency assessment, counseling, warning, probation.

Drugs For any use: varies by situation. For first-time possession: varies by situation—suspension. For subsequent possession: varies by situation. For first-time sale: varies by situation—expulsion. For subsequent sale: expulsion.

For More Information

Contact: Lane Bove, Vice President for Student Affairs, Loyola Marymount University, Loyola Blvd. at W. 80th St., Los Angeles, CA 90045. Telephone: 213-642-2885.

LOYOLA UNIVERSITY, NEW ORLEANS

New Orleans, Louisiana

General Information

Independent Roman Catholic 5-year coed college. Founded 1912. Awards B, M, D. Primary accreditation: regional. Metropolitan setting; 19-acre campus. Total enrollment: 4,952. Faculty: 340 (202 full-time, 138 part-time). Social organizations: 3 national fraternities, 4 national sororities, 2 local fraternities; 15% of eligible undergraduate men and 31% of eligible undergraduate women are members.

Drug and Alcohol Information

Education

On campus Drug and alcohol education/prevention programs offered for: all students. Bacchus chapter: 15 members. College holds an annual alcohol awareness week and drug awareness week.

Identification of Problems

Admissions College application does not ask about prior substance abuse problems.

On campus Current students identified as chemically dependent may remain enrolled, but treatment is required. Training program on identifying students with potential substance abuse problems for: any member of the University community who has relevant contact with students. Written procedures for students and staff if substance abuse is suspected.

Support Services

On campus AA, NA, Al-Anon, ACOA, private counseling.

Employee assistance Program for chemically dependent employees not available. Staff working with drug/alcohol-related issues: 75 part-time.

Disciplinary Actions

Alcohol Results of infractions of alcohol regulations (see Comparative Table of Alcohol Regulations) include chemical dependency assessment, counseling, warning, probation, suspension, expulsion.

Drugs For first-time use, possession, or sale: varies by situation. For subsequent use, possession, or sale: expulsion.

For More Information

Contact: Robert J. Miller, Staff Psychologist, Loyola University, New Orleans, 6363 St. Charles Ave., New Orleans, LA 70118. Telephone: 504-865-3835.

LUBBOCK CHRISTIAN UNIVERSITY

Lubbock, Texas

General Information

Independent 4-year coed college, affiliated with Church of Christ. Founded 1957. Awards A (college transfer and terminal), B. Primary accreditation: regional. City setting; 120-acre campus. Total enrollment: 1,079. Faculty: 110 (60 full-time, 50 part-time). Social organizations: 10 social clubs; 50% of eligible undergraduate men and 50% of eligible undergraduate women are members.

Drug and Alcohol Information

Education

On campus Drug and alcohol education/prevention programs offered for: all students; required for: athletes/coaches.

Identification of Problems

Admissions College application does not ask about prior substance abuse problems.

On campus Current students identified as chemically dependent may remain enrolled, but treatment is required. No training program on identifying students with potential substance abuse problems. Written procedures for students and staff if substance abuse is suspected.

Support Services

On campus No support services on campus.

Off campus AA, NA, support groups, private counseling.

Employee assistance Program for chemically dependent employees not available.

Disciplinary Actions

Alcohol Results of infractions of alcohol regulations (see Comparative Table of Alcohol Regulations) include counseling, warning, probation, suspension, expulsion.

Drugs For first-time use or possession: varies by situation. For first-time sale: suspension, expulsion. For subsequent use, possession, or sale: expulsion.

For More Information

Contact: Steve Eckman, Vice President for Student Services, Lubbock Christian University, 5601 W. 19th St., Lubbock, TX 79407. Telephone: 806-792-3221.

LUTHER COLLEGE

Decorah, Iowa

General Information

Independent 4-year coed college, affiliated with Evangelical Lutheran Church in America. Founded 1861. Awards B. Primary accreditation: regional. Small-town setting; 800-acre campus. Total enrollment: 2,214. Faculty: 183 (145 full-time, 38 part-time). Social organizations: 1 national fraternity, 7 local fraternities, 8 local sororities; 30% of eligible undergraduate men and 25% of eligible undergraduate women are members.

Drug and Alcohol Information

Education

On campus Drug and alcohol education/prevention programs offered for: all students, athletes/coaches, faculty, administration. Authorized group concerned with

Luther College (continued)

responsible drinking. College holds an annual alcohol awareness week and drug awareness week.

Identification of Problems

Admissions College application question about prior substance abuse problems is used for counseling and referral, if student is admitted.

On campus Current students identified as chemically dependent may remain enrolled, but treatment is required. Training program on identifying students with potential substance abuse problems for: resident advisers, administration. Written procedures for students and staff if substance abuse is suspected.

Support Services

On campus AA, Al-Anon, ACOA, private counseling.

Employee assistance Program for chemically dependent employees available. Staff working with drug/alcohol-related issues: 9 part-time.

Disciplinary Actions

Alcohol Results of infractions of alcohol regulations (see Comparative Table of Alcohol Regulations) vary by situation but can include chemical dependency assessment, counseling, warning, probation, suspension, expulsion.

Drugs For first-time use or possession: varies by situation—probation. For subsequent use or possession: varies by situation—probation, suspension. For first-time sale: probation, suspension. For subsequent sale: expulsion.

For More Information

Contact: Orlin Mandsager, Vice President and Dean for Student Life, Luther College, Decorah, IA 52101. Telephone: 319-387-1020.

LYCOMING COLLEGE

Williamsport, Pennsylvania

General Information

Independent United Methodist 4-year coed college. Founded 1812. Awards B. Primary accreditation: regional. Small-town setting; 32-acre campus. Total enrollment: 1,065. Faculty: 98 (73 full-time, 25 part-time). Social organizations: 6 national fraternities, 3 local sororities; 20% of eligible undergraduate men and 20% of eligible undergraduate women are members.

Drug and Alcohol Information

Education

On campus Drug and alcohol education/prevention programs offered for: all students, athletes/coaches, faculty, administration; required for freshmen, social organization members, resident advisers. Authorized group concerned with responsible drinking. College holds an annual alcohol awareness week and drug awareness week.

Identification of Problems

Admissions College application does not ask about prior substance abuse problems.

On campus Current students identified as chemically dependent may remain enrolled, but treatment is required. Training program on identifying students with potential substance abuse problems for: resident advisers, coaches, Greek officers, faculty, administration. Written procedures for students and staff if substance abuse is suspected.

Support Services

On campus Private counseling.

Employee assistance Program for chemically dependent employees not available. Staff working with drug/alcohol-related issues: 8 part-time.

Disciplinary Actions

Alcohol Results of infractions of alcohol regulations (see Comparative Table of Alcohol Regulations) vary by situation but can include probation, fine, completion of alcohol education program. Comments: Group sanctions range from loss of social events to loss of special housing privileges.

Drugs For any use or possession: suspension. For first-time sale: expulsion.

For More Information

Contact: R. Michael O'Brien, Dean of Student Services, Lycoming College, Williamsport, PA 17701. Telephone: 717-321-4039.

LYNDON STATE COLLEGE

Lyndonville, Vermont

General Information

State-supported 5-year coed college. Part of Vermont State Colleges System. Founded 1911. Awards A (college transfer and terminal), B, M. Primary accreditation: regional. Rural setting; 175-acre campus. Total enrollment: 996. Faculty: 85 (55 full-time, 30 part-time). Social organizations: 1 national fraternity, 1 national sorority, 1 local fraternity, 1 local sorority.

Drug and Alcohol Information

Education

On campus Drug and alcohol education/prevention programs offered for: all students, athletes/coaches. College holds an annual alcohol awareness week and drug awareness week.

Identification of Problems

Admissions College application does not ask about prior substance abuse problems.

On campus Training program on identifying students with potential substance abuse problems for: resident advisers. Written procedures for students and staff if substance abuse is suspected.

Support Services

On campus Al-Anon, ACOA.

Employee assistance Program for chemically dependent employees not available. Staff working with drug/alcohol-related issues: 1 part-time.

Disciplinary Actions

Alcohol Results of infractions of alcohol regulations (see Comparative Table of Alcohol Regulations) vary by situation but can include counseling, warning, probation, suspension, expulsion.

Drugs For first-time use: warning, probation. For subsequent use: suspension, expulsion. For first-time possession: probation, suspension. For subsequent possession: expulsion. For any sale: expulsion.

For More Information

Contact: David Kanell, Director of Housing, Lyndon State College, Lyndonville, VT 05851. Telephone: 802-626-9371.

MACALESTER COLLEGE

St. Paul, Minnesota

General Information

Independent Presbyterian 4-year coed college. Founded 1874. Awards B. Primary accreditation: regional. Metropolitan setting; 55-acre campus. Total enrollment: 1,847. Faculty: 214 (127 full-time, 87 part-time).

Drug and Alcohol Information

Education

On campus Drug and alcohol education/prevention programs offered for: all students. Authorized group concerned with responsible drinking. College holds an annual alcohol awareness week and drug awareness week.

Identification of Problems

Admissions College application does not ask about prior substance abuse problems.

On campus Current students identified as chemically dependent may remain enrolled, but treatment is required. Training program on identifying students with potential substance abuse problems for: resident advisers, staff. No written procedures for students and staff if substance abuse is suspected.

Support Services

On campus AA, Al-Anon, ACOA, support groups, private counseling.

Employee assistance Program for chemically dependent employees available. Staff working with drug/alcohol-related issues: 6 part-time.

Disciplinary Actions

Alcohol Results of infractions of alcohol regulations (see Comparative Table of Alcohol Regulations) vary by situation.

Drugs For any use or possession: varies by situation—chemical dependency assessment, counseling. For any sale: expulsion.

For More Information

Contact: Mary Ackerman, Dean, Macalester College, 1600 Grand Ave., St. Paul, MN 55105. Telephone: 612-696-6220.

MACMURRAY COLLEGE

Jacksonville, Illinois

General Information

Independent United Methodist 4-year coed college. Founded 1846. Awards A (college transfer), B. Primary accreditation: regional. Small-town setting; 60-acre campus. Total enrollment: 650. Faculty: 74 (56 full-time, 18 part-time). Social organization: 1 local fraternity.

Drug and Alcohol Information

Education

On campus Drug and alcohol education/prevention programs offered for: all students.

Identification of Problems

Admissions College application does not ask about prior substance abuse problems.

On campus Current students identified as chemically dependent may remain enrolled, but treatment is required. Training program on identifying students with potential substance abuse problems for: resident advisers. No written procedures for students and staff if substance abuse is suspected.

Support Services

On campus ACOA, support groups, private counseling. Staff working with drug/alcohol-related issues: 4 part-time.

Disciplinary Actions

Alcohol Results of infractions of alcohol regulations (see Comparative Table of Alcohol Regulations) vary by situation.

Drugs For first-time use or possession: probation. For subsequent use or possession: suspension. For first-time sale: suspension. For subsequent sale: expulsion.

For More Information

Contact: D. Guffy, Dean of Student Life, MacMurray College, E. College Ave., Jacksonville, IL 62650. Telephone: 217-245-6151.

MADONNA COLLEGE

Livonia, Michigan

General Information

Independent Roman Catholic 5-year coed college. Founded 1947. Awards A (college transfer and terminal), B, M. Primary accreditation: regional. City setting; 49-acre campus. Total enrollment: 3,992. Social organization: 1 national sorority; 1% of eligible undergraduate women are members.

Drug and Alcohol Information

Education

On campus Drug and alcohol education/prevention programs offered for: all students, athletes/coaches, faculty, administration.

Identification of Problems

Admissions College application does not ask about prior substance abuse problems.

On campus Current students identified as chemically dependent may remain enrolled, but treatment is required. No training program on identifying students with potential substance abuse problems. Written procedures for students and staff if substance abuse is suspected.

Support Services

On campus Private counseling, referrals.

Employee assistance Program for chemically dependent employees not available. Staff working with drug/alcohol-related issues: 10 part-time.

Disciplinary Actions

Alcohol Results of infractions of alcohol regulations (see Comparative Table of Alcohol Regulations) include chemical dependency assessment, counseling, warning, probation, suspension, expulsion.

Drugs For first-time use, possession, or sale: counseling. For subsequent use, possession, or sale: suspension.

For More Information

Contact: Craig Prether, Director of Student Activities, Madonna College, 36600 Schoolcraft Road, Livonia, MI 48150. Telephone: 313-591-5056.

MALONE COLLEGE

Canton, Ohio

General Information

Independent 4-year coed college, affiliated with Evangelical Friends Alliance. Founded 1892. Awards A (terminal), B. Primary accreditation: regional. City setting; 78-acre campus. Total enrollment: 1,325. Faculty: 91 (47 full-time, 44 part-time).

Drug and Alcohol Information

Education

On campus Drug and alcohol education/prevention programs offered for: resident advisers, student leaders.

Identification of Problems

Admissions College application question about prior substance abuse problems is used for counseling and referral, if student is admitted; in the admissions decision.

On campus Current students identified as chemically dependent may not remain enrolled. Training program on identifying students with potential substance abuse problems for: resident advisers. No written procedures for students and staff if substance abuse is suspected.

Support Services

On campus Private counseling.

Employee assistance Program for chemically dependent employees not available.

Disciplinary Actions

Alcohol Results of infractions of alcohol regulations (see Comparative Table of Alcohol Regulations) vary by situation but can include chemical dependency assessment, counseling, probation, suspension, expulsion.

Drugs For first-time use or possession: chemical dependency assessment, counseling, suspension. For subsequent use or possession: suspension. For any sale: expulsion.

For More Information

Contact: Jim Prout, Dean of Students, Malone College, 515 25th St., NW, Canton, OH 44709. Telephone: 216-438-9388.

MANCHESTER COLLEGE

North Manchester, Indiana

General Information

Independent 5-year coed college, affiliated with Church of the Brethren. Founded 1889. Awards A (college transfer and terminal), B, M. Primary accreditation: regional. Small-town setting; 200-acre campus. Total enrollment: 1,021. Faculty: 90 (79 full-time, 11 part-time).

Drug and Alcohol Information

Education

On campus Drug and alcohol education/prevention programs offered for: all students, faculty, administration; required for: freshmen, athletes/coaches, resident advisers. Authorized group concerned with responsible drinking. College holds an annual alcohol awareness week.

Identification of Problems

Admissions College application does not ask about prior substance abuse problems.

On campus Current students identified as chemically dependent may remain enrolled, but treatment is required. Training program on identifying students with potential substance abuse problems for: resident advisers, Student Affairs personnel. Written procedures for students and staff if substance abuse is suspected.

Support Services

On campus ACOA, support groups, private counseling.

Employee assistance Program for chemically dependent employees available.

Disciplinary Actions

Alcohol Results of infractions of alcohol regulations (see Comparative Table of Alcohol Regulations) vary by situation but can include chemical dependency assessment, counseling, warning, probation, suspension.

Drugs For first-time use or possession: varies by situation. For subsequent use: chemical dependency assessment, counseling, suspension. For subsequent possession: chemical dependency assessment, suspension. For first-time sale: varies by situation—suspension, expulsion. For subsequent sale: expulsion.

For More Information

Contact: Dr. Stanley B. Escott, Dean of Student Development, Manchester College, North Manchester, IN 46962. Telephone: 219-982-2141.

MANHATTAN COLLEGE

Riverdale, New York

General Information

Independent 5-year coed college. Founded 1853. Awards A (college transfer and terminal), B, M. Primary accreditation: regional. Metropolitan setting; 46-acre campus. Total enrollment: 4,341. Faculty: 410 (269 full-time, 141 part-time). Social organizations: 4 national fraternities, 1 national sorority, 2 local fraternities; 5% of eligible undergraduate men and 5% of eligible undergraduate women are members.

Drug and Alcohol Information

Education

On campus Drug and alcohol education/prevention programs offered for: all students; required for: resident advisers. Authorized group concerned with responsible drinking. College holds an annual alcohol awareness week.

Identification of Problems

Admissions College application does not ask about prior substance abuse problems.

On campus Current students identified as chemically dependent may remain enrolled, but treatment is required. Training program on identifying students with potential substance abuse problems for: resident advisers. Written procedures for students and staff if substance abuse is suspected.

Support Services

On campus Support groups (alcohol support group, campus ministry), private counseling.

Employee assistance Program for chemically dependent employees not available. Staff working with drug/alcohol-related issues: 3 part-time.

Disciplinary Actions

Alcohol Results of infractions of alcohol regulations (see

Comparative Table of Alcohol Regulations) include counseling, warning, probation, suspension, expulsion, fine.

Drugs For first-time use or possession: counseling, suspension. For subsequent use or possession: varies by situation. For any sale: expulsion.

For More Information

Contact: Dr. Cathy L. Sales, Chairperson, Alcohol and Drug Committee, Counseling Center, Manhattan College, Manhattan College Pky., Riverdale, NY 10471. Telephone: 914-920-0395.

MANHATTAN SCHOOL OF MUSIC

New York, New York

General Information

Independent 5-year specialized coed college. Founded 1917. Awards B, M, D. Primary accreditation: regional. Metropolitan setting; 1-acre campus. Total enrollment: 787. Faculty: 180 (25 full-time, 155 part-time).

Drug and Alcohol Information

Education

On campus Drug and alcohol education/prevention programs offered for: all students. Authorized group concerned with responsible drinking.

Identification of Problems

Admissions College application does not ask about prior substance abuse problems.

On campus Current students identified as chemically dependent may remain enrolled, but treatment is required. No training program on identifying students with potential substance abuse problems. No written procedures for students and staff if substance abuse is suspected.

Support Services

On campus Private counseling.

Employee assistance Program for chemically dependent employees not available.

Disciplinary Actions

Alcohol Results of infractions of alcohol regulations (see Comparative Table of Alcohol Regulations) include counseling, warning, probation.

Drugs For first-time use: varies by situation—chemical dependency assessment, counseling. For first-time possession or sale: varies by situation. For subsequent possession or sale: varies by situation.

For More Information

Contact: Richard A. Gortney, Director of Student Services, Manhattan School of Music, 120 Claremont Ave., New York, NY 10027. Telephone: 212-749-2802 Ext. 524.

MANHATTANVILLE COLLEGE

Purchase, New York

General Information

Independent 5-year coed college. Founded 1841. Awards B, M. Primary accreditation: regional. Small-town setting; 120-acre campus. Total enrollment: 1,500. Faculty: 130 (85 full-time, 45 part-time).

Drug and Alcohol Information

Education

On campus Drug and alcohol education/prevention programs offered for: all students. College holds an annual alcohol awareness week and drug awareness week.

Identification of Problems

Admissions College application does not ask about prior substance abuse problems.

On campus Current students identified as chemically dependent may remain enrolled, but treatment is required. Training program on identifying students with potential substance abuse problems for: resident advisers. No written procedures for students and staff if substance abuse is suspected.

Support Services

On campus ACOA, private counseling.

Employee assistance Program for chemically dependent employees not available.

Disciplinary Actions

Alcohol Results of infractions of alcohol regulations (see Comparative Table of Alcohol Regulations) vary by situation but can include counseling, warning, probation, suspension, expulsion.

Drugs For any use, possession, or sale: varies by situation.

For More Information

Contact: Patricia McCaffrey, Director of Health Services, Manhattanville College, 125 Purchase St., Purchase, NY 10577. Telephone: 914-694-2200.

MANKATO STATE UNIVERSITY

Mankato, Minnesota

General Information

State-supported 5-year coed college. Part of Minnesota State University System. Founded 1867. Awards A (college transfer and terminal), B, M. Primary accreditation: regional. Small-town setting; 400-acre campus. Total enrollment: 14,206. Faculty: 680 (580 full-time, 100 part-time). Social organizations: 4 national fraternities, 2 national sororities; 15% of eligible undergraduate men and 13% of eligible undergraduate women are members.

Drug and Alcohol Information

Education

On campus Drug and alcohol education/prevention programs offered for: all students, athletes/coaches, faculty, administration. Authorized group concerned with responsible drinking. College holds an annual alcohol awareness week.

Identification of Problems

Admissions College application does not ask about prior substance abuse problems.

On campus Current students identified as chemically dependent may remain enrolled. Training program on identifying students with potential substance abuse problems for: resident advisers, coaches, Greek officers, faculty, administration. No written procedures for students and staff if substance abuse is suspected.

Mankato State University (continued)

Support Services

On campus AA, NA, Al-Anon, ACOA, private counseling.

Employee assistance Program for chemically dependent employees available. Staff working with drug/alcohol-related issues: 1 full-time.

Disciplinary Actions

Alcohol Results of infractions of alcohol regulations (see Comparative Table of Alcohol Regulations) vary by situation.

Drugs For any use, possession, or sale: varies by situation.

For More Information

Contact: Deb Wood, Alcohol/Drug Education Coordinator, Mankato State University, Box 21, Mankato, MN 56002. Telephone: 507-389-6276.

MANSFIELD UNIVERSITY OF PENNSYLVANIA

Mansfield, Pennsylvania

General Information

State-supported 5-year coed college. Part of State System of Higher Education. Founded 1857. Awards A (terminal), B, M. Primary accreditation: regional. Rural setting; 175-acre campus. Total enrollment: 2,980. Faculty: 185 (177 full-time, 8 part-time). Social organizations: 5 national fraternities, 4 national sororities, 2 local fraternities; 20% of eligible undergraduate men and 20% of eligible undergraduate women are members.

Drug and Alcohol Information

Education

On campus Drug and alcohol education/prevention programs offered for: all students, athletes/coaches, faculty, administration. Authorized group concerned with responsible drinking. College holds an annual alcohol awareness week and drug awareness week.

Identification of Problems

Admissions College application does not ask about prior substance abuse problems.

On campus Current students identified as chemically dependent may remain enrolled, but treatment is required. No training program on identifying students with potential substance abuse problems. Written procedures for students and staff if substance abuse is suspected.

Support Services

On campus Counseling Center.

Employee assistance Program for chemically dependent employees available. Staff working with drug/alcohol-related issues: 1 part-time.

Disciplinary Actions

Alcohol Results of infractions of alcohol regulations (see Comparative Table of Alcohol Regulations) vary by situation but can include chemical dependency assessment, counseling, warning, probation, suspension, expulsion, arrest.

Drugs For first-time use or possession: varies by situation. For subsequent use or possession: varies by situation. For subsequent sale: varies by situation-suspension, expulsion, arrest.

For More Information

Contact: Carmen Bianco, Associate Director of Residence Life, Mansfield University of Pennsylvania, 120 Pinecrest Manor, Mansfield, PA 16933. Telephone: 717-662-4933.

MARIAN COLLEGE

Indianapolis, Indiana

General Information

Independent Roman Catholic 4-year coed college. Founded 1851. Awards A (college transfer and terminal), B. Primary accreditation: regional. Metropolitan setting; 114-acre campus. Total enrollment: 1,215. Faculty: 123 (68 full-time, 55 part-time).

Drug and Alcohol Information

Education

On campus Drug and alcohol education/prevention programs offered for: all students, faculty, administration; required for: resident advisers. Authorized group concerned with responsible drinking. College holds an annual alcohol awareness week.

Identification of Problems

Admissions College application does not ask about prior substance abuse problems.

On campus Current students identified as chemically dependent may remain enrolled, but treatment is required. Training program on identifying students with potential substance abuse problems for: resident advisers. Written procedures for students and staff if substance abuse is suspected.

Support Services

On campus Al-Anon.

Employee assistance Program for chemically dependent employees not available. Staff working with drug/alcohol-related issues: 2 part-time.

Disciplinary Actions

Alcohol Results of infractions of alcohol regulations (see Comparative Table of Alcohol Regulations) include chemical dependency assessment, suspension, assigned work hours.

Drugs For first-time use or possession: varies by situation. For subsequent use or possession: chemical dependency assessment. For any sale: varies by situation.

For More Information

Contact: Dr. William H. Woodman, Dean for Student Affairs, Marian College, 3200 Cold Spring Rd., Indianapolis, IN 46222. Telephone: 317-929-0240.

MARIAN COLLEGE OF FOND DU LAC

Fond du Lac, Wisconsin

General Information

Independent Roman Catholic 5-year coed college. Founded 1936. Awards B, M. Primary accreditation: regional. Small-town setting; 50-acre campus. Total enrollment: 859. Faculty: 81 (49 full-time, 32 part-time).

Drug and Alcohol Information

Education

On campus Drug and alcohol education/prevention programs offered for: all students, athletes/coaches, faculty, administration. Authorized group concerned with responsible drinking. College holds an annual alcohol awareness week and drug awareness week.

Identification of Problems

Admissions College application does not ask about prior substance abuse problems.

On campus Current students identified as chemically dependent may remain enrolled, but treatment is required if the dependency is causing problems. Training program on identifying students with potential substance abuse problems for: resident advisers, coaches, faculty, administration. Written procedures for students and staff if substance abuse is suspected.

Support Services

On campus Referrals.

Employee assistance Program for chemically dependent employees available. Staff working with drug/alcohol-related issues: 10 part-time.

Disciplinary Actions

Alcohol Results of infractions of alcohol regulations (see Comparative Table of Alcohol Regulations) vary by situation.

Drugs For first-time use or possession: probation. For subsequent use or possession: varies by situation. For any sale: expulsion.

For More Information

Contact: William P. Rhudy, Vice President for Student Affairs, Marian College of Fond du Lac, 45 S. National Ave., Fond du Lac, WI 54935. Telephone: 414-923-7600.

MARIETTA COLLEGE

Marietta, Ohio

General Information

Independent 5-year coed college. Founded 1835. Awards B, M. Primary accreditation: regional. Small-town setting; 60-acre campus. Total enrollment: 1,339. Faculty: 115 (98 full-time, 17 part-time). Social organizations: 7 national fraternities, 4 national sororities; 25% of eligible undergraduate men and 40% of eligible undergraduate women are members.

Drug and Alcohol Information

Education

On campus Drug and alcohol education/prevention programs offered for: all students. Bacchus chapter: 20 members. College holds an annual alcohol awareness week.

Identification of Problems

Admissions College application does not ask about prior substance abuse problems.

On campus Current students identified as chemically dependent may remain enrolled, but treatment is required. Training program on identifying students with potential substance abuse problems for: resident advisers, coaches, administration. Written procedures for students and staff if substance abuse is suspected.

Support Services

On campus AA, private counseling.

Employee assistance Program for chemically dependent employees available. Staff working with drug/alcohol-related issues: 2 part-time.

Disciplinary Actions

Alcohol Results of infractions of alcohol regulations (see Comparative Table of Alcohol Regulations) include counseling, probation, fine.

Drugs For first-time use or possession: counseling, probation. For subsequent use or possession: suspension. For first-time sale: suspension. For subsequent sale: expulsion.

For More Information

Contact: Dr. Steve Markwood, Dean of Students, Marietta College, Marietta, OH 45750. Telephone: 614-374-4736.

MARS HILL COLLEGE

Mars Hill, North Carolina

General Information

Independent Baptist 4-year coed college. Founded 1856. Awards B. Primary accreditation: regional. Small-town setting; 180-acre campus. Total enrollment: 1,344. Faculty: 89 (77 full-time, 12 part-time). Social organizations: 3 national fraternities, 2 national sororities, 3 local fraternities, 2 local sororities; 10% of eligible undergraduate men and 5% of eligible undergraduate women are members.

Drug and Alcohol Information

Education

On campus Drug and alcohol education/prevention programs offered for: all students; required for: social organization members, athletes/coaches.

Identification of Problems

Admissions College application does not ask about prior substance abuse problems.

On campus Current students identified as chemically dependent may remain enrolled, but treatment is required if the student's academic or social behavior is affected by the dependency. Training program on identifying students with potential substance abuse problems for: resident advisers. Written procedures for students and staff if substance abuse is suspected.

Support Services

On campus Al-Anon, ACOA, private counseling.

Employee assistance Program for chemically dependent employees not available. Staff working with drug/alcohol-related issues: 2 part-time.

Disciplinary Actions

Alcohol Results of infractions of alcohol regulations (see Comparative Table of Alcohol Regulations) vary by situation but can include counseling, warning, fines, work.

Drugs For first-time use or possession: suspension. For subsequent use or possession: expulsion. For first-time sale: expulsion.

For More Information

Contact: Merry Burgess, Dean of Students, or Nancy Harmon, Director of Counseling, Student Development Office, Mars Hill College, Mars Hill, NC 28754. Telephone: 704-689-1121 or 1196.

MARTIN CENTER COLLEGE

Indianapolis, Indiana

General Information

Independent 4-year coed college. Founded 1977. Awards B. Primary accreditation: regional. Metropolitan setting; 5-acre campus. Total enrollment: 340. Faculty: 32 (15 full-time, 17 part-time).

Drug and Alcohol Information

Education

On campus Drug and alcohol education/prevention programs offered for: all students.

Identification of Problems

Admissions College application does not ask about prior substance abuse problems.

On campus Current students identified as chemically dependent may remain enrolled, but treatment is required. Training program on identifying students with potential substance abuse problems for: everyone in the community. Written procedures for students and staff if substance abuse is suspected.

Support Services

On campus AA, NA, Al-Anon, ACOA, support groups, private counseling, Counseling Center.

Employee assistance Program for chemically dependent employees available. Staff working with drug/alcohol-related issues: 4 part-time.

Disciplinary Actions

Alcohol Results of infractions of alcohol regulations (see Comparative Table of Alcohol Regulations) vary include counseling.

Drugs For any use, possession, or sale: varies by situation.

Additional Information from the College

Martin Center College is a nonresidential college whose student body has an average age in the late thirties. The College offers a B.S. or B.A. in substance abuse, is involved in instructing community groups, and plans to offer a graduate degree in substance abuse soon. The College's new Counseling Center is open to all students, anyone involved with the College, and members of the local community.

For More Information

Contact: Sr. Jane Schilling, Academic Dean, Martin Center College, 2171 Avondale Pl., Indianapolis, IN 46226. Telephone: 317-543-3235.

MARY BALDWIN COLLEGE

Staunton, Virginia

General Information

Independent 4-year women's college, affiliated with Presbyterian Church (U.S.A.). Founded 1842. Awards B. Primary accreditation: regional. Small-town setting; 40-acre campus. Total enrollment: 692. Faculty: 84 (60 full-time, 24 part-time).

Drug and Alcohol Information

Education

On campus Drug and alcohol education/prevention programs offered for: all students. Bacchus chapter: 4 members. College holds an annual alcohol awareness week and drug awareness week.

Identification of Problems

Admissions College application does not ask about prior substance abuse problems.

On campus Current students identified as chemically dependent may remain enrolled, but treatment is required. Training program on identifying students with potential substance abuse problems for: resident advisers, faculty. Written procedures for students and staff if substance abuse is suspected are being developed.

Support Services

On campus Support groups, private counseling.

Employee assistance Program for chemically dependent employees not available. Staff working with drug/alcohol-related issues: 4 part-time.

Disciplinary Actions

Alcohol Results of infractions of alcohol regulations (see Comparative Table of Alcohol Regulations) vary by situation but can include chemical dependency assessment, counseling, warning, probation, suspension, expulsion.

Drugs For any use, possession, or sale: varies by situation.

For More Information

Contact: Lucretia Cavan, Director of Student Activities, Mary Baldwin College, Staunton, VA 24401. Telephone: 703-887-7043.

MARYCREST COLLEGE

Davenport, Iowa

General Information

Independent Roman Catholic 5-year coed college. Founded 1939. Awards A (college transfer), B, M. Primary accreditation: regional. City setting; 30-acre campus. Total enrollment: 1,600.

Drug and Alcohol Information

Education

On campus Drug and alcohol education/prevention programs offered for: all students. Authorized group concerned with responsible drinking. College holds an annual alcohol awareness week.

Identification of Problems

Admissions College application does not ask about prior substance abuse problems.

On campus Current students identified as chemically dependent may remain enrolled, but treatment is required. No training program on identifying students with potential substance abuse problems. No written procedures for students and staff if substance abuse is suspected.

Support Services

On campus Private counseling.

Employee assistance Program for chemically dependent employees not available. Staff working with drug/alcohol-related issues: 4 part-time.

Disciplinary Actions

Alcohol Results of infractions of alcohol regulations (see Comparative Table of Alcohol Regulations) include counseling, warning, probation, suspension.

Drugs For first-time use, possession, or sale: suspension.

For subsequent use, possession, or sale: chemical dependency assessment, counseling, suspension.

For More Information

Contact: Laura Genatempo, Director of Housing/Campus Activities, Marycrest College, 1607 W. 12th St., Davenport, IA 52804. Telephone: 319-326-9204 or 9207.

MARYMOUNT COLLEGE
Tarrytown, New York

General Information
Independent 4-year primarily women's college. Founded 1907. Awards B. Primary accreditation: regional. Small-town setting; 25-acre campus. Total enrollment: 1,247. Faculty: 145 (65 full-time, 80 part-time).

Drug and Alcohol Information
Education

On campus Drug and alcohol education/prevention programs offered for: all students; required for: resident advisers. Authorized group concerned with responsible drinking. College holds an annual alcohol awareness week and drug awareness week.

Identification of Problems

Admissions College application does not ask about prior substance abuse problems.

On campus Current students identified as chemically dependent may remain enrolled, but treatment is required. Training program on identifying students with potential substance abuse problems for: resident advisers. Written procedures for students and staff if substance abuse is suspected.

Support Services

On campus Private counseling.

Employee assistance Program for chemically dependent employees not available.

Disciplinary Actions

Alcohol Results of infractions of alcohol regulations (see Comparative Table of Alcohol Regulations) include probation, suspension, expulsion, fine.

Drugs For first-time use or possession: varies by situation—counseling, warning, suspension. For subsequent use or possession: expulsion. For first-time sale: expulsion.

For More Information

Contact: Dr. Barbara Becker, Dean of Students, Marymount College, Tarrytown, NY 10591. Telephone: 914-631-3200.

MARYMOUNT COLLEGE OF KANSAS
Salina, Kansas

General Information
Independent Roman Catholic 4-year coed college. Founded 1922. Awards A (college transfer and terminal), B. Primary accreditation: regional. Small-town setting; 28-acre campus. Total enrollment: 640. Faculty: 153 (64 full-time, 89 part-time).

Drug and Alcohol Information
Education

On campus Drug and alcohol education/prevention programs required for: freshmen, resident advisers. College holds an annual alcohol awareness week.

Identification of Problems

Admissions College application does not ask about prior substance abuse problems.

On campus Current students identified as chemically dependent may remain enrolled, but treatment is required. Training program on identifying students with potential substance abuse problems for: resident advisers. No written procedures for students and staff if substance abuse is suspected.

Support Services

On campus Support groups, private counseling.

Employee assistance Program for chemically dependent employees not available.

Disciplinary Actions

Alcohol Results of infractions of alcohol regulations (see Comparative Table of Alcohol Regulations) vary by situation.

Drugs For first-time use or possession: varies by situation. For first-time sale: varies by situation—expulsion. For subsequent use, possession, or sale: expulsion.

For More Information

Contact: Becky Predota, Associate Dean of Students, Marymount College of Kansas, Box 5050, Salina, KS 67402. Telephone: 913-825-2101 Ext. 110.

MARYMOUNT MANHATTAN COLLEGE
New York, New York

General Information
Independent 4-year primarily women's college. Founded 1936. Awards B. Primary accreditation: regional. Metropolitan setting; 1-acre campus. Total enrollment: 1,300. Faculty: 155 (62 full-time, 93 part-time).

Drug and Alcohol Information
Education

On campus Drug and alcohol education/prevention programs offered for: all students, faculty, administration. Authorized group concerned with responsible drinking. College holds an annual alcohol awareness week and drug awareness week.

Identification of Problems

Admissions College application does not ask about prior substance abuse problems.

On campus Current students identified as chemically dependent may remain enrolled, but treatment is required. Training program on identifying students with potential substance abuse problems for: resident advisers, administration. Written procedures for students and staff if substance abuse is suspected are currently being developed.

Support Services

On campus Private counseling.

Employee assistance Program for chemically dependent

Marymount Manhattan College (continued)

employees not available. Staff working with drug/alcohol-related issues: 3 part-time.

Disciplinary Actions

Alcohol Results of infractions of alcohol regulations (see Comparative Table of Alcohol Regulations) include counseling, warning, probation, suspension, expulsion.

Drugs For first-time use, possession, or sale: counseling, warning. For subsequent use, possession, or sale: varies by situation.

For More Information

Contact: Rosemarie Dackerman, Dean of Students, Marymount Manhattan College, 221 E. 71st St., New York, NY 10021. Telephone: 212-517-0467.

MARYMOUNT UNIVERSITY

Arlington, Virginia

General Information

Independent 5-year coed college, affiliated with Roman Catholic Church. Founded 1950. Awards A (college transfer and terminal), B, M. Primary accreditation: regional. City setting; 17-acre campus. Total enrollment: 2,977. Faculty: 215 (85 full-time, 130 part-time).

Drug and Alcohol Information

Education

On campus Drug and alcohol education/prevention programs offered for: all students, faculty; required for: freshmen, athletes/coaches, administration, student leaders. College holds an annual alcohol awareness week.

Identification of Problems

Admissions College application does not ask about prior substance abuse problems.

On campus Current students identified as chemically dependent may remain enrolled, but treatment is required. Training program on identifying students with potential substance abuse problems for: resident advisers, administration. Written procedures for students and staff if substance abuse is suspected.

Support Services

On campus Private counseling.

Disciplinary Actions

Alcohol Results of infractions of alcohol regulations (see Comparative Table of Alcohol Regulations) include counseling, probation.

Drugs For first-time use or possession: varies by situation—probation, suspension. For subsequent use or possession: suspension. For first-time sale: expulsion.

For More Information

Contact: Dr. Linda McMahon, Vice President–Student Services, Marymount University, 2807 N. Glebe Rd., Arlington, VA 22207. Telephone: 703-284-1615.

MARYVILLE COLLEGE

Maryville, Tennessee

General Information

Independent Presbyterian 4-year coed college. Founded 1819. Awards B. Primary accreditation: regional. Small-town setting; 350-acre campus. Total enrollment: 787. Faculty: 58 (42 full-time, 16 part-time).

Drug and Alcohol Information

Education

On campus Drug and alcohol education/prevention programs offered for: all students. Authorized group concerned with responsible drinking. College holds an annual alcohol awareness week and drug awareness week.

Identification of Problems

On campus Current students identified as chemically dependent may remain enrolled, but treatment is required. No training program on identifying students with potential substance abuse problems. Written procedures for students and staff if substance abuse is suspected.

Support Services

On campus Private counseling.

Employee assistance Program for chemically dependent employees not available. Staff working with drug/alcohol-related issues: 6 part-time.

Disciplinary Actions

Alcohol Results of infractions of alcohol regulations (see Comparative Table of Alcohol Regulations) include chemical dependency assessment, counseling, warning, probation, suspension, expulsion.

Drugs For any use: varies by situation—chemical dependency assessment, counseling, warning. For any possession or sale: varies by situation.

For More Information

Contact: V. Tolis, Counselor, P.O. Box 2893, Maryville College, Maryville, TN 37801. Telephone: 615-984-0665.

MARYVILLE COLLEGE–SAINT LOUIS

St. Louis, Missouri

General Information

Independent 5-year coed college. Founded 1872. Awards B, M. Primary accreditation: regional. Metropolitan setting; 130-acre campus. Total enrollment: 2,934. Faculty: 214 (68 full-time, 146 part-time).

Drug and Alcohol Information

Education

On campus Drug and alcohol education/prevention programs offered for: all students. College holds an annual alcohol awareness week and drug awareness week.

Identification of Problems

Admissions College application does not ask about prior substance abuse problems.

On campus Current students identified as chemically dependent may remain enrolled. Training program on identifying students with potential substance abuse problems for: resident advisers.

Support Services

On campus Private counseling.

Employee assistance Program for chemically dependent employees not available.

Disciplinary Actions

Alcohol Results of infractions of alcohol regulations (see Comparative Table of Alcohol Regulations) vary by situation.

Drugs For any use: varies by situation. For first-time possession: varies by situation. For subsequent possession: suspension. For any sale: suspension.

For More Information

Contact: Jack Morgan, Vice President for Student Affairs, Maryville College–Saint Louis, 13550 Conway Rd., St. Louis, MO 63141. Telephone: 314-576-9480.

MARY WASHINGTON COLLEGE

Fredericksburg, Virginia

General Information

State-supported 5-year coed college. Founded 1908. Awards B, M. Primary accreditation: regional. Small-town setting; 275-acre campus. Total enrollment: 3,427. Faculty: 196 (163 full-time, 33 part-time).

Drug and Alcohol Information

Education

On campus Drug and alcohol education/prevention programs offered for: all students, faculty; required for: freshmen. Bacchus chapter: 10 members. College holds an annual alcohol awareness week.

Identification of Problems

Admissions College application does not ask about prior substance abuse problems.

On campus Current students identified as chemically dependent may remain enrolled, but treatment is required. Training program on identifying students with potential substance abuse problems for: resident advisers. Written procedures for students and staff if substance abuse is suspected.

Support Services

On campus ACOA, support groups, private counseling.

Employee assistance Program for chemically dependent employees available. Staff working with drug/alcohol-related issues: 6 part-time.

Disciplinary Actions

Alcohol Results of infractions of alcohol regulations (see Comparative Table of Alcohol Regulations) vary by situation but can include chemical dependency assessment, counseling, warning, probation, suspension, educational sessions.

Drugs For first-time use, possession, or sale: suspension, expulsion. Comments: There have been no second infractions.

For More Information

Contact: Suzanne Pickett, Alcohol Educator, 200 Lee Hall, Mary Washington College, 1301 College Ave., Fredericksburg, VA 22401. Telephone: 703-899-4641.

MARYWOOD COLLEGE

Scranton, Pennsylvania

General Information

Independent Roman Catholic 5-year coed college. Founded 1915. Awards B, M. Primary accreditation: regional. City setting; 180-acre campus. Total enrollment: 2,395. Faculty: 219 (124 full-time, 95 part-time).

Drug and Alcohol Information

Education

On campus Drug and alcohol education/prevention programs offered for: all students, faculty, administration. Authorized group concerned with responsible drinking. College holds an annual alcohol awareness week and drug awareness week.

Identification of Problems

On campus Current students identified as chemically dependent may remain enrolled. Comments: A counselor would decide whether treatment is required. Training program on identifying students with potential substance abuse problems for: housing staff.

Support Services

On campus AA, Al-Anon, private counseling, 12-step discussion, children's discussion.

Employee assistance Program for chemically dependent employees not available.

Disciplinary Actions

Alcohol Results of infractions of alcohol regulations (see Comparative Table of Alcohol Regulations) vary by situation but can include chemical dependency assessment, warning, fine.

Drugs For first-time use, possession, or sale: varies by situation. For subsequent use, possession, or sale: suspension.

For More Information

Contact: Patricia Martin, Head Nurse, Health Services, Marywood College, 2300 Adams Ave., Scranton, PA 18509. Telephone: 717-348-6249.

MASSACHUSETTS COLLEGE OF PHARMACY AND ALLIED HEALTH SCIENCES

Boston, Massachusetts

General Information

Independent comprehensive specialized coed institution. Founded 1823. Awards A (terminal), B, M, D (Bachelor of Science in Nursing program for registered nurses only). Primary accreditation: regional. Metropolitan setting; 2-acre campus. Total enrollment: 1,064. Faculty: 122 (64 full-time, 58 part-time). Social organizations: 7 national fraternities, national sororities, local fraternities, local sororities; 35% of eligible undergraduate men and 30% of eligible undergraduate women are members.

Drug and Alcohol Information

Education

On campus Drug and alcohol education/prevention programs offered for: all students. Authorized group

Massachusetts College of Pharmacy and Allied Health Sciences (continued)

concerned with responsible drinking. College holds an annual alcohol awareness week and drug awareness week.

Identification of Problems

Admissions College application does not ask about prior substance abuse problems.

On campus Current students identified as chemically dependent may remain enrolled, but treatment is required. Training program on identifying students with potential substance abuse problems for: resident advisers, Student Impairment Committee. Written procedures for students and staff if substance abuse is suspected.

Support Services

On campus Private counseling, Student Impairment Committee.

Employee assistance Program for chemically dependent employees available. Staff working with drug/alcohol-related issues: 3 part-time.

Disciplinary Actions

Alcohol Results of infractions of alcohol regulations (see Comparative Table of Alcohol Regulations) include chemical dependency assessment, counseling, warning, probation, suspension, expulsion.

Drugs For first-time use or possession: chemical dependency assessment, counseling, probation. For subsequent use or possession: varies by situation. For first-time sale: suspension, expulsion. For subsequent sale: expulsion.

For More Information

Contact: Dale James, Associate Dean, Massachusetts College of Pharmacy and Allied Health Sciences, 179 Longwood Avenue, Boston, MA 02115. Telephone: 617-732-2929.

MAYVILLE STATE UNIVERSITY

Mayville, North Dakota

General Information

State-supported 4-year coed college. Part of State University System. Founded 1889. Awards A (college transfer and terminal), B. Primary accreditation: regional. Rural setting; 60-acre campus. Total enrollment: 755. Faculty: 50 (37 full-time, 13 part-time). Social organizations: local fraternities, local sororities; 40% of eligible undergraduate men and 40% of eligible undergraduate women are members.

Drug and Alcohol Information

Education

On campus Drug and alcohol education/prevention programs offered for: all students; required for: athletes/coaches. College holds an annual alcohol awareness week.

Identification of Problems

Admissions College application does not ask about prior substance abuse problems.

On campus Current students identified as chemically dependent may remain enrolled. No training program on identifying students with potential substance abuse problems. Written procedures for students and staff if substance abuse is suspected.

Support Services

On campus Private counseling.

Employee assistance Program for chemically dependent employees not available. Staff working with drug/alcohol-related issues: 1 part-time.

Disciplinary Actions

Alcohol Results of infractions of alcohol regulations (see Comparative Table of Alcohol Regulations) vary by situation.

Drugs For first-time use or possession: varies by situation—counseling. For first-time sale: suspension. For subsequent use, possession, or sale: varies by situation.

For More Information

Contact: Ray Gerszewski, Vice President, Student Affairs, Mayville State University, Mayville, ND 58257. Telephone: 701-786-4875.

MCPHERSON COLLEGE

McPherson, Kansas

General Information

Independent 4-year coed college, affiliated with Church of the Brethren. Founded 1887. Awards A (college transfer and terminal), B. Primary accreditation: regional. Small-town setting; 26-acre campus. Total enrollment: 485. Faculty: 48 (33 full-time, 15 part-time).

Drug and Alcohol Information

Education

On campus Drug and alcohol education/prevention programs offered for: all students; required for: resident advisers. College holds an annual alcohol awareness week and drug awareness week.

Identification of Problems

Admissions College application does not ask about prior substance abuse problems.

On campus Current students identified as chemically dependent may remain enrolled, but treatment is strongly encouraged and required if problems occur. Training program on identifying students with potential substance abuse problems for: resident advisers, coaches, faculty, administration. Written procedures for students and staff if substance abuse is suspected.

Support Services

On campus Private counseling.

Employee assistance Program for chemically dependent employees not available. Staff working with drug/alcohol-related issues: 4 part-time.

Disciplinary Actions

Alcohol Results of infractions of alcohol regulations (see Comparative Table of Alcohol Regulations) vary by situation but can include chemical dependency assessment, counseling, probation, suspension. Comments: Suspension likely for repeated violations.

Drugs For any use or possession: varies by situation. For any sale: chemical dependency assessment, expulsion.

For More Information

Contact: Sharon L. Knechel, Vice President for Student Services, McPherson College, 1600 E. Euclid, McPherson, KS 67460. Telephone: 316-241-0731.

MEDAILLE COLLEGE

Buffalo, New York

General Information

Independent 4-year coed college. Founded 1875. Awards A (college transfer), B. Primary accreditation: regional. Metropolitan setting; 13-acre campus. Total enrollment: 1,053. Faculty: 70 (37 full-time, 33 part-time).

Drug and Alcohol Information

Education

On campus Drug and alcohol education/prevention programs offered for: all students, faculty, administration. Authorized group concerned with responsible drinking. College holds an annual alcohol awareness week.

Identification of Problems

Admissions College application does not ask about prior substance abuse problems.

On campus Current students identified as chemically dependent may remain enrolled, but treatment is required. No training program on identifying students with potential substance abuse problems.

Support Services

On campus ACOA, support groups, private counseling.

Employee assistance Program for chemically dependent employees not available. Staff working with drug/alcohol-related issues: 1 full-time and 3 part-time.

Disciplinary Actions

Alcohol Results of infractions of alcohol regulations (see Comparative Table of Alcohol Regulations) vary by situation but can include counseling, warning, probation.

Drugs For any use: varies by situation. For first-time possession: chemical dependency assessment, counseling, suspension. For subsequent possession: counseling, suspension. For any sale: expulsion.

For More Information

Contact: Michael McGuire, Associate Dean of Students, Medaille College, 18 Agassiz Circle, Buffalo, NY 14214. Telephone: 716-884-3281 Ext. 219.

MEDICAL UNIVERSITY OF SOUTH CAROLINA

Charleston, South Carolina

General Information

State-supported coed college. Founded 1824. Awards B, M, D. Primary accreditation: regional. City setting. Total enrollment: 2,118. Faculty: 1,795.

Drug and Alcohol Information

Education

On campus Drug and alcohol education/prevention programs offered for: all students, faculty, administration, other employees. Authorized group concerned with responsible drinking.

Identification of Problems

On campus Current students identified as chemically dependent may remain enrolled, but treatment is required. No training program on identifying students with potential substance abuse problems. Written procedures for students and staff if substance abuse is suspected.

Support Services

On campus AA, Al-Anon, support groups, private counseling.

Employee assistance Program for chemically dependent employees available. Staff working with drug/alcohol-related issues: 5 full-time.

Disciplinary Actions

Alcohol Results of infractions of alcohol regulations (see Comparative Table of Alcohol Regulations) include counseling, warning.

Drugs For any use, possession, or sale: varies by situation.

Additional Information from the College

Incoming students fill out a medical and personal history form that asks about substance abuse problems, among other things. Through this questionnaire, and again during orientation, they are informed about services available to them.

For More Information

Contact: Sally Sexton, Head, Substance Abuse Counseling, or Dr. Darlene Shaw, Director of Counseling, Student Life Center, Medical University of South Carolina, 171 Ashley Ave., Charleston, SC 29425. Telephone: 803-792-4930.

MEMPHIS COLLEGE OF ART

Memphis, Tennessee

General Information

Independent 5-year specialized coed college. Founded 1936. Awards B, M. Primary accreditation: regional. Metropolitan setting; 200-acre campus. Total enrollment: 262. Faculty: 40 (12 full-time, 28 part-time).

Drug and Alcohol Information

Education

On campus Drug and alcohol education/prevention programs not offered. Authorized group concerned with responsible drinking.

Identification of Problems

Admissions College application does not ask about prior substance abuse problems.

On campus Current students identified as chemically dependent may remain enrolled, but treatment is required. No training program on identifying students with potential substance abuse problems. Written procedures for students and staff if substance abuse is suspected.

Support Services

On campus Private counseling. Off campus mental health centers and private agencies.

Employee assistance Program for chemically dependent employees not available. Staff working with drug/alcohol-related issues: 1 full-time.

Disciplinary Actions

Alcohol Results of infractions of alcohol regulations (see Comparative Table of Alcohol Regulations) include chemical dependency assessment, counseling, probation, suspension, expulsion.

Drugs For first-time use: chemical dependency assessment, expulsion. For first-time possession: probation.

Memphis College of Art (continued)

For subsequent use or possession: suspension, expulsion. For any sale: suspension, expulsion.

For More Information

Contact: Billy C. Boyd, Counselor, Memphis College of Art, Overton Park, Memphis, TN 38112. Telephone: 901-726-4085.

MEMPHIS STATE UNIVERSITY

Memphis, Tennessee

General Information

State-supported comprehensive coed institution. Part of State University and Community College System of Tennessee. Founded 1912. Awards B, M, D. Primary accreditation: regional. Metropolitan setting; 173-acre campus. Total enrollment: 20,399. Faculty: 1,120 (770 full-time, 350 part-time). Social organizations: 16 national fraternities, 12 national sororities; 8% of eligible undergraduate men and 7% of eligible undergraduate women are members.

Drug and Alcohol Information

Education

On campus Drug and alcohol education/prevention programs offered for: all students. Bacchus chapter: 35 members. College holds an annual alcohol awareness week and drug awareness week.

Identification of Problems

Admissions College application does not ask about prior substance abuse problems.

On campus Current students identified as chemically dependent may remain enrolled. Training program on identifying students with potential substance abuse problems for: resident advisers, administration, counseling staff. Written procedures for students and staff if substance abuse is suspected.

Support Services

On campus AA, Al-Anon, support groups, private counseling, Bacchus.

Employee assistance Program for chemically dependent employees available. Staff working with drug/alcohol-related issues: 10 part-time.

Disciplinary Actions

Alcohol Results of infractions of alcohol regulations (see Comparative Table of Alcohol Regulations) vary by situation.

Drugs For any use, possession, or sale: varies by situation.

For More Information

Contact: Joseph E. Landrum, Assistant Dean for Judicial Affairs, Memphis State University, Memphis, TN 38152. Telephone: 901-678-2298.

MENLO COLLEGE

Atherton, California

General Information

Independent 4-year coed college. Founded 1927. Awards A (college transfer), B. Primary accreditation: regional. Small-town setting; 62-acre campus. Total enrollment: 590. Faculty: 68 (46 full-time, 22 part-time). Social organizations: social clubs; 15% of eligible undergraduate men and 15% of eligible undergraduate women are members.

Drug and Alcohol Information

Education

On campus Drug and alcohol education/prevention programs offered for: all students. Authorized group concerned with responsible drinking. College holds an annual alcohol awareness week and drug awareness week.

Identification of Problems

Admissions College application does not ask about prior substance abuse problems.

On campus Current students identified as chemically dependent may remain enrolled. No training program on identifying students with potential substance abuse problems. No written procedures for students and staff if substance abuse is suspected.

Support Services

On campus AA, NA, private counseling.

Employee assistance Program for chemically dependent employees not available.

Disciplinary Actions

Alcohol Results of infractions of alcohol regulations (see Comparative Table of Alcohol Regulations) vary by situation but can include chemical dependency assessment, counseling, warning, probation, suspension, expulsion.

Drugs For first-time use or possession: counseling. For first-time sale: suspension. For subsequent use, possession, or sale: varies by situation.

For More Information

Contact: Mark Kretovics, Director of Student Affairs, Menlo College, 1000 El Camino Road, Atherton, CA 94025. Telephone: 415-323-6141.

MENNONITE COLLEGE OF NURSING

Bloomington, Illinois

General Information

Independent specialized coed college. Founded 1983. Awards B. Primary accreditation: regional. City setting. Total enrollment: 104. Faculty: 18 (13 full-time, 5 part-time).

Drug and Alcohol Information

Education

On campus Drug and alcohol education/prevention programs offered for: all students, faculty, administration. Authorized group concerned with responsible drinking. College holds an annual alcohol awareness week and drug awareness week.

Identification of Problems

Admissions College application does not ask about prior substance abuse problems.

On campus Current students identified as chemically dependent may not remain enrolled. Training program on identifying students with potential substance abuse problems for: resident advisers, faculty, administration. Written procedures for students and staff if substance abuse is suspected.

Support Services

On campus Support groups, private counseling.

Employee assistance Program for chemically dependent employees available. Staff working with drug/alcohol-related issues: 1 part-time.

Disciplinary Actions

Alcohol Results of infractions of alcohol regulations (see Comparative Table of Alcohol Regulations) vary by situation but can include chemical dependency assessment, counseling, warning, probation, suspension, expulsion.

Drugs For any use, possession, or sale: varies by situation.

For More Information

Contact: Gail A. Lamb, Director of Student Affairs, Mennonite College of Nursing, 804 N. East St., Bloomington, IL 61701. Telephone: 309-829-0715.

MERCER UNIVERSITY ATLANTA

Atlanta, Georgia

General Information

Independent Baptist 5-year coed college. Part of Mercer University. Founded 1968. Awards B, M, D. Primary accreditation: regional. Metropolitan setting; 400-acre campus. Total enrollment: 1,911. Faculty: 126 (83 full-time, 43 part-time).

Drug and Alcohol Information

Education

On campus Drug and alcohol education/prevention programs offered for: all students. Authorized group concerned with responsible drinking.

Identification of Problems

Admissions College application does not ask about prior substance abuse problems.

On campus Current students identified as chemically dependent may remain enrolled. No training program on identifying students with potential substance abuse problems. No written procedures for students and staff if substance abuse is suspected.

Support Services

On campus Private counseling.

Employee assistance Program for chemically dependent employees not available. Staff working with drug/alcohol-related issues: 5 part-time.

Disciplinary Actions

Alcohol Results of infractions of alcohol regulations (see Comparative Table of Alcohol Regulations) vary by situation but can include chemical dependency assessment, counseling, probation, suspension, expulsion.

Drugs For any use or possession: varies by situation. For any sale: expulsion.

For More Information

Contact: Chris Kimbro, Counselor and Director of Orientation, Mercer University Atlanta, 3001 Mercer University Dr., Atlanta, GA 30341. Telephone: 404-986-3316.

MERCY COLLEGE

Dobbs Ferry, New York

General Information

Independent 5-year coed college. Founded 1951. Awards A (college transfer), B, M (M in nursing only). Primary accreditation: regional. Small-town setting; 20-acre campus. Total enrollment: 5,548. Faculty: 640 (212 full-time, 428 part-time).

Drug and Alcohol Information

Education

On campus Drug and alcohol education/prevention programs offered for: all students, athletes/coaches, faculty, administration. College holds an annual alcohol awareness week and drug awareness week.

Identification of Problems

Admissions College application does not ask about prior substance abuse problems.

On campus Current students identified as chemically dependent may remain enrolled. No training program on identifying students with potential substance abuse problems.

Support Services

On campus Private counseling, referrals.

Employee assistance Program for chemically dependent employees available. Staff working with drug/alcohol-related issues: 10 part-time.

Disciplinary Actions

Alcohol Results of infractions of alcohol regulations (see Comparative Table of Alcohol Regulations) vary by situation.

Drugs For any use, possession, or sale: varies by situation.

For More Information

Contact: Ann Rodier, Coordinator, Drug Education Committee, Mercy College, 555 Broadway, Dobbs Ferry, NY 10522. Telephone: 914-693-4500 Ext. 312.

MERRIMACK COLLEGE

North Andover, Massachusetts

General Information

Independent Roman Catholic 4-year coed college. Founded 1947. Awards A (college transfer), B. Primary accreditation: regional. Small-town setting; 220-acre campus. Total enrollment: 2,357. Faculty: 274 (130 full-time, 144 part-time). Social organizations: 6 national fraternities, 2 national sororities; 15% of eligible undergraduate men and 7% of eligible undergraduate women are members.

Drug and Alcohol Information

Education

On campus Drug and alcohol education/prevention programs offered for: all students, athletes/coaches, faculty, administration. College holds an annual alcohol awareness week and drug awareness week.

Identification of Problems

Admissions College application does not ask about prior substance abuse problems.

On campus Current students identified as chemically

Merrimack College (continued)

dependent may remain enrolled. Training program on identifying students with potential substance abuse problems for: resident advisers. No written procedures for students and staff if substance abuse is suspected.

Support Services

On campus AA, ACOA, support groups, private counseling.

Employee assistance Program for chemically dependent employees available.

Disciplinary Actions

Alcohol Results of infractions of alcohol regulations (see Comparative Table of Alcohol Regulations) vary by situation.

Drugs For any use, possession, or sale: varies by situation.

For More Information

Contact: Bruce Baker, Assistant Vice President, Student Services, Merrimack College, North Andover, MA 01845. Telephone: 508-683-7111 Ext. 176.

MESA STATE COLLEGE
Grand Junction, Colorado

General Information

State-supported 4-year coed college. Founded 1925. Awards A (college transfer and terminal), B. Primary accreditation: regional. Small-town setting; 42-acre campus. Total enrollment: 3,958. Faculty: 166 (140 full-time, 26 part-time).

Drug and Alcohol Information

Education

On campus Drug and alcohol education/prevention programs offered for: all students. Authorized group concerned with responsible drinking. College holds an annual alcohol awareness week and drug awareness week.

Identification of Problems

Admissions College application does not ask about prior substance abuse problems. Training program on identifying students with potential substance abuse problems for: resident advisers, director of Student Life Center. Written procedures for students and staff if substance abuse is suspected.

Support Services

On campus AA, Al-Anon, support groups.

Employee assistance Program for chemically dependent employees not available.

Disciplinary Actions

Alcohol Results of infractions of alcohol regulations (see Comparative Table of Alcohol Regulations) vary by situation but can include counseling, warning, probation, suspension, expulsion.

Drugs For first-time use: varies by situation—counseling, warning. For first-time possession: varies by situation—counseling, probation. For subsequent use or possession: counseling. For first-time sale: suspension. For subsequent sale: varies by situation—suspension, expulsion.

For More Information

Contact: Dr. Richard Baca, Director of Student Life Center, Mesa State College, P.O. Box 2647, Grand Junction, CO 81502. Telephone: 303-248-1802.

MESSIAH COLLEGE
Grantham, Pennsylvania

General Information

Independent 4-year coed college, affiliated with Brethren in Christ Church. Founded 1909. Awards B. Primary accreditation: regional. Small-town setting; 310-acre campus. Total enrollment: 2,179. Faculty: 141 (101 full-time, 40 part-time).

Drug and Alcohol Information

Education

On campus Drug and alcohol education/prevention programs offered for: all students; required for: resident advisers. College holds an annual alcohol awareness week.

Identification of Problems

Admissions College application question about prior substance abuse problems is used for counseling and referral, if student is admitted; in the admissions decision.

On campus Current students identified as chemically dependent may remain enrolled, but treatment is required. Training program on identifying students with potential substance abuse problems for: resident advisers. Written procedures for students and staff if substance abuse is suspected.

Support Services

On campus ACOA, private counseling.

Employee assistance Program for chemically dependent employees available.

Disciplinary Actions

Alcohol Results of infractions of alcohol regulations (see Comparative Table of Alcohol Regulations) include chemical dependency assessment, counseling, probation, suspension.

Drugs For any use: chemical dependency assessment, counseling, suspension. For first-time possession: chemical dependency assessment, counseling, probation. For subsequent possession: expulsion. For any sale: expulsion.

Additional Information from the College

Messiah College prohibits the use or possession of alcohol or drugs on or off campus by students and employees. This standard is taken seriously and enforced.

For More Information

Contact: Dr. Jay Barnes, Vice President for Student Development, Messiah College, Grantham, PA 17027. Telephone: 717-691-6017.

METHODIST COLLEGE
Fayetteville, North Carolina

General Information

Independent United Methodist 4-year coed college. Founded 1956. Awards A (college transfer), B. Primary accreditation: regional. City setting; 600-acre campus. Total enrollment: 1,391. Faculty: 95 (65 full-time, 30 part-time). Social organizations: 2 national fraternities, 1 national sorority; 10% of eligible undergraduate men and 8% of eligible undergraduate women are members.

Drug and Alcohol Information

Education

On campus Drug and alcohol education/prevention

programs offered for: all students. College holds an annual alcohol awareness week.

Identification of Problems

Admissions College application does not ask about prior substance abuse problems.

On campus Current students identified as chemically dependent may remain enrolled, but treatment is required. Training program on identifying students with potential substance abuse problems for: resident advisers. Written procedures for students and staff if substance abuse is suspected.

Support Services

On campus ACOA, private counseling.

Employee assistance Program for chemically dependent employees available. Staff working with drug/alcohol-related issues: 1 part-time.

Disciplinary Actions

Alcohol Results of infractions of alcohol regulations (see Comparative Table of Alcohol Regulations) vary by situation but can include counseling, warning, probation, suspension, expulsion, fines.

Drugs For first-time use or possession: varies by situation. For subsequent use or possession: counseling, suspension. For first-time sale: suspension, expulsion. For subsequent sale: expulsion.

For More Information

Contact: Kathy Woltz, Director of Counseling and Career Placement, Methodist College, Box 12185, Fayetteville, NC 28311. Telephone: 919-488-7110.

METROPOLITAN STATE UNIVERSITY

St. Paul, Minnesota

General Information

State-supported coed college. Part of Minnesota State University System. Founded 1971. Awards B, M (offers primarily part-time evening degree programs). Primary accreditation: regional. Metropolitan setting. Total enrollment: 5,799. Faculty: 584 (36 full-time, 548 part-time).

Drug and Alcohol Information

Education

On campus Drug and alcohol education/prevention programs not offered.

Identification of Problems

Admissions College application does not ask about prior substance abuse problems.

On campus No training program on identifying students with potential substance abuse problems. Written procedures for students and staff if substance abuse is suspected.

Support Services

On campus No support services on campus.

Employee assistance Program for chemically dependent employees available.

Additional Information from the College

Metropolitan State University is an upper-division adult university; the average student age is 35. There are no traditional activities or organizations.

For More Information

Contact: Joyce LeClaire, Dean, Metropolitan State University, Suite 121, Metro Square, 121 7th Pl. E., St. Paul, MN 55101. Telephone: 612-296-4444.

MIAMI UNIVERSITY

Oxford, Ohio

General Information

State-supported comprehensive coed institution. Part of Miami University System. Founded 1809. Awards B, M, D. Primary accreditation: regional. Small-town setting; 1,100-acre campus. Total enrollment: 16,044. Faculty: 840 (725 full-time, 115 part-time). Social organizations: 28 national fraternities, 22 national sororities; 33% of eligible undergraduate men and 35% of eligible undergraduate women are members.

Drug and Alcohol Information

Education

On campus Drug and alcohol education/prevention programs offered for: all students; required for: resident advisers. Bacchus chapter: 30 members. College holds an annual alcohol awareness week and drug awareness week.

Identification of Problems

On campus Current students identified as chemically dependent may remain enrolled, but treatment is required. No training program on identifying students with potential substance abuse problems. Written procedures for students and staff if substance abuse is suspected.

Support Services

On campus AA, Al-Anon, ACOA, private counseling.

Employee assistance Program for chemically dependent employees available. Staff working with drug/alcohol-related issues: 1 full-time and about 5 part-time.

Disciplinary Actions

Alcohol Results of infractions of alcohol regulations (see Comparative Table of Alcohol Regulations) vary by situation but can include chemical dependency assessment, counseling, suspension, attendance at a substance abuse education program.

Drugs For any use, possession, or sale: varies by situation. Comments: If a student agrees to a voluntary medical withdrawal in order to participate in a treatment program at the student's own expense, any penalties incurred for disruptive behavior may be waived.

Additional Information from the College

Behavior that is disruptive and traceable to abuse of alcohol or other substances is prohibited and Miami University has specific guidelines to deal with such behavior.

For More Information

Contact: Susan Vaughn, Coordinator of Alcohol and Other Drug Education, Miami University, Oxford, OH 45056. Telephone: 513-529-4010.

MICHIGAN STATE UNIVERSITY
East Lansing, Michigan

General Information

State-supported comprehensive coed institution. Founded 1855. Awards B, M, D. Primary accreditation: regional. Small-town setting; 5,000-acre campus. Total enrollment: 42,695. Faculty: 3,990 (3,655 full-time, 335 part-time). Social organizations: 30 national fraternities, 19 national sororities; 8% of eligible undergraduate men and 8% of eligible undergraduate women are members.

Drug and Alcohol Information

Education

On campus Drug and alcohol education/prevention programs offered for: all students, athletes/coaches. Authorized group concerned with responsible drinking. College holds an annual alcohol awareness week and drug awareness week.

Identification of Problems

Admissions College application does not ask about prior substance abuse problems.

On campus Current students identified as chemically dependent may remain enrolled, but treatment is required. Training program on identifying students with potential substance abuse problems for: resident advisers, Greek officers, administration, students. Written procedures for students and staff if substance abuse is suspected.

Support Services

On campus AA, Al-Anon, ACOA, support groups, private counseling.

Employee assistance Program for chemically dependent employees available. Staff working with drug/alcohol-related issues: 2 full-time.

Disciplinary Actions

Alcohol Results of infractions of alcohol regulations (see Comparative Table of Alcohol Regulations) include chemical dependency assessment, warning, probation, suspension, attendance at alcohol education program.

Drugs For first-time use or possession: removal from residence halls, warning. For subsequent use: removal from residence halls, suspension. For subsequent possession: removal from residence halls, probation. For any sale: removal from residence halls, suspension.

Additional Information from the College

During the past five years, progress has been made in working with students and others in the areas of education, remediation, and enforcement. Last year a Kellogg Foundation Health Promotion grant enabled the University to develop a training institute for alcohol and other drug educators. The focus is to train persons who work with young people, stressing prevention rather than remediation. Many residence hall and other staff members have attended this institute and now conduct alcohol and other drug education programs on campus.

For More Information

Contact: Marie A. Hansen, Assistant Director, Student Life, 101 Student Services, Michigan State University, East Lansing, MI 48824. Telephone: 517-353-5509.

MICHIGAN TECHNOLOGICAL UNIVERSITY
Houghton, Michigan

General Information

State-supported comprehensive coed institution. Founded 1885. Awards A (terminal), B, M, D. Primary accreditation: regional. Small-town setting; 240-acre campus. Total enrollment: 6,250. Faculty: 362 (324 full-time, 38 part-time). Social organizations: 11 national fraternities, 4 national sororities, 5 local fraternities, 3 local sororities, social clubs; 14% of eligible undergraduate men and 13% of eligible undergraduate women are members.

Drug and Alcohol Information

Education

On campus Drug and alcohol education/prevention programs offered for: all students; required for: resident advisers. Authorized group concerned with responsible drinking. College holds an annual alcohol awareness week.

Identification of Problems

Admissions College application does not ask about prior substance abuse problems.

On campus Current students identified as chemically dependent may remain enrolled. Training program on identifying students with potential substance abuse problems for: resident advisers, coaches, Greek officers, faculty, administration. No written procedures for students and staff if substance abuse is suspected.

Support Services

On campus AA, Al-Anon, ACOA, support groups.

Employee assistance Program for chemically dependent employees available. Staff working with drug/alcohol-related issues: 5 part-time.

Disciplinary Actions

Alcohol Results of infractions of alcohol regulations (see Comparative Table of Alcohol Regulations) vary by situation.

Drugs For first-time use: chemical dependency assessment. For subsequent use: varies by situation. For any possession: varies by situation. For any sale: varies by situation—suspension.

For More Information

Contact: Jeanine D. Sewell, Director of Counseling, Michigan Technological University, Houghton, MI 49931. Telephone: 906-487-2538.

MIDAMERICA NAZARENE COLLEGE
Olathe, Kansas

General Information

Independent 4-year coed college, affiliated with Church of the Nazarene. Founded 1966. Awards A (college transfer and terminal), B. Primary accreditation: regional. Small-town setting; 112-acre campus. Total enrollment: 1,121. Faculty: 73 (48 full-time, 25 part-time).

Drug and Alcohol Information

Education

On campus Drug and alcohol education/prevention programs offered for: all students, athletes/coaches.

Identification of Problems

Admissions College application does not ask about prior substance abuse problems.

On campus Current students identified as chemically dependent may remain enrolled only if self-reported. Treatment is required. Training program on identifying students with potential substance abuse problems for: resident advisers. Written procedures for students and staff if substance abuse is suspected.

Support Services

On campus Private counseling.

Employee assistance Program for chemically dependent employees not available. Staff working with drug/alcohol-related issues: 2 part-time.

Disciplinary Actions

Alcohol Results of infractions of alcohol regulations (see Comparative Table of Alcohol Regulations) include counseling, probation, expulsion.

Drugs For any use, possession, or sale: expulsion.

For More Information

Contact: Donald E. Stelting, Vice President for Student Development, MidAmerica Nazarene College, 2030 College Way, Box 17765, Olathe, KS 66061. Telephone: 913-782-3750.

MID-CONTINENT BAPTIST BIBLE COLLEGE

Mayfield, Kentucky

General Information

Independent 4-year coed college, affiliated with Baptist Church. Founded 1949. Awards B. Primary accreditation: regional. Small-town setting. Total enrollment: 105. Faculty: 13 (2 full-time, 11 part-time).

Drug and Alcohol Information

Education

On campus Drug and alcohol education/prevention programs not offered.

Information from the College

Mid-Continent Baptist Bible College is a Christian college. There have never been any drug or alcohol problems on campus, but if a problem occurred, it would be handled on an individual basis.

For More Information

Contact: Yvonne Yates, Registrar, Mid-Continent Baptist Bible College, Route 2, P.O. Box I, Mayfield, KY. Telephone: 502-247-8521.

MILLIGAN COLLEGE

Milligan College, Tennessee

General Information

Independent Christian 4-year coed college. Founded 1866. Awards A (terminal), B. Primary accreditation: regional. Rural setting; 135-acre campus. Total enrollment: 658. Faculty: 57 (44 full-time, 13 part-time).

Drug and Alcohol Information

Education

On campus Drug and alcohol education/prevention programs required for all students, athletes/coaches. College holds an annual alcohol awareness week.

Identification of Problems

Admissions College application does not ask about prior substance abuse problems.

On campus Current students identified as chemically dependent may remain enrolled, but treatment is required. Training program on identifying students with potential substance abuse problems for: resident advisers, coaches. No written procedures for students and staff if substance abuse is suspected.

Support Services

On campus Private counseling, referral.

Employee assistance Program for chemically dependent employees not available.

Disciplinary Actions

Alcohol Results of infractions of alcohol regulations (see Comparative Table of Alcohol Regulations) vary by situation but can include chemical dependency assessment, counseling, warning, probation, suspension, expulsion.

Drugs For any use, possession, or sale: expulsion.

For More Information

Contact: John Derry, Dean of Students, Milligan College, Milligan College, TN 37682. Telephone: 615-929-0116 Ext. 131.

MILLSAPS COLLEGE

Jackson, Mississippi

General Information

Independent United Methodist 5-year coed college. Founded 1890. Awards B, M. Primary accreditation: regional. City setting; 100-acre campus. Total enrollment: 1,445. Faculty: 115 (87 full-time, 28 part-time). Social organizations: 6 national fraternities, 5 national sororities; 62% of eligible undergraduate men and 61% of eligible undergraduate women are members.

Drug and Alcohol Information

Education

On campus Drug and alcohol education/prevention programs offered for: all students, athletes/coaches. Authorized group concerned with responsible drinking. College holds an annual alcohol awareness week and drug awareness week.

Identification of Problems

Admissions College application does not ask about prior substance abuse problems.

On campus Current students identified as chemically dependent may remain enrolled, but treatment is required. Training program on identifying students with potential substance abuse problems for: resident advisers. Written procedures for students and staff if substance abuse is suspected.

Millsaps College (continued)

Support Services

On campus ACOA, private counseling.

Employee assistance Program for chemically dependent employees not available.

Disciplinary Actions

Alcohol Results of infractions of alcohol regulations (see Comparative Table of Alcohol Regulations) vary by situation but can include counseling, warning, probation, fines. Comments: Social organizations may be placed on social probation.

Drugs For first-time use or possession: counseling, probation. For subsequent use or possession: suspension. For any sale: suspension.

Additional Information from the College

The College staff and faculty attempt to work positively with problems of substance abuse. In all cases careful assessment is made before action is taken. Parents are informed of the problem and asked for their input and assistance.

For More Information

Contact: Stuart Good, Dean of Student Affairs, Millsaps College, 1701 N. State St., Jackson, MS 39210. Telephone: 601-354-5201 Ext. 205.

MILLS COLLEGE

Oakland, California

General Information

Independent 5-year women's college. Founded 1852. Awards B, M. Primary accreditation: regional. City setting; 135-acre campus. Total enrollment: 1,050. Faculty: 167 (72 full-time, 95 part-time).

Drug and Alcohol Information

Education

On campus Drug and alcohol education/prevention programs offered for: all students. College holds an annual alcohol awareness week.

Identification of Problems

Admissions College application does not ask about prior substance abuse problems.

On campus Current students identified as chemically dependent may remain enrolled, depending on the situation. Training program on identifying students with potential substance abuse problems for: resident advisers. No written procedures for students and staff if substance abuse is suspected.

Support Services

On campus ACOA, private counseling.

Employee assistance Program for chemically dependent employees not available. Staff working with drug/alcohol-related issues: 6 part-time.

Disciplinary Actions

Alcohol Results of infractions of alcohol regulations (see Comparative Table of Alcohol Regulations) vary by situation. Comments: Infractions reviewed by the administration or student judicial board.

Drugs For any use, possession, or sale: varies by situation.

For More Information

Contact: Sandy Hubler, Director of Student Activities, Mills College, Oakland, CA 94613. Telephone: 415-430-2130.

MILWAUKEE INSTITUTE OF ART AND DESIGN

Milwaukee, Wisconsin

General Information

Independent 4-year specialized coed college. Founded 1974. Awards B. Primary accreditation: regional. Metropolitan setting. Total enrollment: 466. Faculty: 70 (18 full-time, 52 part-time).

Drug and Alcohol Information

Education

On campus Drug and alcohol education/prevention programs offered for: all students, faculty, administration.

Identification of Problems

Admissions College application does not ask about prior substance abuse problems.

On campus Current students identified as chemically dependent may remain enrolled, but treatment is required. Training program on identifying students with potential substance abuse problems for: faculty, administratin, student peer advisers. Written procedures for students and staff if substance abuse is suspected.

Support Services

On campus Private counseling, referrals.

Employee assistance Program for chemically dependent employees not available. Staff working with drug/alcohol-related issues: 3 part-time.

Disciplinary Actions

Alcohol Results of infractions of alcohol regulations (see Comparative Table of Alcohol Regulations) vary by situation but can include warning, suspension, expulsion.

Drugs For any use, possession, or sale: varies by situation.

For More Information

Contact: Judy Luebke, Director of Student Services, Milwaukee Institute of Art and Design, 342 N. Water St., Milwaukee, WI 53202. Telephone: 414-276-7889.

MINNEAPOLIS COLLEGE OF ART AND DESIGN

Minneapolis, Minnesota

General Information

Independent 4-year specialized coed college. Founded 1886. Awards B. Primary accreditation: regional. Metropolitan setting; 7-acre campus. Total enrollment: 713. Faculty: 92 (59 full-time, 33 part-time).

Drug and Alcohol Information

Education

On campus Drug and alcohol education/prevention programs offered for: all students.

Identification of Problems

Admissions College application does not ask about prior substance abuse problems.

On campus Current students identified as chemically dependent may remain enrolled, but treatment is required. Training program on identifying students with potential substance abuse problems for: resident advisers. Written procedures for students and staff if substance abuse is suspected.

Support Services

On campus Support groups, private counseling.

Employee assistance Program for chemically dependent employees not available.

Disciplinary Actions

Alcohol Results of infractions of alcohol regulations (see Comparative Table of Alcohol Regulations) include warning, probation, suspension, expulsion.

Drugs For first-time use: varies by situation—counseling, probation. For subsequent use: varies by situation—counseling, probation, expulsion. For any possession or sale: varies by situation—counseling, probation, expulsion.

For More Information

Contact: Dr. Thomas J. Donahue, Dean of Students, Minneapolis College of Art and Design, 2501 Stevens Ave. S., Minneapolis, MN 55404. Telephone: 612-871-3256.

MINOT STATE UNIVERSITY

Minot, North Dakota

General Information

State-supported 5-year coed college. Founded 1913. Awards A (college transfer and terminal), B, M. Primary accreditation: regional. Small-town setting; 160-acre campus. Total enrollment: 3,304. Faculty: 171 (144 full-time, 27 part-time).

Drug and Alcohol Information

Education

On campus Drug and alcohol education/prevention programs offered for: all students. Authorized group concerned with responsible drinking. College holds an annual alcohol awareness week and drug awareness week.

Identification of Problems

Admissions College application question about prior substance abuse problems is used for counseling and referral, if student is admitted. It is part of the health history.

On campus Current students identified as chemically dependent may remain enrolled, and treatment may or may not be required, depending on the situation. Training program on identifying students with potential substance abuse problems for: resident advisers. Written procedures for students and staff if substance abuse is suspected.

Support Services

On campus AA.

Employee assistance Program for chemically dependent employees not available. Staff working with drug/alcohol-related issues: 4 part-time.

Disciplinary Actions

Alcohol Results of infractions of alcohol regulations (see Comparative Table of Alcohol Regulations) vary by situation but can include probation, fines.

Drugs For any use, possession, or sale: varies by situation.

For More Information

Contact: Dr. Richard Jenkins, Director of Student Affairs, Minot State University, 500 University Ave. W., Minot, ND 58701. Telephone: 701-857-3362.

MISSISSIPPI UNIVERSITY FOR WOMEN

Columbus, Mississippi

General Information

State-supported 5-year primarily women's college. Founded 1884. Awards A (terminal), B, M (M in nursing only). Primary accreditation: regional. Small-town setting; 110-acre campus. Total enrollment: 2,085. Faculty: 126 (101 full-time, 25 part-time). Social organizations: 1 local fraternity, 12 local sororities, 3 two-year clubs; 10% of eligible undergraduate men and 65% of eligible undergraduate women are members.

Drug and Alcohol Information

Education

On campus Drug and alcohol education/prevention programs offered for: all students, athletes/coaches, faculty, administration. Authorized group concerned with responsible drinking. College holds an annual alcohol awareness week and drug awareness week.

Identification of Problems

Admissions College application does not ask about prior substance abuse problems.

On campus Current students identified as chemically dependent may remain enrolled, and treatment may or may not be required. No training program on identifying students with potential substance abuse problems. No written procedures for students and staff if substance abuse is suspected.

Support Services

On campus AA, private counseling.

Employee assistance Program for chemically dependent employees not available.

Disciplinary Actions

Alcohol Results of infractions of alcohol regulations (see Comparative Table of Alcohol Regulations) vary by situation but can include counseling, warning, probation.

Drugs For any use, possession, or sale: varies by situation.

For More Information

Contact: Dr. Joe Dell Brasel, Director of Student Affairs, Mississippi University for Women, Columbus, MS 39701. Telephone: 601-329-7350.

MISSOURI SOUTHERN STATE COLLEGE

Joplin, Missouri

General Information

State-supported 4-year coed college. Founded 1937. Awards A (college transfer and terminal), B. Primary accreditation: regional. Small-town setting; 350-acre campus. Total enrollment: 5,404. Faculty: 237 (170 full-time, 67 part-time).

Missouri Southern State College (continued)

Social organizations: 1 national fraternity, 2 national sororities, 1 local sorority; 1% of eligible undergraduate men and 1% of eligible undergraduate women are members.

Drug and Alcohol Information

Education

On campus Drug and alcohol education/prevention programs offered for: all students; required for: freshmen, athletes/coaches, resident advisers. Authorized group concerned with responsible drinking. College holds an annual alcohol awareness week and drug awareness week.

Identification of Problems

Admissions College application does not ask about prior substance abuse problems.

On campus Current students identified as chemically dependent may remain enrolled, but treatment is required. Training program on identifying students with potential substance abuse problems for: resident advisers, orientation leaders. Written procedures for students and staff if substance abuse is suspected.

Support Services

On campus AA, NA, private counseling.

Employee assistance Program for chemically dependent employees not available. Staff working with drug/alcohol-related issues: 10 part-time.

Disciplinary Actions

Alcohol Results of infractions of alcohol regulations (see Comparative Table of Alcohol Regulations) vary by situation but can include chemical dependency assessment, counseling, warning, probation, suspension, expulsion.

Drugs For first-time use: varies by situation—probation. For first-time possession: probation. For subsequent use or possession: suspension. For any sale: expulsion.

For More Information

Contact: Doug Carnahan, Director of Student Life, Missouri Southern State College, Newman and Duquesne Rd., Joplin, MO 64801. Telephone: 417-625-9522.

MOBILE COLLEGE

Mobile, Alabama

General Information

Independent Baptist 5-year coed college. Founded 1961. Awards A (terminal), B, M. Primary accreditation: regional. City setting; 685-acre campus. Total enrollment: 1,059. Faculty: 83 (53 full-time, 30 part-time).

Drug and Alcohol Information

Education

On campus Drug and alcohol education/prevention programs not offered.

Identification of Problems

Admissions College application does not ask about prior substance abuse problems.

On campus Current students identified as chemically dependent may remain enrolled, but treatment is required. No training program on identifying students with potential substance abuse problems. Written procedures for students and staff if substance abuse is suspected.

Support Services

On campus Private counseling.

Employee assistance Program for chemically dependent employees not available.

Disciplinary Actions

Alcohol Results of infractions of alcohol regulations (see Comparative Table of Alcohol Regulations) vary by situation but can include probation, suspension.

Drugs For first-time use or possession: varies by situation. For subsequent use or possession: suspension. For first-time sale: suspension. For subsequent sale: expulsion.

For More Information

Contact: Dr. Leon Pirkle, Vice President for Student Services, Mobile College, P.O. Box 13220, Mobile, AL 36613. Telephone: 205-675-5990.

MOLLOY COLLEGE

Rockville Centre, New York

General Information

Independent 4-year coed college. Founded 1955. Awards A (college transfer), B. Primary accreditation: regional. Small-town setting; 25-acre campus. Total enrollment: 1,384. Faculty: 175 (100 full-time, 75 part-time). Social organizations: 1 local fraternity, 1 local sorority; 2% of eligible undergraduate men and 1% of eligible undergraduate women are members.

Drug and Alcohol Information

Education

On campus Drug and alcohol education/prevention programs offered for: all students, faculty, administration. Authorized group concerned with responsible drinking. College holds an annual alcohol awareness week and drug awareness week.

Identification of Problems

On campus Current students identified as chemically dependent may remain enrolled, but treatment is required. No training program on identifying students with potential substance abuse problems. Written procedures for students and staff if substance abuse is suspected.

Support Services

On campus Support groups (SADD), private counseling.

Employee assistance Program for chemically dependent employees not available. Staff working with drug/alcohol-related issues: 4 part-time.

Disciplinary Actions

Alcohol Results of infractions of alcohol regulations (see Comparative Table of Alcohol Regulations) vary by situation but can include chemical dependency assessment, counseling, warning, probation, suspension, expulsion.

Drugs For first-time use or possession: chemical dependency assessment, counseling, suspension. For first-time sale: chemical dependency assessment, counseling, expulsion. For subsequent use, possession, or sale: counseling, expulsion.

Additional Information from the College

Drug and alcohol programs at Molloy College are tied into a focus on "Wellness Way." Educational programs emphasize health. For students and staff who have problems, the College offers a comprehensive counseling service and referrals to community agencies.

For More Information

Contact: Sr. Angelica O'Connell, Director of Health Services, Molloy College, 1000 Hempstead Avenue, Rockville Centre, NY 11570. Telephone: 516-678-5000.

MONMOUTH COLLEGE

West Long Branch, New Jersey

General Information

Independent 5-year coed college. Founded 1933. Awards A (college transfer), B, M. Primary accreditation: regional. Small-town setting; 125-acre campus. Total enrollment: 4,430. Faculty: 191 (154 full-time, 37 part-time). Social organizations: 2 national fraternities, 1 national sorority, 2 local fraternities, 1 local sorority; 10% of eligible undergraduate men and 10% of eligible undergraduate women are members.

Drug and Alcohol Information

Education

On campus Drug and alcohol education/prevention programs offered for: all students. Authorized group concerned with responsible drinking. College holds an annual alcohol awareness week and drug awareness week.

Identification of Problems

Admissions College application does not ask about prior substance abuse problems.

On campus Current students identified as chemically dependent may remain enrolled, but treatment is required. Training program on identifying students with potential substance abuse problems for: resident advisers, coaches. Written procedures for students and staff if substance abuse is suspected are currently being drafted.

Support Services

On campus Support groups, private counseling.

Employee assistance Program for chemically dependent employees available.

Disciplinary Actions

Alcohol Results of infractions of alcohol regulations (see Comparative Table of Alcohol Regulations) vary by situation.

Drugs For first-time use or possession: varies by situation—fine. For subsequent use or possession: suspension. For any sale: expulsion.

For More Information

Contact: Margaret Corcoran, Coordinator of Health Services, Monmouth College, West Long Branch, NJ 07764. Telephone: 201-571-3543.

MONTANA COLLEGE OF MINERAL SCIENCE AND TECHNOLOGY

Butte, Montana

General Information

State-supported 5-year coed college. Part of Montana University System. Founded 1895. Awards A (college transfer), B, M. Primary accreditation: regional. Small-town setting; 130-acre campus. Total enrollment: 1,818. Faculty: 122 (101 full-time, 21 part-time).

Drug and Alcohol Information

Education

On campus Drug and alcohol education/prevention programs offered for: all students, athletes/coaches. College holds an annual alcohol awareness week.

Identification of Problems

Admissions College application does not ask about prior substance abuse problems.

On campus Current students identified as chemically dependent may remain enrolled. Training program on identifying students with potential substance abuse problems for: resident advisers, coaches. No written procedures for students and staff if substance abuse is suspected.

Support Services

On campus Private counseling.

Employee assistance Program for chemically dependent employees available. Staff working with drug/alcohol-related issues: 1 part-time.

Disciplinary Actions

Alcohol Results of infractions of alcohol regulations (see Comparative Table of Alcohol Regulations) vary by situation but can include chemical dependency assessment, counseling, warning, probation, suspension, expulsion.

Drugs For any use, possession, or sale: varies by situation.

For More Information

Contact: Paul Beatty, Director of Student Life Programs, Montana College of Mineral Science and Technology, Butte, MT 59701. Telephone: 406-496-4198.

MONTANA STATE UNIVERSITY

Bozeman, Montana

General Information

State-supported comprehensive coed institution. Part of Montana University System. Founded 1893. Awards B, M, D. Primary accreditation: regional. Small-town setting; 1,170-acre campus. Total enrollment: 10,024. Faculty: 550 (433 full-time, 117 part-time). Social organizations: 11 national fraternities, 6 national sororities; 6% of eligible undergraduate men and 5% of eligible undergraduate women are members.

Drug and Alcohol Information

Education

On campus Drug and alcohol education/prevention programs offered for: social organization members; required for: resident advisers. Authorized group concerned with responsible drinking.

Identification of Problems

Admissions College application does not ask about prior substance abuse problems.

On campus Current students identified as chemically dependent may remain enrolled. Training program on identifying students with potential substance abuse problems for: resident advisers. No written procedures for students and staff if substance abuse is suspected.

Support Services

On campus AA, ACOA, private counseling.

Montana State University (continued)

Employee assistance Program for chemically dependent employees available. Staff working with drug/alcohol-related issues: 3 part-time.

Disciplinary Actions

Alcohol Results of infractions of alcohol regulations (see Comparative Table of Alcohol Regulations) vary by situation but can include chemical dependency assessment, counseling, warning, probation, suspension, expulsion.

Drugs For first-time use: varies by situation. For first-time possession: probation, suspension. For first-time sale: suspension, expulsion. For subsequent use, possession, or sale: varies by situation.

Additional Information from the College

Montana State University is working on a grant proposal that would, if funded, provide education/awareness and intervention/prevention programs for faculty, staff, and students.

For More Information

Contact: Denny Klewin, Assistant Dean of Students, Room 120, Strand Union, Montana State University, Bozeman, MT 59717. Telephone: 406-994-2827.

MONTCLAIR STATE COLLEGE

Upper Montclair, New Jersey

General Information

State-supported 5-year coed college. Founded 1908. Awards B, M. Primary accreditation: regional. Small-town setting; 200-acre campus. Total enrollment: 12,720. Faculty: 701 (428 full-time, 273 part-time). Social organizations: national fraternities, 11 local fraternities, 4 local sororities.

Drug and Alcohol Information

Education

On campus Drug and alcohol education/prevention programs offered for: all students. Authorized group concerned with responsible drinking. College holds an annual alcohol awareness week and drug awareness week.

Identification of Problems

Admissions College application does not ask about prior substance abuse problems.

On campus Current students identified as chemically dependent may remain enrolled, but treatment is required. No training program on identifying students with potential substance abuse problems. Written procedures for students and staff if substance abuse is suspected.

Support Services

On campus No support services on campus.

Employee assistance Program for chemically dependent employees not available.

Disciplinary Actions

Alcohol Results of infractions of alcohol regulations (see Comparative Table of Alcohol Regulations) include chemical dependency assessment, counseling, probation, suspension, expulsion.

Drugs For any use, possession, or sale: varies by situation.

For More Information

Contact: Dr. Edward C. Martin, Dean of Students, Office of Student Affairs, Montclair State College, Upper Montclair, NJ 07043. Telephone: 201-893-4118.

MOORHEAD STATE UNIVERSITY

Moorhead, Minnesota

General Information

State-supported 5-year coed college. Part of Minnesota State University System. Founded 1887. Awards A (college transfer and terminal), B, M. Primary accreditation: regional. City setting; 104-acre campus. Total enrollment: 8,435. Social organizations: 2 national fraternities, 3 national sororities, 1 local fraternity; 3% of eligible undergraduate men and 2% of eligible undergraduate women are members.

Drug and Alcohol Information

Education

On campus Drug and alcohol education/prevention programs offered for: all students, athletes/coaches, faculty. College holds an annual alcohol awareness week and drug awareness week.

Identification of Problems

Admissions College application does not ask about prior substance abuse problems.

On campus Current students identified as chemically dependent may remain enrolled. Training program on identifying students with potential substance abuse problems for: resident advisers, coaches, faculty. Written procedures for students and staff if substance abuse is suspected.

Support Services

On campus ACOA, private counseling, group counseling.

Off campus AA, NA, Al-Anon.

Employee assistance Program for chemically dependent employees available. Staff working with drug/alcohol-related issues: 1 full-time.

Disciplinary Actions

Alcohol Results of infractions of alcohol regulations (see Comparative Table of Alcohol Regulations) vary by situation but can include chemical dependency assessment, counseling, warning, probation, suspension, expulsion, alcoholic-related educational program, related community service.

Drugs For any use, possession, or sale: varies by situation.

Additional Information from the College

There are alternative (nonalcohol) bars both in the Student Union and in the town.

For More Information

Contact: Kris Anderson, Coordinator of Chemical Dependency Programs and Services, Hendrix Health Center, Moorhead State University, Moorhead, MN 56560. Telephone: 218-236-2329.

MORAVIAN COLLEGE

Bethlehem, Pennsylvania

General Information

Independent 5-year coed college, affiliated with Moravian

Church. Founded 1742. Awards B, M. Primary accreditation: regional. City setting; 80-acre campus. Total enrollment: 1,659. Faculty: 143 (85 full-time, 58 part-time). Social organizations: 3 local fraternities, 3 local sororities; 18% of eligible undergraduate men and 20% of eligible undergraduate women are members.

Drug and Alcohol Information

Education

On campus Drug and alcohol education/prevention programs offered for: all students, athletes/coaches. Authorized group concerned with responsible drinking.

Identification of Problems

Admissions College application does not ask about prior substance abuse problems.

On campus Current students identified as chemically dependent may not remain enrolled. Comments: If the problem is alcohol-related, students may remain enrolled, but treatment is required. Training program on identifying students with potential substance abuse problems for: resident advisers. Written procedures for students and staff if substance abuse is suspected.

Support Services

On campus ACOA, private counseling.

Off campus AA, Al-Anon, other agencies.

Employee assistance Program for chemically dependent employees not available. Staff working with drug/alcohol-related issues: 4 part-time.

Disciplinary Actions

Alcohol Results of infractions of alcohol regulations (see Comparative Table of Alcohol Regulations) vary by situation but can include chemical dependency assessment, counseling, warning, probation, suspension, community service, fines, restitution, required educational program or project.

Drugs For first-time use, possession, or sale: varies by situation. For subsequent use or possession: varies by situation—chemical dependency assessment, probation, suspension. For subsequent sale: suspension, expulsion.

Additional Information from the College

An Alcohol Task Force has recently revised Moravian College's alcohol policy and is working to develop more awareness programs.

For More Information

Contact: Ralph W. Arend Jr., Dean of Students, Moravian College, Main St. and Elizabeth Ave., Bethlehem, PA 18018. Telephone: 215-861-1503.

MOREHEAD STATE UNIVERSITY

Morehead, Kentucky

General Information

State-supported 5-year coed college. Founded 1922. Awards A (college transfer and terminal), B, M. Primary accreditation: regional. Small-town setting; 809-acre campus. Total enrollment: 7,379. Faculty: 358 (314 full-time, 44 part-time). Social organizations: 13 national fraternities, 6 national sororities; 20% of eligible undergraduate men and 11% of eligible undergraduate women are members.

Drug and Alcohol Information

Education

On campus Drug and alcohol education/prevention programs offered for: all students. College holds an annual alcohol awareness week.

Identification of Problems

Admissions College application does not ask about prior substance abuse problems.

On campus Current students identified as chemically dependent may remain enrolled, but treatment is required. Training program on identifying students with potential substance abuse problems for: resident advisers, Greek officers, hall directors. Written procedures for students and staff if substance abuse is suspected.

Support Services

On campus Private counseling.

Employee assistance Program for chemically dependent employees not available.

Disciplinary Actions

Alcohol Results of infractions of alcohol regulations (see Comparative Table of Alcohol Regulations) vary by situation.

Drugs For first-time use or possession: counseling, warning. For subsequent use or possession: varies by situation—counseling. For any sale: varies by situation.

For More Information

Contact: Madonna Huffman, Residence Education, Howell-McDowell Administration Building, Morehead State University, Morehead, KY 40351. Telephone: 606-783-2070.

MORGAN STATE UNIVERSITY

Baltimore, Maryland

General Information

State-supported comprehensive coed institution. Founded 1867. Awards B, M, D. Primary accreditation: regional. Metropolitan setting; 130-acre campus. Total enrollment: 3,941. Faculty: 203 full-time. Social organizations: 5 national fraternities, 4 national sororities.

Drug and Alcohol Information

Education

On campus Drug and alcohol education/prevention programs offered for: all students, athletes/coaches, faculty, administration; required for: freshmen, resident advisers. Bacchus chapter. College holds an annual alcohol awareness week and drug awareness week.

Identification of Problems

Admissions College application does not ask about prior substance abuse problems.

On campus Current students identified as chemically dependent may remain enrolled, but treatment is required. Training program on identifying students with potential substance abuse problems for: resident advisers, Greek officers, staff, peer educators. Written procedures for students and staff if substance abuse is suspected.

Support Services

On campus AA, ACOA, private counseling.

Employee assistance Program for chemically dependent

Morgan State University (continued)

employees available. Staff working with drug/alcohol-related issues: 1 part-time.

Disciplinary Actions

Alcohol Results of infractions of alcohol regulations (see Comparative Table of Alcohol Regulations) vary by situation but can include chemical dependency assessment, counseling, warning, probation, suspension.

Drugs For any use: varies by situation. For any possession or sale: suspension, expulsion.

For More Information

Contact: Lila L. Curry, Counselor/Coordinator, Substance Abuse Education and Prevention Program, Morgan State University, Cold Spring Ln. and Hillen Rd., Baltimore, MD 21239. Telephone: 301-444-3043.

MORNINGSIDE COLLEGE

Sioux City, Iowa

General Information

Independent United Methodist 5-year coed college. Founded 1894. Awards A (terminal), B, M. Primary accreditation: regional. City setting; 27-acre campus. Total enrollment: 1,216. Faculty: 113 (77 full-time, 36 part-time). Social organizations: 1 national fraternity, 2 national sororities, 1 local fraternity; 17% of eligible undergraduate men and 13% of eligible undergraduate women are members.

Drug and Alcohol Information

Education

On campus Drug and alcohol education/prevention programs offered for: all students. Bacchus chapter. College holds an annual alcohol awareness week and drug awareness week.

Identification of Problems

Admissions College application does not ask about prior substance abuse problems.

On campus Current students identified as chemically dependent may sometimes remain enrolled, but treatment is required. Training program on identifying students with potential substance abuse problems for: resident advisers, administration, Student Services personnel. Written procedures for students and staff if substance abuse is suspected are being developed.

Support Services

On campus AA.

Employee assistance Program for chemically dependent employees not available. Staff working with drug/alcohol-related issues: 5 part-time.

Disciplinary Actions

Alcohol Results of infractions of alcohol regulations (see Comparative Table of Alcohol Regulations) include chemical dependency assessment, counseing, warning, probation, suspension, fines.

Drugs For first-time use or possession: varies by situation. For subsequent use or possession: suspension, expulsion. For any sale: suspension, expulsion.

For More Information

Contact: John Stein, Assistant Director of Housing, Morningside College, 1501 Morningside Ave., Sioux City, IA 51106. Telephone: 712-274-5104.

MORRIS COLLEGE

Sumter, South Carolina

General Information

Independent 4-year coed college, affiliated with Baptist Educational and Missionary Convention of South Carolina. Founded 1908. Awards B. Primary accreditation: regional. Small-town setting; 34-acre campus. Total enrollment: 774. Faculty: 52 (42 full-time, 10 part-time). Social organizations: 5 national fraternities, 4 national sororities; 18% of eligible undergraduate men and 15% of eligible undergraduate women are members.

Drug and Alcohol Information

Education

On campus Drug and alcohol education/prevention programs offered for: all students, athletes/coaches, faculty, administration; required for: freshmen, student leaders. College holds an annual alcohol awareness week and drug awareness week.

Identification of Problems

Admissions College application does not ask about prior substance abuse problems.

On campus Current students identified as chemically dependent may remain enrolled, but treatment is required. Training program on identifying students with potential substance abuse problems for: resident advisers, coaches.

Support Services

Off campus AA, NA, Al-Anon.

Employee assistance Program for chemically dependent employees not available. Staff working with drug/alcohol-related issues: 2 part-time.

Disciplinary Actions

Alcohol Results of infractions of alcohol regulations (see Comparative Table of Alcohol Regulations) include counseling, probation, suspension.

Drugs For first-time use: suspension. For subsequent use: expulsion. For first-time possession: counseling, probation. For subsequent possession: suspension. For first-time sale: expulsion.

For More Information

Contact: Alethia Lewis, Director, Student Development Center, Morris College, N. Main St., Sumter, SC 29150. Telephone: 803-775-9371.

MOUNT HOLYOKE COLLEGE

South Hadley, Massachusetts

General Information

Independent 4-year women's college. Founded 1837. Awards B. Primary accreditation: regional. Small-town setting; 800-acre campus. Total enrollment: 1,947. Faculty: 203 (181 full-time, 22 part-time).

Drug and Alcohol Information

Education

On campus Drug and alcohol education/prevention programs offered for: all students, faculty, administration, many panels, speakers, and groups open to the public. Authorized group concerned with responsible drinking. College holds an annual alcohol awareness week and drug awareness week.

Identification of Problems

Admissions College application does not ask about prior substance abuse problems.

On campus Current students identified as chemically dependent may remain enrolled. Training program on identifying students with potential substance abuse problems for: resident advisers, peer educators. No written procedures for students and staff if substance abuse is suspected.

Support Services

On campus AA, Al-Anon, ACOA, support groups, private counseling.

Employee assistance Program for chemically dependent employees available. Staff working with drug/alcohol-related issues: 1 full-time and 1 part-time.

Disciplinary Actions

Alcohol Results of infractions of alcohol regulations (see Comparative Table of Alcohol Regulations) vary by situation. Comments: Violation of policies may be confronted at the residence hall or organization level by an adviser, the Dean, or by the Council on Student Affairs.

Drugs For any use, possession, or sale: varies by situation.

Additional Information from the College

The Alcohol Awareness Project offers assessment, diagnosis, and counseling in substance abuse and chemical dependency. Education and training are provided for student leaders and all campus groups. An alcohol educator advises the peer education group, Sensible Alcohol Use Campus Educators.

For More Information

Contact: Patricia Hughes, Director of the Alcohol Awareness Project, Mount Holyoke College, South Hadley, MA 01075. Telephone: 413-538-2616.

MOUNT IDA COLLEGE

Newton Centre, Massachusetts

General Information

Independent primarily 2-year coed college. Founded 1899. Awards A (college transfer and terminal), B. Primary accreditation: regional. City setting; 85-acre campus. Total enrollment: 1,650. Faculty: 125 (98 full-time, 27 part-time).

Drug and Alcohol Information

Education

On campus Drug and alcohol education/prevention programs offered for: all students. College holds an annual alcohol awareness week.

Identification of Problems

Admissions College application does not ask about prior substance abuse problems.

On campus Current students identified as chemically dependent may remain enrolled, but treatment is required. Training program on identifying students with potential substance abuse problems for: resident advisers. Written procedures for students and staff if substance abuse is suspected.

Support Services

On campus Private counseling.

Employee assistance Program for chemically dependent employees not available.

Disciplinary Actions

Alcohol Results of infractions of alcohol regulations (see Comparative Table of Alcohol Regulations) include counseling, warning, probation, suspension, expulsion.

Drugs For first-time use or possession: warning. For subsequent use or possession: counseling, probation. For first-time sale: expulsion.

For More Information

Contact: Marcia Winters, Director of Counseling Services, Mount Ida College, 777 Dedham St., Newton Centre, MA 02159. Telephone: 617-969-7000 Ext. 163.

MOUNT MARY COLLEGE

Milwaukee, Wisconsin

General Information

Independent Roman Catholic 5-year women's college. Founded 1913. Awards B, M. Primary accreditation: regional. Metropolitan setting; 80-acre campus. Total enrollment: 1,366. Faculty: 137 (70 full-time, 67 part-time).

Drug and Alcohol Information

Education

On campus Drug and alcohol education/prevention programs offered for: all students, faculty, administration; required for: freshmen, resident advisers.

Identification of Problems

Admissions College application does not ask about prior substance abuse problems.

On campus Current students identified as chemically dependent may remain enrolled, but treatment is required. Training program on identifying students with potential substance abuse problems for: resident advisers, administration. Written procedures for students and staff if substance abuse is suspected.

Support Services

On campus Support groups (12-Step Meetings), private counseling, referrals.

Employee assistance Program for chemically dependent employees not available. Staff working with drug/alcohol-related issues: 5 part-time.

Disciplinary Actions

Alcohol Results of infractions of alcohol regulations (see Comparative Table of Alcohol Regulations) vary by situation but can include chemical dependency assessment, counseling, warning, probation, suspension, expulsion, contacting police.

Drugs For first-time use: chemical dependency assessment, counseling, probation. For subsequent use: expulsion. For any possession: chemical dependency assessment, counseling, probation. For first-time sale: expulsion.

For More Information

Contact: Sr. Shannon Marie Scallon, Dean of Students, Mount Mary College, 2900 N. Menomonee River Pkwy., Milwaukee, WI 53222. Telephone: 414-258-4810 Ext. 220.

MOUNT OLIVE COLLEGE

Mount Olive, North Carolina

General Information

Independent Free Will Baptist 4-year coed college. Founded 1951. Awards A (college transfer and terminal), B. Primary accreditation: regional. Small-town setting; 110-acre campus. Total enrollment: 997. Faculty: 55 (35 full-time, 20 part-time).

Drug and Alcohol Information

Education

On campus Drug and alcohol education/prevention programs offered for: all students, athletes/coaches. College holds an annual alcohol awareness week.

Identification of Problems

Admissions College application does not ask about prior substance abuse problems.

On campus Current students identified as chemically dependent may sometimes remain enrolled. Training program on identifying students with potential substance abuse problems for: resident advisers.

Support Services

On campus Support groups (Mental Health Association), private counseling.

Employee assistance Program for chemically dependent employees not available.

Disciplinary Actions

Alcohol Results of infractions of alcohol regulations (see Comparative Table of Alcohol Regulations) include probation, suspension.

Drugs For any use, possession, or sale: expulsion.

For More Information

Contact: Dr. Tom Johnson, Vice President for Student Affairs, Mount Olive College, Mount Olive, NC 28365. Telephone: 919-658-5056.

MOUNT ST. MARY'S COLLEGE

Los Angeles, California

General Information

Independent Roman Catholic 5-year primarily women's college. Founded 1925. Awards A (college transfer and terminal), B, M. Primary accreditation: regional. Metropolitan setting; 71-acre campus. Total enrollment: 1,203. Faculty: 141 (63 full-time, 78 part-time). Social organization: 1 local sorority.

Drug and Alcohol Information

Education

On campus Drug and alcohol education/prevention programs offered for: all students, faculty, administration. Authorized group concerned with responsible drinking. College holds an annual alcohol awareness week.

Identification of Problems

Admissions College application does not ask about prior substance abuse problems.

On campus Current students identified as chemically dependent may remain enrolled. Training program on identifying students with potential substance abuse problems for: resident advisers. No written procedures for students and staff if substance abuse is suspected.

Support Services

On campus ACOA, private counseling.

Employee assistance Program for chemically dependent employees not available.

Disciplinary Actions

Alcohol Results of infractions of alcohol regulations (see Comparative Table of Alcohol Regulations) vary by situation.

Drugs For any use, possession, or sale: varies by situation.

For More Information

Contact: Betty Glick, Assistant Dean for Student Development, Mount St. Mary's College, 12001 Chalon Rd., Los Angeles, CA 90049. Telephone: 213-471-9507.

MOUNT SAINT MARY'S COLLEGE

Emmitsburg, Maryland

General Information

Independent Roman Catholic 5-year coed college. Founded 1808. Awards B, M. Primary accreditation: regional. Rural setting; 1,500-acre campus. Total enrollment: 1,717. Faculty: 116 (82 full-time, 34 part-time).

Drug and Alcohol Information

Education

On campus Drug and alcohol education/prevention programs offered for: all students, athletes/coaches. Authorized group concerned with responsible drinking. College holds an annual alcohol awareness week and drug awareness week.

Identification of Problems

Admissions College application does not ask about prior substance abuse problems.

On campus Current students identified as chemically dependent may remain enrolled, but treatment is required. Training program on identifying students with potential substance abuse problems for: resident advisers, coaches. Written procedures for students and staff if substance abuse is suspected.

Support Services

On campus AA, ACOA, private counseling.

Employee assistance Program for chemically dependent employees available.

Disciplinary Actions

Alcohol Results of infractions of alcohol regulations (see Comparative Table of Alcohol Regulations) include chemical dependency assessment, counseling, warning, probation, suspension.

Drugs For first-time use: counseling, suspension. For subsequent use: expulsion. For first-time possession: chemical dependency assessment, counseling, probation. For subsequent possession: suspension. For first-time sale: expulsion.

For More Information

Contact: Jeanne Bergeron, Director of Residence Life,

Mount Saint Mary's College, Emmitsburg, MD 21727. Telephone: 301-447-5274.

MOUNT VERNON COLLEGE

Washington, District of Columbia

General Information

Independent 4-year women's college. Founded 1875. Awards A (college transfer), B. Primary accreditation: regional. Metropolitan setting; 26-acre campus. Total enrollment: 530. Faculty: 48 (33 full-time, 15 part-time).

Drug and Alcohol Information

Education

On campus Drug and alcohol education/prevention programs offered for: all students. College holds an annual alcohol awareness week.

Identification of Problems

Admissions College application does not ask about prior substance abuse problems.

On campus Current students identified as chemically dependent may remain enrolled, but treatment is required. No training program on identifying students with potential substance abuse problems. No written procedures for students and staff if substance abuse is suspected.

Support Services

On campus Private counseling. Staff working with drug/alcohol-related issues: 13 part-time.

Disciplinary Actions

Alcohol Results of infractions of alcohol regulations (see Comparative Table of Alcohol Regulations) vary by situation but can include chemical dependency assessment, counseling, warning, probation.

Drugs For first-time use or possession: varies by situation—counseling, warning. For subsequent use or possession: varies by situation. For any sale: suspension, expulsion.

For More Information

Contact: Donna R. Savage, Dean of Students, Mount Vernon College, 2100 Foxhall Rd., N.W., Washington, DC 20007. Telephone: 202-331-3424.

MOUNT VERNON NAZARENE COLLEGE

Mount Vernon, Ohio

General Information

Independent Nazarene 4-year coed college. Founded 1968. Awards A (college transfer and terminal), B. Primary accreditation: regional. Small-town setting; 210-acre campus. Total enrollment: 1,087. Faculty: 77 (69 full-time, 8 part-time).

Drug and Alcohol Information

Education

On campus Drug and alcohol education/prevention programs offered for: all students, athletes/coaches. College holds an annual alcohol awareness week and drug awareness week.

Identification of Problems

Admissions College application question about prior substance abuse problems is used to explain past academic performance; for counseling and referral, if student is admitted.

On campus No training program on identifying students with potential substance abuse problems. Written procedures for students and staff if substance abuse is suspected.

Support Services

On campus Private counseling.

Employee assistance Program for chemically dependent employees not available. Staff working with drug/alcohol-related issues: 2 part-time.

Disciplinary Actions

Alcohol Results of infractions of alcohol regulations (see Comparative Table of Alcohol Regulations) vary by situation but can include suspension.

Drugs For first-time use or possession: varies by situation—suspension, probation. For first-time sale: varies by situation. For subsequent use, possession, or sale: varies by situation—counseling, suspension.

For More Information

Contact: Lora H. Donoho, Athletic Director, Mount Vernon Nazarene College, 800 Martinsburg Rd., Mount Vernon, OH 43050. Telephone: 614-397-1244 Ext. 307–311.

MUHLENBERG COLLEGE

Allentown, Pennsylvania

General Information

Independent 4-year coed college, affiliated with Lutheran Church. Founded 1848. Awards B. Primary accreditation: regional. City setting; 75-acre campus. Total enrollment: 1,597. Faculty: 150 (112 full-time, 38 part-time). Social organizations: 6 national fraternities, 3 national sororities; 50% of eligible undergraduate men and 35% of eligible undergraduate women are members.

Drug and Alcohol Information

Education

On campus Drug and alcohol education/prevention programs offered for: all students. Authorized group concerned with responsible drinking. College holds an annual alcohol awareness week.

Identification of Problems

Admissions College application does not ask about prior substance abuse problems.

On campus Current students identified as chemically dependent may remain enrolled, but treatment is required. Training program on identifying students with potential substance abuse problems for: resident advisers, Greek officers. Written procedures for students and staff if substance abuse is suspected.

Support Services

On campus Al-Anon, private counseling, peer counselors.

Employee assistance Program for chemically dependent employees not available. Staff working with drug/alcohol-related issues: 1 part-time.

Disciplinary Actions

Alcohol Results of infractions of alcohol regulations (see

Muhlenberg College (continued)

Comparative Table of Alcohol Regulations) include counseling, probation, suspension.

Drugs For first-time use: varies by situation—chemical dependency assessment, counseling. For first-time possession: chemical dependency assessment, counseling, warning. For subsequent use or possession: suspension. For any sale: expulsion.

For More Information

Contact: Barry Anthony, Specialist–Drugs and Alcohol, Muhlenberg College, 24th and Chew Sts., Allentown, PA 18104. Telephone: 215-821-3185.

MUNDELEIN COLLEGE

Chicago, Illinois

General Information

Independent 5-year primarily women's college, affiliated with Roman Catholic Church. Founded 1929. Awards B, M. Primary accreditation: regional. Metropolitan setting; 1-acre campus. Total enrollment: 1,010. Faculty: 97 (58 full-time, 39 part-time). Social organizations: national sororities.

Drug and Alcohol Information

Education

On campus Drug and alcohol education/prevention programs offered for: all students, athletes/coaches; required for: freshmen, resident advisers. Authorized group concerned with responsible drinking. College holds an annual alcohol awareness week.

Identification of Problems

Admissions College application does not ask about prior substance abuse problems.

On campus Current students identified as chemically dependent may remain enrolled, but treatment is required. Training program on identifying students with potential substance abuse problems for: resident advisers, staff, student leaders (peer counselors, peer health educators). No written procedures for students and staff if substance abuse is suspected.

Support Services

On campus Private counseling, referrals.

Off campus ACOA.

Employee assistance Program for chemically dependent employees not available. Staff working with drug/alcohol-related issues: 3 part-time.

Disciplinary Actions

Alcohol Results of infractions of alcohol regulations (see Comparative Table of Alcohol Regulations) vary by situation.

Drugs For any use, possession, or sale: varies by situation.

For More Information

Contact: Jean Kartje, Assistant Dean of Students, Mundelein College, 6363 N. Sheridan Rd., Chicago, IL 60660. Telephone: 312-262-8100.

MURRAY STATE UNIVERSITY

Murray, Kentucky

General Information

State-supported 5-year coed college. Founded 1922. Awards A (college transfer and terminal), B, M. Primary accreditation: regional. Small-town setting; 238-acre campus. Total enrollment: 7,628. Faculty: 371 (368 full-time, 3 part-time). Social organizations: 14 national fraternities, 8 national sororities, 1 local sorority; 25% of eligible undergraduate men and 25% of eligible undergraduate women are members.

Drug and Alcohol Information

Education

On campus Drug and alcohol education/prevention programs offered for: all students. Authorized group concerned with responsible drinking. College holds an annual alcohol awareness week and drug awareness week.

Identification of Problems

Admissions

On campus Current students identified as chemically dependent may remain enrolled. Training program on identifying students with potential substance abuse problems for: resident advisers.

Support Services

On campus AA, NA, Al-Anon, ACOA, private counseling.

Employee assistance Program for chemically dependent employees available. Staff working with drug/alcohol-related issues: 4 part-time.

Disciplinary Actions

Alcohol Results of infractions of alcohol regulations (see Comparative Table of Alcohol Regulations) vary by situation but can include chemical dependency assessment, counseling, warning, probation, suspension, expulsion.

Drugs For any use, possession, or sale: varies by situation.

For More Information

Contact: Bill Allbritten, Director, Counseling Center, Ordway Hall, Murray State University, University Station, Murray, KY 42071. Telephone: 502-762-6851.

MUSKEGON COLLEGE

Muskegon, Michigan

General Information

Independent 4-year coed college. Founded 1888. Awards A (college transfer and terminal), B. Primary accreditation: regional and AICS. Small-town setting; 15-acre campus. Total enrollment: 1,700. Faculty: 60 (23 full-time, 37 part-time).

Drug and Alcohol Information

Education

On campus Drug and alcohol education/prevention programs offered for: all students. College holds an annual alcohol awareness week and drug awareness week.

Identification of Problems

Admissions College application does not ask about prior substance abuse problems.

On campus Current students identified as chemically dependent may remain enrolled, but treatment is required. Training program on identifying students with potential substance abuse problems for: resident advisers, faculty. No written procedures for students and staff if substance abuse is suspected.

Support Services

On campus Support groups.

Employee assistance Program for chemically dependent employees not available. Staff working with drug/alcohol-related issues: 2 part-time.

Disciplinary Actions

Alcohol Results of infractions of alcohol regulations (see Comparative Table of Alcohol Regulations) vary by situation.

Drugs For any use, possession, or sale: varies by situation.

For More Information

Contact: Patricia Shafer, Director, Housing and Student Activities, Muskegon College, 141 Hartford St., Muskegon, MI 49442. Telephone: 616-726-4904.

MUSKINGUM COLLEGE

New Concord, Ohio

General Information

Independent 4-year coed college, affiliated with Presbyterian Church (U.S.A.). Founded 1837. Awards B. Primary accreditation: regional. Rural setting; 215-acre campus. Total enrollment: 1,101. Faculty: 115 (77 full-time, 38 part-time). Social organizations: 2 national fraternities, 1 national sorority, 3 local fraternities, 3 local sororities; 55% of eligible undergraduate men and 55% of eligible undergraduate women are members.

Drug and Alcohol Information

Education

On campus Drug and alcohol education/prevention programs offered for: all students; required for: freshmen. Bacchus chapter: 25 members. College holds an annual alcohol awareness week and drug awareness week.

Identification of Problems

Admissions College application does not ask about prior substance abuse problems.

On campus Current students identified as chemically dependent may remain enrolled, but treatment is required. Training program on identifying students with potential substance abuse problems for: resident advisers. Written procedures for students and staff if substance abuse is suspected.

Support Services

On campus Support groups, private counseling.

Off campus AA.

Employee assistance Program for chemically dependent employees not available.

Disciplinary Actions

Alcohol Results of infractions of alcohol regulations (see Comparative Table of Alcohol Regulations) vary by situation but can include counseling, warning, probation, suspension.

Drugs For any use or possession: varies by situation—counseling. For any sale: expulsion.

For More Information

Contact: David R. Skeen, Dean, Student Life, Muskingum College, New Concord, OH 43762. Telephone: 614-826-8141.

NAES COLLEGE

Chicago, Illinois

General Information

Independent 4-year coed college. Founded 1974. Awards B. Primary accreditation: regional. Metropolitan setting. Total enrollment: 50.

Drug and Alcohol Information

Education

On campus Drug and alcohol education/prevention programs offered for: all students, faculty, administration.

Identification of Problems

Admissions College application does not ask about prior substance abuse problems.

On campus Current students identified as chemically dependent may remain enrolled, but treatment is required. Training program on identifying students with potential substance abuse problems for: faculty, administration, students. Written procedures for students and staff if substance abuse is suspected.

Support Services

On campus Private counseling.

Employee assistance Program for chemically dependent employees available. Staff working with drug/alcohol-related issues: 2 part-time.

Disciplinary Actions

Alcohol Results of infractions of alcohol regulations (see Comparative Table of Alcohol Regulations) include chemical dependency assessment, counseling.

Drugs For first-time use: chemical dependency assessment, counseling. For first-time possession or sale: varies by situation. For subsequent use, possession, or sale: varies by situation.

For More Information

Contact: Joe White Eyes, Coordinator of Alcoholism Studies, NAES College, 2838 W. Peterson Ave., Chicago, IL 60659. Telephone: 312-761-5000.

NATIONAL COLLEGE–ST. PAUL CAMPUS

St. Paul, Minnesota

General Information

Proprietary 4-year coed college. Part of National College. Founded 1970. Awards A (college transfer), B. Primary accreditation: regional. Metropolitan setting; 1-acre campus.

National College–St. Paul Campus (continued)

Drug and Alcohol Information

Education

On campus Drug and alcohol education/prevention programs not offered.

Identification of Problems

Admissions College application does not ask about prior substance abuse problems.

On campus Current students identified as chemically dependent may remain enrolled. No training program on identifying students with potential substance abuse problems. No written procedures for students and staff if substance abuse is suspected.

Support Services

On campus Private counseling.

Employee assistance Program for chemically dependent employees not available.

Disciplinary Actions

Alcohol Results of infractions of alcohol regulations (see Comparative Table of Alcohol Regulations) vary by situation but can include counseling. Comments: There has never been any instance of drug use, possession, or sale on campus.

Additional Information from the College

National College–St. Paul Campus is nonresidential. No alcohol is sold or distributed on campus, and no alcohol-related problems have arisen.

For More Information

Contact: Jim Downie, Dean of Students, National College–St. Paul Campus, 1380 Energy Ln., St. Paul, MN 55108. Telephone: 612-644-1265.

NAZARETH COLLEGE IN KALAMAZOO

Kalamazoo, Michigan

General Information

Independent Roman Catholic 5-year coed college. Founded 1924. Awards B, M. Primary accreditation: regional. City setting; 59-acre campus. Total enrollment: 730. Faculty: 97 (42 full-time, 55 part-time).

Drug and Alcohol Information

Education

On campus Drug and alcohol education/prevention programs offered for: all students, athletes/coaches. College holds an annual alcohol awareness week and drug awareness week.

Identification of Problems

Admissions College application does not ask about prior substance abuse problems.

On campus Current students identified as chemically dependent may remain enrolled, but treatment is required. Training program on identifying students with potential substance abuse problems for: resident advisers. Written procedures for students and staff if substance abuse is suspected.

Support Services

On campus Private counseling.

Employee assistance Program for chemically dependent employees not available.

Disciplinary Actions

Alcohol Results of infractions of alcohol regulations (see Comparative Table of Alcohol Regulations) vary by situation but can include chemical dependency assessment, counseling, warning, probation, suspension, expulsion.

Drugs For any use or possession: varies by situation. For any sale: suspension, expulsion.

Additional Information from the College

Infractions involving drug and/or alcohol policies are handled through the judicial system. Counseling services, both on and off campus, are utilized for individuals who demonstrate dependency.

For More Information

Contact: Kenyon Morgan, Director of Counseling Services, Nazareth College in Kalamazoo, 3333 Gull Road, Kalamazoo, MI 49001. Telephone: 616-349-4200.

NAZARETH COLLEGE OF ROCHESTER

Rochester, New York

General Information

Independent 5-year coed college. Founded 1924. Awards B, M. Primary accreditation: regional. Metropolitan setting; 75-acre campus. Total enrollment: 2,935. Faculty: 153 (103 full-time, 50 part-time).

Drug and Alcohol Information

Education

On campus Drug and alcohol education/prevention programs offered for: all students, faculty, administration; required for: athletes/coaches, resident advisers. Authorized group concerned with responsible drinking. College holds an annual alcohol awareness week and drug awareness week.

Identification of Problems

Admissions College application does not ask about prior substance abuse problems.

On campus Current students identified as chemically dependent may remain enrolled. Training program on identifying students with potential substance abuse problems for: resident advisers, coaches, administration. Written procedures for students and staff if substance abuse is suspected.

Support Services

On campus Al-Anon, ACOA, private counseling, Substance Abuse Education Committee.

Employee assistance Program for chemically dependent employees not available. Staff working with drug/alcohol-related issues: 12 part-time.

Disciplinary Actions

Alcohol Results of infractions of alcohol regulations (see Comparative Table of Alcohol Regulations) vary by situation but can include chemical dependency assessment, counseling, warning, probation.

Drugs For any use or possession: varies by situation. For any sale: expulsion.

Additional Information from the College

Nazareth College of Rochester attempts to take a proactive and educational approach to substance abuse issues. The

College community works together to provide alternatives to alcohol and drug use and to see that peer pressure is exerted against, rather than toward, such use.

For More Information

Contact: Jane Liberman, Associate Director of Residential Life, Nazareth College of Rochester, 4245 East Ave., Rochester, NY 14610. Telephone: 716-586-2525 Ext. 700.

NEBRASKA CHRISTIAN COLLEGE

Norfolk, Nebraska

General Information

Independent 4-year coed college, affiliated with Christian Churches and Churches of Christ. Founded 1944. Awards A (terminal), B. Primary accreditation: AABC. Small-town setting; 85-acre campus. Total enrollment: 148. Faculty: 14 (5 full-time, 9 part-time).

Drug and Alcohol Information

Education

On campus Drug and alcohol education/prevention programs not offered.

Identification of Problems

Admissions College application question about prior substance abuse problems is used for counseling and referral, if student is admitted; in the admissions decision.

On campus Current students identified as chemically dependent may not remain enrolled. No training program on identifying students with potential substance abuse problems. Written procedures for students and staff if substance abuse is suspected.

Support Services

On campus ACOA, private counseling.

Employee assistance Program for chemically dependent employees not available. Staff working with drug/alcohol-related issues: 1 part-time.

Disciplinary Actions

Alcohol Results of infractions of alcohol regulations (see Comparative Table of Alcohol Regulations) include suspension, expulsion.

Drugs for first-time use, possession, or sale: suspension, expulsion. For subsequent use, possession, or sale: expulsion.

Additional Information from the College

Students who are suspended or expelled from Nebraska Christian College are referred to local counselors for help.

For More Information

Contact: Chris Lahm, Dean of Students, Nebraska Christian College, 1800 Syracuse Ave., Norfolk, NE 68701. Telephone: 402-371-5960.

NEWBERRY COLLEGE

Newberry, South Carolina

General Information

Independent Lutheran 4-year coed college. Founded 1856. Awards B. Primary accreditation: regional. Small-town setting; 60-acre campus. Total enrollment: 686. Faculty: 62 (39 full-time, 23 part-time). Social organizations: 4 national fraternities, 2 national sororities; 30% of eligible undergraduate men and 31% of eligible undergraduate women are members.

Drug and Alcohol Information

Education

On campus Drug and alcohol education/prevention programs offered for: all students. College holds an annual alcohol awareness week and drug awareness week.

Identification of Problems

Admissions College application does not ask about prior substance abuse problems.

On campus Current students identified as chemically dependent may sometimes remain enrolled, but treatment is required. No training program on identifying students with potential substance abuse problems. Written procedures for students and staff if substance abuse is suspected.

Support Services

On campus Private counseling.

Disciplinary Actions

Alcohol Results of infractions of alcohol regulations (see Comparative Table of Alcohol Regulations) vary by situation but can include warning, fines.

Drugs For first-time use or possession: chemical dependency assessment, counseling, probation. For subsequent use or possession: varies by situation. For first-time sale: suspension, expulsion. For subsequent sale: expulsion.

For More Information

Contact: Susan Bowers, Dean of Women, Newberry College, 2100 College St., Newberry, SC 29108. Telephone: 803-276-5010.

NEW COLLEGE OF CALIFORNIA

San Francisco, California

General Information

Independent 5-year coed college. Founded 1971. Awards A (college transfer), B, M. Primary accreditation: regional. Metropolitan setting. Total enrollment: 365.

Drug and Alcohol Information

Education

On campus Drug and alcohol education/prevention programs offered for: all students, athletes/coaches, faculty. Authorized group concerned with responsible drinking. College holds an annual alcohol awareness week and drug awareness week.

Identification of Problems

Admissions College application does not ask about prior substance abuse problems.

On campus Current students identified as chemically dependent may remain enrolled, but treatment is required. Training program on identifying students with potential substance abuse problems for: faculty advisers. No written procedures now for students and staff if substance abuse is suspected, but such procedures are being developed.

New College of California (continued)

Support Services

On campus AA, private counseling.

Employee assistance Program for chemically dependent employees not available.

Disciplinary Actions

Alcohol Results of infractions of alcohol regulations (see Comparative Table of Alcohol Regulations) include chemical dependency assessment, counseling.

Drugs For any use: counseling. For first-time possession or sale: chemical dependency assessment, counseling. For subsequent possession: chemical dependency assessment, counseling. For subsequent sale: counseling, warning.

Additional Information from the College

The drug/alcohol abuse issue is fundamentally examined in the faculty adviser–student relationship. Referrals may be made to resources on or off campus.

For More Information

Contact: Richard Shapiro, Director of Humanities, New College of California, 50 Fell St., San Francisco, CA 94102. Telephone: 415-626-1694 Ext. 144.

NEW COLLEGE OF THE UNIVERSITY OF SOUTH FLORIDA

Sarasota, Florida

General Information

State-supported 4-year coed college. Part of State University System of Florida. Founded 1960. Awards B. Primary accreditation: regional. City setting; 120-acre campus. Total enrollment: 517. Faculty: 52 (all full-time).

Drug and Alcohol Information

Education

On campus Drug and alcohol education/prevention programs offered for: all students.

Identification of Problems

Admissions College application does not ask about prior substance abuse problems.

On campus Current students identified as chemically dependent may remain enrolled. Training program on identifying students with potential substance abuse problems for: resident advisers. No written procedures for students and staff if substance abuse is suspected.

Support Services

On campus Private counseling.

Employee assistance Program for chemically dependent employees available. Staff working with drug/alcohol-related issues: 3 part-time.

Disciplinary Actions

Alcohol Results of infractions of alcohol regulations (see Comparative Table of Alcohol Regulations) vary by situation.

Drugs For any use, possession, or sale: varies by situation.

For More Information

Contact: Mark Johnson, Associate Director of Student Affairs, New College of the University of South Florida, 5700 N. Tamiami Trail, Sarasota, FL 34243. Telephone: 813-359-4259.

NEW ENGLAND COLLEGE

Henniker, New Hampshire

General Information

Independent 5-year coed college. Founded 1946. Awards B, M. Primary accreditation: regional. Rural setting; 212-acre campus. Total enrollment: 1,260. Faculty: 116 (86 full-time, 30 part-time). Social organizations: 1 national fraternity, 2 local fraternities, 1 local sorority; 20% of eligible undergraduate men are members.

Drug and Alcohol Information

Education

On campus Drug and alcohol education/prevention programs offered for: all students, athletes/coaches; required for: disciplinary cases. Authorized group concerned with responsible drinking. College holds an annual alcohol and drug awareness week.

Identification of Problems

Admissions College application does not ask about prior substance abuse problems.

On campus Current students identified as chemically dependent may remain enrolled depending on the situation and the resources available, but treatment is required. Training program on identifying students with potential substance abuse problems for: resident advisers, coaches, faculty. Written procedures for students and staff if substance abuse is suspected.

Support Services

On campus ACOA, private counseling, drug/alcohol assessment programs.

Off campus AA.

Employee assistance Program for chemically dependent employees not available. Staff working with drug/alcohol-related issues: 5 part-time.

Disciplinary Actions

Alcohol Results of infractions of alcohol regulations (see Comparative Table of Alcohol Regulations) vary by situation but can include chemical dependency assessment, counseling, probation.

Drugs For first-time use: varies by situation—chemical dependency assessment, counseling. For subsequent use: varies by situation. For first-time possession: varies by situation—probation, suspension, expulsion. For first-time sale: varies by situation—suspension, expulsion. For subsequent possession or sale: expulsion.

For More Information

Contact: Ken Gobbo, Associate Dean of Student Affairs, New England College, Henniker, NH 03242. Telephone: 603-428-2241.

NEW HAMPSHIRE COLLEGE

Manchester, New Hampshire

General Information

Independent 5-year coed college. Founded 1932. Awards A (terminal), B, M. Primary accreditation: regional and AICS. City setting; 700-acre campus. Total enrollment: 3,373.

Faculty: 77 (57 full-time, 20 part-time). Social organizations: 4 national fraternities, 1 national sorority, 5 local sororities; 15% of eligible undergraduate men and 15% of eligible undergraduate women are members.

Drug and Alcohol Information

Education

On campus Drug and alcohol education/prevention programs offered for: all students, faculty, administration, professional staff. Authorized group concerned with responsible drinking. College holds an annual alcohol awareness week and drug awareness week.

Identification of Problems

Admissions College application does not ask about prior substance abuse problems.

On campus Current students identified as chemically dependent may remain enrolled, but treatment is required. Training program on identifying students with potential substance abuse problems for: resident advisers, coaches, Greek officers, faculty, administration, all members of the community. Written procedures for students and staff if substance abuse is suspected.

Support Services

On campus Support groups, private counseling.

Employee assistance Program for chemically dependent employees available. Staff working with drug/alcohol-related issues: 2 part-time.

Disciplinary Actions

Alcohol Results of infractions of alcohol regulations (see Comparative Table of Alcohol Regulations) vary by situation.

Drugs For any use or possession: varies by situation. For any sale: expulsion.

For More Information

Contact: Charles Mitchell, Director of Counseling, New Hampshire College, 2500 N. River Rd., Manchester, NH 03104. Telephone: 603-645-9608.

NEW MEXICO INSTITUTE OF MINING AND TECHNOLOGY

Socorro, New Mexico

General Information

State-supported comprehensive coed institution. Founded 1889. Awards A (college transfer), B, M, D. Primary accreditation: regional. Small-town setting; 320-acre campus. Total enrollment: 1,228. Faculty: 98 (95 full-time, 3 part-time).

Drug and Alcohol Information

Education

On campus Drug and alcohol education/prevention programs offered for: all students. Authorized group concerned with responsible drinking. College holds an annual alcohol awareness week.

Identification of Problems

Admissions College application does not ask about prior substance abuse problems.

On campus Current students identified as chemically dependent may remain enrolled, but treatment is required. Training program on identifying students with potential substance abuse problems for: resident advisers, faculty, administration. No written procedures for students and staff if substance abuse is suspected.

Support Services

On campus Private counseling.

Employee assistance Program for chemically dependent employees not available. Staff working with drug/alcohol-related issues: 4 part-time.

Disciplinary Actions

Alcohol Results of infractions of alcohol regulations (see Comparative Table of Alcohol Regulations) include chemical dependency assessment, counseling, probation, suspension, expulsion.

Drugs For any use: varies by situation—counseling. For any possession or sale: varies by situation.

Additional Information from the College

New Mexico Institute of Mining and Technology is in the process of formulating a strong policy on alcohol.

For More Information

Contact: Frank T. Etscorn, Dean of Students, New Mexico Institute of Mining and Technology, Socorro, NM 87801. Telephone: 505-835-5208.

NEW MEXICO STATE UNIVERSITY

Las Cruces, New Mexico

General Information

State-supported comprehensive coed institution. Part of New Mexico State University System. Founded 1888. Awards A (college transfer and terminal), B, M, D. Primary accreditation: regional. City setting; 6,000-acre campus. Total enrollment: 14,284. Faculty: 715 (601 full-time, 114 part-time). Social organizations: 9 national fraternities, 5 national sororities; 6% of eligible undergraduate men and 5% of eligible undergraduate women are members.

Drug and Alcohol Information

Education

On campus Drug and alcohol education/prevention programs offered for: all students, faculty, staff. Authorized group concerned with responsible drinking. College holds an annual alcohol awareness week and drug awareness week.

Identification of Problems

Admissions College application does not ask about prior substance abuse problems.

On campus Current students identified as chemically dependent may remain enrolled, but treatment is required. Training program on identifying students with potential substance abuse problems for: resident advisers, Greek officers. Written procedures for students and staff if substance abuse is suspected.

Support Services

On campus Support groups (group counseling), private counseling, psychiatrist.

Employee assistance Program for chemically dependent employees available. Staff working with drug/alcohol-related issues: 6–10 part-time.

Disciplinary Actions

Alcohol Results of infractions of alcohol regulations (see Comparative Table of Alcohol Regulations) vary by situation but can include counseling, probation.

New Mexico State University (continued)

Drugs For first-time use, possession, or sale: varies by situation—counseling, warning, probation. For subsequent use, possession, or sale: varies by situation.

For More Information

Contact: Stephen Sanchez Jr., Graduate Assistant, New Mexico State University, Box 3923, Las Cruces, NM 88005. Telephone: 505-646-1722.

NEW YORK SCHOOL OF INTERIOR DESIGN

New York, New York

General Information

Independent 4-year specialized coed college. Founded 1916. Awards A (terminal), B. Primary accreditation: New York State Board of Regents. Metropolitan setting. Total enrollment: 726. Faculty: 70 (all part-time).

Drug and Alcohol Information

Education

On campus Drug and alcohol education/prevention programs not offered.

Identification of Problems

Admissions College application does not ask about prior substance abuse problems.

On campus Current students identified as chemically dependent may remain enrolled, but treatment is required. No training program on identifying students with potential substance abuse problems. No written procedures for students and staff if substance abuse is suspected.

Support Services

On campus No support services on campus.

Employee assistance Program for chemically dependent employees not available.

Disciplinary Actions

Alcohol Results of infractions of alcohol regulations (see Comparative Table of Alcohol Regulations) include counseling, warning, probation, suspension, expulsion.

Drugs For any use or possession: varies by situation. For first-time sale: expulsion.

For More Information

Contact: R. Zelazny, Vice President, New York School of Interior Design, 155 E. 56th St., New York, NY 10022. Telephone: 212-753-5365.

NEW YORK UNIVERSITY

New York, New York

General Information

Independent comprehensive coed institution. Founded 1831. Awards A (college transfer and terminal), B, M, D. Primary accreditation: regional. Metropolitan setting; 28-acre campus. Total enrollment: 31,690. Faculty: 5,428 (2,494 full-time, 2,934 part-time). Social organizations: 10 national fraternities, 7 national sororities; 6% of eligible undergraduate men and 5% of eligible undergraduate women are members.

Drug and Alcohol Information

Education

On campus Drug and alcohol education/prevention programs offered for: freshmen, social organization members, athletes/coaches, resident advisers, student leaders. Authorized group concerned with responsible drinking. College holds an annual alcohol awareness week and drug awareness week.

Identification of Problems

Admissions College application does not ask about prior substance abuse problems.

On campus Current students identified as chemically dependent may remain enrolled, but treatment is required. Training program on identifying students with potential substance abuse problems for: resident advisers, coaches, Greek officers, administration. Written procedures for students and staff if substance abuse is suspected.

Support Services

On campus AA, NA, Al-Anon, private counseling.

Employee assistance Program for chemically dependent employees not available. Staff working with drug/alcohol-related issues: 1 full-time and 25 part-time.

Disciplinary Actions

Alcohol Results of infractions of alcohol regulations (see Comparative Table of Alcohol Regulations) vary by situation.

Drugs For any use or possession: varies by situation. For first-time sale: expulsion.

For More Information

Contact: Sara Arthur, Director of Student Life, New York University, 566 La Guardia Pl., Rm. 208, New York, NY 10003. Telephone: 212-998-4953.

NICHOLS COLLEGE

Dudley, Massachusetts

General Information

Independent 5-year coed college. Founded 1815. Awards A (college transfer), B, M. Primary accreditation: regional. Rural setting; 210-acre campus. Total enrollment: 1,209. Faculty: 49 (36 full-time, 13 part-time).

Drug and Alcohol Information

Education

On campus Drug and alcohol education/prevention programs offered for: all students; required for: freshmen. Authorized group concerned with responsible drinking.

Identification of Problems

Admissions College application does not ask about prior substance abuse problems.

On campus Current students identified as chemically dependent may remain enrolled, but treatment is required. Training program on identifying students with potential substance abuse problems for: resident advisers. Written procedures for students and staff if substance abuse is suspected.

Support Services

On campus Private counseling.

Off campus AA, Al-Anon.

Employee assistance Program for chemically dependent

employees available. Staff working with drug/alcohol-related issues: 2 part-time.

Disciplinary Actions

Alcohol Results of infractions of alcohol regulations (see Comparative Table of Alcohol Regulations) vary by situation but can include chemical dependency assessment, counseling, warning, probation, expulsion.

Drugs For first-time use, possession, or sale: urinalysis, unannounced room search, probation. For subsequent sale: expulsion.

Additional Information from the College

As a small, private, residential college, Nichols makes every attempt to supplement on-campus resources with services available in the local community. The College's goals are a drug-free campus and responsible use of alcohol by members of the community.

For More Information

Contact: Roger F. X. Carney, Dean of Student Affairs, Nichols College, Dudley, MA 01570-5000. Telephone: 508-943-1560 Ext. 249.

NORTH ADAMS STATE COLLEGE

North Adams, Massachusetts

General Information

State-supported 5-year coed college. Founded 1894. Awards B, M. Primary accreditation: regional. Small-town setting; 95-acre campus. Total enrollment: 2,584. Faculty: 127 (104 full-time, 23 part-time). Social organizations: 4 national fraternities, 3 national sororities; 15% of eligible undergraduate men and 10% of eligible undergraduate women are members.

Drug and Alcohol Information

Education

On campus Drug and alcohol education/prevention programs offered for: all students, athletes/coaches, faculty, administration; required for: Judicial Board referrals. Authorized group concerned with responsible drinking. College holds an annual alcohol awareness week and drug awareness week.

Identification of Problems

Admissions College application does not ask about prior substance abuse problems.

On campus Current students identified as chemically dependent may remain enrolled. Training program on identifying students with potential substance abuse problems for: resident advisers, coaches, faculty, administration, campus police. Written procedures for students and staff if substance abuse is suspected.

Support Services

On campus ACOA, private counseling.

Employee assistance Program for chemically dependent employees available. Staff working with drug/alcohol-related issues: 2 full-time.

Disciplinary Actions

Alcohol Results of infractions of alcohol regulations (see Comparative Table of Alcohol Regulations) include probation.

Drugs For any use, possession, or sale: referral to the state legal system.

For More Information

Contact: Doreen Forney, Substance Abuse Counselor, North Adams State College, Church St., North Adams, MA 01247. Telephone: 413-664-4511.

NORTH CAROLINA CENTRAL UNIVERSITY

Durham, North Carolina

General Information

State-supported 5-year coed college. Part of University of North Carolina System. Founded 1910. Awards B, M. Primary accreditation: regional. City setting; 109-acre campus. Total enrollment: 5,182. Faculty: 326 (218 full-time, 108 part-time). Social organizations: 4 national fraternities, 4 national sororities, 5 local fraternities, 4 local sororities; 30% of eligible undergraduate men and 30% of eligible undergraduate women are members.

Drug and Alcohol Information

Education

On campus Drug and alcohol education/prevention programs offered for: all students, athletes/coaches, faculty, administration; required for: freshmen. College holds an annual alcohol awareness week and drug awareness week.

Identification of Problems

Admissions College application does not ask about prior substance abuse problems.

On campus Current students identified as chemically dependent may remain enrolled, but treatment is required. Training program on identifying students with potential substance abuse problems for: counselors. Written procedures for students and staff if substance abuse is suspected.

Support Services

On campus Private counseling.

Employee assistance Program for chemically dependent employees not available. Staff working with drug/alcohol-related issues: 2 part-time.

Disciplinary Actions

Alcohol Results of infractions of alcohol regulations (see Comparative Table of Alcohol Regulations) include suspension.

Drugs For first-time use or possession: suspension. For subsequent use or possession: expulsion. For any sale: expulsion.

For More Information

Contact: Dr. Glen R. Martin, Associate Vice Chancellor/Student Affairs, P.O. Box 19688, North Carolina Central University, Durham, NC 27707. Telephone: 919-560-6336.

NORTH CAROLINA STATE UNIVERSITY

Raleigh, North Carolina

General Information

State-supported comprehensive coed institution. Part of University of North Carolina System. Founded 1887. Awards A (terminal), B, M, D. Primary accreditation: regional. City setting; 623-acre campus. Total enrollment:

North Carolina State University (continued)

25,537. Faculty: 1,442. Social organizations: 24 national fraternities, 7 national sororities; 7% of eligible undergraduate men and 8% of eligible undergraduate women are members.

Drug and Alcohol Information

Education

On campus Drug and alcohol education/prevention programs offered for: all students. Authorized group concerned with responsible drinking. College holds an annual alcohol awareness week and drug awareness week.

Identification of Problems

Admissions College application does not ask about prior substance abuse problems.

On campus Current students identified as chemically dependent may remain enrolled. Training program on identifying students with potential substance abuse problems for: resident advisers, coaches. No written procedures for students and staff if substance abuse is suspected.

Support Services

On campus NA, ACOA, support groups, private counseling.

Off campus AA.

Employee assistance Program for chemically dependent employees available. Staff working with drug/alcohol-related issues: 1 full-time and 9 part-time.

Disciplinary Actions

Alcohol Results of infractions of alcohol regulations (see Comparative Table of Alcohol Regulations) vary by situation but can include chemical dependency assessment, counseling, warning, probation, suspension, expulsion.

Drugs For first-time use, possession, or sale: varies by situation. For subsequent use or possession: suspension. For subsequent sale: expulsion.

Additional Information from the College

Academic classes, programs provided by health educators and peer counselors, literature, and film/video material are all available for education and intervention.

For More Information

Contact: Jeanine Atkinson, Substance Abuse Prevention Coordinator, Student Health Service, North Carolina State University, Box 7304, Raleigh, NC 27695.
Telephone: 919-737-2563.

NORTH DAKOTA STATE UNIVERSITY

Fargo, North Dakota

General Information

State-supported comprehensive coed institution. Founded 1890. Awards A (college transfer and terminal), B, M, D. Primary accreditation: regional. City setting; 2,100-acre campus. Total enrollment: 9,534. Faculty: 429 (424 full-time, 5 part-time). Social organizations: 14 national fraternities, 5 national sororities; 16% of eligible undergraduate men and 2% of eligible undergraduate women are members.

Drug and Alcohol Information

Education

On campus Drug and alcohol education/prevention programs offered for: all students; required for: athletes/coaches, resident advisers. Authorized group concerned with responsible drinking. College holds an annual alcohol awareness week and drug awareness week.

Identification of Problems

Admissions College application does not ask about prior substance abuse problems.

On campus Current students identified as chemically dependent may remain enrolled, but treatment is required. Training program on identifying students with potential substance abuse problems for: resident advisers, coaches, Greek officers, faculty, any group or individual upon request. Written procedures for students and staff if substance abuse is suspected.

Support Services

On campus ACOA, support groups through the Center for Student Counseling and Personal Growth, private counseling.

Employee assistance Program for chemically dependent employees available. Staff working with drug/alcohol-related issues: 1 full-time and 6 part-time.

Disciplinary Actions

Alcohol Results of infractions of alcohol regulations (see Comparative Table of Alcohol Regulations) vary by situation but can include chemical dependency assessment, counseling, warning, probation, suspension, expulsion, fine, or community service.

Drugs For any use, possession, or sale: varies by situation.

For More Information

Contact: Peter Bower, Director of Chemically Dependent and Handicapped Student Services, 212K Ceres Hall, North Dakota State University, University Station, Fargo, ND 58105. Telephone: 701-237-7198.

NORTHEASTERN ILLINOIS UNIVERSITY

Chicago, Illinois

General Information

State-supported 5-year coed college. Part of State Colleges and Universities of Illinois System. Founded 1961. Awards B, M. Primary accreditation: regional. Metropolitan setting; 67-acre campus. Total enrollment: 9,846. Faculty: 525 (368 full-time, 157 part-time). Social organizations: 1 national fraternity, men's and women's associations; 10% of eligible undergraduate men and 20% of eligible undergraduate women are members.

Drug and Alcohol Information

Education

On campus Drug and alcohol education/prevention programs offered for: all students, athletes/coaches, faculty, administration. College holds an annual alcohol awareness week and drug awareness week.

Identification of Problems

Admissions College application does not ask about prior substance abuse problems.

On campus Current students identified as chemically

dependent may remain enrolled. Training program on identifying students with potential substance abuse problems for: faculty, administration, academic advisers, prevention/intervention ambassadors. No written procedures for students and staff if substance abuse is suspected.

Support Services

On campus AA, ACOA, support groups, private counseling.

Employee assistance Program for chemically dependent employees available.

Disciplinary Actions

Alcohol Results of infractions of alcohol regulations (see Comparative Table of Alcohol Regulations) vary by situation but can include counseling, warning, probation, suspension, expulsion.

Drugs For any use, possession, or sale: varies by situation.

Additional Information from the College

The University, a completely commuter institution, initiated alcohol and substance abuse prevention efforts several years ago. The program has steadily expanded, and in 1987 the University received a 2-year FIPSE grant to initiate several new prevention-oriented projects. These include an on-going student needs assessment, extensive education workshops and seminars, integration of prevention into existing courses, training of academic advisers, a Prevention Ambassadors program, a prevention resource library, and utilization of alumni employed in the prevention/treatment field in delivering prevention programming. The University is a member of the National Network of Colleges and Universities Committed to the Elimination of Drug and Alcohol Abuse.

For More Information

Contact: R. Kipp Hassell, Dean for Student Development, Northeastern Illinois University, 5500 N. Saint Louis Ave., Chicago, IL 60625. Telephone: 312-583-4050 Ext. 3167.

NORTHEASTERN STATE UNIVERSITY

Tahlequah, Oklahoma

General Information

State-supported 5-year coed college. Founded 1846. Awards B, M, D. Primary accreditation: regional. Small-town setting; 160-acre campus. Total enrollment: 8,707. Faculty: 329 (269 full-time, 60 part-time). Social organizations: 4 national fraternities, 4 national sororities, 3 local fraternities, 2 local sororities; 3% of eligible undergraduate men and 2% of eligible undergraduate women are members.

Drug and Alcohol Information

Education

On campus Drug and alcohol education/prevention programs offered for: all students, athletes/coaches. Bacchus chapter is being organized. College holds an annual alcohol awareness week.

Identification of Problems

Admissions College application does not ask about prior substance abuse problems.

On campus Current students identified as chemically dependent may remain enrolled, but treatment is required. Training program on identifying students with potential substance abuse problems for: all students. Written procedures for students and staff if substance abuse is suspected.

Support Services

On campus Private counseling, Alcohol and Drug Awareness Program.

Employee assistance Program for chemically dependent employees not available. Staff working with drug/alcohol-related issues: 3 part-time.

Disciplinary Actions

Alcohol Results of infractions of alcohol regulations (see Comparative Table of Alcohol Regulations) vary by situation.

Drugs For first-time use or possession: varies by situation. For subsequent use or possession: suspension. For first-time sale: probation, suspension, expulsion. For subsequent sale: suspension, expulsion.

For More Information

Contact: Ernest Robinson, Director, Counseling Center, Haskell Hall, 2nd Fl., Northeastern State University, Tahlequah, OK 74464. Telephone: 918-456-5511 Ext. 3100.

NORTHEASTERN UNIVERSITY

Boston, Massachusetts

General Information

Independent comprehensive coed institution. Founded 1898. Awards A (terminal), B, M, D. Primary accreditation: regional. Metropolitan setting; 55-acre campus. Total enrollment: 32,389. Faculty: 2,996 (763 full-time, 2,233 part-time). Social organizations: 12 national fraternities, 5 national sororities, 3 local fraternities, local sororities; 4% of eligible undergraduate men and 3% of eligible undergraduate women are members.

Drug and Alcohol Information

Education

On campus Drug and alcohol education/prevention programs offered for: all students, faculty, administration; required for: students whose behavior has caused harm. Authorized group concerned with responsible drinking. College holds an annual alcohol awareness week and drug awareness week.

Identification of Problems

On campus Current students identified as chemically dependent may remain enrolled, but treatment is required. Training program on identifying students with potential substance abuse problems for: resident advisers, Greek officers, faculty, administration, Health Center staff. Written procedures for students and staff if substance abuse is suspected.

Support Services

On campus AA, Al-Anon, support groups (Peers Counseling Peers), private counseling, INSTEAD (mandatory program for students with drug/alcohol problems).

Employee assistance Program for chemically dependent employees not available. Staff working with drug/alcohol-related issues: 1 full-time and 9 part-time.

Disciplinary Actions

Alcohol Results of infractions of alcohol regulations (see

Northeastern University (continued)

Comparative Table of Alcohol Regulations) vary by situation but can include warning.

Drugs For first-time use: varies by situation. For subsequent use: varies by situation—chemical dependency assessment, counseling, probation. For first-time possession: varies by situation—chemical dependency assessment, counseling, probation. For subsequent possession: suspension. For any sale: suspension, expulsion.

Additional Information from the College

Peers Counseling Peers (PCP) is a volunteer student group that was recently formed to raise the awareness level on campus. INSTEAD (Involuntary Students Educated Regarding Alcohol and Drugs) is a program of six 1 1/2-hour meetings that is intended to help students with serious drug or alcohol problems. The program does not replace disciplinary actions but supplements them.

For More Information

Contact: Margaret Crooks, Coordinator, Alcohol and Drug Education, Northeastern University, 360 Huntington Ave., Boston, MA 02115. Telephone: 617-437-8715.

NORTHEAST LOUISIANA UNIVERSITY

Monroe, Louisiana

General Information

State-supported 5-year coed college. Founded 1931. Awards A (college transfer and terminal), B, M, D. Primary accreditation: regional. City setting; 227-acre campus. Total enrollment: 10,340. Faculty: 428 (376 full-time, 52 part-time). Social organizations: 6 national fraternities, 4 national sororities; 4% of eligible undergraduate men and 4% of eligible undergraduate women are members.

Drug and Alcohol Information

Education

On campus Drug and alcohol education/prevention programs not offered. College holds an annual alcohol awareness week.

Identification of Problems

Admissions College application does not ask about prior substance abuse problems.

On campus Current students identified as chemically dependent may remain enrolled, but treatment is required. No training program on identifying students with potential substance abuse problems. Written procedures for students and staff if substance abuse is suspected.

Support Services

On campus Private counseling.

Employee assistance Program for chemically dependent employees not available.

Disciplinary Actions

Alcohol Results of infractions of alcohol regulations (see Comparative Table of Alcohol Regulations) include chemical dependency assessment, counseling, probation, fines.

Drugs For first-time use or possession: varies by situation—probation, fines. For subsequent use or possession: suspension. For any sale: suspension.

For More Information

Contact: Thomas E. Murphy, Dean for Student Affairs, Northeast Louisiana University, 700 University Ave., Monroe, LA 71209. Telephone: 318-342-3053.

NORTHEAST MISSOURI STATE UNIVERSITY

Kirksville, Missouri

General Information

State-supported 5-year coed college. Founded 1867. Awards B, M. Primary accreditation: regional. Small-town setting; 140-acre campus. Total enrollment: 6,085. Faculty: 341 (298 full-time, 43 part-time). Social organizations: 16 national fraternities, 8 national sororities, 1 local sorority; 28% of eligible undergraduate men and 14% of eligible undergraduate women are members.

Drug and Alcohol Information

Education

On campus Drug and alcohol education/prevention programs offered for: all students. Authorized group concerned with responsible drinking. College holds an annual alcohol awareness week.

Identification of Problems

Admissions College application does not ask about prior substance abuse problems.

On campus Current students identified as chemically dependent may remain enrolled. No written procedures for students and staff if substance abuse is suspected.

Support Services

On campus ACOA, private counseling.

Employee assistance Program for chemically dependent employees not available.

Disciplinary Actions

Alcohol Results of infractions of alcohol regulations (see Comparative Table of Alcohol Regulations) vary by situation.

Drugs For first-time use or possession: varies by situation. For first-time sale: suspension. Comments: The University has not had to deal with any cases of repeated drug offenses.

For More Information

Contact: Dr. Terry B. Smith, Dean of the Colleges, Northeast Missouri State University, Kirksville, MO 63501. Telephone: 816-785-4111.

NORTHERN ARIZONA UNIVERSITY

Flagstaff, Arizona

General Information

State-supported comprehensive coed institution. Founded 1899. Awards B, M, D. Primary accreditation: regional. Small-town setting; 730-acre campus. Total enrollment: 15,059. Faculty: 899 (524 full-time, 375 part-time). Social organizations: 10 national fraternities, 4 national sororities; 3% of eligible undergraduate men and 3% of eligible undergraduate women are members.

Drug and Alcohol Information

Education

On campus Drug and alcohol education/prevention programs offered for: all students, faculty, administration; required for: athletes/coaches, resident advisers. Authorized group concerned with responsible drinking. College holds an annual alcohol awareness week and drug awareness week.

Identification of Problems

Admissions College application does not ask about prior substance abuse problems.

On campus Current students identified as chemically dependent may remain enrolled. Treatment may or may not be required. Training program on identifying students with potential substance abuse problems for: resident advisers, coaches, Greek officers, faculty, administration, anyone else who is interested. Written procedures for students and staff if substance abuse is suspected.

Support Services

On campus AA, NA, Al-Anon, ACOA, support groups (codependency), private counseling, peer counseling.

Employee assistance Program for chemically dependent employees available. Staff working with drug/alcohol-related issues: 2 full-time.

Disciplinary Actions

Alcohol Results of infractions of alcohol regulations (see Comparative Table of Alcohol Regulations) vary by situation but can include chemical dependency assessment, counseling, warning, probation, suspension, expulsion, attendance at First Offenders' Education class.

Drugs For any use, possession, or sale: varies by situation—chemical dependency assessment, counseling—but always includes arrest.

For More Information

Contact: Cindy Leisse, Coordinator, Project Daylight, Northern Arizona University, P.O. Box 6045, Flagstaff, AZ 86011-6045. Telephone: 602-523-6306.

NORTHERN ILLINOIS UNIVERSITY

De Kalb, Illinois

General Information

State-supported comprehensive coed institution. Founded 1895. Awards B, M, D. Primary accreditation: regional. Small-town setting; 589-acre campus. Total enrollment: 24,255. Faculty: 1,264 (1,085 full-time, 179 part-time). Social organizations: 19 national fraternities, 14 national sororities; 13% of eligible undergraduate men and 9% of eligible undergraduate women are members.

Drug and Alcohol Information

Education

On campus Drug and alcohol education/prevention programs offered for: all students; required for: athletes/coaches. Bacchus chapter: 35 members. College holds an annual alcohol awareness week and drug awareness week.

Identification of Problems

Admissions College application does not ask about prior substance abuse problems.

On campus Current students identified as chemically dependent may remain enrolled; treatment is recommended but not required. Training program on identifying students with potential substance abuse problems for: resident advisers, coaches, Judicial Office staff.

Support Services

On campus AA, ACOA.

Employee assistance Program for chemically dependent employees not available. Staff working with drug/alcohol-related issues: 1 full-time and 10 part-time.

Disciplinary Actions

Alcohol Results of infractions of alcohol regulations (see Comparative Table of Alcohol Regulations) include chemical dependency assessment, 3-week alcohol education class for those not diagnosed as abusers.

Drugs For first-time use, possession, or sale: Judicial Office sanctions vary by situation. Police action is possible. For subsequent use or possession: probation. For subsequent sale: varies by situation—probation, expulsion.

For More Information

Contact: Michael Haines, Coordinator, Health Enhancement Service, Health Service 414, Northern Illinois University, De Kalb, IL 60115. Telephone: 815-753-9745.

NORTHERN KENTUCKY UNIVERSITY

Highland Heights, Kentucky

General Information

State-supported 5-year coed college. Founded 1968. Awards A (terminal), B, M, D. Primary accreditation: regional. Small-town setting; 300-acre campus. Total enrollment: 9,497. Faculty: 539 (307 full-time, 232 part-time). Social organizations: 5 national fraternities, 3 national sororities; 3% of eligible undergraduate men and 2% of eligible undergraduate women are members.

Drug and Alcohol Information

Education

On campus Drug and alcohol education/prevention programs offered for: all students, athletes/coaches. College holds an annual alcohol awareness week and drug awareness week.

Identification of Problems

Admissions College application does not ask about prior substance abuse problems.

On campus Current students identified as chemically dependent may not remain enrolled. No training program on identifying students with potential substance abuse problems. No written procedures for students and staff if substance abuse is suspected.

Support Services

On campus AA, Al-Anon.

Employee assistance Program for chemically dependent employees available.

Disciplinary Actions

Alcohol Results of infractions of alcohol regulations (see Comparative Table of Alcohol Regulations) vary by situation.

Drugs For any use, possession, or sale: varies by situation.

For More Information

Contact: Bill Lamb, Dean of Students, Northern

Northern Kentucky University (continued)

Kentucky University, College Station, Highland Heights, KY 41076. Telephone: 606-572-6376.

NORTHERN MONTANA COLLEGE

Havre, Montana

General Information

State-supported 5-year coed college. Part of Montana University System. Founded 1929. Awards A (college transfer and terminal), B, M. Primary accreditation: regional. Small-town setting; 104-acre campus. Total enrollment: 1,583. Faculty: 103 (69 full-time, 34 part-time).

Drug and Alcohol Information

Education

On campus Drug and alcohol education/prevention programs offered for: all students, athletes/coaches, faculty, administration; required for: resident advisers. Authorized group concerned with responsible drinking. College holds an annual alcohol awareness week and drug awareness week.

Identification of Problems

Admissions College application question about prior substance abuse problems is used for counseling and referral, if student is admitted.

On campus Current students identified as chemically dependent may remain enrolled, but treatment is required. Training program on identifying students with potential substance abuse problems for: resident advisers, coaches, core team. Written procedures for students and staff if substance abuse is suspected.

Support Services

On campus AA, private counseling.

Employee assistance Program for chemically dependent employees available. Staff working with drug/alcohol-related issues: 6 part-time.

Disciplinary Actions

Alcohol Results of infractions of alcohol regulations (see Comparative Table of Alcohol Regulations) include chemical dependency assessment, probation.

Drugs For first-time use, possession, or sale: chemical dependency assessment, counseling, referral to city judge. For subsequent use, possession, or sale: expulsion, referral to legal system.

Additional Information from the College

Northern Montana College has a FIPSE Drug/Alcohol Abuse Prevention Grant.

For More Information

Contact: Robin E. Morris, Coordinator, FIPSE Grant, P.O. Box 7751, Northern Montana College, Havre, MT 59501. Telephone: 406-265-3783.

NORTHERN STATE COLLEGE

Aberdeen, South Dakota

General Information

State-supported 5-year coed college. Founded 1901. Awards A (college transfer and terminal), B, M. Primary accreditation: regional. Small-town setting; 25-acre campus. Total enrollment: 3,029.

Drug and Alcohol Information

Education

On campus Drug and alcohol education/prevention programs offered for: all students, faculty, administration; required for: athletes/coaches, resident advisers. Bacchus chapter. College holds an annual alcohol awareness week.

Identification of Problems

Admissions College application does not ask about prior substance abuse problems.

On campus Current students identified as chemically dependent may remain enrolled. Training program on identifying students with potential substance abuse problems for: resident advisers, coaches. No written procedures for students and staff if substance abuse is suspected.

Support Services

On campus ACOA, private counseling, addictions group.

Employee assistance Program for chemically dependent employees not available. Staff working with drug/alcohol-related issues: 2 part-time.

Disciplinary Actions

Alcohol Results of infractions of alcohol regulations (see Comparative Table of Alcohol Regulations) vary by situation but can include probation, suspension from residence hall.

Drugs For first-time use, possession, or sale: probation. For subsequent use, possession, or sale: varies by situation.

For More Information

Contact: Deb Hofer, Counselor, Counseling and Career Development, Northern State College, S. Jay St., Aberdeen, SD 57401. Telephone: 605-662-2371.

NORTH GEORGIA COLLEGE

Dahlonega, Georgia

General Information

State-supported 5-year coed college. Part of University System of Georgia. Founded 1873. Awards A (terminal), B, M. Primary accreditation: regional. Small-town setting; 140-acre campus. Total enrollment: 2,181. Faculty: 111 (106 full-time, 5 part-time). Social organizations: 4 national fraternities, 3 national sororities, 1 local fraternity, 1 local sorority; 25% of eligible undergraduate men and 13% of eligible undergraduate women are members.

Drug and Alcohol Information

Education

On campus Drug and alcohol education/prevention programs offered for: all students, athletes/coaches, faculty, administration. College holds an annual alcohol awareness week.

Identification of Problems

Admissions College application does not ask about prior substance abuse problems.

On campus Current students identified as chemically dependent may remain enrolled, but treatment is required. Training program on identifying students with potential substance abuse problems for: resident advisers. No written

procedures for students and staff if substance abuse is suspected.

Support Services

On campus AA, Al-Anon, private counseling.

Employee assistance Program for chemically dependent employees available.

Disciplinary Actions

Alcohol Results of infractions of alcohol regulations (see Comparative Table of Alcohol Regulations) include chemical dependency assessment, counseling, probation, suspension.

Drugs For any use: counseling, suspension. For first-time possession: suspension. For subsequent possession: expulsion. For any sale: expulsion.

For More Information

Contact: H. Michael Hyams, Vice President and Dean of Student Affairs, North Georgia College, Dahlonega, GA 30533. Telephone: 404-864-6486.

NORTHLAND COLLEGE

Ashland, Wisconsin

General Information

Independent 4-year coed college, affiliated with United Church of Christ. Founded 1892. Awards B. Primary accreditation: regional. Small-town setting; 130-acre campus. Total enrollment: 647. Faculty: 62 (32 full-time, 30 part-time). Social organizations: 3 national fraternities, 3 local sororities; 12% of eligible undergraduate men and 14% of eligible undergraduate women are members.

Drug and Alcohol Information

Education

On campus Drug and alcohol education/prevention programs offered for: all students. Authorized group concerned with responsible drinking. College holds an annual alcohol awareness week and drug awareness week.

Identification of Problems

Admissions College application does not ask about prior substance abuse problems.

On campus Current students identified as chemically dependent may remain enrolled, but treatment is required. No training program on identifying students with potential substance abuse problems. Written procedures for students and staff if substance abuse is suspected.

Support Services

On campus Private counseling, referral.

Off campus AA, Al-Anon, ACOA.

Employee assistance Program for chemically dependent employees available. Staff working with drug/alcohol-related issues: 5 part-time.

Disciplinary Actions

Alcohol Results of infractions of alcohol regulations (see Comparative Table of Alcohol Regulations) vary by situation but can include chemical dependency assessment, counseling, warning, probation, suspension.

Drugs For any use or possession: varies by situation. For any sale: varies by situation—suspension.

For More Information

Contact: Tom Wojciechowski, Director of Student Development, Northland College, 1411 Ellis Ave., Ashland, WI 54806. Telephone: 715-682-1595.

NORTH PARK COLLEGE

Chicago, Illinois

General Information

Independent 4-year coed college, affiliated with Evangelical Covenant Church of America. Founded 1891. Awards B. Primary accreditation: regional. Metropolitan setting; 30-acre campus. Total enrollment: 1,083. Faculty: 85 (65 full-time, 20 part-time).

Drug and Alcohol Information

Education

On campus Drug and alcohol education/prevention programs offered for: all students, athletes/coaches. Authorized group concerned with responsible drinking. College holds an annual alcohol awareness week.

Identification of Problems

Admissions College application does not ask about prior substance abuse problems.

On campus Current students identified as chemically dependent may remain enrolled, but treatment is required. Training program on identifying students with potential substance abuse problems for: resident advisers, coaches, hall directors, student development staff. Written procedures being developed for students and staff if substance abuse is suspected.

Support Services

On campus Support groups, private counseling, referrals.

Off campus AA, NA, Al-Anon, ACOA.

Employee assistance Program for chemically dependent employees being developed. Staff working with drug/alcohol-related issues: 2 part-time.

Disciplinary Actions

Alcohol Results of infractions of alcohol regulations (see Comparative Table of Alcohol Regulations) vary by situation but can include chemical dependency assessment, counseling, warning, probation, expulsion.

Drugs For any use: varies by situation. For first-time possession: varies by situation. For subsequent possession: varies by situation—suspension. For first-time sale: chemical dependency assessment, expulsion. For subsequent sale: expulsion.

For More Information

Contact: Kathleen Prendergast, Director of Counseling, North Park College, 3225 W. Foster Ave., Chicago, IL 60625. Telephone: 312-583-2700.

NORTHROP UNIVERSITY

Los Angeles, California

General Information

Independent 5-year coed college. Founded 1942. Awards A (terminal), B, M, D. Primary accreditation: regional. Metropolitan setting; 18-acre campus. Total enrollment: 1,813. Faculty: 145. Social organization: 1 national fraternity; 1% of eligible undergraduate men are members.

Drug and Alcohol Information

Education

On campus Drug and alcohol education/prevention

Northrop University (continued)

programs offered for: all students. College holds an annual alcohol awareness week and drug awareness week.

Identification of Problems

Admissions College application does not ask about prior substance abuse problems.

On campus Current students identified as chemically dependent may remain enrolled, but treatment is required. Training program on identifying students with potential substance abuse problems for: resident advisers. No written procedures for students and staff if substance abuse is suspected.

Support Services

Employee assistance Program for chemically dependent employees available.

Disciplinary Actions

Alcohol Results of infractions of alcohol regulations (see Comparative Table of Alcohol Regulations) include counseling, warning, probation, suspension, expulsion.

Drugs For first-time use: warning. For first-time possession or sale: varies by situation—warning. For subsequent use, possession, or sale: expulsion.

For More Information

Contact: Ibrahim Karim, Director, Student Affairs, Northrop University, 5800 W. Arbor Vitae St., Los Angeles, CA 90045. Telephone: 213-337-4456.

NORTHWEST CHRISTIAN COLLEGE

Eugene, Oregon

General Information

Independent interdenominational 5-year coed college. Founded 1895. Awards A (college transfer), B, M. Primary accreditation: regional. City setting; 10-acre campus. Total enrollment: 216. Faculty: 19 (12 full-time, 7 part-time).

Drug and Alcohol Information

Education

On campus Drug and alcohol education/prevention programs offered for: freshmen, resident advisers. Authorized group concerned with responsible drinking. College holds an annual alcohol awareness week.

Identification of Problems

Admissions College application does not ask about prior substance abuse problems.

On campus Current students identified as chemically dependent may remain enrolled, but treatment is required. Training program on identifying students with potential substance abuse problems for: resident advisers. No written procedures for students and staff if substance abuse is suspected.

Support Services

On campus Private counseling, referrals. Off campus AA, NA, Al-Anon, ACOA.

Employee assistance Program for chemically dependent employees not available. Staff working with drug/alcohol-related issues: 4 part-time.

Disciplinary Actions

Alcohol Results of infractions of alcohol regulations (see Comparative Table of Alcohol Regulations) vary by situation but can include chemical dependency assessment, counseling, warning. Comments: Refusal to participate in assessment and counseling could lead to expulsion.

Drugs For first-time use or possession: varies by situation—warning, probation. For subsequent use or possession: varies by situation. For first-time sale: warning, probation. For subsequent sale: expulsion.

For More Information

Contact: David Waggoner, Dean of Students, Northwest Christian College, 828 E. 11th Ave., Eugene, OR 97401. Telephone: 503-687-9456.

NORTHWESTERN COLLEGE

Orange City, Iowa

General Information

Independent 5-year coed college, affiliated with Reformed Church in America. Founded 1882. Awards A (terminal), B, M. Primary accreditation: regional. Rural setting; 40-acre campus. Total enrollment: 965. Faculty: 88 (52 full-time, 36 part-time).

Drug and Alcohol Information

Education

On campus Drug and alcohol education/prevention programs not offered. Authorized group concerned with responsible drinking. College holds an annual alcohol awareness week.

Identification of Problems

Admissions College application does not ask about prior substance abuse problems.

On campus Current students identified as chemically dependent may remain enrolled, but treatment is required. Training program on identifying students with potential substance abuse problems for: resident advisers. No written procedures for students and staff if substance abuse is suspected.

Support Services

On campus Private counseling.

Employee assistance Program for chemically dependent employees not available.

Disciplinary Actions

Alcohol Results of infractions of alcohol regulations (see Comparative Table of Alcohol Regulations) vary by situation but can include chemical dependency assessment, counseling, warning, probation, suspension, expulsion.

Drugs For first-time use, possession, or sale: expulsion.

For More Information

Contact: Steve Beers, Director of Residence Life, Northwestern College, 101 Seventh St., SW, Orange City, IA 51041. Telephone: 712-737-4821.

NORTHWESTERN COLLEGE

St. Paul, Minnesota

General Information

Independent interdenominational 4-year coed college. Founded 1902. Awards A (college transfer and terminal), B. Primary accreditation: regional. Metropolitan setting; 95-

acre campus. Total enrollment: 973. Faculty: 78 (55 full-time, 23 part-time).

Drug and Alcohol Information

Education

On campus Drug and alcohol education/prevention programs not offered.

Identification of Problems

Admissions College application question about prior substance abuse problems is used to explain past academic performance; for counseling and referral, if student is admitted; in the admissions decision.

On campus Current students identified as chemically dependent may remain enrolled, but treatment is required. Training program on identifying students with potential substance abuse problems for: resident advisers. Written procedures for students and staff if substance abuse is suspected.

Support Services

On campus Private counseling.

Employee assistance Program for chemically dependent employees not available.

Disciplinary Actions

Alcohol Results of infractions of alcohol regulations (see Comparative Table of Alcohol Regulations) include counseling, expulsion.

Drugs For first-time use or possession: varies by situation. For subsequent use or possession: expulsion. For any sale: expulsion.

For More Information

Contact: Yngue Magnuson, Dean of Student Affairs, Northwestern College, 3003 N. Snelling Ave., St. Paul, MN 55113. Telephone: 612-631-5100.

NORTHWESTERN UNIVERSITY

Evanston, Illinois

General Information

Independent comprehensive coed institution. Founded 1851. Awards B, M, D. Primary accreditation: regional. City setting; 231-acre campus. Total enrollment: 11,337. Faculty: 729 (693 full-time, 36 part-time). Social organizations: 26 national fraternities, 12 national sororities; 39% of eligible undergraduate men and 41% of eligible undergraduate women are members.

Drug and Alcohol Information

Education

On campus Drug and alcohol education/prevention programs offered for: all students, athletes/coaches, students with discipline problems. Authorized group concerned with responsible drinking.

Identification of Problems

Admissions College application does not ask about prior substance abuse problems.

On campus Current students identified as chemically dependent may remain enrolled. Comments: Whether treatment is required depends on the situation. Training program on identifying students with potential substance abuse problems for: resident advisers, coaches. Written procedures for students and staff if substance abuse is suspected.

Support Services

On campus AA, ACOA, private counseling.

Employee assistance Program for chemically dependent employees not available. Staff working with drug/alcohol-related issues: 1 full-time and 4 part-time.

Disciplinary Actions

Alcohol Results of infractions of alcohol regulations (see Comparative Table of Alcohol Regulations) vary by situation but can include chemical dependency assessment, counseling, warning, probation, suspension, expulsion.

Drugs For any use, possession, or sale: varies by situation.

Additional Information from the College

The new Alcohol/Substance Abuse Education Program at Northwestern University provides a structured educational environment designed to help students to explore attitudes and actions relating to alcohol and drug use. Students may be referred to the program or may refer themselves.

For More Information

Contact: Wendy Janosik, Substance Abuse Coordinator, Searle Student Health Center, Northwestern University, Evanston, IL 60208. Telephone: 312-491-5910.

NORTHWEST MISSOURI STATE UNIVERSITY

Maryville, Missouri

General Information

State-supported 5-year coed college. Founded 1905. Awards B, M. Primary accreditation: regional. Small-town setting; 170-acre campus. Total enrollment: 5,337. Faculty: 288 (256 full-time, 32 part-time). Social organizations: 7 national fraternities, 4 national sororities; 13% of eligible undergraduate men and 11% of eligible undergraduate women are members.

Drug and Alcohol Information

Education

On campus Drug and alcohol education/prevention programs offered for: all students, athletes/coaches, faculty, administration. Bacchus chapter: 25 members. College holds an annual alcohol awareness week.

Identification of Problems

Admissions College application does not ask about prior substance abuse problems.

On campus Current students identified as chemically dependent may remain enrolled, but treatment is required. Training program on identifying students with potential substance abuse problems for: resident advisers, coaches, Greek officers, faculty, administration. Written procedures for students and staff if substance abuse is suspected.

Support Services

On campus AA, Al-Anon, private counseling, CARE program.

Employee assistance Program for chemically dependent employees not available. Staff working with drug/alcohol-related issues: 1 full-time and 7 part-time.

Disciplinary Actions

Alcohol Results of infractions of alcohol regulations (see

Northwest Missouri State University (continued)

Comparative Table of Alcohol Regulations) include probation, suspension.

Drugs For first-time use or possession: probation. For subsequent use or possession: suspension. For any sale: suspension.

Additional Information from the College

Northwest Missouri State University has a comprehensive, campuswide primary prevention program called CARE. This program can deal with crisis situations, but its primary focus is on prevention. CARE offers tools and knowledge for students to make healthy and intelligent decisions about curbing alcohol use and rejecting illegal drugs. A student board, trained advocates, a creative information campaign, interaction and problem-solving groups, relevant assignments in selected courses, and communication with interested community groups and individuals are all part of CARE's activities.

For More Information

Contact: Mindy Brooks, Associate Director, CARE Program, Student Union, Northwest Missouri State University, Maryville, MO 64468. Telephone: 816-562-1241.

NORTHWOOD INSTITUTE

Midland, Michigan

General Information

Independent 4-year coed college. Founded 1959. Awards A (college transfer and terminal), B. Primary accreditation: regional. Small-town setting; 268-acre campus. Total enrollment: 1,785. Faculty: 62 (38 full-time, 24 part-time). Social organizations: 5 national fraternities, 3 national sororities, 3 local fraternities; 25% of eligible undergraduate men and 25% of eligible undergraduate women are members.

Drug and Alcohol Information

Education

On campus Drug and alcohol education/prevention programs offered for: all students; required for: freshmen, athletes/coaches, resident advisers. Authorized group concerned with responsible drinking. College holds an annual alcohol awareness week and drug awareness week.

Identification of Problems

Admissions College application does not ask about prior substance abuse problems.

On campus Current students identified as chemically dependent may remain enrolled, but treatment is required. Training program on identifying students with potential substance abuse problems for: resident advisers, coaches, administration. Written procedures for students and staff if substance abuse is suspected.

Support Services

On campus AA, support groups, private counseling.

Employee assistance Program for chemically dependent employees available. Staff working with drug/alcohol-related issues: 1 full-time.

Disciplinary Actions

Alcohol Results of infractions of alcohol regulations (see Comparative Table of Alcohol Regulations) vary by situation but can include chemical dependency assessment, counseling, warning, probation, suspension, expulsion.

Drugs For any use or possession: varies by situation. For any sale: expulsion.

For More Information

Contact: Henry Chung, Substance Abuse Counselor, Northwood Institute, 3225 Cook Rd., Midland, MI 48640. Telephone: 517-832-4322.

NORTHWOOD INSTITUTE, FLORIDA CAMPUS

West Palm Beach, Florida

General Information

Independent 4-year coed college. Administratively affiliated with Northwood Institute (MI). Founded 1982. Awards A (college transfer), B. Primary accreditation: regional. City setting; 80-acre campus. Total enrollment: 450. Faculty: 23 (12 full-time, 11 part-time).

Drug and Alcohol Information

Education

On campus Drug and alcohol education/prevention programs offered for: all students, faculty, administration; required for: resident advisers. Bacchus chapter. College holds an annual alcohol awareness week and drug awareness week.

Identification of Problems

Admissions College application does not ask about prior substance abuse problems.

On campus Current students identified as chemically dependent may remain enrolled, but treatment is required. Training program on identifying students with potential substance abuse problems for: resident advisers. No written procedures for students and staff if substance abuse is suspected.

Support Services

On campus Al-Anon, private counseling.

Employee assistance Program for chemically dependent employees not available. Staff working with drug/alcohol-related issues: 3 part-time.

Disciplinary Actions

Alcohol Results of infractions of alcohol regulations (see Comparative Table of Alcohol Regulations) vary by situation but can include chemical dependency assessment, counseling, warning, probation, suspension, expulsion.

Drugs For first-time use: varies by situation—chemical dependency assessment, parents notified. For subsequent use: varies by situation—chemical dependency assessment, probation, parents notified. For first-time possession: varies by situation. For subsequent possession: expulsion. For first-time sale: expulsion.

For More Information

Contact: Larraine White, Coordinator, Student Development, Northwood Institute, Florida Campus, 2600 N. Military Trail, West Palm Beach, FL 33409. Telephone: 407-478-5542.

NORWICH UNIVERSITY

Northfield, Vermont

General Information

Independent 5-year coed college. Founded 1819. Awards A (college transfer and terminal), B, M. Primary accreditation: regional. Small-town setting; 1,125-acre campus. Total enrollment: 2,246. Faculty: 242 (201 full-time, 41 part-time).

Drug and Alcohol Information

Education

On campus Drug and alcohol education/prevention programs offered for: all students, athletes/coaches, faculty, administration; required for: freshmen, resident advisers. Authorized group concerned with responsible drinking. College holds an annual alcohol awareness week and drug awareness week.

Identification of Problems

Admissions College application does not ask about prior substance abuse problems.

On campus Current students identified as chemically dependent may remain enrolled, but treatment is required. Training program on identifying students with potential substance abuse problems for: resident advisers, peer assistants. Written procedures for students and staff if substance abuse is suspected.

Support Services

On campus AA, Al-Anon, ACOA, support groups, private counseling.

Employee assistance Program for chemically dependent employees available. Staff working with drug/alcohol-related issues: 5 part-time.

Disciplinary Actions

Alcohol Results of infractions of alcohol regulations (see Comparative Table of Alcohol Regulations) vary by situation but can include chemical dependency assessment, counseling, warning, probation, suspension, expulsion.

Drugs For first-time use, possession, or sale: expulsion.

For More Information

Contact: Paula Gagnon, Dean of Students, Vermont College, Norwich University, Montpelier, VT 05602. Telephone: 802-223-8710.

NOVA UNIVERSITY

Fort Lauderdale, Florida

General Information

Independent comprehensive coed institution. Founded 1964. Awards B, M, D. Primary accreditation: regional. City setting; 200-acre campus. Total enrollment: 7,800. Faculty: 65 (25 full-time, 40 part-time).

Drug and Alcohol Information

Education

On campus Drug and alcohol education/prevention programs offered for: all students; required for: athletes/coaches. Bacchus chapter.

Identification of Problems

Admissions College application does not ask about prior substance abuse problems.

On campus Current students identified as chemically dependent may remain enrolled, but treatment is required. Training program on identifying students with potential substance abuse problems for: resident advisers, coaches. No written procedures for students and staff if substance abuse is suspected.

Support Services

On campus Private counseling, information and referral service. Staff working with drug/alcohol-related issues: 1 part-time.

Disciplinary Actions

Alcohol Results of infractions of alcohol regulations (see Comparative Table of Alcohol Regulations) vary by situation but can include chemical dependency assessment, counseling, warning, probation, suspension.

Drugs For first-time use: varies by situation—counseling, warning, probation. For subsequent use: suspension. For first-time possession: varies by situation. For subsequent possession: suspension, expulsion. For first-time sale: suspension, expulsion. For subsequent sale: expulsion.

For More Information

Contact: Bill Cahill, Director of Behavioral Sciences, Nova University, 3301 College Ave., Fort Lauderdale, FL 33314. Telephone: 305-475-7353.

OAK HILLS BIBLE COLLEGE

Bemidji, Minnesota

General Information

Independent-religious 4-year coed college. Founded 1946. Awards A (college transfer), B. Primary accreditation: AABC (candidate). Rural setting; 180-acre campus. Total enrollment: 126. Faculty: 20 (9 full-time, 11 part-time).

Drug and Alcohol Information

Education

On campus Drug and alcohol education/prevention programs offered for: all students.

Identification of Problems

Admissions College application question about prior substance abuse problems is used for counseling and referral, if student is admitted; in the admissions decision.

On campus Current students identified as chemically dependent may remain enrolled, but treatment is required. No training program on identifying students with potential substance abuse problems. No written procedures for students and staff if substance abuse is suspected.

Support Services

On campus Referrals.

Employee assistance Program for chemically dependent employees not available. Staff working with drug/alcohol-related issues: 4 part-time.

Disciplinary Actions

Alcohol Results of infractions of alcohol regulations (see Comparative Table of Alcohol Regulations) vary by situation. Comments: The focus is on helping, rather than punishing, the student.

Drugs For first-time use: varies by situation—suspension. For subsequent use: varies by situation—chemical dependency assessment, suspension. For any possession: varies by situation. Comments: There has never been a case of a student selling drugs.

Oak Hills Bible College (continued)

Additional Information from the College

Oak Hills Bible College is small. Faculty and administration get to know students well and have been successful in helping a significant number of students get treatment for substance abuse problems.

For More Information

Contact: Daniel Ley, Dean of Student Development, Oak Hills Bible College, 1600 Oak Hills Rd., SW, Bemidji, MN 56601. Telephone: 218-751-8670.

OAKLAND UNIVERSITY

Rochester, Michigan

General Information

State-supported comprehensive coed institution. Founded 1957. Awards B, M, D. Primary accreditation: regional. Small-town setting; 1,500-acre campus. Total enrollment: 12,254. Faculty: 617 (402 full-time, 215 part-time). Social organizations: 4 national fraternities, 4 national sororities, local fraternities, local sororities, eating clubs; 10% of eligible undergraduate men and 10% of eligible undergraduate women are members.

Drug and Alcohol Information

Education

On campus Drug and alcohol education/prevention programs offered for: all students, athletes/coaches; required for: orientation participants. Authorized group concerned with responsible drinking. College holds an annual alcohol awareness week and drug awareness week.

Identification of Problems

Admissions College application does not ask about prior substance abuse problems.

On campus Current students identified as chemically dependent may remain enrolled. Training program on identifying students with potential substance abuse problems for: resident advisers, coaches, administration. Written procedures for students and staff if substance abuse is suspected.

Support Services

On campus NA, ACOA, private counseling, group counseling.

Off campus AA, Al-Anon.

Employee assistance Program for chemically dependent employees available. Staff working with drug/alcohol-related issues: 1 full-time and 4 part-time.

Disciplinary Actions

Alcohol Results of infractions of alcohol regulations (see Comparative Table of Alcohol Regulations) vary by situation but can include chemical dependency assessment, counseling, warning, probation, suspension, expulsion, removal from residence halls.

Drugs For any use: varies by situation. For first-time possession: varies by situation. For subsequent possession: suspension, expulsion. For first-time sale: suspension, expulsion. For subsequent sale: expulsion.

Additional Information from the College

Oakland University has a progressive approach to alcohol and drug problems that includes discipline, counseling, and education. Various support groups participate in the counseling and educational programs, and the University conduct system and police agencies are also involved in the criminal and judicial aspects of such problems. The University's objective is to eradicate substance abuse through creative and diverse approaches.

For More Information

Contact: David Herman, Dean of Students, 144 Oakland Center, Oakland University, Rochester, MI 48309-4401. Telephone: 313-370-3352.

OAKWOOD COLLEGE

Huntsville, Alabama

General Information

Independent Seventh-day Adventist 4-year coed college. Founded 1896. Awards A (terminal), B. Primary accreditation: regional. City setting; 1,200-acre campus. Total enrollment: 1,200. Faculty: 105 (80 full-time, 25 part-time).

Drug and Alcohol Information

Education

On campus Drug and alcohol education/prevention programs offered for: all students, faculty. College holds an annual alcohol awareness week and drug awareness week.

Identification of Problems

Admissions College application does not ask about prior substance abuse problems.

On campus Current students identified as chemically dependent may remain enrolled, but treatment is required. Training program on identifying students with potential substance abuse problems for: faculty, core team of the DARE program. Written procedures for students and staff if substance abuse is suspected.

Support Services

On campus Private counseling, DARE program. Staff working with drug/alcohol-related issues: 12 part-time.

Disciplinary Actions

Alcohol Results of infractions of alcohol regulations (see Comparative Table of Alcohol Regulations) vary by situation but can include counseling, warning, probation, suspension, expulsion, referral to DARE core team.

Drugs For any use: varies by situation. For first-time possession: varies by situation—chemical dependency assessment, probation, suspension. For subsequent possession: counseling, warning, suspension. For any sale: expulsion.

Additional Information from the College

The DARE program, which is new on campus, is currently being evaluated, and additional resources and information to improve it are being sought. There is also a Drug Task Force that has primary responsibility for planning and providing preventive education programs.

For More Information

Contact: Kermit L. Carter, Vice President for Student Services, Ford Hall, Oakwood College, P.O. Box 107, Huntsville, AL 35896. Telephone: 205-837-1630 Ext. 412.

OBERLIN COLLEGE

Oberlin, Ohio

General Information

Independent 5-year coed college. Founded 1833. Awards B, M. Primary accreditation: regional. Small-town setting; 440-acre campus. Total enrollment: 2,857. Faculty: 230 (all full-time).

Drug and Alcohol Information

Education

On campus Drug and alcohol education/prevention programs offered for: all students. Authorized group concerned with responsible drinking. College holds an annual alcohol awareness week.

Identification of Problems

Admissions College application does not ask about prior substance abuse problems.

On campus Current students identified as chemically dependent may remain enrolled, but treatment is required. Training program on identifying students with potential substance abuse problems for: resident advisers, administration, counselors. Written procedures for students and staff if substance abuse is suspected.

Support Services

On campus AA, NA, Al-Anon, ACOA, private counseling.

Employee assistance Program for chemically dependent employees not available.

Disciplinary Actions

Alcohol Results of infractions of alcohol regulations (see Comparative Table of Alcohol Regulations) vary by situation but can include chemical dependency assessment, counseling, warning, probation.

Drugs For any use or possession: varies by situation. For first-time sale: varies by situation. For subsequent sale: varies by situation—chemical dependency assessment, suspension.

For More Information

Contact: Sherry Gutman, Assistant Dean of Students/Residential Life, 104 Peters Hall, Oberlin College, Oberlin, OH 44074. Telephone: 216-775-8471.

OGLETHORPE UNIVERSITY

Atlanta, Georgia

General Information

Independent 5-year coed college. Founded 1835. Awards B, M. Primary accreditation: regional. Metropolitan setting; 95-acre campus. Total enrollment: 1,047. Faculty: 74 (39 full-time, 35 part-time). Social organizations: 4 national fraternities, 2 national sororities; 30% of eligible undergraduate men and 25% of eligible undergraduate women are members.

Drug and Alcohol Information

Education

On campus Drug and alcohol education/prevention programs offered for: all students. Authorized group concerned with responsible drinking. College holds an annual alcohol awareness week and drug awareness week.

Identification of Problems

Admissions College application does not ask about prior substance abuse problems.

On campus Current students identified as chemically dependent may remain enrolled, but treatment is required. No training program on identifying students with potential substance abuse problems. Written procedures for students and staff if substance abuse is suspected.

Support Services

On campus Support groups (Task Force), private counseling, referrals.

Employee assistance Program for chemically dependent employees not available. Staff working with drug/alcohol-related issues: 6 part-time.

Disciplinary Actions

Alcohol Results of infractions of alcohol regulations (see Comparative Table of Alcohol Regulations) vary by situation. Comments: Sanctions are imposed to fit the offense.

Drugs For any use, possession, or sale: varies by situation.

For More Information

Contact: Donald R. Moore, Dean of Community Life, Oglethorpe University, 4484 Peachtree Rd., NE, Atlanta, GA 30319. Telephone: 404-261-1444.

OHIO STATE UNIVERSITY–MARION CAMPUS

Marion, Ohio

General Information

State-supported 4-year coed college. Part of Ohio State University. Founded 1957. Awards A (college transfer), B (also offers some graduate courses). Primary accreditation: regional. Small-town setting; 180-acre campus. Total enrollment: 1,137. Faculty: 33 (25 full-time, 8 part-time).

Drug and Alcohol Information

Education

On campus Drug and alcohol education/prevention programs offered for: all students. Authorized group concerned with responsible drinking. College holds an annual alcohol awareness week and drug awareness week.

Identification of Problems

Admissions College application does not ask about prior substance abuse problems.

On campus Current students identified as chemically dependent may remain enrolled. No training program on identifying students with potential substance abuse problems. Written procedures for students and staff if substance abuse is suspected.

Support Services

On campus AA.

Employee assistance Program for chemically dependent employees available. Staff working with drug/alcohol-related issues: 2 part-time.

Disciplinary Actions

Alcohol Results of infractions of alcohol regulations (see Comparative Table of Alcohol Regulations) vary by situation.

Drugs For any use, possession, or sale: varies by situation.

Ohio State University–Marion Campus (continued)

For More Information

Contact: Melissa Conrath, Assistant Director, Ohio State University–Marion Campus, 1465 Mt. Vernon Ave., Marion, OH 43302. Telephone: 614-389-2361.

OHIO VALLEY COLLEGE

Parkersburg, West Virginia

General Information

Independent primarily 2-year coed college, affiliated with Church of Christ. Founded 1960. Awards A (college transfer and terminal), B. Primary accreditation: regional. Small-town setting; 128-acre campus. Total enrollment: 221. Faculty: 22 (10 full-time, 12 part-time). Social organizations: 4 local fraternities, 4 local sororities; 78% of eligible undergraduate men and 80% of eligible undergraduate women are members.

Drug and Alcohol Information

Education

On campus Drug and alcohol education/prevention programs offered for: all students.

Identification of Problems

Admissions College application question about prior substance abuse problems is used for counseling and referral, if student is admitted; in the admissions decision.

On campus Current students identified as chemically dependent may not remain enrolled. No training program on identifying students with potential substance abuse problems. Written procedures for students and staff if substance abuse is suspected.

Support Services

On campus Private counseling.

Employee assistance Program for chemically dependent employees not available.

Disciplinary Actions

Alcohol Results of infractions of alcohol regulations (see Comparative Table of Alcohol Regulations) include suspension, expulsion.

Drugs For any use, possession, or sale: expulsion.

For More Information

Contact: Dennis Cox, Dean of Student Services, Ohio Valley College, College Pkwy., Parkersburg, WV 26101. Telephone: 304-485-7384.

OKLAHOMA BAPTIST UNIVERSITY

Shawnee, Oklahoma

General Information

Independent Baptist 4-year coed college. Founded 1910. Awards B. Primary accreditation: regional. Small-town setting; 180-acre campus. Total enrollment: 1,967. Faculty: 128 (103 full-time, 25 part-time). Social organizations: 4 local fraternities, 5 local sororities; 25% of eligible undergraduate men and 30% of eligible undergraduate women are members.

Drug and Alcohol Information

Education

On campus Drug and alcohol education/prevention programs offered for: all students. Authorized group concerned with responsible drinking. College holds an annual alcohol awareness week and drug awareness week.

Identification of Problems

Admissions College application does not ask about prior substance abuse problems.

On campus Current students identified as chemically dependent may remain enrolled, but treatment is required. No training program on identifying students with potential substance abuse problems. Written procedures for students and staff if substance abuse is suspected.

Support Services

On campus Private counseling.

Employee assistance Program for chemically dependent employees not available.

Disciplinary Actions

Alcohol Results of infractions of alcohol regulations (see Comparative Table of Alcohol Regulations) include chemical dependency assessment, counseling, warning, probation, suspension, expulsion.

Drugs For first-time use or possession: chemical dependency assessment, probation, suspension. For subsequent use or possession: chemical dependency assessment, suspension, expulsion. For any sale: expulsion.

For More Information

Contact: Dr. Merl A. Jennings, Vice President for Student Development, Oklahoma Baptist University, 500 W. University, Shawnee, OK 74801. Telephone: 405-275-2850.

OKLAHOMA STATE UNIVERSITY

Stillwater, Oklahoma

General Information

State-supported comprehensive coed institution. Part of Oklahoma State University. Founded 1890. Awards B, M, D. Primary accreditation: regional. Small-town setting; 500-acre campus. Total enrollment: 20,764. Faculty: 664 (640 full-time, 24 part-time). Social organizations: 23 national fraternities, 14 national sororities; 11% of eligible undergraduate men and 10% of eligible undergraduate women are members.

Drug and Alcohol Information

Education

On campus Drug and alcohol education/prevention programs offered for: all students, athletes/coaches, violators of student code of conduct. Bacchus chapter: 25 members. College holds an annual alcohol awareness week and drug awareness week.

Identification of Problems

Admissions College application does not ask about prior substance abuse problems.

On campus Current students identified as chemically dependent may remain enrolled. Training program on identifying students with potential substance abuse problems for: resident advisers, coaches, Greek officers.

Written procedures for students and staff if substance abuse is suspected.

Support Services

On campus AA, NA, Al-Anon, support groups (nonmedical detox program).

Employee assistance Program for chemically dependent employees not available. Staff working with drug/alcohol-related issues: 1 full-time and 17 part-time.

Disciplinary Actions

Alcohol Results of infractions of alcohol regulations (see Comparative Table of Alcohol Regulations) vary by situation but can include chemical dependency assessment, counseling, warning, probation, possible group sanctions.

Drugs For any use: varies by situation—chemical dependency assessment. For any possession or sale: varies by situation.

For More Information

Contact: Dr. Patrick M. Murphy, Director, University Counseling Services, 315 Student Union, Oklahoma State University, Stillwater, OK 74078. Telephone: 405-744-5458.

OLD DOMINION UNIVERSITY

Norfolk, Virginia

General Information

State-supported comprehensive coed institution. Founded 1930. Awards B, M, D. Primary accreditation: regional. City setting; 146-acre campus. Total enrollment: 15,656. Faculty: 703 (575 full-time, 128 part-time). Social organizations: 14 national fraternities, 9 national sororities.

Drug and Alcohol Information

Education

On campus Drug and alcohol education/prevention programs offered for: all students. Authorized group concerned with responsible drinking. College holds an annual alcohol awareness week and drug awareness week.

Identification of Problems

Admissions College application does not ask about prior substance abuse problems.

On campus Current students identified as chemically dependent may remain enrolled. Comments: Such students may be referred for treatment, but it is not required. No training program on identifying students with potential substance abuse problems. Written procedures for students and staff if substance abuse is suspected.

Support Services

On campus AA, Al-Anon, ACOA, private counseling.

Employee assistance Program for chemically dependent employees available. Staff working with drug/alcohol-related issues: 2 part-time.

Disciplinary Actions

Alcohol Results of infractions of alcohol regulations (see Comparative Table of Alcohol Regulations) vary by situation but can include chemical dependency assessment, counseling, warning, probation, suspension, expulsion.

Drugs For first-time use: counseling, probation. For first-time possession: probation. For subsequent use or possession: expulsion. For first-time sale: expulsion.

Additional Information from the College

The Resident Directors and the Health Educator at Old Dominion University have recently developed an alcohol education program for first offenders and are now working on a program for repeat offenders.

For More Information

Contact: Mary K. Sefchick, Health Educator, Old Dominion University, 1500 W. 48th St., Norfolk, VA 23529-0486. Telephone: 804-683-3132.

OLIVET COLLEGE

Olivet, Michigan

General Information

Independent 4-year coed college, affiliated with Congregational Christian Church. Founded 1844. Awards B. Primary accreditation: regional. Rural setting; 92-acre campus. Total enrollment: 784. Faculty: 63 (38 full-time, 25 part-time). Social organizations: 3 local fraternities, 3 local sororities; 15% of eligible undergraduate men and 15% of eligible undergraduate women are members.

Drug and Alcohol Information

Education

On campus Drug and alcohol education/prevention programs offered for: all students. Authorized group concerned with responsible drinking. College holds an annual alcohol awareness week and drug awareness week.

Identification of Problems

Admissions College application does not ask about prior substance abuse problems.

On campus Current students identified as chemically dependent may remain enrolled, but treatment is strongly encouraged. Training program on identifying students with potential substance abuse problems for: resident advisers. No written procedures for students and staff if substance abuse is suspected.

Support Services

On campus Private counseling.

Employee assistance Program for chemically dependent employees not available. Staff working with drug/alcohol-related issues: 5 part-time.

Disciplinary Actions

Alcohol Results of infractions of alcohol regulations (see Comparative Table of Alcohol Regulations) vary by situation. Comments: Infractions are assessed by the College's judicial process.

Drugs For any use, possession, or sale: varies by situation.

For More Information

Contact: Dr. Shirley M. Erickson, Dean of Students, Olivet College, Olivet, MI 49076. Telephone: 616-749-7611.

OREGON INSTITUTE OF TECHNOLOGY

Klamath Falls, Oregon

General Information

State-supported 4-year coed college. Founded 1947. Awards A (college transfer and terminal), B. Primary accreditation: regional. Small-town setting; 173-acre campus. Total

Oregon Institute of Technology (continued)

enrollment: 3,026. Faculty: 144 (109 full-time, 35 part-time). Social organizations: 2 national fraternities, 1 local fraternity, 1 local sorority; 20% of eligible undergraduate men and 20% of eligible undergraduate women are members.

Drug and Alcohol Information

Education

On campus Drug and alcohol education/prevention programs offered for: all students, athletes/coaches. Authorized group concerned with responsible drinking. College holds an annual alcohol awareness week and drug awareness week.

Identification of Problems

Admissions College application does not ask about prior substance abuse problems.

On campus Current students identified as chemically dependent may remain enrolled. Comments: Treatment may sometimes be required if student is to remain in a residence hall. No training program on identifying students with potential substance abuse problems. No written procedures for students and staff if substance abuse is suspected.

Support Services

On campus AA, NA, private counseling.

Employee assistance Program for chemically dependent employees available.

Disciplinary Actions

Alcohol Results of infractions of alcohol regulations (see Comparative Table of Alcohol Regulations) vary by situation but can include counseling, warning.

Drugs For any use, possession, or sale: varies by situation.

For More Information

Contact: Marla Edge, Counselor, Oregon Institute of Technology, 3201 Campus Dr., Klamath Falls, OR 97601. Telephone: 503-882-4408.

OREGON STATE UNIVERSITY

Corvallis, Oregon

General Information

State-supported comprehensive coed institution. Founded 1868. Awards B, M, D. Primary accreditation: regional. Small-town setting; 400-acre campus. Total enrollment: 15,637. Faculty: 2,366 (1,684 full-time, 682 part-time). Social organizations: 26 national fraternities, 14 national sororities; 10% of eligible undergraduate men and 7% of eligible undergraduate women are members.

Drug and Alcohol Information

Education

On campus Drug and alcohol education/prevention programs offered for: all students, athletes/coaches, faculty, administration. Bacchus chapter: 10 members. College holds an annual alcohol awareness week and drug awareness week.

Identification of Problems

Admissions College application does not ask about prior substance abuse problems.

On campus Current students identified as chemically dependent may remain enrolled, but treatment will probably be required. Training program on identifying students with potential substance abuse problems for: resident advisers, Greek officers, administration. Written procedures for students and staff if substance abuse is suspected.

Support Services

On campus Support groups, private counseling, University-wide student/faculty/administration committee, health educator, mental health clinic, alcohol abuse course.

Employee assistance Program for chemically dependent employees available. Staff working with drug/alcohol-related issues: 1 full-time and 25 part-time.

Disciplinary Actions

Alcohol Results of infractions of alcohol regulations (see Comparative Table of Alcohol Regulations) vary by situation but can include chemical dependency assessment, counseling, warning, probation, suspension, expulsion.

Drugs For any use, possession, or sale: varies by situation.

Additional Information from the College

Oregon State University uses a variety of education and prevention materials throughout the year and has received several awards for its program efforts.

For More Information

Contact: Cheryl Caraham, Health Educator, Student Health Center, Oregon State University, Corvallis, OR 97331. Telephone: 503-754-2775.

ORLANDO COLLEGE

Orlando, Florida

General Information

Independent 5-year coed college. Part of Summit System of Colleges and Schools. Founded 1918. Awards A (college transfer and terminal), B, M. Primary accreditation: AICS. Metropolitan setting; 6-acre campus. Total enrollment: 846. Faculty: 40 (14 full-time, 26 part-time).

Drug and Alcohol Information

Education

On campus Drug and alcohol education/prevention programs offered for: all students, faculty, administration. College holds an annual alcohol awareness week.

Identification of Problems

Admissions College application does not ask about prior substance abuse problems.

On campus No written procedures for students and staff if substance abuse is suspected.

Support Services

On campus Referrals.

Employee assistance Program for chemically dependent employees not available. Staff working with drug/alcohol-related issues: 3 part-time.

Disciplinary Actions

Alcohol Results of infractions of alcohol regulations (see Comparative Table of Alcohol Regulations) vary by situation but can include warning, suspension.

Drugs For first-time use or possession: warning. For subsequent use or possession: suspension. For first-time sale: varies by situation. For subsequent sale: expulsion.

For More Information

Contact: Michele McArdle, Dean of Education, Orlando College, 5500 Diplomat Circle, Orlando, FL 32810. Telephone: 407-628-5870.

OTIS ART INSTITUTE OF PARSONS SCHOOL OF DESIGN, NEW SCHOOL FOR SOCIAL RESEARCH

Los Angeles, California

General Information

Independent 5-year specialized coed college. Part of New School for Social Research. Founded 1917. Awards B, M. Primary accreditation: regional. Metropolitan setting; 1-acre campus. Total university enrollment: 6,359; total unit enrollment: 854. Faculty: 208 (28 full-time, 180 part-time).

Drug and Alcohol Information

Education

On campus Drug and alcohol education/prevention programs not offered.

Identification of Problems

Admissions College application does not ask about prior substance abuse problems.

On campus Current students identified as chemically dependent may remain enrolled. Treatment is strongly recommended but not required. Training program on identifying students with potential substance abuse problems for: resident advisers, members of the faculty and administration who are on the Student Life Committee. Written procedures for students and staff if substance abuse is suspected are being developed.

Support Services

On campus No support services on campus.

Off campus Private psychiatric hospital provides support services and/or referrals for students and employees. Staff working with drug/alcohol-related issues: 2 part-time.

Disciplinary Actions

Alcohol Results of infractions of alcohol regulations (see Comparative Table of Alcohol Regulations) vary by situation but can include counseling, warning.

Drugs For any use or possession: varies by situation—counseling, warning. Comments: There have been no incidents involving sale of drugs by students.

For More Information

Contact: Cornelia Emerson, Associate Dean, Otis Art Institute of Parsons School of Design, New School for Social Research, 2401 Wilshire Blvd., Los Angeles, CA 90057. Telephone: 213-251-0545.

OUACHITA BAPTIST UNIVERSITY

Arkadelphia, Arkansas

General Information

Independent Baptist 5-year coed college. Founded 1886. Awards B, M. Primary accreditation: regional. Small-town setting; 60-acre campus. Total enrollment: 1,403. Faculty: 101 (85 full-time, 16 part-time). Social organizations: 4 local fraternities, 4 local sororities; 30% of eligible undergraduate men and 30% of eligible undergraduate women are members.

Drug and Alcohol Information

Education

On campus Drug and alcohol education/prevention programs offered for: freshmen, resident advisers; required for: athletes/coaches.

Identification of Problems

Admissions College application does not ask about prior substance abuse problems.

On campus Current students identified as chemically dependent may remain enrolled, but treatment is required. Training program on identifying students with potential substance abuse problems for: resident advisers, coaches. Written procedures for students and staff if substance abuse is suspected.

Support Services

On campus Private counseling.

Employee assistance Program for chemically dependent employees available. Staff working with drug/alcohol-related issues: 2 part-time.

Disciplinary Actions

Alcohol Results of infractions of alcohol regulations (see Comparative Table of Alcohol Regulations) include counseling, probation, suspension.

Drugs For first-time use: counseling, probation. For first-time possession or sale: suspension. For subsequent use, possession, or sale: expulsion.

For More Information

Contact: B. Aldon Dixon, Dean of Students, Ouachita Baptist University, Arkadelphia, AR 71923. Telephone: 501-246-4531.

OUR LADY OF HOLY CROSS COLLEGE

New Orleans, Louisiana

General Information

Independent Roman Catholic 5-year coed college. Founded 1916. Awards A (college transfer), B, M. Primary accreditation: regional. Metropolitan setting; 40-acre campus. Total enrollment: 848. Faculty: 62 (28 full-time, 34 part-time). Social organization: 1 coed fraternity.

Drug and Alcohol Information

Education

On campus Drug and alcohol education/prevention programs offered for: all students, athletes/coaches, faculty, administration, the public. Authorized group concerned with responsible drinking. College holds an annual alcohol awareness week.

Identification of Problems

Admissions College application does not ask about prior substance abuse problems.

On campus Current students identified as chemically dependent may remain enrolled, but treatment is required. Training program on identifying students with potential substance abuse problems for: faculty, administration. No

Our Lady of Holy Cross College (continued)

written procedures for students and staff if substance abuse is suspected.

Support Services

On campus Private counseling.

Employee assistance Program for chemically dependent employees not available.

Disciplinary Actions

Alcohol Results of infractions of alcohol regulations (see Comparative Table of Alcohol Regulations) vary by situation.

Drugs For any use or possession: varies by situation. For any sale: expulsion.

For More Information

Contact: Richard L. MacLennan, Director of Student Affairs and Admissions, Our Lady of Holy Cross College, 4123 Woodland Dr., New Orleans, LA 70131-7399. Telephone: 504-394-7744.

OUR LADY OF THE LAKE UNIVERSITY OF SAN ANTONIO

San Antonio, Texas

General Information

Independent Roman Catholic 5-year coed college. Founded 1911. Awards B, M. Primary accreditation: regional. Metropolitan setting; 75-acre campus. Total enrollment: 2,245. Faculty: 130 (70 full-time, 60 part-time).

Drug and Alcohol Information

Education

On campus Drug and alcohol education/prevention programs offered for: all students. College holds an annual alcohol awareness week and drug awareness week.

Identification of Problems

Admissions College application does not ask about prior substance abuse problems.

On campus Current students identified as chemically dependent may remain enrolled, but treatment is required. Training program on identifying students with potential substance abuse problems for: resident advisers, administration, student life staff. No written procedures for students and staff if substance abuse is suspected.

Support Services

On campus Private counseling.

Employee assistance Program for chemically dependent employees not available.

Disciplinary Actions

Alcohol Results of infractions of alcohol regulations (see Comparative Table of Alcohol Regulations) include counseling, warning, probation, suspension, expulsion.

Drugs For any use, possession, or sale: varies by situation.

For More Information

Contact: Joanna Haley, Coordinator of Counseling Services, Our Lady of the Lake University of San Antonio, 411 S.W. 24th St., San Antonio, TX 78285. Telephone: 512-434-6711.

PACE UNIVERSITY, WHITE PLAINS CAMPUS

White Plains, New York

General Information

Independent 5-year coed college. Part of Pace University. Founded 1923. Awards A (terminal), B, M, D. Primary accreditation: regional. City setting; 32-acre campus. Total enrollment: 4,324. Faculty: 644 (268 full-time, 376 part-time).

Drug and Alcohol Information

Education

On campus Drug and alcohol education/prevention programs offered for: all students, faculty, administration; required for: athletes/coaches, resident advisers. Authorized group concerned with responsible drinking. College holds an annual alcohol awareness week and drug awareness week.

Identification of Problems

Admissions College application does not ask about prior substance abuse problems.

On campus Current students identified as chemically dependent may remain enrolled, but treatment may be required, depending on the situation. Training program on identifying students with potential substance abuse problems for: resident advisers, coaches, Greek officers, faculty, administration. Written procedures for students and staff if substance abuse is suspected.

Support Services

On campus Private counseling.

Employee assistance Program for chemically dependent employees not available. Staff working with drug/alcohol-related issues: 15–20 part-time.

Disciplinary Actions

Alcohol Results of infractions of alcohol regulations (see Comparative Table of Alcohol Regulations) vary by situation but can include chemical dependency assessment, counseling, warning, probation, suspension, expulsion.

Drugs For first-time use: varies by situation—chemical dependency assessment. For first-time possession: varies by situation. For subsequent use or possession: expulsion. For any sale: expulsion.

For More Information

Contact: Geoffrey J. Harter, Associate Dean for Students, Pace University, White Plains Campus, 78 North Broadway, White Plains, NY 10603. Telephone: 914-681-4105.

PACIFIC CHRISTIAN COLLEGE

Fullerton, California

General Information

Independent 5-year coed college, affiliated with Church of Christ. Founded 1928. Awards A (college transfer), B, M. Primary accreditation: regional and AABC. City setting; 11-acre campus. Total enrollment: 557. Faculty: 43 (20 full-time, 23 part-time). Social organizations: 1 local fraternity, 1 local sorority; 5% of eligible undergraduate men and 5% of eligible undergraduate women are members.

Drug and Alcohol Information

Education

On campus Drug and alcohol education/prevention programs not offered. Authorized group concerned with responsible drinking.

Identification of Problems

Admissions College application question about prior substance abuse problems is used in the admissions decision.

On campus Current students identified as chemically dependent may not remain enrolled in most cases, but each is treated individually. Training program on identifying students with potential substance abuse problems for: resident advisers, residence hall directors. Written procedures for students and staff if substance abuse is suspected.

Support Services

On campus Support groups (Bible and prayer), private counseling, accountability groups.

Employee assistance Program for chemically dependent employees not available.

Disciplinary Actions

Alcohol Results of infractions of alcohol regulations (see Comparative Table of Alcohol Regulations) vary by situation but can include probation, suspension, expulsion, eviction from residence halls.

Drugs For any use, possession, or sale: varies by situation—probation, suspension, expulsion, eviction from residence halls.

Additional Information from the College

Pacific Christian College expects that each student's attitude and behavior reflect the character of Jesus Christ at all times. Therefore, students must refrain from any use of alcohol or illegal drugs. All students represent the Lord and PCC wherever they are, and they are expected to exhibit a distinctive Christian life-style in all their activities.

For More Information

Contact: Steve Alley, Dean of Students, Pacific Christian College, 2500 E. Nutwood Ave., Fullerton, CA 92631. Telephone: 714-879-3901 Ext. 228.

PACIFIC COAST BAPTIST BIBLE COLLEGE

San Dimas, California

General Information

Independent 4-year coed college, affiliated with Baptist Bible Fellowship. Founded 1967. Awards A (terminal), B. Primary accreditation: U.S. Department of Education (3IC). City setting; 150-acre campus. Total enrollment: 208.

Drug and Alcohol Information

Education

On campus Drug and alcohol education/prevention programs not offered.

Identification of Problems

Admissions College application question about prior substance abuse problems is used in the admissions decision.

On campus Current students identified as chemically dependent may not remain enrolled. No training program on identifying students with potential substance abuse problems. Written procedures for students and staff if substance abuse is suspected.

Disciplinary Actions

Alcohol Results of infractions of alcohol regulations (see Comparative Table of Alcohol Regulations) include expulsion.

Drugs For any use, possession, or sale: expulsion.

For More Information

Contact: Roger E. Howse, Registrar/Academic Dean, Pacific Coast Baptist Bible College, 1100 S. Valley Ctr., San Dimas, CA 91773. Telephone: 714-599-6843.

PACIFIC NORTHWEST COLLEGE OF ART, OREGON ART INSTITUTE

Portland, Oregon

General Information

Independent 4-year specialized coed college. Founded 1909. Awards B. Primary accreditation: regional. Metropolitan setting. Total enrollment: 204. Faculty: 40 (18 full-time, 22 part-time).

Drug and Alcohol Information

Education

On campus Drug and alcohol education/prevention programs offered for: all students, faculty, administration. College holds an annual alcohol awareness week and drug awareness week.

Identification of Problems

Admissions College application does not ask about prior substance abuse problems.

On campus Current students identified as chemically dependent may remain enrolled, but treatment is required. Training program on identifying students with potential substance abuse problems for: faculty, administration, students. Written procedures for students and staff if substance abuse is suspected.

Support Services

On campus Private counseling, referrals.

Employee assistance Program for chemically dependent employees not available. Staff working with drug/alcohol-related issues: 3 part-time.

Disciplinary Actions

Alcohol Results of infractions of alcohol regulations (see Comparative Table of Alcohol Regulations) vary by situation but can include counseling, expulsion.

Drugs For first-time use: varies by situation—counseling, warning. For first-time possession: varies by situation—counseling. For subsequent use or possession: varies by situation—counseling. For any sale: counseling, expulsion.

For More Information

Contact: Willodean Oswald, Director of Student Services, Pacific Northwest College of Art, Oregon Art Institute, 1219 SW Park Ave., Portland, OR 97205. Telephone: 503-226-4391.

PACIFIC OAKS COLLEGE

Pasadena, California

General Information

Independent specialized coed college. Founded 1945. Awards B, M. Primary accreditation: regional. City setting; 2-acre campus. Total enrollment: 250.

Drug and Alcohol Information

Education

On campus Drug and alcohol education/prevention programs offered for: all students, faculty, administration.

Identification of Problems

Admissions College application does not ask about prior substance abuse problems.

On campus Current students identified as chemically dependent may remain enrolled. No training program on identifying students with potential substance abuse problems. Written procedures for students and staff if substance abuse is suspected.

Support Services

On campus Referrals.

Off campus AA, NA, Al-Anon, ACOA.

Employee assistance Program for chemically dependent employees not available.

Disciplinary Actions

Alcohol Results of infractions of alcohol regulations (see Comparative Table of Alcohol Regulations) vary by situation.

Drugs For first-time use or possession: varies by situation—chemical dependency, assessment, counseling. For subsequent use or possession: varies by situation—expulsion. For any sale: varies by situation—expulsion, police informed.

Additional Information from the College

The student body has an average age of 38, so Pacific Oaks College does not encounter the usual college-age experimentation problems, but more insidious, hidden problems involving denial.

For More Information

Contact: Laila Aaen, Dean, Pacific Oaks College, 5 and 6 Westmoreland Pl., Pasadena, CA 91103. Telephone: 818-397-1321.

PAIER COLLEGE OF ART, INC.

Hamden, Connecticut

General Information

Proprietary 4-year specialized coed college. Founded 1946. Awards A (terminal), B. Primary accreditation: regional (candidate) and NATTS. City setting; 3-acre campus. Total enrollment: 305. Faculty: 45 (6 full-time, 39 part-time).

Drug and Alcohol Information

Education

On campus Drug and alcohol education/prevention programs offered for: all students.

Identification of Problems

Admissions College application does not ask about prior substance abuse problems.

On campus Current students identified as chemically dependent may remain enrolled, but treatment is required. No training program on identifying students with potential substance abuse problems. No written procedures for students and staff if substance abuse is suspected.

Support Services

On campus Private counseling.

Employee assistance Program for chemically dependent employees not available.

Disciplinary Actions

Alcohol Results of infractions of alcohol regulations (see Comparative Table of Alcohol Regulations) vary by situation.

Drugs For any use or possession: varies by situation. For any sale: expulsion.

For More Information

Contact: Catherine DiPersio, Director, Counseling/Placement, Paier College of Art, Inc., 6 Prospect Ct., Hamden, CT 06511. Telephone: 203-288-9580.

PALM BEACH ATLANTIC COLLEGE

West Palm Beach, Florida

General Information

Independent Southern Baptist 4-year coed college. Founded 1968. Awards B. Primary accreditation: regional. City setting; 21-acre campus. Total enrollment: 1,135. Faculty: 81 (40 full-time, 41 part-time).

Drug and Alcohol Information

Education

On campus Drug and alcohol education/prevention programs not offered.

Identification of Problems

Admissions College application does not ask about prior substance abuse problems.

On campus Current students identified as chemically dependent may not remain enrolled. No training program on identifying students with potential substance abuse problems. No written procedures for students and staff if substance abuse is suspected.

Support Services

On campus Private counseling.

Employee assistance Program for chemically dependent employees not available.

Disciplinary Actions

Alcohol Results of infractions of alcohol regulations (see Comparative Table of Alcohol Regulations) include probation, suspension. Comments: By its Christian nature and student rules, the College supports total abstinence, not responsible drinking.

Drugs For first-time use or possession: probation, suspension. For first-time sale: probation, expulsion. For subsequent use, possession, or sale: expulsion.

For More Information

Contact: Dr. Daniel G. MacMillan, Vice President of

Student Development, Palm Beach Atlantic College, P.O. Box 3353, West Palm Beach, FL 33402. Telephone: 407-650-7719.

PAN AMERICAN UNIVERSITY

Edinburg, Texas

General Information

State-supported 5-year coed college. Founded 1927. Awards A (terminal), B, M. Primary accreditation: regional. Rural setting; 200-acre campus. Total enrollment: 11,218. Faculty: 385 (287 full-time, 98 part-time). Social organizations: 5 national fraternities, 2 national sororities.

Drug and Alcohol Information

Education

On campus Drug and alcohol education/prevention programs offered for: all students, athletes/coaches.

Identification of Problems

Admissions College application does not ask about prior substance abuse problems.

On campus Current students identified as chemically dependent may remain enrolled. No training program on identifying students with potential substance abuse problems. No written procedures for students and staff if substance abuse is suspected.

Support Services

On campus Private counseling.

Employee assistance Program for chemically dependent employees not available. Staff working with drug/alcohol-related issues: 1 part-time.

Disciplinary Actions

Alcohol Results of infractions of alcohol regulations (see Comparative Table of Alcohol Regulations) include counseling, warning, probation, suspension, expulsion.

Drugs For first-time use or possession: varies by situation. For first-time sale: varies by situation—suspension, expulsion. For subsequent use, possession, or sale: expulsion.

Additional Information from the College

Representatives of student organizations that plan to sponsor alcohol-related activities must attend an alcohol awareness workshop.

For More Information

Contact: Judy Vinson, Dean of Students, Pan American University, 1201 W. University Dr., Edinburg, TX 78539. Telephone: 512-381-2147.

PARK COLLEGE

Parkville, Missouri

General Information

Independent 5-year coed college, affiliated with Reorganized Church of Jesus Christ of Latter Day Saints. Founded 1875. Awards A (college transfer and terminal), B, M. Primary accreditation: regional. Small-town setting; 800-acre campus. Total enrollment: 653. Faculty: 76 (38 full-time, 38 part-time). Social organizations: 2 coed fraternities; 10% of eligible undergraduate men and 10% of eligible undergraduate women are members.

Drug and Alcohol Information

Education

On campus Drug and alcohol education/prevention programs offered for: all students. College holds an annual alcohol awareness week.

Identification of Problems

Admissions College application does not ask about prior substance abuse problems.

On campus Training program on identifying students with potential substance abuse problems for: resident advisers, counselors. Written procedures for students and staff if substance abuse is suspected.

Support Services

On campus Private counseling.

Employee assistance Program for chemically dependent employees not available.

Disciplinary Actions

Alcohol Results of infractions of alcohol regulations (see Comparative Table of Alcohol Regulations) vary by situation.

Drugs For any use or possession: varies by situation. For first-time sale: varies by situation. For subsequent sale: suspension.

For More Information

Contact: S. L. Sartain, Dean of Students, Park College, Parkville, MO 64152. Telephone: 816-741-2000.

PATTEN COLLEGE

Oakland, California

General Information

Independent interdenominational 4-year coed college. Founded 1944. Awards A (college transfer), B. Primary accreditation: regional. City setting; 5-acre campus. Total enrollment: 200.

Drug and Alcohol Information

Education

On campus Drug and alcohol education/prevention programs not offered.

Identification of Problems

Admissions College application question about prior substance abuse problems is used in the admissions decision.

On campus No training program on identifying students with potential substance abuse problems.

Support Services

On campus No support services on campus.

Employee assistance Program for chemically dependent employees not available.

Disciplinary Actions

Alcohol Results of infractions of alcohol regulations (see Comparative Table of Alcohol Regulations) include expulsion.

Drugs For any use, possession, or sale: expulsion.

Patten College (continued)

Additional Information from the College

Patten College is a Christian college that does not permit any use of drugs or alcohol.

For More Information

Contact: Sharon Hendricks, Director of Admissions, Patten College, 2433 Coolidge Ave., Oakland, CA 94601. Telephone: 415-533-8300.

PEABODY CONSERVATORY OF MUSIC

Baltimore, Maryland

General Information

Independent 5-year specialized coed college. Administratively affiliated with Johns Hopkins University. Founded 1857. Awards B, M, D. Primary accreditation: regional. Metropolitan setting. Total enrollment: 465. Faculty: 100.

Drug and Alcohol Information

Education

On campus Drug and alcohol education/prevention programs offered for: all students.

Identification of Problems

Admissions College application does not ask about prior substance abuse problems.

On campus Current students identified as chemically dependent may remain enrolled, but treatment is required. Training program on identifying students with potential substance abuse problems for: resident advisers. No written procedures for students and staff if substance abuse is suspected.

Support Services

On campus Private counseling.

Employee assistance Program for chemically dependent employees available. Staff working with drug/alcohol-related issues: 1 full-time (at Johns Hopkins).

Disciplinary Actions

Alcohol Results of infractions of alcohol regulations (see Comparative Table of Alcohol Regulations) vary by situation.

Drugs For first-time use: chemical dependency assessment, counseling, warning. For subsequent use: varies by situation. For any possession: varies by situation. For any sale: expulsion.

Additional Information from the College

Peabody Conservatory is a division of the Johns Hopkins University, whose considerable resources are available to Peabody students. The Conservatory's basic approach to substance abuse problems is that education and counseling should, whenever possible, precede the disciplinary process.

For More Information

Contact: Emily F. Frank, Assistant Dean for Student Affairs, Peabody Conservatory of Music, 1 E. Mt. Vernon Pl., Baltimore, MD 21202. Telephone: 301-659-8173.

PEMBROKE STATE UNIVERSITY

Pembroke, North Carolina

General Information

State-supported 5-year coed college. Part of University of North Carolina System. Founded 1887. Awards B, M. Primary accreditation: regional. Rural setting; 100-acre campus. Total enrollment: 2,835. Faculty: 165 (128 full-time, 37 part-time). Social organizations: 4 national fraternities, 6 national sororities, 2 local fraternities; 3% of eligible undergraduate men and 3% of eligible undergraduate women are members.

Drug and Alcohol Information

Education

On campus Drug and alcohol education/prevention programs offered for: all students, faculty, administration. College holds an annual alcohol awareness week and drug awareness week.

Identification of Problems

Admissions College application does not ask about prior substance abuse problems.

On campus Current students identified as chemically dependent may remain enrolled, but treatment is required. No training program on identifying students with potential substance abuse problems. Written procedures for students and staff if substance abuse is suspected.

Support Services

On campus No support services on campus.

Employee assistance Program for chemically dependent employees not available.

Disciplinary Actions

Alcohol Results of infractions of alcohol regulations (see Comparative Table of Alcohol Regulations) include prosecution.

Drugs For first-time use: counseling, warning. For first-time possession: counseling, probation. For subsequent use or possession: suspension. For any sale: suspension.

For More Information

Contact: James B. Chavis, Vice Chancellor for Student Affairs, Pembroke State University, College St., Pembroke, NC 28372. Telephone: 919-521-8000.

PENNSYLVANIA STATE UNIVERSITY AT ERIE, THE BEHREND COLLEGE

Erie, Pennsylvania

General Information

State-related 5-year coed college. Part of Pennsylvania State University. Founded 1926. Awards A (college transfer and terminal), B, M. Primary accreditation: regional. City setting; 422-acre campus. Total enrollment: 2,830. Faculty: 151 (118 full-time, 33 part-time). Social organizations: national fraternities, national sororities, local fraternities, local sororities.

Drug and Alcohol Information

Education

On campus Drug and alcohol education/prevention programs offered for: all students, athletes/coaches, faculty, administration. Bacchus chapter: 10 members. College holds an annual alcohol awareness week and drug awareness week.

Identification of Problems

Admissions College application does not ask about prior substance abuse problems.

On campus Current students identified as chemically dependent may remain enrolled, but treatment is required. Training program on identifying students with potential substance abuse problems for: resident advisers, coaches. Written procedures for students and staff if substance abuse is suspected.

Support Services

On campus Private counseling.

Employee assistance Program for chemically dependent employees not available.

Disciplinary Actions

Alcohol Results of infractions of alcohol regulations (see Comparative Table of Alcohol Regulations) include chemical dependency assessment, counseling, warning, probation, suspension, expulsion.

Drugs For any use, possession, or sale: varies by situation.

For More Information

Contact: Patty McMahon, Nurse Practitioner, Pennsylvania State University at Erie, The Behrend College, Station Rd., Erie, PA 16563. Telephone: 814-898-6217.

PEPPERDINE UNIVERSITY

Malibu, California

General Information

Independent 5-year coed college, affiliated with Church of Christ. Founded 1937. Awards B, M, D. Primary accreditation: regional. Small-town setting; 830-acre campus. Total enrollment: 3,396. Faculty: 279 (132 full-time, 147 part-time). Social organizations: 6 local fraternities, 4 local sororities; 18% of eligible undergraduate men and 12% of eligible undergraduate women are members.

Drug and Alcohol Information

Education

On campus Drug and alcohol education/prevention programs offered for: all students, athletes/coaches, faculty, administration. Authorized group concerned with responsible drinking. College holds an annual alcohol awareness week and drug awareness week.

Identification of Problems

Admissions College application does not ask about prior substance abuse problems.

On campus Current students identified as chemically dependent may remain enrolled, but treatment is required. Training program on identifying students with potential substance abuse problems for: resident advisers, Greek officers.

Support Services

On campus AA, NA, Al-Anon, ACOA, support groups (care groups), private counseling.

Employee assistance Program for chemically dependent employees available. Staff working with drug/alcohol-related issues: 1 full-time and 4 part-time.

Disciplinary Actions

Alcohol Results of infractions of alcohol regulations (see Comparative Table of Alcohol Regulations) vary by situation.

Drugs For any use or possession: varies by situation. For any sale: expulsion.

For More Information

Contact: Dr. John Free, Health and Counseling, Pepperdine University, 24255 Pacific Coast Hwy., Malibu, CA 90265. Telephone: 213-456-4210.

PERU STATE COLLEGE

Peru, Nebraska

General Information

State-supported 5-year coed college. Part of Nebraska State College System. Founded 1867. Awards A (terminal), B, M. Primary accreditation: regional. Rural setting; 118-acre campus. Total enrollment: 1,552. Faculty: 82. Social organizations: 1 national fraternity, 1 local sorority; 5% of eligible undergraduate men and 4% of eligible undergraduate women are members.

Drug and Alcohol Information

Education

On campus Drug and alcohol education/prevention programs offered for: all students; required for: resident advisers. Authorized group concerned with responsible drinking. College holds an annual alcohol awareness week.

Identification of Problems

Admissions College application does not ask about prior substance abuse problems.

On campus Current students identified as chemically dependent may remain enrolled. Training program on identifying students with potential substance abuse problems for: resident advisers. Written procedures for students and staff if substance abuse is suspected.

Support Services

On campus AA, private counseling.

Employee assistance Program for chemically dependent employees available. Staff working with drug/alcohol-related issues: 2 part-time.

Disciplinary Actions

Alcohol Results of infractions of alcohol regulations (see Comparative Table of Alcohol Regulations) vary by situation but can include chemical dependency assessment, counseling, warning, probation, suspension.

Drugs For first-time use or possession: counseling, probation. For subsequent use or possession: varies by situation—chemical dependency assessment, counseling, probation. For any sale: suspension.

For More Information

Contact: Dan Haugland, Director of Residence Life, Peru State College, Peru, NE 68421. Telephone: 402-872-3815 Ext. 2246.

PFEIFFER COLLEGE

Misenheimer, North Carolina

General Information

Independent United Methodist 5-year coed college. Founded 1885. Awards B, M. Primary accreditation: regional. Rural setting; 300-acre campus. Total enrollment: 883. Faculty: 65 (44 full-time, 21 part-time).

Drug and Alcohol Information

Education

On campus Drug and alcohol education/prevention programs offered for: all students. Authorized group concerned with responsible drinking. College holds an annual alcohol awareness week and drug awareness week.

Identification of Problems

Admissions College application does not ask about prior substance abuse problems.

On campus Current students identified as chemically dependent may remain enrolled, but treatment is required. No training program on identifying students with potential substance abuse problems. Written procedures for students and staff if substance abuse is suspected.

Support Services

On campus Private counseling.

Employee assistance Program for chemically dependent employees not available. Staff working with drug/alcohol-related issues: 4 part-time.

Disciplinary Actions

Alcohol Results of infractions of alcohol regulations (see Comparative Table of Alcohol Regulations) vary by situation but can include chemical dependency assessment, counseling, probation, suspension.

Drugs For first-time use or possession: varies by situation (particularly type of drug). For subsequent use or possession: suspension. For any sale: expulsion.

For More Information

Contact: Dr. Thomas B. Westcott, Vice President for Student Affairs, Pfeiffer College, Misenheimer, NC 28109. Telephone: 704-463-7343.

PHILADELPHIA COLLEGE OF PHARMACY AND SCIENCE

Philadelphia, Pennsylvania

General Information

Independent comprehensive coed institution. Founded 1821. Awards B, M, D. Primary accreditation: regional. Metropolitan setting; 15-acre campus. Total enrollment: 1,619. Faculty: 161 (124 full-time, 37 part-time). Social organizations: 5 national fraternities, 3 national sororities; 20% of eligible undergraduate men and 15% of eligible undergraduate women are members.

Drug and Alcohol Information

Education

On campus Drug and alcohol education/prevention programs required for: freshmen, resident advisers, student leaders. Authorized group concerned with responsible drinking.

Identification of Problems

Admissions College application does not ask about prior substance abuse problems.

On campus Current students identified as chemically dependent may remain enrolled, but treatment is required. No training program on identifying students with potential substance abuse problems. Written procedures for students and staff if substance abuse is suspected.

Support Services

On campus Referrals through the Counseling Office.

Off campus AA, NA, Al-Anon, ACOA, other support groups, and private counseling.

Employee assistance Program for chemically dependent employees available. Staff working with drug/alcohol-related issues: 5 part-time.

Disciplinary Actions

Alcohol Results of infractions of alcohol regulations (see Comparative Table of Alcohol Regulations) vary by situation but can include counseling, warning, probation, suspension, expulsion.

Drugs For any use or possession: varies by situation. For any sale: expulsion.

For More Information

Contact: Juana Reina-Morrison, Associate Dean of Students, GH 214, Philadelphia College of Pharmacy and Science, Woodland Ave. at 43rd St., Philadelphia, PA 19104. Telephone: 215-596-8536.

PINE MANOR COLLEGE

Chestnut Hill, Massachusetts

General Information

Independent 4-year women's college. Founded 1911. Awards A (college transfer), B. Primary accreditation: regional. City setting; 79-acre campus. Total enrollment: 620. Faculty: 66 (36 full-time, 30 part-time).

Drug and Alcohol Information

Education

On campus Drug and alcohol education/prevention programs offered for: all students. College holds an annual alcohol awareness week and drug awareness week.

Identification of Problems

Admissions College application does not ask about prior substance abuse problems.

On campus Current students identified as chemically dependent may remain enrolled, but treatment is required. Training program on identifying students with potential substance abuse problems for: resident advisers. Written procedures for students and staff if substance abuse is suspected.

Support Services

On campus Al-Anon, support groups, private counseling.

Employee assistance Program for chemically dependent employees not available.

Disciplinary Actions

Alcohol Results of infractions of alcohol regulations (see Comparative Table of Alcohol Regulations) vary by

situation but can include warning, probation, suspension, expulsion.

Drugs For first-time use: chemical dependency assessment, counseling, probation. For first-time possession: chemical dependency assessment, warning, probation. For subsequent use or possession: suspension. For first-time sale: suspension, expulsion. For subsequent sale: expulsion.

For More Information

Contact: Julie A. Glavin, Dean of Students, Pine Manor College, 400 Heath St., Chestnut Hill, MA 02167. Telephone: 617-731-7108.

PITTSBURG STATE UNIVERSITY

Pittsburg, Kansas

General Information

State-supported 5-year coed college. Founded 1903. Awards A (college transfer and terminal), B, M. Primary accreditation: regional. Small-town setting; 125-acre campus. Total enrollment: 5,609. Faculty: 283 (244 full-time, 39 part-time). Social organizations: 5 national fraternities, 3 national sororities; 6% of eligible undergraduate men and 4% of eligible undergraduate women are members.

Drug and Alcohol Information

Education

On campus Drug and alcohol education/prevention programs offered for: athletes/coaches, resident advisers, orientation classes. Bacchus chapter: 200 members. College holds an annual alcohol awareness week and drug awareness week.

Identification of Problems

Admissions College application does not ask about prior substance abuse problems.

On campus Current students identified as chemically dependent may remain enrolled. Training program on identifying students with potential substance abuse problems for: resident advisers, coaches. Written procedures for students and staff if substance abuse is suspected.

Support Services

On campus AA, NA, Al-Anon, private counseling, referrals.

Employee assistance Program for chemically dependent employees available. Staff working with drug/alcohol-related issues: 5 part-time.

Disciplinary Actions

Alcohol Results of infractions of alcohol regulations (see Comparative Table of Alcohol Regulations) vary by situation.

Drugs For any use, possession, or sale: varies by situation.

For More Information

Contact: Wilma Minton, Vice President for Student Affairs, Pittsburg State University, 1701 S. Broadway, Pittsburg, KS 66762. Telephone: 316-231-7000 Ext. 4233.

PITZER COLLEGE

Claremont, California

General Information

Independent 4-year coed college. Part of The Claremont Colleges. Founded 1963. Awards B. Primary accreditation: regional. Small-town setting; 25-acre campus. Total enrollment: 770. Faculty: 85 (59 full-time, 26 part-time).

Drug and Alcohol Information

Education

On campus Drug and alcohol education/prevention programs offered for: all students, athletes/coaches. Bacchus chapter. College holds an annual alcohol awareness week and drug awareness week.

Identification of Problems

Admissions College application does not ask about prior substance abuse problems.

On campus Current students identified as chemically dependent may remain enrolled, but treatment is required. Continued enrollment depends on medical recommendation. Training program on identifying students with potential substance abuse problems for: resident advisers, administration. No written procedures for students and staff if substance abuse is suspected.

Support Services

On campus AA, NA, Al-Anon, support groups, private counseling.

Employee assistance Program for chemically dependent employees available.

Disciplinary Actions

Alcohol Results of infractions of alcohol regulations (see Comparative Table of Alcohol Regulations) vary by situation but can include chemical dependency assessment, counseling, warning, probation, suspension, expulsion.

Drugs For first-time use: chemical dependency assessment, counseling, warning, probation. For subsequent use: varies by situation—counseling, probation, suspension. For first-time possession: varies by situation—counseling, warning, probation. For subsequent possession: varies by situation. For first-time sale: varies by situation. For subsequent sale: suspension, expulsion.

Additional Information from the College

Pitzer College is currently drafting new policy proposals with regard to drugs and alcohol.

For More Information

Contact: Jack T. F. Ling, Dean of Students, Pitzer College, 1050 N. Mills Ave., Rm. 128, Claremont, CA 91711. Telephone: 714-621-8241.

PLYMOUTH STATE COLLEGE OF THE UNIVERSITY SYSTEM OF NEW HAMPSHIRE

Plymouth, New Hampshire

General Information

State-supported 5-year coed college. Part of University System of New Hampshire. Founded 1871. Awards A (college transfer and terminal), B, M. Primary

Plymouth State College of the University System of New Hampshire (continued)

accreditation: regional. Small-town setting; 80-acre campus. Total enrollment: 3,400. Faculty: 200 (150 full-time, 50 part-time). Social organizations: 5 national fraternities, 6 national sororities, local fraternities, local sororities; 5% of eligible undergraduate men and 5% of eligible undergraduate women are members.

Drug and Alcohol Information

Education

On campus Drug and alcohol education/prevention programs offered for: all students, athletes/coaches; required for: resident advisers, judicial referrals. Authorized group concerned with responsible drinking. College holds an annual alcohol awareness week and drug awareness week.

Identification of Problems

Admissions College application does not ask about prior substance abuse problems.

On campus Current students identified as chemically dependent may remain enrolled. No training program on identifying students with potential substance abuse problems. Written procedures for students and staff if substance abuse is suspected.

Support Services

On campus NA, support groups, private counseling.

Off campus AA, Al-Anon, ACOA.

Employee assistance Program for chemically dependent employees not available. Staff working with drug/alcohol-related issues: 10 part-time.

Disciplinary Actions

Alcohol Results of infractions of alcohol regulations (see Comparative Table of Alcohol Regulations) vary by situation but can include chemical dependency assessment, warning.

Drugs For any use, possession, or sale: varies by situation.

For More Information

Contact: Dr. Michael Fischler, Director, Office of Counseling and Human Relations, Plymouth State College of the University System of New Hampshire, Plymouth, NH 03264. Telephone: 603-536-5000 Ext. 2461.

POINT LOMA NAZARENE COLLEGE

San Diego, California

General Information

Independent 5-year coed college, affiliated with Church of the Nazarene. Founded 1902. Awards B, M. Primary accreditation: regional. Metropolitan setting; 88-acre campus. Total enrollment: 2,165. Faculty: 92 full-time.

Drug and Alcohol Information

Education

On campus Drug and alcohol education/prevention programs offered for: all students, athletes/coaches. College holds an annual alcohol awareness week and drug awareness week.

Identification of Problems

Admissions College application question about prior substance abuse problems is used for counseling and referral, if student is admitted; in the admissions decision.

On campus Current students identified as chemically dependent may remain enrolled, but treatment is required. Training program on identifying students with potential substance abuse problems for: resident advisers, coaches, student leaders. Written procedures for students and staff if substance abuse is suspected.

Support Services

On campus ACOA, support groups, private counseling.

Employee assistance Program for chemically dependent employees not available. Staff working with drug/alcohol-related issues: 4 part-time.

Disciplinary Actions

Alcohol Results of infractions of alcohol regulations (see Comparative Table of Alcohol Regulations) vary by situation but can include chemical dependency assessment, counseling, suspension, expulsion.

Drugs For first-time use or possession: varies by situation. For subsequent use or possession: expulsion. For any sale: expulsion.

Additional Information from the College

Point Loma Nazarene College has a policy of abstinence from drugs and alcohol.

For More Information

Contact: Dana M. Walling, Associate for Student Development, Point Loma Nazarene College, 3900 Lomaland Dr., San Diego, CA 92106. Telephone: 619-221-2253.

POINT PARK COLLEGE

Pittsburgh, Pennsylvania

General Information

Independent 5-year coed college. Founded 1960. Awards A (college transfer and terminal), B, M. Primary accreditation: regional. Metropolitan setting. Total enrollment: 2,812. Faculty: 171 (75 full-time, 96 part-time). Social organizations: 1 national fraternity, 1 local fraternity, 3 local sororities; 5% of eligible undergraduate men and 5% of eligible undergraduate women are members.

Drug and Alcohol Information

Education

On campus Drug and alcohol education/prevention programs offered for: all students; required for: resident advisers. Authorized group concerned with responsible drinking. College holds an annual alcohol awareness week.

Identification of Problems

Admissions College application question about prior substance abuse problems is part of medical history.

On campus Current students identified as chemically dependent may remain enrolled, but treatment is required. Training program on identifying students with potential substance abuse problems for: resident advisers, administration. No written procedures for students and staff if substance abuse is suspected.

Support Services

On campus Private counseling.

Off campus St. Francis Hospital.

Employee assistance Program for chemically dependent

employees not available. Staff working with drug/alcohol-related issues: 1 part-time.

Disciplinary Actions

Alcohol Results of infractions of alcohol regulations (see Comparative Table of Alcohol Regulations) include warning, probation.

Drugs For first-time use: suspension. For subsequent use: expulsion. For first-time possession: probation. For subsequent possession: suspension. For first-time sale: expulsion.

For More Information

Contact: Charles R. Quillin, Dean of Student Development, Point Park College, 201 Wood St., Pittsburgh, PA 15222. Telephone: 412-392-3840.

POLYTECHNIC UNIVERSITY, BROOKLYN CAMPUS

Brooklyn, New York

General Information

Independent comprehensive coed institution. Founded 1854. Awards B, M, D. Primary accreditation: regional. Metropolitan setting; 2-acre campus. Total enrollment: 2,652. Faculty: 393 (195 full-time, 198 part-time). Social organizations: 5 national fraternities; 10% of eligible undergraduate men are members.

Drug and Alcohol Information

Education

On campus Drug and alcohol education/prevention programs required for: freshmen.

Identification of Problems

Admissions College application does not ask about prior substance abuse problems.

On campus Current students identified as chemically dependent may remain enrolled, but treatment is required. No training program on identifying students with potential substance abuse problems. No written procedures for students and staff if substance abuse is suspected.

Support Services

On campus Private counseling.

Employee assistance Program for chemically dependent employees not available. Staff working with drug/alcohol-related issues: 2 part-time.

Disciplinary Actions

Alcohol Results of infractions of alcohol regulations (see Comparative Table of Alcohol Regulations) vary by situation.

Drugs For any use, possession, or sale: varies by situation.

Additional Information from the College

Alcohol and drug use and abuse are covered in the required student life course for freshmen.

For More Information

Contact: Jeffrey Kessler, Dean of Students, Polytechnic University, Brooklyn Campus, 333 Jay St., Brooklyn, NY 11201. Telephone: 718-260-3600.

POLYTECHNIC UNIVERSITY, FARMINGDALE CAMPUS

Farmingdale, New York

General Information

Independent comprehensive coed institution. Founded 1854. Awards B, M, D. Primary accreditation: regional. Small-town setting; 25-acre campus. Total enrollment: 1,095. Faculty: 393 (195 full-time, 198 part-time). Social organization: 1 national fraternity; 8% of eligible undergraduate men are members.

Drug and Alcohol Information

Education

On campus Drug and alcohol education/prevention programs required for: freshmen.

Identification of Problems

Admissions College application does not ask about prior substance abuse problems.

On campus Current students identified as chemically dependent may remain enrolled, but treatment is required. No training program on identifying students with potential substance abuse problems. No written procedures for students and staff if substance abuse is suspected.

Support Services

On campus Private counseling.

Employee assistance Program for chemically dependent employees not available. Staff working with drug/alcohol-related issues: 2 part-time.

Disciplinary Actions

Alcohol Results of infractions of alcohol regulations (see Comparative Table of Alcohol Regulations) vary by situation.

Drugs For any use, possession, or sale: varies by situation.

Additional Information from the College

Alcohol and drug use and abuse are covered in the required student life course for freshmen.

For More Information

Contact: Jeffrey Kessler, Dean of Students, Polytechnic University, Farmingdale Campus, Route 110, Farmingdale, NY 11201. Telephone: 516-454-5150.

POMONA COLLEGE

Claremont, California

General Information

Independent 4-year coed college. Founded 1887. Awards B. Primary accreditation: regional. Small-town setting; 160-acre campus. Total enrollment: 1,402. Faculty: 189 (154 full-time, 35 part-time). Social organizations: 8 local fraternities, local coed fraternities; 13% of eligible undergraduate men and 2% of eligible undergraduate women are members.

Drug and Alcohol Information

Education

On campus Drug and alcohol education/prevention programs offered for: all students, athletes/coaches, faculty, administration; required for: resident advisers, student leaders. Authorized group concerned with responsible

Pomona College (continued)

drinking. College holds an annual alcohol awareness week and drug awareness week.

Identification of Problems

Admissions College application does not ask about prior substance abuse problems.

On campus Training program on identifying students with potential substance abuse problems for: resident advisers, faculty, administration. Written procedures for students and staff if substance abuse is suspected.

Support Services

On campus AA, NA, Al-Anon, support groups, private counseling.

Employee assistance Program for chemically dependent employees available.

Disciplinary Actions

Alcohol Results of infractions of alcohol regulations (see Comparative Table of Alcohol Regulations) vary by situation.

Drugs For any use, possession, or sale: varies by situation.

For More Information

Contact: Richard A. Fass, Vice President and Dean of Students, Pomona College, 333 N. College Way, Claremont, CA 91711. Telephone: 714-621-8017.

PORTLAND STATE UNIVERSITY

Portland, Oregon

General Information

State-supported comprehensive coed institution. Part of Oregon State System of Higher Education. Founded 1946. Awards B, M, D. Primary accreditation: regional. Metropolitan setting; 48-acre campus. Total enrollment: 16,021. Faculty: 726 (476 full-time, 250 part-time). Social organizations: 2 national fraternities, 2 national sororities; 1% of eligible undergraduate men and 1% of eligible undergraduate women are members.

Drug and Alcohol Information

Education

On campus Drug and alcohol education/prevention programs offered for: all students, athletes/coaches, faculty, administration, security personnel. College holds an annual alcohol awareness week and drug awareness week.

Identification of Problems

Admissions College application does not ask about prior substance abuse problems.

On campus Current students identified as chemically dependent may remain enrolled. Training program on identifying students with potential substance abuse problems for: resident advisers, coaches, Greek officers, faculty, administration, security personnel, other support staff. Written procedures for students and staff if substance abuse is suspected.

Support Services

On campus AA, NA, Al-Anon, ACOA, support groups, private counseling, student health service assessment, referral.

Employee assistance Program for chemically dependent employees available. Staff working with drug/alcohol-related issues: 4 part-time.

Disciplinary Actions

Alcohol Results of infractions of alcohol regulations (see Comparative Table of Alcohol Regulations) vary by situation but can include chemical dependency assessment, eviction from campus housing. Comments: Referred to Student Conduct Committee with no specific rules for any infraction.

Drugs For any use, possession, or sale: varies by situation.

For More Information

Contact: Rusty Broderick, Drug Program Coordinator, Health Services, Portland State University, P.O. Box 751, Portland, OR 97207. Telephone: 503-464-3462.

POST COLLEGE

Waterbury, Connecticut

General Information

Independent 4-year coed college. Founded 1890. Awards A (college transfer and terminal), B. Primary accreditation: regional. City setting; 70-acre campus. Total enrollment: 1,654. Faculty: 276 (26 full-time, 250 part-time).

Drug and Alcohol Information

Education

On campus Drug and alcohol education/prevention programs offered for: all students, athletes/coaches, faculty, administration. Authorized group concerned with responsible drinking. College holds an annual alcohol awareness week and drug awareness week.

Identification of Problems

Admissions College application does not ask about prior substance abuse problems.

On campus Current students identified as chemically dependent may remain enrolled, but treatment is required. Training program on identifying students with potential substance abuse problems for: resident advisers, coaches, faculty, administration. Written procedures for students and staff if substance abuse is suspected.

Support Services

On campus AA, Al-Anon, private counseling.

Employee assistance Program for chemically dependent employees not available. Staff working with drug/alcohol-related issues: 1 part-time.

Disciplinary Actions

Alcohol Results of infractions of alcohol regulations (see Comparative Table of Alcohol Regulations) vary by situation but can include counseling, probation, suspension, expulsion, fines.

Drugs For first-time use or possession: varies by situation—counseling, probation, suspension. For first-time sale: varies by situation—counseling, expulsion. For subsequent use, possession, or sale: counseling, expulsion.

For More Information

Contact: Sharon Santel, Counselor, Post College, 800 Country Club Rd., Waterbury, CT 06708. Telephone: 203-755-0121.

PRAIRIE VIEW A&M UNIVERSITY

Prairie View, Texas

General Information

State-supported 5-year coed college. Part of Texas A&M University System. Founded 1878. Awards B, M. Primary accreditation: regional. Small-town setting; 1,400-acre campus. Total enrollment: 5,307. Faculty: 286. Social organizations: 4 national fraternities, 4 national sororities, 5 local fraternities, 4 local sororities; 10% of eligible undergraduate men and 10% of eligible undergraduate women are members.

Drug and Alcohol Information

Education

On campus Drug and alcohol education/prevention programs offered for: all students, athletes/coaches, faculty, administration, staff. Authorized group concerned with responsible drinking. College holds an annual alcohol awareness week and drug awareness week.

Identification of Problems

Admissions College application does not ask about prior substance abuse problems.

On campus Current students identified as chemically dependent may remain enrolled. Comments: Treatment is suggested and encouraged but not required. Training program on identifying students with potential substance abuse problems for: resident advisers. Written procedures for students and staff if substance abuse is suspected.

Support Services

On campus Private counseling, peer counselor, chapel services.

Employee assistance Program for chemically dependent employees not available.

Disciplinary Actions

Alcohol Results of infractions of alcohol regulations (see Comparative Table of Alcohol Regulations) vary by situation.

Drugs For first-time use: counseling, suspension. For subsequent use: suspension. For any possession or sale: suspension.

Additional Information from the College

Although Prairie View A&M University's location limits access to comprehensive drug and alcohol abuse care, referral services are available. The University is sensitive to the issue of alcohol and drug abuse, and the administration actively supports a variety of programs to foster awareness in members of the University community.

For More Information

Contact: Dr. Elaine P. Adams, Vice President for Student Affairs, Prairie View A&M University, P.O. Box 337, Prairie View, TX 77446. Telephone: 409-857-2693 or 2694.

PRESBYTERIAN COLLEGE

Clinton, South Carolina

General Information

Independent Presbyterian 4-year coed college. Founded 1880. Awards B. Primary accreditation: regional. Small-town setting; 175-acre campus. Total enrollment: 1,112. Faculty: 97 (62 full-time, 35 part-time). Social organizations: 6 national fraternities, Women's Social Hall; 50% of eligible undergraduate men and 25% of eligible undergraduate women are members.

Drug and Alcohol Information

Education

On campus Drug and alcohol education/prevention programs offered for: all students, athletes/coaches; required for: freshmen, resident advisers. Authorized group concerned with responsible drinking. College holds an annual alcohol awareness week and drug awareness week.

Identification of Problems

Admissions College application does not ask about prior substance abuse problems.

On campus Current students identified as chemically dependent may remain enrolled, but treatment is required. Training program on identifying students with potential substance abuse problems for: resident advisers, administration. Written procedures for students and staff if substance abuse is suspected.

Support Services

On campus ACOA, private counseling.

Employee assistance Program for chemically dependent employees not available.

Disciplinary Actions

Alcohol Results of infractions of alcohol regulations (see Comparative Table of Alcohol Regulations) vary by situation but can include chemical dependency assessment, counseling, warning, probation, suspension, fines.

Drugs For first-time use or possession: suspension. For subsequent use or possession: expulsion. For any sale: expulsion.

For More Information

Contact: Joseph O. Nixon, Dean of Students, Presbyterian College, S. Broad St., Clinton, SC 29325. Telephone: 803-833-8275.

PRINCETON UNIVERSITY

Princeton, New Jersey

General Information

Independent comprehensive coed institution. Founded 1746. Awards B, M, D. Primary accreditation: regional. Small-town setting; 600-acre campus. Total enrollment: 6,140. Faculty: 800 (672 full-time, 128 part-time). Social organizations: 13 eating clubs; 70% of eligible undergraduate men and 70% of eligible undergraduate women are members.

Drug and Alcohol Information

Education

On campus Drug and alcohol education/prevention programs offered for: all students, faculty, administration; required for: athletes/coaches. Authorized group concerned with responsible drinking. College holds an annual alcohol awareness week and drug awareness week.

Identification of Problems

Admissions College application question about prior substance abuse problems is part of medical history.

On campus Current students identified as chemically dependent may remain enrolled. Training program on

Princeton University (continued)
identifying students with potential substance abuse problems for: administration. Written procedures for students and staff if substance abuse is suspected.

Support Services

On campus AA, NA, ACOA, private counseling.

Employee assistance Program for chemically dependent employees available. Staff working with drug/alcohol-related issues: 1 full-time and 2 part-time.

Disciplinary Actions

Alcohol Results of infractions of alcohol regulations (see Comparative Table of Alcohol Regulations) vary by situation.

Drugs For first-time use: chemical dependency assessment, counseling. For subsequent use: varies by situation. For any possession or sale: varies by situation.

Additional Information from the College

Princeton University offers a wide range of education, consultation, assessment, and assistance programs that deal with alcohol and the problems it can cause.

For More Information

Contact: Kevin Ferry, Director, Alcohol & Drug Program, McCosh Health Center, Room 303, Princeton University, Princeton, NJ 08544. Telephone: 609-452-3350.

PROVIDENCE COLLEGE

Providence, Rhode Island

General Information

Independent Roman Catholic 5-year coed college. Founded 1917. Awards A (terminal), B, M, D. Primary accreditation: regional. City setting; 105-acre campus. Total enrollment: 4,329. Faculty: 279 (243 full-time, 36 part-time).

Drug and Alcohol Information

Education

On campus Drug and alcohol education/prevention programs offered for: all students. College holds an annual alcohol awareness week and drug awareness week.

Identification of Problems

Admissions College application does not ask about prior substance abuse problems.

On campus Current students identified as chemically dependent may remain enrolled, but treatment is required. Training program on identifying students with potential substance abuse problems for: resident advisers, coaches, faculty, administration. No written procedures for students and staff if substance abuse is suspected.

Support Services

On campus AA, ACOA, private counseling.

Employee assistance Program for chemically dependent employees not available.

Disciplinary Actions

Alcohol Results of infractions of alcohol regulations (see Comparative Table of Alcohol Regulations) vary by situation.

Drugs For first-time use: varies by situation—counseling, warning. For subsequent use: varies by situation—warning, probation. For first-time possession: varies by situation—warning, probation. For subsequent possession: varies by situation—counseling, suspension. For first-time sale: varies by situation—suspension, expulsion. For subsequent sale: varies by situation—counseling, suspension, expulsion.

For More Information

Contact: Dr. John Hogan, Coordinator of Personal Counseling, Providence College, River Ave. and Eaton St., Providence, RI 02918. Telephone: 401-865-2343.

PURDUE UNIVERSITY

West Lafayette, Indiana

General Information

State-supported comprehensive coed institution. Part of Purdue University System. Founded 1869. Awards A (college transfer and terminal), B, M, D. Primary accreditation: regional. City setting; 1,565-acre campus. Total enrollment: 34,969. Social organizations: 49 national fraternities, 21 national sororities, 1 local sorority; 20% of eligible undergraduate men and 15% of eligible undergraduate women are members.

Drug and Alcohol Information

Education

On campus Drug and alcohol education/prevention programs offered for: all students, athletes/coaches. Authorized group concerned with responsible drinking. College holds an annual alcohol awareness week.

Identification of Problems

Admissions College application does not ask about prior substance abuse problems.

On campus Current students identified as chemically dependent may remain enrolled. Training program on identifying students with potential substance abuse problems for: resident advisers, available to all students. Written procedures for students and staff if substance abuse is suspected.

Support Services

On campus AA, NA, Al-Anon, ACOA, support groups, private counseling.

Employee assistance Program for chemically dependent employees available. Staff working with drug/alcohol-related issues: 1 (Employee Assistance Program) full-time and 4 part-time.

Disciplinary Actions

Alcohol Results of infractions of alcohol regulations (see Comparative Table of Alcohol Regulations) vary by situation but can include chemical dependency assessment, counseling, warning, probation, suspension, expulsion. Comments: Student organizations that violate the University's alcohol policy can lose recognition.

Drugs For first-time use: varies by situation—warning, probation. For subsequent use: varies by situation—probated suspension, suspension. For first-time possession: varies by situation. For subsequent possession: varies by situation—probated suspension. For any sale: suspension.

For More Information

Contact: Jill Oliver Dill, Counselor, Dean of Students' Office, Hovde Hall, Purdue University, West Lafayette, IN 47907. Telephone: 317-494-1747.

QUINCY COLLEGE
Quincy, Illinois

General Information
Independent Roman Catholic 5-year coed college. Founded 1860. Awards A (terminal), B, M. Primary accreditation: regional. Small-town setting; 73-acre campus. Total enrollment: 1,527. Faculty: 87 (56 full-time, 31 part-time).

Drug and Alcohol Information
Education
On campus Drug and alcohol education/prevention programs offered for: all students. Bacchus chapter: 20 members. College holds an annual alcohol awareness week and drug awareness week.

Identification of Problems
Admissions College application does not ask about prior substance abuse problems.

On campus Current students identified as chemically dependent may remain enrolled, but treatment is required. Training program on identifying students with potential substance abuse problems for: resident advisers, administration. Written procedures for students and staff if substance abuse is suspected.

Support Services
On campus AA, Al-Anon, ACOA, support groups, private counseling.

Employee assistance Program for chemically dependent employees not available. Staff working with drug/alcohol-related issues: 3 part-time.

Disciplinary Actions
Alcohol Results of infractions of alcohol regulations (see Comparative Table of Alcohol Regulations) vary by situation but can include chemical dependency assessment, counseling, warning, probation, suspension.

Drugs For any use: varies by situation. For first-time possession: varies by situation. For subsequent possession: varies by situation—chemical dependency assessment, counseling, probation. For first-time sale: suspension, expulsion. For subsequent sale: expulsion.

For More Information
Contact: Linda Gooley, Dean of Students, Quincy College, 1800 College Ave., Quincy, IL 62301. Telephone: 217-228-5320.

QUINNIPIAC COLLEGE
Hamden, Connecticut

General Information
Independent 5-year coed college. Founded 1929. Awards A (college transfer and terminal), B, M. Primary accreditation: regional. Small-town setting; 160-acre campus. Total enrollment: 2,925. Faculty: 150 full-time. Social organizations: 2 national fraternities, 1 national sorority, 2 local fraternities, 2 local sororities; 15% of eligible undergraduate men and 3% of eligible undergraduate women are members.

Drug and Alcohol Information
Education
On campus Drug and alcohol education/prevention programs offered for: all students. College holds an annual alcohol awareness week and drug awareness week.

Identification of Problems
Admissions College application does not ask about prior substance abuse problems.

On campus Current students identified as chemically dependent may remain enrolled, but treatment is encouraged. Training program on identifying students with potential substance abuse problems for: resident advisers. No written procedures for students and staff if substance abuse is suspected.

Support Services
On campus ACOA.

Employee assistance Program for chemically dependent employees not available. Staff working with drug/alcohol-related issues: 1 part-time.

Disciplinary Actions
Alcohol Results of infractions of alcohol regulations (see Comparative Table of Alcohol Regulations) vary by situation but can include probation, suspension.

Drugs For first-time use or possession: varies by situation—drug education, suspension. For subsequent use or possession: varies by situation—expulsion. For any sale: expulsion. Comments: For first-time use and possession, violators must educate themselves about the dangers of drug use and present a report.

Additional Information from the College
An alcohol education class is being instituted for violators of the alcohol policy.

For More Information
Contact: Maggie Potapchuk, Assistant Dean of Student Affairs, Quinnipiac College, Mount Carmel Ave., Hamden, CT 06518. Telephone: 203-281-8735.

RADFORD UNIVERSITY
Radford, Virginia

General Information
State-supported 5-year coed college. Founded 1910. Awards B, M. Primary accreditation: regional. Small-town setting; 138-acre campus. Total enrollment: 8,764. Faculty: 418. Social organizations: 11 national fraternities, 8 national sororities; 18% of eligible undergraduate men and 10% of eligible undergraduate women are members.

Drug and Alcohol Information
Education
On campus Drug and alcohol education/prevention programs offered for: all students. Bacchus chapter: 50 members. College holds an annual alcohol awareness week.

Identification of Problems
Admissions College application does not ask about prior substance abuse problems.

On campus Current students identified as chemically dependent may remain enrolled. No training program on identifying students with potential substance abuse problems. Written procedures for students and staff if substance abuse is suspected.

Support Services
On campus ACOA, support groups, private counseling.

Employee assistance Program for chemically dependent

Radford University (continued)

employees available. Staff working with drug/alcohol-related issues: 20 part-time.

Disciplinary Actions

Alcohol Results of infractions of alcohol regulations (see Comparative Table of Alcohol Regulations) vary by situation but can include probation, referral to alcohol education class.

Drugs For first-time use or possession: varies by situation—probation. For subsequent use or possession: varies by situation—suspension. For any sale: varies by situation—expulsion.

For More Information

Contact: Ken Lott, Director of Counseling Center, P.O. Box 5787, Radford University, Radford, VA 24142. Telephone: 703-831-5226.

RAMAPO COLLEGE OF NEW JERSEY

Mahwah, New Jersey

General Information

State-supported 4-year coed college. Part of New Jersey State College System. Founded 1969. Awards B. Primary accreditation: regional. Small-town setting; 300-acre campus. Total enrollment: 4,058. Faculty: 218 (120 full-time, 98 part-time).

Drug and Alcohol Information

Education

On campus Drug and alcohol education/prevention programs offered for: all students, athletes/coaches, faculty, administration; required for: resident advisers. College holds an annual alcohol awareness week and drug awareness week.

Identification of Problems

Admissions College application does not ask about prior substance abuse problems.

On campus Current students identified as chemically dependent may remain enrolled. Training program on identifying students with potential substance abuse problems for: resident advisers, coaches, faculty, administration. Written procedures for students and staff if substance abuse is suspected.

Support Services

On campus AA, ACOA, private counseling.

Employee assistance Program for chemically dependent employees available. Staff working with drug/alcohol-related issues: 7 part-time.

Disciplinary Actions

Alcohol Results of infractions of alcohol regulations (see Comparative Table of Alcohol Regulations) vary by situation but can include chemical dependency assessment, counseling, warning, probation, suspension.

Drugs For any use, possession, or sale: varies by situation. Comments: Action to be taken is determined by the campus judicial board.

For More Information

Contact: Pamela M. Bischoff, Dean of Students, Ramapo College, 505 Ramapo Valley Rd., Mahwah, NJ 07430. Telephone: 201-529-7457.

RANDOLPH-MACON WOMAN'S COLLEGE

Lynchburg, Virginia

General Information

Independent Methodist 4-year women's college. Founded 1891. Awards B. Primary accreditation: regional. City setting; 100-acre campus. Total enrollment: 765. Faculty: 87 (74 full-time, 13 part-time).

Drug and Alcohol Information

Education

On campus Drug and alcohol education/prevention programs offered for: all students; required for: freshmen, resident advisers. Authorized group concerned with responsible drinking. College holds an annual alcohol awareness week.

Identification of Problems

Admissions College application does not ask about prior substance abuse problems.

On campus Current students identified as chemically dependent may remain enrolled, but treatment is required. Training program on identifying students with potential substance abuse problems for: resident advisers, administration. Written procedures for students and staff if substance abuse is suspected.

Support Services

On campus AA, ACOA, support groups, private counseling.

Employee assistance Program for chemically dependent employees available. Staff working with drug/alcohol-related issues: 10 part-time.

Disciplinary Actions

Alcohol Results of infractions of alcohol regulations (see Comparative Table of Alcohol Regulations) vary by situation but can include counseling, warning, probation.

Drugs For first-time use: varies by situation—chemical dependency assessment, intervention program. For subsequent use: expulsion. For first-time possession or sale: expulsion.

For More Information

Contact: Amy Jarmon, Dean of Students, Randolph-Macon Woman's College, 2500 Rivermont Ave., Box 836, Lynchburg, VA 24503. Telephone: 804-846-7392.

RAY COLLEGE OF DESIGN

Chicago, Illinois

General Information

Proprietary 4-year coed college. Branch location: Schaumburg. Founded 1916. Awards A (college transfer and terminal), B. Primary accreditation: NATTS. Metropolitan setting. Total enrollment: 506. Faculty: 85 (13 full-time, 72 part-time).

Drug and Alcohol Information

Education

On campus Drug and alcohol education/prevention programs offered for: all students.

Identification of Problems

Admissions College application does not ask about prior substance abuse problems.

On campus No training program on identifying students with potential substance abuse problems. No written procedures for students and staff if substance abuse is suspected.

Support Services

On campus Private counseling.

Employee assistance Program for chemically dependent employees not available.

Disciplinary Actions

Alcohol Results of infractions of alcohol regulations (see Comparative Table of Alcohol Regulations) include probation, expulsion.

Drugs For first-time use or possession: probation. For subsequent use or possession: expulsion. For any sale: expulsion.

For More Information

Contact: Jerry Molepske, Executive Director, Ray College of Design, 401 N. Wabash Ave., Chicago, IL 60611. Telephone: 312-280-3500.

REED COLLEGE

Portland, Oregon

General Information

Independent 5-year coed college. Founded 1909. Awards B, M. Primary accreditation: regional. Metropolitan setting; 98-acre campus. Total enrollment: 1,286. Faculty: 117 (81 full-time, 36 part-time).

Drug and Alcohol Information

Education

On campus Drug and alcohol education/prevention programs offered for: all students. Authorized group concerned with responsible drinking.

Identification of Problems

Admissions College application does not ask about prior substance abuse problems.

On campus Current students identified as chemically dependent may remain enrolled, but treatment is required. Training program on identifying students with potential substance abuse problems for: resident advisers. Written procedures for students and staff if substance abuse is suspected.

Support Services

On campus AA, private counseling.

Employee assistance Program for chemically dependent employees available. Staff working with drug/alcohol-related issues: 4 part-time.

Disciplinary Actions

Alcohol Results of infractions of alcohol regulations (see Comparative Table of Alcohol Regulations) vary by situation but can include chemical dependency assessment, counseling, warning. Comments: If an honor violation is involved, the case goes before the Judicial Board.

Drugs For first-time use, possession, or sale: varies by situation. For subsequent use, possession, or sale: varies by situation—chemical dependency assessment.

For More Information

Contact: Stephen Beardsley-Schoonmaker, Director of Student Activities, Reed College, 3203 S.E. Woodstock Blvd., Portland, OR 97202. Telephone: 503-777-7536.

REGIS COLLEGE

Denver, Colorado

General Information

Independent Roman Catholic 5-year coed college. Founded 1877. Awards B, M. Primary accreditation: regional. Metropolitan setting; 90-acre campus. Total enrollment: 5,100. Faculty: 95 (75 full-time, 20 part-time). Social organizations: 2 national fraternities, 1 national sorority; 15% of eligible undergraduate men and 15% of eligible undergraduate women are members.

Drug and Alcohol Information

Education

On campus Drug and alcohol education/prevention programs offered for: freshmen, athletes/coaches, resident advisers, student leaders. Authorized group concerned with responsible drinking. College holds an annual alcohol awareness week and drug awareness week.

Identification of Problems

Admissions College application does not ask about prior substance abuse problems.

On campus Current students identified as chemically dependent may remain enrolled, but treatment is required. Training program on identifying students with potential substance abuse problems for: resident advisers, Student Life staff. Written procedures for students and staff if substance abuse is suspected.

Support Services

On campus ACOA, support groups, private counseling.

Employee assistance Program for chemically dependent employees available. Staff working with drug/alcohol-related issues: 4 part-time.

Disciplinary Actions

Alcohol Results of infractions of alcohol regulations (see Comparative Table of Alcohol Regulations) vary by situation but can include counseling, warning, probation, suspension, expulsion.

Drugs For first-time use: chemical dependency assessment, probation. For first-time possession: varies by situation—chemical dependency assessment, probation. For subsequent use or possession: suspension. For first-time sale: expulsion.

For More Information

Contact: Tom Reynolds, Vice President for Student Life, Regis College, 3539 West 50th Pkwy., Denver, CO 80221. Telephone: 303-458-4086.

RENO BUSINESS COLLEGE

Reno, Nevada

General Information

Proprietary 4-year coed college. Founded 1902. Awards A (college transfer and terminal), B. Primary accreditation: AICS. City setting. Total enrollment: 252. Faculty: 20 (12 full-time, 8 part-time). Social organizations: 1 national

Reno Business College (continued)

fraternity, 1 national sorority; 25% of eligible undergraduate men and 35% of eligible undergraduate women are members.

Drug and Alcohol Information

Education

On campus Drug and alcohol education/prevention programs offered for: all students.

Identification of Problems

Admissions College application does not ask about prior substance abuse problems.

On campus Current students identified as chemically dependent may remain enrolled, but treatment is required. No training program on identifying students with potential substance abuse problems. Written procedures for students and staff if substance abuse is suspected.

Support Services

On campus Private counseling.

Employee assistance Program for chemically dependent employees not available. Staff working with drug/alcohol-related issues: 5 part-time.

Disciplinary Actions

Alcohol Results of infractions of alcohol regulations (see Comparative Table of Alcohol Regulations) vary by situation but can include counseling, referral to an outside agency.

Drugs For any use, possession, or sale: varies by situation.

Additional Information from the College

Reno Business College has had only isolated incidents of alcohol/drug-related problems, and they were dealt with on an individual basis. The College has not needed to develop a formal policy to deal with these issues.

For More Information

Contact: Lynnda Dee English, Job Placement Director, Reno Business College, 140 Washington St., Reno, NV 89502. Telephone: 702-323-4145.

RENSSELAER POLYTECHNIC INSTITUTE

Troy, New York

General Information

Independent comprehensive coed institution. Founded 1824. Awards B, M, D. Primary accreditation: regional. City setting; 260-acre campus. Total enrollment: 6,371. Faculty: 400 (all full-time). Social organizations: 27 national fraternities, 4 national sororities, 3 coed fraternities; 35% of eligible undergraduate men and 20% of eligible undergraduate women are members.

Drug and Alcohol Information

Education

On campus Drug and alcohol education/prevention programs offered for: all students, athletes/coaches, faculty, administration. College holds an annual alcohol awareness week.

Identification of Problems

On campus No training program on identifying students with potential substance abuse problems. No written procedures for students and staff if substance abuse is suspected.

Support Services

On campus AA, Al-Anon, ACOA, private counseling.

Employee assistance Program for chemically dependent employees available. Staff working with drug/alcohol-related issues: 5 part-time.

Disciplinary Actions

Alcohol Results of infractions of alcohol regulations (see Comparative Table of Alcohol Regulations) vary by situation but can include chemical dependency assessment, counseling, warning, probation, suspension.

Drugs For first-time use: varies by situation—chemical dependency assessment, counseling. For first-time possession: varies by situation—probation, suspension, expulsion. For subsequent use or possession: varies by situation. For first-time sale: expulsion.

For More Information

Contact: Jacqueline Peterson, Associate Dean of Students, Rensselaer Polytechnic Institute, 200 Troy Bldg., Troy, NY 12180. Telephone: 518-276-6266.

RESEARCH COLLEGE OF NURSING

Kansas City, Missouri

General Information

Independent 4-year specialized coed college. Founded 1980. Awards B (jointly with Rockhurst College). Primary accreditation: regional. Metropolitan setting; 66-acre campus. Total enrollment: 105. Faculty: 27 (21 full-time, 6 part-time). Social organizations: 5 national fraternities, 1 local sorority; 60% of eligible undergraduate men and 60% of eligible undergraduate women are members.

Drug and Alcohol Information

Education

On campus Drug and alcohol education/prevention programs offered for: all students.

Identification of Problems

Admissions College application does not ask about prior substance abuse problems.

On campus Current students identified as chemically dependent may remain enrolled, but treatment is required. No training program on identifying students with potential substance abuse problems. No written procedures for students and staff if substance abuse is suspected.

Support Services

Employee assistance Program for chemically dependent employees available. Staff: Qualified staff members are available to deal with cases of drug and alcohol abuse.

Disciplinary Actions

Alcohol Results of infractions of alcohol regulations (see Comparative Table of Alcohol Regulations) include warning, probation.

Drugs For first-time use or possession: varies by situation. For subsequent use or possession: varies by situation—probation, suspension. For first-time sale: varies by situation—expulsion. For subsequent sale: varies by situation—suspension, expulsion.

Additional Information from the College

The Research College of Nursing has not had any serious drug or alcohol problems. The College tends to focus on responsible behavior rather than rules and regulation.

For More Information

Contact: Graham Houston, Director of Student Affairs, Research College of Nursing, 2316 E. Meyer Blvd., Kansas City, MO 64132. Telephone: 816-276-4381.

RHODE ISLAND COLLEGE

Providence, Rhode Island

General Information

State-supported 5-year coed college. Founded 1854. Awards B, M. Primary accreditation: regional. City setting; 125-acre campus. Total enrollment: 8,044. Faculty: 422 (315 full-time, 107 part-time). Social organizations: local fraternities, local sororities; 5% of eligible undergraduate men and 5% of eligible undergraduate women are members.

Drug and Alcohol Information

Education

On campus Drug and alcohol education/prevention programs offered for: all students. College holds an annual alcohol awareness week.

Identification of Problems

Admissions College application does not ask about prior substance abuse problems.

On campus Current students identified as chemically dependent may remain enrolled. Training program on identifying students with potential substance abuse problems for: resident advisers. No written procedures for students and staff if substance abuse is suspected.

Support Services

On campus AA, Al-Anon, ACOA.

Employee assistance Program for chemically dependent employees available. Staff working with drug/alcohol-related issues: 1 part-time.

Disciplinary Actions

Alcohol Results of infractions of alcohol regulations (see Comparative Table of Alcohol Regulations) include chemical dependency assessment, counseling, warning, probation, suspension, expulsion.

Drugs For first-time use or possession: counseling, warning. For subsequent use: chemical dependency assessment, probation. For subsequent possession: probation, suspension. For first-time sale: probation, suspension. For subsequent sale: suspension, expulsion.

For More Information

Contact: Dixon A. McCool, Associate Dean, Rhode Island College, 600 Mount Pleasant Ave., Providence, RI 02908. Telephone: 401-456-8061.

RHODES COLLEGE

Memphis, Tennessee

General Information

Independent Presbyterian 4-year coed college. Founded 1848. Awards B. Primary accreditation: regional. Metropolitan setting; 100-acre campus. Total enrollment: 1,346. Faculty: 149 (106 full-time, 43 part-time). Social organizations: 7 national fraternities, 6 national sororities; 62% of eligible undergraduate men and 65% of eligible undergraduate women are members.

Drug and Alcohol Information

Education

On campus Drug and alcohol education/prevention programs offered for: all students, athletes/coaches; required for: freshmen, resident advisers. Bacchus chapter: 45 members. College holds an annual alcohol awareness week.

Identification of Problems

Admissions College application does not ask about prior substance abuse problems.

On campus Current students identified as chemically dependent may remain enrolled. Training program on identifying students with potential substance abuse problems for: resident advisers. No written procedures for students and staff if substance abuse is suspected.

Support Services

On campus Support groups, private counseling.

Employee assistance Program for chemically dependent employees not available. Staff working with drug/alcohol-related issues: 4 part-time.

Disciplinary Actions

Alcohol Results of infractions of alcohol regulations (see Comparative Table of Alcohol Regulations) include counseling, warning, probation, suspension, expulsion.

Drugs For any use or possession: varies by situation. For any sale: expulsion.

For More Information

Contact: Dr. Libby Robertson, College Counselor, Rhodes College, 2000 N. Pkwy., Memphis, TN 38112. Telephone: 901-726-3800.

RICE UNIVERSITY

Houston, Texas

General Information

Independent comprehensive coed institution. Founded 1891. Awards B, M, D. Primary accreditation: regional. Metropolitan setting; 300-acre campus. Total enrollment: 3,850. Faculty: 454.

Drug and Alcohol Information

Education

On campus Drug and alcohol education/prevention programs offered for: all students.

Identification of Problems

Admissions College application does not ask about prior substance abuse problems.

On campus Current students identified as chemically dependent may remain enrolled. No training program on identifying students with potential substance abuse problems. No written procedures for students and staff if substance abuse is suspected.

Support Services

On campus Private counseling.

Employee assistance Program for chemically dependent employees not available.

Rice University (continued)

Disciplinary Actions

Alcohol Results of infractions of alcohol regulations (see Comparative Table of Alcohol Regulations) vary by situation but can include warning, probation, suspension.

Drugs For any use, possession, or sale: varies by situation.

For More Information

Contact: Lois M. Waldron, Associate Director of Student Activities, Rice University, P.O. Box 1892, Houston, TX 77251. Telephone: 713-527-4097.

RIDER COLLEGE

Lawrenceville, New Jersey

General Information

Independent 5-year coed college. Founded 1865. Awards A (college transfer), B, M. Primary accreditation: regional. Small-town setting; 340-acre campus. Total enrollment: 4,139. Faculty: 275 (200 full-time, 75 part-time). Social organizations: 5 national fraternities, 3 national sororities; 6% of eligible undergraduate men and 4% of eligible undergraduate women are members.

Drug and Alcohol Information

Education

On campus Drug and alcohol education/prevention programs offered for: all students, faculty, administration. College holds an annual alcohol awareness week.

Identification of Problems

Admissions College application does not ask about prior substance abuse problems.

On campus Current students identified as chemically dependent may remain enrolled, but treatment is required. Training program on identifying students with potential substance abuse problems for: resident advisers. Written procedures for students and staff if substance abuse is suspected.

Support Services

On campus AA, private counseling.

Employee assistance Program for chemically dependent employees not available. Staff working with drug/alcohol-related issues: 6 part-time.

Disciplinary Actions

Alcohol Results of infractions of alcohol regulations (see Comparative Table of Alcohol Regulations) include counseling, warning, probation, alcohol awareness class.

Drugs For any use or possession: varies by situation. For any sale: varies by situation—expulsion.

For More Information

Contact: Cassie Iacovelli, Director of Student Activities, Rider College, 2083 Lawrenceville Rd., P.O. Box 6400, Lawrenceville, NJ 08648. Telephone: 609-896-5327.

RINGLING SCHOOL OF ART AND DESIGN

Sarasota, Florida

General Information

Independent 4-year specialized coed college. Founded 1931. Awards B. Primary accreditation: regional. City setting; 26-acre campus. Total enrollment: 480. Faculty: 37 (32 full-time, 5 part-time). Social organization: 1 local fraternity; 15% of eligible undergraduate men are members.

Drug and Alcohol Information

Education

On campus Drug and alcohol education/prevention programs offered for: all students. Bacchus chapter.

Identification of Problems

Admissions College application does not ask about prior substance abuse problems.

On campus Current students identified as chemically dependent may remain enrolled, but treatment is required. Training program on identifying students with potential substance abuse problems for: resident advisers, faculty, administration.

Support Services

On campus No support services on campus.

Off campus AA, NA, Al-Anon, ACOA, other support groups.

Employee assistance Program for chemically dependent employees not available.

Disciplinary Actions

Alcohol Results of infractions of alcohol regulations (see Comparative Table of Alcohol Regulations) vary by situation but can include chemical dependency assessment, probation.

Drugs For first-time use or possession: varies by situation. For subsequent use or possession: expulsion. For any sale: expulsion.

For More Information

Contact: Dan Cormany, Dean of Students, Ringling School of Art and Design, 1111 27th St., Sarasota, FL 34234. Telephone: 813-351-4614.

RIO GRANDE COLLEGE/ COMMUNITY COLLEGE

Rio Grande, Ohio

General Information

Independent 4-year coed college. Founded 1876. Awards A (terminal), B. Primary accreditation: regional. Rural setting; 170-acre campus. Total enrollment: 1,884. Faculty: 108 (72 full-time, 36 part-time). Social organizations: 2 national fraternities, 2 national sororities, 3 local fraternities, 4 local sororities; 15% of eligible undergraduate men and 15% of eligible undergraduate women are members.

Drug and Alcohol Information

Education

On campus Drug and alcohol education/prevention programs offered for: all students. College holds an annual alcohol awareness week and drug awareness week.

Identification of Problems

Admissions College application does not ask about prior substance abuse problems except for transfer applicants.

On campus Current students identified as chemically dependent may remain enrolled, but treatment is required. Training program on identifying students with potential substance abuse problems for: resident advisers, coaches, administration. No written procedures for students and staff if substance abuse is suspected.

Support Services

On campus Private counseling.

Off campus Community mental health agency.

Employee assistance Program for chemically dependent employees not available. Staff working with drug/alcohol-related issues: 5 part-time.

Disciplinary Actions

Alcohol Results of infractions of alcohol regulations (see Comparative Table of Alcohol Regulations) vary by situation but can include counseling, warning, probation, suspension.

Drugs For first-time use or possession: suspension. For subsequent use or possession: expulsion. For any sale: expulsion.

Additional Information from the College

Rio Grande College/Community College has a fine educational program, administered through the Campus Health Center, to deal with substance abuse issues. Support services are available both on and off campus through the Counseling Center.

For More Information

Contact: Dean S. Brown, Vice President, Student Services, Rio Grande College/Community College, Rio Grande, OH 45674. Telephone: 614-245-5353, Ext. 234.

RIPON COLLEGE

Ripon, Wisconsin

General Information

Independent 4-year coed college. Founded 1851. Awards B. Primary accreditation: regional. Small-town setting; 250-acre campus. Total enrollment: 857. Faculty: 164 (92 full-time, 72 part-time). Social organizations: 3 national fraternities, 2 national sororities, 3 local fraternities, 1 local sorority; 67% of eligible undergraduate men and 33% of eligible undergraduate women are members.

Drug and Alcohol Information

Education

On campus Drug and alcohol education/prevention programs offered for: all students. College holds an annual alcohol awareness week.

Identification of Problems

Admissions College application question about prior substance abuse problems is used to explain past academic performance; for counseling and referral, if student is admitted.

On campus Current students identified as chemically dependent may remain enrolled. Training program on identifying students with potential substance abuse problems for: resident advisers. Written procedures for students and staff if substance abuse is suspected.

Support Services

On campus Al-Anon, ACOA, private counseling.

Employee assistance Program for chemically dependent employees available.

Disciplinary Actions

Alcohol Results of infractions of alcohol regulations (see Comparative Table of Alcohol Regulations) vary by situation but can include warning, probation, suspension.

Drugs For first-time use or possession: counseling, warning. For subsequent use or possession: chemical dependency assessment, probation, suspension. For first-time sale: varies by situation—probation, suspension. For subsequent sale: suspension, expulsion.

For More Information

Contact: Sherry Lynch, College Counselor, Ripon College, 300 Seward St., Ripon, WI 54971. Telephone: 414-748-8312.

ROANOKE COLLEGE

Salem, Virginia

General Information

Independent 4-year coed college, affiliated with Evangelical Lutheran Church in America. Founded 1842. Awards B. Primary accreditation: regional. Small-town setting; 68-acre campus. Total enrollment: 1,594. Faculty: 116 (81 full-time, 35 part-time). Social organizations: 4 national fraternities, 3 national sororities; 33% of eligible undergraduate men and 32% of eligible undergraduate women are members.

Drug and Alcohol Information

Education

On campus Drug and alcohol education/prevention programs offered for: all students, athletes/coaches. Authorized group concerned with responsible drinking. College holds an annual alcohol awareness week and drug awareness week.

Identification of Problems

Admissions College application does not ask about prior substance abuse problems.

On campus Current students identified as chemically dependent may remain enrolled, but treatment is required. Training program on identifying students with potential substance abuse problems for: resident advisers, administration, peer facilitators. Written procedures for students and staff if substance abuse is suspected.

Support Services

On campus Private counseling, referral service. Staff working with drug/alcohol-related issues: 7 part-time.

Disciplinary Actions

Alcohol Results of infractions of alcohol regulations (see Comparative Table of Alcohol Regulations) vary by situation but can include chemical dependency assessment, counseling, warning, probation, suspension, papers, fines, community service.

Drugs For first-time use: probation, suspension, community service and/or fine. For subsequent use: varies by situation—chemical dependency assessment, counseling. For first-time possession: probation, community service and/or fine. For subsequent possession: varies by situation—chemical dependency assessment, counseling, probation. For first-time sale: suspension. For subsequent sale: expulsion.

Additional Information from the College

Roanoke College, which is currently evaluating its program, is a member of the Inter-Association Task Force on Alcohol and Other Drug Issues and has actively participated in its national forums.

Roanoke College (continued)

For More Information

Contact: I. Rodney Goins II, Assistant Housing Director, Office of Student Affairs, Roanoke College, Salem, VA 24153. Telephone: 703-375-2309.

ROBERT MORRIS COLLEGE

Coraopolis, Pennsylvania

General Information

Independent 5-year coed college. Founded 1921. Awards A (college transfer and terminal), B, M. Primary accreditation: regional. Small-town setting; 230-acre campus. Total enrollment: 5,429. Social organizations: 4 national fraternities, 5 national sororities, 2 local sororities; 15% of eligible undergraduate men and 6% of eligible undergraduate women are members.

Drug and Alcohol Information

Education

On campus Drug and alcohol education/prevention programs offered for: all students, athletes/coaches, faculty, administration; required for: freshmen. Authorized group concerned with responsible drinking. College holds an annual alcohol awareness week and drug awareness week.

Identification of Problems

Admissions College application does not ask about prior substance abuse problems.

On campus Current students identified as chemically dependent may remain enrolled, but treatment is required. Training program on identifying students with potential substance abuse problems for: resident advisers, Greek officers. Written procedures for students and staff if substance abuse is suspected.

Support Services

On campus Support groups, private counseling.

Employee assistance Program for chemically dependent employees not available. Staff working with drug/alcohol-related issues: 6 part-time.

Disciplinary Actions

Alcohol Results of infractions of alcohol regulations (see Comparative Table of Alcohol Regulations) vary by situation but can include chemical dependency assessment, counseling, warning, probation, suspension, expulsion.

Drugs For any use or possession: varies by situation. For any sale: expulsion.

For More Information

Contact: Jack V. Balderson, Dean of Students, Robert Morris College, Narrows Run Rd., Coraopolis, PA 15108. Telephone: 412-262-8346.

ROBERTS WESLEYAN COLLEGE

Rochester, New York

General Information

Independent 4-year coed college, affiliated with Free Methodist Church of North America. Founded 1866. Awards A (terminal), B. Primary accreditation: regional. Metropolitan setting; 75-acre campus. Total enrollment: 820. Faculty: 79 (44 full-time, 35 part-time).

Drug and Alcohol Information

Education

On campus Drug and alcohol education/prevention programs offered for: all students.

Identification of Problems

Admissions College application does not ask about prior substance abuse problems.

On campus Current students identified as chemically dependent may remain enrolled, but treatment is required. Training program on identifying students with potential substance abuse problems for: resident advisers, administration, student service personnel. Written procedures for students and staff if substance abuse is suspected.

Support Services

On campus Support groups (Counseling Center), private counseling.

Employee assistance Program for chemically dependent employees not available. Staff working with drug/alcohol-related issues: 6 part-time.

Disciplinary Actions

Alcohol Results of infractions of alcohol regulations (see Comparative Table of Alcohol Regulations) vary by situation but can include chemical dependency assessment, counseling, warning, probation, suspension, expulsion, enrollment in rehab program.

Drugs For any use: varies by situation. For first-time possession: varies by situation. For subsequent possession: probation, suspension, expulsion. For first-time sale: suspension, expulsion. For subsequent sale: expulsion.

For More Information

Contact: Dr. Julie Pecnik, Director of Counseling Services, Roberts Wesleyan College, 2301 Westside Dr., Rochester, NY 14624-1997. Telephone: 716-594-9471.

ROCHESTER INSTITUTE OF TECHNOLOGY

Rochester, New York

General Information

Independent 5-year coed college. Founded 1829. Awards A (college transfer), B, M. Primary accreditation: regional. Metropolitan setting; 1,300-acre campus. Total enrollment: 13,181. Faculty: 1,127 (626 full-time, 501 part-time). Social organizations: 10 national fraternities, 3 national sororities, local fraternities, local sororities; 10% of eligible undergraduate men and 3% of eligible undergraduate women are members.

Drug and Alcohol Information

Education

On campus Drug and alcohol education/prevention programs offered for: all students.

Identification of Problems

Admissions College application does not ask about prior substance abuse problems.

On campus Current students identified as chemically dependent may remain enrolled. Training program on identifying students with potential substance abuse

problems for: resident advisers, faculty, administration. No written procedures for students and staff if substance abuse is suspected.

Support Services

On campus AA, ACOA, support groups, private counseling.

Employee assistance Program for chemically dependent employees available. Staff working with drug/alcohol-related issues: 1 full-time and 8 part-time.

Disciplinary Actions

Alcohol Results of infractions of alcohol regulations (see Comparative Table of Alcohol Regulations) vary by situation but can include counseling, warning, probation, suspension, community service, volunteer work.

Drugs For first-time use or possession: varies by situation—counseling, warning, probation. For subsequent use or possession: varies by situation. For first-time sale: suspension. For subsequent sale: varies by situation—suspension, expulsion.

For More Information

Contact: Dr. Elaine Spaull, Assistant Vice President, Rochester Institute of Technology, 1 Lomb Memorial Dr., P.O. Box 9887, Rochester, NY 14623. Telephone: 716-475-2268.

ROCKHURST COLLEGE

Kansas City, Missouri

General Information

Independent Roman Catholic 5-year coed college. Founded 1910. Awards A (college transfer and terminal), B, M. Primary accreditation: regional. Metropolitan setting; 25-acre campus. Total enrollment: 2,034. Faculty: 173 (89 full-time, 84 part-time). Social organizations: 3 national fraternities; 30% of eligible undergraduate men are members.

Drug and Alcohol Information

Education

On campus Drug and alcohol education/prevention programs offered for: all students. Authorized group concerned with responsible drinking. College holds an annual alcohol awareness week.

Identification of Problems

Admissions College application does not ask about prior substance abuse problems.

On campus Current students identified as chemically dependent may remain enrolled. No training program on identifying students with potential substance abuse problems. No written procedures for students and staff if substance abuse is suspected.

Support Services

On campus ACOA, support groups, private counseling.

Employee assistance Program for chemically dependent employees not available. Staff working with drug/alcohol-related issues: 2 part-time.

Disciplinary Actions

Alcohol Results of infractions of alcohol regulations (see Comparative Table of Alcohol Regulations) vary by situation but can include counseling, warning, probation.

Drugs For any use: varies by situation. For first-time possession: varies by situation. For subsequent possession: suspension. For first-time sale: suspension. For subsequent sale: expulsion.

For More Information

Contact: Dr. Dan Birmingham, Director of Counseling Center, Rockhurst College, 5225 Troost Ave., Kansas City, MO 64110. Telephone: 816-926-4125.

ROLLINS COLLEGE

Winter Park, Florida

General Information

Independent 5-year coed college. Founded 1885. Awards B, M. Primary accreditation: regional. Small-town setting; 65-acre campus. Total enrollment: 2,051. Faculty: 131 (all full-time). Social organizations: 4 national fraternities, 4 national sororities, 1 local fraternity, 1 local sorority; 24% of eligible undergraduate men and 30% of eligible undergraduate women are members.

Drug and Alcohol Information

Education

On campus Drug and alcohol education/prevention programs offered for: all students, athletes/coaches, faculty, administration; required for: freshmen, those assigned by Student Hearing Board. Authorized group concerned with responsible drinking. College holds an annual alcohol awareness week and drug awareness week.

Identification of Problems

Admissions College application does not ask about prior substance abuse problems.

On campus Current students identified as chemically dependent may remain enrolled, but treatment is required in most cases. Training program on identifying students with potential substance abuse problems for: resident advisers, coaches, Greek officers and members, faculty, administration, peers/students. Written procedures for students and staff if substance abuse is suspected.

Support Services

On campus AA, ACOA, support groups (recovery group), private counseling, Alcohol/Drug Education Planning Team.

Employee assistance Program for chemically dependent employees not available. Staff working with drug/alcohol-related issues: 4 part-time.

Disciplinary Actions

Alcohol Results of infractions of alcohol regulations (see Comparative Table of Alcohol Regulations) vary by situation but can include chemical dependency assessment, counseling, warning, probation, suspension. Comments: Infractions are investigated by the Student Hearing Board.

Drugs For first-time use or possession: varies by situation. For subsequent use: chemical dependency assessment, counseling, suspension. For first-time possession: varies by situation. For first-time sale: suspension, expulsion. For subsequent possession or sale: expulsion.

For More Information

Contact: Dr. Judith Provost, Director, Counseling and Health Services, Box 2727, Rollins College, Winter Park, FL 32789. Telephone: 407-646-2194.

ROSARY COLLEGE

River Forest, Illinois

General Information

Independent Roman Catholic 5-year coed college. Founded 1848. Awards B, M. Primary accreditation: regional. Small-town setting; 30-acre campus. Total enrollment: 1,625. Faculty: 83 (54 full-time, 29 part-time).

Drug and Alcohol Information

Education

On campus Drug and alcohol education/prevention programs offered for: Counseling Center staff; required for: resident advisers.

Identification of Problems

Admissions College application does not ask about prior substance abuse problems.

On campus Current students identified as chemically dependent may remain enrolled, but treatment is required. Training program on identifying students with potential substance abuse problems for: resident advisers. No written procedures for students and staff if substance abuse is suspected.

Support Services

On campus ACOA, private counseling, residence hall programs.

Employee assistance Program for chemically dependent employees not available. Staff working with drug/alcohol-related issues: 1 part-time.

Disciplinary Actions

Alcohol Results of infractions of alcohol regulations (see Comparative Table of Alcohol Regulations) vary by situation but can include counseling, warning, probation, restriction from residence halls.

Drugs For first-time use or possession: varies by situation—counseling, probation. For first-time sale: varies by situation—probation. For subsequent use, possession, or sale: varies by situation—suspension.

For More Information

Contact: Sr. Michelle Germanson, Dean of Students, Rosary College, 7900 W. Division St., River Forest, IL 60305. Telephone: 312-366-2490 Ext. 263.

ROSE-HULMAN INSTITUTE OF TECHNOLOGY

Terre Haute, Indiana

General Information

Independent 5-year men's college. Founded 1874. Awards B, M. Primary accreditation: regional. Rural setting; 130-acre campus. Total enrollment: 1,360. Faculty: 97 (92 full-time, 5 part-time). Social organizations: 8 national fraternities; 40% of eligible undergraduates are members.

Drug and Alcohol Information

Education

On campus Drug and alcohol education/prevention programs offered for: all students, faculty. College holds an annual alcohol awareness week.

Identification of Problems

Admissions College application does not ask about prior substance abuse problems.

On campus Current students identified as chemically dependent may remain enrolled, but treatment is required. Training program on identifying students with potential substance abuse problems for: resident advisers. No written procedures for students and staff if substance abuse is suspected.

Support Services

On campus Private counseling.

Employee assistance Program for chemically dependent employees not available.

Disciplinary Actions

Alcohol Results of infractions of alcohol regulations (see Comparative Table of Alcohol Regulations) include counseling, warning, probation.

Drugs For first-time use: probation. For subsequent use: suspension. For any possession or sale: expulsion.

For More Information

Contact: Pete Gustafson, Associate Dean of Students, Rose-Hulman Institute of Technology, 5500 Wabash Ave., Terre Haute, IN 47803. Telephone: 812-877-1511.

ROSEMONT COLLEGE

Rosemont, Pennsylvania

General Information

Independent Roman Catholic 4-year women's college. Founded 1921. Awards B. Primary accreditation: regional. Small-town setting; 56-acre campus. Total enrollment: 613. Faculty: 99 (48 full-time, 51 part-time).

Drug and Alcohol Information

Education

On campus Drug and alcohol education/prevention programs offered for: all students, athletes/coaches; required for: freshmen, social organization members, faculty, administration, resident advisers, student leaders.

Identification of Problems

Admissions College application does not ask about prior substance abuse problems.

On campus Current students identified as chemically dependent may remain enrolled, but treatment is required. Training program on identifying students with potential substance abuse problems for: resident advisers. No written procedures for students and staff if substance abuse is suspected.

Support Services

On campus Private counseling.

Employee assistance Program for chemically dependent employees not available. Staff working with drug/alcohol-related issues: 3 part-time.

Disciplinary Actions

Alcohol Results of infractions of alcohol regulations (see Comparative Table of Alcohol Regulations) vary by situation but can include counseling, warning.

Drugs For first-time use: varies by situation—chemical dependency assessment, counseling, warning. For subsequent use: varies by situation. For first-time possession: varies by situation—counseling, warning, probation. For subsequent possession: varies by situation—suspension, expulsion. For first-time sale: probation, suspension, expulsion. For subsequent sale: expulsion.

For More Information

Contact: Ethel C. Levenson, Dean of Students, Rosemont College, Rosemont, PA 19010. Telephone: 215-527-0200 Ext. 402.

RUTGERS, THE STATE UNIVERSITY OF NEW JERSEY, COLLEGE OF ENGINEERING

Piscataway, New Jersey

General Information

State-supported 4-year specialized coed college. Part of Rutgers, The State University of New Jersey. Founded 1864. Awards B. Primary accreditation: regional. Small-town setting; 2,686-acre campus. Total university enrollment: 47,899. Faculty: 132 full-time. Social organizations: 25 national fraternities, 11 national sororities, 5 local fraternities, 2 local sororities.

Drug and Alcohol Information

Education

On campus Drug and alcohol education/prevention programs offered for: all students, athletes/coaches, faculty. Authorized group concerned with responsible drinking. College holds an annual alcohol awareness week and drug awareness week.

Identification of Problems

Admissions College application does not ask about prior substance abuse problems.

On campus Current students identified as chemically dependent may remain enrolled. Training program on identifying students with potential substance abuse problems for: resident advisers, faculty, administration. Written procedures for students and staff if substance abuse is suspected.

Support Services

On campus AA, NA, ACOA, private counseling.

Employee assistance Program for chemically dependent employees available. Staff working with drug/alcohol-related issues: 2 full-time and 2 part-time.

Disciplinary Actions

Alcohol Results of infractions of alcohol regulations (see Comparative Table of Alcohol Regulations) vary by situation but can include chemical dependency assessment, counseling, warning, probation, suspension, expulsion.

Drugs For any use, possession, or sale: varies by situation.

For More Information

Contact: Margaret A. Sheppard, Coordinator, Alcohol and Drug Education and Training, Rutgers, The State University of New Jersey, College of Engineering, P.O. Box 2101, New Brunswick, NJ 08903. Telephone: 201-932-7710.

RUTGERS, THE STATE UNIVERSITY OF NEW JERSEY, COOK COLLEGE

New Brunswick, New Jersey

General Information

State-supported 4-year coed college. Part of Rutgers, The State University of New Jersey. Founded 1921. Awards B. Primary accreditation: regional. Small-town setting; 2,686-acre campus. Total university enrollment: 47,899. Faculty: 95 full-time. Social organizations: 25 national fraternities, 11 national sororities, 5 local fraternities, 2 local sororities.

Drug and Alcohol Information

Education

On campus Drug and alcohol education/prevention programs offered for: all students. College holds an annual alcohol awareness week.

Identification of Problems

Admissions College application does not ask about prior substance abuse problems.

On campus Current students identified as chemically dependent may remain enrolled. Training program on identifying students with potential substance abuse problems for: resident advisers. No written procedures for students and staff if substance abuse is suspected.

Support Services

On campus AA, NA, Al-Anon, private counseling.

Employee assistance Program for chemically dependent employees available. Staff working with drug/alcohol-related issues: 2 full-time and 2 part-time.

Disciplinary Actions

Alcohol Results of infractions of alcohol regulations (see Comparative Table of Alcohol Regulations) include chemical dependency assessment, counseling, warning, probation, suspension.

Drugs For any use or possession: varies by situation. For first-time sale: varies by situation. For subsequent sale: suspension, police notification.

For More Information

Contact: Mike Fitzgerald, Director, Residence Life, Rutgers, The State University of New Jersey, Cook College, P.O. Box 231, New Brunswick, NJ 08903. Telephone: 201-932-9363.

RUTGERS, THE STATE UNIVERSITY OF NEW JERSEY, RUTGERS COLLEGE

New Brunswick, New Jersey

General Information

State-supported 4-year coed college. Part of Rutgers, The State University of New Jersey. Founded 1766. Awards B. Primary accreditation: regional. Small-town setting; 2,686-acre campus. Total university enrollment: 47,899. Faculty (shared by Douglass College, Livingston College, Rutgers College, University College–New Brunswick): 759 full-time. Social organizations: 25 national fraternities, 11 national sororities, 5 local fraternities, 2 local sororities.

Rutgers, The State University of New Jersey, Rutgers College (continued)

Drug and Alcohol Information

Education

On campus Drug and alcohol education/prevention programs offered for: all students, athletes/coaches, administration. Authorized group concerned with responsible drinking. College holds an annual alcohol awareness week and drug awareness week.

Identification of Problems

Admissions College application does not ask about prior substance abuse problems.

On campus Current students identified as chemically dependent may remain enrolled, but treatment is required. Training program on identifying students with potential substance abuse problems for: resident advisers, Greek officers, administration. Written procedures for students and staff if substance abuse is suspected.

Support Services

On campus AA, ACOA, support groups, private counseling.

Employee assistance Program for chemically dependent employees available. Staff working with drug/alcohol-related issues: 4 full-time and 100 part-time.

Disciplinary Actions

Alcohol Results of infractions of alcohol regulations (see Comparative Table of Alcohol Regulations) vary by situation but can include chemical dependency assessment, counseling, warning, probation, suspension, expulsion.

Drugs For first-time use or possession: varies by situation—chemical dependency assessment, probation. For subsequent use: varies by situation—suspension. For subsequent possession: suspension. For any sale: expulsion.

For More Information

Contact: Lisa Laitman, Coordinator, Alcohol Education, Rutgers, The State University of New Jersey, Rutgers College, P.O. Box 2101, New Brunswick, NJ 08903. Telephone: 201-932-7976.

RUTGERS, THE STATE UNIVERSITY OF NEW JERSEY, UNIVERSITY COLLEGE–NEWARK

Newark, New Jersey

General Information

State-supported 4-year coed college. Part of Rutgers, The State University of New Jersey. Founded 1934. Awards B (offers primarily part-time evening degree programs). Primary accreditation: regional. City setting; 31-acre campus. Total university enrollment: 47,899. Faculty: 241 full-time. Social organizations: 5 national fraternities, 3 national sororities.

Drug and Alcohol Information

Education

On campus Drug and alcohol education/prevention programs offered for: all students, athletes/coaches, faculty, administration. College holds an annual alcohol awareness week and drug awareness week.

Identification of Problems

Admissions College application does not ask about prior substance abuse problems.

On campus Current students identified as chemically dependent may remain enrolled. Training program on identifying students with potential substance abuse problems for: resident advisers, coaches, Greek officers, faculty, administration, staff. Written procedures for students and staff if substance abuse is suspected.

Support Services

On campus ACOA, substance abuse program.

Employee assistance Program for chemically dependent employees available. Staff working with drug/alcohol-related issues: 1 full-time.

Disciplinary Actions

Alcohol Results of infractions of alcohol regulations (see Comparative Table of Alcohol Regulations) vary by situation but can include chemical dependency assessment, counseling, warning, probation, suspension, expulsion.

Drugs For any use, possession, or sale: varies by situation.

Additional Information from the College

A University-wide inpatient Alcohol Assistance Program is available at the Hurtado Health Center in New Brunswick. Its goal is to keep the student in school while still in treatment, and students from all Rutgers campuses and other New Jersey colleges are eligible for consideration. The Director, Lisa Laitmain, can be reached at 201-932-7962.

For More Information

Contact: Polly McLaughlin, Newark Campus Coordinator of the Health Education and Alcohol Assistance Program, Rutgers, The State University of New Jersey, University College–Newark, 360 Dr. Martin Luther King Jr., Blvd., Newark, NJ 07102. Telephone: 201-648-5805.

SAGINAW VALLEY STATE UNIVERSITY

University Center, Michigan

General Information

State-supported 5-year coed college. Founded 1963. Awards B, M. Primary accreditation: regional. City setting; 800-acre campus. Total enrollment: 5,870. Faculty: 313 (149 full-time, 164 part-time). Social organizations: 2 national fraternities, 2 national sororities; 1% of eligible undergraduate men and 1% of eligible undergraduate women are members.

Drug and Alcohol Information

Education

On campus Drug and alcohol education/prevention programs offered for: all students, athletes/coaches, faculty, administration, SafeHaven volunteers. Authorized group concerned with responsible drinking. College holds an annual alcohol awareness week and drug awareness week.

Identification of Problems

Admissions College application does not ask about prior substance abuse problems.

On campus Training program on identifying students with potential substance abuse problems for: resident advisers, faculty, administration, SafeHaven volunteers. Written procedures for students and staff if substance abuse is suspected.

Support Services

On campus Al-Anon, ACOA, private counseling, substance abuse consultations and referral.

Employee assistance Program for chemically dependent employees not available. Staff working with drug/alcohol-related issues: 1 part-time.

Disciplinary Actions

Alcohol Results of infractions of alcohol regulations (see Comparative Table of Alcohol Regulations) vary by situation.

Drugs For first-time use: varies by situation. For subsequent use: varies by situation—criminal prosecution. For any possession or sale: varies by situation—criminal prosecution.

Additional Information from the College

The University is committed to implementing a program that will set forth guidelines, provide education, assist with intervention, and provide counseling or referral as appropriate.

For More Information

Contact: Anne Mahoney, SafeHaven Coordinator, Saginaw Valley State University, University Center, MI 48710. Telephone: 517-790-5600.

SAINT ANSELM COLLEGE

Manchester, New Hampshire

General Information

Independent Roman Catholic 4-year coed college. Founded 1889. Awards B. Primary accreditation: regional. City setting; 410-acre campus. Total enrollment: 1,833. Faculty: 145 (110 full-time, 35 part-time). Social organizations: 2 male fraternal societies; 8% of eligible undergraduate men are members.

Drug and Alcohol Information

Education

On campus Drug and alcohol education/prevention programs offered for: all students. College holds an annual alcohol awareness week and drug awareness week.

Identification of Problems

Admissions College application question about prior substance abuse problems is optional and is used for information only.

On campus Current students identified as chemically dependent may remain enrolled, but treatment is required. Training program on identifying students with potential substance abuse problems for: resident advisers. No written procedures for students and staff if substance abuse is suspected.

Support Services

On campus ACOA, support groups, private counseling.

Employee assistance Program for chemically dependent employees not available. Staff working with drug/alcohol-related issues: 1 full-time and 3 part-time.

Disciplinary Actions

Alcohol Results of infractions of alcohol regulations (see Comparative Table of Alcohol Regulations) vary by situation but can include counseling, warning, probation, suspension, expulsion, weekends off campus.

Drugs For first-time use or possession: probation. For subsequent use or possession: expulsion. For any sale: expulsion.

For More Information

Contact: Dr. Connie Richards, Director, College Health Services, Saint Anselm College, Saint Anselm Dr., Manchester, NH 03102-1310. Telephone: 603-641-7000.

SAINT AUGUSTINE'S COLLEGE

Raleigh, North Carolina

General Information

Independent Episcopal 4-year coed college. Founded 1867. Awards B. Primary accreditation: regional. City setting; 110-acre campus. Total enrollment: 1,828. Faculty: 112 (78 full-time, 34 part-time). Social organizations: 4 national fraternities, 2 national sororities, 3 local fraternities, 2 local sororities; 8% of eligible undergraduate men and 3% of eligible undergraduate women are members.

Drug and Alcohol Information

Education

On campus Drug and alcohol education/prevention programs offered for: all students; required for: athletes/coaches.

Identification of Problems

Admissions College application does not ask about prior substance abuse problems.

On campus Current students identified as chemically dependent may not remain enrolled. Training program on identifying students with potential substance abuse problems for: resident advisers, peer counselors. Written procedures for students and staff if substance abuse is suspected.

Support Services

On campus AA, support groups (Drug Action of Wake County).

Employee assistance Program for chemically dependent employees not available. Staff working with drug/alcohol-related issues: 3 part-time.

Disciplinary Actions

Alcohol Results of infractions of alcohol regulations (see Comparative Table of Alcohol Regulations) include probation, suspension.

Drugs For first-time use, possession, or sale: probation. For subsequent use, possession, or sale: suspension.

For More Information

Contact: Gwendolyn Newsome, Acting Director of Student Development, Saint Augustine's College, 1315 Oakwood Ave., Raleigh, NC 27610-2298. Telephone: 919-828-4451.

ST. CHARLES BORROMEO SEMINARY

Philadelphia, Pennsylvania

General Information

Independent Roman Catholic 5-year men's college. Founded 1832. Awards B, M. Primary accreditation: regional.

St. Charles Borromeo Seminary (continued)

Metropolitan setting; 77-acre campus. Total enrollment: 351. Faculty: 18 (10 full-time, 8 part-time).

Drug and Alcohol Information

Education

On campus Drug and alcohol education/prevention programs required for: all students. College holds an annual alcohol awareness week.

Identification of Problems

Admissions College application question about prior substance abuse problems is used for counseling and referral, if student is admitted; in the admissions decision.

On campus Current students identified as chemically dependent may remain enrolled, but treatment is required. No training program on identifying students with potential substance abuse problems. Written procedures for students and staff if substance abuse is suspected.

Support Services

On campus Private counseling.

Employee assistance Program for chemically dependent employees not available.

Disciplinary Actions

Alcohol Results of infractions of alcohol regulations (see Comparative Table of Alcohol Regulations) include chemical dependency assessment, counseling, warning, expulsion.

Drugs For first-time use or possession: chemical dependency assessment, counseling, probation. For subsequent use: chemical dependency assessment, counseling, expulsion. For subsequent possession: varies by situation. For any sale: expulsion.

For More Information

Contact: Rev. William J. Lynn, Dean of Men, College Division, St. Charles Borromeo Seminary, Philadelphia, PA 19151. Telephone: 215-667-3394.

ST. FRANCIS COLLEGE

Brooklyn Heights, New York

General Information

Independent 4-year coed college. Founded 1858. Awards A (college transfer), B. Primary accreditation: regional. Metropolitan setting. Total enrollment: 1,929. Faculty: 128 (57 full-time, 71 part-time). Social organizations: 1 national fraternity, national sororities, 2 local sororities; 5% of eligible undergraduate men and 5% of eligible undergraduate women are members.

Drug and Alcohol Information

Education

On campus Drug and alcohol education/prevention programs offered for: all students, athletes/coaches. Authorized group concerned with responsible drinking. College holds an annual alcohol awareness week.

Identification of Problems

Admissions College application does not ask about prior substance abuse problems.

On campus Current students identified as chemically dependent may remain enrolled, but treatment is required. Training program on identifying students with potential substance abuse problems for: coaches. Written procedures being developed for students and staff if substance abuse is suspected.

Support Services

On campus Private counseling, referral to community agencies.

Employee assistance Program for chemically dependent employees not available.

Disciplinary Actions

Alcohol Results of infractions of alcohol regulations (see Comparative Table of Alcohol Regulations) vary by situation but can include chemical dependency assessment, counseling, warning, probation, suspension, expulsion.

Drugs For first-time use: chemical dependency assessment, counseling, warning. For subsequent use: suspension. For first-time possession: chemical dependency assessment, counseling, probation, For subsequent possession: expulsion. For any sale: expulsion.

For More Information

Contact: Catherine Ford, College Nurse, St. Francis College, 180 Remsen St., Brooklyn Heights, NY 11201. Telephone: 718-522-2300 Ext. 366.

ST. HYACINTH COLLEGE AND SEMINARY

Granby, Massachusetts

General Information

Independent Roman Catholic 4-year specialized men's college. Founded 1927. Awards B. Primary accreditation: regional. Small-town setting; 600-acre campus. Total enrollment: 40. Faculty: 15 (6 full-time, 9 part-time).

Drug and Alcohol Information

Education

On campus Drug and alcohol education/prevention programs offered for: all students, Formation Directors.

Identification of Problems

Admissions College application does not ask about prior substance abuse problems.

On campus Current students identified as chemically dependent may possibly remain enrolled, but treatment is required. No training program on identifying students with potential substance abuse problems. Written procedures for students and staff if substance abuse is suspected.

Support Services

On campus Private counseling.

Employee assistance Program for chemically dependent employees not available.

Disciplinary Actions

Alcohol Results of infractions of alcohol regulations (see Comparative Table of Alcohol Regulations) vary by situation but can include expulsion.

Drugs For first-time use or possession: personalized intervention, counseling, suspension. For subsequent use or possession: varies by situation. For any sale: expulsion.

Additional Information from the College

The College is small and primarily composed of candidates for a religious community. A screening process identifies potential problems before candidates are admitted to the program. Problems are handled on a personalized basis.

For More Information

Contact: Fr. Donald Grzymski, Registrar, St. Hyacinth College and Seminary, Granby, MA 01033. Telephone: 413-467-7191.

ST. JOHN FISHER COLLEGE

Rochester, New York

General Information

Independent 5-year coed college. Founded 1948. Awards B, M. Primary accreditation: regional. Metropolitan setting; 125-acre campus. Total enrollment: 1,987. Faculty: 131 (94 full-time, 37 part-time).

Drug and Alcohol Information

Education

On campus Drug and alcohol education/prevention programs offered for: all students, faculty, administration. Authorized group concerned with responsible drinking. College holds an annual alcohol awareness week and drug awareness week.

Identification of Problems

Admissions College application does not ask about prior substance abuse problems.

On campus Current students identified as chemically dependent may remain enrolled, but treatment is required. Training program on identifying students with potential substance abuse problems for: resident advisers, administration. No written procedures for students and staff if substance abuse is suspected.

Support Services

On campus No support services on campus at this time.

Employee assistance Program for chemically dependent employees available. Staff working with drug/alcohol-related issues: 10 part-time.

Disciplinary Actions

Alcohol Results of infractions of alcohol regulations (see Comparative Table of Alcohol Regulations) include chemical dependency assessment, counseling, warning, probation, suspension, expulsion.

Drugs For first-time use: chemical dependency assessment, counseling, warning. For subsequent use: probation. For first-time possession or sale: counseling, suspension. For subsequent possession or sale: expulsion.

For More Information

Contact: Rev. Paul F. English, Assistant Dean of Students, St. John Fisher College, 3690 East Ave., Rochester, NY 14618. Telephone: 716-385-8281.

ST. JOHN'S COLLEGE

Annapolis, Maryland

General Information

Independent 5-year coed college. Founded 1696. Awards B, M. Primary accreditation: regional. Small-town setting; 36-acre campus. Total enrollment: 467. Faculty: 65 (58 full-time, 7 part-time).

Drug and Alcohol Information

Education

On campus Drug and alcohol education/prevention programs offered for: all students.

Identification of Problems

Admissions College general health question about prior substance abuse problems is used for counseling and referral, if student is admitted.

On campus No training program on identifying students with potential substance abuse problems. Written procedures for students and staff if substance abuse is suspected.

Support Services

On campus Private counseling.

Employee assistance Program for chemically dependent employees not available. Staff working with drug/alcohol-related issues: 10 part-time.

Disciplinary Actions

Alcohol Results of infractions of alcohol regulations (see Comparative Table of Alcohol Regulations) vary by situation.

Drugs For first-time use or possession: varies by situation—warning. For subsequent use or possession: varies by situation.For any sale: expulsion.

Additional Information from the College

The College is very aware of the problems of alcohol and drug abuse and is working toward national solutions. St. John's has a small student body, with a well-organized network of senior residents and other support personnel. There are no off-campus fraternities where drinking might take place.

For More Information

Contact: Dr. John Verdi, Assistant Dean, St. John's College, Annapolis, MD 21404. Telephone: 501-263-2371.

ST. JOHN'S COLLEGE

Santa Fe, New Mexico

General Information

Independent 5-year coed college. Administratively affiliated with St. John's College (MD). Founded 1964. Awards B, M. Primary accreditation: regional. City setting; 300-acre campus. Total enrollment: 430. Faculty: 54 (47 full-time, 7 part-time).

Drug and Alcohol Information

Education

On campus Drug and alcohol education/prevention programs offered for: all students. College holds an annual alcohol awareness week.

Identification of Problems

Admissions College application does not ask about prior substance abuse problems.

On campus Current students identified as chemically dependent may remain enrolled. No training program on identifying students with potential substance abuse problems. Written procedures for students and staff if substance abuse is suspected.

Support Services

On campus Private counseling, resident advisers.

St. John's College (continued)

Employee assistance Program for chemically dependent employees available.

Disciplinary Actions

Alcohol Results of infractions of alcohol regulations (see Comparative Table of Alcohol Regulations) vary by situation but can include counseling, warning, expulsion.

Drugs For any use: varies by situation—expulsion for felony drugs. For any possession or sale: expulsion for felony drugs.

For More Information

Contact: Kathy Mizrahi, Head Resident, St. John's College, 1160 Camino de La Cruz Blanca, Santa Fe, NM 87501. Telephone: 505-982-3691 Ext. 210.

ST. JOHN'S SEMINARY COLLEGE

Camarillo, California

General Information

Independent Roman Catholic 4-year specialized men's college. Administratively affiliated with St John's Seminary (CA). Founded 1939. Awards B. Primary accreditation: regional. City setting; 100-acre campus. Total enrollment: 86.

Drug and Alcohol Information

Education

On campus Drug and alcohol education/prevention programs offered for: all students, faculty, administration.

Identification of Problems

Admissions College application does not ask about prior substance abuse problems.

On campus Current students identified as chemically dependent may remain enrolled, but treatment is required. No training program on identifying students with potential substance abuse problems. Written procedures for students and staff if substance abuse is suspected.

Support Services

On campus Resident psychologist.

Employee assistance Program for chemically dependent employees not available.

Disciplinary Actions

Alcohol Results of infractions of alcohol regulations (see Comparative Table of Alcohol Regulations) vary by situation but can include probation, expulsion.

Drugs For first-time use, possession, or sale: varies by situation. For subsequent use, possession, or sale: expulsion.

For More Information

Contact: Rev. George Sullivan, Director of Students, St. John's Seminary College, 5118 E. Seminary Rd., Camarillo, CA 93010. Telephone: 805-482-4697.

SAINT JOHN'S UNIVERSITY

Collegeville, Minnesota

General Information

Independent Roman Catholic 5-year men's college, coordinate with College of Saint Benedict. Founded 1857. Awards B, M. Primary accreditation: regional. Rural setting; 2,400-acre campus. Total enrollment: 1,998. Faculty: 156 (128 full-time, 28 part-time).

Drug and Alcohol Information

Education

On campus Drug and alcohol education/prevention programs required for: freshmen, athletes/coaches, resident advisers. Bacchus chapter: 20 members. College holds an annual alcohol awareness week and drug awareness week.

Identification of Problems

Admissions College application does not ask about prior substance abuse problems.

On campus Current students identified as chemically dependent may remain enrolled, but treatment is required. Training program on identifying students with potential substance abuse problems for: resident advisers, coaches, faculty residents. Written procedures for students and staff if substance abuse is suspected.

Support Services

On campus AA, ACOA, private counseling.

Employee assistance Program for chemically dependent employees available. Staff working with drug/alcohol-related issues: 1 full-time and 4 part-time.

Disciplinary Actions

Alcohol Results of infractions of alcohol regulations (see Comparative Table of Alcohol Regulations) include chemical dependency assessment/counseling, warning, probation, expulsion.

Drugs For first-time use or possession: varies by situation. For first-time sale: varies by situation—counseling, expulsion. For subsequent use: varies by situation. For subsequent possession: varies by situation—chemical dependency assessment, counseling, suspension. For subsequent sale: expulsion.

For More Information

Contact: Cletus Connors, Director of Residential Program, Saint John's University, Collegeville, MN 56321. Telephone: 612-363-2734.

SAINT JOSEPH'S COLLEGE

Rensselaer, Indiana

General Information

Independent Roman Catholic 5-year coed college. Founded 1889. Awards A (terminal), B, M. Primary accreditation: regional. Small-town setting; 130-acre campus. Total enrollment: 1,001. Faculty: 85 (64 full-time, 21 part-time). Social organizations: 1 national fraternity, 1 local fraternity, 1 local sorority; 2% of eligible undergraduate men and 1% of eligible undergraduate women are members.

Drug and Alcohol Information

Education

On campus Drug and alcohol education/prevention programs offered for: resident advisers, violators of drug and alcohol regulations. Authorized group concerned with responsible drinking. College holds an annual alcohol awareness week.

Identification of Problems

Admissions College application question about prior substance abuse problems is used for counseling and referral, if student is admitted.

On campus Current students identified as chemically dependent may remain enrolled, but treatment is required. Training program on identifying students with potential substance abuse problems for: resident advisers, administration. Written procedures for students and staff if substance abuse is suspected.

Support Services

On campus Support groups, private counseling, alcohol education course.

Employee assistance Program for chemically dependent employees available. Staff working with drug/alcohol-related issues: 3 part-time.

Disciplinary Actions

Alcohol Results of infractions of alcohol regulations (see Comparative Table of Alcohol Regulations) vary by situation but can include chemical dependency assessment, counseling, warning, probation, suspension, expulsion.

Drugs For first-time use: chemical dependency assessment, probation, suspension. For first-time possession: probation. For subsequent use or possession: expulsion. For any sale: expulsion.

For More Information

Contact: William R. Maniscalco, Vice President for Student Affairs, Saint Joseph's College, P.O. Box 910, Rensselaer, IN 47978. Telephone: 219-866-6000 Ext. 351.

SAINT JOSEPH'S COLLEGE

Windham, Maine

General Information

Independent 4-year coed college, affiliated with Roman Catholic Church. Founded 1912. Awards A (terminal), B. Primary accreditation: regional. Rural setting; 285-acre campus. Total enrollment: 622. Faculty: 73 (35 full-time, 38 part-time).

Drug and Alcohol Information

Education

On campus Drug and alcohol education/prevention programs offered for: all students, athletes/coaches. Authorized group concerned with responsible drinking. College holds an annual alcohol awareness week and plans a drug awareness week.

Identification of Problems

On campus Current students identified as chemically dependent may remain enrolled, but treatment is required. Training program on identifying students with potential substance abuse problems for: resident advisers. No written procedures for students and staff if substance abuse is suspected.

Support Services

On campus No support services on campus.

Employee assistance Program for chemically dependent employees not available. Staff working with drug/alcohol-related issues: 5–7 part-time.

Disciplinary Actions

Alcohol Results of infractions of alcohol regulations (see Comparative Table of Alcohol Regulations) vary by situation but can include chemical dependency assessment, counseling, warning, probation, suspension, expulsion, attend or sponsor educational programs.

Drugs For any use, possession, or sale: varies by situation.

For More Information

Contact: Kevin P. Kelly, Assistant Dean of Students, Saint Joseph's College, Windham, ME 04062-1198. Telephone: 207-892-6766.

SAINT JOSEPH SEMINARY COLLEGE

Saint Benedict, Louisiana

General Information

Independent Roman Catholic 4-year men's college. Founded 1891. Awards B. Primary accreditation: regional. Rural setting; 300-acre campus. Total enrollment: 62. Faculty: 29 (all part-time).

Drug and Alcohol Information

Education

On campus Drug and alcohol education/prevention programs not offered. Authorized group concerned with responsible drinking.

Identification of Problems

Admissions College application does not ask about prior substance abuse problems.

On campus Current students identified as chemically dependent may remain enrolled, but treatment is required. No training program on identifying students with potential substance abuse problems. No written procedures for students and staff if substance abuse is suspected.

Support Services

On campus AA, NA, ACOA, support groups, private counseling.

Employee assistance Program for chemically dependent employees not available.

Disciplinary Actions

Alcohol Results of infractions of alcohol regulations (see Comparative Table of Alcohol Regulations) include warning, probation.

Drugs For first-time use: probation. For subsequent use: expulsion. For any possession or sale: expulsion.

Additional Information from the College

Because of the nature of the Seminary College, applicants who have a substance abuse problem are not accepted. The only substance abusers who may be admitted are those who are involved in self-help groups and who have stopped abusing drugs or alcohol.

For More Information

Contact: Thomas A. Siegrist, Director of Admissions/ Registrar, Saint Joseph Seminary College, Saint Benedict, LA 70457. Telephone: 504-892-1800.

SAINT JOSEPH'S UNIVERSITY
Philadelphia, Pennsylvania

General Information
Independent Roman Catholic 5-year coed college. Founded 1851. Awards A (college transfer), B, M. Primary accreditation: regional. Metropolitan setting; 55-acre campus. Total enrollment: 5,715. Faculty: 160 (all full-time). Social organizations: 4 national fraternities, 3 national sororities; 15% of eligible undergraduate men and 7% of eligible undergraduate women are members.

Drug and Alcohol Information
Education
On campus Drug and alcohol education/prevention programs offered for: all students, Greek system. Authorized group concerned with responsible drinking. College holds an annual alcohol awareness week and drug awareness week.

Identification of Problems
Admissions College application does not ask about prior substance abuse problems.

On campus Current students identified as chemically dependent may remain enrolled. Training program on identifying students with potential substance abuse problems for: resident advisers, Greek officers, staff. Written procedures for students and staff if substance abuse is suspected.

Support Services
On campus AA, Al-Anon, ACOA, support groups, private counseling, chemical dependency education—prevention, diagnosis, and referral.

Employee assistance Program for chemically dependent employees not available. Staff working with drug/alcohol-related issues: 1 full-time.

Disciplinary Actions
Alcohol Results of infractions of alcohol regulations (see Comparative Table of Alcohol Regulations) include chemical dependency assessment, counseling, warning, probation, suspension.

Drugs For first-time use: chemical dependency assessment, warning, probation. For first-time possession: counseling, probation. For first-time sale: probation, suspension. For subsequent use: counseling, suspension. For subsequent possession or sale: suspension.

Additional Information from the College
The University implemented a new alcohol policy in 1987–88, which is currently being reviewed in order to determine its effectiveness.

For More Information
Contact: Katherine A. Linstrom, Coordinator, Drug and Alcohol Programs, Saint Joseph's University, 5600 City Ave., Philadelphia, PA 19131. Telephone: 215-660-1090.

ST. LAWRENCE UNIVERSITY
Canton, New York

General Information
Independent 5-year coed college. Founded 1856. Awards B, M. Primary accreditation: regional. Rural setting; 1,000-acre campus. Total enrollment: 2,224. Faculty: 194 (172 full-time, 22 part-time). Social organizations: 7 national fraternities, 4 national sororities, 1 local sorority; 40% of eligible undergraduate men and 50% of eligible undergraduate women are members.

Drug and Alcohol Information
Education
On campus Drug and alcohol education/prevention programs offered for: all students, athletes/coaches, faculty, administration; required for: social organization members. Authorized group concerned with responsible drinking. College holds an annual alcohol awareness week.

Identification of Problems
Admissions College application does not ask about prior substance abuse problems.

On campus Current students identified as chemically dependent may remain enrolled. Training program on identifying students with potential substance abuse problems for: resident advisers, Greek officers. Written procedures for students and staff if substance abuse is suspected.

Support Services
On campus Support groups (SLU Alcohol Support Group), private counseling, employee assistance program.

Employee assistance Program for chemically dependent employees available. Staff working with drug/alcohol-related issues: 6 part-time.

Disciplinary Actions
Alcohol Results of infractions of alcohol regulations (see Comparative Table of Alcohol Regulations) vary by situation but can include chemical dependency assessment, counseling, warning, probation, suspension, expulsion.

Drugs For any use or possession: varies by situation. For any sale: suspension, expulsion.

For More Information
Contact: David Howison, Dean of Student Affairs, Vilas Hall, St. Lawrence University, Canton, NY 13617. Telephone: 315-379-5311.

ST. LOUIS COLLEGE OF PHARMACY
St. Louis, Missouri

General Information
Independent 5-year specialized coed college. Founded 1864. Awards B, M, D. Primary accreditation: regional. Metropolitan setting; 5-acre campus. Total enrollment: 750. Faculty: 54 (35 full-time, 19 part-time). Social organizations: 4 national fraternities, 2 national sororities.

Drug and Alcohol Information
Education
On campus Drug and alcohol education/prevention programs offered for: freshmen. Bacchus chapter: 8 members. College holds an annual alcohol awareness week.

Identification of Problems
Admissions College application question about prior substance abuse problems is used to explain past peformance; for counseling and referral, if student is admitted; in the admissions decision.

On campus Current students identified as chemically

dependent may remain enrolled, but treatment is required. Training program on identifying students with potential substance abuse problems for: resident advisers. Written procedures for students and staff if substance abuse is suspected.

Support Services

On campus No support services on campus.

Employee assistance Program for chemically dependent employees available.

Disciplinary Actions

Alcohol Results of infractions of alcohol regulations (see Comparative Table of Alcohol Regulations) include probation.

Drugs For first-time use or possession: varies by situation. For subsequent use or possession: expulsion. For any sale: expulsion.

For More Information

Contact: Dr. Taylor E. Lindhorst, Dean of Student Affairs, St. Louis College of Pharmacy, 4588 Parkview Pl., St. Louis, Missouri 63110. Telephone: 314-367-8700.

SAINT LOUIS UNIVERSITY

St. Louis, Missouri

General Information

Independent Roman Catholic comprehensive coed institution. Founded 1818. Awards A (college transfer), B, M, D. Primary accreditation: regional. Metropolitan setting; 225-acre campus. Total enrollment: 11,148. Faculty: 904 (384 full-time, 520 part-time). Social organizations: 3 national fraternities, 1 national sorority, 3 local fraternities, 2 local sororities; 16% of eligible undergraduate men and 8% of eligible undergraduate women are members.

Drug and Alcohol Information

Education

On campus Drug and alcohol education/prevention programs offered for: all students, athletes/coaches, administration. Bacchus chapter: 20 members. College holds an annual alcohol awareness week.

Identification of Problems

Admissions College application does not ask about prior substance abuse problems.

On campus Current students identified as chemically dependent may remain enrolled. No training program on identifying students with potential substance abuse problems. No written procedures for students and staff if substance abuse is suspected.

Support Services

On campus AA, NA, Al-Anon, ACOA, private counseling, student health center, campus ministry, and residence hall staff.

Employee assistance Program for chemically dependent employees available. Staff working with drug/alcohol-related issues: 2 part-time.

Disciplinary Actions

Alcohol Results of infractions of alcohol regulations (see Comparative Table of Alcohol Regulations) vary by situation but can include chemical dependency assessment, counseling, warning, probation, suspension, public service.

Drugs For any use, possession, or sale: varies by situation. Comments: Actions may include public service.

Additional Information from the College

Income from a recent $100,000 endowment is designated for an alcohol and drug awareness program and ensures extra financial support for many recent, ongoing prevention/education activities. Anheuser-Busch sponsored the national kickoff of a new collegiate organization, Student Athletes Detest Drugs, in October 1988.

For More Information

Contact: Helen Snyder, Alcohol Education Coordinator, Saint Louis University, 221 N. Grand Blvd., St. Louis, MO 63103. Telephone: 314-658-2323.

SAINT MARTIN'S COLLEGE

Lacey, Washington

General Information

Independent Roman Catholic 5-year coed college. Founded 1895. Awards A (terminal), B, M. Primary accreditation: regional. Small-town setting; 480-acre campus. Total enrollment: 635. Faculty: 50 (38 full-time, 12 part-time). Social organizations: 1 national fraternity, 1 local sorority; 3% of eligible undergraduate men and 3% of eligible undergraduate women are members.

Drug and Alcohol Information

Education

On campus Drug and alcohol education/prevention programs offered for: resident advisers. College holds an annual alcohol awareness week and drug awareness week.

Identification of Problems

Admissions College application does not ask about prior substance abuse problems.

On campus Current students identified as chemically dependent may remain enrolled, but treatment is required. Training program on identifying students with potential substance abuse problems for: resident advisers. Written procedures for students and staff if substance abuse is suspected.

Support Services

On campus AA, Al-Anon.

Employee assistance Program for chemically dependent employees not available. Staff working with drug/alcohol-related issues: 1 full-time and 1 part-time.

Disciplinary Actions

Alcohol Results of infractions of alcohol regulations (see Comparative Table of Alcohol Regulations) include chemical dependency assessment, counseling, warning.

Drugs For first-time use: chemical dependency assessment, counseling, warning. For first-time possession: warning. For subsequent use or possession: suspension. For any sale: expulsion.

For More Information

Contact: Dr. Myron Apilado, Vice President, Saint Martin's College, Lacey, WA 98503. Telephone: 206-438-4367.

SAINT MARY COLLEGE

Leavenworth, Kansas

General Information

Independent Roman Catholic 4-year coed college. Founded 1923. Awards A (college transfer), B. Primary accreditation: regional. Small-town setting; 240-acre campus. Total enrollment: 1,071. Faculty: 107 (39 full-time, 68 part-time).

Drug and Alcohol Information

Education

On campus Drug and alcohol education/prevention programs offered for: all students; required for: resident advisers, student leaders. Authorized group concerned with responsible drinking. College holds an annual alcohol awareness week and drug awareness week.

Identification of Problems

Admissions College application does not ask about prior substance abuse problems.

On campus Current students identified as chemically dependent may remain enrolled, but treatment is encouraged. Training program on identifying students with potential substance abuse problems for: resident advisers, student services staff. Written procedures for students and staff if substance abuse is suspected.

Support Services

On campus Private counseling.

Employee assistance Program for chemically dependent employees not available. Staff working with drug/alcohol-related issues: 3 part-time.

Disciplinary Actions

Alcohol Results of infractions of alcohol regulations (see Comparative Table of Alcohol Regulations) vary by situation but can include chemical dependency assessment, counseling, warning, probation, suspension, expulsion.

Drugs For first-time use: varies by situation—counseling, warning. For subsequent use: varies by situation—probation. For first-time possession: varies by situation—counseling, probation. For subsequent possession: suspension. For first-time sale: varies by situation—counseling, probation, suspension. For subsequent sale: expulsion.

For More Information

Contact: Joann Bangert, RN, Health Director, Saint Mary College, 4100 S. Fourth St. Trafficway, Leavenworth, KS 66048. Telephone: 913-682-5151 Ext. 216.

SAINT MARY-OF-THE-WOODS COLLEGE

Saint Mary-of-the-Woods, Indiana

General Information

Independent Roman Catholic 5-year women's college. Founded 1840. Awards A (college transfer and terminal), B, M. Primary accreditation: regional. City setting; 67-acre campus. Total enrollment: 910. Faculty: 55 (47 full-time, 8 part-time).

Drug and Alcohol Information

Education

On campus Drug and alcohol education/prevention programs offered for: all students, athletes/coaches. Bacchus chapter: 25 members. College holds an annual alcohol awareness week.

Identification of Problems

Admissions College application does not ask about prior substance abuse problems.

On campus Current students identified as chemically dependent may remain enrolled, but treatment is required. Training program on identifying students with potential substance abuse problems for: resident advisers, coaches, administration. Written procedures for students and staff if substance abuse is suspected.

Support Services

On campus Private counseling.

Employee assistance Program for chemically dependent employees not available. Staff working with drug/alcohol-related issues: 4 part-time.

Disciplinary Actions

Alcohol Results of infractions of alcohol regulations (see Comparative Table of Alcohol Regulations) vary by situation but can include warning, probation, suspension, expulsion.

Drugs For first-time use or possession: warning. For subsequent use or possession: probation. For any sale: varies by situation.

For More Information

Contact: Catherine M. Bickel, Director of Residence Life, Saint Mary-of-the-Woods College, Saint Mary-of-the-Woods, IN 47876. Telephone: 812-535-5151.

SAINT MARY'S COLLEGE

Notre Dame, Indiana

General Information

Independent Roman Catholic 4-year women's college. Founded 1844. Awards B. Primary accreditation: regional. City setting; 275-acre campus. Total enrollment: 1,821. Faculty: 180 (121 full-time, 59 part-time).

Drug and Alcohol Information

Education

On campus Drug and alcohol education/prevention programs offered for: all students, athletes/coaches, faculty, administration. Bacchus chapter being formed. Authorized group concerned with responsible drinking. College holds an annual alcohol awareness week and drug awareness week.

Identification of Problems

Admissions College application does not ask about prior substance abuse problems.

On campus Current students identified as chemically dependent may remain enrolled, but treatment is required. Training program on identifying students with potential substance abuse problems for: resident advisers. Written procedures for students and staff if substance abuse is suspected.

Support Services

On campus Private counseling.

Off campus AA, Al-Anon, ACOA.

Employee assistance Program for chemically dependent employees available. Staff working with drug/alcohol-related issues: 1 full-time and 5 part-time.

Disciplinary Actions

Alcohol Results of infractions of alcohol regulations (see Comparative Table of Alcohol Regulations) vary by situation but can include chemical dependency assessment, counseling, probation, expulsion, individual contract.

Drugs For any use, possession, or sale: varies by situation.

For More Information

Contact: Molly Sullivan, Consultant, Saint Mary's College Alcohol Education Council, Saint Mary's College, Notre Dame, IN 46556. Telephone: 219-284-5386.

SAINT MARY'S COLLEGE

Orchard Lake, Michigan

General Information

Independent Roman Catholic 4-year coed college. Founded 1885. Awards A (college transfer), B. Primary accreditation: regional. Small-town setting; 120-acre campus. Total enrollment: 307. Faculty: 35 (15 full-time, 20 part-time). Social organizations: 2 local fraternities, 1 local sorority; 10% of eligible undergraduate men and 10% of eligible undergraduate women are members.

Drug and Alcohol Information

Education

On campus Drug and alcohol education/prevention programs offered in an optional class.

Identification of Problems

Admissions College application does not ask about prior substance abuse problems.

On campus Current students identified as chemically dependent may remain enrolled, but treatment may be required. No training program on identifying students with potential substance abuse problems. No written procedures for students and staff if substance abuse is suspected.

Support Services

On campus No support services on campus.

Employee assistance Program for chemically dependent employees not available.

Disciplinary Actions

Alcohol Results of infractions of alcohol regulations (see Comparative Table of Alcohol Regulations) include warning, probation.

Drugs For first-time use: warning. For subsequent use: chemical dependency assessment. For any possession or sale: expulsion.

For More Information

Contact: Dr. Edward D. Meyer, President, Saint Mary's College, Commerce and Orchard Lake Rds., Orchard Lake, MI 48033. Telephone: 313-683-0504.

SAINT MARY'S COLLEGE OF MINNESOTA

Winona, Minnesota

General Information

Independent Roman Catholic 5-year coed college. Founded 1912. Awards B, M. Primary accreditation: regional. Small-town setting; 350-acre campus. Total enrollment: 1,886. Faculty: 114 (66 full-time, 48 part-time). Social organizations: 2 national fraternities, 3 national sororities; 16% of eligible undergraduate men and 32% of eligible undergraduate women are members.

Drug and Alcohol Information

Education

On campus Drug and alcohol education/prevention programs offered for: all students, athletes/coaches, faculty. Authorized group concerned with responsible drinking. College holds an annual alcohol awareness week.

Identification of Problems

Admissions College application does not ask about prior substance abuse problems.

On campus Current students identified as chemically dependent may remain enrolled. Training program on identifying students with potential substance abuse problems for: resident advisers. Written procedures for students and staff if substance abuse is suspected.

Support Services

On campus AA, ACOA, support groups, private counseling.

Employee assistance Program for chemically dependent employees not available. Staff working with drug/alcohol-related issues: 1 full-time and 2 part-time.

Disciplinary Actions

Alcohol Results of infractions of alcohol regulations (see Comparative Table of Alcohol Regulations) include chemical dependency assessment, counseling, warning, probation.

Drugs For first-time use: varies by situation. For subsequent use: probation, suspension. For first-time possession: varies by situation—counseling. For subsequent possession: varies by situation. For any sale: expulsion.

For More Information

Contact: Brother Dominic Fontaine, Director of Counseling Services, Saint Mary's College of Minnesota, Winona, MN 55987. Telephone: 507-457-1478.

ST. MARY'S UNIVERSITY OF SAN ANTONIO

San Antonio, Texas

General Information

Independent Roman Catholic 5-year coed college. Founded 1852. Awards B, M, D. Primary accreditation: regional. Metropolitan setting; 135-acre campus. Total enrollment: 3,654. Faculty: 216 (140 full-time, 76 part-time). Social organizations: 4 national fraternities, 3 national sororities, 3 local fraternities, 2 local sororities; 25% of eligible undergraduate men and 20% of eligible undergraduate women are members.

Drug and Alcohol Information

Education

On campus Drug and alcohol education/prevention programs offered for: all students, athletes/coaches, faculty, administration. Authorized group concerned with responsible drinking. College holds an annual alcohol awareness week and drug awareness week.

Identification of Problems

Admissions College application does not ask about prior substance abuse problems.

St. Mary's University of San Antonio (continued)

On campus Current students identified as chemically dependent may remain enrolled, but treatment is required. Training program on identifying students with potential substance abuse problems for: resident advisers, coaches, any appropriate group. Written procedures for students and staff if substance abuse is suspected.

Support Services

On campus Support groups, private counseling.

Employee assistance Program for chemically dependent employees not available. Staff working with drug/alcohol-related issues: 5–7 part-time.

Disciplinary Actions

Alcohol Results of infractions of alcohol regulations (see Comparative Table of Alcohol Regulations) vary by situation but can include chemical dependency assessment, counseling, warning, probation, suspension, expulsion.

Drugs For first-time use, possession, or sale: varies by situation—counseling, probation. For subsequent use, possession, or sale: varies by situation—suspension, expulsion.

For More Information

Contact: Charles J. Fey, Dean of Students, St. Mary's University of San Antonio, 1 Camino Santa Maria, San Antonio, TX 78284. Telephone: 512-436-3714.

SAINT MEINRAD COLLEGE

Saint Meinrad, Indiana

General Information

Independent Roman Catholic 4-year men's college. Founded 1857. Awards B. Primary accreditation: regional. Rural setting; 350-acre campus. Total enrollment: 130. Faculty: 41 (16 full-time, 25 part-time).

Drug and Alcohol Information

Education

On campus Drug and alcohol education/prevention programs offered for: all students. College holds an annual alcohol awareness week.

Identification of Problems

Admissions College application does not ask about prior substance abuse problems.

On campus Current students identified as chemically dependent may remain enrolled, but treatment is required. No training program on identifying students with potential substance abuse problems. Written procedures for students and staff if substance abuse is suspected.

Support Services

On campus AA, ACOA, private counseling.

Employee assistance Program for chemically dependent employees available. Staff working with drug/alcohol-related issues: 7 part-time.

Disciplinary Actions

Alcohol Results of infractions of alcohol regulations (see Comparative Table of Alcohol Regulations) vary by situation but can include chemical dependency assessment, warning. Comments: Warning for under-age drinking on first offense, assessment for frequent intoxication.

Drugs For first-time use or possession: probation. For subsequent use or possession: expulsion. For any sale: expulsion.

For More Information

Contact: Rev. Leo Ryska, O.S.B., Provost and Vice-Rector, Saint Meinrad College, Saint Meinrad, IN 47577. Telephone: 812-357-6611.

SAINT MICHAEL'S COLLEGE

Winooski, Vermont

General Information

Independent Roman Catholic 5-year coed college. Founded 1904. Awards B, M. Primary accreditation: regional. Small-town setting; 440-acre campus. Total enrollment: 2,287. Faculty: 151 (115 full-time, 36 part-time).

Drug and Alcohol Information

Education

On campus Drug and alcohol education/prevention programs offered for: all students, athletes/coaches, faculty, administration, parents. Bacchus chapter: 20 members. College holds an annual alcohol awareness week and drug awareness week.

Identification of Problems

Admissions College application does not ask about prior substance abuse problems.

On campus Current students identified as chemically dependent may remain enrolled, but treatment is required. Training program on identifying students with potential substance abuse problems for: resident advisers, coaches, Wellness Committee, student services staffs. Written procedures for students and staff if substance abuse is suspected.

Support Services

On campus AA, Al-Anon, ACOA, support groups (group counseling for chemically dependent students), private counseling.

Employee assistance Program for chemically dependent employees available. Staff working with drug/alcohol-related issues: 15–20 part-time.

Disciplinary Actions

Alcohol Results of infractions of alcohol regulations (see Comparative Table of Alcohol Regulations) vary by situation.

Drugs For any use or possession: varies by situation. For any sale: expulsion.

Additional Information from the College

The College's Wellness Committee has encouraged the implementation of several programs, methods of intervention, and development of educational resources that will reach most students. These programs and resources, in addition to offering professional services, provide students with a broad knowledge base upon which to make good decisions about their personal use of alcohol and other drugs.

For More Information

Contact: Michael Samara, Vice President for Student Affairs, Saint Michael's College, Winooski, VT 05404. Telephone: 802-655-2000 Ext. 2567.

ST. NORBERT COLLEGE

De Pere, Wisconsin

General Information

Independent Roman Catholic 5-year coed college. Founded 1898. Awards B, M. Primary accreditation: regional. Small-town setting; 40-acre campus. Total enrollment: 1,851. Faculty: 143 (118 full-time, 25 part-time). Social organizations: 3 national fraternities, 2 local fraternities, 3 local sororities; 17% of eligible undergraduate men and 11% of eligible undergraduate women are members.

Drug and Alcohol Information

Education

On campus Drug and alcohol education/prevention programs offered for: all students; required for: athletes/coaches, resident advisers, student leaders. Bacchus chapter: 45–60 members.

Identification of Problems

Admissions College application does not ask about prior substance abuse problems.

On campus Current students identified as chemically dependent may remain enrolled, but treatment is required. Training program on identifying students with potential substance abuse problems for: resident advisers, administration. Written procedures for students and staff if substance abuse is suspected.

Support Services

On campus Support groups, private counseling.

Employee assistance Program for chemically dependent employees not available. Staff working with drug/alcohol-related issues: 1 full-time and 3 part-time.

Disciplinary Actions

Alcohol Results of infractions of alcohol regulations (see Comparative Table of Alcohol Regulations) vary by situation but can include chemical dependency assessment, counseling, warning, probation, suspension, expulsion.

Drugs For first-time use or possession: counseling, warning, probation. For subsequent use or possession: varies by situation. For first-time sale: probation, suspension. For subsequent sale: suspension. Comments: Actions vary depending on type and amount of drug.

For More Information

Contact: Dr. R. C. Rankin, Vice President, Student Life, St. Norbert College, De Pere, WI 54115. Telephone: 414-337-3055.

ST. OLAF COLLEGE

Northfield, Minnesota

General Information

Independent Lutheran 4-year coed college. Founded 1874. Awards B. Primary accreditation: regional. Small-town setting; 350-acre campus. Total enrollment: 3,121. Faculty: 382 (225 full-time, 157 part-time).

Drug and Alcohol Information

Education

On campus Drug and alcohol education/prevention programs offered for: all students, athletes/coaches. Authorized group concerned with responsible drinking. College holds an annual alcohol awareness week and drug awareness week.

Identification of Problems

Admissions College application does not ask about prior substance abuse problems.

On campus Current students identified as chemically dependent may remain enrolled, but treatment is required. Training program on identifying students with potential substance abuse problems for: resident advisers, coaches, administration. Written procedures for students and staff if substance abuse is suspected.

Support Services

On campus AA, support groups, private counseling.

Employee assistance Program for chemically dependent employees available. Staff working with drug/alcohol-related issues: several part-time.

Disciplinary Actions

Alcohol Results of infractions of alcohol regulations (see Comparative Table of Alcohol Regulations) include chemical dependency assessment, counseling, warning.

Drugs For first-time use, possession, or sale: counseling, warning. For subsequent use, possession, or sale: varies by situation.

For More Information

Contact: Eric Engwall, Head Resident and Alcohol Education Facilitator, St. Olaf College, Northfield, MN 55057. Telephone: 507-663-2965.

ST. PAUL BIBLE COLLEGE

St. Bonifacius, Minnesota

General Information

Independent 4-year coed college, affiliated with Christian and Missionary Alliance Church. Founded 1916. Awards A (college transfer and terminal), B. Primary accreditation: regional and AABC. Rural setting; 193-acre campus. Total enrollment: 528. Faculty: 48 (31 full-time, 17 part-time).

Drug and Alcohol Information

Education

On campus Drug and alcohol education/prevention programs not offered.

Identification of Problems

Admissions College application does not ask about prior substance abuse problems.

On campus Current students identified as chemically dependent may not remain enrolled. No training program on identifying students with potential substance abuse problems.

Support Services

On campus No support services on campus.

Off campus Support; counseling.

Employee assistance Program for chemically dependent employees not available.

Disciplinary Actions

Alcohol Results of infractions of alcohol regulations (see Comparative Table of Alcohol Regulations) include expulsion.

Drugs For any use or sale: expulsion. For first-time possession: suspension. For subsequent possession: expulsion.

St. Paul Bible College (continued)

For More Information

Contact: D. E. Jenkins, Dean of Students, St. Paul Bible College, 6425 County Rd. 30, St. Bonifacius, MN 55375. Telephone: 612-446-4100.

ST. THOMAS UNIVERSITY

Miami, Florida

General Information

Independent Roman Catholic 5-year coed college. Founded 1961. Awards B, M. Primary accreditation: regional. Metropolitan setting; 140-acre campus. Total enrollment: 2,500. Faculty: 202 (68 full-time, 134 part-time). Social organizations: 1 national fraternity, 1 local fraternity, 1 local sorority.

Drug and Alcohol Information

Education

On campus Drug and alcohol education/prevention programs offered for: all students, athletes/coaches. Authorized group concerned with responsible drinking. College holds an annual alcohol awareness week and drug awareness week.

Identification of Problems

Admissions College application does not ask about prior substance abuse problems.

On campus Current students identified as chemically dependent may remain enrolled, but treatment is required. Training program on identifying students with potential substance abuse problems for: resident advisers, student life personnel. Written procedures being developed for students and staff if substance abuse is suspected.

Support Services

On campus Support groups, private counseling.

Employee assistance Program for chemically dependent employees not available. Staff working with drug/alcohol-related issues: 3 part-time.

Disciplinary Actions

Alcohol Results of infractions of alcohol regulations (see Comparative Table of Alcohol Regulations) vary by situation but can include counseling, warning, probation, suspension, expulsion.

Drugs For any use, possession, or sale: expulsion.

For More Information

Contact: George Edmondson, Acting Dean/Student Affairs, St. Thomas University, 16400 NW 32nd Ave., Miami, FL 33054. Telephone: 305-625-6000 Ext. 206.

SALEM COLLEGE

Winston-Salem, North Carolina

General Information

Independent Moravian 4-year women's college. Founded 1772. Awards B. Primary accreditation: regional. City setting; 57-acre campus. Total enrollment: 667. Faculty: 79 (55 full-time, 24 part-time).

Drug and Alcohol Information

Education

On campus Drug and alcohol education/prevention programs offered for: all students. Authorized group concerned with responsible drinking. College holds an annual alcohol awareness week and drug awareness week.

Identification of Problems

Admissions College application does not ask about prior substance abuse problems.

On campus Current students identified as chemically dependent may remain enrolled, but treatment is required. Training program on identifying students with potential substance abuse problems for: resident advisers, peer counselors. No written procedures for students and staff if substance abuse is suspected.

Support Services

On campus Private counseling.

Employee assistance Program for chemically dependent employees not available. Staff working with drug/alcohol-related issues: 1 part-time.

Disciplinary Actions

Alcohol Results of infractions of alcohol regulations (see Comparative Table of Alcohol Regulations) vary by situation.

Drugs For any use, possession, or sale: varies by situation.

Additional Information from the College

A Drug Prevention Committee consisting of faculty, staff, and students oversees all alcohol- and drug-related programming/training on campus. The College also has access to a resource library of films and videos and on-campus centers offering videos, programs, and pamphlets.

For More Information

Contact: Tyrell S. Rice, Director, Learning Resource Center and Counseling Center, Salem College, Salem Station, Winston-Salem, NC 27108. Telephone: 919-721-2625.

SALEM COLLEGE

Salem, West Virginia

General Information

Independent 5-year coed college. Founded 1888. Awards A (college transfer and terminal), B, M. Primary accreditation: regional. Rural setting; 100-acre campus. Total enrollment: 750. Faculty: 57 (47 full-time, 10 part-time). Social organizations: 3 national fraternities, 2 local fraternities, 3 local sororities; 30% of eligible undergraduate men and 30% of eligible undergraduate women are members.

Drug and Alcohol Information

Education

On campus Drug and alcohol education/prevention programs offered for: all students, athletes/coaches, faculty. College holds an annual alcohol awareness week and drug awareness week.

Identification of Problems

Admissions College application does not ask about prior substance abuse problems.

On campus Current students identified as chemically dependent may remain enrolled, but treatment is required.

Training program on identifying students with potential substance abuse problems for: resident advisers, coaches, faculty, administration. Written procedures for students and staff if substance abuse is suspected.

Support Services

On campus Private counseling.

Employee assistance Program for chemically dependent employees not available. Staff working with drug/alcohol-related issues: 2 part-time.

Disciplinary Actions

Alcohol Results of infractions of alcohol regulations (see Comparative Table of Alcohol Regulations) vary by situation but can include counseling, warning, probation, suspension. Comments: Warning for first offense, counseling/probationary suspension for second offense.

Drugs For first-time use: probation. For first-time possession: varies by situation. For subsequent use or possession: suspension. For any sale: expulsion.

For More Information

Contact: Perry L. Cain, Counselor, Student Support Services, Salem College, Salem, WV 26426. Telephone: 304-782-5290.

SALEM STATE COLLEGE

Salem, Massachusetts

General Information

State-supported 5-year coed college. Founded 1854. Awards B, M. Primary accreditation: regional. Small-town setting; 62-acre campus. Total enrollment: 8,654. Faculty: 323 (302 full-time, 21 part-time). Social organizations: local fraternities, local sororities; 20% of eligible undergraduate men and 30% of eligible undergraduate women are members.

Drug and Alcohol Information

Education

On campus Drug and alcohol education/prevention programs offered for: all students, faculty, administration; required for: athletes/coaches, resident advisers. College holds an annual alcohol awareness week and drug awareness week.

Identification of Problems

Admissions College application does not ask about prior substance abuse problems.

On campus Current students identified as chemically dependent may remain enrolled. Training program on identifying students with potential substance abuse problems for: resident advisers, coaches, faculty, administration. No written procedures for students and staff if substance abuse is suspected.

Support Services

On campus AA, Al-Anon, support groups (counseling center).

Employee assistance Program for chemically dependent employees available. Staff working with drug/alcohol-related issues: 5 part-time.

Disciplinary Actions

Alcohol Results of infractions of alcohol regulations (see Comparative Table of Alcohol Regulations) vary by situation but can include counseling, warning, probation, suspension, expulsion.

Drugs For first-time use: varies by situation. For first-time possession: probation, suspension, expulsion. For subsequent use or possession: suspension. For any sale: expulsion.

For More Information

Contact: Dr. James Stoll, Director, Counseling and Health Services, Salem State College, 352 Lafayette St., Salem, MA 01970. Telephone: 508-741-6410.

SALVE REGINA COLLEGE

Newport, Rhode Island

General Information

Independent Roman Catholic 5-year coed college. Founded 1934. Awards A (college transfer), B, M. Primary accreditation: regional. Small-town setting; 65-acre campus. Total enrollment: 2,252. Faculty: 203 (100 full-time, 103 part-time).

Drug and Alcohol Information

Education

On campus Drug and alcohol education/prevention programs offered for: all students; required for: freshmen.

Identification of Problems

Admissions College application does not ask about prior substance abuse problems.

On campus Current students identified as chemically dependent may remain enrolled, but treatment is required. Training program on identifying students with potential substance abuse problems for: resident advisers, coaches. No written procedures for students and staff if substance abuse is suspected.

Support Services

On campus AA, support groups, private counseling.

Employee assistance Program for chemically dependent employees not available. Staff working with drug/alcohol-related issues: 3 part-time.

Disciplinary Actions

Alcohol Results of infractions of alcohol regulations (see Comparative Table of Alcohol Regulations) vary by situation but can include counseling, warning, probation, suspension.

Drugs For any use, possession, or sale: varies by situation.

Additional Information from the College

The College feels strongly about the destructive consequences of alcohol and drug abuse, and addresses these issues through a combination of educational programs, practical rules and regulations, and the expectation that students are involved with the development of their best selves while enrolled. Each situation is judged on an individual basis, with consideration given to the needs of the student.

For More Information

Contact: John Rok, Dean of Students, Salve Regina College, Ochre Point Ave., Newport, RI 02840. Telephone: 401-847-6650 Ext. 515.

SAMFORD UNIVERSITY

Birmingham, Alabama

General Information

Independent Baptist 5-year coed college. Founded 1841. Awards A (terminal), B, M, D. Primary accreditation: regional. Metropolitan setting; 280-acre campus. Total enrollment: 4,089. Faculty: 271 (184 full-time, 87 part-time). Social organizations: 5 national fraternities, 6 national sororities; 20% of eligible undergraduate men and 20% of eligible undergraduate women are members.

Drug and Alcohol Information

Education

On campus Drug and alcohol education/prevention programs offered for: all students; required for: social organization members, resident advisers. College holds an annual alcohol awareness week and drug awareness week.

Identification of Problems

Admissions College application does not ask about prior substance abuse problems.

On campus Current students identified as chemically dependent may remain enrolled, but treatment is required. Training program on identifying students with potential substance abuse problems for: resident advisers, administration. Written procedures for students and staff if substance abuse is suspected.

Support Services

On campus Private counseling.

Employee assistance Program for chemically dependent employees available. Staff working with drug/alcohol-related issues: 1 part-time.

Disciplinary Actions

Alcohol Results of infractions of alcohol regulations (see Comparative Table of Alcohol Regulations) include probation, suspension.

Drugs For first-time use, possession, or sale: probation, suspension. For subsequent use, possession, or sale: expulsion.

For More Information

Contact: Martha Ann Cox, Vice President, Dean of Students, Samford University, Birmingham, AL 35229. Telephone: 205-870-2736.

SAM HOUSTON STATE UNIVERSITY

Huntsville, Texas

General Information

State-supported 5-year coed college. Founded 1879. Awards B, M, D. Primary accreditation: regional. Small-town setting; 211-acre campus. Total enrollment: 11,550. Faculty: 387 (305 full-time, 82 part-time). Social organizations: 6 national fraternities, 6 national sororities, 8 local fraternities, 3 local sororities; 9% of eligible undergraduate men and 8% of eligible undergraduate women are members.

Drug and Alcohol Information

Education

On campus Drug and alcohol education/prevention programs offered for: all students, athletes/coaches. Authorized group concerned with responsible drinking. College holds an annual alcohol awareness week and drug awareness week.

Identification of Problems

Admissions College application does not ask about prior substance abuse problems.

On campus Current students identified as chemically dependent may remain enrolled. Training program on identifying students with potential substance abuse problems for: resident advisers, Greek officers. No written procedures for students and staff if substance abuse is suspected.

Support Services

On campus AA, NA, Al-Anon, ACOA, private counseling.

Employee assistance Program for chemically dependent employees not available. Staff working with drug/alcohol-related issues: more than 5 part-time.

Disciplinary Actions

Alcohol Results of infractions of alcohol regulations (see Comparative Table of Alcohol Regulations) vary by situation but can include chemical dependency assessment, counseling, warning, probation, suspension, expulsion.

Drugs For any use, possession, or sale: suspension.

Additional Information from the College

The University has established a committee of faculty, staff, and students to address the concerns of alcohol and drug abuse. This committee develops programs, reviews policies, and supports other organizations that promote alcohol and drug abuse education. Educational programs are available for all students and student organizations.

For More Information

Contact: Kathy L. Bowman, Assistant Dean of Student Life, Sam Houston State University, P.O. Box 2237, Sam Houston Station, Huntsville, TX 77341. Telephone: 409-294-1783.

SAMUEL MERRITT COLLEGE OF NURSING

Oakland, California

General Information

Independent 4-year specialized coed college. Founded 1909. Awards B (jointly with Saint Mary's College of California). Primary accreditation: regional. City setting. Total enrollment: 149. Faculty: 19 (15 full-time, 4 part-time).

Drug and Alcohol Information

Education

On campus Drug and alcohol education/prevention programs required for: all students.

Identification of Problems

Admissions College application question about prior substance abuse problems is used in the admissions decision.

On campus Current students identified as chemically dependent may remain enrolled, but treatment is required. No training program on identifying students with potential substance abuse problems. Written procedures for students and staff if substance abuse is suspected.

Support Services

On campus Support groups.

Employee assistance Program for chemically dependent employees not available.

Disciplinary Actions

Alcohol Results of infractions of alcohol regulations (see Comparative Table of Alcohol Regulations) include probation, suspension, expulsion.

Drugs For any use, possession, or sale: expulsion.

For More Information

Contact: David Wallace, Ph.D., Dean, Samuel Merritt College of Nursing, 370 Hawthorne Ave., Oakland, CA 94609. Telephone: 415-420-6193.

SAN FRANCISCO ART INSTITUTE

San Francisco, California

General Information

Independent 5-year specialized coed college. Founded 1871. Awards B, M. Primary accreditation: regional. Metropolitan setting; 3-acre campus. Total enrollment: 723.

Drug and Alcohol Information

Education

On campus Drug and alcohol education/prevention programs offered for: all students.

Identification of Problems

Admissions College application does not ask about prior substance abuse problems.

On campus Current students identified as chemically dependent may remain enrolled. No training program on identifying students with potential substance abuse problems. No written procedures for students and staff if substance abuse is suspected.

Support Services

On campus AA, private counseling.

Employee assistance Program for chemically dependent employees not available. Staff working with drug/alcohol-related issues: 2 part-time.

Disciplinary Actions

Alcohol Results of infractions of alcohol regulations (see Comparative Table of Alcohol Regulations) include counseling, warning, probation, suspension, expulsion.

Drugs For first-time use or possession: counseling, warning, probation. For subsequent use or possession: counseling, probation, suspension. For first-time sale: suspension, expulsion. For subsequent sale: expulsion.

For More Information

Contact: Linda Vega, Director of Student Affairs, San Francisco Art Institute, 800 Chestnut St., San Francisco, CA 94133. Telephone: 415-771-7020.

SANGAMON STATE UNIVERSITY

Springfield, Illinois

General Information

State-supported coed college. Founded 1969. Awards B, M. Primary accreditation: regional. City setting; 746-acre campus. Total enrollment: 3,942. Faculty: 185 (140 full-time, 45 part-time).

Drug and Alcohol Information

Education

On campus Drug and alcohol education/prevention programs offered for: all students; required for: athletes/coaches. College holds an annual alcohol awareness week.

Identification of Problems

Admissions College application does not ask about prior substance abuse problems.

On campus Current students identified as chemically dependent may remain enrolled, but treatment is required. Training program on identifying students with potential substance abuse problems for: resident advisers, coaches, administration. Written procedures for students and staff if substance abuse is suspected.

Support Services

On campus Private counseling.

Employee assistance Program for chemically dependent employees available. Staff working with drug/alcohol-related issues: 2 part-time.

Disciplinary Actions

Alcohol Results of infractions of alcohol regulations (see Comparative Table of Alcohol Regulations) include chemical dependency assessment, counseling, warning, probation.

Drugs For first-time use and possession: chemical dependency assessment, counseling, warning. For subsequent use or possession: suspension. For first-time sale: suspension, expulsion. For subsequent sale: expulsion.

For More Information

Contact: Homer L. Butler, Dean of Student Services, Sangamon State University, Springfield, IL 62794. Telephone: 217-786-6581.

SANTA CLARA UNIVERSITY

Santa Clara, California

General Information

Independent Roman Catholic 5-year coed college. Founded 1851. Awards B, M, D. Primary accreditation: regional. City setting; 104-acre campus. Total enrollment: 7,802. Faculty: 545 (345 full-time, 200 part-time). Social organizations: 5 national fraternities, 3 national sororities; 6% of eligible undergraduate men and 5% of eligible undergraduate women are members.

Drug and Alcohol Information

Education

On campus Drug and alcohol education/prevention programs offered for: all students, students involved in alcohol-related conduct code violations. College holds an annual alcohol awareness week and drug awareness week.

Santa Clara University (continued)

Identification of Problems

Admissions

On campus Current students identified as chemically dependent may remain enrolled. Training program on identifying students with potential substance abuse problems for: resident advisers, administration. No written procedures for students and staff if substance abuse is suspected.

Support Services

On campus ACOA, private counseling.

Employee assistance Program for chemically dependent employees not available. Staff working with drug/alcohol-related issues: 1 part-time.

Disciplinary Actions

Alcohol Results of infractions of alcohol regulations (see Comparative Table of Alcohol Regulations) vary by situation.

Drugs For any use, possession, or sale: varies by situation.

Additional Information from the College

While 1 part-time staff member works directly with alcohol and drug issues, staff members in the Housing and Residence Life Office, Counseling Services and Programs Center, and Office of the Dean of Students are also very involved in programming, counseling, and intervention.

For More Information

Contact: Dr. Charles Erekson, Dean of Students, Santa Clara University, Santa Clara, CA 95053. Telephone: 408-554-4366.

SAVANNAH STATE COLLEGE

Savannah, Georgia

General Information

State-supported 5-year coed college. Part of University System of Georgia. Founded 1890. Awards A (terminal), B, M. Primary accreditation: regional. City setting. Total enrollment: 1,932. Faculty: 149 (135 full-time, 14 part-time). Social organizations: 4 national fraternities, 4 national sororities, 6 local fraternities, 5 local sororities; 35% of eligible undergraduate men and 38% of eligible undergraduate women are members.

Drug and Alcohol Information

Education

On campus Drug and alcohol education/prevention programs offered for: all students, faculty, administration. Authorized group concerned with responsible drinking. College holds an annual alcohol awareness week and drug awareness week.

Identification of Problems

Admissions College application does not ask about prior substance abuse problems.

On campus Current students identified as chemically dependent may remain enrolled unless they are a clear and present danger. Treatment is required. Training program on identifying students with potential substance abuse problems for: resident advisers. Written procedures for students and staff if substance abuse is suspected.

Support Services

On campus Support groups (Counseling Center, Residence Life Program).

Employee assistance Program for chemically dependent employees not available. Staff working with drug/alcohol-related issues: 3 part-time.

Disciplinary Actions

Alcohol Results of infractions of alcohol regulations (see Comparative Table of Alcohol Regulations) vary by situation but can include chemical dependency assessment, counseling. Comments: Chemical dependency assessment and counseling may be conditions required for continuation.

Drugs For first-time use: varies by situation—chemical dependency assessment. For first-time possession or sale: varies by situation. For subsequent use, possession, or sale: varies by situation—chemical dependency assessment, suspension.

For More Information

Contact: Henton Thomas, Director of Comprehensive Counseling, Savannah State College, State College Branch, Savannah, GA 31404. Telephone: 912-356-2202.

SCHOOL OF THE ASSOCIATED ARTS

St. Paul, Minnesota

General Information

Independent 4-year coed college. Founded 1924. Awards B. Primary accreditation: NATTS. Metropolitan setting; 2-acre campus. Total enrollment: 134. Faculty: 29 (4 full-time, 25 part-time).

Drug and Alcohol Information

Education

On campus Drug and alcohol education/prevention programs offered for: all students, faculty, administration. College holds an annual drug awareness week.

Identification of Problems

Admissions College application does not ask about prior substance abuse problems.

On campus Current students identified as chemically dependent may remain enrolled, but treatment is required. Training program on identifying students with potential substance abuse problems for: administration, psychologist. Written procedures for students and staff if substance abuse is suspected.

Support Services

On campus AA, Al-Anon.

Employee assistance Program for chemically dependent employees not available.

Disciplinary Actions

Alcohol Results of infractions of alcohol regulations (see Comparative Table of Alcohol Regulations) include counseling, warning.

Drugs For first-time use or possession: counseling, warning. For subsequent use or possession: chemical dependency assessment, counseling. For any sale: expulsion.

For More Information

Contact: Mary Cramer, Counselor, School of the

Associated Arts, 344 Summit Ave., St. Paul, MN 55102. Telephone: 612-224-3416.

SCHOOL OF THE MUSEUM OF FINE ARTS

Boston, Massachusetts

General Information

Independent 5-year specialized coed college. Administratively affiliated with Tufts University. Founded 1876. Awards B, M. Primary accreditation: NASAD. Metropolitan setting; 14-acre campus. Total enrollment: 664. Faculty: 61 (51 full-time, 10 part-time).

Drug and Alcohol Information

Education

On campus Drug and alcohol education/prevention programs offered for: all students, faculty, administration. College holds an annual alcohol awareness week and drug awareness week.

Identification of Problems

Admissions College application does not ask about prior substance abuse problems.

On campus Current students identified as chemically dependent may remain enrolled. No training program on identifying students with potential substance abuse problems. Written procedures for students and staff if substance abuse is suspected.

Support Services

On campus Private counseling.

Employee assistance Program for chemically dependent employees available. Staff working with drug/alcohol-related issues: 5 part-time.

Disciplinary Actions

Alcohol Results of infractions of alcohol regulations (see Comparative Table of Alcohol Regulations) vary by situation.

Drugs For any use, possession, or sale: varies by situation.

For More Information

Contact: John L. Thompson, Dean of Students, School of the Museum of Fine Arts, 230 The Fenway, Boston, MA 02115. Telephone: 617-267-6100 Ext. 615.

SCHOOL OF THE OZARKS

Point Lookout, Missouri

General Information

Independent 4-year coed college. Founded 1906. Awards B. Primary accreditation: regional. Small-town setting; 960-acre campus. Total enrollment: 1,310. Faculty: 98 (88 full-time, 10 part-time).

Drug and Alcohol Information

Education

On campus Drug and alcohol education/prevention programs offered for: all students.

Identification of Problems

Admissions College application does not ask about prior substance abuse problems.

On campus Current students identified as chemically dependent may remain enrolled, but treatment is required. Training program on identifying students with potential substance abuse problems for: resident advisers. No written procedures for students and staff if substance abuse is suspected.

Support Services

On campus ACOA.

Employee assistance Program for chemically dependent employees not available.

Disciplinary Actions

Alcohol Results of infractions of alcohol regulations (see Comparative Table of Alcohol Regulations) include probation, suspension, expulsion.

Drugs For first-time use or possession: suspension. For subsequent use or possession: expulsion. For any sale: expulsion.

For More Information

Contact: Paul Blisard, Director-Counseling Center, School of the Ozarks, Point Lookout, MO 65726. Telephone: 417-334-6411.

SCRIPPS COLLEGE

Claremont, California

General Information

Independent 4-year women's college. Part of The Claremont Colleges. Founded 1926. Awards B. Primary accreditation: regional. Small-town setting; 26-acre campus. Total enrollment: 607. Faculty: 84 (53 full-time, 31 part-time).

Drug and Alcohol Information

Education

On campus Drug and alcohol education/prevention programs offered for: all students; required for: freshmen, resident advisers, student leaders. College holds an annual alcohol awareness week.

Identification of Problems

On campus

On campus Current students identified as chemically dependent may remain enrolled, but treatment is required. Training program on identifying students with potential substance abuse problems for: resident advisers. Written procedures for students and staff if substance abuse is suspected.

Support Services

On campus ACOA, private counseling.

Employee assistance Program for chemically dependent employees available. Staff working with drug/alcohol-related issues: 2 part-time.

Disciplinary Actions

Alcohol Results of infractions of alcohol regulations (see Comparative Table of Alcohol Regulations) vary by situation.

Drugs For any use: varies by situation. For first-time possession: varies by situation. For subsequent possession: expulsion. For any sale: expulsion.

Additional Information from the College

Counseling, health center, and student health education groups provide support and resources for drug and alcohol-related issues and are shared with the four other

Scripps College (continued)

Claremont Colleges. The five-college alcohol policy is being revised and a Chapter of Bacchus is planned for one of the campuses in 1989.

For More Information

Contact: Alice Moy, Assistant Dean, Balch Hall 10A, Scripps College, Claremont, CA 91711. Telephone: 714-621-8277.

SEATTLE PACIFIC UNIVERSITY

Seattle, Washington

General Information

Independent Free Methodist 5-year coed college. Founded 1891. Awards B, M. Primary accreditation: regional. Metropolitan setting; 35-acre campus. Total enrollment: 3,356. Faculty: 240 (130 full-time, 110 part-time).

Drug and Alcohol Information

Education

On campus Drug and alcohol education/prevention programs offered for: all students, athletes/coaches, faculty, administration; required for: resident advisers, student leaders. Authorized group concerned with responsible drinking. College holds an annual alcohol awareness week and drug awareness week.

Identification of Problems

Admissions College application does not ask about prior substance abuse problems.

On campus Current students identified as chemically dependent probably may not remain enrolled, but treatment is required. Training program on identifying students with potential substance abuse problems for: resident advisers. Written procedures for students and staff if substance abuse is suspected.

Support Services

On campus ACOA, private counseling, off-campus referrals.

Employee assistance Program for chemically dependent employees not available. Staff working with drug/alcohol-related issues: 15 part-time.

Disciplinary Actions

Alcohol Results of infractions of alcohol regulations (see Comparative Table of Alcohol Regulations) vary by situation.

Drugs For any use, possession, or sale: varies by situation.

Additional Information from the College

It is exceptional for a private Christian liberal arts college/university that has a policy of abstinence to do the proactive alcohol and drug abuse programming that Seattle Pacific University does. All student leaders attend a fall retreat where they receive alcohol and drug abuse training. An alcohol and drug awareness committee is comprised of faculty, staff, and students.

For More Information

Contact: Wendy Fisher, Personal Development Counselor, Seattle Pacific University, 3rd Ave. W. at W. Nickerson, Seattle, WA 98119. Telephone: 206-281-2016.

SETON HILL COLLEGE

Greensburg, Pennsylvania

General Information

Independent Roman Catholic 4-year primarily women's college. Founded 1883. Awards B. Primary accreditation: regional. Small-town setting; 200-acre campus. Total enrollment: 870. Faculty: 84 (48 full-time, 36 part-time).

Drug and Alcohol Information

Education

On campus Drug and alcohol education/prevention programs offered for: all students, athletes/coaches, administration; required for: freshmen. Authorized group concerned with responsible drinking. College holds an annual alcohol awareness week and drug awareness week.

Identification of Problems

Admissions College application does not ask about prior substance abuse problems.

On campus Current students identified as chemically dependent may remain enrolled, but treatment is required. Training program on identifying students with potential substance abuse problems for: resident advisers, administration, student leaders. Written procedures for students and staff if substance abuse is suspected.

Support Services

On campus ACOA, support groups, private counseling.

Off campus AA, Al-Anon.

Employee assistance Program for chemically dependent employees not available. Staff working with drug/alcohol-related issues: 2 part-time.

Disciplinary Actions

Alcohol Results of infractions of alcohol regulations (see Comparative Table of Alcohol Regulations) vary by situation but can include chemical dependency assessment, counseling, warning, probation, suspension. Comments: Individual needs are considered.

Drugs For any use, possession, or sale: expulsion.

For More Information

Contact: Karen Boros, Counselor, Seton Hill College, Greensburg, PA 15601. Telephone: 412-834-2200.

SHAWNEE STATE UNIVERSITY

Portsmouth, Ohio

General Information

State-supported 4-year coed college. Founded 1986. Awards A (college transfer and terminal), B. Primary accreditation: regional. Small-town setting; 20-acre campus. Total enrollment: 2,967. Faculty: 233 (83 full-time, 150 part-time). Social organizations: 1 local fraternity, 1 local sorority.

Drug and Alcohol Information

Education

On campus Drug and alcohol education/prevention programs offered for: all students, athletes/coaches. College holds an annual alcohol awareness week and drug awareness week.

Identification of Problems

Admissions College application does not ask about prior substance abuse problems.

On campus Current students identified as chemically dependent may remain enrolled. No training program on identifying students with potential substance abuse problems. No written procedures for students and staff if substance abuse is suspected.

Support Services

On campus Private counseling.

Employee assistance Program for chemically dependent employees available.

Disciplinary Actions

Alcohol Results of infractions of alcohol regulations (see Comparative Table of Alcohol Regulations) vary by situation.

Drugs For any use, possession, or sale: varies by situation.

For More Information

Contact: Paul Crabtree, Ph.D., Director, Counseling and Assessment, Shawnee State University, 940 Second St., Portsmouth, OH 45662. Telephone: 614-354-3205 Ext. 251.

SHELDON JACKSON COLLEGE
Sitka, Alaska

General Information

Independent Presbyterian 4-year coed college. Founded 1878. Awards A (college transfer and terminal), B. Primary accreditation: regional. Small-town setting; 345-acre campus. Total enrollment: 290. Faculty: 33 (26 full-time, 7 part-time).

Drug and Alcohol Information

Education

On campus Drug and alcohol education/prevention programs offered for: all students. College holds an annual alcohol awareness week and drug awareness week.

Identification of Problems

Admissions College application does not ask about prior substance abuse problems.

On campus Current students identified as chemically dependent may remain enrolled, but treatment is required. No training program on identifying students with potential substance abuse problems. Written procedures for students and staff if substance abuse is suspected.

Support Services

On campus No support services on campus.

Employee assistance Program for chemically dependent employees not available. Staff working with drug/alcohol-related issues: 3 part-time.

Disciplinary Actions

Alcohol Results of infractions of alcohol regulations (see Comparative Table of Alcohol Regulations) vary by situation but can include chemical dependency assessment, counseling, warning, probation, suspension.

Drugs For first-time use or possession: chemical dependency assessment, counseling, probation. For subsequent use or possession: suspension. For first-time sale: suspension. For subsequent sale: expulsion.

For More Information

Contact: Bill Stenberg, Vice President for Student Services, Sheldon Jackson College, 801 Lincoln St., Sitka, AK 99835. Telephone: 907-747-5241.

SHENANDOAH COLLEGE AND CONSERVATORY
Winchester, Virginia

General Information

Independent United Methodist 5-year coed college. Founded 1875. Awards A (terminal), B, M. Primary accreditation: regional. Small-town setting; 62-acre campus. Total enrollment: 1,007. Faculty: 130 (70 full-time, 60 part-time). Social organizations: 2 national fraternities, 1 national sorority, 1 local fraternity, 1 local sorority.

Drug and Alcohol Information

Education

On campus Drug and alcohol education/prevention programs offered for: all students, athletes/coaches, faculty, administration; required for: freshmen. Authorized group concerned with responsible drinking. College holds an annual alcohol awareness week and drug awareness week.

Identification of Problems

Admissions College application question about prior substance abuse problems is used to explain past academic performance; for counseling and referral, if student is admitted; in the admissions decision.

On campus Current students identified as chemically dependent may remain enrolled, but treatment is required. Training program on identifying students with potential substance abuse problems for: resident advisers, faculty. Written procedures for students and staff if substance abuse is suspected.

Support Services

On campus ACOA, support groups, private counseling.

Employee assistance Program for chemically dependent employees not available. Staff working with drug/alcohol-related issues: 2 part-time.

Disciplinary Actions

Alcohol Results of infractions of alcohol regulations (see Comparative Table of Alcohol Regulations) vary by situation but can include chemical dependency assessment, counseling, warning, probation, suspension, expulsion.

Drugs For first-time use or possession: varies by situation. For subsequent use or possession: suspension. For any sale: expulsion.

Additional Information from the College

The College is Methodist-related, and abstinence is encouraged in regard to consumption of alcoholic beverages.

For More Information

Contact: Dr. William Berghaus, Vice President for Student Affairs, Shenandoah College and Conservatory, Winchester, VA 22601. Telephone: 703-665-4520.

SHEPHERD COLLEGE

Shepherdstown, West Virginia

General Information

State-supported 4-year coed college. Founded 1871. Awards A (college transfer and terminal), B. Primary accreditation: regional. Small-town setting; 165-acre campus. Total enrollment: 4,020. Faculty: 172 (112 full-time, 60 part-time). Social organizations: 5 national fraternities, 4 national sororities, 1 local fraternity, 2 local sororities; 25% of eligible undergraduate men and 25% of eligible undergraduate women are members.

Drug and Alcohol Information

Education

On campus Drug and alcohol education/prevention programs offered for: all students; required for: freshmen, athletes/coaches. College holds an annual alcohol awareness week and drug awareness week.

Identification of Problems

Admissions College application does not ask about prior substance abuse problems.

On campus Current students identified as chemically dependent may remain enrolled, but treatment is required. No training program on identifying students with potential substance abuse problems. Written procedures for students and staff if substance abuse is suspected.

Support Services

On campus AA, ACOA, private counseling.

Employee assistance Program for chemically dependent employees not available.

Disciplinary Actions

Alcohol Results of infractions of alcohol regulations (see Comparative Table of Alcohol Regulations) include chemical dependency assessment, counseling, warning, probation, suspension, expulsion.

Drugs For first-time use or possession: chemical dependency assessment, counseling, probation. For subsequent use or possession: varies by situation. For any sale: suspension, expulsion.

For More Information

Contact: Harry C. Young Jr., Acting Dean of Student Affairs, Shepherd College, Shepherdstown, WV 25443. Telephone: 304-876-2511 Ext. 214.

SHIMER COLLEGE

Waukegan, Illinois

General Information

Independent 4-year coed college. Founded 1853. Awards B. Primary accreditation: regional (candidate). City setting. Total enrollment: 100. Faculty: 10 (8 full-time, 2 part-time).

Drug and Alcohol Information

Education

On campus Drug and alcohol education/prevention programs offered for: all students; required for: freshmen.

Identification of Problems

Admissions College application does not ask about prior substance abuse problems.

On campus Current students identified as chemically dependent may remain enrolled, but treatment is required. No training program on identifying students with potential substance abuse problems. No written procedures for students and staff if substance abuse is suspected.

Support Services

On campus Private counseling.

Employee assistance Program for chemically dependent employees not available.

Disciplinary Actions

Alcohol Results of infractions of alcohol regulations (see Comparative Table of Alcohol Regulations) vary by situation.

Drugs For any use, possession, or sale: varies by situation.

For More Information

Contact: David Shiner, Dean, Shimer College, P.O. Box A500, Waukegan, IL 60079. Telephone: 312-623-8400.

SHIPPENSBURG UNIVERSITY OF PENNSYLVANIA

Shippensburg, Pennsylvania

General Information

State-supported 5-year coed college. Part of State System of Higher Education. Founded 1871. Awards B, M. Primary accreditation: regional. Rural setting; 200-acre campus. Total enrollment: 6,352. Faculty: 359 (311 full-time, 48 part-time). Social organizations: 10 national fraternities, 7 national sororities, 2 local fraternities, 5 local sororities; 15% of eligible undergraduate men and 15% of eligible undergraduate women are members.

Drug and Alcohol Information

Education

On campus Drug and alcohol education/prevention programs offered for: all students, athletes/coaches. Authorized group concerned with responsible drinking. College holds an annual alcohol awareness week.

Identification of Problems

Admissions College application does not ask about prior substance abuse problems.

On campus Current students identified as chemically dependent may remain enrolled, but treatment is required. Training program on identifying students with potential substance abuse problems for: resident advisers, coaches, Greek officers, faculty, administration. Written procedures for students and staff if substance abuse is suspected.

Support Services

On campus AA, Al-Anon, ACOA, private counseling.

Employee assistance Program for chemically dependent employees available.

Disciplinary Actions

Alcohol Results of infractions of alcohol regulations (see Comparative Table of Alcohol Regulations) vary by situation but can include chemical dependency assessment, counseling, warning, probation, suspension, expulsion.

Drugs For any use, possession, or sale: varies by situation.

For More Information

Contact: Dr. Betty Lu Morgan, Associate Dean of

Students, Shippensburg University of Pennsylvania, Shippensburg, PA 17257. Telephone: 717-532-1535.

SIENA HEIGHTS COLLEGE

Adrian, Michigan

General Information

Independent Roman Catholic 5-year coed college. Founded 1919. Awards A (college transfer and terminal), B, M. Primary accreditation: regional. Small-town setting; 140-acre campus. Total enrollment: 1,599. Faculty: 110 (70 full-time, 40 part-time).

Drug and Alcohol Information

Education

On campus Drug and alcohol education/prevention programs offered for: all students, faculty, administration, violators of drug and alcohol policies. Bacchus chapter: 12 members. Authorized group concerned with responsible drinking. College holds an annual alcohol awareness week and drug awareness week.

Identification of Problems

Admissions College application does not ask about prior substance abuse problems.

On campus Current students identified as chemically dependent may remain enrolled, but treatment is required. Training program on identifying students with potential substance abuse problems for: resident advisers, coaches, Greek officers, faculty, administration, staff. Written procedures for students and staff if substance abuse is suspected.

Support Services

On campus AA, Al-Anon, ACOA, private counseling.

Employee assistance Program for chemically dependent employees available. Staff working with drug/alcohol-related issues: 1 full-time and 1 part-time.

Disciplinary Actions

Alcohol Results of infractions of alcohol regulations (see Comparative Table of Alcohol Regulations) include chemical dependency assessment, counseling, probation, suspension.

Drugs For first-time use, possession, or sale: suspension from residence hall. For subsequent use: varies by situation. For subsequent possession or sale: suspension, expulsion.

For More Information

Contact: Frederick A. Dobens, Dean of Students, Siena Heights College, 1247 E. Siena Heights Dr., Adrian, MI 49221-1796. Telephone: 517-263-0731 Ext. 251.

SIERRA NEVADA COLLEGE

Incline Village, Nevada

General Information

Independent 4-year coed college. Founded 1969. Awards B. Primary accreditation: regional. Small-town setting; 20-acre campus. Total enrollment: 302. Faculty: 52 (10 full-time, 42 part-time).

Drug and Alcohol Information

Education

On campus Drug and alcohol education/prevention programs not offered.

Identification of Problems

Admissions College application does not ask about prior substance abuse problems.

On campus Current students identified as chemically dependent may remain enrolled. No training program on identifying students with potential substance abuse problems. No written procedures for students and staff if substance abuse is suspected.

Support Services

On campus No support services on campus.

Employee assistance Program for chemically dependent employees not available.

Disciplinary Actions

Alcohol Results of infractions of alcohol regulations (see Comparative Table of Alcohol Regulations) include warning.

Drugs For first-time use or possession: warning. For subsequent use or possession; suspension. For first-time sale: suspension. For subsequent sale: expulsion.

For More Information

Contact: David Fenimore, Dean of Students, Sierra Nevada College, P.O. Box 4269, Incline Village, NV 89450. Telephone: 702-831-1314.

SIMPSON COLLEGE

Indianola, Iowa

General Information

Independent Methodist 4-year coed college. Founded 1860. Awards B. Primary accreditation: regional. Small-town setting; 63-acre campus. Total enrollment: 1,710. Faculty: 134 (67 full-time, 67 part-time). Social organizations: 3 national fraternities, 3 national sororities, 1 local fraternity; 36% of eligible undergraduate men and 35% of eligible undergraduate women are members.

Drug and Alcohol Information

Education

On campus Drug and alcohol education/prevention programs offered for: all students. Bacchus chapter: 15 members. College holds an annual alcohol awareness week.

Identification of Problems

Admissions College application does not ask about prior substance abuse problems.

On campus Current students identified as chemically dependent may remain enrolled, but treatment is required. No training program on identifying students with potential substance abuse problems. No written procedures for students and staff if substance abuse is suspected.

Support Services

On campus AA.

Employee assistance Program for chemically dependent employees available.

Disciplinary Actions

Alcohol Results of infractions of alcohol regulations (see Comparative Table of Alcohol Regulations) vary by situation but can include chemical dependency assessment, counseling, warning, probation, suspension.

Drugs For first-time use or possession: chemical dependency assessment, counseling, probation. For

Simpson College (continued)

subsequent use or possession: suspension. For any sale: suspension.

For More Information

Contact: Jim Thorius, Vice President for Student Development, Simpson College, 701 N. C St., Indianola, IA 50125. Telephone: 515-961-1667.

SIOUX FALLS COLLEGE

Sioux Falls, South Dakota

General Information

Independent American Baptist 5-year coed college. Founded 1883. Awards A (college transfer), B, M. Primary accreditation: regional. City setting; 14-acre campus. Total enrollment: 900. Faculty: 66 (40 full-time, 26 part-time).

Drug and Alcohol Information

Education

On campus Drug and alcohol education/prevention programs offered for: all students. College holds an annual alcohol awareness week and drug awareness week.

Identification of Problems

Admissions College application does not ask about prior substance abuse problems.

On campus Current students identified as chemically dependent may remain enrolled, but treatment is required. Training program on identifying students with potential substance abuse problems for: resident advisers. Written procedures for students and staff if substance abuse is suspected.

Support Services

On campus Private counseling.

Employee assistance Program for chemically dependent employees not available.

Disciplinary Actions

Alcohol Results of infractions of alcohol regulations (see Comparative Table of Alcohol Regulations) include chemical dependency assessment, warning.

Drugs For first-time use, possession, or sale: varies by situation—counseling, warning. For subsequent use, possession, or sale: expulsion.

For More Information

Contact: Barbara Dewald, Assistant Dean of Students, Sioux Falls College, 1501 S. Prairie Ave., Sioux Falls, SD 57105. Telephone: 605-331-6594.

SLIPPERY ROCK UNIVERSITY OF PENNSYLVANIA

Slippery Rock, Pennsylvania

General Information

State-supported 5-year coed college. Part of State System of Higher Education. Founded 1889. Awards B, M. Primary accreditation: regional. Rural setting; 611-acre campus. Total enrollment: 7,360. Faculty: 381 (369 full-time, 12 part-time). Social organizations: 10 national fraternities, 8 national sororities; 16% of eligible undergraduate men and 13% of eligible undergraduate women are members.

Drug and Alcohol Information

Education

On campus Drug and alcohol education/prevention programs offered for: all students, athletes/coaches, faculty, administration, first-time alcohol offenders. Authorized group concerned with responsible drinking (SADD). College holds an annual alcohol awareness week and drug awareness week.

Identification of Problems

Admissions College application does not ask about prior substance abuse problems. Drug and alcohol questions appear on health history form.

On campus Current students identified as chemically dependent may remain enrolled. Training program on identifying students with potential substance abuse problems for: resident advisers, administration, health center staff. Written procedures for students and staff if substance abuse is suspected.

Support Services

On campus AA, ACOA, support groups, private counseling.

Employee assistance Program for chemically dependent employees available. Staff working with drug/alcohol-related issues: 2+ part-time.

Disciplinary Actions

Alcohol Results of infractions of alcohol regulations (see Comparative Table of Alcohol Regulations) vary by situation but can include chemical dependency assessment, counseling, warning, probation, suspension, expulsion.

Drugs For first-time use, possession, or sale: varies by situation—chemical dependency assessement, counseling, probation. For subsequent use, possession, or sale: varies by situation.

Additional Information from the College

The University's drug and alcohol program is designed as an educational process, not as a disciplinary action. Should subsequent violations occur, disciplinary action may be taken.

For More Information

Contact: Dr. Alan Rusnak, Director, Counseling Center, Maltby Center, Slippery Rock University of Pennsylvania, Slippery Rock, PA 16057. Telephone: 412-794-7255.

SMITH COLLEGE

Northampton, Massachusetts

General Information

Independent 5-year women's college. Founded 1871. Awards B, M, D. Primary accreditation: regional. Small-town setting; 125-acre campus. Total enrollment: 2,834. Faculty: 296 (247 full-time, 49 part-time).

Drug and Alcohol Information

Education

On campus Drug and alcohol education/prevention programs offered for: all students. Authorized group concerned with responsible drinking. College holds an annual alcohol awareness week and will hold a drug awareness week this year.

Identification of Problems

Admissions College application does not ask about prior substance abuse problems.

On campus Current students identified as chemically dependent may remain enrolled. Training program on identifying students with potential substance abuse problems for: resident advisers, Alcohol Peers. Written procedures for students and staff if substance abuse is suspected.

Support Services

On campus AA, ACOA, private counseling.

Employee assistance Program for chemically dependent employees not available. Staff working with drug/alcohol-related issues: 5 part-time.

Disciplinary Actions

Alcohol Results of infractions of alcohol regulations (see Comparative Table of Alcohol Regulations) vary by situation.

Drugs For any use, possession, or sale: varies by situation.

For More Information

Contact: Connie Peterson, Health Educator, Health Services, Smith College, Northampton, MA 01063. Telephone: 413-585-2824.

SONOMA STATE UNIVERSITY

Rohnert Park, California

General Information

State-supported 5-year coed college. Part of California State University System. Founded 1961. Awards B, M. Primary accreditation: regional. Small-town setting; 220-acre campus. Total enrollment: 6,697. Faculty: 318 (161 full-time, 157 part-time). Social organizations: 4 local fraternities, 3 local sororities; 5% of eligible undergraduate men and 2% of eligible undergraduate women are members.

Drug and Alcohol Information

Education

On campus Drug and alcohol education/prevention programs offered for: all students, athletes/coaches, faculty, administration, educational equity participants. College holds an annual alcohol awareness week and drug awareness week.

Identification of Problems

Admissions College application does not ask about prior substance abuse problems.

On campus Current students identified as chemically dependent may remain enrolled. Training program on identifying students with potential substance abuse problems for: resident advisers, coaches, Greek officers, faculty, administration. No written procedures for students and staff if substance abuse is suspected.

Support Services

On campus AA, NA, Al-Anon, ACOA, private counseling.

Employee assistance Program for chemically dependent employees available.

Disciplinary Actions

Alcohol Results of infractions of alcohol regulations (see Comparative Table of Alcohol Regulations) vary by situation.

Drugs For any use, possession, or sale: varies by situation.

For More Information

Contact: Ann Strack, Coordinator, Alcohol and Drug Education Program, Sonoma State University, 1801 E. Cotati Ave., Rohnert Park, CA 94928. Telephone: 707-664-2850.

SOUTH CAROLINA STATE COLLEGE

Orangeburg, South Carolina

General Information

State-supported 5-year coed college. Founded 1896. Awards B, M, D. Primary accreditation: regional. Small-town setting; 147-acre campus. Total enrollment: 4,399. Faculty: 269 (262 full-time, 7 part-time). Social organizations: 4 national fraternities, 4 national sororities, 4 local fraternities, 4 local sororities; 10% of eligible undergraduate men and 12% of eligible undergraduate women are members.

Drug and Alcohol Information

Education

On campus Drug and alcohol education/prevention programs offered for: all students, athletes/coaches, faculty, administration, members of the community. Bacchus chapter: 30 members. College holds an annual alcohol awareness week and drug awareness week.

Identification of Problems

Admissions College application does not ask about prior substance abuse problems.

On campus Current students identified as chemically dependent may remain enrolled, but treatment is required. Training program on identifying students with potential substance abuse problems for: resident advisers, peer counselors. No written procedures for students and staff if substance abuse is suspected.

Support Services

On campus Counseling Center, Commission on Alcohol and Drugs.

Employee assistance Program for chemically dependent employees available.

Disciplinary Actions

Alcohol Results of infractions of alcohol regulations (see Comparative Table of Alcohol Regulations) vary by situation but can include chemical dependency assessment, counseling, warning, probation, suspension, expulsion.

Drugs For any use, possession, or sale: varies by situation. Comments: As a historically black institution, South Carolina State College approaches drug problems with a culturally sensitive perspective.

For More Information

Contact: Dr. Robert Mays, Counseling Psychologist, South Carolina State College, P.O. Box 2008, Orangeburg, SC 29117. Telephone: 803-536-7245.

SOUTH DAKOTA SCHOOL OF MINES AND TECHNOLOGY

Rapid City, South Dakota

General Information

State-supported comprehensive coed institution. Founded 1885. Awards B, M, D. Primary accreditation: regional. City setting; 120-acre campus. Total enrollment: 2,062. Faculty: 126 (92 full-time, 34 part-time). Social organizations: 5 national fraternities, 1 national sorority, 1 local fraternity, 2 local sororities; 24% of eligible undergraduate men and 28% of eligible undergraduate women are members.

Drug and Alcohol Information

Education

On campus Drug and alcohol education/prevention programs offered for: all students, athletes/coaches, faculty, administration, staff. Authorized group concerned with responsible drinking. College holds an annual alcohol awareness week.

Identification of Problems

Admissions College application does not ask about prior substance abuse problems.

On campus Current students identified as chemically dependent may remain enrolled, but treatment is required. Training program on identifying students with potential substance abuse problems for: resident advisers, coaches, Greek officers, faculty, administratin, staff. No written procedures for students and staff if substance abuse is suspected.

Support Services

On campus Private counseling.

Employee assistance Program for chemically dependent employees not available.

Disciplinary Actions

Alcohol Results of infractions of alcohol regulations (see Comparative Table of Alcohol Regulations) vary by situation but can include counseling, warning. Conference required with Dean and/or Assistant Dean of Students.

Drugs For first-time use or possession: varies by situation—counseling, warning, probation. For subsequent use or possession: probation. For any sale: suspension.

Additional Information from the College

The School contracts with an off-campus agency for substance use awareness sessions. The agency representative and personnel in the Dean of Students Office are referral sources for substance use problems.

For More Information

Contact: Carol L. Kiefer, Assistant Dean of Students, South Dakota School of Mines and Technology, 501 E. Saint Joseph, Rapid City, SD 57701. Telephone: 605-394-2416.

SOUTH DAKOTA STATE UNIVERSITY

Brookings, South Dakota

General Information

State-supported comprehensive coed institution. Founded 1881. Awards A (college transfer), B, M, D. Primary accreditation: regional. Rural setting; 228-acre campus. Total enrollment: 6,871. Faculty: 490 (332 full-time, 158 part-time). Social organizations: 4 national fraternities, 2 national sororities, 1 local fraternity; 5% of eligible undergraduate men and 2% of eligible undergraduate women are members.

Drug and Alcohol Information

Education

On campus Drug and alcohol education/prevention programs offered for: all students. Authorized group concerned with responsible drinking. College holds an annual alcohol awareness week.

Identification of Problems

Admissions College application does not ask about prior substance abuse problems.

On campus Current students identified as chemically dependent may remain enrolled. Training program on identifying students with potential substance abuse problems for: resident advisers, Greek officers, counselors, physicians. Written procedures for students and staff if substance abuse is suspected.

Support Services

On campus AA, private counseling, referral to off-campus services.

Employee assistance Program for chemically dependent employees not available. Staff working with drug/alcohol-related issues: 4 part-time.

Disciplinary Actions

Alcohol Results of infractions of alcohol regulations (see Comparative Table of Alcohol Regulations) include chemical dependency assessment, counseling, warning, appropriate judicial sanctions (behavioral contracts).

Drugs For any use: varies by situation. For first-time possession or sale: probation, suspension, expulsion. For subsequent possession or sale: varies by situation.

Additional Information from the College

The primary emphasis is on education/awareness. Frequent use of community services occurs through the referral system, which may originate with health service, counseling, or residence hall staff, or academic advisers.

For More Information

Contact: Don Smith, Director, Student Health and Counseling, 202 W. Hall, Box 510, South Dakota State University, Brookings, SD 57007. Telephone: 605-688-4157.

SOUTHEASTERN COLLEGE OF THE ASSEMBLIES OF GOD

Lakeland, Florida

General Information

Independent 4-year coed college, affiliated with Assemblies of God. Founded 1935. Awards B. Primary accreditation: regional and AABC. City setting; 57-acre campus. Total enrollment: 1,155. Faculty: 71 (51 full-time, 20 part-time).

Drug and Alcohol Information

Education

On campus Drug and alcohol education/prevention programs offered for: all students.

Identification of Problems

Admissions College application question about prior substance abuse problems is used for counseling and referral, if student is admitted; in the admissions decision.

On campus Current students identified as chemically dependent may not remain enrolled. No training program on identifying students with potential substance abuse problems. No written procedures for students and staff if substance abuse is suspected.

Support Services

On campus Private counseling.

Employee assistance Program for chemically dependent employees not available.

Disciplinary Actions

Alcohol Results of infractions of alcohol regulations (see Comparative Table of Alcohol Regulations) vary by situation but can include counseling, probation, suspension.

Drugs For any use, possession, or sale: suspension.

Additional Information from the College

The College is a Christian institution and has very few drug/alcohol incidents. The focus is on helping those in the community who have these problems and on keeping students informed of the issues and how to deal with them.

For More Information

Contact: Charles W. Spong, Vice President, Southeastern College of the Assemblies of God, 1000 Longfellow Blvd., Lakeland, FL 33801. Telephone: 813-665-4404.

SOUTHEASTERN LOUISIANA UNIVERSITY

Hammond, Louisiana

General Information

State-supported 5-year coed college. Founded 1925. Awards A (terminal), B, M. Primary accreditation: regional. Small-town setting; 365-acre campus. Total enrollment: 8,655. Faculty: 377 (271 full-time, 106 part-time). Social organizations: 7 national fraternities, 5 national sororities, 2 local fraternities, 2 local sororities; 10% of eligible undergraduate men and 10% of eligible undergraduate women are members.

Drug and Alcohol Information

Education

On campus Drug and alcohol education/prevention programs offered for: all students; required for: athletes/coaches, resident advisers. College holds an annual alcohol awareness week.

Identification of Problems

Admissions College application does not ask about prior substance abuse problems.

On campus Current students identified as chemically dependent may remain enrolled, but treatment is required. Training program on identifying students with potential substance abuse problems for: resident advisers, coaches, housing staff. No written procedures for students and staff if substance abuse is suspected.

Support Services

On campus Private counseling.

Employee assistance Program for chemically dependent employees not available. Staff working with drug/alcohol-related issues: 4 part-time.

Disciplinary Actions

Alcohol Results of infractions of alcohol regulations (see Comparative Table of Alcohol Regulations) include chemical dependency assessment, counseling, warning, probation.

Drugs For first-time use or possession: varies by situation—counseling, probation. For first-time sale: varies by situation—suspension. For subsequent use, possession, or sale: suspension.

For More Information

Contact: Dr. Tom Terrell, Director, Counseling Center, Southeastern Louisiana University, P.O. Box 387, Hammond, LA 70402. Telephone: 504-549-3894.

SOUTHEASTERN MASSACHUSETTS UNIVERSITY

North Dartmouth, Massachusetts

General Information

State-supported 5-year coed college. Part of Massachusetts State University System. Founded 1895. Awards B, M. Primary accreditation: regional. Small-town setting; 710-acre campus. Total enrollment: 6,162. Faculty: 440 (359 full-time, 81 part-time). Social organizations: 1 national fraternity, 1 national sorority; 1% of eligible undergraduate men and 1% of eligible undergraduate women are members.

Drug and Alcohol Information

Education

On campus Drug and alcohol education/prevention programs offered for: all students, athletes/coaches, faculty, administration. Authorized group concerned with responsible drinking. College holds an annual alcohol awareness week and drug awareness week.

Identification of Problems

Admissions College application question about prior substance abuse problems.

On campus Current students identified as chemically dependent may remain enrolled, but treatment is required. Training program on identifying students with potential substance abuse problems for: resident advisers and anyone else who is interested. No written procedures for students and staff if substance abuse is suspected.

Support Services

On campus AA, ACOA, private counseling.

Employee assistance Program for chemically dependent employees available. Staff working with drug/alcohol-related issues: 1 part-time.

Disciplinary Actions

Alcohol Results of infractions of alcohol regulations (see Comparative Table of Alcohol Regulations) vary by situation.

Drugs For first-time use: counseling, warning. For first-time possession: varies by situation—counseling, warning. For subsequent use or possession: counseling, probation. For any sale: varies by situation. Comments: For any sale, police are notified and student is prosecuted to the full extent of the law.

Southeastern Massachusetts University (continued)

For More Information

Contact: Richard Potter, Alcohol/Drug Education Coordinator, Southeastern Massachusetts University, Old Westport Rd., North Dartmouth, MA 02747. Telephone: 508-999-8983.

SOUTHEASTERN OKLAHOMA STATE UNIVERSITY

Durant, Oklahoma

General Information

State-supported 5-year coed college. Founded 1909. Awards B, M. Primary accreditation: regional. Small-town setting; 170-acre campus. Total enrollment: 3,632. Faculty: 174 (154 full-time, 20 part-time). Social organizations: 2 national fraternities, 2 national sororities; 3% of eligible undergraduate men and 1% of eligible undergraduate women are members.

Drug and Alcohol Information

Education

On campus Drug and alcohol education/prevention programs offered for: all students.

Identification of Problems

Admissions College application does not ask about prior substance abuse problems.

On campus Current students identified as chemically dependent may remain enrolled. No training program on identifying students with potential substance abuse problems. Written procedures for students and staff if substance abuse is suspected.

Support Services

On campus AA, support groups (mental health center), private counseling.

Employee assistance Program for chemically dependent employees not available.

Disciplinary Actions

Alcohol Results of infractions of alcohol regulations (see Comparative Table of Alcohol Regulations) vary by situation but can include counseling, warning. Comments: Suspension on first offense possible if infraction affects other students.

Drugs For first-time use, possession, or sale: probation, suspension. For subsequent use, possession, or sale: probation, suspension, expulsion.

For More Information

Contact: Lahoma E. Clark, Guidance Counselor, Southeastern Oklahoma State University, Durant, OK 74701. Telephone: 405-924-0121 Ext. 555.

SOUTHEAST MISSOURI STATE UNIVERSITY

Cape Girardeau, Missouri

General Information

State-supported 5-year coed college. Founded 1873. Awards A (terminal), B, M. Primary accreditation: regional. Small-town setting; 200-acre campus. Total enrollment: 8,778. Faculty: 500 (420 full-time, 80 part-time). Social organizations: 10 national fraternities, 8 national sororities; 13% of eligible undergraduate men and 12% of eligible undergraduate women are members.

Drug and Alcohol Information

Education

On campus Drug and alcohol education/prevention programs offered for: all students; required for: alcohol policy violators. Authorized group concerned with responsible drinking. College holds an annual alcohol awareness week.

Identification of Problems

Admissions College application does not ask about prior substance abuse problems.

On campus Current students identified as chemically dependent may remain enrolled. Training program on identifying students with potential substance abuse problems for: resident advisers, staff. No written procedures for students and staff if substance abuse is suspected.

Support Services

On campus AA, Al-Anon, ACOA, private counseling.

Employee assistance Program for chemically dependent employees not available. Staff working with drug/alcohol-related issues: 1 part-time.

Disciplinary Actions

Alcohol Results of infractions of alcohol regulations (see Comparative Table of Alcohol Regulations) include chemical dependency assessment, counseling, probation, suspension, expulsion, alcohol/drug education class.

Drugs For first-time use or possession: chemical dependency assessment, suspension (held in abeyance if student contracts for treatment). For subsequent use or possession: suspension, expulsion. For any sale: expulsion.

For More Information

Contact: Patricia Murray, Coordinator, Alcohol/Drug Education Services, Southeast Missouri State University, Cape Girardeau, MO 63701. Telephone: 314-651-2270.

SOUTHERN ARKANSAS UNIVERSITY

Magnolia, Arkansas

General Information

State-supported 5-year coed college. Part of Southern Arkansas University System. Founded 1909. Awards A (college transfer and terminal), B, M. Primary accreditation: regional. Small-town setting; 781-acre campus. Total enrollment: 2,159. Faculty: 116. Social organizations: 5 national fraternities, 2 national sororities, 3 local sororities; 10% of eligible undergraduate men and 8% of eligible undergraduate women are members.

Drug and Alcohol Information

Education

On campus Drug and alcohol education/prevention programs offered for: all students; required for: freshmen. Authorized group concerned with responsible drinking. College holds an annual alcohol awareness week and drug awareness week.

Identification of Problems

Admissions College application does not ask about prior substance abuse problems.

On campus Current students identified as chemically dependent may remain enrolled, but treatment is required. Training program on identifying students with potential substance abuse problems for: resident advisers. Written procedures for students and staff if substance abuse is suspected.

Support Services

On campus Private counseling.

Employee assistance Program for chemically dependent employees available.

Disciplinary Actions

Alcohol Results of infractions of alcohol regulations (see Comparative Table of Alcohol Regulations) include counseling, warning, probation, suspension.

Drugs For first-time use or possession: varies by situation. For subsequent use or possession: counseling, suspension. For first-time sale: suspension. For subsequent sale: expulsion.

For More Information

Contact: Dean J. Marshall, Assistant Dean for Activities, Southern Arkansas University, Box 1421, Magnolia, AR 71753. Telephone: 501-235-4041.

SOUTHERN CALIFORNIA INSTITUTE OF ARCHITECTURE

Santa Monica, California

General Information

Independent 5-year specialized coed college. Founded 1972. Awards B, M. City setting. Total enrollment: 389. Faculty: 79 (40 full-time, 39 part-time).

Drug and Alcohol Information

Education

On campus Drug and alcohol education/prevention programs not offered.

Identification of Problems

Admissions College application does not ask about prior substance abuse problems.

On campus Current students identified as chemically dependent may not remain enrolled. No training program on identifying students with potential substance abuse problems. No written procedures for students and staff if substance abuse is suspected.

Support Services

On campus No support services on campus.

Employee assistance Program for chemically dependent employees not available. Staff working with drug/alcohol-related issues: 1 part-time.

Disciplinary Actions

Alcohol Results of infractions of alcohol regulations (see Comparative Table of Alcohol Regulations) vary by situation.

Drugs For first-time use or possession: suspension. For subsequent use or possession: expulsion. For any sale: expulsion.

For More Information

Contact: Bill Simonian, Counselor, Southern California Institute of Architecture, 1800 Berkeley St., Santa Monica, CA 90404. Telephone: 213-829-3482.

SOUTHERN ILLINOIS UNIVERSITY AT CARBONDALE

Carbondale, Illinois

General Information

State-supported comprehensive coed institution. Part of Southern Illinois University. Founded 1869. Awards A (terminal), B, M, D. Primary accreditation: regional. Rural setting; 900-acre campus. Total enrollment: 24,227. Social organizations: 16 national fraternities, 9 national sororities, local fraternities, local sororities; 6% of eligible undergraduate men and 6% of eligible undergraduate women are members.

Drug and Alcohol Information

Education

On campus Drug and alcohol education/prevention programs offered for: all students, athletes/coaches, high-risk groups. Authorized group concerned with responsible drinking. College holds an annual alcohol awareness week and drug awareness week.

Identification of Problems

Admissions College application does not ask about prior substance abuse problems.

On campus Current students identified as chemically dependent may remain enrolled. Training program on identifying students with potential substance abuse problems for: resident advisers. No written procedures for students and staff if substance abuse is suspected.

Support Services

On campus ACOA, support groups (alcohol education, Rethinking about Drinking), individual, group counseling.

Employee assistance Program for chemically dependent employees not available. Staff working with drug/alcohol-related issues: 3 full-time and 3 part-time.

Disciplinary Actions

Alcohol Results of infractions of alcohol regulations (see Comparative Table of Alcohol Regulations) include chemical dependency assessment, counseling, warning, probation.

Drugs For first-time use or possession: warning. For first-time sale: varies by situation. For subsequent use, possession, or sale: varies by situation.

For More Information

Contact: Cheryl Presley, Coordinator, Drug Prevention Program, Wellness Center, Southern Illinois University at Carbondale, Carbondale, IL 62901. Telephone: 618-536-4441.

SOUTHERN ILLINOIS UNIVERSITY AT EDWARDSVILLE
Edwardsville, Illinois

General Information
State-supported comprehensive coed institution. Part of Southern Illinois University. Founded 1957. Awards B, M, D. Primary accreditation: regional. Rural setting; 2,600-acre campus. Total enrollment: 11,352. Faculty: 743 (560 full-time, 183 part-time). Social organizations: 8 national fraternities, 5 national sororities, 4 local fraternities, 2 local sororities.

Drug and Alcohol Information
Education
On campus Drug and alcohol education/prevention programs offered for: all students; required for: athletes/coaches, faculty, administration, resident advisers, all new residents. Authorized group concerned with responsible drinking. College holds an annual alcohol awareness week and drug awareness week.

Identification of Problems
Admissions College application does not ask about prior substance abuse problems.

On campus Current students identified as chemically dependent may remain enrolled. Training program on identifying students with potential substance abuse problems for: resident advisers, coaches, Greek officers, faculty, administration. Written procedures for students and staff if substance abuse is suspected.

Support Services
On campus AA, private counseling, resource advocates.

Employee assistance Program for chemically dependent employees being planned. Staff working with drug/alcohol-related issues: 1 full-time and 30 part-time.

Disciplinary Actions
Alcohol Results of infractions of alcohol regulations (see Comparative Table of Alcohol Regulations) include warning, probation, suspension.

Drugs For first-time use, possession, or sale: varies by situation—suspension. For subsequent use, possession, or sale: suspension, expulsion.

Additional Information from the College
The Alcohol and Drug Awareness Program provides substance abuse education, consultation, and referral to all students, faculty, and staff. Educational presentations are made to all segments of the University on a regular basis. Cooperative efforts have been undertaken with Student Government to provide nonalcoholic student events and substance abuse education. Orientation programs incorporate drug and alcohol information. Special mandatory orientation programs emphasizing drug and alcohol issues have been implemented for athletes and new residents of University housing.

For More Information
Contact: Daniel Herbst, Health Service Counselor, Box 1055, Southern Illinois University at Edwardsville, Edwardsville, IL 62026. Telephone: 618-692-2855.

SOUTHERN METHODIST UNIVERSITY
Dallas, Texas

General Information
Independent comprehensive coed institution. Founded 1911. Awards B, M, D. Primary accreditation: regional. Metropolitan setting; 164-acre campus. Total enrollment: 8,944. Faculty: 471 full-time. Social organizations: 15 national fraternities, 12 national sororities; 45% of eligible undergraduate men and 52% of eligible undergraduate women are members.

Drug and Alcohol Information
Education
On campus Drug and alcohol education/prevention programs offered for: all students; required for: freshmen. Bacchus chapter: 20 members. College holds an annual alcohol awareness week and drug awareness week.

Identification of Problems
Admissions College application does not ask about prior substance abuse problems.

On campus Current students identified as chemically dependent may remain enrolled. Training program on identifying students with potential substance abuse problems for: resident advisers, coaches, Greek officers, student helpers. Written procedures for students and staff if substance abuse is suspected.

Support Services
On campus AA, ACOA, support groups.

Employee assistance Program for chemically dependent employees not available. Staff working with drug/alcohol-related issues: 1 full-time and 3 part-time.

Disciplinary Actions
Alcohol Results of infractions of alcohol regulations (see Comparative Table of Alcohol Regulations) vary by situation but can include chemical dependency assessment, counseling.

Drugs For first-time use: probation. For subsequent use: varies by situation. For any possession or sale: suspension.

For More Information
Contact: Sam Brito, Coordinator, Alcohol/Drug Prevention Program, Hughes-Trigg Student Building, Southern Methodist University, Dallas, TX 75275. Telephone: 214-692-4564.

SOUTHERN OREGON STATE COLLEGE
Ashland, Oregon

General Information
State-supported 5-year coed college. Founded 1926. Awards A (terminal), B, M. Primary accreditation: regional. Small-town setting; 175-acre campus. Total enrollment: 4,853. Faculty: 288 (188 full-time, 100 part-time).

Drug and Alcohol Information
Education
On campus Drug and alcohol education/prevention

programs offered for: all students. College holds an annual alcohol awareness week and drug awareness week.

Identification of Problems

Admissions College application does not ask about prior substance abuse problems.

On campus Current students identified as chemically dependent may remain enrolled, but treatment is required. Training program on identifying students with potential substance abuse problems for: resident advisers, coaches, faculty, administration. Written procedures for students and staff if substance abuse is suspected.

Support Services

On campus AA, NA, Al-Anon, ACOA, support groups.

Employee assistance Program for chemically dependent employees available. Staff working with drug/alcohol-related issues: 2 part-time.

Disciplinary Actions

Alcohol Results of infractions of alcohol regulations (see Comparative Table of Alcohol Regulations) include chemical dependency assessment, counseling, warning, probation, suspension, expulsion.

Drugs For first-time use: For any use, possession, or sale: varies by situation—chemical dependency assessment, warning, probation. For subsequent use: varies by situation—suspension, expulsion. For first-time possession: varies by situation—warning, probation. For subsequent possession: varies by situation—probation, suspension. For first-time sale: varies by situation—probation, suspension, expulsion. For subsequent sale: varies by situation—suspension, expulsion.

For More Information

Contact: Joseph Fischer, Director of Residential Life, Southern Oregon State College, Siskiyou Blvd., Ashland, OR 97520. Telephone: 503-482-6377.

SOUTHERN VERMONT COLLEGE

Bennington, Vermont

General Information

Independent 4-year coed college. Founded 1926. Awards A (college transfer), B. Primary accreditation: regional. Small-town setting; 371-acre campus. Total enrollment: 635. Faculty: 56 (27 full-time, 29 part-time).

Drug and Alcohol Information

Education

On campus Drug and alcohol education/prevention programs offered for: all students, athletes/coaches, faculty, administration; required for: resident advisers. Authorized group concerned with responsible drinking. College holds an annual alcohol awareness week and drug awareness week.

Identification of Problems

Admissions College application does not ask about prior substance abuse problems.

On campus Current students identified as chemically dependent may remain enrolled, but treatment may be required. Training program on identifying students with potential substance abuse problems for: resident advisers. Written procedures being developed for students and staff to follow if substance abuse is suspected.

Support Services

On campus AA, Al-Anon, support groups. Staff working with drug/alcohol-related issues: 1 full-time and about 10 part-time.

Disciplinary Actions

Alcohol Results of infractions of alcohol regulations (see Comparative Table of Alcohol Regulations) include warning, probation, suspension, expulsion.

Drugs For any use, possession, or sale: varies by situation.

Additional Information from the College

It is expected that programming and policy will be developed in 1988–89, the first year that the College has had a full-time substance abuse specialist on campus.

For More Information

Contact: Laurie Waisel, Substance Abuse Program Coordinator, Southern Vermont College, Monument Rd., Bennington, VT 05201. Telephone: 802-442-5427.

SOUTHWESTERN ASSEMBLIES OF GOD COLLEGE

Waxahachie, Texas

General Information

Independent 4-year coed college, affiliated with Assemblies of God. Founded 1927. Awards A (college transfer and terminal), B. Primary accreditation: AABC. Small-town setting; 70-acre campus. Total enrollment: 622.

Drug and Alcohol Information

Education

On campus Drug and alcohol education/prevention programs offered for: all students.

Identification of Problems

Admissions College application question about prior substance abuse problems is used in the admissions decision.

On campus Current students identified as chemically dependent may not remain enrolled. No training program on identifying students with potential substance abuse problems. Written procedures for students and staff if substance abuse is suspected.

Support Services

On campus No support services on campus.

Disciplinary Actions

Alcohol Results of infractions of alcohol regulations (see Comparative Table of Alcohol Regulations) include probation, suspension, expulsion.

Drugs For any use or possession: suspension. For any sale: expulsion.

For More Information

Contact: Peggy McDaniel, College Counselor, Southwestern Assemblies of God College, 1200 Sycamore St., Waxahachie, TX 75165. Telephone: 214-937-4010.

SOUTHWESTERN COLLEGE
Phoenix, Arizona

General Information
Independent Conservative Baptist 4-year coed college. Founded 1960. Awards A (college transfer), B. Primary accreditation: regional (candidate) and AABC. Metropolitan setting; 17-acre campus. Total enrollment: 147. Faculty: 34 (9 full-time, 25 part-time).

Drug and Alcohol Information
Education
On campus Drug and alcohol education/prevention programs required for: freshmen.

Identification of Problems
Admissions College application question about prior substance abuse problems is used to explain past academic performance; for counseling and referral, if student is admitted; in the admissions decision.

On campus Current students identified as chemically dependent may not remain enrolled. Training program on identifying students with potential substance abuse problems for: resident advisers. Written procedures for students and staff if substance abuse is suspected.

Support Services
On campus No support services on campus.

Employee assistance Program for chemically dependent employees available.

Disciplinary Actions
Alcohol Results of infractions of alcohol regulations (see Comparative Table of Alcohol Regulations) include probation, suspension, expulsion.

Drugs For first-time use or possession: probation. For subsequent use or possession: suspension. For any sale: suspension.

For More Information
Contact: Joel Wilson, Dean of Students, Southwestern College, 2625 E. Cactus Rd., Phoenix, AZ 85032. Telephone: 602-992-6101.

SOUTHWESTERN COLLEGE
Winfield, Kansas

General Information
Independent United Methodist 5-year coed college. Founded 1885. Awards B, M (M in education). Primary accreditation: regional. Small-town setting; 38-acre campus. Total enrollment: 663. Faculty: 72 (50 full-time, 22 part-time). Social organizations: 3 local fraternities, 3 local sororities; 65% of eligible undergraduate men and 75% of eligible undergraduate women are members.

Drug and Alcohol Information
Education
On campus Drug and alcohol education/prevention programs offered for: all students. College holds an annual alcohol awareness week.

Identification of Problems
Admissions College application does not ask about prior substance abuse problems.

On campus Current students identified as chemically dependent may remain enrolled, but treatment is required. No training program on identifying students with potential substance abuse problems. Written procedures for students and staff if substance abuse is suspected.

Support Services
On campus No support services on campus.

Employee assistance Program for chemically dependent employees not available.

Disciplinary Actions
Alcohol Results of infractions of alcohol regulations (see Comparative Table of Alcohol Regulations) vary by situation but can include chemical dependency assessment. Comments: An organization may be put on probation.

Drugs For first-time use or possession: chemical dependency assessment. For subsequent use or possession: varies by situation. For any sale: varies by situation—expulsion.

For More Information
Contact: Dr. Sue Robinson, Dean of Students, Southwestern College, 100 College St., Winfield, KS 67156. Telephone: 316-221-4150 Ext. 277.

SOUTHWESTERN UNIVERSITY
Georgetown, Texas

General Information
Independent Methodist 4-year coed college. Founded 1840. Awards B. Primary accreditation: regional. Small-town setting; 500-acre campus. Total enrollment: 1,171. Faculty: 111 (75 full-time, 36 part-time). Social organizations: 4 national fraternities, 4 national sororities; 44% of eligible undergraduate men and 41% of eligible undergraduate women are members.

Drug and Alcohol Information
Education
On campus Drug and alcohol education/prevention programs not offered. Authorized group concerned with responsible drinking.

Identification of Problems
Admissions College application does not ask about prior substance abuse problems.

On campus Current students identified as chemically dependent may remain enrolled. Training program on identifying students with potential substance abuse problems for: resident advisers. No written procedures for students and staff if substance abuse is suspected.

Support Services
On campus ACOA.

Employee assistance Program for chemically dependent employees not available.

Disciplinary Actions
Alcohol Results of infractions of alcohol regulations (see Comparative Table of Alcohol Regulations) vary by situation.

Drugs For any use: varies by situation. For first-time possession: varies by situation—probation. For subsequent possession: suspension. For any sale: expulsion.

For More Information

Contact: Roger Ballou, Dean of Students, Southwestern University, University Ave., Georgetown, TX 78626. Telephone: 512-863-1582.

SOUTHWEST MISSOURI STATE UNIVERSITY

Springfield, Missouri

General Information

State-supported 5-year coed college. Founded 1905. Awards A (terminal), B, M. Primary accreditation: regional. City setting; 163-acre campus. Total enrollment: 17,561. Faculty: 803 (607 full-time, 196 part-time). Social organizations: 15 national fraternities, 6 national sororities; 14% of eligible undergraduate men and 8% of eligible undergraduate women are members.

Drug and Alcohol Information

Education

On campus Drug and alcohol education/prevention programs offered for: all students. Bacchus chapter: 5 members. College holds an annual alcohol awareness week and drug awareness week.

Identification of Problems

Admissions College application does not ask about prior substance abuse problems.

On campus Current students identified as chemically dependent may remain enrolled. Training program on identifying students with potential substance abuse problems for: resident advisers. No written procedures for students and staff if substance abuse is suspected.

Support Services

On campus AA, ACOA, private counseling.

Employee assistance Program for chemically dependent employees not available. Staff working with drug/alcohol-related issues: 1 full-time and 10 part-time.

Disciplinary Actions

Alcohol Results of infractions of alcohol regulations (see Comparative Table of Alcohol Regulations) vary by situation but can include chemical dependency assessment, counseling, warning, probation, suspension, expulsion.

Drugs For first-time use: varies by situation—chemical dependency assessment, probation. For subsequent use: varies by situation—chemical dependency assessment, suspension. For first-time possession: chemical dependency assessment, probation. For subsequent possession: chemical dependency assessment, suspension. For any sale: expulsion.

For More Information

Contact: Dr. Sarah Bickel, Dean of Student Life, Southwest Missouri State University, 901 S. National, Springfield, MO 65804. Telephone: 417-836-5527.

SOUTHWEST TEXAS STATE UNIVERSITY

San Marcos, Texas

General Information

State-supported 5-year coed college. Part of Texas State University System. Founded 1899. Awards A (terminal), B, M. Primary accreditation: regional. Small-town setting; 317-acre campus. Total enrollment: 19,731. Social organizations: 13 national fraternities, 9 national sororities.

Drug and Alcohol Information

Education

On campus Drug and alcohol education/prevention programs offered for: all students, athletes/coaches, faculty, administration. Authorized group concerned with responsible drinking. College holds an annual alcohol awareness week and drug awareness week.

Identification of Problems

Admissions College application question about prior substance abuse problems is used to explain past academic performance; for counseling and referral, if student is admitted; in the admissions decision.

On campus Current students identified as chemically dependent may remain enrolled. Comments: May be referred for counseling/education. Training program on identifying students with potential substance abuse problems for: resident advisers, peer network members. Written procedures for students and staff if substance abuse is suspected.

Support Services

On campus AA, ACOA, support groups, private counseling, free, confidential alcohol/drug abuse counseling and referral.

Employee assistance Program for chemically dependent employees available. Staff working with drug/alcohol-related issues: 1 full-time and 12 part-time.

Disciplinary Actions

Alcohol Results of infractions of alcohol regulations (see Comparative Table of Alcohol Regulations) vary by situation but can include chemical dependency assessment, counseling, education component referral.

Drugs For first-time use, possession, or sale: chemical dependency assessment, suspension. For subsequent use, possession, or sale: expulsion.

Additional Information from the College

The University received an FIPSE grant for 1988–90.

For More Information

Contact: H. H. Howze, Director, Alcohol and Drug Education and Prevention Training Center, Medina Hall 204, Southwest Texas State University, San Marcos, TX 78666. Telephone: 512-245-3601.

SPALDING UNIVERSITY

Louisville, Kentucky

General Information

Independent 5-year coed college, affiliated with Roman Catholic Church. Founded 1814. Awards A (terminal), B, M, D. Primary accreditation: regional. Metropolitan setting; 5-acre campus. Total enrollment: 1,141. Faculty: 91 (61 full-time, 30 part-time).

Drug and Alcohol Information

Education

On campus Drug and alcohol education/prevention programs offered for: all students, faculty, administration. College holds an annual alcohol awareness week and drug awareness week.

Spalding University (continued)

Identification of Problems

Admissions College application does not ask about prior substance abuse problems.

On campus Current students identified as chemically dependent may remain enrolled, but treatment is required. Training program on identifying students with potential substance abuse problems for: resident advisers. Written procedures for students and staff if substance abuse is suspected.

Support Services

On campus Private counseling.

Employee assistance Program for chemically dependent employees available.

Disciplinary Actions

Alcohol Results of infractions of alcohol regulations (see Comparative Table of Alcohol Regulations) vary by situation but can include counseling, warning, probation, suspension, expulsion.

Drugs For any use: varies by situation. For first-time possession: varies by situation—suspension. For first-time sale: varies by situation—expulsion. For subsequent possession or sale: expulsion.

Additional Information from the College

Any drug or alcohol problem is evaluated on an individual basis. Counseling and treatment are the first steps taken.

For More Information

Contact: Sr. Eileen Mary Meyer, Dean of Students, Spalding University, 851 S. 4th St., Louisville, KY 40203. Telephone: 502-585-9911.

SPELMAN COLLEGE

Atlanta, Georgia

General Information

Independent 4-year women's college. Founded 1881. Awards B. Primary accreditation: regional. Metropolitan setting; 32-acre campus. Total enrollment: 1,742. Faculty: 167 (109 full-time, 58 part-time). Social organizations: 4 national sororities; 8% of eligible undergraduates are members.

Drug and Alcohol Information

Education

On campus Drug and alcohol education/prevention programs offered for: freshmen. Authorized group concerned with responsible drinking. College holds an annual alcohol awareness week and drug awareness week.

Identification of Problems

Admissions College application does not ask about prior substance abuse problems.

On campus Current students identified as chemically dependent might be allowed to remain enrolled. Treatment may be required. No training program on identifying students with potential substance abuse problems. Written procedures for students and staff if substance abuse is suspected.

Support Services

On campus No support services on campus.

Disciplinary Actions

Alcohol Results of infractions of alcohol regulations (see Comparative Table of Alcohol Regulations) vary by situation.

Drugs For any use, possession, or sale: varies by situation.

For More Information

Contact: Cheryl McGinnis, Counselor, Spelman College, 350 Spelman Ln., SW, Atlanta, GA 30314. Telephone: 404-681-3643.

SPRINGFIELD COLLEGE

Springfield, Massachusetts

General Information

Independent 5-year coed college. Founded 1885. Awards B, M, D. Primary accreditation: regional. City setting; 167-acre campus. Total enrollment: 2,502. Faculty: 259 (159 full-time, 100 part-time).

Drug and Alcohol Information

Education

On campus Drug and alcohol education/prevention programs offered for: all students, athletes/coaches, faculty, administration. Bacchus chapter: 30 members. College holds an annual alcohol awareness week and drug awareness week.

Identification of Problems

Admissions College application does not ask about prior substance abuse problems.

On campus Current students identified as chemically dependent may remain enrolled. No training program on identifying students with potential substance abuse problems. No written procedures for students and staff if substance abuse is suspected.

Support Services

On campus AA, ACOA, private counseling.

Employee assistance Program for chemically dependent employees not available.

Disciplinary Actions

Alcohol Results of infractions of alcohol regulations (see Comparative Table of Alcohol Regulations) vary by situation but can include counseling, warning, probation, suspension, expulsion, fines.

Drugs For any use, possession, or sale: varies by situation.

For More Information

Contact: Sidney Chastain, Assistant Dean of Students, Springfield College, 263 Alden St., Springfield, MA 01109. Telephone: 413-788-3100.

SPRING GARDEN COLLEGE

Philadelphia, Pennsylvania

General Information

Independent 4-year coed college. Founded 1851. Awards A (college transfer and terminal), B. Primary accreditation: regional. Metropolitan setting; 33-acre campus. Total enrollment: 1,224. Faculty: 100 (60 full-time, 40 part-time). Social organizations: 3 local fraternities, 2 local sororities; 10% of eligible undergraduate men and 5% of eligible undergraduate women are members.

Drug and Alcohol Information

Education

On campus Drug and alcohol education/prevention programs offered for: all students. College holds an annual alcohol awareness week and drug awareness week.

Identification of Problems

Admissions College application does not ask about prior substance abuse problems.

On campus Current students identified as chemically dependent may remain enrolled. No training program on identifying students with potential substance abuse problems. No written procedures for students and staff if substance abuse is suspected.

Support Services

On campus Private counseling.

Employee assistance Program for chemically dependent employees not available.

Disciplinary Actions

Alcohol Results of infractions of alcohol regulations (see Comparative Table of Alcohol Regulations) vary by situation but can include warning, suspension.

Drugs For first-time use: counseling, warning, probation. For subsequent use: probation, suspension, expulsion. For first-time possession: counseling, warning. For subsequent possession: warning, probation, suspension. For first-time sale: probation, suspension. For subsequent sale: expulsion.

For More Information

Contact: Peter Rondinaro, Director, Student Development, Spring Garden College, 7500 Germantown Ave., Philadelphia, PA 19119. Telephone: 215-248-7910.

SPRING HILL COLLEGE

Mobile, Alabama

General Information

Independent Roman Catholic 5-year coed college. Founded 1830. Awards B, M. Primary accreditation: regional. City setting; 500-acre campus. Total enrollment: 1,036. Faculty: 87 (68 full-time, 19 part-time). Social organizations: 3 national fraternities, 2 national sororities, 2 local fraternities, 1 local sorority; 45% of eligible undergraduate men and 47% of eligible undergraduate women are members.

Drug and Alcohol Information

Education

On campus Drug and alcohol education/prevention programs offered for: all students, athletes/coaches, faculty, administration, employees. Authorized group concerned with responsible drinking. College holds an annual alcohol awareness week and drug awareness week.

Identification of Problems

Admissions College application question about prior substance abuse problems is used for counseling and referral, if student is admitted.

On campus Current students identified as chemically dependent may remain enrolled, but treatment is required. Training program on identifying students with potential substance abuse problems for: resident advisers, coaches, Greek officers, faculty, administration, employees. Written procedures for students and staff if substance abuse is suspected.

Support Services

On campus Support groups, private counseling.

Employee assistance Program for chemically dependent employees available. Staff working with drug/alcohol-related issues: 6 part-time.

Disciplinary Actions

Alcohol Results of infractions of alcohol regulations (see Comparative Table of Alcohol Regulations) vary by situation but can include chemical dependency assessment, counseling, warning, probation, suspension, expulsion.

Drugs For first-time use or possession: varies by situation. For subsequent use or possession: suspension. For any sale: expulsion.

For More Information

Contact: Elbert LaLande, Director of Student Development, Spring Hill College, 4000 Dauphin St., Mobile, AL 36608. Telephone: 205-460-2351.

STATE UNIVERSITY OF NEW YORK AT ALBANY

Albany, New York

General Information

State-supported comprehensive coed institution. Part of State University of New York System. Founded 1844. Awards B, M, D. Primary accreditation: regional. City setting; 500-acre campus. Total enrollment: 16,219. Faculty: 946 (668 full-time, 278 part-time). Social organizations: 15 national fraternities, 5 national sororities, 5 local fraternities, 6 local sororities; 20% of eligible undergraduate men and 10% of eligible undergraduate women are members.

Drug and Alcohol Information

Education

On campus Drug and alcohol education/prevention programs offered for: all students, athletes/coaches. Authorized group concerned with responsible drinking.

Identification of Problems

Admissions College application does not ask about prior substance abuse problems.

On campus Current students identified as chemically dependent may remain enrolled. Training program on identifying students with potential substance abuse problems for: resident advisers, coaches, Greek officers, faculty, administration. Written procedures for students and staff if substance abuse is suspected.

Support Services

On campus AA, Al-Anon, ACOA, support groups, counseling center, peer counseling.

Employee assistance Program for chemically dependent employees available. Staff working with drug/alcohol-related issues: 2 part-time.

Disciplinary Actions

Alcohol Results of infractions of alcohol regulations (see Comparative Table of Alcohol Regulations) include counseling, warning, probation, suspension, expulsion.

Drugs For first-time use: varies by situation—counseling, warning, probation. For first-time possession: varies by situation—counseling, probation, suspension. For first-time sale: varies by situation—suspension, expulsion. For subsequent use, possession, or sale: varies by situation.

State University of New York at Albany (continued)

Additional Information from the College

Matters relating to alcohol and drug abuse are taken very seriously by the University. Students are offered 'due process' in all matters relating to application of sanctions for violating the University's code of behavior.

For More Information

Contact: James Doellefeld, Assistant Vice President, Campus Life, State University of New York at Albany, 1400 Washington Ave., Albany, NY 12222. Telephone: 518-442-5566.

STATE UNIVERSITY OF NEW YORK AT BUFFALO

Buffalo, New York

General Information

State-supported comprehensive coed institution. Part of State University of New York System. Founded 1846. Awards B, M, D. Primary accreditation: regional. Metropolitan setting; 1,376-acre campus. Total enrollment: 24,942. Faculty: 2,005 (1,399 full-time, 606 part-time). Social organizations: 18 national fraternities, 6 national sororities, local fraternities, local sororities; 8% of eligible undergraduate men and 4% of eligible undergraduate women are members.

Drug and Alcohol Information

Education

On campus Drug and alcohol education/prevention programs offered for: all students, athletes/coaches; required for: freshmen, resident advisers. Auhthorized group concerned with responsible drinking. College holds an annual alcohol awareness week and drug awareness week.

Identification of Problems

Admissions College application does not ask about prior substance abuse problems.

On campus Current students identified as chemically dependent may remain enrolled, but treatment is required. Training program on identifying students with potential substance abuse problems for: resident advisers, Greek officers. No written procedures for students and staff if substance abuse is suspected.

Support Services

On campus AA, ACOA, support groups (SADD), private counseling.

Employee assistance Program for chemically dependent employees available. Staff working with drug/alcohol-related issues: 1 part-time.

Disciplinary Actions

Alcohol Results of infractions of alcohol regulations (see Comparative Table of Alcohol Regulations) include chemical dependency assessment, counseling, warning, probation, suspension of privileges, dismissal from residence halls.

Drugs For any use, possession, or sale: varies by situation.

For More Information

Contact: Sarah Bihr, Associate Director, Health Sciences, 215 Michael Hall, State University of New York at Buffalo, Buffalo, NY 14260. Telephone: 716-831-3316.

STATE UNIVERSITY OF NEW YORK AT STONY BROOK

Stony Brook, New York

General Information

State-supported comprehensive coed institution. Part of State University of New York System. Founded 1957. Awards B, M, D. Primary accreditation: regional. Small-town setting; 1,100-acre campus. Total enrollment: 14,799. Faculty: 1,465 (1,105 full-time, 360 part-time). Social organizations: national fraternities, national sororities.

Drug and Alcohol Information

Education

On campus Drug and alcohol education/prevention programs offered for: all students, faculty, administration; required for: social organization members, resident advisers, student leaders. Authorized group concerned with responsible drinking. College holds an annual alcohol awareness week and drug awareness week.

Identification of Problems

Admissions College application does not ask about prior substance abuse problems.

On campus Current students identified as chemically dependent may remain enrolled. No training program on identifying students with potential substance abuse problems. Written procedures for students and staff if substance abuse is suspected.

Support Services

On campus AA, NA, Al-Anon, ACOA, private counseling, SADD.

Employee assistance Program for chemically dependent employees available.

Disciplinary Actions

Alcohol Results of infractions of alcohol regulations (see Comparative Table of Alcohol Regulations) vary by situation but can include chemical dependency assessment, counseling, warning, probation, suspension, expulsion. Comments: Student organizations may be suspended or have their right to reserve space for events entailed for a period of time.

Drugs For first-time use or possession: varies by situation. For subsequent use or possession: varies by situation—suspension, expulsion. For first-time sale: suspension, expulsion. For subsequent sale: expulsion.

For More Information

Contact: Gary G.S. Mis, Associate Dean of Students, 347 Administration, State University of New York at Stony Brook, Stony Brook, NY 11794. Telephone: 516-632-6705.

STATE UNIVERSITY OF NEW YORK COLLEGE AT BROCKPORT

Brockport, New York

General Information

State-supported 5-year coed college. Part of State University of New York System. Founded 1867. Awards B, M. Primary accreditation: regional. Small-town setting; 591-acre campus. Total enrollment: 7,371. Faculty: 555 (349 full-time, 206 part-time). Social organizations: 7 national fraternities,

6 national sororities; 3% of eligible undergraduate men and 2% of eligible undergraduate women are members.

Drug and Alcohol Information

Education

On campus Drug and alcohol education/prevention programs offered for: all students, athletes/coaches, faculty, administration. Authorized group concerned with responsible drinking.

Identification of Problems

Admissions College application does not ask about prior substance abuse problems.

On campus Current students identified as chemically dependent may remain enrolled. Training program on identifying students with potential substance abuse problems for: resident advisers, coaches, Greek officers. Written procedures for students and staff if substance abuse is suspected.

Support Services

On campus AA, private counseling.

Employee assistance Program for chemically dependent employees available. Staff working with drug/alcohol-related issues: 1 full-time and 25 part-time.

Disciplinary Actions

Alcohol Results of infractions of alcohol regulations (see Comparative Table of Alcohol Regulations) vary by situation.

Drugs For first-time use: chemical dependency assessment, counseling, probation. For first-time use or possession: varies by situation. For first-time possession: varies by situation. For first-time sale: suspension, expulsion. For subsequent sale: expulsion.

For More Information

Contact: Joseph F. Franek Jr., Director of Residential Life, State University of New York College at Brockport, Brockport, NY 14420. Telephone: 716-395-2122.

STATE UNIVERSITY OF NEW YORK COLLEGE AT FREDONIA

Fredonia, New York

General Information

State-supported 5-year coed college. Part of State University of New York System. Founded 1867. Awards B, M. Primary accreditation: regional. Small-town setting; 235-acre campus. Total enrollment: 4,994. Faculty: 310 (262 full-time, 48 part-time). Social organizations: 3 national fraternities, 2 national sororities, 2 local sororities; 1% of eligible undergraduate men and 1% of eligible undergraduate women are members.

Drug and Alcohol Information

Education

On campus Drug and alcohol education/prevention programs offered for: all students. Authorized group concerned with responsible drinking. College holds an annual combined alcohol awareness week and drug awareness week.

Identification of Problems

Admissions College application does not ask about prior substance abuse problems.

On campus Current students identified as chemically dependent may remain enrolled, but treatment is required. Training program on identifying students with potential substance abuse problems for: resident advisers. Written procedures for students and staff if substance abuse is suspected.

Support Services

On campus AA, Al-Anon, support groups, private counseling.

Employee assistance Program for chemically dependent employees available. Staff working with drug/alcohol-related issues: over 20 part-time.

Disciplinary Actions

Alcohol Results of infractions of alcohol regulations (see Comparative Table of Alcohol Regulations) vary by situation.

Drugs For first-time use and possession: counseling, warning, probation. For subsequent use, possession, or sale: varies by situation. For first-time sale: suspension, expulsion.

For More Information

Contact: Dr. Joan Gibson, Counselor, State University of New York College at Fredonia, Fredonia, NY 14063. Telephone: 716-673-3424.

STATE UNIVERSITY OF NEW YORK COLLEGE AT GENESEO

Geneseo, New York

General Information

State-supported 5-year coed college. Part of State University of New York System. Founded 1867. Awards B, M. Primary accreditation: regional. Rural setting; 225-acre campus. Total enrollment: 4,957. Faculty: 282 (252 full-time, 30 part-time). Social organizations: 5 national fraternities, 1 national sorority, 2 local fraternities, 6 local sororities; 21% of eligible undergraduate men and 19% of eligible undergraduate women are members.

Drug and Alcohol Information

Education

On campus Drug and alcohol education/prevention programs offered for: all students, athletes/coaches. College holds an annual alcohol awareness week and drug awareness week.

Identification of Problems

Admissions College application does not ask about prior substance abuse problems. There is a question on the Medical Information form used by the College Health Service. The information is requested after admission.

On campus Current students identified as chemically dependent may remain enrolled, but treatment is required. Training program on identifying students with potential substance abuse problems for: resident advisers, residence life staff. Written procedures for students and staff if substance abuse is suspected.

State University of New York College at Geneseo (continued)

Support Services

On campus AA, private counseling.

Employee assistance Program for chemically dependent employees available. Staff working with drug/alcohol-related issues: numerous part-time.

Disciplinary Actions

Alcohol Results of infractions of alcohol regulations (see Comparative Table of Alcohol Regulations) vary by situation.

Drugs For any use, possession, or sale: varies by situation. Comments: The disciplinary procedure is based on a student's right to due process. Each incident is adjudicated.

For More Information

Contact: K. Hayes Sugarman, Assistant Vice President and Dean of Students, State University of New York College at Geneseo, Geneseo, NY 14454. Telephone: 716-245-5706.

STATE UNIVERSITY OF NEW YORK COLLEGE AT NEW PALTZ

New Paltz, New York

General Information

State-supported 5-year coed college. Part of State University of New York System. Founded 1828. Awards B, M. Primary accreditation: regional. Rural setting; 216-acre campus. Total enrollment: 8,128. Faculty: 455 (307 full-time, 148 part-time). Social organizations: 7 national fraternities, 6 national sororities, 4 local fraternities, 2 local sororities; 5% of eligible undergraduate men and 4% of eligible undergraduate women are members.

Drug and Alcohol Information

Education

On campus Drug and alcohol education/prevention programs offered for: all students, athletes/coaches. Bacchus chapter. Additional group concerned with responsible drinking. College holds an annual alcohol awareness week and drug awareness week.

Identification of Problems

Admissions College application does not ask about prior substance abuse problems.

On campus Current students identified as chemically dependent may remain enrolled, but treatment is required. Training program on identifying students with potential substance abuse problems for: resident advisers, administration, orientation and faculty advisers. Written procedures for students and staff if substance abuse is suspected.

Support Services

On campus ACOA, support groups, private counseling.

Off campus AA, Al-Anon.

Employee assistance Program for chemically dependent employees available. Staff working with drug/alcohol-related issues: 3 part-time.

Disciplinary Actions

Alcohol Results of infractions of alcohol regulations (see Comparative Table of Alcohol Regulations) include warning, probation, suspension.

Drugs For first-time use: varies by situation—chemical dependency assessment, counseling, suspension. For subsequent use: varies by situation. For first-time possession: suspension, expulsion. For subsequent possession: expulsion. For any sale: expulsion.

For More Information

Contact: Michael Nuccitelli, Alcohol Programmer, Psychological Counseling Center, State University of New York College at New Paltz, New Paltz, NY 12561. Telephone: 914-257-2250.

STATE UNIVERSITY OF NEW YORK COLLEGE AT OLD WESTBURY

Old Westbury, New York

General Information

State-supported 4-year coed college. Part of State University of New York System. Founded 1965. Awards B. Primary accreditation: regional. Small-town setting; 605-acre campus. Total enrollment: 3,946. Faculty: 188 (138 full-time, 50 part-time). Social organizations: 1 national fraternity, local fraternities, local sororities.

Drug and Alcohol Information

Education

On campus Drug and alcohol education/prevention programs offered for: all students. College holds an annual alcohol awareness week.

Identification of Problems

Admissions College application does not ask about prior substance abuse problems.

On campus Current students identified as chemically dependent may remain enrolled. Training program on identifying students with potential substance abuse problems for: resident advisers. No written procedures for students and staff if substance abuse is suspected.

Support Services

On campus AA, Al-Anon.

Employee assistance Program for chemically dependent employees available. Staff working with drug/alcohol-related issues: 1 full-time and 2 part-time.

Disciplinary Actions

Alcohol Results of infractions of alcohol regulations (see Comparative Table of Alcohol Regulations) vary by situation.

Drugs For any use or possession: varies by situation. For any sale: arrest.

For More Information

Contact: Myrna DeCuba, Project Director, Drug Education/Prevention, Bldg. #10 Academic Village, State University of New York College at Old Westbury, Old Westbury, NY 11568. Telephone: 516-876-3326.

STATE UNIVERSITY OF NEW YORK COLLEGE AT POTSDAM

Potsdam, New York

General Information

State-supported 5-year coed college. Part of State University of New York System. Founded 1816. Awards B, M. Primary accreditation: regional. Small-town setting; 240-acre campus. Total enrollment: 4,273. Faculty: 263 (245 full-time, 18 part-time). Social organizations: 2 national fraternities, 1 national sorority, 4 local fraternities, 6 local sororities; 10% of eligible undergraduate men and 10% of eligible undergraduate women are members.

Drug and Alcohol Information

Education

On campus Drug and alcohol education/prevention programs offered for: all students, athletes/coaches, faculty, administration. Authorized group concerned with responsible drinking. College holds an annual alcohol awareness week.

Identification of Problems

Admissions College application does not ask about prior substance abuse problems.

On campus Current students identified as chemically dependent may remain enrolled, but treatment is required. No training program on identifying students with potential substance abuse problems. No written procedures for students and staff if substance abuse is suspected.

Support Services

On campus AA, support groups, private counseling.

Employee assistance Program for chemically dependent employees available. Staff working with drug/alcohol-related issues: 8–12 part-time.

Disciplinary Actions

Alcohol Results of infractions of alcohol regulations (see Comparative Table of Alcohol Regulations) vary by situation.

Drugs For any use, possession, or sale: varies by situation.

For More Information

Contact: Susan Thomas, Director, Counseling Center, State University of New York College at Potsdam, Pierrepont Ave., Potsdam, NY 13676. Telephone: 315-267-2330.

STATE UNIVERSITY OF NEW YORK COLLEGE AT PURCHASE

Purchase, New York

General Information

State-supported 5-year coed college. Part of State University of New York System. Founded 1967. Awards B, M. Primary accreditation: regional. Small-town setting; 550-acre campus. Total enrollment: 2,410. Faculty: 284 (135 full-time, 149 part-time).

Drug and Alcohol Information

Education

On campus Drug and alcohol education/prevention programs offered for: all students, faculty, administration, staff.

Identification of Problems

Admissions College application does not ask about prior substance abuse problems.

On campus Current students identified as chemically dependent may sometimes remain enrolled, but treatment may be required. Training program on identifying students with potential substance abuse problems for: resident advisers, administration. No written procedures for students and staff if substance abuse is suspected.

Support Services

On campus AA, ACOA, private counseling.

Employee assistance Program for chemically dependent employees available.

Disciplinary Actions

Alcohol Results of infractions of alcohol regulations (see Comparative Table of Alcohol Regulations) vary by situation but can include chemical dependency assessment, counseling, warning, probation, suspension, expulsion.

Drugs For any use, possession, or sale: varies by situation.

For More Information

Contact: Dr. Paul Grayson, Director of Counseling, State University of New York College at Purchase, 735 Anderson Hill Rd., Purchase, NY 10577-1400. Telephone: 914-253-5196.

STATE UNIVERSITY OF NEW YORK COLLEGE OF ENVIRONMENTAL SCIENCE AND FORESTRY

Syracuse, New York

General Information

State-supported coed college. Part of State University of New York System. Founded 1911. Awards B, M, D. Primary accreditation: regional. Metropolitan setting; 12-acre campus. Total enrollment: 1,222. Faculty: 122 (110 full-time, 12 part-time). Social organizations: 25 national fraternities, 13 national sororities, 1 local fraternity; 25% of eligible undergraduate men and 25% of eligible undergraduate women are members.

Drug and Alcohol Information

Education

On campus Drug and alcohol education/prevention programs offered for: all students. College holds an annual alcohol awareness week and drug awareness week.

Identification of Problems

Admissions College application does not ask about prior substance abuse problems.

On campus Current students identified as chemically dependent may remain enrolled, but treatment is required. No training program on identifying students with potential substance abuse problems. No written procedures for students and staff if substance abuse is suspected.

State University of New York College of Environmental Science and Forestry (continued)

Support Services

On campus AA, Al-Anon, ACOA, support groups, private counseling.

Off campus City support groups.

Employee assistance Program (referral) for chemically dependent employees available.

Disciplinary Actions

Alcohol Results of infractions of alcohol regulations (see Comparative Table of Alcohol Regulations) vary by situation but can include counseling, warning, probation, suspension.

Drugs For any use, possession, or sale: varies by situation.

Additional Information from the College

The College is very close to Syracuse University and fully utilizes its programs and support services.

For More Information

Contact: Thomas O. Slocum, Director of Counseling, 110 Bray Hall, State University of New York College of Environmental Science and Forestry, Syracuse, NY 13210. Telephone: 315-470-6660.

STATE UNIVERSITY OF NEW YORK COLLEGE OF TECHNOLOGY AT UTICA/ ROME

Utica, New York

General Information

State-supported coed college. Part of State University of New York System. Founded 1966. Awards B, M. Primary accreditation: regional. City setting; 800-acre campus. Total enrollment: 2,620. Faculty: 172 (84 full-time, 88 part-time). Social organizations: 2 national fraternities, 1 local sorority; 5% of eligible undergraduate men and 2% of eligible undergraduate women are members.

Drug and Alcohol Information

Education

On campus Drug and alcohol education/prevention programs offered for: all students, faculty, administration. Authorized group concerned with responsible drinking. College holds an annual alcohol awareness week.

Identification of Problems

Admissions College application does not ask about prior substance abuse problems.

On campus Current students identified as chemically dependent may remain enrolled. Training program on identifying students with potential substance abuse problems for: administration. Written procedures for students and staff if substance abuse is suspected.

Support Services

On campus AA, private counseling.

Employee assistance Program for chemically dependent employees available.

Disciplinary Actions

Alcohol Results of infractions of alcohol regulations (see Comparative Table of Alcohol Regulations) include counseling, warning, probation, suspension, expulsion.

Drugs For first-time use or possession: varies by situation—counseling, probation, suspension. For subsequent use or possession: expulsion. For any sale: expulsion.

For More Information

Contact: David Garrett, Director, Student Activities, State University of New York College of Technology at Utica/ Rome, Marcy Campus, P.O. Box 3050, Utica, NY 13504. Telephone: 315-792-7530.

STATE UNIVERSITY OF NEW YORK HEALTH SCIENCE CENTER AT SYRACUSE

Syracuse, New York

General Information

State-supported comprehensive coed institution. Part of State University of New York System. Founded 1950. Awards A (terminal), B, M, D. Primary accreditation: regional. Metropolitan setting; 25-acre campus. Total enrollment: 980. Faculty: 353 full-time.

Drug and Alcohol Information

Education

On campus Drug and alcohol education/prevention programs offered for: all students, faculty, administration; required for: resident advisers. College holds an annual alcohol awareness week and drug awareness week.

Identification of Problems

Admissions College application does not ask about prior substance abuse problems.

On campus Current students identified as chemically dependent may remain enrolled. Comments: Each case handled individually. No training program on identifying students with potential substance abuse problems. Written procedures for students and staff if substance abuse is suspected.

Support Services

On campus Private counseling, student affairs staff for referrals.

Employee assistance Program for chemically dependent employees available.

Disciplinary Actions

Alcohol Results of infractions of alcohol regulations (see Comparative Table of Alcohol Regulations) vary by situation but can include chemical dependency assessment, counseling, warning, probation, suspension, expulsion.

Drugs For any use, possession, or sale: varies by situation.

For More Information

Contact: Donald F. Midlam, Assistant Dean for Student Services, State University of New York Health Science Center at Syracuse, 155 Elizabeth Blackwell St., Syracuse, NY 13210. Telephone: 315-473-4816.

STEPHEN F. AUSTIN STATE UNIVERSITY

Nacogdoches, Texas

General Information

State-supported 5-year coed college. Founded 1923. Awards B, M, D. Primary accreditation: regional. Small-town setting; 400-acre campus. Total enrollment: 12,564. Faculty: 450 (325 full-time, 125 part-time).

Drug and Alcohol Information

Education

On campus Drug and alcohol education/prevention programs offered for: all students; required for: alcohol/discipline cases. College holds an annual alcohol awareness week and drug awareness week.

Identification of Problems

Admissions College application does not ask about prior substance abuse problems.

On campus Current students identified as chemically dependent may remain enrolled unless found in possession of drugs. No training program on identifying students with potential substance abuse problems. Written procedures for students and staff if substance abuse is suspected.

Support Services

On campus AA, ACOA.

Employee assistance Program for chemically dependent employees available. Staff working with drug/alcohol-related issues: 1 full-time and 1 part-time.

Disciplinary Actions

Alcohol Results of infractions of alcohol regulations (see Comparative Table of Alcohol Regulations) include probation, suspension, alcohol awareness classes.

Drugs For any use, possession, or sale: suspension.

For More Information

Contact: Julie Schuller, Counselor, Box 13030, Stephen F. Austin State University, 1936 North St., Nacogdoches, TX 75962. Telephone: 409-568-2401.

STETSON UNIVERSITY

DeLand, Florida

General Information

Independent Baptist 5-year coed college. Founded 1883. Awards B, M, D. Primary accreditation: regional. Small-town setting; 117-acre campus. Total enrollment: 2,975. Faculty: 164 (141 full-time, 23 part-time). Social organizations: 8 national fraternities, 7 national sororities; 44% of eligible undergraduate men and 42% of eligible undergraduate women are members.

Drug and Alcohol Information

Education

On campus Drug and alcohol education/prevention programs offered for: all students, athletes/coaches, faculty, administration. Bacchus chapter: 45 members. College holds an annual alcohol awareness week and drug awareness week.

Identification of Problems

Admissions College application question about prior substance abuse problems is used for counseling and referral, if student is admitted.

On campus Current students identified as chemically dependent may remain enrolled, but treatment is required. Training program on identifying students with potential substance abuse problems for: resident advisers, coaches, Greek officers. Written procedures for students and staff if substance abuse is suspected.

Support Services

On campus Support groups, private counseling.

Employee assistance Program for chemically dependent employees available.

Disciplinary Actions

Alcohol Results of infractions of alcohol regulations (see Comparative Table of Alcohol Regulations) vary by situation but can include chemical dependency assessment, counseling, warning, probation, suspension.

Drugs For any use, possession, or sale: varies by situation.

For More Information

Contact: Carol Nak, Counselor, Stetson University, Campus Box 8365, DeLand, FL 32720. Telephone: 904-734-4121 Ext. 215.

STEVENS INSTITUTE OF TECHNOLOGY

Hoboken, New Jersey

General Information

Independent comprehensive coed institution. Founded 1870. Awards B, M, D. Primary accreditation: regional. Small-town setting; 55-acre campus. Total enrollment: 3,200. Faculty: 250 (140 full-time, 110 part-time). Social organizations: 10 national fraternities, 2 national sororities; 35% of eligible undergraduate men and 30% of eligible undergraduate women are members.

Drug and Alcohol Information

Education

On campus Drug and alcohol education/prevention programs offered for: all students, athletes/coaches; required for: freshmen, resident advisers, Greek leaders. Authorized group concerned with responsible drinking. College holds an annual alcohol awareness week and drug awareness week.

Identification of Problems

Admissions College application does not ask about prior substance abuse problems.

On campus Current students identified as chemically dependent may remain enrolled, but treatment is required. Training program on identifying students with potential substance abuse problems for: resident advisers, coaches, Greek officers. Written procedures for students if substance abuse is suspected.

Support Services

On campus AA, Al-Anon, support groups (counseling center group), private counseling, referral to local groups in hospital and in mental health clinic.

Employee assistance Program for chemically dependent employees available. Staff working with drug/alcohol-related issues: 8 part-time.

Stevens Institute of Technology (continued)

Disciplinary Actions

Alcohol Results of infractions of alcohol regulations (see Comparative Table of Alcohol Regulations) vary by situation but can include counseling, warning, probation, suspension.

Drugs For any use or possession: varies by situation. For any sale: expulsion.

Additional Information from the College

Dean's Office and Health Center staffs stay current by regular attendance at conferences and programs and by interaction with statewide professional organizations. In the past year, a tremendous effort has been made to provide alcohol awareness and education programs for Greek organization members.

For More Information

Contact: Henry C. Tomkiewicz, Assistant Dean for Student Affairs, Stevens Institute of Technology, Castle Point Station, Hoboken, NJ 07030. Telephone: 201-420-5206.

STILLMAN COLLEGE

Tuscaloosa, Alabama

General Information

Independent 4-year coed college, affiliated with Presbyterian Church. Founded 1876. Awards B. Primary accreditation: regional. City setting; 100-acre campus. Total enrollment: 748. Social organizations: 4 national fraternities, 4 national sororities, 1 local fraternity; 6% of eligible undergraduate men and 6% of eligible undergraduate women are members.

Drug and Alcohol Information

Education

On campus Drug and alcohol education/prevention programs offered for: all students, faculty, administration. College holds an annual alcohol awareness week and drug awareness week.

Identification of Problems

Admissions College application does not ask about prior substance abuse problems.

On campus Current students identified as chemically dependent may remain enrolled. No training program on identifying students with potential substance abuse problems. No written procedures for students and staff if substance abuse is suspected.

Support Services

On campus Private counseling.

Employee assistance Program for chemically dependent employees not available.

Disciplinary Actions

Alcohol Results of infractions of alcohol regulations (see Comparative Table of Alcohol Regulations) include counseling, warning, probation, suspension, expulsion.

Drugs For any use, possession, or sale: varies by situation.

For More Information

Contact: Darnell Williams, Director of the Student Development Center, Stillman College, Tuscaloosa, AL 35403. Telephone: 205-349-4240.

STOCKTON STATE COLLEGE

Pomona, New Jersey

General Information

State-supported 4-year coed college. Part of New Jersey State College System. Founded 1971. Awards B. Primary accreditation: regional. Rural setting; 1,600-acre campus. Total enrollment: 5,297. Faculty: 243 (173 full-time, 70 part-time). Social organizations: 8 national fraternities, 7 national sororities, 3 local fraternities, 3 local sororities; 5% of eligible undergraduate men and 5% of eligible undergraduate women are members.

Drug and Alcohol Information

Education

On campus Drug and alcohol education/prevention programs offered for: all students. Authorized group concerned with responsible drinking. College holds an annual alcohol awareness week and drug awareness week.

Identification of Problems

Admissions College application does not ask about prior substance abuse problems.

On campus Current students identified as chemically dependent may remain enrolled, but treatment is required. Training program on identifying students with potential substance abuse problems for: resident advisers, Greek officers, student leaders. Written procedures for students and staff if substance abuse is suspected.

Support Services

On campus Al-Anon, ACOA, private counseling.

Employee assistance Program for chemically dependent employees available. Staff working with drug/alcohol-related issues: 1 full-time and 10–12 part-time.

Disciplinary Actions

Alcohol Results of infractions of alcohol regulations (see Comparative Table of Alcohol Regulations) vary by situation but can include counseling, warning, probation, suspension, completion of an alcohol awareness course.

Drugs For first-time use: varies by situation—chemical dependency assessment, counseling, suspension. For first-time use: suspension. For first-time possession: varies by situation—probation. For subsequent possession: suspension. For first-time sale: varies by situation. For subsequent sale: expulsion, legal charges.

Additional Information from the College

An innovative student development program with a 12-hour alcohol/drug awareness component is required of student workers, RAs, and others employed within the Division of Student Services. In addition, students who intend to join a Greek organization must complete the course.

Drugs Dr. Joseph Marchetti, Dean of Students, Stockton State College, Pomona, NJ 08240. Telephone: 609-652-4645.

SUL ROSS STATE UNIVERSITY

Alpine, Texas

General Information

State-supported 5-year coed college. Founded 1917. Awards A (terminal), B, M. Primary accreditation: regional. Small-town setting; 640-acre campus. Total enrollment: 2,313.

Faculty: 118 (92 full-time, 26 part-time). Social organization: 1 national sorority.

Drug and Alcohol Information

Education

On campus Drug and alcohol education/prevention programs offered for: all students, faculty, administration, staff. College holds an annual alcohol awareness week and drug awareness week.

Identification of Problems

Admissions College application does not ask about prior substance abuse problems.

On campus Current students identified as chemically dependent may remain enrolled. No training program on identifying students with potential substance abuse problems. No written procedures for students and staff if substance abuse is suspected.

Support Services

On campus Private counseling.

Employee assistance Program for chemically dependent employees available. Staff working with drug/alcohol-related issues: 3 part-time.

Disciplinary Actions

Alcohol Results of infractions of alcohol regulations (see Comparative Table of Alcohol Regulations) vary by situation.

Drugs For first-time use, possession, or sale: suspension. For subsequent use, possesion, or sale: expulsion.

Additional Information from the College

The University's alcohol and drug programs are in their early stages. More services and better educational programs are anticipated in the next few years.

For More Information

Contact: Kristin Sayre, Director of Student Development, Sul Ross State University, Box C-121, Alpine, TX 79832. Telephone: 915-837-8037.

SUSQUEHANNA UNIVERSITY

Selinsgrove, Pennsylvania

General Information

Independent 4-year coed college, affiliated with Lutheran Church. Founded 1858. Awards B. Primary accreditation: regional. Small-town setting; 190-acre campus. Total enrollment: 1,476. Faculty: 143 (104 full-time, 39 part-time). Social organizations: 5 national fraternities, 4 national sororities; 30% of eligible undergraduate men and 30% of eligible undergraduate women are members.

Drug and Alcohol Information

Education

On campus Drug and alcohol education/prevention programs offered for: all students, peer educator group. Bacchus chapter: 12 members. College holds an annual alcohol awareness week.

Identification of Problems

Admissions College application does not ask about prior substance abuse problems.

On campus Current students identified as chemically dependent may remain enrolled, but treatment is required. Training program on identifying students with potential substance abuse problems for: resident advisers, peer educator group. Written procedures for students and staff if substance abuse is suspected.

Support Services

On campus ACOA, support groups (peer educator program), private counseling.

Employee assistance Program for chemically dependent employees not available. Staff working with drug/alcohol-related issues: 1 part-time.

Disciplinary Actions

Alcohol Results of infractions of alcohol regulations (see Comparative Table of Alcohol Regulations) vary by situation but can include chemical dependency assessment, counseling, warning, probation, suspension, expulsion, alcohol education program, group sanctions imposed on fraternities.

Drugs For first-time use or possession: varies by situation—chemical dependency assessment. For subsequent use or possession: varies by situation. For first-time sale: referral to local law enforcement, suspension, expulsion. For subsequent sale: suspension, expulsion.

Additional Information from the College

The University believes its step-level discipline system for alcohol violations is effective. A more detailed policy for drug violations should be available by fall 1989.

For More Information

Contact: Dr. A. F. Kreisler, Director of Counseling, Susquehanna University, University Ave., Selinsgrove, PA 17870. Telephone: 717-372-4238.

SWEET BRIAR COLLEGE

Sweet Briar, Virginia

General Information

Independent 4-year women's college. Founded 1901. Awards B. Primary accreditation: regional. Rural setting; 3,300-acre campus. Total enrollment: 598. Faculty: 65 (43 full-time, 22 part-time).

Drug and Alcohol Information

Education

On campus Drug and alcohol education/prevention programs offered for: all students. Authorized group concerned with responsible drinking. College holds an annual alcohol awareness week and drug awareness week.

Identification of Problems

On campus Current students identified as chemically dependent may remain enrolled, but treatment is required. Training program on identifying students with potential substance abuse problems for: resident advisers, administration (Student Affairs). Written procedures for students and staff if substance abuse is suspected.

Support Services

On campus Support groups, private counseling.

Employee assistance Program for chemically dependent employees not available. Staff working with drug/alcohol-related issues: 3–4 part-time.

Disciplinary Actions

Alcohol Results of infractions of alcohol regulations (see Comparative Table of Alcohol Regulations) vary by

Sweet Briar College (continued)

situation but can include chemical dependency assessment, counseling, warning, probation, suspension.

Drugs For first-time use: varies by situation—counseling, warning. For subsequent use: varies by situation—counseling, warning, probation. For first-time possession: varies by situation—counseling, warning, probation. For subsequent possession: varies by situation—counseling, probation, suspension. For first-time sale: varies by situation—suspension, expulsion. For subsequent sale: varies by situation—expulsion.

For More Information

Contact: Robert H. Barlow, Dean of Student Affairs, Sweet Briar College, P.O. Box H, Sweet Briar, VA 24595. Telephone: 804-381-6134.

SYRACUSE UNIVERSITY

Syracuse, New York

General Information

Independent comprehensive coed institution. Founded 1870. Awards B, M, D. Primary accreditation: regional. City setting; 600-acre campus. Total enrollment: 16,821. Faculty: 1,050 (944 full-time, 106 part-time). Social organizations: 26 national fraternities, 14 national sororities, local fraternities, local sororities, minority organizations.

Drug and Alcohol Information

Education

On campus Drug and alcohol education/prevention programs offered for: all students, athletes/coaches, faculty, administration. Authorized group concerned with responsible drinking. College holds an annual alcohol awareness week.

Identification of Problems

Admissions College application does not ask about prior substance abuse problems.

On campus Current students identified as chemically dependent may remain enrolled, but treatment may be required. No training program on identifying students with potential substance abuse problems. No written procedures for students and staff if substance abuse is suspected.

Support Services

On campus AA, Al-Anon, ACOA, individual and group counseling.

Employee assistance Program for chemically dependent employees available. Staff working with drug/alcohol-related issues: 2 part-time.

Disciplinary Actions

Alcohol Results of infractions of alcohol regulations (see Comparative Table of Alcohol Regulations) vary by situation but can include chemical dependency assessment, counseling, warning, probation.

Drugs For first-time use: varies by situation. For subsequent use: varies by situation—probation, suspension. For first-time possession: varies by situation—warning, probation, suspension. For subsequent possession: suspension. For first-time sale: suspension. For subsequent sale: suspension, expulsion.

Additional Information from the College

A clearly written alcohol policy is included in the rules and regulations given to every student each year. This policy is reinforced in the residence halls. Since the alcohol policy applies to University property and events only, Greek organizations have their own alcohol policy.

For More Information

Contact: Elizabeth A. Coccia, Staff Therapist, Syracuse University, 111 Waverly Ave., Syracuse, NY 13244. Telephone: 315-443-4715.

TABOR COLLEGE

Hillsboro, Kansas

General Information

Independent Mennonite Brethren 4-year coed college. Founded 1908. Awards A (college transfer and terminal), B. Primary accreditation: regional. Small-town setting; 26-acre campus. Total enrollment: 476. Faculty: 48 (30 full-time, 18 part-time).

Drug and Alcohol Information

Education

On campus Drug and alcohol education/prevention programs offered for: all students, athletes/coaches. College holds an annual alcohol awareness week and drug awareness week.

Identification of Problems

Admissions College application does not ask about prior substance abuse problems.

On campus Current students identified as chemically dependent may remain enrolled, but treatment is required. Training program on identifying students with potential substance abuse problems for: resident advisers. Written procedures for students and staff if substance abuse is suspected.

Support Services

On campus Private counseling.

Employee assistance Program for chemically dependent employees not available. Staff working with drug/alcohol-related issues: 18 part-time.

Disciplinary Actions

Alcohol Results of infractions of alcohol regulations (see Comparative Table of Alcohol Regulations) include chemical dependency assessment, counseling, warning, probation, expulsion.

Drugs For any use or possession: varies by situation. For any sale: expulsion.

For More Information

Contact: Judy Hiebert, Assistant Dean of Student Development, Tabor College, 400 S. Jefferson, Hillsboro, KS 67063. Telephone: 316-947-3121.

TARKIO COLLEGE

Tarkio, Missouri

General Information

Independent Presbyterian 4-year coed college. Founded 1883. Awards A (terminal), B. Primary accreditation: regional. Rural setting; 60-acre campus. Total enrollment: 784. Faculty: 54 (49 full-time, 5 part-time). Social organizations: 3 national fraternities, 2 local fraternities, 4 local sororities; 20% of eligible undergraduate men and 20% of eligible undergraduate women are members.

Drug and Alcohol Information

Education

On campus Drug and alcohol education/prevention programs offered for: freshmen, athletes/coaches, resident advisers, student leaders. College holds an annual alcohol awareness week and drug awareness week.

Identification of Problems

Admissions College application does not ask about prior substance abuse problems.

On campus Current students identified as chemically dependent may remain enrolled, but treatment is required. Training program on identifying students with potential substance abuse problems for: resident advisers, coaches, administration. Written procedures for students and staff if substance abuse is suspected.

Support Services

On campus AA, support groups, private counseling.

Employee assistance Program for chemically dependent employees not available. Staff working with drug/alcohol-related issues: 4 full-time and 2 part-time.

Disciplinary Actions

Alcohol Results of infractions of alcohol regulations (see Comparative Table of Alcohol Regulations) include chemical dependency assessment, counseling, probation, suspension.

Drugs For first-time use: varies by situation. For subsequent use: chemical dependency assessment, expulsion. For any possession or sale: expulsion.

For More Information

Contact: Gary Mekelburg, Athletic Director-Dean of Students, Tarkio College, 13th and McNary, Tarkio, MO 64491. Telephone: 816-736-4131.

TEMPLE UNIVERSITY

Philadelphia, Pennsylvania

General Information

State-related comprehensive coed institution. Founded 1884. Awards A (college transfer and terminal), B, M, D. Primary accreditation: regional. Metropolitan setting; 76-acre campus. Total enrollment: 28,056. Faculty: 2,062 (1,662 full-time, 400 part-time). Social organizations: national fraternities, national sororities; 3% of eligible undergraduate men and 3% of eligible undergraduate women are members.

Drug and Alcohol Information

Education

On campus Drug and alcohol education/prevention programs offered for: all students, athletes/coaches, faculty, administration. Bacchus chapter planned for 1989. Authorized group concerned with responsible drinking. College holds an annual alcohol awareness week and drug awareness week.

Identification of Problems

Admissions College application does not ask about prior substance abuse problems.

On campus Current students identified as chemically dependent may remain enrolled. Training program on identifying students with potential substance abuse problems for: resident advisers, coaches, Greek officers, faculty, administration, Drug and Alcohol Task Force. Written procedures for students and staff if substance abuse is suspected.

Support Services

On campus AA, NA, ACOA, support groups (Drug/Alcohol Recovery Support Group), private counseling, Counseling Center support groups, Cocaine Anonymous.

Employee assistance Program for chemically dependent employees not available but is being planned for 1989. Staff working with drug/alcohol-related issues: 1 full-time and 2 part-time.

Disciplinary Actions

Alcohol Results of infractions of alcohol regulations (see Comparative Table of Alcohol Regulations) vary by situation but can include chemical dependency assessment, counseling, warning, probaton, suspension, expulsion.

Drugs For any use, possession, or sale: varies by situation.

For More Information

Contact: F. Robert Schiraldi, Drug & Alcohol Program Counselor/Coordinator, Temple University, 1802 N. Park Mall, Philadelphia, PA 19122. Telephone: 215-787-7503.

TEMPLE UNIVERSITY, AMBLER CAMPUS

Ambler, Pennsylvania

General Information

State-related 5-year coed college. Part of Temple University. Founded 1910. Awards A (terminal), B, M, D. Primary accreditation: regional. Small-town setting; 186-acre campus. Total enrollment: 4,516. Social organizations: 1 national fraternity, 1 local sorority.

Drug and Alcohol Information

Education

On campus Drug and alcohol education/prevention programs offered for: all students, faculty, administration. College holds an annual alcohol awareness week and drug awareness week.

Identification of Problems

Admissions College application does not ask about prior substance abuse problems.

On campus Current students identified as chemically dependent may remain enrolled. Training program on identifying students with potential substance abuse problems for: resident advisers, coaches. No written procedures for students and staff if substance abuse is suspected.

Support Services

On campus AA, NA, ACOA, private counseling, peer counselors.

Employee assistance Program for chemically dependent employees not available. Staff working with drug/alcohol-related issues: 1 full-time.

Disciplinary Actions

Alcohol Results of infractions of alcohol regulations (see Comparative Table of Alcohol Regulations) include chemical dependency assessment, counseling, warning, probation, suspension, expulsion.

Drugs For any use, possession, or sale: varies by situation.

Temple University, Ambler Campus (continued)

Additional Information from the College

There is a University-wide Drug and Alcohol Task Force for policy recommendations and program planning.

For More Information

Contact: F. Robert Schiraldi, Coordinator of Drug and Alcohol Referral and Education, University Health Services, Temple University, Ambler Campus, Meeting House Road, Ambler, PA 19002. Telephone: 215-787-7503.

TENNESSEE TECHNOLOGICAL UNIVERSITY

Cookeville, Tennessee

General Information

State-supported comprehensive coed institution. Part of State University and Community College System of Tennessee. Founded 1915. Awards A (terminal), B, M, D. Primary accreditation: regional. Small-town setting; 235-acre campus. Total enrollment: 8,006. Faculty: 674 (339 full-time, 335 part-time). Social organizations: 15 national fraternities, 5 national sororities, 2 local fraternities; 16% of eligible undergraduate men and 10% of eligible undergraduate women are members.

Drug and Alcohol Information

Education

On campus Drug and alcohol education/prevention programs offered for: all students. Authorized group concerned with responsible drinking. College holds an annual alcohol awareness week.

Identification of Problems

Admissions College application does not ask about prior substance abuse problems.

On campus Whether current students identified as chemically dependent may remain enrolled varies by situation. Training program on identifying students with potential substance abuse problems for: resident advisers, Greek officers. No written procedures for students and staff if substance abuse is suspected.

Support Services

On campus NA, private counseling.

Employee assistance Program for chemically dependent employees not available.

Disciplinary Actions

Alcohol Results of infractions of alcohol regulations (see Comparative Table of Alcohol Regulations) vary by situation.

Drugs For any use or possession: varies by situation. For first-time sale: suspension. For subsequent sale: varies by situation.

For More Information

Contact: Marc Burnett, Assistant Vice President for Student Services, Tennessee Technological University, Box 5135, Cookeville, TN 38505. Telephone: 615-372-3236.

TEXAS A&M UNIVERSITY

College Station, Texas

General Information

State-supported comprehensive coed institution. Part of Texas A&M University System. Founded 1876. Awards B, M, D. Primary accreditation: regional. City setting; 5,142-acre campus. Total enrollment: 39,163. Faculty: 2,151 (1,792 full-time, 359 part-time). Social organizations: 26 national fraternities, 11 national sororities; 8% of eligible undergraduate men and 9% of eligible undergraduate women are members.

Drug and Alcohol Information

Education

On campus Drug and alcohol education/prevention programs offered for: all students, athletes/coaches, faculty, administration, staff. Bacchus chapter: 7 members. College holds an annual alcohol awareness week and drug awareness week.

Identification of Problems

Admissions College application does not ask about prior substance abuse problems.

On campus Current students identified as chemically dependent may remain enrolled, but treatment may be required. Training program on identifying students with potential substance abuse problems for: resident advisers, Greek officers, faculty, administration, students. Written procedures for students and staff if substance abuse is suspected.

Support Services

On campus AA, NA, ACOA, support groups, private counseling, Center for Drug Prevention and Education.

Employee assistance Program for chemically dependent employees not available. Staff working with drug/alcohol-related issues: 2 full-time and 11 part-time.

Disciplinary Actions

Alcohol Results of infractions of alcohol regulations (see Comparative Table of Alcohol Regulations) vary by situation.

Drugs For first-time use, possession, or sale: suspension. For subsequent use, possession, or sale: expulsion.

Additional Information from the College

Texas A&M University recognizes the need to serve the student in areas of personal as well as academic growth. The Center for Drug Prevention and Education (CDPE) strives to serve the student by preventing drug abuse through education and information. The Center for Drug Prevention and Education is responsible for the following areas: drug prevention programming, resource development and dissemination, early intervention and referral, research and evaluation, and training and consultation.

For More Information

Contact: Dennis Reardon, Ph.D., Coordinator of the Center for Drug Prevention and Education, Department of Student Affairs, Texas A&M University, College Station, TX 77843-1257. Telephone: 409-845-0280.

TEXAS A&M UNIVERSITY AT GALVESTON

Galveston, Texas

General Information

State-supported 4-year specialized coed college. Part of Texas A&M University System. Founded 1971. Awards B. Primary accreditation: regional. City setting; 100-acre campus. Total enrollment: 743. Faculty: 60 (49 full-time, 11 part-time). Social organizations: sailing club, diving club, swimming club.

Drug and Alcohol Information

Education

On campus Drug and alcohol education/prevention programs offered for: all students, faculty, administration. Authorized group concerned with responsible drinking.

Identification of Problems

Admissions College application does not ask about prior substance abuse problems.

On campus Current students identified as chemically dependent may remain enrolled. Training program on identifying students with potential substance abuse problems for: resident advisers. Written procedures for students and staff if substance abuse is suspected.

Support Services

On campus Private counseling.

Employee assistance Program for chemically dependent employees available. Staff working with drug/alcohol-related issues: 3 part-time.

Disciplinary Actions

Alcohol Results of infractions of alcohol regulations (see Comparative Table of Alcohol Regulations) vary by situation but can include chemical dependency assessment, counseling, warning, probation, suspension, expulsion.

Drugs For first-time use, possession, or sale: suspension. For subsequent use, possession, or sale: varies by situation. Comments: Subsequent drug offenses would probably result in expulsion or dismissal.

For More Information

Contact: Linda Van Meter, Coordinator of Counseling Services, Texas A&M University at Galveston, P.O. Box 1675, Galveston, TX 77553. Telephone: 409-740-4587.

TEXAS CHRISTIAN UNIVERSITY

Fort Worth, Texas

General Information

Independent comprehensive coed institution, affiliated with Christian Church (Disciples of Christ). Founded 1873. Awards B, M, D. Primary accreditation: regional. Metropolitan setting; 237-acre campus. Total enrollment: 6,993. Faculty: 385 (310 full-time, 75 part-time). Social organizations: 10 national fraternities, 12 national sororities, 1 local fraternity; 42% of eligible undergraduate men and 50% of eligible undergraduate women are members.

Drug and Alcohol Information

Education

On campus Drug and alcohol education/prevention programs offered for: all students, athletes/coaches, faculty, administration. Bacchus chapter. College holds an annual alcohol awareness week and drug awareness week.

Identification of Problems

Admissions College application does not ask about prior substance abuse problems.

On campus Current students identified as chemically dependent may remain enrolled, but treatment is required. Training program on identifying students with potential substance abuse problems for: resident advisers, coaches, Greek officers, faculty, administration, peer counselors. Written procedures for students and staff if substance abuse is suspected.

Support Services

On campus ACOA, support groups, private counseling.

Employee assistance Program for chemically dependent employees not available. Staff working with drug/alcohol-related issues: 3 full-time and 2 part-time.

Disciplinary Actions

Alcohol Results of infractions of alcohol regulations (see Comparative Table of Alcohol Regulations) include chemical dependency assessment, counseling, warning, probation, suspension.

Drugs For first-time use or possession: varies by situation—probation. For subsequent use or possession: suspension. For any sale: expulsion.

Additional Information from the College

Texas Christian emphasizes education, not control, in its alcohol and drug programs, which are available to student groups, residence halls, classes, and athletic teams. There is peer counseling and training for faculty and staff. Individual assessments can be made with referrals to appropriate resources on or off campus. An extensive resource library is available. The programs which are set in an overall context of health and healthy life-styles, are continually evaluated to monitor their impact and effectiveness.

For More Information

Contact: Barbara Herman, Coordinator of Drug and Alcohol Education, Box 32902, Texas Christian University, 2800 S. University Dr., Fort Worth, TX 76129. Telephone: 817-921-7100.

TEXAS COLLEGE

Tyler, Texas

General Information

Independent 4-year coed college, affiliated with Christian Methodist Episcopal Church. Founded 1894. Awards B. Primary accreditation: regional. City setting; 63-acre campus. Total enrollment: 478. Social organizations: 3 national fraternities, 3 national sororities; 10% of eligible undergraduate men and 25% of eligible undergraduate women are members.

Drug and Alcohol Information

Education

On campus Drug and alcohol education/prevention programs offered for: all students, athletes/coaches, faculty,

Texas College (continued)

administration. Authorized group concerned with responsible drinking. College holds an annual alcohol awareness week and drug awareness week.

Identification of Problems

Admissions College application does not ask about prior substance abuse problems.

On campus Current students identified as chemically dependent may not remain enrolled. No training program on identifying students with potential substance abuse problems. Written procedures for students and staff if substance abuse is suspected.

Support Services

On campus AA, NA, ACOA, private counseling.

Employee assistance Program for chemically dependent employees available. Staff working with drug/alcohol-related issues: 4 full-time and 5 part-time.

Disciplinary Actions

Alcohol Results of infractions of alcohol regulations (see Comparative Table of Alcohol Regulations) include counseling, probation, suspension.

Drugs For first-time use or possession: varies by situation. For subsequent use: varies by situation—chemical dependency assessment, suspension, expulsion. For subsequent possession: suspension, expulsion. For any sale: expulsion.

For More Information

Contact: Janice Starks, Nurse, Texas College, 2404 N. Grand Ave., Tyler, TX 75702. Telephone: 214-593-8311.

TEXAS LUTHERAN COLLEGE

Seguin, Texas

General Information

Independent 4-year coed college, affiliated with Evangelical Lutheran Church. Founded 1891. Awards B. Primary accreditation: regional. Small-town setting; 150-acre campus. Total enrollment: 1,006. Faculty: 79 (63 full-time, 16 part-time). Social organizations: 5 local fraternities, 4 local sororities; 20% of eligible undergraduate men and 20% of eligible undergraduate women are members.

Drug and Alcohol Information

Education

On campus Drug and alcohol education/prevention programs offered for: all students, athletes/coaches, faculty. Authorized group concerned with responsible drinking. College holds an annual alcohol awareness week and drug awareness week.

Identification of Problems

On campus Current students identified as chemically dependent may remain enrolled, but treatment may be required. Training program on identifying students with potential substance abuse problems for: resident advisers, coaches, Greek officers, faculty, administration. Written procedures for students and staff if substance abuse is suspected.

Support Services

On campus AA, NA, ACOA, private counseling.

Employee assistance Program for chemically dependent employees not available. Staff working with drug/alcohol-related issues: 1 part-time.

Disciplinary Actions

Alcohol Results of infractions of alcohol regulations (see Comparative Table of Alcohol Regulations) vary by situation but can include chemical dependency assessment, counseling, warning, probation, suspension, expulsion.

Drugs For first-time use: varies by situation—counseling. For subsequent use: varies by situation. For any possession: varies by situation. For first-time sale: suspension. For subsequent sale: expulsion.

For More Information

Contact: Anne Costas, WellWay Program Coordinator, Texas Lutheran College, 1000 W. Court St., Seguin, TX 78155. Telephone: 512-379-4161 Ext. 260.

TEXAS TECH UNIVERSITY

Lubbock, Texas

General Information

State-supported comprehensive coed institution. Founded 1923. Awards B, M, D. Primary accreditation: regional. City setting; 1,839-acre campus. Total enrollment: 24,605. Faculty: 1,611 (883 full-time, 728 part-time). Social organizations: 24 national fraternities, 14 national sororities, 1 local fraternity, 1 local sorority; 12% of eligible undergraduate men and 10% of eligible undergraduate women are members.

Drug and Alcohol Information

Education

On campus Drug and alcohol education/prevention programs offered for: all students, faculty. Bacchus chapter. Authorized group concerned with responsible drinking. College holds an annual alcohol awareness week and drug awareness week.

Identification of Problems

Admissions College application does not ask about prior substance abuse problems.

On campus Training program on identifying students with potential substance abuse problems for: resident advisers, hall directors. Written procedures for students and staff if substance abuse is suspected.

Support Services

On campus AA, NA, support groups, private counseling.

Employee assistance Program for chemically dependent employees available. Staff working with drug/alcohol-related issues: 1 full-time and 2 part-time.

Disciplinary Actions

Alcohol Results of infractions of alcohol regulations (see Comparative Table of Alcohol Regulations) vary by situation.

Drugs For any use, possession, or sale: varies by situation.

Additional Information from the College

Programming and activities will increase using funds from a recently-awarded FIPSE grant for the prevention of substance abuse on campus.

For More Information

Contact: Brenda Arkell, Assistant to the Dean of Students, Texas Tech University, P.O. Box 4259, Lubbock, TX 79409. Telephone: 806-742-2192.

TEXAS WOMAN'S UNIVERSITY

Denton, Texas

General Information

State-supported comprehensive primarily women's institution. Founded 1901. Awards B, M, D. Primary accreditation: regional. City setting; 270-acre campus. Total enrollment: 8,898. Faculty: 476 (382 full-time, 94 part-time). Social organizations: 5 national sororities, 2 local sororities; 5% of eligible undergraduate women are members.

Drug and Alcohol Information

Education

On campus Drug and alcohol education/prevention programs offered for: all students, faculty, administration. Authorized group concerned with responsible drinking. College holds an annual alcohol awareness week and drug awareness week.

Identification of Problems

Admissions College application does not ask about prior substance abuse problems.

On campus Current students identified as chemically dependent may remain enrolled. Training program on identifying students with potential substance abuse problems for: resident advisers. Written procedures for students and staff if substance abuse is suspected.

Support Services

On campus Support groups, private counseling.

Employee assistance Program for chemically dependent employees not available.

Disciplinary Actions

Alcohol Results of infractions of alcohol regulations (see Comparative Table of Alcohol Regulations) include chemical dependency assessment, counseling, warning, probation, suspension.

Drugs For any use, possession, or sale: expulsion.

For More Information

Contact: Dr. Don Rosen, Director, Counseling Center, Texas Woman's University, P.O. Box 22305, Denton, TX 76204. Telephone: 817-898-3801.

THOMAS COLLEGE

Waterville, Maine

General Information

Independent 5-year coed college. Founded 1894. Awards A (college transfer and terminal), B, M. Primary accreditation: regional. Small-town setting; 70-acre campus. Total enrollment: 1,068. Faculty: 58 (25 full-time, 33 part-time). Social organizations: 1 national fraternity, 1 national sorority, 2 local fraternities, 2 local sororities; 20% of eligible undergraduate men and 15% of eligible undergraduate women are members.

Drug and Alcohol Information

Education

On campus Drug and alcohol education/prevention programs offered for: all students. College holds an annual alcohol awareness week.

Identification of Problems

On campus Current students identified as chemically dependent may remain enrolled, but treatment is required. Training program on identifying students with potential substance abuse problems for: resident advisers, administration. Written procedures for students and staff if substance abuse is suspected.

Support Services

On campus Private counseling.

Employee assistance Program for chemically dependent employees not available. Staff working with drug/alcohol-related issues: 3 part-time.

Disciplinary Actions

Alcohol Results of infractions of alcohol regulations (see Comparative Table of Alcohol Regulations) include warning, probation.

Drugs For first-time use, possession, or sale: varies by situation. For subsequent use: probation. For subsequent possession: varies by situation. For subsequent sale: expulsion.

For More Information

Contact: Rob Bongiovanni, Dean of Student Affairs, Thomas College, West River Rd., Waterville, ME 04901. Telephone: 207-873-0771.

THOMAS MORE COLLEGE

Crestview Hills, Kentucky

General Information

Independent Roman Catholic 4-year coed college. Founded 1921. Awards A (college transfer), B. Primary accreditation: regional. City setting; 160-acre campus. Total enrollment: 1,120. Faculty: 120 (67 full-time, 53 part-time). Social organizations: 1 national fraternity, 1 national sorority, 1 local fraternity, 1 local sorority; 25% of eligible undergraduate men and 22% of eligible undergraduate women are members.

Drug and Alcohol Information

Education

On campus Drug and alcohol education/prevention programs offered for: all students; required for: athletes/coaches, resident advisers. Authorized group concerned with responsible drinking. College holds an annual alcohol awareness week.

Identification of Problems

Admissions College application does not ask about prior substance abuse problems.

On campus Current students identified as chemically dependent may remain enrolled. Training program on identifying students with potential substance abuse problems for: resident advisers, coaches. No written procedures for students and staff if substance abuse is suspected.

Support Services

On campus Private counseling.

Employee assistance Program for chemically dependent employees not available.

Disciplinary Actions

Alcohol Results of infractions of alcohol regulations (see Comparative Table of Alcohol Regulations) vary by

Thomas More College (continued)

situation but can include counseling, warning, probation, suspension, expulsion.

Drugs For first-time use: warning, probation. For subsequent use: probation. For first-time possession: probation. For subsequent possession: suspension. For any sale: expulsion.

For More Information

Contact: Dr. Richard Herdlein, Vice President for Student Development, Thomas More College, Crestview Hills, KY 41017. Telephone: 606-344-3317.

TIFFIN UNIVERSITY

Tiffin, Ohio

General Information

Independent 4-year coed college. Founded 1888. Awards A (college transfer and terminal), B. Primary accreditation: regional. Small-town setting; 8-acre campus. Total enrollment: 777. Faculty: 47 (25 full-time, 22 part-time). Social organizations: 1 national fraternity, 1 national sorority, 1 local fraternity, 2 local sororities; 15% of eligible undergraduate men and 14% of eligible undergraduate women are members.

Drug and Alcohol Information

Education

On campus Drug and alcohol education/prevention programs offered for: all students; required for: freshmen, athletes/coaches, resident advisers. Authorized group concerned with responsible drinking. College holds an annual alcohol awareness week.

Identification of Problems

Admissions College application does not ask about prior substance abuse problems.

On campus Current students identified as chemically dependent may remain enrolled, but treatment is required. No training program on identifying students with potential substance abuse problems. Written procedures for students and staff if substance abuse is suspected.

Support Services

On campus Private counseling.

Employee assistance Program for chemically dependent employees not available. Staff working with drug/alcohol-related issues: 2 part-time.

Disciplinary Actions

Alcohol Results of infractions of alcohol regulations (see Comparative Table of Alcohol Regulations) include chemical dependency assessment, counseling, warning, probation, suspension.

Drugs For first-time use: counseling, warning, probation. For subsequent use: varies by situation—probation, suspension. For first-time possession: counseling, probation, suspension. For subsequent possession: varies by situation—probation, suspension, expulsion. For first-time sale: suspension, expulsion. For subsequent sale: expulsion.

Additional Information from the College

A drug and alcohol abuse prevention information/education session is included in freshman orientation activities in early September.

For More Information

Contact: Walter E. Zielinski, Dean of Students, Tiffin University, Tiffin, OH 44883. Telephone: 419-447-6442 Ext. 22.

TOCCOA FALLS COLLEGE

Toccoa Falls, Georgia

General Information

Independent interdenominational 4-year coed college. Founded 1907. Awards A (college transfer), B. Primary accreditation: regional and AABC. Small-town setting; 1,100-acre campus. Total enrollment: 769. Faculty: 50 (46 full-time, 4 part-time).

Drug and Alcohol Information

Education

On campus Drug and alcohol education/prevention programs offered for: all students.

Identification of Problems

Admissions College application question about prior substance abuse problems is used in the admissions decision.

On campus Current students identified as chemically dependent may not remain enrolled. Training program on identifying students with potential substance abuse problems for: resident advisers.

Support Services

On campus Private counseling, campus pastor.

Employee assistance Program for chemically dependent employees not available.

Disciplinary Actions

Alcohol Results of infractions of alcohol regulations (see Comparative Table of Alcohol Regulations) include expulsion.

Drugs For any use, possession, or sale: expulsion.

For More Information

Contact: Kenneth Sanders, Dean of Students, Toccoa Falls College, Toccoa Falls, GA 30598. Telephone: 404-886-6831.

TOWSON STATE UNIVERSITY

Towson, Maryland

General Information

State-supported 5-year coed college. Part of Maryland State Colleges and Universities System. Founded 1866. Awards B, M. Primary accreditation: regional. City setting; 326-acre campus. Total enrollment: 15,169. Faculty: 957 (490 full-time, 467 part-time). Social organizations: 15 national fraternities, 10 national sororities, 1 local sorority; 5% of eligible undergraduate men and 5% of eligible undergraduate women are members.

Drug and Alcohol Information

Education

On campus Drug and alcohol education/prevention programs offered for: all students. Authorized group concerned with responsible drinking. College holds an annual alcohol awareness week and drug awareness week.

Identification of Problems

Admissions College application does not ask about prior substance abuse problems.

On campus Current students identified as chemically dependent may remain enrolled. No training program on identifying students with potential substance abuse problems. No written procedures for students and staff if substance abuse is suspected.

Support Services

On campus AA, NA, ACOA, support groups (SADD).

Employee assistance Program for chemically dependent employees not available. Staff working with drug/alcohol-related issues: 1 full-time.

Disciplinary Actions

Alcohol Results of infractions of alcohol regulations (see Comparative Table of Alcohol Regulations) include warning.

Drugs For first-time use or possession: warning. For subsequent use or possession: varies by situation. For any sale: expulsion.

Additional Information from the College

The University has a drug/alcohol committee consisting of 1 counselor and 1 faculty member. A drug education teacher offers two drug education courses for 60 students per semester. 'Tailgate' parties are outlawed, but this rule is being reconsidered.

For More Information

Contact: Alice Randolph-Prince, Professor of Health Sciences, Towson State University, Towson, MD 21204. Telephone: 301-321-2378.

TREVECCA NAZARENE COLLEGE

Nashville, Tennessee

General Information

Independent Nazarene 5-year coed college. Founded 1901. Awards A (terminal), B, M. Primary accreditation: regional. Metropolitan setting; 80-acre campus. Total enrollment: 1,727.

Drug and Alcohol Information

Education

On campus Drug and alcohol education/prevention programs offered for: all students, faculty, administration.

Identification of Problems

Admissions College application question about prior substance abuse problems is used for counseling and referral, if student is admitted; in the admissions decision.

On campus Current students identified as chemically dependent may not remain enrolled. No training program on identifying students with potential substance abuse problems. Written procedures for students and staff if substance abuse is suspected.

Support Services

On campus Private counseling.

Employee assistance Program for chemically dependent employees not available.

Disciplinary Actions

Alcohol Results of infractions of alcohol regulations (see Comparative Table of Alcohol Regulations) include counseling, probation.

Drugs For any use or sale: expulsion. For first-time possession: counseling, probation. For subsequent possession: expulsion.

Additional Information from the College

The College recognizes the danger to others and the ethical responsibilities associated with the use of alcohol and drugs and insists that members of the College community abstain. Medical use of drugs may be permitted when prescribed by a licensed practicing physician.

For More Information

Contact: Steve Harris, Dean of Students, Trevecca Nazarene College, 333 Murfreesboro Rd., Nashville, TN 37210. Telephone: 615-248-1245.

TRINITY CHRISTIAN COLLEGE

Palos Heights, Illinois

General Information

Independent 4-year coed college, affiliated with Christian Reformed Church. Founded 1959. Awards B. Primary accreditation: regional. Small-town setting; 50-acre campus. Total enrollment: 550. Faculty: 63 (38 full-time, 25 part-time).

Drug and Alcohol Information

Education

On campus Drug and alcohol education/prevention programs offered for: all students, faculty, administration. Authorized group concerned with responsible drinking.

Identification of Problems

Admissions College application does not ask about prior substance abuse problems.

On campus Current students identified as chemically dependent may remain enrolled, but treatment is required. Training program on identifying students with potential substance abuse problems for: resident advisers. Written procedures for students and staff if substance abuse is suspected.

Support Services

On campus Support groups, private counseling.

Employee assistance Program for chemically dependent employees available.

Disciplinary Actions

Alcohol Results of infractions of alcohol regulations (see Comparative Table of Alcohol Regulations) vary by situation but can include chemical dependency assessment, counseling. Comments: Alcohol/drug educational assessment required for those who violate policy.

Drugs For first-time use or possession: chemical dependency assessment, counseling, warning. For subsequent use or possession: suspension. For first-time sale: suspension. For subsequent sale: expulsion. Comments: Drug/alcohol educational assessment required for those who violate policy.

For More Information

Contact: David Larsen, Dean of Students, Trinity Christian College, 6601 W. College Dr., Palos Heights, IL 60463. Telephone: 312-597-3000.

TRI-STATE UNIVERSITY
Angola, Indiana

General Information
Independent 4-year coed college. Founded 1884. Awards A (college transfer and terminal), B. Primary accreditation: regional. Small-town setting; 300-acre campus. Total enrollment: 1,054. Faculty: 75 (72 full-time, 3 part-time). Social organizations: 8 national fraternities, 2 local fraternities, 3 local sororities; 13% of eligible undergraduate men and 2% of eligible undergraduate women are members.

Drug and Alcohol Information
Education
On campus Drug and alcohol education/prevention programs offered for: freshmen, resident advisers; required for: athletes/coaches.

Identification of Problems
Admissions College application does not ask about prior substance abuse problems.

On campus Current students identified as chemically dependent may remain enrolled, but treatment is required. Training program on identifying students with potential substance abuse problems for: resident advisers, coaches. Written procedures for students and staff if substance abuse is suspected.

Support Services
On campus No support services on campus.

Employee assistance Program for chemically dependent employees not available.

Disciplinary Actions
Alcohol Results of infractions of alcohol regulations (see Comparative Table of Alcohol Regulations) vary by situation.

Drugs For any use or possession: varies by situation. For any sale: suspension, expulsion.

For More Information
Contact: Robert Imhoff, Dean of Students, Tri-State University, Angola, IN 46703. Telephone: 219-665-4167.

TROY STATE UNIVERSITY AT DOTHAN
Dothan, Alabama

General Information
State-supported 5-year coed college. Part of Troy State University System. Founded 1962. Awards A (college transfer), B, M. Primary accreditation: regional. Small-town setting; 4-acre campus. Total enrollment: 1,735. Faculty: 82 (41 full-time, 41 part-time).

Drug and Alcohol Information
Education
On campus Drug and alcohol education/prevention programs offered for: all students. College holds an annual alcohol awareness week and drug awareness week.

Identification of Problems
Admissions College application does not ask about prior substance abuse problems.

On campus Current students identified as chemically dependent may remain enrolled, but treatment may be required. Comments: Varies by severity of addiction. No training program on identifying students with potential substance abuse problems. Written procedures for students and staff if substance abuse is suspected.

Support Services
Off campus Referral made to community agencies.

Employee assistance Program for chemically dependent employees not available. Staff working with drug/alcohol-related issues: 1 part-time.

Disciplinary Actions
Alcohol Results of infractions of alcohol regulations (see Comparative Table of Alcohol Regulations) vary by situation. Comments: Review by Student Affairs Committee.

Drugs For any use, possession, or sale: varies by situation.

Additional Information from the College
The University is a commuter campus. There are a limited number of University-sponsored activities and no on-campus housing.

For More Information
Contact: Pamela Williamson, Director of Counseling Services, Troy State University at Dothan, 227 N. Foster St., Dothan, AL 36303. Telephone: 205-792-8783 Ext. 225.

TUSCULUM COLLEGE
Greeneville, Tennessee

General Information
Independent Presbyterian 5-year coed college. Founded 1794. Awards B, M. Primary accreditation: regional. Small-town setting; 140-acre campus. Total enrollment: 716. Faculty: 133 (43 full-time, 90 part-time).

Drug and Alcohol Information
Education
On campus Drug and alcohol education/prevention programs offered for: all students. College holds an annual alcohol awareness week and drug awareness week.

Identification of Problems
Admissions College application does not ask about prior substance abuse problems.

On campus Current students identified as chemically dependent may remain enrolled, but treatment is required. Training program on identifying students with potential substance abuse problems for: resident advisers. Written procedures for students and staff if substance abuse is suspected.

Support Services
On campus Support groups (peer counseling center), private counseling.

Employee assistance Program for chemically dependent employees not available. Staff working with drug/alcohol-related issues: 4 part-time.

Disciplinary Actions
Alcohol Results of infractions of alcohol regulations (see Comparative Table of Alcohol Regulations) include chemical dependency assessment, probation, suspension (third offense).

Drugs For first-time use: suspension. For subsequent use:

expulsion. For first-time possession: probation. For subsequent possession: suspension. For any sale: expulsion.

Additional Information from the College

The College has a crisis intervention team that exchanges information when behavior indicates a potential problem. The team consists of the director of enrollment, the dean of liberal arts studies, resident directors, and psychology department instructors.

For More Information

Contact: Joseph Corfield, Assistant Director of Student Services, Tusculum College, Box 5090, Tusculum Station, Greeneville, TN 37743. Telephone: 615-638-1111.

TUSKEGEE UNIVERSITY

Tuskegee, Alabama

General Information

Independent 5-year coed college. Founded 1881. Awards B, M, D. Primary accreditation: regional. Small-town setting; 5,000-acre campus. Total enrollment: 3,400. Faculty: 307 (285 full-time, 22 part-time). Social organizations: 4 national fraternities, 4 national sororities, 12 non-Greek organizations; 7% of eligible undergraduate men and 10% of eligible undergraduate women are members.

Drug and Alcohol Information

Education

On campus Drug and alcohol education/prevention programs offered for: freshmen, all students, social organization members, athletes/coaches, faculty, administration, resident advisers, student leaders, community. Authorized group concerned with responsible drinking. College holds an annual alcohol awareness week and drug awareness week.

Identification of Problems

Admissions College application does not ask about prior substance abuse problems.

On campus Current students identified as chemically dependent may remain enrolled. No training program on identifying students with potential substance abuse problems. Written procedures for students and staff if substance abuse is suspected.

Support Services

On campus No support services on campus.

Off campus AA.

Employee assistance Program for chemically dependent employees not available.

Disciplinary Actions

Alcohol Results of infractions of alcohol regulations (see Comparative Table of Alcohol Regulations) vary by situation but can include counseling, warning, probation.

Drugs For any use, possession, or sale: varies by situation.

Additional Information from the College

A task force has been providing weekly and monthly substance abuse programs for students, faculty, staff, and community for about ten years. The University does an excellent job with limited resources and currently is drafting a proposal for federal funding.

For More Information

Contact: Emma R. Boone, Counselor, Tuskegee University, Tuskegee, AL 36088. Telephone: 205-727-8147.

UNION COLLEGE

Barbourville, Kentucky

General Information

Independent United Methodist 5-year coed college. Founded 1879. Awards A (college transfer and terminal), B, M. Primary accreditation: regional. Small-town setting; 110-acre campus. Total enrollment: 1,147. Faculty: 61 (46 full-time, 15 part-time). Social organizations: 1 local fraternity, 2 local sororities; 10% of eligible undergraduate men and 20% of eligible undergraduate women are members.

Drug and Alcohol Information

Education

On campus Drug and alcohol education/prevention programs offered for: all students, athletes/coaches. Authorized group concerned with responsible drinking.

Identification of Problems

Admissions College application does not ask about prior substance abuse problems.

On campus Current students identified as chemically dependent may remain enrolled, but treatment is required. Training program on identifying students with potential substance abuse problems for: resident advisers. Written procedures for students and staff if substance abuse is suspected.

Support Services

On campus Private counseling. Off campus AA.

Employee assistance Program for chemically dependent employees not available.

Disciplinary Actions

Alcohol Results of infractions of alcohol regulations (see Comparative Table of Alcohol Regulations) vary by situation but can include counseling, warning, fines, suspension.

Drugs For first-time use or possession: counseling, probation. For subsequent use or possession: counseling, suspension. For any sale: expulsion.

For More Information

Contact: Donna Jancarek, Counselor, Union College, 310 College St., Barbourville, KY 40906. Telephone: 606-546-4151 Ext. 293.

UNION COLLEGE

Schenectady, New York

General Information

Independent 5-year coed college. Founded 1795. Awards B, M, D. Primary accreditation: regional. City setting; 100-acre campus. Total enrollment: 2,395. Faculty: 197 (169 full-time, 28 part-time). Social organizations: 18 national fraternities, 4 national sororities; 46% of eligible undergraduate men and 25% of eligible undergraduate women are members.

Drug and Alcohol Information

Education

On campus Drug and alcohol education/prevention programs offered for: all students. Authorized group concerned with responsible drinking. College holds an annual alcohol awareness week.

Union College (continued)

Identification of Problems

Admissions College application does not ask about prior substance abuse problems.

On campus Current students identified as chemically dependent may remain enrolled, but treatment is required. Training program on identifying students with potential substance abuse problems for: resident advisers, administration. Written procedures for students and staff if substance abuse is suspected.

Support Services

On campus AA, NA, Al-Anon, private counseling.

Employee assistance Staff working with drug/alcohol-related issues: 5 part-time.

Disciplinary Actions

Alcohol Results of infractions of alcohol regulations (see Comparative Table of Alcohol Regulations) include chemical dependency assessment, counseling, warning, probation, suspension, expulsion.

Drugs For first-time use or possessionL varies by situation. For first-time sale: suspension, expulsion. For subsequent use: probation, suspension, expulsion. For subsequent possession: expulsion. For subsequent sale: expulsion.

For More Information

Contact: Joseph Mammola, Dean of Students, Union College, Schenectady, NY 12308. Telephone: 518-370-6116.

UNITED STATES INTERNATIONAL UNIVERSITY

San Diego, California

General Information

Independent comprehensive coed institution. Part of International University (other campuses in London, Mexico City, Nairobi). Founded 1952. Awards A (college transfer), B, M, D. Primary accreditation: regional. Metropolitan setting; 200-acre campus. Total enrollment: 3,307. Faculty: 245 (95 full-time, 150 part-time).

Drug and Alcohol Information

Education

On campus Drug and alcohol education/prevention programs offered for: all students, athletes/coaches, faculty, administration, graduate staff. Authorized group concerned with responsible drinking. College holds an annual alcohol awareness week.

Identification of Problems

Admissions College application does not ask about prior substance abuse problems.

On campus Current students identified as chemically dependent may remain enrolled, but treatment is required. Training program on identifying students with potential substance abuse problems for: resident advisers. No written procedures for students and staff if substance abuse is suspected.

Support Services

On campus AA, NA, ACOA, private counseling, peer/group counseling.

Employee assistance Program for chemically dependent employees not available. Staff working with drug/alcohol-related issues: 1 full-time and several part-time.

Disciplinary Actions

Alcohol Results of infractions of alcohol regulations (see Comparative Table of Alcohol Regulations) vary by situation but can include chemical dependency assessment, counseling, warning, probation, suspension, expulsion.

Drugs For any use, possession, or sale: varies by situation.

Additional Information from the College

The Drug Prevention Program is new and is expected to be expanded significantly by next year. As a comprehensive program it includes alcohol and other drug education, peer educators, and peer counselors.

For More Information

Contact: Joy Covert, Director, Drug Prevention Program, United States International University, 10455 Pomerado Road, San Diego, CA 92131. Telephone: 619-693-4504.

UNITED STATES MERCHANT MARINE ACADEMY

Kings Point, New York

General Information

Federally supported 4-year specialized coed college. Founded 1943. Awards B. Primary accreditation: regional. Small-town setting; 80-acre campus. Total enrollment: 844. Faculty: 74 (64 full-time, 10 part-time).

Drug and Alcohol Information

Education

On campus Drug and alcohol education/prevention programs offered for: all students. Authorized group concerned with responsible drinking. College holds an annual alcohol awareness week and drug awareness week.

Identification of Problems

Admissions College application question about prior substance abuse problems is used in the admissions decision.

On campus Current students identified as chemically dependent may not remain enrolled. Training program on identifying students with potential substance abuse problems for: administration. Written procedures for students and staff if substance abuse is suspected.

Support Services

On campus AA, private counseling.

Employee assistance Program for chemically dependent employees available. Staff working with drug/alcohol-related issues: 1 part-time.

Disciplinary Actions

Alcohol Results of infractions of alcohol regulations (see Comparative Table of Alcohol Regulations) include counseling, warning, probation, suspension, expulsion.

Drugs For any use, possession, or sale: expulsion.

For More Information

Contact: Robert L. Safarik, Commandant of Midshipmen, United States Merchant Marine Academy, Kings Point, NY 11024. Telephone: 516-773-5338.

UNIVERSITY OF AKRON

Akron, Ohio

General Information

State-supported comprehensive coed institution. Founded 1870. Awards A (terminal), B, M, D. Primary accreditation: regional. City setting; 160-acre campus. Total enrollment: 27,818. Faculty: 1,647 (837 full-time, 810 part-time). Social organizations: 15 national fraternities, 10 national sororities, 1 local fraternity; 3% of eligible undergraduate men and 2% of eligible undergraduate women are members.

Drug and Alcohol Information

Education

On campus Drug and alcohol education/prevention programs offered for: freshmen, social organization members, resident advisers, student leaders; required for: athletes/coaches. Authorized group concerned with responsible drinking. College holds an annual alcohol awareness week.

Identification of Problems

Admissions College application does not ask about prior substance abuse problems.

On campus Current students identified as chemically dependent may remain enrolled. Training program on identifying students with potential substance abuse problems for: resident advisers, coaches, Greek officers. No written procedures for students and staff if substance abuse is suspected.

Support Services

On campus Support groups (counseling center).

Employee assistance Program for chemically dependent employees available. Staff working with drug/alcohol-related issues: 1 full-time and 6 part-time.

Disciplinary Actions

Alcohol Results of infractions of alcohol regulations (see Comparative Table of Alcohol Regulations) vary by situation.

Drugs For any use or possession: varies by situation. For first-time sale: suspension, expulsion. For subsequent sale: expulsion.

For More Information

Contact: Dr. S. Marc Silling, Psychologist/Coordinator of Testing, University of Akron, 302 Buchtel Mall, Akron, OH 44325. Telephone: 216-375-7084.

UNIVERSITY OF ALABAMA AT BIRMINGHAM

Birmingham, Alabama

General Information

State-supported comprehensive coed institution. Part of University of Alabama System. Founded 1966. Awards B, M, D. Primary accreditation: regional. Metropolitan setting; 265-acre campus. Total enrollment: 14,245. Social organizations: 11 national fraternities, 7 national sororities; 7% of eligible undergraduate men and 3% of eligible undergraduate women are members.

Drug and Alcohol Information

Education

On campus Drug and alcohol education/prevention programs offered for: all students, athletes/coaches, faculty, administration, community. Authorized group concerned with responsible drinking. College holds an annual alcohol awareness week and drug awareness week.

Identification of Problems

Admissions College application does not ask about prior substance abuse problems.

On campus Current students identified as chemically dependent may remain enrolled. No training program on identifying students with potential substance abuse problems. No written procedures for students and staff if substance abuse is suspected.

Support Services

On campus Private counseling.

Employee assistance Program for chemically dependent employees available. Staff working with drug/alcohol-related issues: 2 part-time.

Disciplinary Actions

Alcohol Results of infractions of alcohol regulations (see Comparative Table of Alcohol Regulations) vary by situation. Comments: Consideration is given to extenuating circumstances.

Drugs For first-time use: chemical dependency assessment, counseling, suspension. For first-time possession or sale: varies by situation. For subsequent use, possession, or sale: expulsion.

Additional Information from the College

Alcohol and drug programs and activities are reviewed annually; revisions usually occur to increase comprehensiveness and effectiveness.

For More Information

Contact: Marianne Dreyspring, Student Affairs Specialist, University of Alabama at Birmingham, University Center, Box 9, Birmingham, AL 35294. Telephone: 205-934-8020.

UNIVERSITY OF ALABAMA IN HUNTSVILLE

Huntsville, Alabama

General Information

State-supported comprehensive coed institution. Part of University of Alabama System. Founded 1950. Awards B, M, D. Primary accreditation: regional. City setting; 345-acre campus. Total enrollment: 7,474. Faculty: 466 (300 full-time, 166 part-time). Social organizations: 4 national fraternities, 4 national sororities; 5% of eligible undergraduate men and 5% of eligible undergraduate women are members.

Drug and Alcohol Information

Education

On campus Drug and alcohol education/prevention programs offered for: all students, athletes/coaches. Authorized group concerned with responsible drinking. College holds an annual alcohol awareness week.

Identification of Problems

Admissions College application does not ask about prior substance abuse problems.

University of Alabama in Huntsville (continued)

On campus Current students identified as chemically dependent may remain enrolled. Training program on identifying students with potential substance abuse problems for: administration. Written procedures for students and staff if substance abuse is suspected.

Support Services

On campus Private counseling.

Employee assistance Program for chemically dependent employees not available. Staff working with drug/alcohol-related issues: 2 part-time.

Disciplinary Actions

Alcohol Results of infractions of alcohol regulations (see Comparative Table of Alcohol Regulations) include counseling, warning, probation, suspension.

Drugs For first-time use: counseling, warning, probation. For subsequent use: warning, probation, suspension. For first-time possession: probation, suspension. For subsequent possession: suspension, expulsion. For first-time sale: suspension, expulsion. For subsequent sale: expulsion.

For More Information

Contact: Dr. Gary M. Biller, Director of Student Development, University of Alabama in Huntsville, Huntsville, AL 35899. Telephone: 205-895-6203.

UNIVERSITY OF ALASKA ANCHORAGE

Anchorage, Alaska

General Information

State-supported 5-year coed college. Part of University of Alaska System. Founded 1954. Awards A (college transfer and terminal), B, M. Primary accreditation: regional. City setting; 350-acre campus. Total enrollment: 13,200. Faculty: 851 (345 full-time, 506 part-time). Social organization: 1 national fraternity.

Drug and Alcohol Information

Education

On campus Drug and alcohol education/prevention programs offered for: all students, athletes/coaches, faculty, administration. Authorized group concerned with responsible drinking. College holds an annual alcohol awareness week and drug awareness week.

Identification of Problems

Admissions College application does not ask about prior substance abuse problems.

On campus Current students identified as chemically dependent may remain enrolled. No training program on identifying students with potential substance abuse problems. No written procedures for students and staff if substance abuse is suspected.

Support Services

On campus AA, NA, support groups, private counseling.

Employee assistance Program for chemically dependent employees available.

Disciplinary Actions

Alcohol Results of infractions of alcohol regulations (see Comparative Table of Alcohol Regulations) vary by situation.

Drugs For any use, possession, or sale: varies by situation.

For More Information

Contact: Steve Butler, Director of Student Life, University of Alaska Anchorage, 3211 Providence Dr., Anchorage, AK 99508. Telephone: 907-786-4814.

UNIVERSITY OF ALASKA FAIRBANKS

Fairbanks, Alaska

General Information

State-supported comprehensive coed institution. Part of University of Alaska System. Founded 1917. Awards A (terminal), B, M, D. Primary accreditation: regional. Small-town setting; 2,250-acre campus. Total enrollment: 4,278. Faculty: 524 (436 full-time, 88 part-time).

Drug and Alcohol Information

Education

On campus Drug and alcohol education/prevention programs offered for: all students, athletes/coaches; required for: administration, resident advisers. Authorized group concerned with responsible drinking. College holds an annual alcohol awareness week and drug awareness week.

Identification of Problems

Admissions College application does not ask about prior substance abuse problems.

On campus Current students identified as chemically dependent may remain enrolled, but treatment is required. Training program on identifying students with potential substance abuse problems for: resident advisers, administration. Written procedures for students and staff if substance abuse is suspected.

Support Services

On campus AA, ACOA, support groups, private couseling.

Employee assistance Program for chemically dependent employees not available. Staff working with drug/alcohol-related issues: 8–10 part-time.

Disciplinary Actions

Alcohol Results of infractions of alcohol regulations (see Comparative Table of Alcohol Regulations) include chemical dependency assessment, counseling, warning, probation, suspension, expulsion, work detail sanctions.

Drugs For first-time use: varies by situation—counseling, probation. For subsequent use: varies by situation. For first-time possession: varies by situation—counseling, warning, probation. For subsequent possession: varies by situation. For first-time sale: suspension, expulsion. For subsequent sale: expulsion.

For More Information

Contact: Bill Connor, Director of Health and Counseling, Center for Health and Counseling, University of Alaska Fairbanks, Fairbanks, AK 99775. Telephone: 907-474-7043.

UNIVERSITY OF ALASKA SOUTHEAST

Juneau, Alaska

General Information

State-supported 5-year coed college. Part of University of

Alaska System. Founded 1972. Awards A (college transfer and terminal), B, M. Primary accreditation: regional. Small-town setting; 10-acre campus. Total enrollment: 3,484. Faculty: 93 (all full-time).

Drug and Alcohol Information

Education

On campus Drug and alcohol education/prevention programs offered for: all students. Authorized group concerned with responsible drinking. College holds an annual alcohol awareness week and drug awareness week.

Identification of Problems

Admissions College application does not ask about prior substance abuse problems.

On campus Current students identified as chemically dependent may remain enrolled. No training program on identifying students with potential substance abuse problems. No written procedures for students and staff if substance abuse is suspected.

Support Services

On campus AA, support groups.

Employee assistance Program for chemically dependent employees not available.

Disciplinary Actions

Alcohol Results of infractions of alcohol regulations (see Comparative Table of Alcohol Regulations) include counseling, probation, suspension, expulsion.

Drugs For first-time use or possession: counseling, probation. For subsequent use or possession: suspension. For first-time sale: suspension, expulsion. For subsequent sale: expulsion.

For More Information

Contact: Mary Lou Follett, Counselor, University of Alaska Southeast, 11120 Glacier Hwy., Juneau, AK 99801. Telephone: 907-789-4560.

UNIVERSITY OF ARIZONA

Tucson, Arizona

General Information

State-supported comprehensive coed institution. Founded 1885. Awards B, M, D. Primary accreditation: regional. Metropolitan setting; 325-acre campus. Total enrollment: 34,725. Faculty: 1,865 (1,214 full-time, 651 part-time). Social organizations: 22 national fraternities, 13 national sororities; 12% of eligible undergraduate men and 12% of eligible undergraduate women are members.

Drug and Alcohol Information

Education

On campus Drug and alcohol education/prevention programs offered for: all students, athletes/coaches. Authorized group concerned with responsible drinking. College holds an annual alcohol awareness week and drug awareness week.

Identification of Problems

Admissions College application does not ask about prior substance abuse problems.

On campus Current students identified as chemically dependent may remain enrolled. Training program on identifying students with potential substance abuse problems for: resident advisers. Written procedures for students and staff if substance abuse is suspected.

Support Services

On campus AA, Al-Anon, ACOA, support groups.

Employee assistance Program for chemically dependent employees not available. Staff working with drug/alcohol-related issues: 1 full-time and 1 part-time.

Disciplinary Actions

Alcohol Results of infractions of alcohol regulations (see Comparative Table of Alcohol Regulations) vary by situation but can include chemical dependency assessment, counseling, warning, probation, suspension.

Drugs For first-time use or possession: varies by situation. For first-time sale: suspension, expulsion. For subsequent use or possession: suspension, expulsion. For subsequent sale: expulsion.

For More Information

Contact: Carolyn Collins, Health Educator, Student Health Service, University of Arizona, Tucson, AZ 85721. Telephone: 602-621-6497.

UNIVERSITY OF ARKANSAS

Fayetteville, Arkansas

General Information

State-supported comprehensive coed institution. Part of University of Arkansas System. Founded 1871. Awards A (terminal), B, M, D. Primary accreditation: regional. Small-town setting; 329-acre campus. Total enrollment: 13,856. Social organizations: 22 national fraternities, 12 national sororities; 18% of eligible undergraduate men and 18% of eligible undergraduate women are members.

Drug and Alcohol Information

Education

On campus Drug and alcohol education/prevention programs offered for: all students, athletes/coaches, faculty, administration. Authorized group concerned with responsible drinking. College holds an annual alcohol awareness week and drug awareness week.

Identification of Problems

On campus Current students identified as chemically dependent may not remain enrolled. Training program on identifying students with potential substance abuse problems for: resident advisers, coaches, Greek officers, faculty, administration, available to all. Written procedures for students and staff if substance abuse is suspected.

Support Services

On campus AA, NA, Al-Anon, ACOA, support groups, private counseling.

Employee assistance Program for chemically dependent employees not available. Staff working with drug/alcohol-related issues: 2 full-time.

Disciplinary Actions

Alcohol Results of infractions of alcohol regulations (see Comparative Table of Alcohol Regulations) vary by situation.

Drugs For any use or possession: varies by situation. For any sale: expulsion.

For More Information

Contact: Ed Mink, Substance Abuse Prevention

University of Arkansas (continued)

Coordinator, University of Arkansas, 600 Razorback Road, Fayetteville, AR 72701. Telephone: 501-575-6376 or 4749.

UNIVERSITY OF ARKANSAS AT LITTLE ROCK

Little Rock, Arkansas

General Information

State-supported 5-year coed college. Part of University of Arkansas System. Founded 1927. Awards A (college transfer and terminal), B, M. Primary accreditation: regional. City setting; 150-acre campus. Total enrollment: 10,152. Faculty: 680 (453 full-time, 227 part-time). Social organizations: 5 national fraternities, 4 national sororities; 3% of eligible undergraduate men and 2% of eligible undergraduate women are members.

Drug and Alcohol Information

Education

On campus Drug and alcohol education/prevention programs offered for: all students. College holds an annual alcohol awareness week and drug awareness week.

Identification of Problems

Admissions College application does not ask about prior substance abuse problems.

On campus Current students identified as chemically dependent may remain.enrolled. Training program on identifying students with potential substance abuse problems for: Greek officers, faculty, administration.

Support Services

On campus AA, ACOA.

Employee assistance Program for chemically dependent employees available. Staff working with drug/alcohol-related issues: 6 part-time.

Disciplinary Actions

Alcohol Results of infractions of alcohol regulations (see Comparative Table of Alcohol Regulations) vary by situation but can include counseling, warning, probation, workshop requirement, DWI school in the community.

Drugs For any use or possession: varies by situation. For any sale: suspension.

For More Information

Contact: Barbara Taegel, Dean of Students, University of Arkansas at Little Rock, 2801 S. University Ave., Little Rock, AR 72204. Telephone: 501-569-3175.

UNIVERSITY OF ARKANSAS AT MONTICELLO

Monticello, Arkansas

General Information

State-supported 4-year coed college. Part of University of Arkansas System. Founded 1909. Awards A (terminal), B. Primary accreditation: regional. Small-town setting; 400-acre campus. Total enrollment: 1,934. Faculty: 117 (100 full-time, 17 part-time). Social organizations: 5 national fraternities, 2 national sororities; 20% of eligible undergraduate men and 22% of eligible undergraduate women are members.

Drug and Alcohol Information

Education

On campus Drug and alcohol education/prevention programs offered for: all students, athletes/coaches. Authorized group concerned with responsible drinking.

Identification of Problems

Admissions College application does not ask about prior substance abuse problems.

On campus Current students identified as chemically dependent may remain enrolled. No training program on identifying students with potential substance abuse problems. Written procedures for students and staff if substance abuse is suspected.

Support Services

On campus Private counseling.

Employee assistance Program for chemically dependent employees not available. Staff working with drug/alcohol-related issues: 7 part-time.

Disciplinary Actions

Alcohol Results of infractions of alcohol regulations (see Comparative Table of Alcohol Regulations) include warning,probation.

Drugs For any use, possession, or sale: suspension.

For More Information

Contact: Gary Gaston, Dean of Students, University of Arkansas at Monticello, P.O. Box 3466, Monticello, AR 71655. Telephone: 501-460-1045.

UNIVERSITY OF BRIDGEPORT

Bridgeport, Connecticut

General Information

Independent 5-year coed college. Founded 1927. Awards A (college transfer and terminal), B, M, D. Primary accreditation: regional. City setting; 86-acre campus. Total enrollment: 5,376. Faculty: 375 (194 full-time, 181 part-time). Social organizations: 2 national fraternities, 2 national sororities, 3 local fraternities, 3 local sororities; 2% of eligible undergraduate men and 2% of eligible undergraduate women are members.

Drug and Alcohol Information

Education

On campus Drug and alcohol education/prevention programs offered for: all students, athletes/coaches, faculty, administration; required for: resident advisers, student life staff. College holds an annual alcohol awareness week and drug awareness week.

Identification of Problems

Admissions College application does not ask about prior substance abuse problems.

On campus Current students identified as chemically dependent may remain enrolled, but treatment may be required. Training program on identifying students with potential substance abuse problems for: resident advisers, student services personnel. Written procedures for students and staff if substance abuse is suspected.

Support Services

On campus AA, private counseling.

Employee assistance Program for chemically dependent employees not available. Staff working with drug/alcohol-related issues: 1 part-time.

Disciplinary Actions

Alcohol Results of infractions of alcohol regulations (see Comparative Table of Alcohol Regulations) vary by situation but can include chemical dependency assessment, counseling, warning, probation, suspension, expulsion.

Drugs For first-time use or possession: varies by situation. For subsequent use or possession: expulsion. For any sale: expulsion.

For More Information

Contact: Daniel Stracka, Dean of Student Life, University of Bridgeport, 85 Park Ave., Bridgeport, CT 06601. Telephone: 203-576-4461.

UNIVERSITY OF CALIFORNIA, DAVIS

Davis, California

General Information

State-supported comprehensive coed institution. Part of University of California System. Founded 1906. Awards B, M, D. Primary accreditation: regional. Small-town setting; 3,600-acre campus. Total enrollment: 21,838. Faculty: 1,520 (1,279 full-time, 241 part-time). Social organizations: 23 national fraternities, 13 national sororities, 1 local fraternity; 14% of eligible undergraduate men and 12% of eligible undergraduate women are members.

Drug and Alcohol Information

Education

On campus Drug and alcohol education/prevention programs offered for: all students, athletes/coaches, any student group upon request. Authorized group concerned with responsible drinking. College holds an annual alcohol awareness week and drug awareness week.

Identification of Problems

Admissions College application does not ask about prior substance abuse problems.

On campus Current students identified as chemically dependent may remain enrolled, but treatment is recommended. Training program on identifying students with potential substance abuse problems for: resident advisers, coaches, DRInC (Drink Responsibly in College) and other peer counselor volunteers. No written procedures for students and staff if substance abuse is suspected, but an EAP training program is available for campus supervisory staff.

Support Services

On campus AA, Al-Anon, ACOA, support groups, private counseling.

Off campus AA, Al-Anon, ACOA.

Employee assistance Program for chemically dependent employees available. Staff working with drug/alcohol-related issues: 3 part-time.

Disciplinary Actions

Alcohol Results of infractions of alcohol regulations (see Comparative Table of Alcohol Regulations) vary by situation but can include chemical dependency assessment, counseling, warning, probation, suspension, expulsion.

Drugs For first-time use or possession: probation, suspension. For subsequent use or possession: probation, suspension, dismissal. For any sale: suspension, dismissal.

Additional Information from the College

The University's new Assistant Director for Health Promotion will assess current resources and efforts in alcohol and substance abuse prevention education in coordination with other campus and community resources.

For More Information

Contact: Pat Lindsay, M.P.H., Assistant Director for Health Promotion, Cowell Student Health Center, University of California, Davis, Davis, CA 95616. Telephone: 916-752-4142.

UNIVERSITY OF CALIFORNIA, LOS ANGELES

Los Angeles, California

General Information

State-supported comprehensive coed institution. Part of University of California System. Founded 1919. Awards B, M, D. Primary accreditation: regional. Metropolitan setting; 411-acre campus. Total enrollment: 35,730. Faculty: 3,150. Social organizations: 27 national fraternities, 16 national sororities, 6 local fraternities, 6 local sororities; 26% of eligible undergraduate men and 25% of eligible undergraduate women are members.

Drug and Alcohol Information

Education

On campus Drug and alcohol education/prevention programs offered for: all students; required for: athletes/coaches, resident advisers. Authorized group concerned with responsible drinking. College holds an annual alcohol awareness week and drug awareness week.

Identification of Problems

Admissions College application does not ask about prior substance abuse problems.

On campus Current students identified as chemically dependent may remain enrolled, but treatment may be required. Training program on identifying students with potential substance abuse problems for: resident advisers, Greek officers. Written procedures for students and staff if substance abuse is suspected.

Support Services

On campus AA, Al-Anon, ACOA, support groups, private counseling.

Employee assistance Program for chemically dependent employees available. Staff working with drug/alcohol-related issues: 1 full-time and 5 part-time.

Disciplinary Actions

Alcohol Results of infractions of alcohol regulations (see Comparative Table of Alcohol Regulations) vary by situation but can include chemical dependency assessment, counseling, probation.

Drugs For first-time use or possession: chemical dependency assessment, probation. For subsequent use: varies by situation—probation, suspension, expulsion. For subsequent possession: suspension. For any sale: expulsion.

For More Information

Contact: Cece Freeman, Substance Abuse Prevention Coordinator, Student Health Service, University of

University of California, Los Angeles (continued)

California, Los Angeles, 405 Hilgard Ave., Los Angeles, CA 90024-1703. Telephone: 213-825-7164.

UNIVERSITY OF CALIFORNIA, SANTA CRUZ

Santa Cruz, California

General Information

State-supported comprehensive coed institution. Part of University of California System. Founded 1965. Awards B, M, D. Primary accreditation: regional. Small-town setting; 2,000-acre campus. Total enrollment: 8,589. Faculty: 449 (305 full-time, 144 part-time).

Drug and Alcohol Information

Education

On campus Drug and alcohol education/prevention programs offered for: all students, athletes/coaches, faculty, administration; required for: resident advisers, student leaders. Authorized group concerned with responsible drinking. College holds an annual alcohol awareness week and drug awareness week.

Identification of Problems

Admissions College application does not ask about prior substance abuse problems.

On campus Current students identified as chemically dependent may remain enrolled, but treatment is required. Training program on identifying students with potential substance abuse problems for: resident advisers, coaches, staff. Written procedures for students and staff if substance abuse is suspected.

Support Services

On campus AA, NA, Al-Anon, ACOA, private counseling.

Employee assistance Program for chemically dependent employees available. Staff working with drug/alcohol-related issues: 1 part-time.

Disciplinary Actions

Alcohol Results of infractions of alcohol regulations (see Comparative Table of Alcohol Regulations) vary by situation but can include chemical dependency assessment, counseling, warning, probation, suspension, expulsion.

Drugs For first-time use or possession: varies by situation—counseling, warning. For subsequent use or possession: probation. For first-time sale: counseling, probation. For subsequent sale: varies by situation—suspension, expulsion.

Additional Information from the College

The University has a committee composed of members of each college on campus, which is currently reviewing proposals and guidelines regarding a postsecondary drug and alcohol education network.

For More Information

Contact: Jay Lang, Substance Abuse Prevention Coordinator, University of California, Santa Cruz, Santa Cruz, CA 95064. Telephone: 408-429-4866.

UNIVERSITY OF CENTRAL ARKANSAS

Conway, Arkansas

General Information

State-supported 5-year coed college. Founded 1907. Awards A (college transfer and terminal), B, M. Primary accreditation: regional. Small-town setting; 220-acre campus. Total enrollment: 6,698. Faculty: 263 (201 full-time, 62 part-time). Social organizations: 10 national fraternities, 8 national sororities; 30% of eligible undergraduate men and 20% of eligible undergraduate women are members.

Drug and Alcohol Information

Education

On campus Drug and alcohol education/prevention programs offered for: all students, faculty, administration. Bacchus chapter is being formed. College holds an annual alcohol awareness week.

Identification of Problems

Admissions College application does not ask about prior substance abuse problems.

On campus Current students identified as chemically dependent may remain enrolled. Training program on identifying students with potential substance abuse problems for: resident advisers. Written procedures for students and staff if substance abuse is suspected.

Support Services

On campus No support services on campus.

Employee assistance Program for chemically dependent employees not available. Staff working with drug/alcohol-related issues: 1 part-time.

Disciplinary Actions

Alcohol Results of infractions of alcohol regulations (see Comparative Table of Alcohol Regulations) vary by situation but can include warning, probation, suspension.

Drugs For first-time use: varies by situation—probation. For subsequent use: suspension. For first-time possession: suspension. For subsequent possession: expulsion. For any sale: expulsion.

For More Information

Contact: John W. Smith, Dean of Students, University of Central Arkansas, Conway, AR 72032. Telephone: 501-450-3133.

UNIVERSITY OF CENTRAL FLORIDA

Orlando, Florida

General Information

State-supported comprehensive coed institution. Part of State University System of Florida. Founded 1963. Awards A (college transfer), B, M, D. Primary accreditation: regional. Metropolitan setting; 1,227-acre campus. Total enrollment: 18,094. Faculty: 754 (480 full-time, 274 part-time). Social organizations: national fraternities, national sororities, local fraternities, local sororities; 11% of eligible undergraduate men and 9% of eligible undergraduate women are members.

Drug and Alcohol Information

Education

On campus Drug and alcohol education/prevention programs offered for: all students, athletes/coaches. Bacchus chapter forming. Authorized group concerned with responsible drinking. College holds an annual alcohol awareness week and drug awareness week.

Identification of Problems

Admissions College application does not ask about prior substance abuse problems.

On campus Current students identified as chemically dependent may remain enrolled, but treatment is required. No training program on identifying students with potential substance abuse problems. No written procedures for students and staff if substance abuse is suspected.

Support Services

On campus AA, private counseling, alcohol and substance abuse program as part of Wellness Program of the Student Health Center.

Employee assistance Program for chemically dependent employees available. Staff working with drug/alcohol-related issues: 5 part-time.

Disciplinary Actions

Alcohol Results of infractions of alcohol regulations (see Comparative Table of Alcohol Regulations) vary by situation but can include counseling, warning, probation, suspension, expulsion.

Drugs For any use or possessioon: varies by situation. For any sale: suspension, expulsion.

For More Information

Contact: Terrie Langford, Health Education–Health Resource Center, University of Central Florida, P.O. Box 25000, Orlando, FL 32816. Telephone: 407-275-3846.

UNIVERSITY OF CENTRAL TEXAS

Killeen, Texas

General Information

Independent coed college. Founded 1973. Awards B, M. Primary accreditation: regional. City setting; 545-acre campus. Total enrollment: 593. Faculty: 25 (11 full-time, 14 part-time).

Drug and Alcohol Information

Education

On campus Drug and alcohol education/prevention programs not offered.

Identification of Problems

Admissions College application does not ask about prior substance abuse problems.

On campus Current students identified as chemically dependent are dealt with on a case-by-case basis. No training program on identifying students with potential substance abuse problems. No written procedures for students and staff if substance abuse is suspected.

Support Services

On campus No support services on campus.

Employee assistance Program for chemically dependent employees not available. Staff working with drug/alcohol-related issues: 4 part-time off campus.

Disciplinary Actions

Alcohol Results of infractions of alcohol regulations (see Comparative Table of Alcohol Regulations) vary by situation.

Drugs For any use, possession, or sale: varies by situation.

Additional Information from the College

The University is a nonresidential upper-division and graduate institution, and the average age of its students is 34. Students live independently and come to campus for classes only.

For More Information

Contact: Dr. Charles E. Urbanic, Vice President for Academic Affairs, University of Central Texas, Highway 190 West, P.O. Box 1416, Killeen, TX 76540. Telephone: 817-526-1170.

UNIVERSITY OF CHARLESTON

Charleston, West Virginia

General Information

Independent 5-year coed college. Founded 1888. Awards A (college transfer and terminal), B, M. Primary accreditation: regional. City setting; 40-acre campus. Total enrollment: 1,407. Faculty: 118 (56 full-time, 62 part-time). Social organizations: 4 national fraternities, 1 local fraternity, 1 local sorority; 10% of eligible undergraduate men and 3% of eligible undergraduate women are members.

Drug and Alcohol Information

Education

On campus Drug and alcohol education/prevention programs offered for: all students, athletes/coaches, faculty, administration; required for: resident advisers. Authorized group concerned with responsible drinking. College holds an annual alcohol awareness week and drug awareness week.

Identification of Problems

Admissions College application does not ask about prior substance abuse problems.

On campus Current students identified as chemically dependent may remain enrolled, but treatment is required. Training program on identifying students with potential substance abuse problems for: resident advisers, administration, student affairs staff, counseling services staff. Written procedures for students and staff if substance abuse is suspected.

Support Services

On campus Support groups, private counseling, student assistance program.

Employee assistance Program for chemically dependent employees not available.

Disciplinary Actions

Alcohol Results of infractions of alcohol regulations (see Comparative Table of Alcohol Regulations) include chemical dependency assessment, counseling, warning, probation, suspension, expulsion.

Drugs For first-time use: varies by situation—chemical dependency assessment, counseling, probation. For subsequent use: varies by situation—chemical dependency

University of Charleston (continued)

assessment, counseling, suspension. For any possession: varies by situation—chemical dependency assessment, counseling, suspension. For any sale: varies by situation—expulsion.

Additional Information from the College

An alcohol task force has been organized to address alcohol issues. Plans include applying for grant money for alcohol programming. The University is participating in a West Virginia University alcohol survey.

For More Information

Contact: Diana Hackney, Vice President for Student Affairs, University of Charleston, 2300 MacCorkle Ave., SE, Charleston, WV 25304. Telephone: 304-357-4809.

UNIVERSITY OF CINCINNATI

Cincinnati, Ohio

General Information

State-supported comprehensive coed institution. Part of University of Cincinnati System. Founded 1819. Awards A (college transfer and terminal), B, M, D. Primary accreditation: regional. Metropolitan setting; 270-acre campus. Total enrollment: 26,475. Faculty: 1,457 (1,075 full-time, 382 part-time). Social organizations: 23 national fraternities, 13 national sororities, 1 local sorority; 11% of eligible undergraduate men and 10% of eligible undergraduate women are members.

Drug and Alcohol Information

Education

On campus Drug and alcohol education/prevention programs offered for: all students, athletes/coaches, faculty. Authorized group concerned with responsible drinking. College holds an annual alcohol awareness week and drug awareness week.

Identification of Problems

Admissions College application does not ask about prior substance abuse problems.

On campus Current students identified as chemically dependent may remain enrolled. Training program on identifying students with potential substance abuse problems for: resident advisers, coaches, Greek officers. No written procedures for students and staff if substance abuse is suspected.

Support Services

On campus AA, NA, Al-Anon, ACOA, private counseling.

Employee assistance Program for chemically dependent employees available. Staff working with drug/alcohol-related issues: 1 part-time.

Disciplinary Actions

Alcohol Results of infractions of alcohol regulations (see Comparative Table of Alcohol Regulations) include chemical dependency assessment, counseling, warning, probation, suspension, expulsion.

Drugs For any use, possession, or sale: varies by situation. Comments: Policy is being rewritten.

For More Information

Contact: Bob Canning, Alcohol and Substance Abuse Coordinator, University of Cincinnati, 340 Tangeman University Center, Mail Location #136, Cincinnati, OH 45221. Telephone: 513-556-6115.

UNIVERSITY OF COLORADO AT DENVER

Denver, Colorado

General Information

State-supported comprehensive coed institution. Part of University of Colorado System. Founded 1912. Awards B, M, D. Primary accreditation: regional. Metropolitan setting; 169-acre campus. Total enrollment: 10,096. Faculty: 624 (324 full-time, 300 part-time).

Drug and Alcohol Information

Education

On campus Drug and alcohol education/prevention programs offered for: all students. Authorized group concerned with responsible drinking. College holds an annual alcohol awareness week.

Identification of Problems

Admissions College application does not ask about prior substance abuse problems.

On campus Current students identified as chemically dependent may remain enrolled. No training program on identifying students with potential substance abuse problems. No written procedures for students and staff if substance abuse is suspected.

Support Services

On campus AA.

Employee assistance Program for chemically dependent employees not available.

Disciplinary Actions

Alcohol Results of infractions of alcohol regulations (see Comparative Table of Alcohol Regulations) include chemical dependency assessment, counseling, warning, probation, suspension, expulsion.

Drugs For first-time use: counseling, warning. For subsequent use: probation. For first-time possession: probation. For subsequent possession: suspension. For any sale: expulsion.

For More Information

Contact: Dr. George H. Wayne, Assistant Dean, University of Colorado at Denver, 1200 Larimer St., Box 137, Denver, CO 80204. Telephone: 303-556-2321.

UNIVERSITY OF CONNECTICUT AT WATERBURY

Waterbury, Connecticut

General Information

State-supported 4-year coed college. Part of University of Connecticut System. Founded 1946. Awards B (nontraditional upper-level program; also offers first 2 years of most baccalaureate programs available at the main campus in Storrs). Primary accreditation: regional. City setting; 3-acre campus. Total enrollment: 608. Faculty: 58 (26 full-time, 32 part-time).

Drug and Alcohol Information

Education

On campus Drug and alcohol education/prevention programs offered for: all students. College holds an annual alcohol awareness week.

Identification of Problems

Admissions College application does not ask about prior substance abuse problems.

On campus No training program on identifying students with potential substance abuse problems. No written procedures for students and staff if substance abuse is suspected.

Support Services

On campus No support services on campus.

Employee assistance Program for chemically dependent employees available.

Disciplinary Actions

Alcohol Results of infractions of alcohol regulations (see Comparative Table of Alcohol Regulations) vary by situation.

Drugs For any use, possession, or sale: varies by situation.

For More Information

Contact: Susan Brandt, Assistant to the Dean of Students, University of Connecticut at Waterbury, 32 Hillside Ave., Waterbury, CT 06710. Telephone: 203-757-1231.

UNIVERSITY OF DALLAS

Irving, Texas

General Information

Independent Roman Catholic comprehensive coed institution. Founded 1956. Awards B, M, D. Primary accreditation: regional. City setting; 750-acre campus. Total enrollment: 2,649. Faculty: 102 (68 full-time, 34 part-time).

Drug and Alcohol Information

Education

On campus Drug and alcohol education/prevention programs offered for: all students. Bacchus chapter: 7 members. College holds an annual alcohol awareness week and drug awareness week.

Identification of Problems

Admissions College application does not ask about prior substance abuse problems.

On campus Current students identified as chemically dependent may remain enrolled, but treatment is required. No training program on identifying students with potential substance abuse problems. No written procedures for students and staff if substance abuse is suspected.

Support Services

On campus Private counseling, referral in community.

Employee assistance Program for chemically dependent employees available. Staff working with drug/alcohol-related issues: 5 part-time.

Disciplinary Actions

Alcohol Results of infractions of alcohol regulations (see Comparative Table of Alcohol Regulations) vary by situation.

Drugs For any use, possession, or sale: varies by situation.

For More Information

Contact: Dr. Lisa L. Grubbs, Assistant Dean of Students, University of Dallas, 1845 E. Northgate Dr., Irving, TX 75062. Telephone: 214-721-5394.

UNIVERSITY OF DAYTON

Dayton, Ohio

General Information

Independent Roman Catholic comprehensive coed institution. Founded 1850. Awards B, M, D. Primary accreditation: regional. City setting; 80-acre campus. Total enrollment: 11,090. Faculty: 693 (389 full-time, 304 part-time). Social organizations: 9 national fraternities, 6 national sororities, 8 local fraternities, 3 local sororities, 1 local co-ed fraternity; 9% of eligible undergraduate men and 6% of eligible undergraduate women are members.

Drug and Alcohol Information

Education

On campus Drug and alcohol education/prevention programs offered for: all students, athletes/coaches, faculty, administration. Bacchus chapter: 6 members. College holds an annual alcohol awareness week.

Identification of Problems

Admissions College application does not ask about prior substance abuse problems.

On campus Current students identified as chemically dependent may remain enrolled. Training program on identifying students with potential substance abuse problems for: resident advisers, coaches. Written procedures for students and staff if substance abuse is suspected.

Support Services

On campus AA, private counseling, referral to inpatient program.

Employee assistance Program for chemically dependent employees not available. Staff working with drug/alcohol-related issues: 1 full-time and 15 part-time.

Disciplinary Actions

Alcohol Results of infractions of alcohol regulations (see Comparative Table of Alcohol Regulations) vary by situation but can include chemical dependency assessment, counseling, warning, probation, suspension, expulsion.

Drugs For any use or possession: varies by situation—chemical dependency assessment, counseling. For any sale: expulsion. Comments: Selling is treated as a criminal matter.

For More Information

Contact: L. B. Fred, Director of Special Programs, University of Dayton, 300 College Pk., Dayton, OH 45469. Telephone: 513-229-2229.

UNIVERSITY OF DELAWARE

Newark, Delaware

General Information

State-related comprehensive coed institution. Founded 1743. Awards A (college transfer), B, M, D. Primary accreditation: regional. Small-town setting; 1,100-acre campus. Total enrollment: 17,197. Faculty: 930 (878 full-time, 52 part-time). Social organizations: 15 national fraternities, 10

University of Delaware (continued)

national sororities; 14% of eligible undergraduate men and 9% of eligible undergraduate women are members.

Drug and Alcohol Information

Education

On campus Drug and alcohol education/prevention programs offered for: all students, athletes/coaches, administration. Authorized group concerned with responsible drinking. College holds an annual alcohol awareness week and drug awareness week.

Identification of Problems

Admissions College application does not ask about prior substance abuse problems.

On campus Current students identified as chemically dependent may remain enrolled, but treatment is required. Training program on identifying students with potential substance abuse problems for: resident advisers, coaches, Greek officers, administration. Written procedures for students and staff if substance abuse is suspected.

Support Services

On campus AA, NA, Al-Anon, ACOA, private counseling.

Employee assistance Program for chemically dependent employees available. Staff working with drug/alcohol-related issues: 1 full-time and 14 part-time.

Disciplinary Actions

Alcohol Results of infractions of alcohol regulations (see Comparative Table of Alcohol Regulations) vary by situation but can include chemical dependency assessment, counseling, probation, suspension.

Drugs For first-time use or possession: varies by situation—chemical dependency assessment, counseling, probation. For subsequent use or possession: suspension. For any sale: suspension.

For More Information

Contact: Joyce Walter, Coordinator of Wellspring, Laurel Hall, University of Delaware, Newark, DE 19716. Telephone: 302-451-8992.

UNIVERSITY OF DETROIT

Detroit, Michigan

General Information

Independent Roman Catholic comprehensive coed institution. Founded 1877. Awards B, M, D. Primary accreditation: regional. Metropolitan setting; 70-acre campus. Total enrollment: 6,021. Faculty: 159. Social organizations: 7 national fraternities, 7 local fraternities, 3 local sororities; 22% of eligible undergraduate men and 13% of eligible undergraduate women are members.

Drug and Alcohol Information

Education

On campus Drug and alcohol education/prevention programs offered for: all students, athletes/coaches. Authorized group concerned with responsible drinking. College holds an annual alcohol awareness week and drug awareness week.

Identification of Problems

Admissions College application does not ask about prior substance abuse problems.

On campus Current students identified as chemically dependent may remain enrolled, but treatment is required. No training program on identifying students with potential substance abuse problems.

Support Services

On campus Private counseling.

Off campus AA, NA, Al-Anon, ACOA, support groups.

Employee assistance Program for chemically dependent employees not available.

Disciplinary Actions

Alcohol Results of infractions of alcohol regulations (see Comparative Table of Alcohol Regulations) vary by situation but can include counseling, warning, probation, suspension, expulsion.

Drugs For first-time use or possession: varies by situation. For subsequent use or possession: suspension, expulsion. For any sale: expulsion.

For More Information

Contact: R. W. Davidson, Vice President of Student Services, University of Detroit, 4001 W. McNichols Rd., Detroit, MI 48221. Telephone: 313-927-1591.

UNIVERSITY OF DUBUQUE

Dubuque, Iowa

General Information

Independent Presbyterian 5-year coed college. Founded 1852. Awards A (college transfer), B, M, D. Primary accreditation: regional. City setting; 56-acre campus. Total enrollment: 1,248. Faculty: 66 (52 full-time, 14 part-time). Social organizations: 1 national fraternity, 1 national sorority, 4 local fraternities, 3 local sororities; 20% of eligible undergraduate men and 15% of eligible undergraduate women are members.

Drug and Alcohol Information

Education

On campus Drug and alcohol education/prevention programs offered for: all students, athletes/coaches; required for: resident advisers, student services staff. Bacchus chapter. College holds an annual alcohol awareness week and drug awareness week.

Identification of Problems

Admissions College application does not ask about prior substance abuse problems.

On campus Current students identified as chemically dependent may remain enrolled, but treatment is required. Training program on identifying students with potential substance abuse problems for: resident advisers, administration, student services staff. Written procedures for students and staff if substance abuse is suspected.

Support Services

On campus No support services on campus.

Off campus AA, NA, Al-Anon, ACOA, support groups, private counseling.

Employee assistance Program for chemically dependent employees not available.

Disciplinary Actions

Alcohol Results of infractions of alcohol regulations (see Comparative Table of Alcohol Regulations) vary by situation but can include chemical dependency assessment, counseling, warning, probation, suspension, expulsion.

Drugs For first-time use or possession: chemical dependency assessment, counseling, probation. For subsequent use or possession: suspension, expulsion. For any sale: suspension, expulsion.

For More Information

Contact: Richard R. Nelson, Director of Student Development, University of Dubuque, 2000 University Ave., Dubuque, IA 52001. Telephone: 319-589-3128.

UNIVERSITY OF FLORIDA

Gainesville, Florida

General Information

State-supported comprehensive coed institution. Part of State University System of Florida. Founded 1853. Awards B, M, D. Primary accreditation: regional. City setting; 2,000-acre campus. Total enrollment: 34,021. Faculty: 4,233 (3,956 full-time, 277 part-time). Social organizations: 30 national fraternities, 20 national sororities; 30% of eligible undergraduate men and 25% of eligible undergraduate women are members.

Drug and Alcohol Information

Education

On campus Drug and alcohol education/prevention programs offered for: all students, administration. Bacchus chapter: over 30 members. College holds an annual alcohol awareness week and drug awareness week.

Identification of Problems

Admissions College application does not ask about prior substance abuse problems.

On campus Training program on identifying students with potential substance abuse problems for: resident advisers, coaches, Greek officers, administration. Written procedures for students and staff if substance abuse is suspected.

Support Services

On campus AA, NA, Al-Anon, ACOA, private counseling.

Employee assistance Program for chemically dependent employees available. Staff working with drug/alcohol-related issues: many part-time.

Disciplinary Actions

Alcohol Results of infractions of alcohol regulations (see Comparative Table of Alcohol Regulations) vary by situation but can include chemical dependency assessment, counseling, warning, probation, suspension, expulsion.

Drugs For any use, possession, or sale: varies by situation.

For More Information

Contact: Liz Broughton, Assistant Dean for Student Services, 124 Tigert Hall, University of Florida, Gainesville, FL 32611. Telephone: 904-392-1261.

UNIVERSITY OF GEORGIA

Athens, Georgia

General Information

State-supported comprehensive coed institution. Part of University System of Georgia. Founded 1785. Awards A (terminal), B, M, D. Primary accreditation: regional. Small-town setting; 1,502-acre campus. Total enrollment: 27,176. Faculty: 2,637 (2,435 full-time, 202 part-time). Social organizations: 29 national fraternities, 21 national sororities, local fraternities, local sororities; 8% of eligible undergraduate men and 14% of eligible undergraduate women are members.

Drug and Alcohol Information

Education

On campus Drug and alcohol education/prevention programs offered for: all students, administration; required for: athletes/coaches, resident advisers. Bacchus chapter: 10 members. Authorized group concerned with responsible drinking. College holds an annual alcohol awareness week and drug awareness week.

Identification of Problems

Admissions College application does not ask about prior substance abuse problems.

On campus Current students identified as chemically dependent may remain enrolled. Training program on identifying students with potential substance abuse problems for: resident advisers, coaches, Greek officers, faculty, administration, judicial programs. No written procedures for students and staff if substance abuse is suspected.

Support Services

On campus AA, NA, ACOA, private counseling.

Employee assistance Program for chemically dependent employees not available. Staff working with drug/alcohol-related issues: 1 full-time and 6 part-time.

Disciplinary Actions

Alcohol Results of infractions of alcohol regulations (see Comparative Table of Alcohol Regulations) vary by situation but can include chemical dependency assessment, counseling, warning, probation, community service.

Drugs For any use, possession, or sale: varies by situation. Comments: The University does not distinguish between alcohol and drugs.

Additional Information from the College

Teaching About Prevention of Substance Abuse (TAPS) is designed for students, faculty, and staff to increase awareness of alcohol- and drug-related issues. TAPS includes education, training, and consultation, and is neither prohibitionist nor pro-use. The program strives to help members of the University community explore their personal values related to drinking and drug use and to examine the ways in which their attitudes and behaviors affect others. Short-term counseling and referral are also available for anyone experiencing problems related to substance abuse.

For More Information

Contact: Carole Middlebrooks, Coordinator of Alcohol and Drug Education, University of Georgia, Athens, GA 30602. Telephone: 404-542-2273.

UNIVERSITY OF GUAM

Mangilao, Guam

General Information

Territory-supported 5-year coed college. Founded 1952. Awards A (terminal), B, M. Primary accreditation: regional. Rural setting; 100-acre campus. Total enrollment: 2,096. Faculty: 215.

University of Guam (continued)

Drug and Alcohol Information

Education

On campus Drug and alcohol education/prevention programs required for: all students, athletes/coaches, faculty, administration, campus security guards.

Identification of Problems

Admissions College application does not ask about prior substance abuse problems.

On campus Current students identified as chemically dependent may remain enrolled, but treatment is required. Training program on identifying students with potential substance abuse problems for: resident advisers, coaches, faculty, administration. Written procedures for students and staff if substance abuse is suspected.

Support Services

On campus Private counseling, peer counseling (Project Freedom).

Employee assistance Program for chemically dependent employees not available. Staff working with drug/alcohol-related issues: 1 full-time and 2 part-time.

Disciplinary Actions

Alcohol Results of infractions of alcohol regulations (see Comparative Table of Alcohol Regulations) include chemical dependency assessment, counseling, warning, probation, suspension.

Drugs For first-time use: varies by situation. For subsequent use: expulsion. For any possession or sale: expulsion.

Additional Information from the College

Project Freedom is a comprehensive, multifaceted program serving students, faculty, and staff. Prevention activities are campuswide, creative, and broad ranging, including academic, social-cultural, and financial components. The program's philosophy emphasizes taking personal responsibility for avoiding substance abuse. To establish a drug-free learning community, specific goals of the program include a campuswide substance abuse and disciplinary policy, extensive dissemination of drug information, and a campuswide referral network.

For More Information

Contact: Francesca K. Remengesau, Coordinator, Project Freedom, University of Guam, UOG Station, Mangilao, GU 96923. Telephone: 671-734-2939.

UNIVERSITY OF HARTFORD

West Hartford, Connecticut

General Information

Independent comprehensive coed institution. Founded 1877. Awards A (college transfer and terminal), B, M, D. Primary accreditation: regional. Small-town setting; 300-acre campus. Total enrollment: 7,710. Faculty: 608 (316 full-time, 292 part-time). Social organizations: 6 national fraternities, 3 national sororities; 7% of eligible undergraduate men and 5% of eligible undergraduate women are members.

Drug and Alcohol Information

Education

On campus Drug and alcohol education/prevention programs offered for: all students, athletes/coaches, faculty, administration. Bacchus chapter: 25 members. College holds an annual alcohol awareness week and drug awareness week.

Identification of Problems

Admissions College application does not ask about prior substance abuse problems.

On campus Current students identified as chemically dependent may remain enrolled, but treatment may be required. Training program on identifying students with potential substance abuse problems for: resident advisers, coaches, Greek officers, selected students. Written procedures for students and staff if substance abuse is suspected.

Support Services

On campus AA, NA, private counseling, referral.

Employee assistance Program for chemically dependent employees available. Staff working with drug/alcohol-related issues: approximately 10 part-time.

Disciplinary Actions

Alcohol Results of infractions of alcohol regulations (see Comparative Table of Alcohol Regulations) vary by situation but can include chemical dependency assessment, counseling, warning, probation, suspension, expulsion, fines.

Drugs For any use, possession, or sale: varies by situation.

Additional Information from the College

Each case is treated individually. There are no automatic sanctions for any violators. Students may be suspended with readmission contingent on involvement in a qualified substance abuse counseling or rehabilitation program.

For More Information

Contact: Marcia Mathews, Health Educator/Nurse Practitioner, Health Services, University of Hartford, 200 Bloomfield Ave., West Hartford, CT 06117. Telephone: 203-243-4601.

UNIVERSITY OF HAWAII AT HILO

Hilo, Hawaii

General Information

State-supported 4-year coed college. Part of University of Hawaii System. Founded 1970. Awards A (college transfer and terminal), B. Primary accreditation: regional. Small-town setting; 78-acre campus. Total enrollment: 2,812. Faculty: 200 (117 full-time, 83 part-time).

Drug and Alcohol Information

Education

On campus Drug and alcohol education/prevention programs offered for: all students. College holds an annual alcohol awareness week and drug awareness week.

Identification of Problems

Admissions College application does not ask about prior substance abuse problems.

On campus Current students identified as chemically dependent may remain enrolled, but treatment is recommended. Training program on identifying students with potential substance abuse problems for: resident advisers. No written procedures for students and staff if substance abuse is suspected.

Support Services

On campus Support groups, private counseling.

Employee assistance Program for chemically dependent employees not available. Staff working with drug/alcohol-related issues: 20 part-time.

Disciplinary Actions

Alcohol Results of infractions of alcohol regulations (see Comparative Table of Alcohol Regulations) vary by situation but can include counseling, warning, probation, suspension, expulsion.

Drugs For first-time use or possession: varies by situation—counseling, probation. For subsequent use or possession: varies by situation. For any sale: varies by situation.

For More Information

Contact: Paul Kopecky, Dean of Student Services, University of Hawaii at Hilo, Hilo, HI 96720. Telephone: 808-933-3334.

UNIVERSITY OF HAWAII–WEST OAHU COLLEGE

Pearl City, Hawaii

General Information

State-supported coed college. Part of University of Hawaii System. Founded 1976. Awards B. Primary accreditation: regional. Small-town setting. Total enrollment: 492. Faculty: 20 (10 full-time, 10 part-time).

Drug and Alcohol Information

Education

On campus Drug and alcohol education/prevention programs offered for: all students. College holds an annual alcohol awareness week.

Identification of Problems

Admissions College application does not ask about prior substance abuse problems.

On campus Current students identified as chemically dependent may remain enrolled. No training program on identifying students with potential substance abuse problems. No written procedures for students and staff if substance abuse is suspected.

Support Services

On campus Private counseling.

Employee assistance Program for chemically dependent employees not available.

Disciplinary Actions

Alcohol Results of infractions of alcohol regulations (see Comparative Table of Alcohol Regulations) vary by situation but can include warning, probation, suspension, expulsion.

Drugs For any use, possession, or sale: varies by situation.

For More Information

Contact: Stella Asahara, Student Services Coordinator, University of Hawaii–West Oahu College, 96-043 Ala Ike, Pearl City, HI 96782. Telephone: 808-456-5921.

UNIVERSITY OF HOUSTON

Houston, Texas

General Information

State-supported comprehensive coed institution. Part of University of Houston System. Founded 1927. Awards B, M, D. Primary accreditation: regional. Metropolitan setting; 540-acre campus. Total enrollment: 30,372. Faculty: 2,025 (925 full-time, 1,100 part-time). Social organizations: 17 national fraternities, 10 national sororities, local fraternities, local sororities.

Drug and Alcohol Information

Education

On campus Drug and alcohol education/prevention programs offered for: all students, faculty, staff. College holds an annual alcohol awareness week.

Identification of Problems

Admissions College application does not ask about prior substance abuse problems.

On campus Current students identified as chemically dependent may remain enrolled. No training program on identifying students with potential substance abuse problems. No written procedures for students and staff if substance abuse is suspected.

Support Services

On campus AA, Al-Anon, ACOA.

Employee assistance Program for chemically dependent employees not available.

Disciplinary Actions

Alcohol Results of infractions of alcohol regulations (see Comparative Table of Alcohol Regulations) vary by situation but can include chemical dependency assessment, counseling, warning, probation, suspension, expulsion.

Drugs For any use, possession, or sale: varies by situation.

For More Information

Contact: Dr. Gerald Osborne, Director of Counseling, University of Houston, 4800 Calhoun Blvd., Houston, TX 77004. Telephone: 713-749-1736.

UNIVERSITY OF HOUSTON–CLEAR LAKE

Houston, Texas

General Information

State-supported coed college. Part of University of Houston System. Founded 1971. Awards B, M. Primary accreditation: regional. Metropolitan setting; 487-acre campus. Total enrollment: 7,196. Faculty: 321 (199 full-time, 122 part-time).

Drug and Alcohol Information

Education

On campus Drug and alcohol education/prevention programs offered for: all students, faculty, administration. College holds an annual alcohol awareness week and drug awareness week.

Identification of Problems

Admissions College application does not ask about prior substance abuse problems.

University of Houston–Clear Lake (continued)

On campus Current students identified as chemically dependent may remain enrolled. No training program on identifying students with potential substance abuse problems. No written procedures for students and staff if substance abuse is suspected.

Support Services

On campus ACOA, private counseling.

Employee assistance Program for chemically dependent employees not available. Staff working with drug/alcohol-related issues: 1 part-time.

Disciplinary Actions

Alcohol Results of infractions of alcohol regulations (see Comparative Table of Alcohol Regulations) include counseling, warning, probation. Comments: Organization may lose recognition or privileges.

Drugs For any use, possession, or sale: varies by situation.

Additional Information from the College

Substance abuse problems at the University differ from those at other schools because there are no freshmen or sophomore students. Under-age use of alcohol is generally not a problem, and abuse on campus is less common. However, driving after drinking is an issue.

For More Information

Contact: Wanda Mercer, Assistant Vice President, Student Life, University of Houston–Clear Lake, 2700 Bay Area Blvd., Houston, TX 77058. Telephone: 713-488-9224.

UNIVERSITY OF HOUSTON–DOWNTOWN

Houston, Texas

General Information

State-supported 4-year coed college. Part of University of Houston System. Founded 1974. Awards B. Primary accreditation: regional. Metropolitan setting; 20-acre campus. Total enrollment: 7,414. Faculty: 347 (147 full-time, 200 part-time). Social organizations: 1 national fraternity, 1 national sorority; 1% of eligible undergraduate men and 1% of eligible undergraduate women are members.

Drug and Alcohol Information

Education

On campus Drug and alcohol education/prevention programs offered for: all students, faculty, administration. Authorized group concerned with responsible drinking. College holds an annual alcohol awareness week and drug awareness week.

Identification of Problems

Admissions College application does not ask about prior substance abuse problems.

On campus Current students identified as chemically dependent may remain enrolled, but treatment is required. Training program on identifying students with potential substance abuse problems under development for: resident advisers, faculty, administration, student leaders. No written procedures for students and staff if substance abuse is suspected.

Support Services

On campus AA, private counseling, wellness program (under development).

Employee assistance Program for chemically dependent employees not available. Staff working with drug/alcohol-related issues: 3 part-time.

Disciplinary Actions

Alcohol Results of infractions of alcohol regulations (see Comparative Table of Alcohol Regulations) vary by situation but can include chemical dependency assessment, counseling, warning, probation, suspension, expulsion.

Drugs For first-time use or possession: varies by situation—counseling. For subsequent use or possession: suspension, expulsion. For any sale: expulsion.

Additional Information from the College

The University is developing a wellness program to aid faculty, staff, and students in identifying and dealing with substance abuse issues. Grant proposals are being written to help integrate substance abuse awareness into the curriculum.

For More Information

Contact: Dr. Richard Padilla, Dean of Student Affairs, University of Houston–Downtown, 1 Main St., Houston, TX 77002. Telephone: 713-221-8100.

UNIVERSITY OF IDAHO

Moscow, Idaho

General Information

State-supported comprehensive coed institution. Founded 1889. Awards B, M, D. Primary accreditation: regional. Small-town setting; 1,200-acre campus. Total enrollment: 9,444. Faculty: 546 (480 full-time, 66 part-time). Social organizations: 17 national fraternities, 8 national sororities; 22% of eligible undergraduate men and 18% of eligible undergraduate women are members.

Drug and Alcohol Information

Education

On campus Drug and alcohol education/prevention programs offered for: all students, athletes/coaches. Bacchus chapter: 35 members. College holds an annual alcohol awareness week.

Identification of Problems

Admissions College application does not ask about prior substance abuse problems.

On campus Current students identified as chemically dependent may remain enrolled, but treatment is required. Training program on identifying students with potential substance abuse problems for: resident advisers, Greek officers, student services staff. Written procedures for students and staff if substance abuse is suspected.

Support Services

On campus AA, private counseling.

Employee assistance Program for chemically dependent employees not available. Staff working with drug/alcohol-related issues: 4 part-time.

Disciplinary Actions

Alcohol Results of infractions of alcohol regulations (see Comparative Table of Alcohol Regulations) vary by situation. Comments: Infractions generally result in disciplinary action, community service, fines, and education programs.

Drugs For first-time use or possession: varies by situation—chemical dependency assessment, probation. For subsequent use: probation, suspension. For subsequent possession: suspension. For first-time sale: suspension. For subsequent sale: suspension, expulsion.

For More Information

Contact: Diane Milhollin, Coordinator of Disabled Student Services, Student Advisory Services, University of Idaho, Moscow, ID 83843. Telephone: 208-885-6757.

UNIVERSITY OF ILLINOIS AT CHICAGO

Chicago, Illinois

General Information

State-supported comprehensive coed institution. Part of University of Illinois System. Founded 1965. Awards B, M, D. Primary accreditation: regional. Metropolitan setting; 170-acre campus. Total enrollment: 24,087. Faculty: 2,665 (1,820 full-time, 845 part-time). Social organizations: 7 national fraternities, 3 national sororities.

Drug and Alcohol Information

Education

On campus Drug and alcohol education/prevention programs offered for: all students, athletes/coaches. Authorized group concerned with responsible drinking. College holds an annual alcohol awareness week and drug awareness week.

Identification of Problems

Admissions College application does not ask about prior substance abuse problems.

On campus Training program on identifying students with potential substance abuse problems for: resident advisers, coaches. Written procedures for students and staff if substance abuse is suspected.

Support Services

On campus AA.

Employee assistance Program for chemically dependent employees available. Staff working with drug/alcohol-related issues: 1 full-time and 4–5 part-time.

Disciplinary Actions

Alcohol Results of infractions of alcohol regulations (see Comparative Table of Alcohol Regulations) vary by situation but can include counseling, warning, probation, suspension, expulsion.

Drugs For any use, possession, or sale: varies by situation.

For More Information

Contact: Paul J. Johnston, Director, Student Counseling Service, Univerity of Illinois at Chicago, P.O. Box 4348 (M/C 333), Chicago, IL 60607. Telephone: 312-996-3487.

UNIVERSITY OF IOWA

Iowa City, Iowa

General Information

State-supported comprehensive coed institution. Founded 1847. Awards B, M, D. Primary accreditation: regional. City setting; 1,880-acre campus. Total enrollment: 29,230. Faculty: 1,600. Social organizations: 30 national fraternities, 20 national sororities; 15% of eligible undergraduate men and 16% of eligible undergraduate women are members.

Drug and Alcohol Information

Education

On campus Drug and alcohol education/prevention programs offered for: all students, athletes/coaches, faculty, administration. Authorized group concerned with responsible drinking. College holds an annual alcohol awareness week and drug awareness week.

Identification of Problems

Admissions College application does not ask about prior substance abuse problems.

On campus Current students identified as chemically dependent may remain enrolled, but treatment is required. Training program on identifying students with potential substance abuse problems for: resident advisers, Greek officers. No written procedures for students and staff if substance abuse is suspected.

Support Services

On campus AA, NA, Al-Anon, ACOA, support groups (Alatots), private counseling.

Employee assistance Program for chemically dependent employees available. Staff working with drug/alcohol-related issues: 1 full-time and 4 part-time.

Disciplinary Actions

Alcohol Results of infractions of alcohol regulations (see Comparative Table of Alcohol Regulations) vary by situation but can include chemical dependency assessment.

Drugs For any use, possession, or sale: varies by situation.

For More Information

Contact: Lisa Broek, Health Educator, Steindler Building, University of Iowa, Iowa City, IA 52242. Telephone: 319-335-8392.

UNIVERSITY OF KENTUCKY

Lexington, Kentucky

General Information

State-supported comprehensive coed institution. Founded 1865. Awards B, M, D. Primary accreditation: regional. City setting; 716-acre campus. Total enrollment: 22,336. Faculty: 1,879 (1,520 full-time, 359 part-time). Social organizations: 23 national fraternities, 15 national sororities; 17% of eligible undergraduate men and 16% of eligible undergraduate women are members.

Drug and Alcohol Information

Education

On campus Drug and alcohol education/prevention programs offered for: all students, athletes/coaches. Bacchus chapter: 12 members. College holds an annual alcohol awareness week and drug awareness week.

Identification of Problems

Admissions College application does not ask about prior substance abuse problems.

On campus Current students identified as chemically dependent may remain enrolled. Training program on identifying students with potential substance abuse problems for: resident advisers, coaches, Greek officers, faculty, administration, anyone upon request. No written procedures for students and staff if substance abuse is suspected.

University of Kentucky (continued)

Support Services

On campus AA, NA, Al-Anon, ACOA, support groups, private counseling.

Employee assistance Program for chemically dependent employees available. Staff working with drug/alcohol-related issues: 2 full-time and 5–6 part-time.

Disciplinary Actions

Alcohol Results of infractions of alcohol regulations (see Comparative Table of Alcohol Regulations) vary by situation but can include chemical dependency assessment, counseling, warning, probation, suspension, expulsion.

Drugs For first-time use: varies by situation—warning, probation. For first-time possession: varies by situation—counseling, warning, probation. For subsequent use or possession: varies by situation—probation, suspension, expulsion. For first-time sale: varies by situation—suspension, expulsion. For subsequent sale: varies by situation—expulsion.

For More Information

Contact: Mary Brinkman, Health Education Coordinator, 575 Patterson Office Tower, University of Kentucky, Lexington, KY 40506-0027. Telephone: 606-257-6597.

UNIVERSITY OF LOWELL

Lowell, Massachusetts

General Information

State-supported comprehensive coed institution. Founded 1894. Awards A (college transfer), B, M, D. Primary accreditation: regional. City setting; 100-acre campus. Total enrollment: 11,456. Faculty: 636 (524 full-time, 112 part-time).

Drug and Alcohol Information

Education

On campus Drug and alcohol education/prevention programs offered for: all students, athletes/coaches. Authorized group concerned with responsible drinking. College holds an annual alcohol awareness week and drug awareness week.

Identification of Problems

Admissions College application does not ask about prior substance abuse problems.

On campus Current students identified as chemically dependent may remain enrolled, but treatment is required. Training program on identifying students with potential substance abuse problems for: resident advisers, administration, campus police. Written procedures for students and staff if substance abuse is suspected.

Support Services

On campus AA, Al-Anon, ACOA, counseling center.

Employee assistance Program for chemically dependent employees available.

Disciplinary Actions

Alcohol Results of infractions of alcohol regulations (see Comparative Table of Alcohol Regulations) vary by situation but can include chemical dependency assessment, counseling, warning, probation, suspension, expulsion, withdrawal of recognition to groups, inluding suspension of charter and loss of privileges.

Drugs For any use or possession: varies by situation. For any sale: probation, suspension, expulsion.

For More Information

Contact: Dr. Noel Cartwright, Director of Counseling/Career Development, University of Lowell, 1 University Ave., Lowell, MA 01854. Telephone: 508-452-5000 Ext. 2390.

UNIVERSITY OF MAINE

Orono, Maine

General Information

State-supported comprehensive coed institution. Part of University of Maine System. Founded 1865. Awards A (college transfer and terminal), B, M, D. Primary accreditation: regional. Small-town setting; 3,298-acre campus. Total enrollment: 10,967. Faculty: 900 (768 full-time, 132 part-time). Social organizations: 16 national fraternities, 9 national sororities, 1 local fraternity; 18% of eligible undergraduate men and 11% of eligible undergraduate women are members.

Drug and Alcohol Information

Education

On campus Drug and alcohol education/prevention programs offered for: all students, faculty, administration; required for: freshmen, athletes/coaches, resident advisers. Authorized group concerned with responsible drinking. College holds an annual alcohol awareness week and drug awareness week.

Identification of Problems

Admissions College application question about prior substance abuse problems is used to explain past academic performance.

On campus Current students identified as chemically dependent may remain enrolled, but treatment is required. Training program on identifying students with potential substance abuse problems for: resident advisers, coaches, Greek officers, faculty, administration. Written procedures for students and staff if substance abuse is suspected.

Support Services

On campus AA, NA, Al-Anon, ACOA, support groups, private counseling, comprehensive substance abuse services.

Employee assistance Program for chemically dependent employees available. Staff working with drug/alcohol-related issues: 1 full-time and 3 part-time.

Disciplinary Actions

Alcohol Results of infractions of alcohol regulations (see Comparative Table of Alcohol Regulations) vary by situation but can include chemical dependency assessment, counseling, warning, probation, suspension, expulsion. Comments: Multitiered approach includes increasingly intensive educational and treatment interventions.

Drugs For first-time use, possession, or sale: varies by situation—counseling, probation. For subsequent use or possession: chemical dependency assessment, counseling. For subsequent sale: expulsion.

Additional Information from the College

The comprehensive substance abuse services program provides prevention programming, training, consultation, referral, assessment, treatment, speakers, and student, staff, and faculty training. This program is also engaged in ongoing research concerning determinants of substance abuse, incidence of substance use and abuse, programming, efficacy, and prevention and intervention strategies. The "Late Night Local," a student-run safe transportation service provided without charge.

For More Information

Contact: Dr. Robert Dana, Coordinator, Substance Abuse Services, University of Maine, Orono, ME 04469. Telephone: 207-581-4016.

UNIVERSITY OF MAINE AT AUGUSTA

Augusta, Maine

General Information

State-supported 4-year coed college. Part of University of Maine System. Founded 1965. Awards A (college transfer and terminal), B. Primary accreditation: regional. Small-town setting; 165-acre campus. Total enrollment: 3,824. Faculty: 218 (68 full-time, 150 part-time).

Drug and Alcohol Information

Education

On campus Drug and alcohol education/prevention programs offered for: all students, athletes/coaches, faculty, administration, community members. Authorized group concerned with responsible drinking. College holds an annual alcohol awareness week and drug awareness week.

Identification of Problems

Admissions College application does not ask about prior substance abuse problems.

On campus Current students identified as chemically dependent may remain enrolled. No training program on identifying students with potential substance abuse problems. No written procedures for students and staff if substance abuse is suspected.

Support Services

On campus ACOA, support groups.

Employee assistance Program for chemically dependent employees not available. Staff working with drug/alcohol-related issues: 3 part-time.

Disciplinary Actions

Alcohol Results of infractions of alcohol regulations (see Comparative Table of Alcohol Regulations) include counseling, probation, suspension, expulsion.

Drugs For first-time use: counseling, referral. For subsequent use: varies by situation. For first-time possession or sale: probation, suspension, expulsion. For subsequent possession or sale: expulsion.

For More Information

Contact: Jon Schlenker, Dean, University of Maine at Augusta, University Heights, Augusta, ME 04330. Telephone: 207-622-7131.

UNIVERSITY OF MAINE AT FARMINGTON

Farmington, Maine

General Information

State-supported 4-year coed college. Part of University of Maine System. Founded 1864. Awards A (college transfer and terminal), B. Primary accreditation: regional. Small-town setting; 32-acre campus. Total enrollment: 2,427. Faculty: 159 (110 full-time, 49 part-time). Social organizations: 1 local fraternity, 1 local sorority; 5% of eligible undergraduate men and 5% of eligible undergraduate women are members.

Drug and Alcohol Information

Education

On campus Drug and alcohol education/prevention programs offered for: all students, faculty, administration. Bacchus chapter: 20 members. College holds an annual alcohol awareness week.

Identification of Problems

Admissions College application does not ask about prior substance abuse problems.

On campus Current students identified as chemically dependent may remain enrolled. Training program on identifying students with potential substance abuse problems for: resident advisers. Written procedures for students and staff if substance abuse is suspected.

Support Services

On campus AA, NA, Al-Anon, ACOA, support groups, private counseling.

Employee assistance Program for chemically dependent employees not available. Staff working with drug/alcohol-related issues: 1 part-time.

Disciplinary Actions

Alcohol Results of infractions of alcohol regulations (see Comparative Table of Alcohol Regulations) vary by situation but can include chemical dependency assessment, counseling, warning, probation, suspension.

Drugs For first-time use or possession: chemical dependency assessment, counseling, probation. For subsequent use or possession: suspension. For any sale: suspension.

For More Information

Contact: Bill Geller, Executive Director of Educational Services, University of Maine at Farmington, Farmington, ME 04938. Telephone: 207-778-3501.

UNIVERSITY OF MAINE AT FORT KENT

Fort Kent, Maine

General Information

State-supported 4-year coed college. Part of University of Maine System. Founded 1878. Awards A (college transfer and terminal), B. Primary accreditation: regional. Rural setting; 52-acre campus. Total enrollment: 714. Faculty: 30 (28 full-time, 2 part-time). Social organizations: 2 national fraternities, 1 national sorority; 12% of eligible undergraduate men and 3% of eligible undergraduate women are members.

Drug and Alcohol Information

Education

On campus Drug and alcohol education/prevention programs offered for: all students. College holds an annual alcohol awareness week and drug awareness week.

University of Maine at Fort Kent (continued)

Identification of Problems

Admissions College application does not ask about prior substance abuse problems.

On campus Current students identified as chemically dependent may remain enrolled, but treatment is required. Training program on identifying students with potential substance abuse problems for: resident advisers.

Support Services

On campus AA, Al-Anon, ACOA, private counseling.

Employee assistance Program for chemically dependent employees not available.

Disciplinary Actions

Alcohol Results of infractions of alcohol regulations (see Comparative Table of Alcohol Regulations) vary by situation.

Drugs For first-time use or possession: warning, probation. For first-time sale: warning, suspension. For subsequent use, possession, or sale: counseling, suspension.

For More Information

Contact: Dr. J. J. Nabors, Dean of Student Affairs, University of Maine at Fort Kent, Fort Kent, ME 04743. Telephone: 207-834-3162.

UNIVERSITY OF MAINE AT MACHIAS

Machias, Maine

General Information

State-supported 4-year coed college. Part of University of Maine System. Founded 1909. Awards A (college transfer and terminal), B. Primary accreditation: regional. Rural setting; 47-acre campus. Total enrollment: 851. Faculty: 54 (35 full-time, 19 part-time). Social organizations: 2 national fraternities, 1 national sorority, 1 local fraternity, 2 local sororities; 17% of eligible undergraduate men and 12% of eligible undergraduate women are members.

Drug and Alcohol Information

Education

On campus Drug and alcohol education/prevention programs offered for: all students, athletes/coaches, faculty, administration. College holds an annual alcohol awareness week.

Identification of Problems

Admissions College application does not ask about prior substance abuse problems.

On campus Current students identified as chemically dependent may remain enrolled, but treatment is recommended. Training program on identifying students with potential substance abuse problems for: resident advisers, coaches, faculty, administration. No written procedures for students and staff if substance abuse is suspected.

Support Services

On campus Support groups, private counseling.

Employee assistance Program for chemically dependent employees available. Staff working with drug/alcohol-related issues: 4 part-time.

Disciplinary Actions

Alcohol Results of infractions of alcohol regulations (see Comparative Table of Alcohol Regulations) include counseling, probation, removal from residence halls. Comments: Social organizations violating regulations cannot have social functions for one year.

Drugs For any use, possession, or sale: referral to police.

For More Information

Contact: Debra Anderson, Director of Counseling, University of Maine at Machias, 9 O'Brien Ave., Machias, ME 04654. Telephone: 207-255-3313 Ext. 331.

UNIVERSITY OF MARY

Bismarck, North Dakota

General Information

Independent Roman Catholic 5-year coed college. Founded 1959. Awards B, M. Primary accreditation: regional. Small-town setting; 107-acre campus. Total enrollment: 1,352. Faculty: 87 (61 full-time, 26 part-time).

Drug and Alcohol Information

Education

On campus Drug and alcohol education/prevention programs offered for: all students, faculty, administration; required for: freshmen, athletes/coaches, resident advisers. Bacchus chapter: about 20 members. College holds an annual alcohol awareness week and drug awareness week.

Identification of Problems

Admissions College application does not ask about prior substance abuse problems.

On campus Current students identified as chemically dependent may remain enrolled, but treatment is required. Training program on identifying students with potential substance abuse problems for: resident advisers, coaches, faculty. Written procedures for students and staff if substance abuse is suspected.

Support Services

On campus AA, support groups (Christian ministry), private counseling.

Employee assistance Program for chemically dependent employees not available. Staff working with drug/alcohol-related issues: 6 part-time.

Disciplinary Actions

Alcohol Results of infractions of alcohol regulations (see Comparative Table of Alcohol Regulations) vary by situation but can include chemical dependency assessment, counseling, warning, probation, suspension, expulsion.

Drugs For first-time use, possession, or sale: varies by situation. For subsequent use, possession, or sale: varies by situation—chemical dependency assessment, suspension, expulsion.

For More Information

Contact: Charles Hanson, Vice President for Student Development, University of Mary, 7500 University Dr., Bismarck, ND 58504. Telephone: 701-255-7500 Ext. 416.

UNIVERSITY OF MARY HARDIN-BAYLOR

Belton, Texas

General Information

Independent Southern Baptist 5-year coed college. Founded 1845. Awards B, M. Primary accreditation: regional. Small-town setting; 100-acre campus. Total enrollment: 1,511. Faculty: 75.

Drug and Alcohol Information

Education

On campus Drug and alcohol education/prevention programs required for: freshmen, resident advisers.

Identification of Problems

Admissions College application does not ask about prior substance abuse problems.

On campus Current students identified as chemically dependent may not remain enrolled. Training program on identifying students with potential substance abuse problems for: resident advisers. Written procedures for students and staff if substance abuse is suspected.

Support Services

On campus No support services on campus.

Employee assistance Program for chemically dependent employees not available.

Disciplinary Actions

Alcohol Results of infractions of alcohol regulations (see Comparative Table of Alcohol Regulations) include suspension.

Drugs For any use, possession, or sale: expulsion.

For More Information

Contact: Ray Martin, Dean of Students, University of Mary Hardin-Baylor, M H-B Station, Belton, TX 76513. Telephone: 817-939-5811 Ext. 227.

UNIVERSITY OF MARYLAND AT BALTIMORE

Baltimore, Maryland

General Information

State-supported coed college. Part of University of Maryland System. Founded 1807. Awards B, M, D. Primary accreditation: regional. Metropolitan setting; 30-acre campus. Total enrollment: 4,563. Faculty: 187 (139 full-time, 48 part-time).

Drug and Alcohol Information

Education

On campus Drug and alcohol education/prevention programs offered for: all students, faculty, administration. Authorized group concerned with responsible drinking.

Identification of Problems

Admissions College application does not ask about prior substance abuse problems.

On campus Current students identified as chemically dependent may remain enrolled, but treatment is required. No training program on identifying students with potential substance abuse problems. Written procedures for students and staff if substance abuse is suspected.

Support Services

On campus ACOA, private counseling, EAP.

Employee assistance Program for chemically dependent employees available. Staff working with drug/alcohol-related issues: 1 full-time.

Disciplinary Actions

Alcohol Results of infractions of alcohol regulations (see Comparative Table of Alcohol Regulations) include warning.

For More Information

Contact: Carrie Burmaster, Employee Assistance Program Manager, University of Maryland at Baltimore, 621 W. Lombard St., Baltimore, MD 21201. Telephone: 301-328-8404.

UNIVERSITY OF MARYLAND BALTIMORE COUNTY

Baltimore, Maryland

General Information

State-supported comprehensive coed institution. Part of University of Maryland System. Founded 1966. Awards B, M, D. Primary accreditation: regional. Metropolitan setting; 475-acre campus. Total enrollment: 9,868. Faculty: 575 (350 full-time, 225 part-time). Social organizations: 8 national fraternities, 6 national sororities, 2 local sororities; 5% of eligible undergraduate men and 5% of eligible undergraduate women are members.

Drug and Alcohol Information

Education

On campus Drug and alcohol education/prevention programs offered for: all students; required for: athletes/coaches. Authorized group concerned with responsible drinking. College holds an annual alcohol awareness week and drug awareness week.

Identification of Problems

Admissions College application does not ask about prior substance abuse problems.

On campus Current students identified as chemically dependent may remain enrolled. Training program on identifying students with potential substance abuse problems for: resident advisers, coaches, student affairs staff. Written procedures for students and staff if substance abuse is suspected.

Support Services

On campus ACOA, private counseling.

Employee assistance Program for chemically dependent employees not available. Staff working with drug/alcohol-related issues: 1 full-time and several part-time.

Disciplinary Actions

Alcohol Results of infractions of alcohol regulations (see Comparative Table of Alcohol Regulations) include counseling, warning, closing an event, judicial charges, prohibition from sponsoring events for up to one year.

Drugs For first-time use or possession: counseling, warning. For first-time sale: counseling, warning, probation. For subsequent use: counseling, warning, probation. For subsequent possession or sale: varies by situation.

University of Maryland Baltimore County (continued)

For More Information

Contact: Lisa Dieter-Borisky, Assistant Director for Health Education, Student Health Services, University of Maryland Baltimore County, 5401 Wilkens Ave., Baltimore, MD 21228. Telephone: 301-455-2542.

UNIVERSITY OF MARYLAND EASTERN SHORE

Princess Anne, Maryland

General Information

State-supported comprehensive coed institution. Part of University of Maryland System. Founded 1886. Awards B, M, D. Primary accreditation: regional. Rural setting; 540-acre campus. Total enrollment: 1,559. Faculty: 130 (95 full-time, 35 part-time). Social organizations: national fraternities, national sororities, local fraternities, local sororities; 25% of eligible undergraduate men and 18% of eligible undergraduate women are members.

Drug and Alcohol Information

Education

On campus Drug and alcohol education/prevention programs offered for: all students, athletes/coaches, faculty, administration, voluntary participation. College holds an annual alcohol awareness week and drug awareness week.

Identification of Problems

Admissions College application does not ask about prior substance abuse problems.

On campus Current students identified as chemically dependent may remain enrolled, but treatment is required. Training program on identifying students with potential substance abuse problems for: resident advisers, coaches, Greek officers, faculty, administration, voluntary participation. Written procedures for students and staff if substance abuse is suspected.

Support Services

On campus Private counseling, referral.

Employee assistance Program for chemically dependent employees available. Staff working with drug/alcohol-related issues: 2 part-time.

Disciplinary Actions

Alcohol Results of infractions of alcohol regulations (see Comparative Table of Alcohol Regulations) vary by situation but can include counseling.

Drugs For any use: suspension. For any possession: varies by situation. For any sale: turned over to criminal authorities.

For More Information

Contact: Dr. Beatrice Hamilton-Obaid, Counseling Center Director, University of Maryland Eastern Shore, Princess Anne, MD 21853. Telephone: 301-651-2200 Ext. 343.

UNIVERSITY OF MARYLAND UNIVERSITY COLLEGE

College Park, Maryland

General Information

State-supported 5-year coed college. Part of University of Maryland System. Founded 1947. Awards B, M (offers primarily part-time evening and weekend degree programs). Primary accreditation: regional. Total enrollment: 36,258.

Drug and Alcohol Information

Education

On campus Drug and alcohol education/prevention programs offered for: all students, faculty, administration.

Identification of Problems

Admissions College application does not ask about prior substance abuse problems.

On campus Current students identified as chemically dependent may remain enrolled. No training program on identifying students with potential substance abuse problems. Written procedures for students and staff if substance abuse is suspected.

Support Services

On campus Private counseling.

Employee assistance Program for chemically dependent employees available.

Disciplinary Actions

Alcohol Results of infractions of alcohol regulations (see Comparative Table of Alcohol Regulations) vary by situation. Comments: Judicial proceedings are initiated under University Student Conduct Code.

Additional Information from the College

University of Maryland University College provides evening and weekend programs for adult, part-time students.

For More Information

Contact: Barbara Mayo-Wells, Associate Vice President, Student Services, University of Maryland University College, University Blvd. at Adelphi Rd., College Park, MD 20742. Telephone: 800-888-UMUC Ext. 7289.

UNIVERSITY OF MICHIGAN

Ann Arbor, Michigan

General Information

State-supported comprehensive coed institution. Founded 1817. Awards B, M, D. Primary accreditation: regional. City setting; 2,580-acre campus. Total enrollment: 35,220. Faculty: 3,619 (all full-time). Social organizations: national fraternities, national sororities, local fraternities, local sororities; 14% of eligible undergraduate men and 20% of eligible undergraduate women are members.

Drug and Alcohol Information

Education

On campus Drug and alcohol education/prevention programs offered for: all students. Authorized group concerned with responsible drinking. College holds an annual alcohol awareness week.

Identification of Problems

Admissions College application does not ask about prior substance abuse problems. Prospective students can indicate if they are in recovery.

On campus Current students identified as chemically dependent may remain enrolled. Training program on identifying students with potential substance abuse problems for: resident advisers, coaches. No written

procedures for students and staff if substance abuse is suspected.

Support Services

On campus AA, NA, ACOA, private counseling.

Employee assistance Program for chemically dependent employees available. Staff working with drug/alcohol-related issues: 1 full-time.

Disciplinary Actions

Alcohol Results of infractions of alcohol regulations (see Comparative Table of Alcohol Regulations) vary by situation but can include expulsion.

Drugs For first-time use: varies by situation—counseling. For subsequent use: varies by situation—probation. For any possession: varies by situation. For any sale: varies by situation—expulsion.

For More Information

Contact: Henry Johnson, Vice President of Student Services, 3000 Michigan Union, University of Michigan, Ann Arbor, MI 48109. Telephone: 313-764-7423.

UNIVERSITY OF MICHIGAN–DEARBORN

Dearborn, Michigan

General Information

State-supported 5-year coed college. Part of University of Michigan System. Founded 1959. Awards B, M. Primary accreditation: regional. City setting; 210-acre campus. Total enrollment: 6,573. Faculty: 370 (193 full-time, 177 part-time). Social organizations: 6 local fraternities, 3 local sororities; 4% of eligible undergraduate men and 7% of eligible undergraduate women are members.

Drug and Alcohol Information

Education

On campus Drug and alcohol education/prevention programs offered for: students in residence halls, social organization members. College holds an annual alcohol awareness week and drug awareness week.

Identification of Problems

Admissions College application does not ask about prior substance abuse problems.

On campus Current students identified as chemically dependent may remain enrolled. No training program on identifying students with potential substance abuse problems. No written procedures for students and staff if substance abuse is suspected.

Support Services

On campus Private counseling, referrals.

Employee assistance Program for chemically dependent employees available. Staff working with drug/alcohol-related issues: 1 part-time.

Disciplinary Actions

Alcohol Results of infractions of alcohol regulations (see Comparative Table of Alcohol Regulations) vary by situation but can include chemical dependency assessment, counseling, warning, probation, suspension, expulsion.

Drugs For any use, possession, or sale: varies by situation.

For More Information

Contact: Margaret Flannery, Assistant Director of Counseling, University of Michigan–Dearborn, 4901 Evergreen Rd., Dearborn, MI 48128. Telephone: 313-593-5430.

UNIVERSITY OF MICHIGAN–FLINT

Flint, Michigan

General Information

State-supported 5-year coed college. Part of University of Michigan System. Founded 1956. Awards B, M. Primary accreditation: regional. City setting; 42-acre campus. Total enrollment: 6,305. Faculty: 211 (160 full-time, 51 part-time). Social organizations: 2 national fraternities, 4 national sororities.

Drug and Alcohol Information

Education

On campus Drug and alcohol education/prevention programs offered for: all students, faculty, administration. College holds an annual alcohol awareness week.

Identification of Problems

Admissions College application does not ask about prior substance abuse problems.

On campus Current students identified as chemically dependent may remain enrolled. No training program on identifying students with potential substance abuse problems. Written procedures for students and staff if substance abuse is suspected.

Support Services

On campus Private counseling.

Employee assistance Program for chemically dependent employees available. Staff working with drug/alcohol-related issues: 2 part-time.

Disciplinary Actions

Alcohol Results of infractions of alcohol regulations (see Comparative Table of Alcohol Regulations) include counseling.

Drugs For any use, possession, or sale: varies by situation.

Additional Information from the College

No BYOB or outside sources of liquor allowed. Student organizations subject to alcohol guidelines. Group accountability rather than individual culpability for off-campus events. Enforcement off campus by local police agencies. Heavy use is made of community resources through referrals.

For More Information

Contact: Irene Roach, Nurse, University of Michigan–Flint, Flint, MI 48502-2186. Telephone: 313-762-3456.

UNIVERSITY OF MINNESOTA, DULUTH

Duluth, Minnesota

General Information

State-supported 5-year coed college. Part of University of Minnesota System. Founded 1948. Awards B, M. Primary accreditation: regional. City setting; 250-acre campus. Total enrollment: 7,435. Social organizations: 1 national

University of Minnesota, Duluth (continued)

fraternity, 1 national sorority, 4 local fraternities, 3 local sororities; 15% of eligible undergraduate men and 16% of eligible undergraduate women are members.

Drug and Alcohol Information

Education

On campus Drug and alcohol education/prevention programs offered for: all students; required for: athletes/coaches. Authorized group concerned with responsible drinking. College holds an annual alcohol awareness week.

Identification of Problems

On campus Current students identified as chemically dependent may remain enrolled.

Support Services

On campus AA, ACOA.

Employee assistance Program for chemically dependent employees available. Staff working with drug/alcohol-related issues: 1 part-time.

Disciplinary Actions

Alcohol Results of infractions of alcohol regulations (see Comparative Table of Alcohol Regulations) vary by situation but can include chemical dependency assessment, group education.

Drugs For any use, possession, or sale: varies by situation.

For More Information

Contact: William Long, Counselor, Student Health and Counseling Center, University of Minnesota, Duluth, 10 University Drive, Duluth, MN 55812. Telephone: 218-723-1759.

UNIVERSITY OF MINNESOTA, MORRIS

Morris, Minnesota

General Information

State-supported 4-year coed college. Part of University of Minnesota System. Founded 1959. Awards B. Primary accreditation: regional. Small-town setting; 130-acre campus. Total enrollment: 1,959. Faculty: 142 (127 full-time, 15 part-time). Social organizations: 2 national fraternities, 2 local sororities; 87% of eligible undergraduate men and 90% of eligible undergraduate women are members.

Drug and Alcohol Information

Education

On campus Drug and alcohol education/prevention programs offered for: all students, athletes/coaches, faculty, administration, community members. Authorized group concerned with responsible drinking. College holds an annual alcohol awareness week.

Identification of Problems

Admissions College application does not ask about prior substance abuse problems.

On campus Current students identified as chemically dependent may remain enrolled. Training program on identifying students with potential substance abuse problems for: resident advisers. Written procedures for students and staff if substance abuse is suspected.

Support Services

On campus ACOA, support groups, counseling services.

Off campus AA.

Employee assistance Program for chemically dependent employees available. Staff working with drug/alcohol-related issues: 2 part-time.

Disciplinary Actions

Alcohol Results of infractions of alcohol regulations (see Comparative Table of Alcohol Regulations) vary by situation but can include counseling, warning, probation, suspension.

Drugs For any use, possession, or sale: varies by situation—warning, Campus Police involvement.

For More Information

Contact: Lois Flagstad-Kramer, Counselor, Student Counseling Service, University of Minnesota, Morris, 235 Behmler Hall, Morris, MN 56267. Telephone: 612-589-2211 Ext. 6060.

UNIVERSITY OF MINNESOTA, TWIN CITIES CAMPUS

Minneapolis, Minnesota

General Information

State-supported comprehensive coed institution. Part of University of Minnesota System. Founded 1851. Awards B, M, D. Primary accreditation: regional. Metropolitan setting; 1,000-acre campus. Total enrollment: 38,172. Faculty: 2,836 (2,446 full-time, 390 part-time). Social organizations: 27 national fraternities, 16 national sororities.

Drug and Alcohol Information

Education

On campus Drug and alcohol education/prevention programs offered for: all students, faculty, administration; required for: athletes/coaches, resident advisers. Authorized group concerned with responsible drinking. College holds an annual alcohol awareness week and drug awareness week.

Identification of Problems

Admissions College application does not ask about prior substance abuse problems.

On campus Current students identified as chemically dependent may remain enrolled. Comments: Treatment is required if student is an athlete and wishes to remain an athlete. Training program on identifying students with potential substance abuse problems for: resident advisers, coaches, student groups. Written procedures for students and staff if substance abuse is suspected.

Support Services

On campus AA, Al-Anon, ACOA, support groups, private counseling, student health insurance covers out-patient chemical dependency treatment in full.

Employee assistance Program for chemically dependent employees available for union and civil service employees. Faculty program is in the development stage. Staff working with drug/alcohol-related issues: 1 full-time.

Disciplinary Actions

Alcohol Results of infractions of alcohol regulations (see Comparative Table of Alcohol Regulations) vary by

situation but can include chemical dependency assessment, counseling.

Drugs For any use: varies by situation—chemical dependency assessment, counseling. For any possession or sale: varies by situation.

Additional Information from the College

Over the past twelve years there has been a significant improvement in the attitude and interest of various campus populations regarding drug and alcohol abuse prevention. For example, Greek organizations voluntarily decided to have nonalcoholic rush parties, and some have coordinated with the University's Chemical Health Coordinator to plan intervention with house members. The Chemical Awareness Promotion through Peers (CAPP) program has brought positive changes.

For More Information

Contact: Julie E. Hynes, Chemical Health Counselor, Boynton Health Service, University of Minnesota, Twin Cities Campus, 410 Church St., Minneapolis, MN 55455. Telephone: 612-884-2045.

UNIVERSITY OF MISSOURI–COLUMBIA

Columbia, Missouri

General Information

State-supported comprehensive coed institution. Part of University of Missouri System. Founded 1839. Awards B, M, D. Primary accreditation: regional. City setting; 1,335-acre campus. Total enrollment: 23,434. Faculty: 1,549 (1,517 full-time, 32 part-time). Social organizations: 32 national fraternities, 16 national sororities; 20% of eligible undergraduate men and 20% of eligible undergraduate women are members.

Drug and Alcohol Information

Education

On campus Drug and alcohol education/prevention programs offered for: all students, athletes/coaches. Authorized group concerned with responsible drinking. College holds an annual alcohol awareness week.

Identification of Problems

Admissions College application does not ask about prior substance abuse problems.

On campus Current students identified as chemically dependent may remain enrolled. Training program on identifying students with potential substance abuse problems for: resident advisers. No written procedures for students and staff if substance abuse is suspected.

Support Services

On campus AA, ACOA.

Employee assistance Program for chemically dependent employees available. Staff working with drug/alcohol-related issues: 3 part-time, plus counseling staff.

Disciplinary Actions

Alcohol Results of infractions of alcohol regulations (see Comparative Table of Alcohol Regulations) vary by situation.

Drugs For any use, possession, or sale: varies by situation.

For More Information

Contact: Kim Dude, Assistant Director of Residential Life, University of Missouri–Columbia, 15 Defoe Hall, Columbia, MO 65211. Telephone: 314-882-2834.

UNIVERSITY OF MISSOURI–KANSAS CITY

Kansas City, Missouri

General Information

State-supported comprehensive coed institution. Part of University of Missouri System. Founded 1933. Awards B, M, D. Primary accreditation: regional. Metropolitan setting; 300-acre campus. Total enrollment: 11,756. Faculty: 952 (612 full-time, 340 part-time). Social organizations: 8 national fraternities, 5 national sororities, 1 local sorority; 3% of eligible undergraduate men and 2% of eligible undergraduate women are members.

Drug and Alcohol Information

Education

On campus Drug and alcohol education/prevention programs offered for: all students. Bacchus chapter: 20 members. College holds an annual alcohol awareness week.

Identification of Problems

Admissions College application does not ask about prior substance abuse problems.

On campus Current students identified as chemically dependent may remain enrolled. Training program on identifying students with potential substance abuse problems for: resident advisers. No written procedures for students and staff if substance abuse is suspected.

Support Services

On campus Private counseling.

Employee assistance Program for chemically dependent employees not available. Staff working with drug/alcohol-related issues: 3 part-time.

Disciplinary Actions

Alcohol Results of infractions of alcohol regulations (see Comparative Table of Alcohol Regulations) include warning, probation, suspension.

Drugs For first-time use or possession: probation. For first-time sale: varies by situation. For subsequent use, possession, or sale: varies by situation.

Additional Information from the College

The University has minimal drug- and alcohol-related programming because it has only one small residence hall and few Greek organizations. The Bacchus chapter is growing and the professional schools are increasingly interested in this topic. Therefore, a more sophisticated program is imminent.

For More Information

Contact: Dr. Larry H. Dietz, Associate Vice Chancellor, University of Missouri–Kansas City, 5100 Rockhill Rd., Kansas City, MO 64110. Telephone: 816-276-1141.

UNIVERSITY OF MISSOURI–ROLLA

Rolla, Missouri

General Information

State-supported comprehensive coed institution. Part of University of Missouri System. Founded 1870. Awards B, M, D. Primary accreditation: regional. Small-town setting; 260-acre campus. Total enrollment: 5,724. Faculty: 381 (344 full-time, 37 part-time). Social organizations: 20 national fraternities, 3 national sororities, 2 eating clubs; 35% of eligible undergraduate men and 10% of eligible undergraduate women are members.

Drug and Alcohol Information

Education

On campus Drug and alcohol education/prevention programs offered for: all students; being developed for: faculty, administration; required for: athletes/coaches. Bacchus chapter: 10–15 members. College holds an annual alcohol awareness week.

Identification of Problems

Admissions College application does not ask about prior substance abuse problems.

On campus Current students identified as chemically dependent may remain enrolled. Training programs on identifying students with potential substance abuse problems exist or are being developed for: resident advisers, coaches, Greek officers and residents, faculty, administration. No written procedures for students and staff if substance abuse is suspected.

Support Services

On campus AA, support groups (CODA), private counseling.

Off campus NA, Al-Anon, ACOA.

Employee assistance Program for chemically dependent employees available. Staff working with drug/alcohol-related issues: 1 full-time and 4 part-time.

Disciplinary Actions

Alcohol Results of infractions of alcohol regulations (see Comparative Table of Alcohol Regulations) vary by situation.

Drugs For any use, possession, or sale: varies by situation.

Additional Information from the College

The University has made much progress in the last year and is currently assessing campus drug and alcohol problems and networking with other resources in and out of Missouri. A campus-community committee is examining substance abuse issues for future programming and policies.

For More Information

Contact: Camille Consolvo, Counseling Psychologist, Counseling Center, 106 Rolla Bldg., University of Missouri–Rolla, Rolla, MO 65401. Telephone: 314-341-4211.

UNIVERSITY OF MONTANA

Missoula, Montana

General Information

State-supported comprehensive coed institution. Part of Montana University System. Founded 1893. Awards A (college transfer), B, M, D. Primary accreditation: regional. City setting; 200-acre campus. Total enrollment: 8,879. Faculty: 483 (397 full-time, 86 part-time). Social organizations: 8 national fraternities, 4 national sororities; 11% of eligible undergraduate men and 6% of eligible undergraduate women are members.

Drug and Alcohol Information

Education

On campus Drug and alcohol education/prevention programs offered for: all students, faculty, administration; required for: athletes/coaches, resident advisers. Authorized group concerned with responsible drinking. College holds an annual alcohol awareness week and drug awareness week.

Identification of Problems

Admissions College application does not ask about prior substance abuse problems.

On campus Current students identified as chemically dependent may remain enrolled, but treatment is required. Training program on identifying students with potential substance abuse problems is being developed for: resident advisers, coaches, Greek officers, faculty, administration, peer advisers. Written procedures are being developed for students and staff if substance abuse is suspected.

Support Services

On campus AA, ACOA, support groups, private counseling.

Employee assistance Program for chemically dependent employees available. Staff working with drug/alcohol-related issues: 1 full-time and 5 part-time.

Disciplinary Actions

Alcohol Results of infractions of alcohol regulations (see Comparative Table of Alcohol Regulations) vary by situation but can include chemical dependency assessment, counseling, warning, probation, suspension, expulsion.

Drugs For first-time use: chemical dependency assessment, counseling, warning. For subsequent use: probation, suspension. For first-time possession: probation. For subsequent possession: suspension, expulsion. For first-time sale: suspension, expulsion. For subsequent sale: expulsion.

For More Information

Contact: Joanne Blake, Drug and Alcohol Coordinator, Counseling Center, University of Montana, Missoula, MT 59812. Telephone: 406-243-4711.

UNIVERSITY OF NEBRASKA AT OMAHA

Omaha, Nebraska

General Information

State-supported 5-year coed college. Part of University of Nebraska System. Founded 1908. Awards A (college transfer and terminal), B, M. Primary accreditation: regional. Metropolitan setting; 88-acre campus. Total enrollment: 14,194. Faculty: 534 (434 full-time, 100 part-time). Social organizations: 9 national fraternities, 6 national sororities; 7% of eligible undergraduate men and 7% of eligible undergraduate women are members.

Drug and Alcohol Information

Education

On campus Drug and alcohol education/prevention

programs offered for: all students. College holds an annual alcohol awareness week and drug awareness week.

Identification of Problems

Admissions College application does not ask about prior substance abuse problems.

On campus Current students identified as chemically dependent may remain enrolled, but treatment is required. Training program on identifying students with potential substance abuse problems for: faculty, administration, health staff. Written procedures for students and staff if substance abuse is suspected.

Support Services

On campus AA, Al-Anon, ACOA, private counseling.

Employee assistance Program for chemically dependent employees available. Staff working with drug/alcohol-related issues: 1–2 full-time and 4 part-time.

Disciplinary Actions

Alcohol Results of infractions of alcohol regulations (see Comparative Table of Alcohol Regulations) vary by situation but can include chemical dependency assessment, counseling, suspension, expulsion.

Drugs For first-time use, possession, or sale: varies by situation. For subsequent use, possession, or sale: expulsion.

Additional Information from the College

Received FIPSE grant for two-year program called "Let's Intervene for Tomorrow-University Project" (LIFT-UP), a University-wide effort to combat drug and alcohol abuse.

For More Information

Contact: Joe L. Davis, Assistant Vice Chancellor, University of Nebraska at Omaha, 60th and Dodge Sts., Omaha, NE 68182. Telephone: 402-554-2409.

UNIVERSITY OF NEBRASKA MEDICAL CENTER

Omaha, Nebraska

General Information

State-supported coed college. Part of University of Nebraska System. Founded 1869. Awards B, M, D. Primary accreditation: regional. Metropolitan setting; 51-acre campus. Total enrollment: 2,279. Faculty: 155 (85 full-time, 70 part-time). Social organizations: 2 national fraternities, 2 national sororities; 10% of eligible undergraduate men and 10% of eligible undergraduate women are members.

Drug and Alcohol Information

Education

On campus Drug and alcohol education/prevention programs offered for: all students, faculty, peer support leaders. Authorized group concerned with responsible drinking.

Identification of Problems

Admissions College application does not ask about prior substance abuse problems.

On campus Current students identified as chemically dependent may remain enrolled, but treatment is required. Training program on identifying students with potential substance abuse problems for: peer counselors. Written procedures for students and staff if substance abuse is suspected.

Support Services

On campus AA, Al-Anon, ACOA, private counseling.

Employee assistance Program for chemically dependent employees available. Staff working with drug/alcohol-related issues: 2 part-time.

Disciplinary Actions

Alcohol Results of infractions of alcohol regulations (see Comparative Table of Alcohol Regulations) vary by situation but can include chemical dependency assessment, counseling, warning.

Drugs For any use: varies by situation—chemical dependency assessment, counseling. For any possession: chemical dependency assessment, counseling. For first-time sale: suspension, expulsion. For subsequent sale: expulsion.

For More Information

Contact: Dave Carver, Ph.D., Director, Student Counseling, University of Nebraska Medical Center, 42nd and Dewey Avenue, Omaha, NE 68105. Telephone: 402-559-7276.

UNIVERSITY OF NEVADA–RENO

Reno, Nevada

General Information

State-supported comprehensive coed institution. Part of University of Nevada System. Founded 1874. Awards B, M, D. Primary accreditation: regional. City setting; 200-acre campus. Total enrollment: 9,772. Faculty: 445 (335 full-time, 110 part-time). Social organizations: 8 national fraternities, 5 national sororities, 1 local fraternity; 9% of eligible undergraduate men and 7% of eligible undergraduate women are members.

Drug and Alcohol Information

Education

On campus Drug and alcohol education/prevention programs offered for: all students, faculty, administration; required for: social organization members, athletes/coaches, resident advisers, student leaders. Bacchus chapter: 12 members. College holds an annual alcohol awareness week and drug awareness week.

Identification of Problems

Admissions College application does not ask about prior substance abuse problems.

On campus Training program on identifying students with potential substance abuse problems for: resident advisers, coaches, Greek officers, faculty, administration. Written procedures being developed for students and staff if substance abuse is suspected.

Support Services

On campus Support groups, private counseling, liaison contact with community services.

Off campus AA, NA, Al-Anon, ACOA.

Employee assistance Program for chemically dependent employees available. Staff working with drug/alcohol-related issues: 1 part-time.

Disciplinary Actions

Alcohol Results of infractions of alcohol regulations (see Comparative Table of Alcohol Regulations) vary by situation. Comments: Policy is being reevaluated.

Drugs Comments: Policy is being developed.

University of Nevada–Reno (continued)

Additional Information from the College

The University has joined the Network of Colleges and Universities Committed to the Elimination of Drug and Alcohol Abuse.

For More Information

Contact: Garry E. Rubinstein, Coordinator of Substance Abuse Prevention Program, 209 Thompson Student Services Center, University of Nevada–Reno, Reno, NV 89557. Telephone: 702-784-4648.

UNIVERSITY OF NEW ENGLAND

Biddeford, Maine

General Information

Independent 5-year coed college. Founded 1939. Awards A (terminal), B, M, D. Primary accreditation: regional. Small-town setting; 127-acre campus. Total enrollment: 1,071. Faculty: 92 (60 full-time, 32 part-time).

Drug and Alcohol Information

Education

On campus Drug and alcohol education/prevention programs offered for: all students, athletes/coaches, faculty, administration. Authorized group concerned with responsible drinking. College holds an annual alcohol awareness week.

Identification of Problems

Admissions College application does not ask about prior substance abuse problems.

On campus Current students identified as chemically dependent may remain enrolled, but treatment is required. Training program on identifying students with potential substance abuse problems for: faculty, staff, peer educators. Written procedures for students and staff if substance abuse is suspected.

Support Services

On campus AA, Al-Anon, ACOA, support groups (peer educators), private counseling.

Employee assistance Program for chemically dependent employees not available. Staff working with drug/alcohol-related issues: 2 part-time.

Disciplinary Actions

Alcohol Results of infractions of alcohol regulations (see Comparative Table of Alcohol Regulations) vary by situation but can include chemical dependency assessment, counseling, warning, probation.

Drugs For first-time use or possession: warning. For subsequent use or possession: varies by situation—probation. For first-time sale: suspension. For subsequent sale: expulsion.

For More Information

Contact: Dr. Jeri Keane, Director of the Counseling and Career Center, University of New England, 11 Hills Beach Rd., Biddeford, ME 04005. Telephone: 207-282-0171.

UNIVERSITY OF NEW HAMPSHIRE

Durham, New Hampshire

General Information

State-supported comprehensive coed institution. Part of University System of New Hampshire. Founded 1866. Awards A (terminal), B, M, D. Primary accreditation: regional. Small-town setting; 200-acre campus. Total enrollment: 11,131. Faculty: 778 (578 full-time, 200 part-time). Social organizations: 14 national fraternities, 7 national sororities, 1 local fraternity; 22% of eligible undergraduate men and 10% of eligible undergraduate women are members.

Drug and Alcohol Information

Education

On campus Drug and alcohol education/prevention programs offered for: all students, athletes/coaches, faculty, administration. College holds its own annual alcohol awareness week and drug awareness week.

Identification of Problems

Admissions College application does not ask about prior substance abuse problems.

On campus Current students identified as chemically dependent may remain enrolled. Training program on identifying students with potential substance abuse problems for: resident advisers, coaches, Greek officers, key administrators and faculty who work with students. Written procedures for students and staff if substance abuse is suspected.

Support Services

On campus AA, NA, Al-Anon, ACOA, private counseling, therapy groups.

Employee assistance Program for chemically dependent employees available. Staff working with drug/alcohol-related issues: 1 full-time.

Disciplinary Actions

Alcohol Results of infractions of alcohol regulations (see Comparative Table of Alcohol Regulations) vary by situation but can include chemical dependency assessment, counseling, warning, probation, suspension, expulsion.

Drugs For any use, possession, or sale: varies by situation.

For More Information

Contact: K. Gildea-Dinzeo, Associate Director, Health Service, University of New Hampshire, 12 Ballard St., Durham, NH 03824. Telephone: 603-862-3823.

UNIVERSITY OF NEW HAVEN

West Haven, Connecticut

General Information

Independent 5-year coed college. Founded 1920. Awards A (college transfer and terminal), B, M, D. Primary accreditation: regional. City setting; 74-acre campus. Total enrollment: 6,044. Faculty: 428 (153 full-time, 275 part-time). Social organizations: 2 national fraternities, national sororities, 1 local fraternity, 3 local sororities; 7% of eligible undergraduate men and 4% of eligible undergraduate women are members.

Drug and Alcohol Information

Education

On campus Drug and alcohol education/prevention programs offered for: all students, athletes/coaches. Authorized group concerned with responsible drinking. College holds an annual alcohol awareness week and drug awareness week.

Identification of Problems

Admissions College application does not ask about prior substance abuse problems.

On campus Current students identified as chemically dependent may remain enrolled, but treatment is required. Training program on identifying students with potential substance abuse problems for: resident advisers, coaches. Written procedures for students and staff if substance abuse is suspected.

Support Services

On campus No support services on campus.

Off campus AA, NA, Al-Anon, ACOA.

Employee assistance Program for chemically dependent employees not available.

Disciplinary Actions

Alcohol Results of infractions of alcohol regulations (see Comparative Table of Alcohol Regulations) include chemical dependency assessment, counseing, warning, probation, suspension, expulsion.

Drugs For first-time use or possession: varies by situation. For subsequent use or possession: suspension. For any sale: legal action, expulsion.

For More Information

Contact: Dr. Deborah Everhart, Director of Counseling Services, University of New Haven, 300 Orange Avenue, West Haven, CT 06516. Telephone: 203-932-7332.

UNIVERSITY OF NEW MEXICO

Albuquerque, New Mexico

General Information

State-supported comprehensive coed institution. Founded 1889. Awards A (college transfer and terminal), B, M, D. Primary accreditation: regional. City setting; 600-acre campus. Total enrollment: 24,158. Faculty: 2,047 (1,204 full-time, 843 part-time). Social organizations: 10 national fraternities, 6 national sororities; 2% of eligible undergraduate men and 2% of eligible undergraduate women are members.

Drug and Alcohol Information

Education

On campus Drug and alcohol education/prevention programs offered for: all students, faculty, administration; required for: resident advisers. Authorized group concerned with responsible drinking. College holds an annual alcohol awareness week.

Identification of Problems

Admissions College application does not ask about prior substance abuse problems.

On campus Current students identified as chemically dependent may remain enrolled. Training program on identifying students with potential substance abuse problems for: resident advisers, Greek officers, faculty, administration. Written procedures for students and staff if substance abuse is suspected.

Support Services

On campus AA, Al-Anon, ACOA, support groups, private counseling.

Employee assistance Program for chemically dependent employees available. Staff working with drug/alcohol-related issues: 4 full-time and 2 part-time.

Disciplinary Actions

Alcohol Results of infractions of alcohol regulations (see Comparative Table of Alcohol Regulations) include counseling, warning, probation, suspension.

Drugs For first-time use or possession: counseling, warning, probation. For subsequent use or possession: suspension, expulsion. For first-time sale: probation, suspension, expulsion. For subsequent sale: expulsion.

For More Information

Contact: Susan Corban, Assistant Director of Student Activities, University of New Mexico, Albuquerque, NM 87131. Telephone: 505-277-4706.

UNIVERSITY OF NORTH CAROLINA AT CHAPEL HILL

Chapel Hill, North Carolina

General Information

State-supported comprehensive coed institution. Part of University of North Carolina System. Founded 1795. Awards B, M, D. Primary accreditation: regional. Small-town setting; 474-acre campus. Total enrollment: 23,579. Social organizations: 28 national fraternities, 15 national sororities; 20% of eligible undergraduate men and 20% of eligible undergraduate women are members.

Drug and Alcohol Information

Education

On campus Drug and alcohol education/prevention programs offered for: all students, athletes/coaches, faculty, administration. Authorized group concerned with responsible drinking.

Identification of Problems

Admissions College application question about prior medical problems is used for counseling and referral, if student is admitted.

On campus Current students identified as chemically dependent may remain enrolled, but treatment is required. Training program on identifying students with potential substance abuse problems for: resident advisers, coaches. Written procedures for students and staff if substance abuse is suspected.

Support Services

On campus AA, support groups, private counseling.

Employee assistance Program for chemically dependent employees not available. Staff working with drug/alcohol-related issues: 1 full-time and 10–20 part-time.

Disciplinary Actions

Alcohol Results of infractions of alcohol regulations (see Comparative Table of Alcohol Regulations) vary by situation but can include warning, probation.

Drugs For first-time use, possession, or sale: varies by

University of North Carolina at Chapel Hill (continued)

situation—chemical dependency assessment, probation, suspension. For subsequent use, possession, or sale: suspension, expulsion.

For More Information

Contact: Frederic W. Schroeder Jr., Dean of Students, University of North Carolina at Chapel Hill, Chapel Hill, NC 27514. Telephone: 919-966-4041.

UNIVERSITY OF NORTH CAROLINA AT CHARLOTTE

Charlotte, North Carolina

General Information

State-supported 5-year coed college. Part of University of North Carolina System. Founded 1946. Awards B, M. Primary accreditation: regional. City setting; 1,000-acre campus. Total enrollment: 12,031. Faculty: 875 (645 full-time, 230 part-time). Social organizations: 9 national fraternities, 7 national sororities, local fraternities; 10% of eligible undergraduate men and 7% of eligible undergraduate women are members.

Drug and Alcohol Information

Education

On campus Drug and alcohol education/prevention programs offered for: all students, faculty, administration; required for: athletes/coaches, resident advisers, student leaders. Authorized group concerned with responsible drinking. College holds an annual alcohol awareness week.

Identification of Problems

Admissions College application does not ask about prior substance abuse problems.

On campus Current students identified as chemically dependent may remain enrolled, but treatment may be required. Training program on identifying students with potential substance abuse problems for: resident advisers, coaches, Greek officers. Written procedures for students and staff if substance abuse is suspected.

Support Services

On campus AA, ACOA, support groups, private counseling.

Employee assistance Program for chemically dependent employees available. Staff working with drug/alcohol-related issues: many part-time.

Disciplinary Actions

Alcohol Results of infractions of alcohol regulations (see Comparative Table of Alcohol Regulations) vary by situation but can include counseling, warning, probation, suspension, expulsion.

Drugs For any use, possession, or sale: varies by situation. Comments: Community service may be required.

For More Information

Contact: Dr. Jody Harpster, Dean of Students, University of North Carolina at Charlotte, 217 King Blvd., Charlotte, NC 28213. Telephone: 704-547-2375.

UNIVERSITY OF NORTH CAROLINA AT GREENSBORO

Greensboro, North Carolina

General Information

State-supported comprehensive coed institution. Part of University of North Carolina System. Founded 1891. Awards B, M, D. Primary accreditation: regional. City setting; 175-acre campus. Total enrollment: 11,174. Faculty: 678 (565 full-time, 113 part-time). Social organizations: 7 national fraternities, 6 national sororities; 15% of eligible undergraduate men and 15% of eligible undergraduate women are members.

Drug and Alcohol Information

Education

On campus Drug and alcohol education/prevention programs offered for: all students, athletes/coaches. Authorized group concerned with responsible drinking. College holds an annual alcohol awareness week and drug awareness week.

Identification of Problems

Admissions College application does not ask about prior substance abuse problems.

On campus Current students identified as chemically dependent may remain enrolled. Training program on identifying students with potential substance abuse problems for: resident advisers, coaches, Greek officers, faculty, administration. Written procedures for students and staff if substance abuse is suspected.

Support Services

On campus AA, Al-Anon, Counseling Center.

Employee assistance Program for chemically dependent employees available. Staff working with drug/alcohol-related issues: several part-time.

Disciplinary Actions

Alcohol Results of infractions of alcohol regulations (see Comparative Table of Alcohol Regulations) vary by situation.

Drugs For any use, possession, or sale: varies by situation. Comments: Actions taken depend on the category of the drugs involved.

For More Information

Contact: Robert T. Tomlinson, Director of Residence Life, University of North Carolina at Greensboro, 1000 Spring Garden Street, Greensboro, NC 27412-5001. Telephone: 919-334-5636.

UNIVERSITY OF NORTH CAROLINA AT WILMINGTON

Wilmington, North Carolina

General Information

State-supported 5-year coed college. Part of University of North Carolina System. Founded 1947. Awards B, M. Primary accreditation: regional. City setting; 650-acre campus. Total enrollment: 6,553. Faculty: 377 (323 full-time, 54 part-time). Social organizations: 9 national fraternities, 6 national sororities; 8% of eligible undergraduate men and 5% of eligible undergraduate women are members.

Drug and Alcohol Information

Education

On campus Drug and alcohol education/prevention programs offered for: all students, athletes/coaches, faculty, administration. Authorized group concerned with responsible drinking. College holds an annual alcohol awareness week and drug awareness week.

Identification of Problems

Admissions College application does not ask about prior substance abuse problems.

On campus Current students identified as chemically dependent may remain enrolled, but treatment is required. Training program on identifying students with potential substance abuse problems for: resident advisers. Written procedures for students and staff if substance abuse is suspected.

Support Services

On campus AA, ACOA, support groups, private counseling.

Employee assistance Program for chemically dependent employees not available. Staff working with drug/alcohol-related issues: 2 full-time and 2 part-time.

Disciplinary Actions

Alcohol Results of infractions of alcohol regulations (see Comparative Table of Alcohol Regulations) include chemical dependency assessment, counseling, probation.

Drugs For first-time use: chemical dependency assessment, counseling, probation. For subsequent use: varies by situation—counseling, probation, suspension. For first-time possession: suspension. For subsequent possession: expulsion. For any sale: expulsion.

For More Information

Contact: Pat Leonard, Dean of Students, University of North Carolina at Wilmington, 602 S. College Rd., Wilmington, NC 28403. Telephone: 919-395-3119.

UNIVERSITY OF NORTH TEXAS

Denton, Texas

General Information

State-supported comprehensive coed institution. Founded 1890. Awards B, M, D. Primary accreditation: regional. City setting; 424-acre campus. Total enrollment: 24,498. Faculty: 888 (723 full-time, 165 part-time). Social organizations: 16 national fraternities, 10 national sororities, local fraternities, local sororities.

Drug and Alcohol Information

Education

On campus Drug and alcohol education/prevention programs offered for: all students, athletes/coaches, faculty, administration. Bacchus chapter: 20 members. College holds an annual alcohol awareness week and drug awareness week.

Identification of Problems

Admissions College application does not ask about prior substance abuse problems.

On campus Current students identified as chemically dependent may remain enrolled. Training program on identifying students with potential substance abuse problems for: resident advisers, coaches, Greek officers, faculty, administration. Written procedures for students and staff if substance abuse is suspected.

Support Services

On campus AA, NA, Al-Anon, ACOA, support groups, private counseling.

Employee assistance Program for chemically dependent employees available. Staff working with drug/alcohol-related issues: 2 full-time and 1 part-time.

Disciplinary Actions

Alcohol Results of infractions of alcohol regulations (see Comparative Table of Alcohol Regulations) vary by situation.

Drugs For any use, possession, or sale: expulsion.

For More Information

Contact: Dr. Tom Overton, Director, Counseling Center, Suite 321 University, University of North Texas, P.O. Box 13797, Denton, TX 76203. Telephone: 817-565-2741.

UNIVERSITY OF NOTRE DAME

Notre Dame, Indiana

General Information

Independent Roman Catholic comprehensive coed institution. Founded 1842. Awards B, M, D. Primary accreditation: regional. City setting; 1,250-acre campus. Total enrollment: 9,700. Faculty: 800.

Drug and Alcohol Information

Education

On campus Drug and alcohol education/prevention programs offered for: all students; required for: freshmen, athletes/coaches, resident advisers. Bacchus chapter: 25 members. College holds an annual alcohol awareness week and drug awareness week.

Identification of Problems

Admissions College application does not ask about prior substance abuse problems.

On campus Current students identified as chemically dependent may remain enrolled, but treatment is required. Training program on identifying students with potential substance abuse problems for: resident advisers, coaches, administration. Written procedures for students and staff if substance abuse is suspected.

Support Services

On campus AA, ACOA, private counseling.

Employee assistance Program for chemically dependent employees available. Staff working with drug/alcohol-related issues: 2 full-time and 3 part-time.

Disciplinary Actions

Alcohol Results of infractions of alcohol regulations (see Comparative Table of Alcohol Regulations) vary by situation but can include chemical dependency assessment, counseling, warning, probation, suspension, expulsion.

Drugs For any use or possession: varies by situation. For any sale: expulsion.

For More Information

Contact: Carolyn Kelly, Coordinator of Drug and Alcohol

University of Notre Dame (continued)

Education, University of Notre Dame, 210 LaFortune, Notre Dame, IN 46556. Telephone: 219-239-7970.

UNIVERSITY OF OKLAHOMA

Norman, Oklahoma

General Information

State-supported comprehensive coed institution. Founded 1890. Awards B, M, D. Primary accreditation: regional. City setting; 2,100-acre campus. Total enrollment: 20,632. Faculty: 870 (780 full-time, 90 part-time). Social organizations: 26 national fraternities, 16 national sororities; 21% of eligible undergraduate men and 25% of eligible undergraduate women are members.

Drug and Alcohol Information

Education

On campus Drug and alcohol education/prevention programs offered for: all students, athletes/coaches, faculty, administration. Authorized group concerned with responsible drinking. College holds an annual alcohol awareness week and drug awareness week.

Identification of Problems

Admissions College application does not ask about prior substance abuse problems.

On campus Current students identified as chemically dependent may remain enrolled. Training program on identifying students with potential substance abuse problems for: resident advisers, coaches, Greek officers, faculty, administration.

Support Services

On campus AA, support groups, private counseling, University Mental Health Service/Hospital.

Employee assistance Program for chemically dependent employees available. Staff working with drug/alcohol-related issues: Several part-time.

Disciplinary Actions

Alcohol Results of infractions of alcohol regulations (see Comparative Table of Alcohol Regulations) vary by situation but can include chemical dependency assessment, counseling, warning, probation.

Drugs For first-time use or possession: varies by situation. For subsequent use or possession: varies by situation—chemical dependency assessment, counseling, probation. For any sale: varies by situation—counseling, expulsion.

For More Information

Contact: David F. Schrage, Assistant Vice President for Student Affairs and Director of Housing Programs, University of Oklahoma, Norman, OK 73069. Telephone: 405-325-2511.

UNIVERSITY OF OREGON

Eugene, Oregon

General Information

State-supported comprehensive coed institution. Founded 1872. Awards B, M, D. Primary accreditation: regional. City setting; 250-acre campus. Total enrollment: 18,530. Faculty: 1,133 (715 full-time, 418 part-time). Social organizations: 16 national fraternities, 11 national sororities; 18% of eligible undergraduate men and 18% of eligible undergraduate women are members.

Drug and Alcohol Information

Education

On campus Drug and alcohol education/prevention programs offered for: all students, athletes/coaches, faculty, administration, recovering students. Authorized group concerned with responsible drinking. College holds an annual alcohol awareness week and drug awareness week.

Identification of Problems

Admissions College application does not ask about prior substance abuse problems.

On campus Current students identified as chemically dependent may remain enrolled, but stipulations may be attached to enrollment. Training program on identifying students with potential substance abuse problems for: resident advisers, coaches, Greek officers, faculty, administration. Written procedures for students and staff if substance abuse is suspected.

Support Services

On campus AA, NA, ACOA, support groups, private counseling, student "choice" groups.

Employee assistance Program for chemically dependent employees not available. Staff working with drug/alcohol-related issues: 2–5 full-time and 10–20 part-time.

Disciplinary Actions

Alcohol Results of infractions of alcohol regulations (see Comparative Table of Alcohol Regulations) vary by situation.

Drugs For any use, possession, or sale: varies by situation. Comments: Due process is followed. Sanctions are not set at an inflexible level.

For More Information

Contact: Gregg Lobisser, Associate Dean of Students, University of Oregon, 364 Oregon Hall, Eugene, OR 97403. Telephone: 503-686-3105.

UNIVERSITY OF OSTEOPATHIC MEDICINE AND HEALTH SCIENCES

Des Moines, Iowa

General Information

Independent coed college. Founded 1898. Awards B, M, D. Primary accreditation: regional. City setting; 20-acre campus. Total enrollment: 1,002. Faculty: 108 (68 full-time, 40 part-time).

Drug and Alcohol Information

Education

On campus Drug and alcohol education/prevention programs offered for: all students; required for: freshmen. College holds an annual alcohol awareness week and drug awareness week.

Identification of Problems

Admissions College application question about prior substance abuse problems is used in the admissions decision.

On campus Current students identified as chemically dependent may remain enrolled, but treatment is required.

Training program on identifying students with potential substance abuse problems for: coaches, faculty. No written procedures for students and staff if substance abuse is suspected.

Support Services

On campus Private counseling.

Employee assistance Program for chemically dependent employees not available.

Disciplinary Actions

Alcohol Results of infractions of alcohol regulations (see Comparative Table of Alcohol Regulations) vary by situation.

Drugs For first-time use: chemical dependency assessment. For first-time possession: suspension, expulsion. For subsequent use or possession: expulsion. For any sale: expulsion.

For More Information

Contact: Lawrence Jacobson, D.O., Dean of Academic Affairs, University of Osteopathic Medicine and Health Sciences, 3200 Grand Ave., Des Moines, IA 50312. Telephone: 515-271-1415.

UNIVERSITY OF PITTSBURGH

Pittsburgh, Pennsylvania

General Information

State-related comprehensive coed institution. Part of University of Pittsburgh System. Founded 1787. Awards B, M, D. Primary accreditation: regional. Metropolitan setting; 132-acre campus. Total enrollment: 28,524. Faculty: 2,960 (2,430 full-time, 530 part-time). Social organizations: 21 national fraternities, 14 national sororities; 10% of eligible undergraduate men and 6% of eligible undergraduate women are members.

Drug and Alcohol Information

Education

On campus Drug and alcohol education/prevention programs offered for: all students, athletes/coaches, faculty, administration. Authorized group concerned with responsible drinking. College holds an annual alcohol awareness week and drug awareness week.

Identification of Problems

Admissions College application does not ask about prior substance abuse problems.

On campus Current students identified as chemically dependent may remain enrolled. Training program on identifying students with potential substance abuse problems for: resident advisers, coaches, Greek officers. No written procedures for students and staff if substance abuse is suspected.

Support Services

On campus AA, NA, ACOA, support groups, private counseling, medical school, Western Psychiatric Institute and Clinic.

Off campus Numerous agencies.

Employee assistance Program for chemically dependent employees not available. Individuals referred to Western Psychiatric Institute and Clinic. Staff working with drug/alcohol-related issues: 24 part-time.

Disciplinary Actions

Alcohol Results of infractions of alcohol regulations (see Comparative Table of Alcohol Regulations) vary by situation but can include chemical dependency assessment, counseling, warning, protection, suspension, expulsion. Comments: A panel of students recommends sanctions.

Drugs For any use or possession: varies by situation. For any sale: varies by situation—suspension, expulsion. Comments: Campus police enforce federal and state drug laws.

Additional Information from the College

Those who require serious and/or long-term therapy are referred to the University of Pittsburgh School of Medicine and the Western Psychiatric Institute and Clinic, located on campus, or to any of a number of nearby hospitals, clinics, and helping agencies. Several of the University's clinical programs are nationally recognized. Sponsored student life programs are alcohol-free on the undergraduate level. Students have an abundant selection of wholesome social and recreational programs for their leisure time.

For More Information

Contact: Shirley Haberman, Health Educator, Student Health Service, 204 Brackenridge Hall, University of Pittsburgh, Pittsburgh, PA 15260. Telephone: 412-648-1250.

UNIVERSITY OF PITTSBURGH AT BRADFORD

Bradford, Pennsylvania

General Information

State-related 4-year coed college. Part of University of Pittsburgh System. Founded 1963. Awards A (terminal), B. Primary accreditation: regional. Small-town setting; 125-acre campus. Total enrollment: 993. Faculty: 89 (64 full-time, 25 part-time). Social organizations: 1 national fraternity, 2 local fraternities, 1 local sorority; 8% of eligible undergraduate men and 5% of eligible undergraduate women are members.

Drug and Alcohol Information

Education

On campus Drug and alcohol education/prevention programs offered for: all students, athletes/coaches. Authorized group concerned with responsible drinking. College holds an annual alcohol awareness week and drug awareness week.

Identification of Problems

Admissions College application does not ask about prior substance abuse problems.

On campus Current students identified as chemically dependent may remain enrolled, but treatment is required. Training program on identifying students with potential substance abuse problems for: resident advisers. Written procedures for students and staff if substance abuse is suspected.

Support Services

On campus AA, private counseling.

Employee assistance Program for chemically dependent employees not available. Staff working with drug/alcohol-related issues: 1 part-time.

Disciplinary Actions

Alcohol Results of infractions of alcohol regulations (see

University of Pittsburgh at Bradford (continued)

Comparative Table of Alcohol Regulations) include counseling, warning, probation, suspension, expulsion.

Drugs For any use or possession: varies by situation. For any sale: suspension, expulsion.

For More Information

Contact: Dr. James Evans, Dean of Student Affairs, University of Pittsburgh at Bradford, Campus Dr., Bradford, PA 16701. Telephone: 814-362-7650.

UNIVERSITY OF PITTSBURGH AT GREENSBURG

Greensburg, Pennsylvania

General Information

State-related 4-year coed college. Part of University of Pittsburgh System. Founded 1963. Awards B. Primary accreditation: regional. Small-town setting; 160-acre campus. Total enrollment: 1,520. Faculty: 91 (50 full-time, 41 part-time). Social organizations: 1 national fraternity, 1 national sorority; 10% of eligible undergraduate men and 5% of eligible undergraduate women are members.

Drug and Alcohol Information

Education

On campus Drug and alcohol education/prevention programs offered for: all students; required for: resident advisers. College holds an annual alcohol awareness week and drug awareness week.

Identification of Problems

Admissions College application does not ask about prior substance abuse problems.

On campus Current students identified as chemically dependent may remain enrolled, but treatment is required. Training program on identifying students with potential substance abuse problems for: resident advisers. No written procedures for students and staff if substance abuse is suspected.

Support Services

On campus Private counseling.

Employee assistance Program for chemically dependent employees not available.

Disciplinary Actions

Alcohol Results of infractions of alcohol regulations (see Comparative Table of Alcohol Regulations) vary by situation but can include counseling, warning, probation, suspension.

Drugs For first-time use or possession: varies by situation—counseling, warning, probation. For subsequent use: counseling, probation, suspension. For subsequent possession: varies by situation. For first-time sale: varies by situation—probation, suspension. For subsequent sale: suspension, expulsion.

For More Information

Contact: Helen Connors, Counselor, University of Pittsburgh at Greensburg, 1150 Mt. Pleasant, Greensburg, PA 15601. Telephone: 412-837-7040.

UNIVERSITY OF PORTLAND

Portland, Oregon

General Information

Independent Roman Catholic 5-year coed college. Founded 1901. Awards B, M. Primary accreditation: regional. Metropolitan setting; 95-acre campus. Total enrollment: 2,367. Faculty: 187 (120 full-time, 67 part-time). Social organizations: 3 local fraternities, 2 local sororities; 15% of eligible undergraduate men and 15% of eligible undergraduate women are members.

Drug and Alcohol Information

Education

On campus Drug and alcohol education/prevention programs offered for: all students, athletes/coaches. Authorized group concerned with responsible drinking.

Identification of Problems

Admissions College application does not ask about prior substance abuse problems.

On campus Current students identified as chemically dependent may remain enrolled, but treatment may be required. Training program on identifying students with potential substance abuse problems for: resident advisers, coaches. No written procedures for students and staff if substance abuse is suspected.

Support Services

On campus AA, NA, private counseling.

Employee assistance Program for chemically dependent employees not available but will be available soon. Staff working with drug/alcohol-related issues: 4 part-time.

Disciplinary Actions

Alcohol Results of infractions of alcohol regulations (see Comparative Table of Alcohol Regulations) vary by situation but can include chemical dependency assessment, counseling, warning, probation, suspension, expulsion.

Drugs For any use, possession, or sale: varies by situation.

Additional Information from the College

The University has a progressive policy regarding substance abuse. The Student Assistance Plan for intervention, assessment, and treatment is part of a holistic approach to student health problems that includes financial and academic policies to support the student in need.

For More Information

Contact: Louise Allen, Director of the University Health Center, University of Portland, 5000 N. Willamette Blvd., Portland, OR 97203. Telephone: 503-283-7134.

UNIVERSITY OF PUERTO RICO, HUMACAO UNIVERSITY COLLEGE

Humacao, Puerto Rico

General Information

Commonwealth-supported 4-year coed college. Part of University of Puerto Rico System. Founded 1962. Awards A (college transfer and terminal), B. Primary accreditation: regional. Small-town setting; 62-acre campus. Total enrollment: 3,825. Faculty: 234 (210 full-time, 24 part-time).

Drug and Alcohol Information

Education

On campus Drug and alcohol education/prevention programs offered for: all students, faculty, administration. College holds an annual alcohol awareness week.

Identification of Problems

Admissions College application does not ask about prior substance abuse problems.

On campus Current students identified as chemically dependent may remain enrolled. No training program on identifying students with potential substance abuse problems. No written procedures for students and staff if substance abuse is suspected.

Support Services

On campus No support services on campus.

Employee assistance Program for chemically dependent employees not available. Staff working with drug/alcohol-related issues: 1 full-time.

Disciplinary Actions

Alcohol Results of infractions of alcohol regulations (see Comparative Table of Alcohol Regulations) include suspension.

Drugs For first-time use: counseling, warning. For first-time possession or sale: varies by situation. For subsequent use, possession, or sale: varies by situation.

For More Information

Contact: Josefina Sánchez, Director of Drug Prevention Program, University of Puerto Rico, Humacao University College, CUM Station, Humacao, PR 00661. Telephone: 809-852-2525 Ext. 230.

UNIVERSITY OF PUERTO RICO, MAYAGÜEZ CAMPUS

Mayagüez, Puerto Rico

General Information

Commonwealth-supported comprehensive coed institution. Part of University of Puerto Rico System. Founded 1911. Awards A (terminal), B, M, D. Primary accreditation: regional. City setting; 305-acre campus. Total enrollment: 9,432. Faculty: 676 (647 full-time, 29 part-time). Social organizations: 8 national fraternities, 3 national sororities, 1 local fraternity, 1 local sorority.

Drug and Alcohol Information

Education

On campus Drug and alcohol education/prevention programs offered for: all students.

Identification of Problems

Admissions College application does not ask about prior substance abuse problems.

On campus Current students identified as chemically dependent may remain enrolled, but treatment is required. Training program on identifying students with potential substance abuse problems for: health and counseling personnel. No written procedures for students and staff if substance abuse is suspected.

Support Services

On campus Private counseling, referrals.

Employee assistance Program for chemically dependent employees not available. Staff working with drug/alcohol-related issues: 4 part-time.

Disciplinary Actions

Alcohol Results of infractions of alcohol regulations (see Comparative Table of Alcohol Regulations) include counseling, warning.

Drugs For first-time use, possession, or sale: varies by situation—counseling, warning. For subsequent use, possession, or sale: varies by situation—counseling, probation.

For More Information

Contact: Rosie Torres de Calderón, Health Services Department Director, University of Puerto Rico, Mayagüez Campus, P.O. Box 5000, Mayagüez, Puerto Rico 00709-5000. Telephone: 809-832-4040 Ext. 3405.

UNIVERSITY OF PUGET SOUND

Tacoma, Washington

General Information

Independent Methodist 5-year coed college. Founded 1888. Awards B, M. Primary accreditation: regional. City setting; 72-acre campus. Total enrollment: 3,344. Faculty: 216 (195 full-time, 21 part-time). Social organizations: 6 national fraternities, 6 national sororities; 36% of eligible undergraduate men and 30% of eligible undergraduate women are members.

Drug and Alcohol Information

Education

On campus Drug and alcohol education/prevention programs offered for: all students, athletes/coaches. Bacchus chapter: 18 members. College holds an annual alcohol awareness week.

Identification of Problems

Admissions College application does not ask about prior substance abuse problems.

On campus Current students identified as chemically dependent may remain enrolled, but treatment is required. Training program on identifying students with potential substance abuse problems for: resident advisers. Written procedures for students and staff if substance abuse is suspected.

Support Services

On campus ACOA, support groups, private counseling.

Employee assistance Program for chemically dependent employees not available. Staff working with drug/alcohol-related issues: 1 full-time and 8 part-time.

Disciplinary Actions

Alcohol Results of infractions of alcohol regulations (see Comparative Table of Alcohol Regulations) vary by situation but can include chemical dependency assessment, counseling, warning, probation, suspension, expulsion.

Drugs For first-time use: varies by situation. For subsequent use: probation, suspension, expulsion. For any possession or sale: expulsion.

For More Information

Contact: Judith Jaynes, Ph.D., Substance Abuse Educator, University of Puget Sound, 1500 N. Warner St., Tacoma, WA 98416. Telephone: 206-756-3372.

UNIVERSITY OF REDLANDS

Redlands, California

General Information

Independent 5-year coed college. Founded 1907. Awards B, M. Primary accreditation: regional. Small-town setting; 130-acre campus. Total enrollment: 2,900. Faculty: 120 (100 full-time, 20 part-time). Social organizations: 5 local fraternities, 4 local sororities; 20% of eligible undergraduate men and 20% of eligible undergraduate women are members.

Drug and Alcohol Information

Education

On campus Drug and alcohol education/prevention programs offered for: all students, students with disciplinary problems; required for: freshmen, resident advisers. Bacchus chapter: 10 members. Authorized group concerned with responsible drinking. College holds an annual alcohol awareness week.

Identification of Problems

Admissions College application does not ask about prior substance abuse problems.

On campus Current students identified as chemically dependent may remain enrolled, but treatment is required. Training program on identifying students with potential substance abuse problems for: resident advisers, faculty, administration. Written procedures for students and staff if substance abuse is suspected.

Support Services

On campus ACOA, support groups, private counseling.

Employee assistance Program for chemically dependent employees not available. Staff working with drug/alcohol-related issues: 1 full-time and 1 part-time.

Disciplinary Actions

Alcohol Results of infractions of alcohol regulations (see Comparative Table of Alcohol Regulations) vary by situation but can include counseling, warning, probation.

Drugs For first-time use: counseling, probation. For subsequent use: suspension. For first-time possession: suspension. For subsequent possession: expulsion. For any sale: expulsion.

Additional Information from the College

The designated server program as instituted by the University of Redlands is not only one of the most innovative in the country but also one of the most effective. By providing trained personnel at on-campus parties, the University receives the assurance that alcohol is being administered in a responsible and legal manner. Designated servers have two functions: to check identification of people who wish to drink alcohol at a party and to actually serve the alcohol. This system, when used properly, dramatically reduces the number of incidents of underage drinking at school social events and encourages responsible drinking by all of the participants.

For More Information

Contact: Eileen Granosky, Director of Counseling, University of Redlands, 1200 E. Colton Ave., Redlands, CA 92373. Telephone: 714-793-2790.

UNIVERSITY OF RHODE ISLAND

Kingston, Rhode Island

General Information

State-supported comprehensive coed institution. Part of Rhode Island State System of Higher Education. Founded 1892. Awards A (terminal), B, M, D. Primary accreditation: regional. Small-town setting; 1,200-acre campus. Total enrollment: 11,874. Faculty: 804 (784 full-time, 20 part-time). Social organizations: 16 national fraternities, 8 national sororities; 16% of eligible undergraduate men and 14% of eligible undergraduate women are members.

Drug and Alcohol Information

Education

On campus Drug and alcohol education/prevention programs offered for: all students, athletes/coaches. College holds an annual alcohol awareness week and drug awareness week.

Identification of Problems

Admissions College application does not ask about prior substance abuse problems.

On campus Current students identified as chemically dependent may remain enrolled. Training program on identifying students with potential substance abuse problems for: resident advisers, coaches, Greek officers, peer advisers. Written procedures for students and staff if substance abuse is suspected.

Support Services

On campus Support groups, private counseling, referrals.

Employee assistance Program for chemically dependent employees available. Staff working with drug/alcohol-related issues: 2 full-time and 10–20 part-time.

Disciplinary Actions

Alcohol Results of infractions of alcohol regulations (see Comparative Table of Alcohol Regulations) vary by situation but can include counseling, warning, probation, suspension for repeated violations, education session.

Drugs For first-time use: varies by situation—education seminar, counseling. For subsequent use: varies by situation—counseling. For any possession or sale: varies by situation.

Additional Information from the College

A recently received $98,000 FIPSE grant will fund increased educational alcohol- and drug-related programming.

For More Information

Contact: Dr. Thomas R. Dougan, Assistant Vice President for Campus Life, University of Rhode Island, 337 Memorial Union, Kingston, RI 02881. Telephone: 401-792-2427.

UNIVERSITY OF RICHMOND

Richmond, Virginia

General Information

Independent Baptist 5-year coed college. Founded 1830. Awards B, M. Primary accreditation: regional. Metropolitan setting; 350-acre campus. Total enrollment: 4,956. Faculty: 297 (210 full-time, 87 part-time). Social organizations: 11 national fraternities, 6 national sororities; 55% of eligible undergraduate men and 40% of eligible undergraduate women are members.

Drug and Alcohol Information

Education

On campus Drug and alcohol education/prevention programs offered for: all students, violators of alcohol/drug policies. Bacchus chapter: 10 members. College holds an annual alcohol awareness week.

Identification of Problems

Admissions College application does not ask about prior substance abuse problems.

On campus Current students identified as chemically dependent may remain enrolled. No training program on identifying students with potential substance abuse problems. Written procedures for students and staff if substance abuse is suspected.

Support Services

On campus Private counseling.

Employee assistance Program for chemically dependent employees not available. Staff working with drug/alcohol-related issues: 8 part-time.

Disciplinary Actions

Alcohol Results of infractions of alcohol regulations (see Comparative Table of Alcohol Regulations) include counseling, warning, probation, fines.

Drugs For first-time use or possession: counseling, probation. For subsequent use or possession: suspension. For first-time sale: suspension. For subsequent sale: expulsion.

For More Information

Contact: Dr. Warren Hopkins, Director of Counseling and Psychological Services, University of Richmond, Richmond, VA 23173. Telephone: 804-289-8119.

UNIVERSITY OF ROCHESTER

Rochester, New York

General Information

Independent comprehensive coed institution. Founded 1850. Awards B, M, D. Primary accreditation: regional. Metropolitan setting; 530-acre campus. Total enrollment: 8,114. Faculty: 655 (575 full-time, 80 part-time). Social organizations: 16 national fraternities, 5 national sororities; 45% of eligible undergraduate men and 16% of eligible undergraduate women are members.

Drug and Alcohol Information

Education

On campus Drug and alcohol education/prevention programs offered for: all students, athletes/coaches, faculty administration. Authorized group concerned with responsible drinking.

Identification of Problems

Admissions College application does not ask about prior substance abuse problems.

On campus Current students identified as chemically dependent may remain enrolled, depending on circumstances, but treatment is required. Training program on identifying students with potential substance abuse problems being developed.

Support Services

On campus ACOA, support groups, private counseling.

Employee assistance Program for chemically dependent employees available. Staff working with drug/alcohol-related issues: 1 full-time and many part-time.

Disciplinary Actions

Alcohol Results of infractions of alcohol regulations (see Comparative Table of Alcohol Regulations) vary by situation but can include chemical dependency assessment, counseling, warning, probation, suspension, expulsion.

Drugs For any use, possession, or sale: varies by situation.

For More Information

Contact: Nadine Simpson, Health Educator for Substance Abuse Programs, University Health Service, University of Rochester, Wilson Blvd., Rochester, NY 14627. Telephone: 716-275-2662.

UNIVERSITY OF SAN DIEGO

San Diego, California

General Information

Independent Roman Catholic comprehensive coed institution. Founded 1949. Awards B, M, D. Primary accreditation: regional. Metropolitan setting; 180-acre campus. Total enrollment: 5,858. Faculty: 405 (231 full-time, 174 part-time). Social organizations: 3 national fraternities, 3 national sororities; 12% of eligible undergraduate men and 12% of eligible undergraduate women are members.

Drug and Alcohol Information

Education

On campus Drug and alcohol education/prevention programs offered for: all students. Bacchus chapter. College holds an annual alcohol awareness week and drug awareness week.

Identification of Problems

Admissions College application does not ask about prior substance abuse problems.

On campus Current students identified as chemically dependent may remain enrolled, but treatment is required. Training program on identifying students with potential substance abuse problems for: resident advisers, coaches, faculty, administration. Written procedures for students and staff if substance abuse is suspected.

Support Services

On campus AA, NA, support groups (student-only AA).

Employee assistance Program for chemically dependent employees available. Staff working with drug/alcohol-related issues: 1 full-time and 1 part-time.

Disciplinary Actions

Alcohol Results of infractions of alcohol regulations (see Comparative Table of Alcohol Regulations) include chemical dependency assessment, counseling, warning, probation, suspension.

Drugs For first-time use: varies by situation. For subsequent use: suspension. For first-time possession: chemical dependency assessment, counseling, probation. For subsequent possession: suspension. For first-time sale: chemical dependency assessment, counseling, expulsion. For subsequent sale: expulsion.

For More Information

Contact: Sr. Annette Schmeling, Special Projects

University of San Diego (continued)

Coordinator, University of San Diego, UC 232 Alcala Park, San Diego, CA 92110. Telephone: 619-260-4590.

UNIVERSITY OF SCIENCE AND ARTS OF OKLAHOMA

Chickasha, Oklahoma

General Information

State-supported 4-year coed college. Founded 1908. Awards B. Primary accreditation: regional. Small-town setting; 75-acre campus. Total enrollment: 1,373. Faculty: 75 (54 full-time, 21 part-time).

Drug and Alcohol Information

Education

On campus Drug and alcohol education/prevention programs offered for: all students, athletes/coaches. Authorized group concerned with responsible drinking. College holds an annual alcohol awareness week.

Identification of Problems

Admissions College application does not ask about prior substance abuse problems.

On campus Current students identified as chemically dependent may remain enrolled, but treatment is required. Training program on identifying students with potential substance abuse problems for: anyone who wishes to attend. No written procedures for students and staff if substance abuse is suspected.

Support Services

On campus No support services on campus.

Off campus AA, NA.

Employee assistance Program for chemically dependent employees not available. Staff working with drug/alcohol-related issues: 3–5 part-time.

Disciplinary Actions

Alcohol Results of infractions of alcohol regulations (see Comparative Table of Alcohol Regulations) vary by situation. Comments: Student services director counsels student and determines if other actions are appropriate.

Drugs For any use: varies by situation. For first-time possession: counseling, warning. For subsequent possession: chemical dependency assessment, counseling, probation. For any sale: suspension.

For More Information

Contact: Hope Layman, Director of Health Services, University of Science and Arts of Oklahoma, P.O. Box 82598, Chickasha, OK 73018. Telephone: 405-224-3140 Ext. 331.

UNIVERSITY OF SOUTH CAROLINA

Columbia, South Carolina

General Information

State-supported comprehensive coed institution. Part of University of South Carolina System. Founded 1801. Awards B, M, D. Primary accreditation: regional. City setting; 242-acre campus. Total enrollment: 26,435. Faculty: 1,360 (1,069 full-time, 291 part-time). Social organizations: 20 national fraternities, 12 national sororities; 14% of eligible undergraduate men and 14% of eligible undergraduate women are members.

Drug and Alcohol Information

Education

On campus Drug and alcohol education/prevention programs offered for: all students; required for athletes/coaches, student organization representatives for campus events with alcohol. Bacchus (combined with GAMMA) chapter: 75 members. College holds an annual alcohol awareness week and drug awareness week.

Identification of Problems

Admissions College application does not ask about prior substance abuse problems.

On campus Current students identified as chemically dependent may remain enrolled. Training program on identifying students with potential substance abuse problems for: resident advisers, coaches. No written procedures for students and staff if substance abuse is suspected.

Support Services

On campus AA, NA, Al-Anon, ACOA, private counseling.

Employee assistance Program for chemically dependent employees available. Staff working with drug/alcohol-related issues: 3 full-time and 13 part-time.

Disciplinary Actions

Alcohol Results of infractions of alcohol regulations (see Comparative Table of Alcohol Regulations) vary by situation but can include chemical dependency assessment, counseling, warning, probation, suspension, expulsion.

Drugs For any use, possession, or sale: varies by situation.

Additional Information from the College

The Office of Alcohol and Drug Programs offers prevention, education, and intervention services using campus and community treatment and support resources. The School of Medicine provides education and clinical research and houses the Office of Alcohol and Drug Studies. The athletic program operates a drug screening and education program. The Personnel Division provides employee assistance services. The various components of alcohol- and drug-related programs are cooperative and mutually supportive. An advisory committee on alcohol and drug-related policies and programs is currently being developed.

For More Information

Contact: Katherine Turner Altman, Director, Office of Alcohol and Drug Programs, Campus Activities Center, Russell House, University of South Carolina, Columbia, SC 29208. Telephone: 803-777-6688.

UNIVERSITY OF SOUTH CAROLINA AT AIKEN

Aiken, South Carolina

General Information

State-supported 4-year coed college. Part of University of South Carolina System. Founded 1961. Awards A (terminal), B. Primary accreditation: regional. Small-town setting; 144-acre campus. Total enrollment: 2,528. Faculty: 217 (120 full-time, 97 part-time). Social organizations: 5 national fraternities, 4 national sororities; 1% of eligible undergraduate men and 1% of eligible undergraduate women are members.

Drug and Alcohol Information

Education

On campus Drug and alcohol education/prevention programs not offered at the present time. Authorized group concerned with responsible drinking. College holds an annual alcohol awareness week and drug awareness week.

Identification of Problems

Admissions College application does not ask about prior substance abuse problems.

On campus Current students identified as chemically dependent may remain enrolled, but treatment is required. No training program on identifying students with potential substance abuse problems. Written procedures for students and staff if substance abuse is suspected.

Support Services

On campus Private counseling.

Employee assistance Program for chemically dependent employees available. Staff working with drug/alcohol-related issues: 1 full-time and 3 part-time.

Disciplinary Actions

Alcohol Results of infractions of alcohol regulations (see Comparative Table of Alcohol Regulations) include counseling, warning, probation.

Drugs For first-time use or possession: varies by situation—counseling, probation, suspension. For subsequent use: counseling, probation, suspension. For subsequent possession: varies by situation. For any sale: varies by situation—counseling, expulsion.

For More Information

Contact: Gayle Lofgren, Counselor, University of South Carolina at Aiken, 171 University Pkwy., Aiken, SC 29801. Telephone: 803-648-6851 Ext. 3487.

UNIVERSITY OF SOUTHERN CALIFORNIA

Los Angeles, California

General Information

Independent comprehensive coed institution. Founded 1880. Awards B, M, D. Primary accreditation: regional. Metropolitan setting; 165-acre campus. Total enrollment: 29,590. Faculty: 3,289 (2,021 full-time, 1,268 part-time). Social organizations: 28 national fraternities, 15 national sororities; 25% of eligible undergraduate men and 25% of eligible undergraduate women are members.

Drug and Alcohol Information

Education

On campus Drug and alcohol education/prevention programs offered for: all students, athletes/coaches. Authorized group concerned with responsible drinking. College holds an annual alcohol awareness week and drug awareness week.

Identification of Problems

Admissions College application does not ask about prior substance abuse problems.

On campus Current students identified as chemically dependent may remain enrolled. Treatment is not required but is encouraged and available. No training program on identifying students with potential substance abuse problems. Written procedures for students and staff if substance abuse is suspected.

Support Services

On campus AA, ACOA, support groups, private counseling.

Employee assistance Program for chemically dependent employees available. Staff working with drug/alcohol-related issues: many part-time.

Disciplinary Actions

Alcohol Results of infractions of alcohol regulations (see Comparative Table of Alcohol Regulations) vary by situation.

Drugs For any use, possession, or sale: varies by situation.

For More Information

Contact: Lynn Mountain, Health Educator, University of Southern California, 849 W. 34th St., Los Angeles, CA 90089-0311. Telephone: 213-743-7093.

UNIVERSITY OF SOUTHERN COLORADO

Pueblo, Colorado

General Information

State-supported 5-year coed college. Part of Colorado State University System. Founded 1933. Awards B, M. Primary accreditation: regional. City setting; 800-acre campus. Total enrollment: 3,953. Faculty: 240 (170 full-time, 70 part-time).

Drug and Alcohol Information

Education

On campus Drug and alcohol education/prevention programs offered for: all students; required for: athletes/coaches. Bacchus chapter: 10 members. College holds an annual alcohol awareness week and drug awareness week.

Identification of Problems

Admissions College application does not ask about prior substance abuse problems, except with reference to prior felony incidents and their adjudication.

On campus Current students identified as chemically dependent may remain enrolled, but treatment may be required. Training program on identifying students with potential substance abuse problems for: resident advisers, coaches, administration, Student Activities Board members. Written procedures for students and staff if substance abuse is suspected.

Support Services

On campus AA, NA, ACOA, support groups, private counseling, referral agencies.

Employee assistance Program for chemically dependent employees available. Staff working with drug/alcohol-related issues: 6 part-time.

Disciplinary Actions

Alcohol Results of infractions of alcohol regulations (see Comparative Table of Alcohol Regulations) vary by situation.

Drugs For any use, possession, or sale: varies by situation. Comments: All incidents are adjudicated via a formal or informal hearing process. Use of drugs is viewed as very detrimental to the well-being of the student and the University.

University of Southern Colorado (continued)

Additional Information from the College

The University has comprehensive guidelines for the use of alcoholic beverages and policies and procedures to prevent substance abuse on campus. Disciplinary procedures are outlined in the Standards of Conduct and Residence Hall Procedures and Policies handbooks.

For More Information

Contact: Dr. Richard H. Hill, Dean of Student Services, University of Southern Colorado, 2200 Bonforte Blvd., Pueblo, CO 81001. Telephone: 719-549-2586.

UNIVERSITY OF SOUTHERN INDIANA

Evansville, Indiana

General Information

State-supported 5-year coed college. Founded 1965. Awards A (terminal), B, M. Primary accreditation: regional. City setting; 300-acre campus. Total enrollment: 5,265. Faculty: 247 (126 full-time, 121 part-time). Social organizations: 5 national fraternities, 3 national sororities; 9% of eligible undergraduate men and 4% of eligible undergraduate women are members.

Drug and Alcohol Information

Education

On campus Drug and alcohol education/prevention programs offered for: all students. Authorized group concerned with responsible drinking. College holds an annual alcohol awareness week.

Identification of Problems

Admissions College application does not ask about prior substance abuse problems.

On campus Current students identified as chemically dependent may remain enrolled, but treatment is required. Training program on identifying students with potential substance abuse problems for: resident advisers. Written procedures for students and staff if substance abuse is suspected.

Support Services

On campus AA, support groups (Substance Abuse Team composed of students, faculty, and staff), private counseling.

Employee assistance Program for chemically dependent employees available. Staff working with drug/alcohol-related issues: 1 part-time.

Disciplinary Actions

Alcohol Results of infractions of alcohol regulations (see Comparative Table of Alcohol Regulations) vary by situation but can include chemical dependency assessment, counseling, warning, probation, suspension, expulsion.

Drugs For first-time use or possession: varies by situation—chemical dependency assessment, counseling, probation. For subsequent use or possession: varies by situation. For any sale: expulsion.

For More Information

Contact: Jim Browning, Director of Counseling, University of Southern Indiana, 8600 University Blvd., Evansville, IN 47712. Telephone: 812-464-1867.

UNIVERSITY OF SOUTHERN MISSISSIPPI

Hattiesburg, Mississippi

General Information

State-supported comprehensive coed institution. Founded 1910. Awards B, M, D. Primary accreditation: regional. Small-town setting; 840-acre campus. Total enrollment: 11,051. Faculty: 668 (585 full-time, 83 part-time). Social organizations: 14 national fraternities, 12 national sororities; 15% of eligible undergraduate men and 13% of eligible undergraduate women are members.

Drug and Alcohol Information

Education

On campus Drug and alcohol education/prevention programs offered for: all students, athletes/coaches, faculty, administration. Authorized group concerned with responsible drinking (GAMMA).

Identification of Problems

Admissions College application does not ask about prior substance abuse problems.

On campus Current students identified as chemically dependent may remain enrolled. Training program on identifying students with potential substance abuse problems for: resident advisers, volunteer trainers with the Drug Prevention Program. Written procedures for students and staff if substance abuse is suspected.

Support Services

On campus AA, NA, ACOA, private counseling, Drug Prevention Program.

Employee assistance Program for chemically dependent employees available. Staff working with drug/alcohol-related issues: 1 full-time and 3 part-time.

Disciplinary Actions

Alcohol Results of infractions of alcohol regulations (see Comparative Table of Alcohol Regulations) include chemical dependency assessment, suspension. Comments: If violation results in disciplinary action, student must attend 12 hours of an alcohol education class similar to what the state requires for DUI.

Drugs For first-time use: varies by situation. For first-time possession: counseling, probation, suspension. For first-time sale: suspension, expulsion. For subsequent use or possession: suspension, expulsion. For subsequent sale: expulsion.

Additional Information from the College

The University recently received a Mississippi Highway Safety Grant to implement the Salute the Sober Driver Program for reducing drunk driving among students.

For More Information

Contact: Dr. Joanne Stevens, Director, Drug Prevention Program, University of Southern Mississippi, Southern Station, Box 10031, Hattiesburg, MS 39406. Telephone: 601-266-4454.

UNIVERSITY OF SOUTH FLORIDA
Tampa, Florida

General Information
State-supported comprehensive coed institution. Part of State University System of Florida. Founded 1956. Awards A (college transfer), B, M, D. Primary accreditation: regional. Metropolitan setting; 1,695-acre campus. Total enrollment: 30,003. Faculty: 1,422 (1,231 full-time, 191 part-time). Social organizations: 17 national fraternities, 9 national sororities, 1 local sorority; 10% of eligible undergraduate men and 7% of eligible undergraduate women are members.

Drug and Alcohol Information
Education
On campus Drug and alcohol education/prevention programs offered for: all students, athletes/coaches. Bacchus chapter: 25 members. College holds an annual alcohol awareness week and drug awareness week.

Identification of Problems
Admissions College application does not ask about prior substance abuse problems.

On campus Current students identified as chemically dependent may remain enrolled. Training program on identifying students with potential substance abuse problems for: resident advisers, coaches. No written procedures for students and staff if substance abuse is suspected.

Support Services
On campus AA, NA, Al-Anon, ACOA, private counseling.

Employee assistance Program for chemically dependent employees not available.

Disciplinary Actions
Alcohol Results of infractions of alcohol regulations (see Comparative Table of Alcohol Regulations) vary by situation but can include chemical dependency assessment, counseling, warning, probation, suspension, expulsion.

Drugs For first-time use: varies by situation—probation. For subsequent use—varies by situation. For first-time possession: varies by situation. For subsequent possession: suspension, expulsion. For any sale: suspension, expulsion.

For More Information
Contact: Troy Collier, Associate Dean of Students, University of South Florida, 4202 E. Fowler Ave., Tampa, FL 33617. Telephone: 813-974-2151.

UNIVERSITY OF SOUTHWESTERN LOUISIANA
Lafayette, Louisiana

General Information
State-supported comprehensive coed institution. Founded 1898. Awards A (college transfer and terminal), B, M, D. Primary accreditation: regional. City setting; 735-acre campus. Total enrollment: 15,037. Faculty: 677. Social organizations: 16 national fraternities, 10 national sororities; 7% of eligible undergraduate men and 5% of eligible undergraduate women are members.

Drug and Alcohol Information
Education
On campus Drug and alcohol education/prevention programs offered for: all students. Bacchus chapter: 30 members. College holds an annual alcohol awareness week.

Identification of Problems
Admissions College application does not ask about prior substance abuse problems.

On campus Current students identified as chemically dependent may remain enrolled, depending on the situation, but treatment is required. Training program on identifying students with potential substance abuse problems for: resident advisers, coaches, Greek officers, University police. Written procedures for students and staff if substance abuse is suspected.

Support Services
On campus Support groups, private counseling.

Employee assistance Program for chemically dependent employees not available. Staff working with drug/alcohol-related issues: 23 part-time.

Disciplinary Actions
Alcohol Results of infractions of alcohol regulations (see Comparative Table of Alcohol Regulations) vary by situation but can include chemical dependency assessment, counseling, warning, probation, suspension, expulsion.

Drugs For any use, possession, or sale: varies by situation.

For More Information
Contact: Dr. Doug Blair, Director of Counseling and Testing Center, University of Southwestern Louisiana, P.O. Box 44710, Lafayette, LA 70504. Telephone: 318-231-6480.

UNIVERSITY OF TENNESSEE AT CHATTANOOGA
Chattanooga, Tennessee

General Information
State-supported 5-year coed college. Part of University of Tennessee System. Founded 1886. Awards B, M. Primary accreditation: regional. City setting; 60-acre campus. Total enrollment: 7,526. Faculty: 314 (284 full-time, 30 part-time). Social organizations: 7 national fraternities, 7 national sororities; 7% of eligible undergraduate men and 7% of eligible undergraduate women are members.

Drug and Alcohol Information
Education
On campus Drug and alcohol education/prevention programs offered for: freshmen, social organization members, athletes/coaches, resident advisers. College holds an annual alcohol awareness week and drug awareness week.

Identification of Problems
Admissions College application does not ask about prior substance abuse problems.

On campus Current students identified as chemically dependent may remain enrolled, but treatment is required. Training program on identifying students with potential substance abuse problems for: resident advisers, administration. No written procedures for students and staff if substance abuse is suspected.

University of Tennessee at Chattanooga (continued)

Support Services

On campus AA, NA, private counseling.

Employee assistance Program for chemically dependent employees not available. Staff working with drug/alcohol-related issues: 4 part-time.

Disciplinary Actions

Alcohol Results of infractions of alcohol regulations (see Comparative Table of Alcohol Regulations) vary by situation but can include warning.

Drugs For first-time use or possession: varies by situation—probation. For first-time sale: varies by situation—suspension. For subsequent use, possession, or sale: varies by situation.

For More Information

Contact: Richard E. MacDougall, Assistant Vice Chancellor, University of Tennessee at Chattanooga, 615 McCallie Ave., Chattanooga, TN 37403. Telephone: 615-755-4246.

UNIVERSITY OF TENNESSEE, KNOXVILLE

Knoxville, Tennessee

General Information

State-supported comprehensive coed institution. Part of University of Tennessee System. Founded 1794. Awards B, M, D. Primary accreditation: regional. City setting; 417-acre campus. Total enrollment: 24,361. Faculty: 1,173 (1,119 full-time, 54 part-time). Social organizations: 27 national fraternities, 16 national sororities; 8% of eligible undergraduate men and 16% of eligible undergraduate women are members.

Drug and Alcohol Information

Education

On campus Drug and alcohol education/prevention programs offered for: all students, athletes/coaches. College holds an annual alcohol awareness week and drug awareness week.

Identification of Problems

Admissions College application does not ask about prior substance abuse problems.

On campus Current students identified as chemically dependent may remain enrolled. Training program on identifying students with potential substance abuse problems for: resident advisers. Written procedures for students and staff if substance abuse is suspected.

Support Services

On campus AA, NA, ACOA, private counseling.

Employee assistance Program for chemically dependent employees available. Staff working with drug/alcohol-related issues: 2 part-time.

Disciplinary Actions

Alcohol Results of infractions of alcohol regulations (see Comparative Table of Alcohol Regulations) include chemical dependency assessment, warning, probation, suspension.

Drugs For first-time use: chemical dependency assessment, counseling, probation. For subsequent use: probation, suspension. For first-time possession: suspension. For subsequent possession: expulsion. For any sale: expulsion.

For More Information

Contact: Richard F. Nash, Director, Student Counseling, University of Tennessee, Knoxville, 900 Volunteer Blvd., Knoxville, TN 37996. Telephone: 615-974-2196.

UNIVERSITY OF TENNESSEE, MEMPHIS

Memphis, Tennessee

General Information

State-supported coed college. Part of University of Tennessee System. Founded 1911. Awards B, M, D. Primary accreditation: regional. Metropolitan setting. Total enrollment: 1,773. Faculty: 779 (620 full-time, 159 part-time).

Drug and Alcohol Information

Education

On campus Drug and alcohol education/prevention programs offered for: all students. Authorized group concerned with responsible drinking. College holds an annual alcohol awareness week.

Identification of Problems

Admissions College application question about prior substance abuse problems is used in the admissions decision.

On campus Current students identified as chemically dependent may remain enrolled, but treatment is required. Training program on identifying students with potential substance abuse problems for: AIMS (Aid to Impaired Medical Students). Written procedures for students and staff if substance abuse is suspected.

Support Services

On campus ACOA, support groups, private counseling.

Employee assistance Program for chemically dependent employees not available.

Disciplinary Actions

Alcohol Results of infractions of alcohol regulations (see Comparative Table of Alcohol Regulations) include counseling, warning, probation.

Drugs For any use, possession, or sale: varies by situation.

For More Information

Contact: Pam Moon, Assistant Vice Chancellor of Student Life, University of Tennessee, Memphis, 800 Madison Ave., Memphis, TN 38163. Telephone: 901-528-5610.

UNIVERSITY OF TEXAS AT ARLINGTON

Arlington, Texas

General Information

State-supported comprehensive coed institution. Part of University of Texas System. Founded 1895. Awards B, M, D. Primary accreditation: regional. City setting; 300-acre campus. Total enrollment: 23,383. Faculty: 870 (590 full-time, 280 part-time). Social organizations: 15 national fraternities, 9 national sororities; 10% of eligible undergraduate men and 8% of eligible undergraduate women are members.

Drug and Alcohol Information

Education

On campus Drug and alcohol education/prevention programs offered for: all students, athletes/coaches, faculty, administration. College holds an annual alcohol awareness week and drug awareness week.

Identification of Problems

Admissions College application does not ask about prior substance abuse problems.

On campus Current students identified as chemically dependent may remain enrolled. Training program on identifying students with potential substance abuse problems for: resident advisers, faculty, administration, student leaders. Written procedures for students and staff if substance abuse is suspected.

Support Services

On campus Private counseling, UTA Recovering Students Association.

Employee assistance Program for chemically dependent employees available. Staff working with drug/alcohol-related issues: 2 full-time and 1 part-time.

Disciplinary Actions

Alcohol Results of infractions of alcohol regulations (see Comparative Table of Alcohol Regulations) include counseling, warning, probation, suspension.

Drugs For any use or possession: suspension. For any sale: expulsion.

For More Information

Contact: Joy Ford Murray, Substance Abuse Specialist, University of Texas at Arlington, P.O. Box 19329, Arlington, TX 76019. Telephone: 817-794-5152.

UNIVERSITY OF TEXAS AT AUSTIN

Austin, Texas

General Information

State-supported comprehensive coed institution. Part of University of Texas System. Founded 1883. Awards B, M, D. Primary accreditation: regional. City setting; 300-acre campus. Total enrollment: 50,107. Faculty: 2,301 (1,631 full-time, 670 part-time). Social organizations: national fraternities, local fraternities, local sororities; 14% of eligible undergraduate men and 14% of eligible undergraduate women are members.

Drug and Alcohol Information

Education

On campus Drug and alcohol education/prevention programs offered for: all students, athletes/coaches. Authorized group concerned with responsible drinking. College holds an annual alcohol awareness week and drug awareness week.

Identification of Problems

Admissions College application does not ask about prior substance abuse problems.

On campus Current students identified as chemically dependent may remain enrolled. Training program on identifying students with potential substance abuse problems for: resident advisers, coaches, Student Health and Counseling Center staff, others upon request. Written procedures for students and staff if substance abuse is suspected.

Support Services

On campus AA, Al-Anon, ACOA, private counseling, assessment and referral.

Employee assistance Program for chemically dependent employees not available. Staff working with drug/alcohol-related issues: 2 full-time and 2 part-time.

Disciplinary Actions

Alcohol Results of infractions of alcohol regulations (see Comparative Table of Alcohol Regulations) include chemical dependency assessment, counseling, warning.

Drugs For first-time use, possession, or sale: suspension. For subsequent use, possession, or sale: suspension, expulsion.

For More Information

Contact: Dr. Jerry Horton, Coordinator of Campus Alcohol and Drug Education Program, University of Texas Student Health Center, University of Texas at Austin, P.O. Box 7339, Austin, TX 78713. Telephone: 512-471-6252.

UNIVERSITY OF TEXAS HEALTH SCIENCE CENTER AT SAN ANTONIO

San Antonio, Texas

General Information

State-supported specialized coed college. Part of University of Texas System. Founded 1976. Awards B, M, D. Primary accreditation: regional. Metropolitan setting; 100-acre campus. Total enrollment: 2,219. Faculty: 118 (100 full-time, 18 part-time).

Drug and Alcohol Information

Education

On campus Drug and alcohol education/prevention programs offered for: most students. College holds an annual alcohol awareness week and drug awareness week.

Identification of Problems

Admissions College application does not ask about prior substance abuse problems.

On campus Training program on identifying students with potential substance abuse problems being developed for: faculty, administration, peer advisers, advocates. Written procedures are being developed for students and staff if substance abuse is suspected.

Support Services

On campus Private counseling.

Employee assistance Program for chemically dependent employees not available. Staff working with drug/alcohol-related issues: 2 full-time.

Disciplinary Actions

Alcohol Results of infractions of alcohol regulations (see Comparative Table of Alcohol Regulations) include suspension.

Drugs For first-time use, possession, or sale: varies by situation—suspension. For subsequent violations: policy being developed.

Additional Information from the College

A Substance Abuse Prevention Program, funded by a

University of Texas Health Science Center at San Antonio (continued)

FIPSE grant, will serve the students of all University of Texas Health Science Center campuses. An ad hoc committee on substance use and abuse is currently writing policy.

For More Information

Contact: Diane Williams, RN, Substance Abuse Prevention Program Director, University of Texas Health Science Center at San Antonio, 7703 Floyd Curl Dr., San Antonio, TX 78284. Telephone: 512-567-6774.

UNIVERSITY OF TEXAS MEDICAL BRANCH AT GALVESTON

Galveston, Texas

General Information

State-supported coed college. Part of University of Texas System. Founded 1891. Awards B, M, D. Primary accreditation: regional. City setting. Total enrollment: 1,705. Faculty: 609 (559 full-time, 50 part-time). Social organizations: 6 national fraternities; 15% of eligible undergraduate men and 10% of eligible undergraduate women are members.

Drug and Alcohol Information

Education

On campus Drug and alcohol education/prevention programs offered for: all students, residents and fellows. Authorized group concerned with responsible drinking. College holds an annual alcohol awareness week and drug awareness week.

Identification of Problems

Admissions College application does not ask about prior substance abuse problems.

On campus Current students identified as chemically dependent may remain enrolled. No training program on identifying students with potential substance abuse problems. No written procedures for students and staff if substance abuse is suspected.

Support Services

On campus AA, NA, Al-Anon, ACOA, support groups, private counseling.

Employee assistance Program for chemically dependent employees available. Staff working with drug/alcohol-related issues: 2 full-time and 25 part-time.

Disciplinary Actions

Alcohol Results of infractions of alcohol regulations (see Comparative Table of Alcohol Regulations) include warning, probation, suspension, expulsion.

Drugs For any use, possession, or sale: expulsion.

For More Information

Contact: Alice Wygant, Project Director, Alchohol and Drug Awareness Program, University of Texas Medical Branch at Galveston, M-17, 301 University Blvd., Galveston, TX 77550. Telephone: 409-761-1462.

UNIVERSITY OF TEXAS OF THE PERMIAN BASIN

Odessa, Texas

General Information

State-supported coed college. Part of University of Texas System. Founded 1969. Awards B, M. Primary accreditation: regional. City setting; 600-acre campus. Total enrollment: 2,132. Faculty: 105 (56 full-time, 49 part-time).

Drug and Alcohol Information

Education

On campus Drug and alcohol education/prevention programs not offered.

Identification of Problems

Admissions College application does not ask about prior substance abuse problems.

On campus No training program on identifying students with potential substance abuse problems. No written procedures for students and staff if substance abuse is suspected.

Support Services

On campus No support services on campus.

Disciplinary Actions

Alcohol Results of infractions of alcohol regulations (see Comparative Table of Alcohol Regulations) vary by situation.

Drugs For first-time use, possession, or sale: varies by situation—suspension, expulsion. For subsequent use, possession, or sale: varies by situation.

For More Information

Contact: Teresa Brockman, Assistant Dean of Student Life, University of Texas of the Permian Basin, P.O. Box 8422-UTPB, Odessa, TX 79762. Telephone: 915-367-2125.

UNIVERSITY OF THE ARTS

Philadelphia, Pennsylvania

General Information

Independent 5-year coed college. Founded 1876. Awards A (college transfer and terminal), B, M. Primary accreditation: regional. Metropolitan setting. Total enrollment: 1,371. Faculty: 355 (94 full-time, 261 part-time).

Drug and Alcohol Information

Education

On campus Drug and alcohol education/prevention programs offered for: student leaders; required for: freshmen, resident advisers.

Identification of Problems

Admissions College application does not ask about prior substance abuse problems.

On campus Current students identified as chemically dependent may remain enrolled, but treatment is required. Training program on identifying students with potential substance abuse problems for: resident advisers, Student Services staff. Written procedures for students and staff if substance abuse is suspected.

Support Services

On campus AA, private counseling, therapeutic referral.

Employee assistance Program for chemically dependent employees not available.

Disciplinary Actions

Alcohol Results of infractions of alcohol regulations (see Comparative Table of Alcohol Regulations) vary by situation but can include counseling, warning, probation, suspension, expulsion.

Drugs For first-time use: varies by situation—counseling, suspension. For subsequent use: varies by situation. For first-time possession: varies by situation—counseling, probation, suspension. For subsequent possession: varies by situation. For any sale: expulsion.

For More Information

Contact: Dr. Victor S. Zarzycki, Dean of Students, University of the Arts, Broad and Pine Sts., Philadelphia, PA 19102. Telephone: 215-875-1110.

UNIVERSITY OF THE SOUTH

Sewanee, Tennessee

General Information

Independent Episcopal 5-year coed college. Founded 1857. Awards B, M, D. Primary accreditation: regional. Rural setting; 10,000-acre campus. Total enrollment: 1,171. Faculty: 111 (81 full-time, 30 part-time). Social organizations: 11 national fraternities, 6 local sororities; 67% of eligible undergraduate men and 57% of eligible undergraduate women are members.

Drug and Alcohol Information

Education

On campus Drug and alcohol education/prevention programs offered for: all students, athletes/coaches; required for: freshmen, social organization members, resident advisers, student leaders. Bacchus chapter: 50 members. College holds an annual alcohol awareness week and drug awareness week.

Identification of Problems

Admissions College application question about prior substance abuse problems is used to explain past academic performance; for counseling and referral, if student is admitted.

On campus Current students identified as chemically dependent may remain enrolled, but treatment is required. Training program on identifying students with potential substance abuse problems for: resident advisers, Greek officers, administration. Written procedures for students and staff if substance abuse is suspected.

Support Services

On campus AA, ACOA, private counseling, counseling services.

Employee assistance Program for chemically dependent employees available.

Disciplinary Actions

Alcohol Results of infractions of alcohol regulations (see Comparative Table of Alcohol Regulations) vary by situation.

Drugs For first-time use: chemical dependency assessment, counseling, probation. For first-time possession: counseling, probation. For subsequent use or possession: chemical dependency assessment, suspension. For any sale: expulsion.

For More Information

Contact: Robert W. Pearigen, Dean of Men, University of the South, Sewanee, TN 37375. Telephone: 615-598-5931.

UNIVERSITY OF TULSA

Tulsa, Oklahoma

General Information

Independent comprehensive coed institution, affiliated with Presbyterian Church. Founded 1894. Awards B, M, D. Primary accreditation: regional. Metropolitan setting; 140-acre campus. Total enrollment: 4,431. Faculty: 400 (328 full-time, 72 part-time). Social organizations: 7 national fraternities, 7 national sororities; 20% of eligible undergraduate men and 24% of eligible undergraduate women are members.

Drug and Alcohol Information

Education

On campus Drug and alcohol education/prevention programs offered for: all students, athletes/coaches, faculty, administration. Authorized group concerned with responsible drinking. College holds an annual alcohol awareness week.

Identification of Problems

Admissions College application does not ask about prior substance abuse problems.

On campus Current students identified as chemically dependent may remain enrolled, but treatment is required. Training program on identifying students with potential substance abuse problems for: resident advisers, coaches.

Support Services

On campus Private counseling.

Disciplinary Actions

Alcohol Results of infractions of alcohol regulations (see Comparative Table of Alcohol Regulations) vary by situation.

Drugs For any use or possession: varies by situation. For first-time sale: suspension. For subsequent sale: expulsion.

For More Information

Contact: Dr. Tom Brian, Director of Counseling Center, University of Tulsa, 600 S. College, Tulsa, OK 74104. Telephone: 918-631-2200.

UNIVERSITY OF VIRGINIA

Charlottesville, Virginia

General Information

State-related comprehensive coed institution. Founded 1819. Awards B, M, D. Primary accreditation: regional. Small-town setting; 2,000-acre campus. Total enrollment: 17,198. Faculty: 1,804 (1,604 full-time, 200 part-time). Social organizations: 39 national fraternities, 21 national sororities; 31% of eligible undergraduate men and 30% of eligible undergraduate women are members.

University of Virginia (continued)

Drug and Alcohol Information

Education

On campus Drug and alcohol education/prevention programs offered for: all students; required for: freshmen, athletes/coaches, resident advisers. Authorized group concerned with responsible drinking. College holds an annual alcohol awareness week.

Identification of Problems

Admissions College application does not ask about prior substance abuse problems.

On campus Current students identified as chemically dependent may remain enrolled, but treatment may be required. Training program on identifying students with potential substance abuse problems for: resident advisers, coaches, Greek officers, faculty, freshman groups upon request. No written procedures for students and staff if substance abuse is suspected.

Support Services

On campus ACOA, private counseling.

Employee assistance Program for chemically dependent employees available. Staff working with drug/alcohol-related issues: 29 full-time.

Disciplinary Actions

Alcohol Results of infractions of alcohol regulations (see Comparative Table of Alcohol Regulations) vary by situation but can include chemical dependency assessment, counseling, warning, probation, suspension, expulsion.

Drugs For any use, possession, or sale: varies by situation.

For More Information

Contact: Susan Grossman, Prevention Coordinator, Institute of Substance Abuse Studies, University of Virginia, Charlottesville, VA 22906. Telephone: 804-924-5276.

UNIVERSITY OF WASHINGTON

Seattle, Washington

General Information

State-supported comprehensive coed institution. Founded 1861. Awards B, M, D. Primary accreditation: regional. Metropolitan setting; 680-acre campus. Total enrollment: 33,460. Faculty: 3,118. Social organizations: 31 national fraternities, 18 national sororities; 18% of eligible undergraduate men and 17% of eligible undergraduate women are members.

Drug and Alcohol Information

Education

On campus Drug and alcohol education/prevention programs offered for: all students, faculty, administration; required for: athletes/coaches, resident advisers. Authorized group concerned with responsible drinking. College holds an annual alcohol and substance awareness week.

Identification of Problems

Admissions College application does not ask about prior substance abuse problems.

On campus Whether current students identified as chemically dependent may remain enrolled is handled on a case-by-case basis. Training program on identifying students with potential substance abuse problems for: resident advisers, coaches, Greek officers, administration, selected student leaders representing on- and off-campus living groups. Written procedures for students and staff if substance abuse is suspected.

Support Services

On campus AA, ACOA, support groups (Counseling Center, campus health service, University Hospital), private counseling.

Off campus Al-Anon.

Employee assistance Program for chemically dependent employees available. Staff working with drug/alcohol-related issues: numerous full- and part-time.

Disciplinary Actions

Alcohol Results of infractions of alcohol regulations (see Comparative Table of Alcohol Regulations) vary by situation but can include criminal citation.

Drugs For any use, possession, or sale: varies by situation.

Additional Information from the College

A committee of students and staff members was established to develop and implement a broad range of ongoing substance education programs, including observance of Alcohol and Substance Awareness Week each October, distribution of a brochure describing effects of various drugs and listing campus and community sources of assistance, and seminars conducted by experts for student living groups. Moreover, the committee has organized training sessions to prepare selected students, about 200 to date, to serve as "preventive helpers" and informed referral sources for students with substance abuse problems.

For More Information

Contact: Patricia Woehrlin, Assistant to the Vice President, 476 Schmitz Hall, PB-10, University of Washington, Seattle, WA 98195. Telephone: 206-543-9958.

UNIVERSITY OF WEST FLORIDA

Pensacola, Florida

General Information

State-supported 5-year coed college. Part of State University System of Florida. Founded 1963. Awards B, M. Primary accreditation: regional. City setting; 1,000-acre campus. Total enrollment: 7,170. Faculty: 383 (270 full-time, 113 part-time). Social organizations: 3 national fraternities, 3 national sororities; 10% of eligible undergraduate men and 10% of eligible undergraduate women are members.

Drug and Alcohol Information

Education

On campus Drug and alcohol education/prevention programs offered for: all students, athletes/coaches. Bacchus chapter: 12 members. College holds an annual alcohol awareness week and drug awareness week.

Identification of Problems

Admissions College application does not ask about prior substance abuse problems.

On campus Current students identified as chemically dependent may remain enrolled. Training program on identifying students with potential substance abuse problems for: resident advisers, coaches, Greek officers. Written procedures for students and staff if substance abuse is suspected.

Support Services

On campus AA, ACOA, private counseling.

Employee assistance Program for chemically dependent employees available. Staff working with drug/alcohol-related issues: 1 full-time.

Disciplinary Actions

Alcohol Results of infractions of alcohol regulations (see Comparative Table of Alcohol Regulations) include counseling, warning, probation, suspension, expulsion.

Drugs For any use, possession, or sale: varies by situation.

For More Information

Contact: Gregory E. Dziadon, Coordinator, Student Affairs, University of West Florida, Bldg. 22, Rm. 207, 11000 University Pkwy., Pensacola, FL 32514-5750. Telephone: 904-474-2384.

UNIVERSITY OF WISCONSIN–MADISON

Madison, Wisconsin

General Information

State-supported comprehensive coed institution. Part of University of Wisconsin System. Founded 1848. Awards B, M, D. Primary accreditation: regional. City setting; 900-acre campus. Total enrollment: 40,949. Faculty: 2,290 (2,200 full-time, 90 part-time). Social organizations: 27 national fraternities, 10 national sororities, eating clubs; 5% of eligible undergraduate men and 5% of eligible undergraduate women are members.

Drug and Alcohol Information

Education

On campus Drug and alcohol education/prevention programs offered for: all students, athletes/coaches. Authorized group concerned with responsible drinking.

Identification of Problems

Admissions College application question about prior substance abuse problems is used for counseling and referral, if student is admitted. There is an optional question concerning disabilities in general.

On campus Current students identified as chemically dependent may remain enrolled, but treatment is sometimes required. Training program on identifying students with potential substance abuse problems for: resident advisers, coaches and trainers, Greek officers, House Fellows, advisers, student leaders, counselors. Written procedures for students and staff if substance abuse is suspected.

Support Services

On campus AA, NA, Al-Anon, ACOA, support groups, private counseling.

Employee assistance Program for chemically dependent employees available. Staff working with drug/alcohol-related issues: 1 full-time and 1 part-time.

Disciplinary Actions

Alcohol Results of infractions of alcohol regulations (see Comparative Table of Alcohol Regulations) vary by situation but can include chemical dependency assessment, counseling, warning, probation, suspension, expulsion.

Drugs For first-time use or possession: varies by situation—warning. For subsequent use or possession: counseling, probation. For first-time sale: suspension. For subsequent sale: expulsion.

Additional Information from the College

The University has recently completed a Comprehensive Campus Plan that calls for a campuswide steering committee and additional staff, including a coordinator and a prevention, intervention, curriculum, and Employee Assistance Program specialist.

For More Information

Contact: Courtie Demarest, Assistant Dean of Students, University of Wisconsin–Madison, 117 Bascom Hall, 500 Lincoln Dr., Madison, WI 53706. Telephone: 608-263-2535.

UNIVERSITY OF WISCONSIN–MILWAUKEE

Milwaukee, Wisconsin

General Information

State-supported comprehensive coed institution. Part of University of Wisconsin System. Founded 1956. Awards B, M, D. Primary accreditation: regional. Metropolitan setting; 90-acre campus. Total enrollment: 25,212. Faculty: 1,263 (807 full-time, 456 part-time). Social organizations: 4 national fraternities, 4 national sororities, 2 local fraternities.

Drug and Alcohol Information

Education

On campus Drug and alcohol education/prevention programs offered for: all students, athletes/coaches, faculty, administration. Bacchus chapter: 10 members. College holds an annual alcohol awareness week and drug awareness week.

Identification of Problems

Admissions College application does not ask about prior substance abuse problems.

On campus Current students identified as chemically dependent may remain enrolled. Training program on identifying students with potential substance abuse problems for: resident advisers, Health Center personnel.

Support Services

On campus AA, NA, support groups, private counseling.

Employee assistance Program for chemically dependent employees available. Staff working with drug/alcohol-related issues: 7 part-time.

Disciplinary Actions

Alcohol Results of infractions of alcohol regulations (see Comparative Table of Alcohol Regulations) include chemical dependency assessment, counseling, warning, probation, suspension, expulsion.

Drugs For any use, possession, or sale: varies by situation.

For More Information

Contact: Robert Trotalli, Assistant Dean of Students, University of Wisconsin–Milwaukee, P.O. Box 413, Milwaukee, WI 53201. Telephone: 414-229-3758.

UNIVERSITY OF WISCONSIN–PLATTEVILLE

Platteville, Wisconsin

General Information

State-supported 5-year coed college. Part of University of Wisconsin System. Founded 1866. Awards A (college transfer), B, M. Primary accreditation: regional. Small-town setting; 380-acre campus. Total enrollment: 5,353. Faculty: 280 (250 full-time, 30 part-time). Social organizations: 8 national fraternities, 3 national sororities; 5% of eligible undergraduate men and 3% of eligible undergraduate women are members.

Drug and Alcohol Information

Education

On campus Drug and alcohol education/prevention programs offered for: resident advisers, any group upon request. College holds an annual alcohol awareness week and drug awareness week.

Identification of Problems

Admissions College application does not ask about prior substance abuse problems.

On campus Current students identified as chemically dependent may remain enrolled. No training program on identifying students with potential substance abuse problems. Written procedures for students and staff if substance abuse is suspected.

Support Services

On campus AA, ACOA, private counseling, Student Assistance Program.

Employee assistance Program for chemically dependent employees available. Staff working with drug/alcohol-related issues: 1 part-time.

Disciplinary Actions

Alcohol Results of infractions of alcohol regulations (see Comparative Table of Alcohol Regulations) include chemical dependency assessment, counseling, warning, probation.

Drugs For any use, possession, or sale: varies by situation.

For More Information

Contact: Ruth A. Wimer, Coordinator, Student Assistance Program, University of Wisconsin–Platteville, 1 University Plaza, Platteville, WI 53818. Telephone: 608-342-1865.

UNIVERSITY OF WISCONSIN–RIVER FALLS

River Falls, Wisconsin

General Information

State-supported 5-year coed college. Part of University of Wisconsin System. Founded 1874. Awards B, M. Primary accreditation: regional. Small-town setting; 117-acre campus. Total enrollment: 5,544. Faculty: 295 (275 full-time, 20 part-time). Social organizations: 5 national fraternities, 2 national sororities, 1 local sorority; 5% of eligible undergraduate men and 3% of eligible undergraduate women are members.

Drug and Alcohol Information

Education

On campus Drug and alcohol education/prevention programs offered for: all students. Bacchus chapter: 12 members. College holds an annual alcohol awareness week.

Identification of Problems

Admissions College application does not ask about prior substance abuse problems.

On campus Current students identified as chemically dependent may remain enrolled, but treatment is required. Training program on identifying students with potential substance abuse problems for: resident advisers. Written procedures for students and staff if substance abuse is suspected.

Support Services

On campus AA, Al-Anon, ACOA, private counseling.

Employee assistance Program for chemically dependent employees available. Staff working with drug/alcohol-related issues: 3 part-time.

Disciplinary Actions

Alcohol Results of infractions of alcohol regulations (see Comparative Table of Alcohol Regulations) include chemical dependency assessment, counseling, warning, probation.

Drugs For first-time use: varies by situation—chemical dependency assessment, warning, probation. For subsequent use: varies by situation—chemical dependency assessment, probation. For first-time possession: varies by situation—warning. For subsequent possession: varies by situation—probation. For first-time sale: probation. For subsequent sale: suspension.

For More Information

Contact: Lorna Dilts, Substance Abuse Counselor, University of Wisconsin–River Falls, River Falls, WI 54022. Telephone: 715-425-3822.

UNIVERSITY OF WISCONSIN–WHITEWATER

Whitewater, Wisconsin

General Information

State-supported 5-year coed college. Part of University of Wisconsin System. Founded 1868. Awards A (college transfer), B, M. Primary accreditation: regional. Small-town setting; 380-acre campus. Total enrollment: 10,458. Faculty: 496 (421 full-time, 75 part-time). Social organizations: 7 national fraternities, 6 national sororities; 12% of eligible undergraduate men and 10% of eligible undergraduate women are members.

Drug and Alcohol Information

Education

On campus Drug and alcohol education/prevention programs offered for: all students. Bacchus chapter being organized. Authorized group concerned with responsible drinking. College holds an annual alcohol awareness week and drug awareness week.

Identification of Problems

Admissions College application does not ask about prior substance abuse problems.

On campus Current students identified as chemically dependent may remain enrolled, but treatment is required.

Training program on identifying students with potential substance abuse problems for: resident advisers. Written procedures for students and staff if substance abuse is suspected.

Support Services

On campus AA, NA, Al-Anon, ACOA, private counseling.

Employee assistance Program for chemically dependent employees available. Staff working with drug/alcohol-related issues: 4 part-time.

Disciplinary Actions

Alcohol Results of infractions of alcohol regulations (see Comparative Table of Alcohol Regulations) vary by situation but can include counseling.

Drugs For any use, possession, or sale: varies by situation.

Additional Information from the College

The Safety Studies Department has 3 professors with doctoral degrees who have been teaching many "Alcohol and Other Drugs" courses for fourteen years. The department offers 8–10 sections of a 3-credit Alcohol and Other Drugs course every semester as an elective. More than 10 percent of the student population take the course each year. Safety Studies professors are most cooperative in helping residence hall assistants set up alcohol programs. Other instructors who teach chemical dependency counseling courses also supervise interns and direct ACOA and other groups on campus.

For More Information

Contact: W. C. Blankenship, Acting Coordinator, SAP/EAP Program, University of Wisconsin–Whitewater, 800 W. Main St., Whitewater, WI 53190. Telephone: 414-472-1490.

UTAH STATE UNIVERSITY

Logan, Utah

General Information

State-supported comprehensive coed institution. Founded 1888. Awards B, M, D. Primary accreditation: regional. Small-town setting; 332-acre campus. Total enrollment: 12,132. Faculty: 524. Social organizations: 7 national fraternities, 3 national sororities.

Drug and Alcohol Information

Education

On campus Drug and alcohol education/prevention programs offered for: all students, adult children of alcoholics. College holds an annual combined alcohol awareness week and drug awareness week.

Identification of Problems

Admissions College application does not ask about prior substance abuse problems.

On campus Current students identified as chemically dependent may remain enrolled, but treatment may be required. Training program on identifying students with potential substance abuse problems for: resident advisers, Greek officers, faculty, administration, students. Written procedures for students and staff if substance abuse is suspected.

Support Services

On campus AA, NA, Al-Anon, ACOA, private counseling, Life Skills.

Employee assistance Program for chemically dependent employees not available. Staff working with drug/alcohol-related issues: 1 full-time and 1 part-time.

Disciplinary Actions

Alcohol Results of infractions of alcohol regulations (see Comparative Table of Alcohol Regulations) vary by situation but can include warning, probation, suspension, expulsion.

Drugs For first-time use: varies by situation—warning. For first-time possession: counseling, warning, probation. For subsequent use or possession: varies by situation. For any sale: varies by situation.

Additional Information from the College

The University is currently rewriting its alcohol and drug policies and creating an institution-wide referral system.

For More Information

Contact: JoAnn Autry, Program Administrator, Alcohol and Drug Education/Prevention Program, Utah State University, TSC Rm. 304, Logan, UT 84322-0110. Telephone: 801-750-1010.

VALLEY CITY STATE UNIVERSITY

Valley City, North Dakota

General Information

State-supported 4-year coed college. Founded 1890. Awards A (college transfer and terminal), B. Primary accreditation: regional. Small-town setting; 55-acre campus. Total enrollment: 1,154. Faculty: 66 (56 full-time, 10 part-time). Social organizations: 2 local fraternities, 4 local sororities; 6% of eligible undergraduate men and 6% of eligible undergraduate women are members.

Drug and Alcohol Information

Education

On campus Drug and alcohol education/prevention programs offered for: all students, faculty, administration; required for: athletes/coaches. Authorized group concerned with responsible drinking. College holds an annual alcohol awareness week and drug awareness week.

Identification of Problems

Admissions College application does not ask about prior substance abuse problems.

On campus Current students identified as chemically dependent may remain enrolled. Training program on identifying students with potential substance abuse problems for: resident advisers, coaches, administration. Written procedures for students and staff if substance abuse is suspected.

Support Services

On campus AA, NA, Al-Anon, support groups, private counseling.

Employee assistance Program for chemically dependent employees not available. Staff working with drug/alcohol-related issues: 3 part-time.

Disciplinary Actions

Alcohol Results of infractions of alcohol regulations (see Comparative Table of Alcohol Regulations) vary by situation but can include chemical dependency assessment, counseling, warning, probation, suspension, expulsion.

Drugs For first-time use or possession: varies by situation. For first-time sale: varies by situation—suspension,

Valley City State University (continued)

expulsion. For subsequent use, possession, or sale: suspension, expulsion.

For More Information

Contact: Bruce Nichols, Student Affairs, Valley City State University, Valley City, ND 58072. Telephone: 701-845-7413.

VALLEY FORGE CHRISTIAN COLLEGE

Phoenixville, Pennsylvania

General Information

Independent 4-year specialized coed college, affiliated with Assemblies of God. Founded 1938. Awards B. Primary accreditation: AABC. Small-town setting; 77-acre campus. Total enrollment: 506. Faculty: 27 (17 full-time, 10 part-time).

Drug and Alcohol Information

Education

On campus Drug and alcohol education/prevention programs offered for: freshmen, athletes/coaches, resident advisers. College holds an annual drug awareness week.

Identification of Problems

Admissions College application question about prior substance abuse problems is used for counseling and referral, if student is admitted; in the admissions decision.

On campus Current students identified as chemically dependent may not remain enrolled. No training program on identifying students with potential substance abuse problems. Written procedures for students and staff if substance abuse is suspected.

Support Services

On campus Private counseling.

Employee assistance Program for chemically dependent employees not available. Staff working with drug/alcohol-related issues: 1 full-time and 2 part-time.

Disciplinary Actions

Alcohol Results of infractions of alcohol regulations (see Comparative Table of Alcohol Regulations) include counseling, expulsion.

Drugs For first-time use: counseling, probation, suspension. For first-time possession: counseling, expulsion. For subsequent use or possession: expulsion. For any sale: expulsion.

For More Information

Contact: Ray Trask, Dean of Student Affairs, Valley Forge Christian College, Charlestown Rd., Phoenixville, PA 19460. Telephone: 215-935-0450.

VALPARAISO UNIVERSITY

Valparaiso, Indiana

General Information

Independent 5-year coed college, affiliated with Lutheran Church–Missouri Synod. Founded 1859. Awards B, M, D. Primary accreditation: regional. Small-town setting; 310-acre campus. Total enrollment: 3,952. Faculty: 368 (277 full-time, 91 part-time). Social organizations: 13 national fraternities, 8 local sororities; 42% of eligible undergraduate men and 39% of eligible undergraduate women are members.

Drug and Alcohol Information

Education

On campus Drug and alcohol education/prevention programs offered for: all students, athletes/coaches, faculty, administration; required for: freshmen, social organization members, resident advisers. Authorized group concerned with responsible drinking. College holds an annual alcohol awareness week and drug awareness week.

Identification of Problems

On campus Current students identified as chemically dependent may not remain enrolled. Training program on identifying students with potential substance abuse problems for: resident advisers, Greek officers, faculty, administration. Written procedures for students and staff if substance abuse is suspected.

Support Services

On campus ACOA, support groups, private counseling.

Employee assistance Program for chemically dependent employees not available. Staff working with drug/alcohol-related issues: 1 part-time.

Disciplinary Actions

Alcohol Results of infractions of alcohol regulations (see Comparative Table of Alcohol Regulations) vary by situation but can include chemical dependency assessment, counseling, warning, probation, suspension, expulsion.

Drugs For first-time use or possession: varies by situation. For subsequent use or possession: suspension. For first-time sale: suspension. For subsequent sale: expulsion.

For More Information

Contact: Daryll D. Hersemann, Vice President of Student Affairs, Valparaiso University, Valparaiso, IN 46383. Telephone: 219-464-5411.

VANDERBILT UNIVERSITY

Nashville, Tennessee

General Information

Independent comprehensive coed institution. Founded 1873. Awards B, M, D. Primary accreditation: regional. Metropolitan setting; 330-acre campus. Total enrollment: 9,021. Faculty: 1,154 (607 full-time, 547 part-time). Social organizations: 15 national fraternities, 12 national sororities, 1 local sorority; 37% of eligible undergraduate men and 45% of eligible undergraduate women are members.

Drug and Alcohol Information

Education

On campus Drug and alcohol education/prevention programs offered for: all students, selected offenders; required for: freshmen. Authorized group concerned with responsible drinking (SADD).

Identification of Problems

Admissions College application does not ask about prior substance abuse problems.

On campus Current students identified as chemically dependent may remain enrolled, but treatment is required. Training program on identifying students with potential substance abuse problems for: resident advisers. Written

procedures for students and staff if substance abuse is suspected.

Support Services

On campus AA, NA, Al-Anon, private counseling, student health services, psychological counseling center.

Employee assistance Program for chemically dependent employees available. Staff working with drug/alcohol-related issues: 5 full-time and 9 part-time.

Disciplinary Actions

Alcohol Results of infractions of alcohol regulations (see Comparative Table of Alcohol Regulations) vary by situation but can include chemical dependency assessment, counseling, warning, probation, suspension, expulsion.

Drugs For any use or possession: varies by situation—chemical dependency assessment, counseling. For any sale: varies by situation.

For More Information

Contact: Dr. John Greene, Director of Student Health, Zerfoss Bldg., Medical Center N., Vanderbilt University, Nashville, TN 37232-8710. Telephone: 615-322-2426.

VILLA MARIA COLLEGE

Erie, Pennsylvania

General Information

Independent Roman Catholic 5-year primarily women's college. Founded 1925. Awards A (terminal), B, M. Primary accreditation: regional. City setting; 45-acre campus. Total enrollment: 686. Faculty: 71 (50 full-time, 21 part-time).

Drug and Alcohol Information

Education

On campus Drug and alcohol education/prevention programs offered for: all students, athletes/coaches; required for: freshmen, resident advisers. College holds an annual alcohol awareness week.

Identification of Problems

Admissions College application does not ask about prior substance abuse problems.

On campus Current students identified as chemically dependent may remain enrolled, but treatment is sometimes required. Training program on identifying students with potential substance abuse problems for: resident advisers. Written procedures for students and staff if substance abuse is suspected.

Support Services

On campus ACOA, private counseling.

Employee assistance Program for chemically dependent employees not available.

Disciplinary Actions

Alcohol Results of infractions of alcohol regulations (see Comparative Table of Alcohol Regulations) vary by situation but can include chemical dependency assessment, counseling, warning.

Drugs For any use, possession, or sale: varies by situation.

For More Information

Contact: Dr. Barbara Reagle, Dean of Students, Villa Maria College, 2551 W. 8th St., Erie, PA 16505. Telephone: 814-838-1966 Ext. 252.

VILLANOVA UNIVERSITY

Villanova, Pennsylvania

General Information

Independent Roman Catholic comprehensive coed institution. Founded 1842. Awards A (college transfer), B, M, D. Primary accreditation: regional. Small-town setting; 240-acre campus. Total enrollment: 11,728. Faculty: 920 (550 full-time, 370 part-time). Social organizations: 9 national fraternities, 7 national sororities, 3 local fraternities; 20% of eligible undergraduate men and 20% of eligible undergraduate women are members.

Drug and Alcohol Information

Education

On campus Drug and alcohol education/prevention programs offered for: all students, faculty, administration; required for: freshmen, social organization members, athletes/coaches, resident advisers, student leaders. Authorized group concerned with responsible drinking. College holds an annual alcohol awareness week and drug awareness week.

Identification of Problems

Admissions College application does not ask about prior substance abuse problems.

On campus Current students identified as chemically dependent may remain enrolled, but treatment is required. Training program on identifying students with potential substance abuse problems for: resident advisers, coaches, Greek officers, faculty. Written procedures for students and staff if substance abuse is suspected.

Support Services

On campus ACOA, support groups, private counseling.

Employee assistance Program for chemically dependent employees available. Staff working with drug/alcohol-related issues: 3 full-time and 2 part-time.

Disciplinary Actions

Alcohol Results of infractions of alcohol regulations (see Comparative Table of Alcohol Regulations) vary by situation but can include chemical dependency assessment, counseling, warning, probation, suspension.

Drugs For first-time use: varies by situation—counseling, probation. For subsequent use: chemical dependency assessment, counseling, suspension. For first-time possession: chemical dependency assessment, counseling, suspension. For subsequent possession: expulsion. For any sale: expulsion.

For More Information

Contact: Janice M. Janosik, Director of Alcohol/Drug Programs, Stanford Hall, Villanova University, Villanova, PA 19085. Telephone: 215-645-7407.

VIRGINIA COMMONWEALTH UNIVERSITY

Richmond, Virginia

General Information

State-supported comprehensive coed institution. Founded 1838. Awards A (terminal), B, M, D. Primary accreditation: regional. Metropolitan setting; 64-acre campus. Total enrollment: 20,645. Faculty: 2,186 (1,594 full-time, 592 part-time). Social organizations: 14 national fraternities, 7

Virginia Commonwealth University (continued)

national sororities, 2 local fraternities, 1 local sorority; 4% of eligible undergraduate men and 1% of eligible undergraduate women are members.

Drug and Alcohol Information

Education

On campus Drug and alcohol education/prevention programs offered for: all students, athletes/coaches, faculty, administration. Bacchus chapter: 4 members. Also another group concerned with responsible drinking (REBOS). College holds an annual alcohol awareness week.

Identification of Problems

Admissions College application does not ask about prior substance abuse problems.

On campus Current students identified as chemically dependent may remain enrolled, but treatment is required. No training program on identifying students with potential substance abuse problems. No written procedures for students and staff if substance abuse is suspected.

Support Services

On campus AA, ACOA, support groups (REBOS), University Counseling Services, Center for Psychological Services and Development.

Employee assistance Program for chemically dependent employees available. Staff working with drug/alcohol-related issues: 1 full-time and 3–4 part-time.

Disciplinary Actions

Alcohol Results of infractions of alcohol regulations (see Comparative Table of Alcohol Regulations) include probation, suspension.

Drugs For first-time use or possession: varies by situation—counseling, suspension. For subsequent use or possession: expulsion. For any sale: expulsion.

For More Information

Contact: Kathleen J. Scott, Ph.D., Senior Staff Psychologist, University Counseling Services, Virginia Commonwealth University, P.O. Box 238–MCV Station, Richmond, VA 23298-0238. Telephone: 804-786-3964.

VIRGINIA MILITARY INSTITUTE

Lexington, Virginia

General Information

State-supported 4-year men's college. Founded 1839. Awards B. Primary accreditation: regional. Small-town setting; 133-acre campus. Total enrollment: 1,310. Faculty: 92.

Drug and Alcohol Information

Education

On campus Drug and alcohol education/prevention programs offered for: all students, athletes/coaches; required for: freshmen. Authorized group concerned with responsible drinking.

Identification of Problems

Admissions College application does not ask about prior substance abuse problems.

On campus Current students identified as chemically dependent may remain enrolled, but treatment is required. Training program on identifying students with potential substance abuse problems for: Drug and Alcohol Abuse Committee, peer alcohol and drug educators. No written procedures for students and staff if substance abuse is suspected.

Support Services

On campus AA, private counseling.

Employee assistance Program for chemically dependent employees not available. Staff working with drug/alcohol-related issues: 4 part-time.

Disciplinary Actions

Alcohol Results of infractions of alcohol regulations (see Comparative Table of Alcohol Regulations) include counseling, probation, suspension, expulsion.

Drugs For any use, possession, or sale: expulsion.

For More Information

Contact: LTC William J. Stockwell, Chairman, Alcohol and Drug Abuse Program, Physical Education Department, Virginia Military Institute, Lexington, VA 24450. Telephone: 703-463-6317.

VIRGINIA POLYTECHNIC INSTITUTE AND STATE UNIVERSITY

Blacksburg, Virginia

General Information

State-supported comprehensive coed institution. Founded 1872. Awards A (terminal), B, M, D. Primary accreditation: regional. Small-town setting; 2,600-acre campus. Total enrollment: 22,361. Faculty: 1,607 (1,507 full-time, 100 part-time). Social organizations: 31 national fraternities, 14 national sororities, 2 local fraternities; 13% of eligible undergraduate men and 15% of eligible undergraduate women are members.

Drug and Alcohol Information

Education

On campus Drug and alcohol education/prevention programs offered for: all students, athletes/coaches. Authorized group concerned with responsible drinking. College holds an annual alcohol awareness week and drug awareness week.

Identification of Problems

Admissions College application does not ask about prior substance abuse problems.

On campus Current students identified as chemically dependent may remain enrolled, but treatment is required. Training program on identifying students with potential substance abuse problems for: resident advisers, coaches, administration. Written procedures for students and staff if substance abuse is suspected.

Support Services

On campus AA, Al-Anon, ACOA, support groups.

Employee assistance Program for chemically dependent employees available. Staff working with drug/alcohol-related issues: 3 part-time.

Disciplinary Actions

Alcohol Results of infractions of alcohol regulations (see Comparative Table of Alcohol Regulations) vary by situation but can include chemical dependency assessment, counseling, warning, probation, suspension.

Drugs For first-time use, possession, or sale: suspension. For subsequent use, possession, or sale: expulsion.

For More Information

Contact: Dr. Steven Janosik, Associate Director for Residence Life, Virginia Polytechnic Institute and State University, Blacksburg, VA 24061-0428. Telephone: 703-231-6204.

VIRGINIA STATE UNIVERSITY

Petersburg, Virginia

General Information

State-supported 5-year coed college. Founded 1882. Awards B, M. Primary accreditation: regional. Small-town setting; 210-acre campus. Total enrollment: 3,855. Faculty: 236 (176 full-time, 60 part-time). Social organizations: 4 national fraternities, 4 national sororities, local fraternities, local sororities; 10% of eligible undergraduate men and 10% of eligible undergraduate women are members.

Drug and Alcohol Information

Education

On campus Drug and alcohol education/prevention programs offered for: all students. College holds an annual alcohol awareness week and drug awareness week.

Identification of Problems

Admissions College application does not ask about prior substance abuse problems.

On campus Current students identified as chemically dependent may remain enrolled. No training program on identifying students with potential substance abuse problems.

Support Services

On campus Private counseling.

Employee assistance Program for chemically dependent employees not available. Staff working with drug/alcohol-related issues: 5 part-time.

Disciplinary Actions

Alcohol Results of infractions of alcohol regulations (see Comparative Table of Alcohol Regulations) include suspension.

Drugs For first-time use: chemical dependency assessment, counseling. For subsequent use: varies by situation—counseling. For any possession or sale: expulsion.

For More Information

Contact: Abraham D. Maven, Acting Director of the Counseling Center, Box 6, Virginia State University, Petersburg, VA 23803. Telephone: 804-520-5562.

VIRGINIA WESLEYAN COLLEGE

Norfolk, Virginia

General Information

Independent United Methodist 4-year coed college. Founded 1961. Awards B. Primary accreditation: regional. City setting; 300-acre campus. Total enrollment: 1,261. Faculty: 94 (55 full-time, 39 part-time). Social organizations: 3 national fraternities, 2 national sororities, 1 local fraternity; 10% of eligible undergraduate men and 5% of eligible undergraduate women are members.

Drug and Alcohol Information

Education

On campus Drug and alcohol education/prevention programs offered for: all students; required for: freshmen, resident advisers. College holds an annual alcohol awareness week and drug awareness week.

Identification of Problems

Admissions College application does not ask about prior substance abuse problems.

On campus Current students identified as chemically dependent may remain enrolled, but treatment is required. Training program on identifying students with potential substance abuse problems for: resident advisers, administration. Written procedures for students and staff if substance abuse is suspected.

Support Services

On campus Private counseling.

Employee assistance Program for chemically dependent employees not available. Staff working with drug/alcohol-related issues: 2 part-time.

Disciplinary Actions

Alcohol Results of infractions of alcohol regulations (see Comparative Table of Alcohol Regulations) vary by situation but can include chemical dependency assessment, counseling, warning, probation, attendance at an educational program, community service work.

Drugs For first-time use or possession: counseling, probation. For subsequent use or possession: suspension. For any sale: expulsion.

For More Information

Contact: Joy Houff, RN, Director of Health Services, Virginia Wesleyan College, Wesleyan Dr., Norfolk, VA 23502. Telephone: 804-455-3343.

VITERBO COLLEGE

La Crosse, Wisconsin

General Information

Independent Roman Catholic 5-year coed college. Founded 1890. Awards B, M. Primary accreditation: regional. City setting; 5-acre campus. Total enrollment: 1,067. Faculty: 89 (73 full-time, 16 part-time).

Drug and Alcohol Information

Education

On campus Drug and alcohol education/prevention programs offered for: all students, athletes/coaches. Authorized group concerned with responsible drinking. College holds an annual alcohol awareness week.

Identification of Problems

Admissions College application does not ask about prior substance abuse problems.

On campus No training program on identifying students with potential substance abuse problems. No written procedures for students and staff if substance abuse is suspected.

Viterbo College (continued)

Support Services

On campus Private counseling.

Employee assistance Program for chemically dependent employees not available.

Disciplinary Actions

Alcohol Results of infractions of alcohol regulations (see Comparative Table of Alcohol Regulations) include chemical dependency assessment, counseling, warning, suspension.

Drugs For first-time use or possession: fines, probation. For subsequent use or possession: expulsion. For any sale: expulsion.

Additional Information from the College

AA and ACOA groups are being established on campus.

For More Information

Contact: Jane Van Aelstyn, Project Director, Viterbo College, 815 S. Ninth St., La Crosse, WI 54601. Telephone: 608-784-0040.

WAGNER COLLEGE

Staten Island, New York

General Information

Independent 5-year coed college. Founded 1883. Awards B, M. Primary accreditation: regional. Metropolitan setting; 86-acre campus. Total enrollment: 1,767. Faculty: 147 (66 full-time, 81 part-time). Social organizations: 1 national fraternity, 2 national sororities, 7 local fraternities, 2 local sororities; 20% of eligible undergraduate men and 20% of eligible undergraduate women are members.

Drug and Alcohol Information

Education

On campus Drug and alcohol education/prevention programs offered for: all students, athletes/coaches; required for: resident advisers. Bacchus chapter. College holds an annual alcohol awareness week and drug awareness week.

Identification of Problems

Admissions College application does not ask about prior substance abuse problems.

On campus Current students identified as chemically dependent may remain enrolled, but treatment is required. Training program on identifying students with potential substance abuse problems for: resident advisers. Written procedures for students and staff if substance abuse is suspected.

Support Services

On campus NA, private counseling.

Employee assistance Program for chemically dependent employees not available. Staff working with drug/alcohol-related issues: 5 full-time.

Disciplinary Actions

Alcohol Results of infractions of alcohol regulations (see Comparative Table of Alcohol Regulations) vary by situation but can include counseling, warning, probation, suspension, expulsion.

Drugs For first-time use or possession: probation. For subsequent use or possession: suspension. For any sale: expulsion.

For More Information

Contact: Joann Mangarelli, Assistant Dean–Students, Wagner College, 631 Howard Ave., Staten Island, NY 10301. Telephone: 718-390-3421.

WAKE FOREST UNIVERSITY

Winston-Salem, North Carolina

General Information

Independent comprehensive coed institution, affiliated with Baptist Church. Founded 1834. Awards B, M, D. Primary accreditation: regional. City setting; 470-acre campus. Total enrollment: 5,337. Faculty: 306 (244 full-time, 62 part-time). Social organizations: 13 national fraternities, 1 national sorority, 7 local sororities; 40% of eligible undergraduate men and 45% of eligible undergraduate women are members.

Drug and Alcohol Information

Education

On campus Drug and alcohol education/prevention programs offered for: all students, athletes/coaches; required for: freshmen. Authorized group concerned with responsible drinking. College holds an annual alcohol awareness week and drug awareness week.

Identification of Problems

Admissions College application does not ask about prior substance abuse problems.

On campus Current students identified as chemically dependent may remain enrolled, but treatment is required. Training program on identifying students with potential substance abuse problems for: resident advisers, coaches, Greek officers, student health staff. No written procedures for students and staff if substance abuse is suspected.

Support Services

On campus NA, ACOA, private counseling.

Employee assistance Program for chemically dependent employees not available. Staff working with drug/alcohol-related issues: 1 full-time and 2 part-time.

Disciplinary Actions

Alcohol Results of infractions of alcohol regulations (see Comparative Table of Alcohol Regulations) include chemical dependency assessment, counseling, warning, probation.

Drugs For first-time use or possession: varies by situation. For first-time sale: warning, probation. For subsequent use, possession, or sale: varies by situation.

For More Information

Contact: Cashin Hunt, Health Educator, Wake Forest University, P.O. Box 7386, Winston–Salem, NC 27109. Telephone: 919-761-5937.

WALLA WALLA COLLEGE

College Place, Washington

General Information

Independent Seventh-day Adventist 5-year coed college. Founded 1892. Awards A (college transfer and terminal), B, M. Primary accreditation: regional. Small-town setting; 77-acre campus. Total enrollment: 1,515. Faculty: 168 (119 full-time, 49 part-time).

Drug and Alcohol Information

Education

On campus Drug and alcohol education/prevention programs offered for: all students; required for: resident advisers. Authorized group concerned with responsible drinking. College holds an annual alcohol awareness week and drug awareness week.

Identification of Problems

Admissions College application question about prior substance abuse problems is used as part of health assessment.

On campus Current students identified as chemically dependent may remain enrolled, but treatment is required. Training program on identifying students with potential substance abuse problems for: resident advisers, student administrative personnel. Written procedures for students and staff if substance abuse is suspected.

Support Services

On campus AA, ACOA, support groups (recovery support), private counseling.

Employee assistance Program for chemically dependent employees available. Staff working with drug/alcohol-related issues: 1 full-time.

Disciplinary Actions

Alcohol Results of infractions of alcohol regulations (see Comparative Table of Alcohol Regulations) include chemical dependency assessment, counseling, suspension.

Drugs For first-time use or possession: chemical dependency assessment, counseling, suspension. For subsequent use or possession: varies by situation—chemical dependency assessment, counseling. For any sale: expulsion.

Additional Information from the College

Although only an estimated 40 percent of the students use alcohol and other drugs, the College is very concerned about high dependency rates in like populations, so a very proactive student assistance program has been initiated.

For More Information

Contact: Wendy Hernandez, RN, Director, Student Health Services, Walla Walla College, 204 S. College, College Place, WA 99324. Telephone: 509-527-2425.

WALSH COLLEGE

Canton, Ohio

General Information

Independent Roman Catholic 5-year coed college. Founded 1958. Awards A (college transfer and terminal), B, M. Primary accreditation: regional. City setting; 58-acre campus. Total enrollment: 1,381. Faculty: 104 (43 full-time, 61 part-time).

Drug and Alcohol Information

Education

On campus Drug and alcohol education/prevention programs offered for: all students, faculty, administration; required for: freshmen, athletes/coaches, resident advisers. Authorized group concerned with responsible drinking. College holds an annual alcohol awareness week and drug awareness week.

Identification of Problems

Admissions College application does not ask about prior substance abuse problems.

On campus Current students identified as chemically dependent may remain enrolled, but treatment is required. Training program on identifying students with potential substance abuse problems for: resident advisers, coaches, faculty, administration, student leaders. Written procedures for students and staff if substance abuse is suspected.

Support Services

On campus Private counseling.

Off campus AA, NA, Al-Anon, ACOA, support groups, private counseling.

Employee assistance Program for chemically dependent employees not available. Staff working with drug/alcohol-related issues: 5 part-time.

Disciplinary Actions

Alcohol Results of infractions of alcohol regulations (see Comparative Table of Alcohol Regulations) vary by situation but can include chemical dependency assessment, counseling, warning, probation, suspension, expulsion.

Drugs For any use or possession: varies by situation. For any sale: expulsion.

Additional Information from the College

A revised policy will be completed by February 1989. A random testing program is in effect for athletes. In all cases, Walsh College utilizes counseling to help the student and his/her family cope with the issue.

For More Information

Contact: Richard W. Waite, Dean of Students, Walsh College, 2020 Easton St., NW, Canton, OH 44720. Telephone: 216-499-7090 Ext. 301.

WARNER PACIFIC COLLEGE

Portland, Oregon

General Information

Independent 5-year coed college, affiliated with Church of God. Founded 1937. Awards A (college transfer and terminal), B, M. Primary accreditation: regional. Metropolitan setting; 15-acre campus. Total enrollment: 412. Faculty: 46 (29 full-time, 17 part-time).

Drug and Alcohol Information

Education

On campus Drug and alcohol education/prevention programs not offered.

Identification of Problems

Admissions College application does not ask about prior substance abuse problems.

On campus Current students identified as chemically dependent may remain enrolled, but treatment is required. Training program on identifying students with potential substance abuse problems for: resident advisers, administration. Written procedures for students and staff if substance abuse is suspected.

Support Services

On campus Support groups, private counseling.

Employee assistance Program for chemically dependent employees not available. Staff working with drug/alcohol-related issues: 2–5 part-time.

Warner Pacific College (continued)

Disciplinary Actions

Alcohol Results of infractions of alcohol regulations (see Comparative Table of Alcohol Regulations) vary by situation but include counseling. Comments: The counseling approach is followed by appropriate action based on student's attitude and plans.

Drugs For first-time use: varies by situation. For first-time possession: counseling, warning, probation. For subsequent use: probation, suspension. For subsequent possession or sale: probation, suspension, expulsion.

For More Information

Contact: Arthur M. Kelly, Vice President–Student Life, Warner Pacific College, 2219 SE 68th Ave., Portland, OR 97215. Telephone: 503-775-4364.

WARNER SOUTHERN COLLEGE

Lake Wales, Florida

General Information

Independent 4-year coed college, affiliated with Church of God. Founded 1968. Awards A (college transfer and terminal), B. Primary accreditation: regional. Rural setting; 350-acre campus. Total enrollment: 364. Faculty: 24 (17 full-time, 7 part-time).

Drug and Alcohol Information

Education

On campus Drug and alcohol education/prevention programs offered for: all students, athletes/coaches, faculty, administration.

Identification of Problems

Admissions College application question about prior substance abuse problems is used for counseling and referral, if student is admitted; in the admissions decision.

On campus Current students identified as chemically dependent may remain enrolled, but treatment is required. Training program on identifying students with potential substance abuse problems for: resident advisers, coaches. No written procedures for students and staff if substance abuse is suspected.

Support Services

On campus Private counseling.

Employee assistance Program for chemically dependent employees not available.

Disciplinary Actions

Alcohol Results of infractions of alcohol regulations (see Comparative Table of Alcohol Regulations) vary by situation but can include counseling, warning, probation, suspension, expulsion.

Drugs For first-time use, possession, or sale: counseling, probation. For subsequent use, possession, or sale: expulsion.

Additional Information from the College

Since Warner Southern College is a Christian college, in the Holiness tradition, drugs and alcohol are not acceptable in the life-style of its students.

For More Information

Contact: Thomas Walton, Dean of Students, Warner Southern College, 5301 US Hwy. 27 South, Lake Wales, FL 33853. Telephone: 813-638-2535.

WARREN WILSON COLLEGE

Swannanoa, North Carolina

General Information

Independent 5-year coed college, affiliated with Presbyterian Church (U.S.A.). Founded 1894. Awards B, M. Primary accreditation: regional. Rural setting; 1,070-acre campus. Total enrollment: 523. Faculty: 68 (29 full-time, 39 part-time).

Drug and Alcohol Information

Education

On campus Drug and alcohol education/prevention programs offered for: anyone who wishes to attend; required for: students under disciplinary action. College has held an annual alcohol awareness week.

Identification of Problems

Admissions College application does not ask about prior substance abuse problems.

On campus Current students identified as chemically dependent may remain enrolled, but treatment is required. Training program on identifying students with potential substance abuse problems for: resident advisers.

Support Services

On campus ACOA.

Employee assistance Program for chemically dependent employees available. Staff working with drug/alcohol-related issues: 5 part-time.

Disciplinary Actions

Alcohol Results of infractions of alcohol regulations (see Comparative Table of Alcohol Regulations) vary by situation but can include chemical dependency assessment, counseling, warning, probation, suspension, expulsion.

Drugs For any use, possession, or sale: expulsion.

For More Information

Contact: Scot A. Wilson, Student Affairs Assistant, Warren Wilson College, 701 Warren Wilson Road, Swannanoa, NC 28778. Telephone: 704-298-3325 Ext. 277.

WASHINGTON AND JEFFERSON COLLEGE

Washington, Pennsylvania

General Information

Independent 4-year coed college. Founded 1781. Awards B. Primary accreditation: regional. Small-town setting; 35-acre campus. Total enrollment: 1,192. Faculty: 96 (83 full-time, 13 part-time). Social organizations: 10 national fraternities, 4 national sororities; 53% of eligible undergraduate men and 65% of eligible undergraduate women are members.

Drug and Alcohol Information

Education

On campus Drug and alcohol education/prevention programs offered for: all students, athletes/coaches. College holds an annual alcohol awareness week.

Identification of Problems

Admissions College application does not ask about prior substance abuse problems.

On campus Current students identified as chemically dependent may remain enrolled, but treatment is required. No training program on identifying students with potential substance abuse problems. Written procedures for students and staff if substance abuse is suspected.

Support Services

On campus Support groups (peer counselors), private counseling.

Employee assistance Program for chemically dependent employees not available. Staff working with drug/alcohol-related issues: 3 part-time.

Disciplinary Actions

Alcohol Results of infractions of alcohol regulations (see Comparative Table of Alcohol Regulations) vary by situation but can include chemical dependency assessment, counseling, warning, suspension.

Drugs For first-time use or possession: varies by situation. For subsequent use or possession: expulsion. For any sale: expulsion.

For More Information

Contact: Mary Jane Jones, Assistant Dean of Students, Washington and Jefferson College, Washington, PA 15301. Telephone: 412-223-6008.

WASHINGTON AND LEE UNIVERSITY

Lexington, Virginia

General Information

Independent 5-year coed college. Founded 1749. Awards B, D. Primary accreditation: regional. Small-town setting; 322-acre campus. Total enrollment: 1,990. Faculty: 161. Social organizations: 16 national fraternities; 80% of eligible undergraduate men are members.

Drug and Alcohol Information

Education

On campus Drug and alcohol education/prevention programs offered for: all students, athletes/coaches; required for: freshmen. Authorized group concerned with responsible drinking. College holds an annual alcohol awareness week and drug awareness week.

Identification of Problems

Admissions College application does not ask about prior substance abuse problems.

On campus Whether current students identified as chemically dependent may remain enrolled depends on circumstances. For students who remain enrolled treatment is required. Training program on identifying students with potential substance abuse problems for: resident advisers, peer counselors. No written procedures for students and staff if substance abuse is suspected.

Support Services

On campus Support groups, private counseling.

Off campus AA, Na.

Employee assistance Program for chemically dependent employees not available. Staff working with drug/alcohol-related issues: 2 part-time.

Disciplinary Actions

Alcohol Results of infractions of alcohol regulations (see Comparative Table of Alcohol Regulations) vary by situation.

Drugs For any use, possession, or sale: varies by situation.

For More Information

Contact: Dr. Anne C. Schroer-Lamont, Associate Dean of Students, Washington and Lee University, Lexington, VA 24450. Telephone: 703-463-8750.

WASHINGTON COLLEGE

Chestertown, Maryland

General Information

Independent 5-year coed college. Founded 1782. Awards B, M. Primary accreditation: regional. Small-town setting; 104-acre campus. Total enrollment: 988. Faculty: 81 (63 full-time, 18 part-time). Social organizations: 3 national fraternities, 3 national sororities, 1 local fraternity; 25% of eligible undergraduate men and 25% of eligible undergraduate women are members.

Drug and Alcohol Information

Education

On campus Drug and alcohol education/prevention programs not offered. Authorized group concerned with responsible drinking. College holds an annual alcohol awareness week.

Identification of Problems

Admissions College application does not ask about prior substance abuse problems.

On campus Current students identified as chemically dependent may remain enrolled. No training program on identifying students with potential substance abuse problems. No written procedures for students and staff if substance abuse is suspected.

Support Services

On campus ACOA.

Employee assistance Program for chemically dependent employees not available. Staff working with drug/alcohol-related issues: 1 part-time.

Disciplinary Actions

Alcohol Results of infractions of alcohol regulations (see Comparative Table of Alcohol Regulations) include counseling, warning, probation.

Drugs For first-time use: varies by situation—counseling, warning. For subsequent use: varies by situation. For any possession or sale: varies by situation. Comments: Policy currently being developed.

For More Information

Contact: Maureen Kelley-McIntire, Dean of Students, Washington College, Chestertown, MD 21620. Telephone: 301-778-0160.

WASHINGTON STATE UNIVERSITY
Pullman, Washington

General Information
State-supported comprehensive coed institution. Founded 1892. Awards B, M, D. Primary accreditation: regional. Rural setting; 620-acre campus. Total enrollment: 16,352. Faculty: 881 (808 full-time, 73 part-time). Social organizations: 25 national fraternities, 14 national sororities; 20% of eligible undergraduate men and 20% of eligible undergraduate women are members.

Drug and Alcohol Information
Education
On campus Drug and alcohol education/prevention programs offered for: all students; required for: athletes/coaches. Bacchus chapter: 30 members. College holds an annual alcohol awareness week.

Identification of Problems
Admissions College application does not ask about prior substance abuse problems.

On campus Current students identified as chemically dependent may remain enrolled, but treatment is required. Training program on identifying students with potential substance abuse problems for: resident advisers, coaches. Written procedures for students and staff if substance abuse is suspected.

Support Services
On campus AA, ACOA, support groups, private counseling.

Employee assistance Program for chemically dependent employees available. Staff working with drug/alcohol-related issues: 1 full-time and 4 part-time.

Disciplinary Actions
Alcohol Results of infractions of alcohol regulations (see Comparative Table of Alcohol Regulations) vary by situation but can include chemical dependency assessment, counseling, warning, probation, suspension, expulsion. Comments: Discipline boards determine sanctions.

Drugs For first-time use: chemical dependency assessment, counseling, warning. For first-time possession: counseling, warning, probation. For first-time sale: varies by situation. For subsequent use: suspension, expulsion. For subsequent possession or sale: expulsion.

Additional Information from the College
The University has made substantial progress in the last three years in the development and implementation of its alcohol policies. The impact on behavior has been significant.

For More Information
Contact: John Miller, Substance Abuse Counselor, AD Annex, Rm. 300, Washington State University, Pullman, WA 99163-4531. Telephone: 509-335-4511.

WAYNESBURG COLLEGE
Waynesburg, Pennsylvania

General Information
Independent 5-year coed college, affiliated with Presbyterian Church (U.S.A.). Founded 1849. Awards A (college transfer and terminal), B, M. Primary accreditation: regional. Small-town setting; 30-acre campus. Total enrollment: 1,031. Faculty: 80 (52 full-time, 28 part-time). Social organizations: 4 national fraternities, 3 national sororities; 40% of eligible undergraduate men and 35% of eligible undergraduate women are members.

Drug and Alcohol Information
Education
On campus Drug and alcohol education/prevention programs offered for: all students; required for: athletes/coaches, resident advisers. College holds an annual alcohol awareness week.

Identification of Problems
Admissions College application does not ask about prior substance abuse problems.

On campus Current students identified as chemically dependent may remain enrolled, but treatment is required. Training program on identifying students with potential substance abuse problems for: resident advisers, coaches. Written procedures for students and staff if substance abuse is suspected.

Support Services
On campus Private counseling, group counseling after assessment.

Employee assistance Program for chemically dependent employees not available. Staff working with drug/alcohol-related issues: 1 part-time.

Disciplinary Actions
Alcohol Results of infractions of alcohol regulations (see Comparative Table of Alcohol Regulations) vary by situation but can include chemical dependency assessment, probation, suspension, fine.

Drugs For first-time use or possession: suspension. For subsequent use or possession: expulsion. For any sale: expulsion.

For More Information
Contact: Julie Rea, Coordinator of Alcohol and Drug Program, Waynesburg College, Waynesburg, PA 15370. Telephone: 412-627-8191.

WAYNE STATE COLLEGE
Wayne, Nebraska

General Information
State-supported 5-year coed college. Part of Nebraska State College System. Founded 1910. Awards B, M. Primary accreditation: regional. Small-town setting; 127-acre campus. Total enrollment: 2,873. Faculty: 151 (93 full-time, 58 part-time). Social organizations: 2 national fraternities, 2 national sororities; 5% of eligible undergraduate men and 5% of eligible undergraduate women are members.

Drug and Alcohol Information
Education
On campus Drug and alcohol education/prevention programs offered for: all students, athletes/coaches. Authorized group concerned with responsible drinking. College holds an annual alcohol awareness week.

Identification of Problems
Admissions College application does not ask about prior substance abuse problems.

On campus Current students identified as chemically dependent may remain enrolled, but treatment is required. Training program on identifying students with potential substance abuse problems for: resident advisers, coaches. Written procedures for students and staff if substance abuse is suspected.

Support Services

On campus AA, private counseling.

Employee assistance Program for chemically dependent employees not available. Staff working with drug/alcohol-related issues: 3 part-time.

Disciplinary Actions

Alcohol Results of infractions of alcohol regulations (see Comparative Table of Alcohol Regulations) vary by situation but can include chemical dependency assessment, counseling, warning, probation, suspension, expulsion.

Drugs For first-time use or possession: chemical dependency assessment, probation. For subsequent use or possession: chemical dependency assessment, counseling, suspension. For first-time sale: suspension. For subsequent sale: expulsion.

For More Information

Contact: Curt Frye, Interim Dean of Students, Wayne State College, Wayne, NE 68787. Telephone: 402-375-2200.

WAYNE STATE UNIVERSITY

Detroit, Michigan

General Information

State-supported comprehensive coed institution. Founded 1868. Awards B, M, D. Primary accreditation: regional. Metropolitan setting; 184-acre campus. Total enrollment: 30,751. Faculty: 1,980 (1,400 full-time, 580 part-time). Social organizations: 15 national fraternities, 11 national sororities, 1 local fraternity.

Drug and Alcohol Information

Education

On campus Drug and alcohol education/prevention programs offered for: all students. Authorized group concerned with responsible drinking. College holds an annual alcohol awareness week and drug awareness week.

Identification of Problems

Admissions College application does not ask about prior substance abuse problems.

On campus Current students identified as chemically dependent may remain enrolled. No training program on identifying students with potential substance abuse problems. No written procedures for students and staff if substance abuse is suspected.

Support Services

On campus AA, NA.

Employee assistance Program for chemically dependent employees not available.

Disciplinary Actions

Alcohol Results of infractions of alcohol regulations (see Comparative Table of Alcohol Regulations) vary by situation.

Drugs For any use, possession, or sale: varies by situation.

Additional Information from the College

The University is completely commuter, does not have a health center, and refers most serious problems to community agencies. Most students work or have a family or both, and the average age is 28.

For More Information

Contact: David Johnson, Director, Student Center and Program Activities, 341 Student Center, Wayne State University, Detroit, MI 48202. Telephone: 313-577-3482.

WEBER STATE COLLEGE

Ogden, Utah

General Information

State-supported 5-year coed college. Part of Utah System of Higher Education. Founded 1889. Awards A (college transfer and terminal), B, M. Primary accreditation: regional. City setting; 375-acre campus. Total enrollment: 12,146. Faculty: 417 (395 full-time, 22 part-time). Social organizations: 2 national fraternities, 1 national sorority, 1 local fraternity, 2 local sororities; 5% of eligible undergraduate men and 5% of eligible undergraduate women are members.

Drug and Alcohol Information

Education

On campus Drug and alcohol education/prevention programs offered for: all students, athletes/coaches, faculty, administration. Authorized group concerned with responsible drinking. College holds an annual drug awareness week.

Identification of Problems

Admissions College application does not ask about prior substance abuse problems.

On campus Current students identified as chemically dependent may remain enrolled. Training program on identifying students with potential substance abuse problems for: resident advisers, coaches, Greek officers, faculty, administration, peer counselors. Written procedures for students and staff if substance abuse is suspected.

Support Services

On campus AA, NA, ACOA, private counseling.

Employee assistance Program for chemically dependent employees available. Staff working with drug/alcohol-related issues: 2 full-time and 6 part-time.

Disciplinary Actions

Alcohol Results of infractions of alcohol regulations (see Comparative Table of Alcohol Regulations) vary by situation but can include chemical dependency assessment, counseling, warning, probation, suspension, expulsion.

Drugs For any use or possession: varies by situation. For first-time sale: counseling, expulsion. For subsequent sale: expulsion.

For More Information

Contact: Grant Protzman, Planning and Development Officer, Weber State College, 3750 Harrison Blvd., Ogden, UT 84408. Telephone: 801-626-6886.

WEBSTER UNIVERSITY

St. Louis, Missouri

General Information

Independent 5-year coed college. Founded 1915. Awards B,

Webster University (continued)

M, D. Primary accreditation: regional. Metropolitan setting; 23-acre campus. Total enrollment: 9,049. Faculty: 353 (103 full-time, 250 part-time).

Drug and Alcohol Information

Education

On campus Drug and alcohol education/prevention programs offered for: all students, athletes/coaches, faculty, administration. Authorized group concerned with responsible drinking. College holds an annual alcohol awareness week and drug awareness week.

Identification of Problems

Admissions College application does not ask about prior substance abuse problems.

On campus Current students identified as chemically dependent may remain enrolled. Training program on identifying students with potential substance abuse problems for: resident advisers. Written procedures for students and staff if substance abuse is suspected.

Support Services

On campus AA, private counseling.

Employee assistance Program for chemically dependent employees not available. Staff working with drug/alcohol-related issues: 2 full-time and 2 part-time.

Disciplinary Actions

Alcohol Results of infractions of alcohol regulations (see Comparative Table of Alcohol Regulations) include counseling, warning.

Drugs For first-time use, possession, or sale: varies by situation—warning. For subsequent use, possession, or sale: varies by situation—counseling.

For More Information

Contact: Patrick Stack, Director of Counseling, Webster University, 470 E. Lockwood Ave., St. Louis, MO 63119. Telephone: 314-968-6922.

WELLESLEY COLLEGE

Wellesley, Massachusetts

General Information

Independent 4-year women's college. Founded 1870. Awards B. Primary accreditation: regional. Small-town setting; 500-acre campus. Total enrollment: 2,239. Faculty: 330 (227 full-time, 103 part-time).

Drug and Alcohol Information

Education

On campus Drug and alcohol education/prevention programs offered for: all students.

Identification of Problems

Admissions College application does not ask about prior substance abuse problems.

On campus Current students identified as chemically dependent may remain enrolled, but treatment may be required. Training program on identifying students with potential substance abuse problems for: resident advisers. Written procedures are being developed for students and staff if substance abuse is suspected.

Support Services

On campus Al-Anon, support groups, private counseling.

Employee assistance Program for chemically dependent employees not available. Staff working with drug/alcohol-related issues: many part-time.

Disciplinary Actions

Alcohol Results of infractions of alcohol regulations (see Comparative Table of Alcohol Regulations) vary by situation but can include warning, probation.

Drugs For any use, possession, or sale: varies by situation.

For More Information

Contact: Nancy Gleason, Senior Social Worker, Stone Center, Wellesley College, Wellesley, MA 02181. Telephone: 617-235-0320 Ext. 2839.

WELLS COLLEGE

Aurora, New York

General Information

Independent 4-year women's college. Founded 1868. Awards B. Primary accreditation: regional. Rural setting; 360-acre campus. Total enrollment: 450. Faculty: 61 (44 full-time, 17 part-time).

Drug and Alcohol Information

Education

On campus Drug and alcohol education/prevention programs offered for: all students. Authorized group concerned with responsible drinking. College holds an annual alcohol awareness week.

Identification of Problems

Admissions College application does not ask about prior substance abuse problems.

On campus Current students identified as chemically dependent may remain enrolled, but treatment is required. Training program on identifying students with potential substance abuse problems for: resident advisers, administration, security and health services personnel. Written procedures for students and staff if substance abuse is suspected.

Support Services

On campus AA, ACOA, support groups, private counseling.

Employee assistance Program for chemically dependent employees available.

Disciplinary Actions

Alcohol Results of infractions of alcohol regulations (see Comparative Table of Alcohol Regulations) vary by situation. Comments: Penalty is determined by a judicial board.

Drugs For any use or possession: varies by situation. For any sale: expulsion.

For More Information

Contact: Ruth B. Sullivan, Dean of Students, Wells College, Aurora, NY 13026. Telephone: 315-364-3311.

WENTWORTH INSTITUTE OF TECHNOLOGY

Boston, Massachusetts

General Information

Independent 4-year coed college. Founded 1904. Awards A (college transfer and terminal), B. Primary accreditation: regional. Metropolitan setting; 35-acre campus. Total enrollment: 3,290. Faculty: 154 (124 full-time, 30 part-time).

Drug and Alcohol Information

Education

On campus Drug and alcohol education/prevention programs offered for: all students. College holds an annual alcohol awareness week and drug awareness week.

Identification of Problems

Admissions College application does not ask about prior substance abuse problems.

On campus Current students identified as chemically dependent may remain enrolled, but treatment is required. Training program on identifying students with potential substance abuse problems for: resident advisers. Written procedures for students and staff if substance abuse is suspected are under review.

Support Services

On campus Private counseling.

Employee assistance Program for chemically dependent employees not available.

Disciplinary Actions

Alcohol Results of infractions of alcohol regulations (see Comparative Table of Alcohol Regulations) include chemical dependency assessment, counseling, warning, probation, suspension.

Drugs For any use or possession: varies by situation. For first-time sale: community service, suspension, expulsion. For subsequent sale: suspension, expulsion.

For More Information

Contact: Russell Watjen, Ph.D., Vice President for Student Affairs, Wentworth Institute of Technology, 550 Huntington Ave., Boston, MA 02115. Telephone: 617-442-9010 Ext. 269.

WESLEYAN COLLEGE

Macon, Georgia

General Information

Independent Methodist 4-year women's college. Founded 1836. Awards B. Primary accreditation: regional. City setting; 240-acre campus. Total enrollment: 544. Faculty: 65 (40 full-time, 25 part-time).

Drug and Alcohol Information

Education

On campus Drug and alcohol education/prevention programs offered for: all students. Authorized group concerned with responsible drinking. College holds an annual alcohol awareness week.

Identification of Problems

Admissions College application does not ask about prior substance abuse problems.

On campus Current students identified as chemically dependent may remain enrolled, but treatment is required. Training program on identifying students with potential substance abuse problems for: resident advisers. No written procedures for students and staff if substance abuse is suspected.

Support Services

On campus Private counseling.

Employee assistance Program for chemically dependent employees not available. Staff working with drug/alcohol-related issues: 2 part-time.

Disciplinary Actions

Alcohol Results of infractions of alcohol regulations (see Comparative Table of Alcohol Regulations) include counseling, warning, probation, suspension. Comments: Students may be required to conduct alcohol education presentations on campus.

Drugs For first-time use: varies by situation—warning. For subsequent use—varies by situation. For first-time possession: varies by situation—counseling. For subsequent possession: varies by situation. For any sale: varies by situation—suspension.

For More Information

Contact: Lizann Provan, Director of Wellness, Wesleyan College, 4760 Forsyth Rd., Macon, GA 31297. Telephone: 912-474-7057 Ext. 165.

WESLEYAN UNIVERSITY

Middletown, Connecticut

General Information

Independent comprehensive coed institution. Founded 1831. Awards B, M, D. Primary accreditation: regional. Small-town setting; 130-acre campus. Total enrollment: 2,938. Faculty: 346 (285 full-time, 61 part-time). Social organizations: 7 national fraternities, 2 national sororities, 2 local fraternities, 6 eating clubs; 10% of eligible undergraduate men and 2% of eligible undergraduate women are members.

Drug and Alcohol Information

Education

On campus Drug and alcohol education/prevention programs offered for: all students, faculty, administration. Authorized group concerned with responsible drinking. College holds an annual alcohol awareness week and drug awareness week.

Identification of Problems

Admissions College application does not ask about prior substance abuse problems.

On campus Current students identified as chemically dependent may remain enrolled. Training program on identifying students with potential substance abuse problems for: resident advisers, administration. No written procedures for students and staff if substance abuse is suspected.

Support Services

On campus AA, Al-Anon, support groups, private counseling.

Employee assistance Program for chemically dependent employees not available. Staff working with drug/alcohol-related issues: 1 full-time and 12 part-time.

Wesleyan University (continued)

Disciplinary Actions

Alcohol Results of infractions of alcohol regulations (see Comparative Table of Alcohol Regulations) vary by situation as determined by a student judiciary board.

Drugs For any use, possession, or sale: varies by situation.

For More Information

Contact: Daniel S. Burt, Assistant Dean, Wesleyan University, Middletown, CT 06457. Telephone: 203-347-9411 Ext. 3055.

WESLEY COLLEGE

Dover, Delaware

General Information

Independent United Methodist 4-year coed college. Founded 1873. Awards A (college transfer and terminal), B. Primary accreditation: regional. Small-town setting; 20-acre campus. Total enrollment: 1,200. Faculty: 98 (50 full-time, 48 part-time). Social organizations: 3 national fraternities, 3 national sororities, 3 local fraternities; 65% of eligible undergraduate men and 65% of eligible undergraduate women are members.

Drug and Alcohol Information

Education

On campus Drug and alcohol education/prevention programs offered for: all students; required for: freshmen. College holds an annual alcohol awareness week.

Identification of Problems

Admissions College application does not ask about prior substance abuse problems.

On campus Current students identified as chemically dependent may remain enrolled, but treatment is required. Training program on identifying students with potential substance abuse problems for: resident advisers. Written procedures for students and staff if substance abuse is suspected.

Support Services

On campus AA, Al-Anon, ACOA, support groups, private counseling.

Off campus Narcotics Anonymous.

Employee assistance Program for chemically dependent employees not available. Staff working with drug/alcohol-related issues: 9 part-time.

Disciplinary Actions

Alcohol Results of infractions of alcohol regulations (see Comparative Table of Alcohol Regulations) vary by situation but can include counseling, warning, probation, suspension, expulsion.

Drugs For first-time use: varies by situation—counseling, suspension. For subsequent use: varies by situation—probation, suspension, expulsion. For first-time possession: suspension. For subsequent possession: varies by situation. For any sale: expulsion.

For More Information

Contact: Alice R. Rasmussen, Dean of Students, Wesley College, Dover, DE 19901. Telephone: 302-736-2435.

WEST CHESTER UNIVERSITY OF PENNSYLVANIA

West Chester, Pennsylvania

General Information

State-supported 5-year coed college. Part of State System of Higher Education. Founded 1871. Awards A (college transfer and terminal), B, M. Primary accreditation: regional. Small-town setting; 547-acre campus. Total enrollment: 11,475. Faculty: 549 (483 full-time, 66 part-time). Social organizations: 10 national fraternities, 8 national sororities; 5% of eligible undergraduate men and 5% of eligible undergraduate women are members.

Drug and Alcohol Information

Education

On campus Drug and alcohol education/prevention programs offered for: all students; required for: freshmen. Bacchus chapter: 10 members. College holds an annual alcohol awareness week.

Identification of Problems

Admissions College application does not ask about prior substance abuse problems.

On campus Current students identified as chemically dependent may remain enrolled. Training program on identifying students with potential substance abuse problems for: resident advisers, Greek officers, administration. No written procedures for students and staff if substance abuse is suspected.

Support Services

On campus AA, support groups, private counseling.

Employee assistance Program for chemically dependent employees not available. Staff working with drug/alcohol-related issues: 1 full-time.

Disciplinary Actions

Alcohol Results of infractions of alcohol regulations (see Comparative Table of Alcohol Regulations) vary by situation but can include counseling, warning, probation, suspension, expulsion.

Drugs For first-time use, possession, or sale: warning, probation. For subsequent use, possession, or sale: varies by situation—counseling, probation, suspension.

For More Information

Contact: Jacqueline S. Hodes, Director of Alcohol/Drug Education, West Chester University of Pennsylvania, 240 Sykes Union, West Chester, PA 19383. Telephone: 215-436-3305.

WESTERN CAROLINA UNIVERSITY

Cullowhee, North Carolina

General Information

State-supported 5-year coed college. Part of University of North Carolina System. Founded 1889. Awards B, M. Primary accreditation: regional. Rural setting; 300-acre campus. Total enrollment: 6,055. Faculty: 379 (309 full-time, 70 part-time). Social organizations: 15 national fraternities, 8 national sororities; 24% of eligible undergraduate men and 11% of eligible undergraduate women are members.

Drug and Alcohol Information

Education

On campus Drug and alcohol education/prevention programs offered for: all students, faculty, administration; required for: freshmen, athletes/coaches, resident advisers. Bacchus chapter: 15 members. College holds an annual alcohol awareness week and drug awareness week.

Identification of Problems

Admissions College application question about prior substance abuse problems is used for counseling and referral, if student is admitted; in the admissions decision.

On campus Current students identified as chemically dependent may remain enrolled, but treatment is required. Training program on identifying students with potential substance abuse problems for: resident advisers, coaches, Greek officers, administration. Written procedures for students and staff if substance abuse is suspected.

Support Services

On campus AA, NA, Al-Anon, private counseling.

Employee assistance Program for chemically dependent employees available. Staff working with drug/alcohol-related issues: 10–12 part-time.

Disciplinary Actions

Alcohol Results of infractions of alcohol regulations (see Comparative Table of Alcohol Regulations) vary by situation but can include chemical dependency assessment, counseling, warning, probation, suspension.

Drugs For first-time use and possession: varies by situation. For subsequent use or possession: varies by situation—expulsion. For any sale: expulsion. Comments: The action taken depends on the drug involved.

For More Information

Contact: Randy Rice, Director of Housing, Dodson Annex, Western Carolina University, Cullowhee, NC 28723. Telephone: 704-227-7303.

WESTERN CONNECTICUT STATE UNIVERSITY

Danbury, Connecticut

General Information

State-supported 5-year coed college. Part of Connecticut State University System. Founded 1903. Awards A (college transfer), B, M. Primary accreditation: regional. City setting; 340-acre campus. Total enrollment: 6,380. Faculty: 248 (175 full-time, 73 part-time). Social organizations: 1 national fraternity, 1 local fraternity, 1 local sorority; 2% of eligible undergraduate men and 2% of eligible undergraduate women are members.

Drug and Alcohol Information

Education

On campus Drug and alcohol education/prevention programs offered for: all students. College holds an annual alcohol awareness week and drug awareness week.

Identification of Problems

Admissions College application does not ask about prior substance abuse problems.

On campus Current students identified as chemically dependent may remain enrolled. No training program on identifying students with potential substance abuse problems. Written procedures for students and staff if substance abuse is suspected.

Support Services

On campus Private counseling.

Employee assistance Program for chemically dependent employees available.

Disciplinary Actions

Alcohol Results of infractions of alcohol regulations (see Comparative Table of Alcohol Regulations) vary by situation.

Drugs For any use or possession: varies by situation. For any sale: suspension.

For More Information

Contact: Joan Apple Lemoine, Dean of Student Affairs, Western Connecticut State University, 181 White St., Danbury, CT 06810. Telephone: 203-797-4392.

WESTERN ILLINOIS UNIVERSITY

Macomb, Illinois

General Information

State-supported 5-year coed college. Part of Board of Governors of State Colleges and Universities. Founded 1899. Awards B, M. Primary accreditation: regional. Small-town setting; 1,056-acre campus. Total enrollment: 12,500. Faculty: 626 (586 full-time, 40 part-time). Social organizations: 18 national fraternities, 10 national sororities, local fraternities; 9% of eligible undergraduate men and 5% of eligible undergraduate women are members.

Drug and Alcohol Information

Education

On campus Drug and alcohol education/prevention programs offered for: all students, athletes/coaches, faculty, administration. Bacchus chapter: 45 members. College holds an annual alcohol awareness and drug awareness week.

Identification of Problems

Admissions College application does not ask about prior substance abuse problems.

On campus Current students identified as chemically dependent may remain enrolled. Training program on identifying students with potential substance abuse problems for: resident advisers, faculty, administration. Written procedures for students and staff if substance abuse is suspected.

Support Services

On campus AA, NA, Al-Anon, ACOA, private counseling.

Employee assistance Program for chemically dependent employees available. Staff working with drug/alcohol-related issues: 4 part-time.

Disciplinary Actions

Alcohol Results of infractions of alcohol regulations (see Comparative Table of Alcohol Regulations) include counseling, warning.

Drugs For any use, possession, or sale: varies by situation.

For More Information

Contact: Charles R. O'Brien, Director, University

Western Illinois University (continued)

Counseling Center, Memorial Hall, Western Illinois University, Adams St., Macomb, IL 61455. Telephone: 309-298-2453.

WESTERN INTERNATIONAL UNIVERSITY

Phoenix, Arizona

General Information

Independent 5-year coed college. Founded 1978. Awards A (college transfer), B, M. Primary accreditation: regional. Metropolitan setting; 4-acre campus. Total enrollment: 1,146. Faculty: 66 (all full-time).

Drug and Alcohol Information

Education

On campus Drug and alcohol education/prevention programs not offered.

Identification of Problems

Admissions College application does not ask about prior substance abuse problems.

On campus Current students identified as chemically dependent may remain enrolled. No training program on identifying students with potential substance abuse problems. No written procedures for students and staff if substance abuse is suspected.

Support Services

On campus No support services on campus.

Disciplinary Actions

Alcohol Results of infractions of alcohol regulations (see Comparative Table of Alcohol Regulations) include counseling, warning, probation, suspension.

Drugs For first-time use, possession, or sale: warning. For subsequent use, possession, or sale: probation.

For More Information

Contact: Elena B. Pattison, Director of Admissions/Student Affairs, Western International University, 10202 N. 19th Ave., Phoenix, AZ 85021. Telephone: 602-943-2311.

WESTERN NEW MEXICO UNIVERSITY

Silver City, New Mexico

General Information

State-supported 5-year coed college. Founded 1893. Awards A (college transfer and terminal), B, M. Primary accreditation: regional. Small-town setting; 83-acre campus. Total enrollment: 1,680. Faculty: 90 (64 full-time, 26 part-time).

Drug and Alcohol Information

Education

On campus Drug and alcohol education/prevention programs offered for: all students, faculty, administration, self-referrals. College holds an annual alcohol awareness week.

Identification of Problems

Admissions College application does not ask about prior substance abuse problems.

On campus Current students identified as chemically dependent may remain enrolled, but treatment is required. No training program on identifying students with potential substance abuse problems. No written procedures for students and staff if substance abuse is suspected.

Support Services

On campus Support groups, private counseling, referrals.

Employee assistance Program for chemically dependent employees not available.

Disciplinary Actions

Alcohol Results of infractions of alcohol regulations (see Comparative Table of Alcohol Regulations) include suspension.

Drugs For first-time use: warning. For subsequent use: suspension, expulsion. For first-time possession or sale: suspension. For subsequent possession or sale: expulsion.

For More Information

Contact: Antonio Macias, Director of Student Development, Western New Mexico University, College Blvd., Silver City, NM 88061. Telephone: 505-538-6134.

WESTERN OREGON STATE COLLEGE

Monmouth, Oregon

General Information

State-supported 5-year coed college. Founded 1856. Awards A (terminal), B, M. Primary accreditation: regional. Rural setting; 122-acre campus. Total enrollment: 3,980. Faculty: 221 (188 full-time, 33 part-time).

Drug and Alcohol Information

Education

On campus Drug and alcohol education/prevention programs offered for: all students, athletes/coaches; parents, alumni, community members; required for: resident advisers. Authorized group concerned with responsible drinking. College holds its own annual alcohol awareness week and drug awareness week.

Identification of Problems

Admissions College application does not ask about prior substance abuse problems.

On campus Current students identified as chemically dependent may remain enrolled. Training program on identifying students with potential substance abuse problems for: resident advisers. No written procedures for students and staff if substance abuse is suspected.

Support Services

On campus Support groups (Counseling Center).

Employee assistance Program for chemically dependent employees not available.

Disciplinary Actions

Alcohol Results of infractions of alcohol regulations (see Comparative Table of Alcohol Regulations) vary by situation but can include chemical dependency assessment, counseling, warning, probation, suspension, expulsion.

Drugs For first-time use or possession: chemical

dependency assessment, probation. For subsequent use or possession: suspension, expulsion. For any sale: expulsion.

For More Information

Contact: Dr. Merlin Darby, Director, Counseling Center, Western Oregon State College, Monmouth, OR 97361. Telephone: 503-838-1220 Ext. 396.

WESTERN WASHINGTON UNIVERSITY

Bellingham, Washington

General Information

State-supported 5-year coed college. Founded 1893. Awards B, M. Primary accreditation: regional. Small-town setting; 225-acre campus. Total enrollment: 9,838. Faculty: 456 (370 full-time, 86 part-time).

Drug and Alcohol Information

Education

On campus Drug and alcohol education/prevention programs offered for: all students, athletes/coaches, administration. College holds an annual alcohol awareness week.

Identification of Problems

Admissions College application does not ask about prior substance abuse problems.

On campus Current students identified as chemically dependent may remain enrolled. Training program on identifying students with potential substance abuse problems for: resident advisers, coaches, administration. Written procedures are being developed for students and staff if substance abuse is suspected.

Support Services

On campus ACOA, private counseling.

Employee assistance Program for chemically dependent employees available. Staff working with drug/alcohol-related issues: 1 full-time and 3 part-time.

Disciplinary Actions

Alcohol Results of infractions of alcohol regulations (see Comparative Table of Alcohol Regulations) include chemical dependency assessment, warning, probation, suspension, removal from residence hall.

Drugs For any use, possession, or sale: varies by situation.

Additional Information from the College

A FIPSE grant was received in September 1988. Additional on-campus support services are planned.

For More Information

Contact: Connie Copeland, Director of Student Life, Old Main 390, Western Washington University, Bellingham, WA 98225. Telephone: 206-676-3846.

WESTFIELD STATE COLLEGE

Westfield, Massachusetts

General Information

State-supported 5-year coed college. Founded 1838. Awards B, M. Primary accreditation: regional. Small-town setting; 227-acre campus. Total enrollment: 5,311. Faculty: 204 (166 full-time, 38 part-time).

Drug and Alcohol Information

Education

On campus Drug and alcohol education/prevention programs offered for: all students. Authorized group concerned with responsible drinking. College holds an annual alcohol awareness week and drug awareness week.

Identification of Problems

Admissions College application does not ask about prior substance abuse problems.

On campus Current students identified as chemically dependent may remain enrolled, but treatment is required. Training program on identifying students with potential substance abuse problems for: resident advisers, administration. No written procedures for students and staff if substance abuse is suspected.

Support Services

On campus Private counseling, Counseling Center.

Employee assistance Program for chemically dependent employees available. Staff working with drug/alcohol-related issues: 5 part-time.

Disciplinary Actions

Alcohol Results of infractions of alcohol regulations (see Comparative Table of Alcohol Regulations) vary by situation but can include counseling, warning, probation, suspension.

Drugs For first-time use or possession: counseling, probation. For subsequent use or possession: counseling, suspension. For first-time sale: counseling, suspension, probation or return. For subsequent sale: expulsion.

For More Information

Contact: Peter D. Mazza, Dean, Student Services, Westfield State College, Western Avenue, Westfield, MA 01086. Telephone: 413-568-3311.

WEST LIBERTY STATE COLLEGE

West Liberty, West Virginia

General Information

State-supported 4-year coed college. Founded 1837. Awards A (terminal), B. Primary accreditation: regional. Rural setting; 150-acre campus. Total enrollment: 2,435. Faculty: 143 (128 full-time, 15 part-time). Social organizations: 2 national fraternities, 3 national sororities, 5 local fraternities; 10% of eligible undergraduate men and 11% of eligible undergraduate women are members.

Drug and Alcohol Information

Education

On campus Drug and alcohol education/prevention programs offered for: all students, athletes/coaches, faculty, administration. Authorized group concerned with responsible drinking.

Identification of Problems

Admissions College application does not ask about prior substance abuse problems.

On campus Current students identified as chemically dependent may remain enrolled, but treatment is required. Training program on identifying students with potential substance abuse problems for: resident advisers, coaches,

West Liberty State College (continued)

administration. Written procedures for students and staff if substance abuse is suspected.

Support Services

On campus Private counseling.

Employee assistance Program for chemically dependent employees not available. Staff working with drug/alcohol-related issues: 1 part-time.

Disciplinary Actions

Alcohol Results of infractions of alcohol regulations (see Comparative Table of Alcohol Regulations) include counseling, warning, probation, suspension, expulsion.

Drugs For first-time use or possession: suspension. For subsequent use or possession: expulsion. For any sale: expulsion.

For More Information

Contact: Tammy West, Counselor, West Liberty State College, West Liberty, WV 26074. Telephone: 304-336-8018.

WESTMINSTER CHOIR COLLEGE

Princeton, New Jersey

General Information

Independent 5-year specialized coed college. Founded 1926. Awards B, M. Primary accreditation: regional. Small-town setting; 23-acre campus. Total enrollment: 347. Faculty: 63 (42 full-time, 21 part-time).

Drug and Alcohol Information

Education

On campus Drug and alcohol education/prevention programs offered for: all students, faculty, administration. College holds an annual alcohol awareness week and drug awareness week.

Identification of Problems

Admissions College application does not ask about prior substance abuse problems.

On campus Current students identified as chemically dependent may not remain enrolled. Training program on identifying students with potential substance abuse problems for: resident advisers. Written procedures for students and staff if substance abuse is suspected.

Support Services

On campus Private counseling, referral.

Off campus Counseling.

Employee assistance Program for chemically dependent employees not available. Staff working with drug/alcohol-related issues: 2 part-time.

Disciplinary Actions

Alcohol Results of infractions of alcohol regulations (see Comparative Table of Alcohol Regulations) include warning. Comments: Three warnings in one calendar year require Judicial Board hearing.

Drugs For any use or sale: expulsion. For any possession: suspension, expulsion.

For More Information

Contact: Dr. Martin J. Stamm, Acting Dean of Students, Westminster Choir College, Princeton, NJ 08540. Telephone: 609-921-7100 Ext. 263.

WESTMINSTER COLLEGE OF SALT LAKE CITY

Salt Lake City, Utah

General Information

Independent 5-year coed college. Founded 1875. Awards B, M. Primary accreditation: regional. Metropolitan setting; 27-acre campus. Total enrollment: 1,856. Faculty: 61 (56 full-time, 5 part-time).

Drug and Alcohol Information

Education

On campus Drug and alcohol education/prevention programs offered for: athletes/coaches, resident advisers. College holds an annual alcohol awareness week.

Identification of Problems

Admissions College application does not ask about prior substance abuse problems.

On campus Current students identified as chemically dependent may remain enrolled. No training program on identifying students with potential substance abuse problems. No written procedures for students and staff if substance abuse is suspected.

Support Services

On campus Private counseling.

Employee assistance Program for chemically dependent employees not available. Staff working with drug/alcohol-related issues: 3–4 part-time.

Disciplinary Actions

Alcohol Results of infractions of alcohol regulations (see Comparative Table of Alcohol Regulations) vary by situation but can include chemical dependency assessment, counseling, warning, probation.

Drugs For first-time use: varies by situation. For first-time possession: chemical dependency assessment, counseling, warning. For first-time sale: counseling, warning, probation. For subsequent use, possession, or sale: varies by situation.

For More Information

Contact: Gary D. Fitzer, Dean of Students, Westminster College of Salt Lake City, 1840 S. 1300 East, Salt Lake City, UT 84105. Telephone: 801-488-4132.

WEST SUBURBAN COLLEGE OF NURSING

Oak Park, Illinois

General Information

Independent 4-year specialized coed college. Founded 1914. Awards B (jointly with Concordia College, IL). Primary accreditation: regional. City setting. Total enrollment: 99. Faculty: 15 (13 full-time, 2 part-time).

Drug and Alcohol Information

Education

On campus Drug and alcohol education/prevention programs not offered.

Identification of Problems

Admissions College application does not ask about prior substance abuse problems.

On campus No training program on identifying students with potential substance abuse problems. Written procedures for students and staff if substance abuse is suspected.

Support Services

On campus Private counseling.

Employee assistance Program for chemically dependent employees not available.

Disciplinary Actions

Alcohol Results of infractions of alcohol regulations (see Comparative Table of Alcohol Regulations) include counseling, warning, probation, suspension, expulsion.

Drugs For any use, possession, or first-time sale: varies by situation. For subsequent sale: expulsion.

Additional Information from the College

The size and nature of the student body (58 percent commuter) allows a very individualized response to any substance abuse concerns, as well as a very limited number of such instances.

For More Information

Contact: Barbara Minogue, Dean of Students, West Suburban College of Nursing, Erie at Austin, Oak Park, IL 60302. Telephone: 312-383-6200 Ext. 6505.

WEST TEXAS STATE UNIVERSITY

Canyon, Texas

General Information

State-supported 5-year coed college. Founded 1909. Awards B, M. Primary accreditation: regional. Small-town setting; 128-acre campus. Total enrollment: 5,756. Faculty: 313 (185 full-time, 128 part-time). Social organizations: 5 national fraternities, 4 national sororities; 10% of eligible undergraduate men and 10% of eligible undergraduate women are members.

Drug and Alcohol Information

Education

On campus Drug and alcohol education/prevention programs offered for: all students; required for: violators of campus alcohol policy. College holds an annual alcohol awareness week.

Identification of Problems

Admissions College application does not ask about prior substance abuse problems.

On campus Current students identified as chemically dependent may remain enrolled, but treatment is required. No training program on identifying students with potential substance abuse problems. Written procedures for students and staff if substance abuse is suspected.

Support Services

On campus ACOA, support groups, private counseling.

Employee assistance Program for chemically dependent employees not available.

Disciplinary Actions

Alcohol Results of infractions of alcohol regulations (see Comparative Table of Alcohol Regulations) include counseling, probation, suspension, expulsion.

Drugs For first-time use or possession: varies by situation. For subsequent use: probation, suspension, expulsion. For subsequent possession: suspension, expulsion. For any sale: suspension, expulsion.

For More Information

Contact: Melanie Kritser, Director of Student Programming, West Texas State University, Canyon, TX 79016. Telephone: 806-656-2344.

WEST VIRGINIA UNIVERSITY

Morgantown, West Virginia

General Information

State-supported comprehensive coed institution. Founded 1867. Awards B, M, D. Primary accreditation: regional. Small-town setting; 1,000-acre campus. Total enrollment: 18,746. Faculty: 1,313 (1,206 full-time, 107 part-time). Social organizations: 22 national fraternities, 11 national sororities; 19% of eligible undergraduate men and 19% of eligible undergraduate women are members.

Drug and Alcohol Information

Education

On campus Drug and alcohol education/prevention programs offered for: all students, athletes/coaches, faculty, administration. Authorized group concerned with responsible drinking. College holds an annual alcohol awareness week and drug awareness week.

Identification of Problems

Admissions College application does not ask about prior substance abuse problems.

On campus Current students identified as chemically dependent may remain enrolled, but treatment is required. Training program on identifying students with potential substance abuse problems for: resident advisers, Greek officers, administration, Peer Educators. Written procedures for students and staff if substance abuse is suspected.

Support Services

On campus ACOA, support groups, private counseling, DUI therapy groups.

Employee assistance Program for chemically dependent employees available. Staff working with drug/alcohol-related issues: 1 full-time.

Disciplinary Actions

Alcohol Results of infractions of alcohol regulations (see Comparative Table of Alcohol Regulations) include chemical dependency assessment, counseling, warning, probation, alcohol education.

Drugs For first-time use: chemical dependency assessment, counseling, warning. For subsequent use: varies by situation—counseling, suspension. For first-time possession: varies by situation. For subsequent possession: suspension, expulsion. For first-time sale: suspension, expulsion. For subsequent sale: expulsion.

For More Information

Contact: Nicolene L. Cavendish, Addiction Specialist, West Virginia University, 6121 Health Sciences Center, Morgantown, WV 26506. Telephone: 304-293-2301.

WEST VIRGINIA WESLEYAN COLLEGE
Buckhannon, West Virginia

General Information
Independent Methodist 5-year coed college. Founded 1890. Awards B, M. Primary accreditation: regional. Small-town setting; 80-acre campus. Total enrollment: 1,484. Faculty: 99 (78 full-time, 21 part-time). Social organizations: 6 national fraternities, 4 national sororities; 33% of eligible undergraduate men and 33% of eligible undergraduate women are members.

Drug and Alcohol Information
Education
On campus Drug and alcohol education/prevention programs offered for: all students, athletes/coaches, faculty; required for: freshmen, resident advisers. Authorized group concerned with responsible drinking. College holds an annual alcohol awareness week.

Identification of Problems
Admissions College application does not ask about prior substance abuse problems.

On campus Current students identified as chemically dependent may remain enrolled, but treatment is required. Training program on identifying students with potential substance abuse problems for: resident advisers, Greek officers, faculty. No written procedures for students and staff if substance abuse is suspected.

Support Services
On campus Support groups (recovery group), private counseling.

Employee assistance Program for chemically dependent employees not available. Staff working with drug/alcohol-related issues: 2 part-time.

Disciplinary Actions
Alcohol Results of infractions of alcohol regulations (see Comparative Table of Alcohol Regulations) vary by situation but can include chemical dependency assessment, counseling, probation, suspension.

Drugs For first-time use, possession, or sale: varies by situation. For subsequent use: medical withdrawal from college, suspension. For subsequent possession or sale: expulsion.

Additional Information from the College
Recently received $100,000 FIPSE drug prevention grant. Drug prevention and wellness programs are to expand in 1989. Student assistants in program. Work with fraternities and sororities has increased. Guidelines for off-campus events are being established. Alcohol/drug policy revisions focused on enforcement are expected in 1989.

For More Information
Contact: Michael Kuba, Director, Counseling, West Virginia Wesleyan College, College Ave., Buckhannon, WV 26201. Telephone: 304-473-8000 Ext. 8090.

WHEELING JESUIT COLLEGE
Wheeling, West Virginia

General Information
Independent Roman Catholic 5-year coed college. Founded 1954. Awards B, M. Primary accreditation: regional. Small-town setting; 65-acre campus. Total enrollment: 1,030. Faculty: 75 (65 full-time, 10 part-time).

Drug and Alcohol Information
Education
On campus Drug and alcohol education/prevention programs offered for: all students; required for: athletes/coaches. Authorized group concerned with responsible drinking. College holds an annual alcohol awareness week and drug awareness week.

Identification of Problems
Admissions College application does not ask about prior substance abuse problems.

On campus Current students identified as chemically dependent may remain enrolled, but treatment is required. Training program on identifying students with potential substance abuse problems for: resident advisers, administration. No written procedures for students and staff if substance abuse is suspected.

Support Services
On campus AA, support groups (Campus Ministries), private counseling.

Employee assistance Program for chemically dependent employees not available. Staff working with drug/alcohol-related issues: 3 part-time.

Disciplinary Actions
Alcohol Results of infractions of alcohol regulations (see Comparative Table of Alcohol Regulations) vary by situation but can include chemical dependency assessment, counseling, warning, probation, fines.

Drugs For first-time use or possession: counseling, probation (one week), suspension. For subsequent use or possession: counseling, probation (one semester), suspension. For any sale: expulsion.

For More Information
Contact: Dr. James H. Thomas Jr., Dean of Student Development, Wheeling Jesuit College, Wheeling, WV 26003. Telephone: 304-243-2210.

WHEELOCK COLLEGE
Boston, Massachusetts

General Information
Independent 5-year primarily women's college. Founded 1888. Awards B, M. Primary accreditation: regional. Metropolitan setting; 5-acre campus. Total enrollment: 985. Faculty: 117 (42 full-time, 75 part-time).

Drug and Alcohol Information
Education
On campus Drug and alcohol education/prevention programs offered for: all students; required for: freshmen.

Identification of Problems
Admissions College application does not ask about prior substance abuse problems.

On campus Current students identified as chemically dependent may remain enrolled. No training program on identifying students with potential substance abuse problems. No written procedures for students and staff if substance abuse is suspected.

Support Services

On campus ACOA.

Employee assistance Program for chemically dependent employees not available. Staff working with drug/alcohol-related issues: 1 part-time.

Disciplinary Actions

Alcohol Results of infractions of alcohol regulations (see Comparative Table of Alcohol Regulations) include warning, probation, suspension, expulsion.

Drugs For first-time use: warning. For subsequent use: expulsion. For first-time possession or sale: removal from residence hall. For subsequent possession or sale: expulsion.

For More Information

Contact: Kathy Woolf Jonas, Dean of Students, Wheelock College, 37 Pilgrim Rd., Boston, MA 02215. Telephone: 617-734-5200 Ext. 118.

WHITMAN COLLEGE

Walla Walla, Washington

General Information

Independent 4-year coed college. Founded 1859. Awards B. Primary accreditation: regional. Small-town setting; 45-acre campus. Total enrollment: 1,230. Faculty: 121 (93 full-time, 28 part-time). Social organizations: 5 national fraternities, 4 national sororities, 1 local sorority; 50% of eligible undergraduate men and 50% of eligible undergraduate women are members.

Drug and Alcohol Information

Education

On campus Drug and alcohol education/prevention programs offered for: all students; required for: freshmen, social organization members, athletes/coaches, resident advisers. Authorized group concerned with responsible drinking. College holds an annual alcohol awareness week and drug awareness week.

Identification of Problems

Admissions College application does not ask about prior substance abuse problems.

On campus Current students identified as chemically dependent may remain enrolled. Training program on identifying students with potential substance abuse problems for: resident advisers, administration. Written procedures for students and staff if substance abuse is suspected.

Support Services

On campus ACOA, support groups, private counseling.

Employee assistance Program for chemically dependent employees not available.

Disciplinary Actions

Alcohol Results of infractions of alcohol regulations (see Comparative Table of Alcohol Regulations) vary by situation but can include chemical dependency assessment, counseling, warning, probation, suspension. Comments: Seriousness of sanction increases with frequency of infraction.

Drugs For first-time use: varies by situation—chemical dependency assessment, counseling, warning. For subsequent use: varies by situation—chemical dependency assessment, counseling. For first-time possession: varies by situation—warning. For subsequent possession: varies by situation. For first-time sale: varies by situation—probation, suspension. For subsequent sale: varies by situation—expulsion.

Additional Information from the College

Although there is no Bacchus chapter on campus, the College subscribes to its philosophy of "responsible use" of alcohol. Harsher penalties for drug abuse reflect differences in law and potential harm to students.

For More Information

Contact: Patti Picha, Director of Student Activities, Whitman College, Walla Walla, WA 99362. Telephone: 509-527-5367.

WICHITA STATE UNIVERSITY

Wichita, Kansas

General Information

State-supported comprehensive coed institution. Founded 1895. Awards A (college transfer and terminal), B, M, D. Primary accreditation: regional. City setting; 330-acre campus. Total enrollment: 17,267. Faculty: 852 (605 full-time, 247 part-time). Social organizations: 13 national fraternities, 8 national sororities; 2% of eligible undergraduate men and 2% of eligible undergraduate women are members.

Drug and Alcohol Information

Education

On campus Drug and alcohol education/prevention programs offered for: all students. Authorized group concerned with responsible drinking. College holds an annual alcohol awareness week and drug awareness week.

Identification of Problems

Admissions College application does not ask about prior substance abuse problems.

On campus Current students identified as chemically dependent may remain enrolled. Training program on identifying students with potential substance abuse problems for: resident advisers, Greek officers. No written procedures for students and staff if substance abuse is suspected.

Support Services

On campus AA, ACOA, support groups.

Employee assistance Program for chemically dependent employees available. Staff working with drug/alcohol-related issues: several part-time.

Disciplinary Actions

Alcohol Results of infractions of alcohol regulations (see Comparative Table of Alcohol Regulations) vary by situation.

Drugs For first-time use or possesion: probation. For subsequent use or possession: suspension. For any sale: expulsion.

For More Information

Contact: John H. Schuh, Associate Vice President, Wichita State University, Wichita, KS 67208. Telephone: 316-689-3032.

WILLAMETTE UNIVERSITY

Salem, Oregon

General Information

Independent United Methodist 5-year coed college. Founded 1842. Awards B, M, D. Primary accreditation: regional. City setting; 59-acre campus. Total enrollment: 2,098. Faculty: 138 (104 full-time, 34 part-time). Social organizations: 5 national fraternities, 3 national sororities; 40% of eligible undergraduate men and 32% of eligible undergraduate women are members.

Drug and Alcohol Information

Education

On campus Drug and alcohol education/prevention programs offered for: all students. College holds an annual alcohol awareness week and drug awareness week.

Identification of Problems

Admissions College application does not ask about prior substance abuse problems.

On campus Current students identified as chemically dependent may remain enrolled, but treatment is required. Training program on identifying students with potential substance abuse problems for: resident advisers, Greek officers, administration, student leaders.

Support Services

On campus AA, ACOA, private counseling, Alcohol Consumption Education Committee.

Employee assistance Program for chemically dependent employees available. Staff working with drug/alcohol-related issues: 6 part-time.

Disciplinary Actions

Alcohol Results of infractions of alcohol regulations (see Comparative Table of Alcohol Regulations) include chemical dependency assessment.

Drugs For first-time use or possession: varies by situation—counseling, warning. For subsequent use: chemical dependency assessment, probation. For subsequent possession: varies by situation—probation, suspension. For first-time sale: suspension. For subsequent sale: expulsion.

Additional Information from the College

A student identified as having a substance abuse problem is required to receive a professional evaluation. Subsequently the University, the student, and the community treatment agency work together. Willamette University encourages students to make responsible choices about alcohol use through educational programming and personal contact with staff members. Each student is considered as an individual in an individual set of circumstances.

For More Information

Contact: Dr. Tim J. Pierson, Director of Residence Life, Willamette University, 900 State St., Salem, OR 97301. Telephone: 503-370-6212.

WILLIAM JENNINGS BRYAN COLLEGE

Dayton, Tennessee

General Information

Independent interdenominational 4-year coed college. Founded 1930. Awards A (terminal), B. Primary accreditation: regional. Small-town setting; 100-acre campus. Total enrollment: 517. Faculty: 39 (28 full-time, 11 part-time).

Drug and Alcohol Information

Education

On campus Drug and alcohol education/prevention programs not offered.

Identification of Problems

Admissions College application question about prior substance abuse problems is used in the admissions decision.

On campus Current students identified as chemically dependent may not remain enrolled. No training program on identifying students with potential substance abuse problems. Written procedures for students and staff if substance abuse is suspected.

Support Services

On campus Private counseling.

Employee assistance Program for chemically dependent employees not available. Staff working with drug/alcohol-related issues: 5 part-time.

Disciplinary Actions

Alcohol Results of infractions of alcohol regulations (see Comparative Table of Alcohol Regulations) include counseling, warning, probation, suspension, expulsion.

Drugs For first-time use, possession, or sale: probation, suspension, expulsion. For subsequent use, possession, or sale: expulsion.

For More Information

Contact: Paul H. Ardelean, Dean of Students, Box 7000, William Jennings Bryan College, Dayton, TN 37321. Telephone: 615-775-2041 Ext. 230.

WILLIAM PATERSON COLLEGE OF NEW JERSEY

Wayne, New Jersey

General Information

State-supported 5-year coed college. Part of New Jersey State College System. Founded 1855. Awards B, M. Primary accreditation: regional. Small-town setting; 250-acre campus. Total enrollment: 9,232. Faculty: 333 (311 full-time, 22 part-time). Social organizations: national fraternities, national sororities, local fraternities, local sororities.

Drug and Alcohol Information

Education

On campus Drug and alcohol education/prevention programs offered for: all students, athletes/coaches. Authorized group concerned with responsible drinking. College holds an annual alcohol awareness week and drug awareness week.

Identification of Problems

On campus Current students identified as chemically dependent may remain enrolled. Training program on identifying students with potential substance abuse problems for: resident advisers. Written procedures for students and staff if substance abuse is suspected.

Support Services

On campus AA, private counseling.

Employee assistance Program for chemically dependent employees not available. Staff working with drug/alcohol-related issues: 2 part-time.

Disciplinary Actions

Alcohol Results of infractions of alcohol regulations (see Comparative Table of Alcohol Regulations) include counseling, warning, probation, suspension, expulsion, mandatory six-week course. Comments: The six-week course is required for alcohol-related violators.

Drugs For first-time use or possession: varies by situation. For subsequent use or possession: counseling, suspension, expulsion. For any sale: expulsion. Comments: A six-week course is available for students to assess whether they have an alcohol/drug problem and to discuss what they feel they can do to resolve it.

For More Information

Contact: Barbara Milne, Director, Student Programs, William Paterson College of New Jersey, 300 Pompton Rd., Wayne, NJ 07470. Telephone: 201-595-2491.

WILLIAM PENN COLLEGE

Oskaloosa, Iowa

General Information

Independent 4-year coed college, affiliated with Society of Friends. Founded 1873. Awards B. Primary accreditation: regional. Small-town setting; 40-acre campus. Total enrollment: 675. Faculty: 57 (36 full-time, 21 part-time). Social organizations: 1 national fraternity, 3 local fraternities, 3 local sororities.

Drug and Alcohol Information

Education

On campus Drug and alcohol education/prevention programs offered for: all students. College holds an annual alcohol awareness week.

Identification of Problems

Admissions College application question about prior substance abuse problems is used for counseling and referral, if student is admitted.

On campus Current students identified as chemically dependent may remain enrolled, but treatment is required. Training program on identifying students with potential substance abuse problems for: resident advisers. Written procedures for students and staff if substance abuse is suspected.

Support Services

On campus Private counseling.

Off campus Community mental health counselors.

Employee assistance Program for chemically dependent employees not available. Staff working with drug/alcohol-related issues: 4 part-time.

Disciplinary Actions

Alcohol Results of infractions of alcohol regulations (see Comparative Table of Alcohol Regulations) include chemical dependency assessment, counseling, warning, probation, suspension.

Drugs For first-time use or possession: warning. For subsequent use or possession: varies by situation. For first-time sale: counseling, probation. For subsequent sale: suspension.

For More Information

Contact: Ronald D. Shafer, Dean of Student Services, William Penn College, Oskaloosa, IA 52577. Telephone: 515-673-1083.

WILLIAM SMITH COLLEGE

Geneva, New York

General Information

Independent 4-year women's college, coordinate with Hobart College. Founded 1908. Awards B. Primary accreditation: regional. Small-town setting; 180-acre campus. Total enrollment: 800. Faculty: 170 (138 full-time, 32 part-time).

Drug and Alcohol Information

Education

On campus Drug and alcohol education/prevention programs offered for: all students; required for: freshmen, athletes/coaches, resident advisers. Authorized group concerned with responsible drinking. College usually holds an annual alcohol awareness week and drug awareness week.

Identification of Problems

Admissions College application does not ask about prior substance abuse problems.

On campus Current students identified as chemically dependent may remain enrolled, but treatment is required. Training program on identifying students with potential substance abuse problems for: resident advisers, coaches, Greek officers, administration. Written procedures for students and staff if substance abuse is suspected.

Support Services

On campus Support groups, private counseling.

Employee assistance Program for chemically dependent employees available from a local agency. Staff working with drug/alcohol-related issues: 1–2 full-time and several part-time.

Disciplinary Actions

Alcohol Results of infractions of alcohol regulations (see Comparative Table of Alcohol Regulations) vary by situation but can include chemical dependency assessment, counseling, warning, probation, suspension, expulsion. Comments: Counseling and a chemical dependency assessment occurs in all cases. Probation, suspension, or expulsion occur if behavior warrants.

Drugs For any use or possession: varies by situation. For any sale: varies by situation—usually expulsion.

For More Information

Contact: John Leonard, Counselor/Substance Abuse Counselor, Hubbs Health Center, William Smith College, Geneva, NY 14456. Telephone: 315-789-5500 Ext. 346.

WILMINGTON COLLEGE

New Castle, Delaware

General Information

Independent 5-year coed college. Founded 1967. Awards A (terminal), B, M. Primary accreditation: regional. City setting; 13-acre campus. Total enrollment: 1,482. Faculty: 103 (18 full-time, 85 part-time). Social organization: 1

Wilmington College (continued)

national fraternity; 7% of eligible undergraduate men are members.

Drug and Alcohol Information

Education

On campus Drug and alcohol education/prevention programs being developed for: all students, athletes/coaches, faculty, administration. College will hold an annual alcohol awareness week and drug awareness week.

Identification of Problems

Admissions College application does not ask about prior substance abuse problems.

On campus Current students identified as chemically dependent may remain enrolled, but treatment is required. Training program on identifying students with potential substance abuse problems being developed. Written procedures being developed for students and staff if substance abuse is suspected.

Support Services

On campus Private counseling.

Employee assistance Program for chemically dependent employees available. Staff working with drug/alcohol-related issues: 3 part-time.

Disciplinary Actions

Alcohol Results of infractions of alcohol regulations (see Comparative Table of Alcohol Regulations) vary by situation but can include counseling. Comments: Can be referred to Student Discipline/Assistance Committee.

Drugs For any use or possession: varies by situation—counseling. For any sale: varies by situation.

Additional Information from the College

The College has received an $80,500 FIPSE grant to develop a model program for drug and alcohol abuse prevention, using the state's Above the Influence culture-based strategy.

For More Information

Contact: Sue Eriksen, Above the Influence Drug Program Coordinator, Wilmington College, 320 Dupont Hwy., New Castle, DE 19720. Telephone: 302-328-9401.

WINGATE COLLEGE

Wingate, North Carolina

General Information

Independent Baptist 5-year coed college. Founded 1895. Awards A (college transfer and terminal), B, M. Primary accreditation: regional. Small-town setting; 330-acre campus. Total enrollment: 1,729. Faculty: 98 (77 full-time, 21 part-time).

Drug and Alcohol Information

Education

On campus Drug and alcohol education/prevention programs offered for: freshmen, athletes/coaches, resident advisers.

Identification of Problems

Admissions College application does not ask about prior substance abuse problems.

On campus Training program on identifying students with potential substance abuse problems for: resident advisers. No written procedures for students and staff if substance abuse is suspected.

Support Services

On campus Private counseling.

Employee assistance Program for chemically dependent employees not available. Staff working with drug/alcohol-related issues: 3 part-time.

Disciplinary Actions

Alcohol Results of infractions of alcohol regulations (see Comparative Table of Alcohol Regulations) include counseling, warning, probation.

Drugs For first-time use or possession: suspension, expulsion. For subsequent use or possession: expulsion. For any sale: expulsion.

For More Information

Contact: Lynn Moss, Associate Dean, Dickson-Palmer Center, Wingate College, Wingate, NC 28174. Telephone: 704-233-8243, 8249, 8245.

WINSTON-SALEM STATE UNIVERSITY

Winston-Salem, North Carolina

General Information

State-supported 4-year coed college. Part of University of North Carolina System. Founded 1892. Awards B. Primary accreditation: regional. City setting; 81-acre campus. Total enrollment: 2,532. Faculty: 186 (143 full-time, 43 part-time). Social organizations: 4 national fraternities, 5 national sororities, 2 local fraternities, 3 local sororities.

Drug and Alcohol Information

Education

On campus Drug and alcohol education/prevention programs required for: all students. Authorized group concerned with responsible drinking. College holds an annual alcohol awareness week and drug awareness week.

Identification of Problems

Admissions College application does not ask about prior substance abuse problems.

On campus Written procedures for students and staff if substance abuse is suspected.

Support Services

On campus Private counseling, referrals. Staff working with drug/alcohol-related issues: 2 part-time.

Disciplinary Actions

Alcohol Results of infractions of alcohol regulations (see Comparative Table of Alcohol Regulations) include suspension.

Drugs For any use, possession, or sale: suspension.

For More Information

Contact: Elaine Browne, Director of Student Activities, P.O. Box 13154. Winston-Salem State University, Winston-Salem, NC 27110. Telephone: 919-750-3350.

WINTHROP COLLEGE

Rock Hill, South Carolina

General Information

State-supported 5-year coed college. Founded 1886. Awards B, M. Primary accreditation: regional. Small-town setting; 85-acre campus. Total enrollment: 5,351. Faculty: 386 (299 full-time, 87 part-time). Social organizations: 9 national fraternities, 8 national sororities; 13% of eligible undergraduate men and 10% of eligible undergraduate women are members.

Drug and Alcohol Information

Education

On campus Drug and alcohol education/prevention programs offered for: all students, adult children of alcoholics; required for: athletes/coaches. Authorized group concerned with responsible drinking. College holds an annual alcohol awareness week and drug awareness week.

Identification of Problems

Admissions College application does not ask about prior substance abuse problems.

On campus Current students identified as chemically dependent may remain enrolled. Training program on identifying students with potential substance abuse problems for: resident advisers, coaches, others upon request. No written procedures for students and staff if substance abuse is suspected.

Support Services

On campus ACOA, support groups, private counseling.

Off campus AA, NA.

Employee assistance Program for chemically dependent employees available. Staff working with drug/alcohol-related issues: 1 full-time and 2 part-time.

Disciplinary Actions

Alcohol Results of infractions of alcohol regulations (see Comparative Table of Alcohol Regulations) include counseling, warning, probation.

Drugs For first-time use or possession: probation. For subsequent use or possession: varies by situation. For any sale: varies by situation.

Additional Information from the College

There are no AA or NA groups on campus because students prefer to go off campus to maintain anonymity.

For More Information

Contact: William Wells, Ph.D., Director, Counseling and Health Center, 203 Crawford Health Center, Winthrop College, Rock Hill, SC 29733. Telephone: 803-323-2233.

WITTENBERG UNIVERSITY

Springfield, Ohio

General Information

Independent 4-year coed college, affiliated with Evangelical Lutheran Church. Founded 1845. Awards B. Primary accreditation: regional. City setting; 71-acre campus. Total enrollment: 2,250. Faculty: 179 (154 full-time, 25 part-time). Social organizations: 7 national fraternities, 8 national sororities; 39% of eligible undergraduate men and 47% of eligible undergraduate women are members.

Drug and Alcohol Information

Education

On campus Drug and alcohol education/prevention programs offered for: all students. Bacchus chapter: 30 members. College holds an annual alcohol awareness week and drug awareness week.

Identification of Problems

Admissions College application does not ask about prior substance abuse problems.

On campus Current students identified as chemically dependent may remain enrolled, but treatment is required. Training program on identifying students with potential substance abuse problems for: resident advisers, student services. Written procedures for students and staff if substance abuse is suspected.

Support Services

On campus AA, ACOA, private counseling.

Employee assistance Program for chemically dependent employees not available. Staff working with drug/alcohol-related issues: 1 part-time.

Disciplinary Actions

Alcohol Results of infractions of alcohol regulations (see Comparative Table of Alcohol Regulations) vary by situation but can include chemical dependency assessment, counseling.

Drugs For first-time use or possession: varies by situation. For subsequent use or possession: varies by situation—chemical dependency assessment, counseling, suspension. For any sale: expulsion.

For More Information

Contact: Richard R. Scott, Dean of Students, Wittenberg University, P.O. Box 720, Springfield, OH 45501. Telephone: 513-327-7800.

WOFFORD COLLEGE

Spartanburg, South Carolina

General Information

Independent 4-year coed college, affiliated with United Methodist Church. Founded 1854. Awards B. Primary accreditation: regional. City setting; 110-acre campus. Total enrollment: 1,135. Faculty: 82 (63 full-time, 19 part-time). Social organizations: 8 national fraternities, 3 national sororities; 55% of eligible undergraduate men and 55% of eligible undergraduate women are members.

Drug and Alcohol Information

Education

On campus Drug and alcohol education/prevention programs offered for: all students. Authorized group concerned with responsible drinking. College holds an annual alcohol awareness week and drug awareness week.

Identification of Problems

Admissions College application does not ask about prior substance abuse problems.

On campus Current students identified as chemically dependent may remain enrolled, but treatment is required. Training program on identifying students with potential substance abuse problems for: resident advisers, coaches. Written procedures for students and staff if substance abuse is suspected.

Wofford College (continued)

Support Services

On campus No support services on campus.

Off campus Community programs.

Employee assistance Program for chemically dependent employees not available. Staff working with drug/alcohol-related issues: 4 part-time.

Disciplinary Actions

Alcohol Results of infractions of alcohol regulations (see Comparative Table of Alcohol Regulations) vary by situation but can include chemical dependency assessment, counseling, warning, probation, suspension.

Drugs For first-time use, possession, or sale: varies by situation. For subsequent use, possession, or sale: varies by situation—suspension.

For More Information

Contact: J. M. Preston, Vice President for Student Affairs, Wofford College, Spartanburg, SC 29301. Telephone: 803-585-4821.

WOODBURY UNIVERSITY
Burbank, California

General Information

Independent 5-year coed college. Founded 1884. Awards B, M. Primary accreditation: regional. City setting; 22-acre campus. Total enrollment: 858. Faculty: 83 (26 full-time, 57 part-time). Social organizations: 1 national fraternity, 1 local sorority; 3% of eligible undergraduate men and 3% of eligible undergraduate women are members.

Drug and Alcohol Information

Education

On campus Drug and alcohol education/prevention programs offered for: all students. Authorized group concerned with responsible drinking. College holds an annual alcohol awareness week.

Identification of Problems

Admissions College application does not ask about prior substance abuse problems.

On campus Current students identified as chemically dependent may remain enrolled. Comments: Continued enrollment depends upon situation. No training program on identifying students with potential substance abuse problems. Written procedures for students and staff if substance abuse is suspected.

Support Services

On campus Private counseling, campus nurse.

Employee assistance Program for chemically dependent employees not available.

Disciplinary Actions

Alcohol Results of infractions of alcohol regulations (see Comparative Table of Alcohol Regulations) vary by situation. Comments: Action taken depends on the decision of the Dean's Council.

Drugs For first-time use or possession: varies by situation. For first-time sale: varies by situation—expulsion. For subsequent use or possession: varies by situation—probation, suspension. For subsequent sale: expulsion.

For More Information

Contact: Dr. Jim Carter, Dean of Student Services, Woodbury University, 7500 Glenoaks Boulevard, Burbank, CA 91510-7846. Telephone: 818-767-0888.

WORCESTER POLYTECHNIC INSTITUTE
Worcester, Massachusetts

General Information

Independent comprehensive coed institution. Founded 1865. Awards B, M, D. Primary accreditation: regional. City setting; 62-acre campus. Total enrollment: 3,812. Faculty: 210 full-time. Social organizations: 12 national fraternities, 3 national sororities; 45% of eligible undergraduate men and 55% of eligible undergraduate women are members.

Drug and Alcohol Information

Education

On campus Drug and alcohol education/prevention programs offered for: all students. Authorized group concerned with responsible drinking. College holds an annual alcohol awareness week.

Identification of Problems

Admissions College application does not ask about prior substance abuse problems.

On campus Current students identified as chemically dependent may remain enrolled, but treatment is required. Comments: Requirement for treatment depends on the situation. Training program on identifying students with potential substance abuse problems for: resident advisers. No written procedures for students and staff if substance abuse is suspected.

Support Services

On campus Peer Educators.

Employee assistance Program for chemically dependent employees available. Staff working with drug/alcohol-related issues: 1 part-time.

Disciplinary Actions

Alcohol Results of infractions of alcohol regulations (see Comparative Table of Alcohol Regulations) vary by situation but can include chemical dependency assesment, counseling, warning, probation.

Drugs For any use, possession, or sale: varies by situation.

For More Information

Contact: Judy M. Robinson, Director of Residential Life, Worcester Polytechnic Institute, Worcester, MA 01609. Telephone: 508-831-5114.

WORCESTER STATE COLLEGE
Worcester, Massachusetts

General Information

State-supported 5-year coed college. Founded 1874. Awards B, M. Primary accreditation: regional. City setting; 55-acre campus. Total enrollment: 4,800. Faculty: 202 (172 full-time, 30 part-time).

Drug and Alcohol Information

Education

On campus Drug and alcohol education/prevention programs offered for: all students, faculty, administraton. College holds an annual alcohol awareness week.

Identification of Problems

Admissions College application does not ask about prior substance abuse problems.

On campus Current students identified as chemically dependent may remain enrolled. No training program on identifying students with potential substance abuse problems. No written procedures for students and staff if substance abuse is suspected.

Support Services

On campus ACOA, private counseling.

Employee assistance Program for chemically dependent employees available.

Disciplinary Actions

Alcohol Results of infractions of alcohol regulations (see Comparative Table of Alcohol Regulations) vary by situation but can include chemical dependency assessment, counseling, warning, probation, suspension, expulsion.

Drugs For any use, possession, or sale: varies by situation.

Additional Information from the College

Staff members from the Counseling and Placement, Security, Residence Life, and Student Activities offices all deal with alcohol/drug issues as they arise.

For More Information

Contact: Charles Oroszko, Assistant Director–Counseling and Placement Center, Worcester State College, 486 Chandler St., Worcester, MA 01602. Telephone: 508-793-8072.

WRIGHT STATE UNIVERSITY

Dayton, Ohio

General Information

State-supported comprehensive coed institution. Founded 1964. Awards A (terminal), B, M, D. Primary accreditation: regional. Metropolitan setting; 645-acre campus. Total enrollment: 17,104. Faculty: 950 (700 full-time, 250 part-time). Social organizations: 6 national fraternities, 6 national sororities, 3 local fraternities, 1 local sorority; 3% of eligible undergraduate men and 3% of eligible undergraduate women are members.

Drug and Alcohol Information

Education

On campus Drug and alcohol education/prevention programs offered for: all students, athletes/coaches. Authorized group concerned with responsible drinking. College holds an annual alcohol awareness week and drug awareness week.

Identification of Problems

Admissions College application does not ask about prior substance abuse problems.

On campus Current students identified as chemically dependent may remain enrolled, but treatment is required. Training program on identifying students with potential substance abuse problems for: resident advisers, coaches. No written procedures for students and staff if substance abuse is suspected.

Support Services

On campus AA, ACOA, private counseling.

Employee assistance Program for chemically dependent employees not available. Staff working with drug/alcohol-related issues: 1 part-time.

Disciplinary Actions

Alcohol Results of infractions of alcohol regulations (see Comparative Table of Alcohol Regulations) vary by situation.

Drugs For first-time use: varies by situation—counseling, warning. For first-time possession: varies by situation. For subsequent use: varies by situation—chemical dependency assessment, counseling, probation. For subsequent possession: varies by situation—suspension. For any sale: suspension, expulsion. Comments: Actions taken for possession vary according to the amount of the drug involved.

Additional Information from the College

The Alcohol Policy Guidelines Committee, in conjunction with the Office of Student Development, is expanding its role to include advising and developing a substance abuse awareness and education program. Current policies are being reviewed, and a practical referral system for substance abuse problems is being developed. Programs are expected to be further refined by fall 1989.

For More Information

Contact: Katie Deedrick, Assistant Director, Student Development, Wright State University, Colonel Glenn Highway, Dayton, OH 45435. Telephone: 513-873-2711.

YALE UNIVERSITY

New Haven, Connecticut

General Information

Independent comprehensive coed institution. Founded 1701. Awards B, M, D. Primary accreditation: regional. City setting; 185-acre campus. Total enrollment: 10,998. Faculty: 718. Social organizations: senior societies.

Drug and Alcohol Information

Education

On campus Drug and alcohol education/prevention programs offered for: all students, athletes/coaches. Authorized group concerned with responsible drinking. College holds an annual alcohol awareness week.

Identification of Problems

Admissions College application does not ask about prior substance abuse problems.

On campus Current students identified as chemically dependent may remain enrolled. Training program on identifying students with potential substance abuse problems for: resident advisers, coaches.

Support Services

On campus AA, Al-Anon, ACOA, private counseling.

Employee assistance Program for chemically dependent employees not available. Staff working with drug/alcohol-related issues: 1 full-time and 2–3 part-time.

Disciplinary Actions

Alcohol Results of infractions of alcohol regulations (see

Yale University (continued)

Comparative Table of Alcohol Regulations) include chemical dependency assessment, counseling.

Drugs For first-time use: varies by situation—counseling. For first-time possession or sale: varies by situation. For subsequent use, possession, or sale: varies by situation.

For More Information

Contact: Patricia Pierce, Associate Dean, Box 1604 A Yale Station, Yale University, New Haven, CT 06520. Telephone: 203-432-2916.

YORK COLLEGE OF PENNSYLVANIA

York, Pennsylvania

General Information

Independent 5-year coed college. Founded 1787. Awards A (college transfer and terminal), B, M. Primary accreditation: regional and AICS. City setting; 80-acre campus. Total enrollment: 4,789. Faculty: 273 (110 full-time, 163 part-time). Social organizations: 4 national fraternities, 2 national sororities, 5 local fraternities, 5 local sororities, student clubs; 33% of eligible undergraduate men and 11% of eligible undergraduate women are members.

Drug and Alcohol Information

Education

On campus Drug and alcohol education/prevention programs offered for: freshmen, athletes/coaches, resident advisers; required for: freshmen, athletes/coaches, resident advisers. Bacchus chapter. Other group also concerned with responsible drinking. College holds an annual alcohol awareness week.

Identification of Problems

Admissions College application does not ask about prior substance abuse problems.

On campus Current students identified as chemically dependent may remain enrolled, but treatment is required. Training program on identifying students with potential substance abuse problems for: resident advisers, coaches, Greek officers, faculty, administration. Written procedures for students and staff if substance abuse is suspected.

Support Services

On campus AA, Al-Anon, ACOA, support groups, private counseling.

Employee assistance Program for chemically dependent employees available. Staff working with drug/alcohol-related issues: 10 part-time.

Disciplinary Actions

Alcohol Results of infractions of alcohol regulations (see Comparative Table of Alcohol Regulations) vary by situation but can include counseling, warning, probation, suspension, expulsion.

Drugs For first-time use: varies by situation—counseling, warning. For first-time possession: varies by situation—warning. For subsequent use or possession: varies by situation—counseling, probation. For any sale: suspension.

For More Information

Contact: Kelly Barclay, Assistant Director of Resident Life, York College of Pennsylvania, York, PA 17313. Telephone: 717-846-7788 Ext. 468.

YORK COLLEGE OF THE CITY UNIVERSITY OF NEW YORK

Jamaica, New York

General Information

State and locally supported 4-year coed college. Part of City University of New York System. Founded 1967. Awards B. Primary accreditation: regional. Metropolitan setting; 50-acre campus. Total enrollment: 4,826. Faculty: 200 (150 full-time, 50 part-time).

Drug and Alcohol Information

Education

On campus Drug and alcohol education/prevention programs offered for: all students, athletes/coaches, faculty, administration. Authorized group concerned with responsible drinking. College holds an annual alcohol awareness week and drug awareness week.

Identification of Problems

Admissions College application does not ask about prior substance abuse problems.

On campus Current students identified as chemically dependent may remain enrolled. Training program on identifying students with potential substance abuse problems for: CUNY Substance Abuse Committee. Written procedures for students and staff if substance abuse is suspected.

Support Services

On campus AA, private counseling, group counseling.

Employee assistance Program for chemically dependent employees available. Staff working with drug/alcohol-related issues: 3 full-time.

Disciplinary Actions

Alcohol Results of infractions of alcohol regulations (see Comparative Table of Alcohol Regulations) include counseling, warning.

Drugs For first-time use: varies by situation—chemical dependency assessment, counseling, warning. For first-time possession: varies by situation. For first-time sale: varies by situation—probation, suspension. For subsequent use, possession, or sale: varies by situation.

For More Information

Contact: Vernon Haley, Dean of Student Development, York College of the City University of New York, 94-20 Guy R. Brewer Blvd., Jamaica, NY 11451. Telephone: 718-262-2282.

YOUNGSTOWN STATE UNIVERSITY

Youngstown, Ohio

General Information

State-supported 5-year coed college. Founded 1908. Awards A (college transfer and terminal), B, M. Primary accreditation: regional. City setting; 92-acre campus. Total enrollment: 14,710. Faculty: 887 (461 full-time, 426 part-time). Social organizations: 10 national fraternities, 5 national sororities; 2% of eligible undergraduate men and 1% of eligible undergraduate women are members.

Drug and Alcohol Information

Education

On campus Drug and alcohol education/prevention programs offered for: all students, faculty, administration. Authorized group concerned with responsible drinking. College holds an annual alcohol awareness week and drug awareness week.

Identification of Problems

Admissions College application does not ask about prior substance abuse problems.

On campus Current students identified as chemically dependent may remain enrolled. Training program on identifying students with potential substance abuse problems for: resident advisers, peer support groups. No written procedures for students and staff if substance abuse is suspected.

Support Services

On campus ACOA, support groups (organization of recovering students), private counseling, substance abuse services.

Employee assistance Program for chemically dependent employees not available. Staff working with drug/alcohol-related issues: 1 full-time.

Disciplinary Actions

Alcohol Results of infractions of alcohol regulations (see Comparative Table of Alcohol Regulations) vary by situation.

Drugs For any use, possession, or sale: varies by situation.

For More Information

Contact: Jain Savage, Coordinator, Health Enhancement Services, Youngstown State University, Youngstown, OH 44555. Telephone: 216-742-3322.

Comparative Table of Alcohol Regulations

	Alcohol is not permitted on campus.	Social events with alcohol are prohibited.	Social events with alcohol must be registered with the college.	All social events with alcohol must be BYOB.	Nonalcoholic alternatives must be provided where alcohol is served.	Food must be provided where alcohol is served.	Students must show proof of legal drinking age to attend a function with alcohol.	A responsible person of age must chaperone at social events with alcohol.	A limit on the quantity of alcohol per person at social events is specified.	Alcohol cannot be served at sporting events.	Drinking is restricted to designated areas.	Drinking games are prohibited.	Social organizations may not have alcohol at social events.	Social organizations are held responsible for infractions of alcohol regulations at their social events.
Acad of Art Coll	✓													
Adams State Coll	✓													
Adelphi U			✓		✓	✓	✓	✓		✓	✓	✓	✓	✓
Agnes Scott Coll			✓		✓	✓		✓		✓	✓	✓		✓
Alaska Pacific U	✓													
Albany Coll of Pharmacy of Union U			✓		✓	✓		✓		✓		✓		✓
Albany State Coll	✓													
Alderson-Broaddus Coll	✓									✓		✓	✓	✓
Alfred U			✓		✓	✓	✓	✓		✓	✓	✓		
Alice Lloyd Coll	✓													
Allegheny Coll			✓		✓	✓	✓			✓	✓	✓	✓	✓
Allentown Coll of St Francis de Sales			✓		✓	✓	✓	✓	✓	✓	✓	✓		✓
Alma Coll			✓		✓	✓			✓	✓		✓		✓
Alverno Coll			✓				✓	✓						
Amber U	✓													
Anderson U	✓													
Andrews U	✓													
Antioch U Santa Barbara		✓			✓	✓	✓				✓	✓		
Antioch U Seattle														
Appalachian Bible Coll	✓													
Aquinas Coll		✓								✓	✓	✓		✓
Arizona State U			✓		✓	✓	✓	✓	✓	✓	✓	✓		✓
Arkansas Baptist Coll	✓													✓
Arkansas State U	✓													
Arkansas Tech U	✓													
Armstrong State Coll			✓		✓	✓	✓	✓			✓	✓	✓	✓
Art Inst of Southern California			✓				✓				✓			
Atlanta Coll of Art			✓		✓	✓	✓	✓			✓			

A "dry" rush is required for social organizations.	The sponsoring of events by alcoholic beverage companies is prohibited.	Alcoholic beverage advertising is prohibited.	The group selling of alcohol for profit is prohibited.	Comments
✓	✓	✓	✓	
	✓	✓	✓	
				Alcohol prohibited in dorms.
✓	✓	✓	✓	
✓	✓	✓	✓	
✓	✓	✓	✓	
	✓	✓	✓	
✓		✓	✓	
				Alcohol use also prohibited off campus.
	✓	✓	✓	Alcohol is served only at public events.
				No formal policy; alcohol not served at campus functions.
	✓	✓	✓	
✓				
				County is dry.
			✓	

	Alcohol is not permitted on campus.	Social events with alcohol are prohibited.	Social events with alcohol must be registered with the college.	All social events must be BYOB.	Nonalcoholic alternatives must be provided where alcohol is served.	Food must be provided where alcohol is served.	Students must show proof of legal drinking age to attend a function with alcohol.	A responsible person of age must chaperone at social events with alcohol.	A limit on the quantity of alcohol per person at social events is specified.	Alcohol cannot be served at sporting events.	Drinking is restricted to designated areas.	Drinking games are prohibited.	Social organizations may not have alcohol at social events.	Social organizations are held responsible for infractions of alcohol regulations at their social events.
Atlantic Union Coll	✓													
Auburn U	✓													
Augsburg Coll			✓		✓	✓	✓	✓	✓	✓	✓	✓		✓
Augustana Coll (IL)	✓													
Augustana Coll (SD)	✓													
Aurora U	✓													
Austin Coll			✓		✓	✓	✓	✓	✓	✓	✓			✓
Austin Peay State U	✓													
Averett Coll	✓													✓
Azusa Pacific U	✓													
Baker Coll	✓													
Baker Coll of Owosso	✓													
Baldwin-Wallace Coll			✓		✓	✓			✓	✓	✓	✓		✓
Ball State U			✓		✓	✓	✓	✓		✓	✓	✓		✓
Baptist Bible Coll of Pennsylvania	✓													
Baptist Coll at Charleston	✓													
Bard Coll			✓		✓	✓		✓		✓				
Barnard Coll			✓		✓	✓		✓			✓			✓
Bartlesville Wesleyan Coll	✓													
Baruch Coll of the City U of New York			✓				✓							
Bassist Coll	✓													
Bayamón Central U	✓													
Baylor U	✓													✓
Belhaven Coll	✓													
Bellarmine Coll			✓	✓	✓	✓		✓	✓			✓		✓
Bellevue Coll			✓		✓		✓	✓	✓					
Bellin Coll of Nursing	✓													
Belmont Abbey Coll			✓		✓	✓	✓	✓	✓	✓	✓	✓		✓
Bemidji State U	✓													✓

A "dry" rush is required for social organizations.	The sponsoring of events by alcoholic beverage companies is prohibited.	Alcoholic beverage advertising is prohibited.	The group selling of alcohol for profit is prohibited.	Comments
		✓	✓	
				Chaperones, proof of age required at off-campus events.
✓		✓	✓	
✓	✓	✓		Two proofs of age required to obtain alcohol at regulated parties.
✓	✓		✓	
	✓	✓	✓	
	✓			Nearly all campus events are alcohol-free.
				Beer and wine are the only alcoholic beverages permitted.
				The legal drinking age is 18.
	✓	✓	✓	
			✓	
	✓	✓	✓	City of Belmont is dry.

Comparative Table of Alcohol Regulations

	Alcohol is not permitted on campus.	Social events with alcohol are prohibited.	Social events with alcohol must be registered with the college.	All social events with alcohol must be BYOB.	Nonalcoholic alternatives must be provided where alcohol is served.	Food must be provided where alcohol is served.	Students must show proof of legal drinking age to attend a function with alcohol.	A responsible person of age must chaperone at social events with alcohol.	A limit on the quantity of alcohol per person at social events is specified.	Alcohol cannot be served at sporting events.	Drinking is restricted to designated areas.	Drinking games are prohibited.	Social organizations may not have alcohol at social events.	Social organizations are held responsible for infractions of alcohol regulations at their social events.
Benedict Coll	✓													
Benedictine Coll		✓								✓	✓	✓		✓
Bennington Coll		✓									✓			
Bentley Coll			✓		✓	✓	✓	✓		✓	✓			✓
Berklee Coll of Music												✓		✓
Berry Coll	✓													
Bethany Coll (KS)	✓													✓
Bethany Coll (WV)			✓		✓				✓	✓	✓			✓
Bethel Coll (KS)	✓													
Bethel Coll (MN)	✓													✓
Beth-El Coll of Nursing	✓													
Bethune-Cookman Coll	✓													
Biola U	✓													
Birmingham-Southern Coll				✓	✓	✓	✓	✓		✓	✓			✓
Blackburn Coll			✓		✓	✓	✓	✓		✓	✓	✓	✓	✓
Black Hills State Coll	✓													✓
Bloomfield Coll			✓		✓	✓		✓	✓		✓	✓		✓
Bloomsburg U of Pennsylvania	✓													✓
Bluefield State Coll	✓													
Blue Mountain Coll	✓													
Bluffton Coll	✓													
Boise Bible Coll	✓													
Boise State U		✓								✓	✓	✓		✓
Boston Coll			✓		✓	✓	✓	✓	✓	✓	✓			✓
Bowdoin Coll										✓	✓			✓
Bowie State U						✓	✓	✓	✓	✓	✓		✓	✓
Bowling Green State U			✓		✓	✓	✓	✓	✓		✓	✓		✓
Bradford Coll			✓	✓	✓	✓		✓	✓		✓			✓
Bradley U					✓	✓					✓	✓		

A "dry" rush is required for social organizations.	The sponsoring of events by alcoholic beverage companies is prohibited.	Alcoholic beverage advertising is prohibited	The group selling of alcohol for profit is prohibited.	Comments
	✓	✓	✓	
	✓			
✓			✓	
	✓	✓		Students of legal age may have alcohol in their rooms.
✓			✓	
	✓	✓	✓	Rules apply to events sponsored by students 21 or over.
			✓	
			✓	
✓	✓	✓	✓	
✓			✓	As a rule, social events including alcoholic beverages are prohibited.
✓	✓	✓	✓	
			✓	
✓			✓	

Comparative Table of Alcohol Regulations

	Alcohol is not permitted on campus.	Social events with alcohol are prohibited.	Social events with alcohol must be registered with the college.	All social events must be BYOB.	Nonalcoholic alternatives must be provided where alcohol is served.	Food must be provided where alcohol is served.	Students must show proof of legal drinking age to attend a function with alcohol.	A responsible person of age must chaperone at social events with alcohol.	A limit on the quantity of alcohol per person at social events is specified.	Alcohol cannot be served at sporting events.	Drinking is restricted to designated areas.	Drinking games are prohibited.	Social organizations may not have alcohol at social events.	Social organizations are held responsible for infractions of alcohol regulations at their social events.
Brescia Coll	✓													✓
Briar Cliff Coll			✓		✓	✓	✓	✓		✓	✓			
Bridgewater State Coll			✓		✓		✓		✓	✓	✓	✓		✓
Brigham Young U–Hawaii Cmps	✓													
Brown U			✓		✓	✓	✓	✓	✓	✓	✓			✓
Bryn Mawr Coll					✓	✓	✓			✓	✓	✓		✓
Buena Vista Coll					✓		✓	✓		✓	✓	✓		✓
Burlington Coll					✓									
Butler U			✓		✓	✓	✓	✓	✓	✓	✓			✓
Cabrini Coll			✓		✓	✓			✓	✓				
Caldwell Coll			✓		✓	✓	✓	✓		✓	✓	✓		✓
California Baptist Coll	✓													✓
California Inst of Tech			✓		✓	✓		✓		✓				✓
California Inst of the Arts			✓		✓	✓								
California Maritime Acad	✓													✓
Calif Polytechnic State U, San Luis Obispo	✓													✓
California State Polytechnic U, Pomona			✓		✓	✓			✓	✓	✓		✓	
California State U, Bakersfield			✓					✓				✓		✓
California State U, Dominguez Hills			✓		✓						✓			✓
California State U, Fresno			✓		✓	✓	✓	✓			✓	✓	✓	
California State U, Fullerton					✓		✓				✓	✓		✓
California State U, Sacramento			✓		✓						✓			✓
California State U, San Bernardino			✓		✓		✓	✓			✓	✓		✓
California State U, Stanislaus							✓			✓	✓			
California U of Pennsylvania	✓													
Cameron U	✓													✓
Campbellsville Coll	✓													✓
Campbell U	✓													

A "dry" rush is required for social organizations.	The sponsoring of events by alcoholic beverage companies is prohibited.	Alcoholic beverage advertising is prohibited.	The group selling of alcohol for profit is prohibited.	Comments
				Alcohol may be served, subject to restrictions, at certain events.
		✓	✓	
✓	✓	✓	✓	
✓	✓	✓	✓	
	✓	✓	✓	Alcohol not served at events when undergraduates are invited.
			✓	
✓	✓	✓	✓	A list of guidelines must be approved before serving alcohol.
		✓	✓	
	✓	✓	✓	
	✓	✓	✓	
	✓	✓	✓	
				Exceptions may be made with special permission—once or twice a year.
				Exceptions are occasional receptions, 4–5 tailgate parties per year.
			✓	Alcohol permitted in rooms of students over 21, at beer bar in Union.
✓				
✓			✓	
✓			✓	
✓	✓		✓	
✓			✓	
✓			✓	

Comparative Table of Alcohol Regulations

	Alcohol is not permitted on campus.	Social events with alcohol are prohibited.	All social events with alcohol must be registered with the college.	All social events must be BYOB.	Nonalcoholic alternatives must be provided where alcohol is served.	Food must be provided where alcohol is served.	Students must show proof of legal drinking age to attend a function with alcohol.	A responsible person of age must chaperone at social events with alcohol.	A limit on the quantity of alcohol per person at social events is specified.	Alcohol cannot be served at sporting events.	Drinking is restricted to designated areas.	Drinking games are prohibited.	Social organizations may not have alcohol at social events.	Social organizations are held responsible for infractions of alcohol regulations at their social events.
Canisius Coll			✓		✓	✓		✓	✓			✓		✓
Capital U			✓		✓	✓			✓	✓	✓	✓		✓
Capitol Coll			✓		✓	✓		✓	✓		✓			✓
Cardinal Stritch Coll			✓		✓	✓	✓	✓		✓	✓	✓		✓
Carleton Coll			✓		✓	✓	✓			✓	✓			
Carlow Coll	✓													✓
Carnegie Mellon U			✓		✓	✓	✓	✓		✓				✓
Carroll Coll													✓	✓
Carson-Newman Coll	✓													
Carthage Coll	✓													✓
Case Western Reserve U			✓		✓	✓	✓		✓		✓	✓		✓
Catawba Coll			✓		✓	✓	✓	✓		✓	✓	✓		
Cedar Crest Coll			✓		✓	✓	✓		✓		✓			
Cedarville Coll	✓													
Centenary Coll			✓		✓	✓	✓	✓	✓	✓	✓	✓		✓
Central Connecticut State U	✓													
Central Methodist Coll	✓													
Central Michigan U					✓	✓					✓	✓		✓
Central State U	✓													✓
Central U of Iowa	✓													✓
Central Washington U		✓								✓	✓			
Centre Coll			✓		✓	✓				✓	✓	✓		✓
Chaminade U of Honolulu			✓		✓	✓	✓		✓	✓	✓			✓
Chapman Coll			✓		✓	✓	✓	✓	✓	✓	✓			✓
Chatham Coll		✓								✓				✓
Cheyney U of Pennsylvania	✓													
Christ Coll Irvine		✓								✓	✓	✓		
Christian Brothers Coll			✓		✓	✓			✓	✓		✓		✓
The Citadel, The Military Coll of SC		✓			✓		✓					✓		✓

A "dry" rush is required for social organizations.	The sponsoring of events by alcoholic beverage companies is prohibited.	Alcoholic beverage advertising is prohibited.	The group selling of alcohol for profit is prohibited.	Comments
	✓		✓	
		✓		Students of age may have alcohol in their rooms.
			✓	
	✓			
	✓		✓	
✓		✓		
			✓	
✓				
	✓	✓	✓	
	✓	✓	✓	
✓		✓	✓	No alcohol is sold on campus except on monitored "Pub Nights."
				Alcohol may be served on rare occasions at special functions.
✓	✓		✓	CMU's alcohol policy is being revised.
	✓	✓	✓	A student 21 or older may consume alcohol only in his or her room.
	✓	✓	✓	
		✓	✓	
✓	✓	✓	✓	
	✓		✓	
	✓	✓	✓	Students of legal age may use alcohol in their apartments.
✓	✓	✓	✓	
			✓	Alcohol not sold to students on campus; may be served rarely.

Comparative Table of Alcohol Regulations

	Alcohol is not permitted on campus.	Social events with alcohol are prohibited.	Social events with alcohol must be registered with the college.	All social events must be BYOB.	Nonalcoholic alternatives must be provided where alcohol is served.	Food must be provided where alcohol is served.	Students must show proof of legal drinking age to attend a function with alcohol.	A responsible person of age must chaperone at social events with alcohol.	A limit on the quantity of alcohol per person at social events is specified.	Alcohol cannot be served at sporting events.	Drinking is restricted to designated areas.	Drinking games are prohibited.	Social organizations may not have alcohol at social events.	Social organizations are held responsible for infractions of alcohol regulations at their social events.
City Coll of the City U of New York			✓				✓							✓
Claflin Coll	✓													
Clarion U of Pennsylvania	✓													
Cleary Coll	✓													✓
Cogswell Polytechnical Coll			✓		✓	✓	✓	✓	✓		✓	✓		✓
Coker Coll			✓	✓	✓	✓	✓			✓	✓	✓		
Colby Coll			✓		✓	✓	✓		✓	✓	✓	✓		✓
Colgate U			✓		✓	✓	✓	✓	✓		✓	✓		✓
Coll Misericordia			✓		✓	✓	✓	✓		✓	✓	✓		✓
Coll of Aeronautics	✓													
Coll of Boca Raton			✓			✓	✓	✓		✓		✓	✓	
Coll of Charleston			✓	✓	✓	✓	✓	✓	✓	✓	✓	✓		✓
Coll of Great Falls			✓		✓	✓	✓	✓			✓			✓
Coll of Idaho			✓		✓	✓	✓				✓	✓		
Coll of Insurance							✓				✓			
Coll of Mount Saint Vincent			✓		✓	✓	✓			✓	✓	✓		✓
Coll of New Rochelle			✓		✓	✓	✓	✓	✓	✓	✓	✓	✓	✓
Coll of Notre Dame			✓		✓	✓	✓	✓	✓		✓			✓
Coll of Saint Benedict			✓		✓	✓		✓	✓	✓	✓	✓		✓
Coll of St Catherine			✓		✓	✓		✓			✓			✓
Coll of Saint Elizabeth			✓		✓	✓	✓	✓		✓	✓	✓		✓
Coll of Saint Mary			✓		✓	✓	✓	✓						✓
Coll of St Scholastica			✓		✓			✓			✓	✓		
Coll of St Thomas			✓		✓	✓	✓	✓	✓	✓	✓	✓	✓	✓
Coll of Santa Fe		✓			✓	✓	✓			✓	✓	✓	✓	✓
Coll of Staten Island of the City U of NY	✓													
Coll of the Southwest	✓													
Coll of William and Mary			✓		✓	✓	✓		✓		✓	✓		✓

A "dry" rush is required for social organizations.	The sponsoring of events by alcoholic beverage companies is prohibited.	Alcoholic beverage advertising is prohibited.	The group selling of alcohol for profit is prohibited.	Comments
			✓	Wine and beer are allowed on campus only by special permission.
	✓	✓		
		✓	✓	
	✓	✓	✓	
✓			✓	
	✓	✓	✓	
	✓	✓	✓	Students of age may consume alcohol only in their rooms.
✓	✓	✓	✓	Only beer may be brought to campus social events.
		✓	✓	Events where alcohol is served are limited.
			✓	
				No alcohol permitted at official student functions on or off campus.
		✓	✓	
	✓	✓	✓	Complete guide to alcohol policies available to students.
		✓	✓	
✓		✓	✓	
	✓	✓	✓	
			✓	
			✓	
✓	✓		✓	
✓	✓	✓	✓	
✓		✓	✓	

Comparative Table of Alcohol Regulations

	Alcohol is not permitted on campus.	Social events with alcohol are prohibited.	Social events with alcohol must be registered with the college.	All social events with alcohol must be BYOB.	Nonalcoholic alternatives must be provided where alcohol is served.	Food must be provided where alcohol is served.	Students must show proof of legal drinking age to attend a function with alcohol.	A responsible person of age must chaperone at social events with alcohol.	A limit on the quantity of alcohol per person at social events is specified.	Alcohol cannot be served at sporting events.	Drinking is restricted to designated areas.	Drinking games are prohibited.	Social organizations may not have alcohol at social events.	Social organizations are held responsible for infractions of alcohol regulations at their social events.
Coll of Wooster			✓		✓	✓	✓		✓	✓	✓			✓
Colorado Tech Coll					✓	✓	✓	✓						✓
Columbia Christian Coll	✓													✓
Columbia Coll (CA)	✓													
Columbia Coll (IL)		✓												
Columbia Coll (MO)	✓													
Columbia Coll (NY)			✓		✓	✓	✓	✓		✓		✓		✓
Columbus Coll	✓													✓
Columbus Coll of Art and Design	✓													
Combs Coll of Music	✓													
Concordia Coll (MI)	✓													
Concordia Coll (MN)	✓													✓
Concordia Coll (MN)	✓													
Concordia Coll (NY)		✓								✓	✓	✓		✓
Concordia Lutheran Coll		✓								✓	✓	✓		✓
Concordia Teachers Coll	✓													
Conservatory of Music of Puerto Rico	✓													
Converse Coll			✓		✓	✓	✓	✓	✓		✓	✓		
Cooper Union for the Advancement of Science & Art			✓		✓	✓	✓		✓		✓			✓
Cornell Coll			✓		✓	✓	✓		✓	✓	✓			
Cornell U			✓		✓	✓		✓		✓		✓		✓
Cornish Coll of the Arts			✓				✓							✓
Covenant Coll	✓													
Culver-Stockton Coll	✓													
Dakota Wesleyan U	✓													✓
Dana Coll	✓													
Daniel Webster Coll			✓		✓					✓	✓			
Dartmouth Coll			✓		✓	✓	✓	✓		✓	✓			✓

A "dry" rush is required for social organizations.	The sponsoring of events by alcoholic beverage companies is prohibited.	Alcoholic beverage advertising is prohibited.	The group selling of alcohol for profit is prohibited.	Comments
✓	✓		✓	Sponsoring groups attend education program, then submit contract.
		✓		
	✓	✓	✓	
	✓	✓	✓	
	✓	✓	✓	Beer and wine are served in the campus pub.
		✓	✓	
		✓	✓	
				Groups must obtain state-issued banquet permits to serve alcohol.
			✓	Possession and use of alcohol allowed only in residence hall rooms.
✓				

Comparative Table of Alcohol Regulations

	Alcohol is not permitted on campus.	Social events with alcohol are prohibited.	Social events with alcohol are registered with the college.	All social events with alcohol must be BYOB.	Nonalcoholic alternatives must be provided where alcohol is served.	Food must be provided where alcohol is served.	Students must show proof of legal drinking age to attend a function with alcohol.	A responsible person of age must chaperone at social events with alcohol.	A limit on the quantity of alcohol per person at social events is specified.	Alcohol cannot be served at sporting events.	Drinking is restricted to designated areas.	Drinking games are prohibited.	Social organizations may not have alcohol at social events.	Social organizations are held responsible for infractions of alcohol regulations at their social events.
Davidson Coll			✓		✓	✓	✓	✓		✓	✓	✓		✓
Davis & Elkins Coll			✓		✓	✓	✓		✓	✓	✓	✓		✓
Deaconess Coll of Nursing	✓													
Defiance Coll			✓		✓	✓	✓	✓	✓	✓	✓			✓
Delaware Valley Coll			✓		✓	✓	✓	✓	✓	✓	✓	✓	✓	✓
Denison U			✓		✓	✓	✓		✓	✓	✓	✓		✓
Detroit Coll of Business–Flint	✓													
DeVry Inst of Tech (CA)	✓													✓
DeVry Inst of Tech (GA)	✓													
DeVry Inst of Tech (IL)	✓													✓
DeVry Inst of Tech (MO)	✓													
Dickinson Coll			✓		✓	✓	✓		✓	✓		✓		✓
Divine Word Coll			✓		✓	✓	✓	✓			✓	✓		✓
Doane Coll		✓					✓			✓	✓	✓		
Dominican Coll of San Rafael			✓		✓	✓	✓	✓			✓	✓		✓
Dordt Coll	✓													
Drake U			✓		✓	✓	✓	✓		✓	✓	✓		✓
D'Youville Coll			✓		✓	✓		✓			✓	✓		✓
Earlham Coll	✓													
East Carolina U			✓		✓	✓	✓	✓	✓	✓	✓	✓		✓
East Coast Bible Coll	✓													
Eastern Christian Coll	✓													
Eastern Coll	✓													
Eastern Illinois U							✓	✓				✓		
Eastern Mennonite Coll	✓													
Eastern Michigan U							✓			✓	✓			✓
Eastern Montana Coll			✓		✓	✓	✓	✓						✓
Eastern New Mexico U	✓													
Eastern Washington U			✓					✓			✓			✓

A "dry" rush is required for social organizations.	The sponsoring of events by alcoholic beverage companies is prohibited.	Alcoholic beverage advertising is prohibited.	The group selling of alcohol for profit is prohibited.	Comments
		✓		
✓	✓			
	✓	✓		
		✓	✓	
✓	✓	✓	✓	
✓	✓	✓	✓	Groups serving alcohol at social events must employ trained servers.
	✓	✓		
✓	✓		✓	An appointed Alcohol Task Force is reviewing College policies.
✓			✓	
			✓	
✓	✓			
✓			✓	
			✓	
			✓	Alcohol may be consumed by students of legal age only in their rooms.
✓			✓	

Comparative Table of Alcohol Regulations

	Alcohol is not permitted on campus.	Social events with alcohol are prohibited.	Social events with alcohol must be registered with the college.	All social events with alcohol must be BYOB.	Nonalcoholic alternatives must be provided where alcohol is served.	Food must be provided where alcohol is served.	Students must show proof of legal drinking age to attend a function with alcohol.	A responsible person of age must chaperone at social events with alcohol.	A limit on the quantity of alcohol per person at social events is specified.	Alcohol cannot be served at sporting events.	Drinking is restricted to designated areas.	Drinking games are prohibited.	Social organizations may not have alcohol at social events.	Social organizations are held responsible for infractions of alcohol regulations at their social events.
East Stroudsburg U of Pennsylvania	✓													
East Texas Baptist U	✓													
East Texas State U at Texarkana	✓													
Eckerd Coll				✓						✓	✓			✓
Edgewood Coll			✓		✓	✓	✓	✓		✓	✓	✓		✓
Edinboro U of Pennsylvania	✓													✓
Elizabethtown Coll	✓													
Elmhurst Coll			✓		✓	✓		✓		✓	✓	✓		✓
Elmira Coll			✓		✓		✓		✓		✓			✓
Elms Coll		✓			✓	✓								
Elon Coll			✓		✓	✓	✓	✓	✓	✓	✓	✓		✓
Embry-Riddle Aeronautical U			✓		✓	✓	✓	✓	✓		✓	✓		✓
Embry-Riddle Aeronautical U, Coll of Continuing Ed			✓		✓	✓		✓		✓	✓	✓		✓
Emmanuel Coll	✓													
Emmanuel Coll Sch of Christian Ministries	✓													
Emmaus Bible Coll	✓													✓
Emory & Henry Coll	✓													
Emporia State U			✓		✓	✓	✓	✓		✓	✓	✓		
Evergreen State Coll			✓		✓	✓	✓	✓		✓	✓		✓	✓
Fairfield U			✓				✓	✓		✓	✓	✓		
Fashion Inst of Tech	✓													✓
Ferris State U		✓								✓	✓		✓	✓
Fisk U	✓													
Fitchburg State Coll			✓		✓	✓	✓	✓	✓	✓	✓	✓		✓
Flagler Coll	✓													
Flaming Rainbow U	✓													
Florida Atlantic U			✓		✓	✓	✓	✓	✓		✓	✓		✓

A "dry" rush is required for social organizations.	The sponsoring of events by alcoholic beverage companies is prohibited.	Alcoholic beverage advertising is prohibited.	The group selling of alcohol for profit is prohibited.	Comments
	✓	✓	✓	
			✓	
✓			✓	
			✓	
				Students of legal age may possess and consume alcohol in their rooms.
✓	✓	✓	✓	
	✓	✓		
✓	✓	✓		
✓			✓	
			✓	Student-sponsored events that include alcohol are prohibited.
	✓	✓	✓	
✓		✓	✓	Containers holding over 1 gallon of alcohol are prohibited.
	✓	✓	✓	
✓			✓	

Comparative Table of Alcohol Regulations

	Alcohol is not permitted on campus.	Social events with alcohol are prohibited.	Social events with alcohol are registered with the college.	All social events with alcohol must be BYOB.	Nonalcoholic alternatives must be provided where alcohol is served.	Food must be provided where alcohol is served.	Students must show proof of legal drinking age to attend a function with alcohol.	A responsible person of age must chaperone at social events with alcohol.	A limit on the quantity of alcohol per person at social events is specified.	Alcohol cannot be served at sporting events.	Drinking is restricted to designated areas.	Drinking games are prohibited.	Social organizations may not have alcohol at social events.	Social organizations are held responsible for infractions of alcohol regulations at their social events.
Florida Inst of Tech		✓								✓	✓	✓		✓
Florida International U										✓	✓			✓
Florida State U					✓	✓	✓			✓	✓			✓
Fontbonne Coll			✓		✓	✓	✓			✓				
Fordham U			✓		✓	✓	✓			✓	✓			✓
Fort Hays State U			✓		✓	✓	✓			✓	✓	✓		✓
Fort Valley State Coll	✓													
Framingham State Coll			✓		✓	✓	✓	✓		✓	✓			✓
Franklin and Marshall Coll			✓		✓	✓				✓	✓	✓		
Franklin Coll of Indiana			✓		✓	✓				✓	✓	✓		✓
Franklin Pierce Coll			✓		✓	✓	✓				✓	✓		✓
Franklin U	✓													
Fresno Pacific Coll	✓													
Friends U	✓													✓
Furman U	✓													
Gallaudet U			✓			✓	✓				✓	✓		✓
Gannon U	✓													
Geneva Coll	✓													
George Mason U			✓		✓	✓	✓			✓	✓			✓
Georgetown Coll	✓													✓
Georgia Inst of Tech					✓	✓	✓	✓		✓	✓	✓		✓
Georgian Court Coll			✓		✓	✓	✓			✓	✓			✓
Georgia Southern Coll			✓		✓	✓	✓	✓		✓	✓	✓		✓
Georgia State U	✓													
Gettysburg Coll			✓		✓	✓		✓	✓	✓	✓			✓
Glassboro State Coll			✓		✓	✓	✓	✓		✓	✓	✓		
Glenville State Coll			✓		✓	✓	✓	✓		✓		✓		✓
GMI Engineering & Management Inst	✓													✓
Goddard Coll		✓												

A "dry" rush is required for social organizations.	The sponsoring of events by alcoholic beverage companies is prohibited.	Alcoholic beverage advertising is prohibited.	The group selling of alcohol for profit is prohibited.	Comments
✓			✓	
✓			✓	
✓			✓	
				Campus sale limited to beer and wine.
			✓	
			✓	
			✓	
		✓	✓	
✓	✓	✓	✓	
		✓	✓	
	✓	✓	✓	
		✓	✓	
				Georgetown College is located in a dry county.
✓	✓	✓	✓	
✓	✓	✓	✓	
✓	✓	✓	✓	
✓	✓		✓	Kegs are prohibited.
✓		✓	✓	
			✓	

Comparative Table of Alcohol Regulations

	Alcohol is not permitted on campus.	Social events with alcohol are prohibited.	Social events with alcohol must be registered with the college.	All social events with alcohol must be BYOB.	Nonalcoholic alternatives must be provided where alcohol is served.	Food must be provided where alcohol is served.	Students must show proof of legal drinking age to attend a function with alcohol.	A responsible person of age must chaperone at social events with alcohol.	A limit on the quantity of alcohol per person at social events is specified.	Alcohol cannot be served at sporting events.	Drinking is restricted to designated areas.	Drinking games are prohibited.	Social organizations may not have alcohol at social events.	Social organizations are held responsible for infractions of alcohol regulations at their social events.
Golden Gate U	✓													✓
Goldey-Beacom Coll			✓	✓						✓	✓			
Gonzaga U			✓		✓	✓	✓	✓	✓	✓	✓	✓		✓
Gordon Coll	✓													
Goshen Coll	✓													✓
Governors State U			✓					✓			✓			✓
Grambling State U	✓													✓
Grand View Coll					✓	✓	✓	✓		✓	✓	✓		✓
Green Mountain Coll		✓			✓	✓	✓		✓	✓	✓	✓	✓	
Grinnell Coll			✓		✓					✓	✓			
Grove City Coll	✓													✓
Guilford Coll					✓						✓			✓
Hamilton Coll			✓		✓	✓				✓				✓
Hampden-Sydney Coll			✓		✓	✓	✓		✓	✓	✓	✓		✓
Hannibal-LaGrange Coll	✓													
Hardin-Simmons U	✓													✓
Hartwick Coll		✓					✓			✓	✓	✓		✓
Henderson State U	✓													
Hendrix Coll		✓								✓	✓	✓		
Heritage Coll			✓		✓			✓	✓		✓			
Hillsdale Free Will Baptist Coll	✓													
Hofstra U			✓		✓	✓	✓	✓			✓			
Holy Family Coll	✓													
Holy Names Coll			✓		✓	✓	✓	✓	✓	✓	✓	✓		✓
Hood Coll			✓		✓	✓	✓	✓			✓	✓		✓
Houghton Coll	✓													
Howard Payne U	✓													
Howard U			✓		✓	✓		✓		✓	✓	✓		✓
Humboldt State U			✓		✓	✓	✓	✓	✓	✓	✓	✓		✓

A "dry" rush is required for social organizations.	The sponsoring of events by alcoholic beverage companies is prohibited.	Alcoholic beverage advertising is prohibited.	The group selling of alcohol for profit is prohibited.	Comments
		✓	✓	Students of legal age may use alcohol in their private quarters only.
			✓	
			✓	
		✓	✓	
	✓	✓	✓	Alcohol is allowed in private rooms of students of legal age.
		✓	✓	
	✓	✓	✓	
	✓	✓	✓	
	✓	✓	✓	
		✓	✓	
✓			✓	
			✓	Alcohol is served on campus only twice a year.
	✓	✓	✓	
		✓	✓	
		✓		Students of legal age may use alcohol in their residence hall rooms.

Comparative Table of Alcohol Regulations

	Alcohol is not permitted on campus.	Social events with alcohol are prohibited.	Social events with alcohol must be registered with the college.	All social events with alcohol must be BYOB.	Nonalcoholic alternatives must be provided where alcohol is served.	Food must be provided where alcohol is served.	Students must show proof of legal drinking age to attend a function with alcohol.	A responsible person of age must chaperone at social events with alcohol.	A limit on the quantity of alcohol per person at social events is specified.	Alcohol cannot be served at sporting events.	Drinking is restricted to designated areas.	Drinking games are prohibited.	Social organizations may not have alcohol at social events.	Social organizations are held responsible for infractions of alcohol regulations at their social events.
Huntingdon Coll	✓													✓
Huntington Coll	✓													
Husson Coll			✓		✓	✓	✓		✓	✓	✓			✓
Idaho State U	✓													
Illinois Benedictine Coll			✓		✓	✓	✓	✓	✓	✓	✓	✓	✓	✓
Illinois Inst of Tech			✓		✓	✓	✓	✓			✓	✓		✓
Illinois State U					✓	✓				✓	✓			✓
Immaculata Coll	✓													✓
Incarnate Word Coll			✓				✓	✓		✓	✓	✓		✓
Indiana Inst of Tech	✓													✓
Indiana State U			✓								✓	✓	✓	✓
Indiana U Bloomington	✓													
Indiana U East	✓													
Indiana U of Pennsylvania	✓													
Indiana U Southeast	✓													✓
Indiana Wesleyan U	✓													✓
Inter Amer U of PR, Arecibo Region Coll	✓													✓
Inter American U of PR, Metro Cmps	✓													✓
Intl Acad of Merchandising & Design		✓												
International Bible Coll	✓													
Iowa State U of Science and Tech					✓	✓	✓		✓		✓	✓		✓
Iowa Wesleyan Coll											✓			
Jacksonville State U	✓													
Jacksonville U			✓		✓	✓	✓	✓		✓	✓			✓
Jamestown Coll	✓													
Jersey City State Coll			✓		✓	✓	✓	✓	✓	✓	✓	✓		✓
Jewish Theological Sem of America			✓		✓	✓	✓							✓
John Bastyr Coll			✓		✓	✓	✓	✓			✓	✓		

A "dry" rush is required for social organizations.	The sponsoring of events by alcoholic beverage companies is prohibited.	Alcoholic beverage advertising is prohibited.	The group selling of alcohol for profit is prohibited.	Comments
	✓	✓		
	✓	✓	✓	
✓				
✓		✓	✓	
✓	✓		✓	
✓		✓		
✓	✓	✓	✓	
	✓	✓	✓	

Comparative Table of Alcohol Regulations

	Alcohol is not permitted on campus.	Social events with alcohol are prohibited.	Social events with alcohol are registered with the college.	All social events with alcohol must be BYOB.	Nonalcoholic alternatives must be provided where alcohol is served.	Food must be provided where alcohol is served.	Students must show proof of legal drinking age to attend a function with alcohol.	A responsible person of age must chaperone at social events with alcohol.	A limit on the quantity of alcohol per person at social events is specified.	Alcohol cannot be served at sporting events.	Drinking is restricted to designated areas.	Drinking games are prohibited.	Social organizations may not have alcohol at social events.	Social organizations are held responsible for infractions of alcohol regulations at their social events.
John Brown U	✓													
John Carroll U			✓			✓	✓	✓		✓	✓	✓		
Johnson & Wales U	✓													
Johnson C Smith U	✓													
Jones Coll	✓													
Judson Coll	✓													
Kalamazoo Coll			✓		✓	✓			✓	✓	✓			✓
Kansas State U							✓			✓				✓
Kean Coll of New Jersey			✓		✓	✓	✓	✓		✓	✓	✓		✓
Kearney State Coll	✓													
Keene State Coll			✓		✓	✓	✓	✓		✓	✓			✓
Kendall Coll	✓													
Kennesaw State Coll	✓													✓
Kent State U			✓		✓	✓	✓		✓	✓	✓	✓		✓
Kentucky Christian Coll	✓													
Kentucky State U	✓													
Kentucky Wesleyan Coll	✓													
Keuka Coll			✓		✓	✓	✓	✓	✓	✓	✓	✓		✓
King Coll	✓													
Knox Coll			✓		✓	✓	✓	✓		✓		✓		✓
Kutztown U of Pennsylvania	✓													✓
Lafayette Coll			✓		✓	✓	✓			✓	✓	✓		✓
LaGrange Coll	✓													
Lake Forest Coll			✓		✓	✓				✓	✓	✓		✓
Lake Superior State U			✓		✓	✓	✓			✓	✓			✓
Lander Coll	✓													✓
Lane Coll	✓													
Langston U	✓													✓
Laredo State U	✓													

A "dry" rush is required for social organizations.	The sponsoring of events by alcoholic beverage companies is prohibited.	Alcoholic beverage advertising is prohibited.	The group selling of alcohol for profit is prohibited.	Comments
✓				
	✓	✓	✓	
✓				
✓			✓	Alcohol is served only in the College Pub and Faculty Lounge.
		✓		
	✓			
	✓	✓	✓	
✓			✓	
✓	✓	✓	✓	
	✓		✓	
			✓	

Comparative Table of Alcohol Regulations

	Alcohol is not permitted on campus.	Social events with alcohol are prohibited.	Social events with alcohol are registered with the college.	All social events with alcohol must be BYOB.	Nonalcoholic alternatives must be provided where alcohol is served.	Food must be provided where alcohol is served.	Students must show proof of legal drinking age to attend a function with alcohol.	A responsible person of age must chaperone at social events with alcohol.	A limit on the quantity of alcohol per person at social events is specified.	Alcohol cannot be served at sporting events.	Drinking is restricted to designated areas.	Drinking games are prohibited.	Social organizations may not have alcohol at social events.	Social organizations are held responsible for infractions of alcohol regulations at their social events.
La Salle U			✓		✓	✓	✓	✓	✓	✓	✓	✓		✓
Lawrence U			✓		✓	✓	✓	✓		✓	✓			✓
Lees-McRae Coll	✓													
Lehigh U			✓		✓	✓				✓	✓	✓		✓
Lehman Coll of the City U of New York			✓		✓		✓	✓	✓					
Lenoir-Rhyne Coll			✓		✓	✓				✓	✓	✓		✓
Lewis-Clark State Coll	✓													
Liberty U	✓													
Limestone Coll	✓													✓
Lincoln Memorial U			✓		✓	✓	✓	✓		✓	✓		✓	
Lindenwood Coll			✓		✓	✓		✓	✓	✓	✓	✓		✓
Linfield Coll			✓		✓	✓				✓	✓			✓
Lock Haven U of Pennsylvania	✓													
Long Island U, C W Post Cmps			✓		✓		✓	✓		✓	✓	✓		✓
Long Island U, Southampton Cmps			✓		✓	✓	✓	✓	✓	✓	✓	✓		✓
Longwood Coll			✓		✓	✓	✓	✓	✓		✓	✓		✓
Loras Coll			✓		✓	✓		✓		✓	✓	✓		✓
Louisiana Coll	✓													✓
Loyola Coll					✓	✓		✓		✓	✓			
Loyola Marymount U			✓		✓	✓	✓	✓	✓	✓	✓	✓		✓
Loyola U, New Orleans			✓		✓	✓		✓			✓	✓		✓
Lubbock Christian U	✓													
Luther Coll		✓								✓	✓	✓		✓
Lycoming Coll			✓		✓	✓			✓	✓	✓	✓		✓
Lyndon State Coll		✓								✓				
Macalester Coll			✓		✓	✓			✓	✓	✓			
MacMurray Coll		✓								✓	✓			
Madonna Coll	✓													
Malone Coll	✓													✓

A "dry" rush is required for social organizations.	The sponsoring of events by alcoholic beverage companies is prohibited.	Alcoholic beverage advertising is prohibited.	The group selling of alcohol for profit is prohibited.	Comments
		✓	✓	
✓				
✓	✓		✓	
	✓	✓		
✓		✓	✓	
✓			✓	
✓			✓	
✓				
	✓	✓	✓	
	✓	✓		
✓	✓		✓	
	✓	✓	✓	
✓		✓		
✓	✓	✓		
✓			✓	
		✓		
	✓	✓	✓	

Comparative Table of Alcohol Regulations

	Alcohol is not permitted on campus.	Social events with alcohol are prohibited.	Social events with alcohol must be registered with the college.	All social events must be BYOB.	Nonalcoholic alternatives must be provided where alcohol is served.	Food must be provided where alcohol is served.	Students must show proof of legal drinking age to attend a function with alcohol.	A responsible person of age must chaperone at social events with alcohol.	A limit on the quantity of alcohol per person at social events is specified.	Alcohol cannot be served at sporting events.	Drinking is restricted to designated areas.	Drinking games are prohibited.	Social organizations may not have alcohol at social events.	Social organizations are held responsible for infractions of alcohol regulations at their social events.
Manchester Coll	✓													
Manhattan Coll			✓		✓	✓	✓	✓		✓	✓	✓		✓
Manhattan Sch of Music			✓		✓	✓	✓	✓	✓		✓	✓		
Manhattanville Coll			✓		✓	✓				✓	✓	✓		✓
Mankato State U	✓													
Mansfield U of Pennsylvania	✓													✓
Marian Coll	✓													✓
Marian Coll of Fond du Lac			✓		✓	✓	✓	✓		✓	✓	✓		✓
Marietta Coll			✓		✓	✓	✓	✓	✓	✓	✓	✓		✓
Mars Hill Coll	✓													✓
Martin Ctr Coll	✓													
Mary Baldwin Coll			✓								✓			
Marycrest Coll			✓		✓	✓	✓	✓		✓	✓	✓		
Marymount Coll			✓		✓	✓	✓	✓		✓	✓	✓		
Marymount Coll of Kansas	✓													
Marymount Manhattan Coll	✓													
Marymount U			✓		✓	✓		✓	✓	✓	✓	✓		
Maryville Coll			✓	✓		✓	✓	✓		✓	✓	✓		✓
Maryville College–Saint Louis			✓		✓	✓	✓	✓			✓			
Mary Washington Coll			✓		✓	✓	✓		✓	✓	✓	✓		
Marywood Coll	✓													
MA Coll of Pharm & Allied Health Sci			✓		✓	✓	✓	✓			✓	✓		✓
Mayville State U	✓													
McPherson Coll	✓													
Medaille Coll			✓		✓	✓	✓	✓	✓			✓		✓
Medical U of South Carolina			✓		✓		✓	✓						✓
Memphis Coll of Art	✓													
Memphis State U	✓													✓
Menlo Coll			✓		✓	✓				✓				✓

A "dry" rush is required for social organizations.	The sponsoring of events by alcoholic beverage companies is prohibited.	Alcoholic beverage advertising is prohibited.	The group selling of alcohol for profit is prohibited.	Comments
		✓		
				Alcohol is available on campus three times a year.
			✓	
✓	✓	✓	✓	
			✓	
	✓	✓	✓	
	✓	✓	✓	
	✓	✓	✓	
		✓		
	✓	✓		
	✓	✓	✓	
✓			✓	

	Alcohol is not permitted on campus.	Social events with alcohol are prohibited.	Social events with alcohol must be registered with the college.	All social events must be BYOB.	Nonalcoholic alternatives must be provided where alcohol is served.	Food must be provided where alcohol is served.	Students must show proof of legal drinking age to attend a function with alcohol.	A responsible person of age must chaperone at social events with alcohol.	A limit on the quantity of alcohol per person at social events is specified.	Alcohol cannot be served at sporting events.	Drinking is restricted to designated areas.	Drinking games are prohibited.	Social organizations may not have alcohol at social events.	Social organizations are held responsible for infractions of alcohol regulations at their social events.
Mennonite Coll of Nursing	✓													
Mercer U Atlanta	✓													
Mercy Coll			✓		✓	✓	✓	✓	✓		✓	✓		
Merrimack Coll					✓	✓	✓	✓	✓		✓			✓
Mesa State Coll			✓			✓	✓	✓	✓	✓	✓	✓	✓	
Messiah Coll	✓													✓
Methodist Coll	✓													
Metropolitan State U	✓													
Miami U			✓		✓	✓	✓		✓	✓	✓	✓		✓
Michigan State U		✓									✓		✓	✓
Michigan Tech U					✓	✓				✓	✓			
MidAmerica Nazarene Coll	✓													
Milligan Coll	✓													✓
Millsaps Coll		✓								✓	✓	✓		✓
Mills Coll			✓		✓	✓	✓	✓		✓	✓			✓
Milwaukee Inst of Art and Design	✓													
Minneapolis Coll of Art and Design			✓		✓	✓	✓	✓	✓				✓	✓
Minot State U	✓													
Mississippi U for Women	✓													✓
Missouri Southern State Coll	✓													✓
Mobile Coll	✓													✓
Molloy Coll			✓		✓	✓	✓	✓		✓	✓	✓		✓
Monmouth Coll			✓		✓	✓	✓	✓		✓	✓	✓		✓
Montana Coll of Mineral Sci & Tech			✓		✓	✓	✓	✓	✓	✓	✓			✓
Montana State U	✓													✓
Montclair State Coll			✓		✓	✓	✓	✓		✓	✓	✓	✓	✓
Moorhead State U	✓													✓
Moravian Coll			✓		✓	✓		✓		✓	✓	✓		✓
Morehead State U	✓													

A "dry" rush is required for social organizations.	The sponsoring of events by alcoholic beverage companies is prohibited.	Alcoholic beverage advertising is prohibited.	The group selling of alcohol for profit is prohibited.	Comments
	✓		✓	
	✓			
✓				
✓	✓	✓	✓	Students 21 and over may drink in residence hall rooms.
	✓		✓	Need special license for group sale of alcohol.
✓	✓	✓		
		✓	✓	
			✓	No alcohol on campus except for special occasions and some housing.
	✓	✓		
✓			✓	
			✓	
	✓		✓	
✓	✓	✓	✓	

Comparative Table of Alcohol Regulations

	Alcohol is not permitted on campus.	Social events with alcohol are prohibited.	Social events with alcohol must be registered with the college.	All social events must be BYOB.	Nonalcoholic alternatives must be provided where alcohol is served.	Food must be provided where alcohol is served.	Students must show proof of legal drinking age to attend a function with alcohol.	A responsible person of age must chaperone at social events with alcohol.	A limit on the quantity of alcohol per person at social events is specified.	Alcohol cannot be served at sporting events.	Drinking is restricted to designated areas.	Drinking games are prohibited.	Social organizations may not have alcohol at social events.	Social organizations are held responsible for infractions of alcohol regulations at their social events.
Morgan State U	✓													✓
Morningside Coll		✓								✓	✓	✓	✓	✓
Morris Coll	✓													
Mount Holyoke Coll			✓		✓	✓	✓				✓			✓
Mount Ida Coll		✓									✓		✓	
Mount Mary Coll			✓		✓	✓	✓			✓	✓	✓		✓
Mount Olive Coll	✓													✓
Mount St Mary's Coll			✓		✓	✓	✓	✓			✓			✓
Mount Saint Mary's Coll					✓	✓	✓	✓	✓	✓	✓	✓	✓	✓
Mount Vernon Coll			✓		✓	✓		✓				✓		
Mount Vernon Nazarene Coll	✓													
Muhlenberg Coll			✓		✓	✓	✓		✓	✓	✓	✓		✓
Mundelein Coll			✓		✓	✓	✓	✓	✓		✓			
Murray State U	✓													
Muskegon Coll	✓													
Muskingum Coll			✓		✓	✓	✓	✓		✓	✓	✓		✓
NAES Coll	✓													
National College–St Paul Cmps	✓													✓
Nazareth Coll in Kalamazoo			✓		✓	✓	✓	✓		✓	✓			
Nazareth Coll of Rochester			✓		✓	✓	✓	✓		✓	✓			✓
Nebraska Christian Coll	✓													
Newberry Coll			✓		✓	✓	✓			✓	✓			✓
New Coll of California				✓	✓	✓	✓	✓		✓		✓		✓
New Coll of the U of South Florida							✓							✓
New England Coll			✓		✓	✓	✓			✓	✓	✓		✓
New Hampshire Coll			✓		✓	✓	✓		✓	✓	✓	✓		✓
New Mexico Inst of Mining and Tech							✓							
New Mexico State U		✓					✓			✓			✓	✓
New York Sch of Interior Design			✓		✓		✓	✓						✓

A "dry" rush is required for social organizations.	The sponsoring of events by alcoholic beverage companies is prohibited.	Alcoholic beverage advertising is prohibited.	The group selling of alcohol for profit is prohibited.	Comments
			✓	
		✓		Hand stamp or wrist band required for legal-age drinkers.
	✓	✓	✓	
	✓	✓	✓	
	✓	✓		
	✓	✓	✓	
✓	✓	✓	✓	
✓		✓	✓	
	✓	✓	✓	Students of legal age may have alcohol in their rooms only.
			✓	
✓		✓	✓	Students of legal age may consume only beer or wine in their rooms.
	✓	✓	✓	
✓	✓	✓	✓	
✓	✓	✓		
	✓	✓		
✓			✓	

Comparative Table of Alcohol Regulations

	Alcohol is not permitted on campus.	Social events with alcohol are prohibited.	Social events with alcohol must be registered with the college.	All social events must be BYOB.	Nonalcoholic alternatives must be provided where alcohol is served.	Food must be provided where alcohol is served.	Students must show proof of legal drinking age to attend a function with alcohol.	A responsible person of age must chaperone at social events with alcohol.	A limit on the quantity of alcohol per person at social events is specified.	Alcohol cannot be served at sporting events.	Drinking is restricted to designated areas.	Drinking games are prohibited.	Social organizations may not have alcohol at social events.	Social organizations are held responsible for infractions of alcohol regulations at their social events.
New York U			✓		✓	✓	✓	✓				✓		✓
Nichols Coll		✓			✓	✓	✓			✓	✓	✓		✓
North Adams State Coll			✓		✓	✓	✓	✓	✓	✓	✓			
North Carolina Central U			✓				✓	✓		✓	✓			✓
North Carolina State U			✓		✓	✓	✓	✓		✓	✓	✓	✓	✓
North Dakota State U	✓													✓
Northeastern Illinois U			✓				✓	✓		✓	✓	✓		✓
Northeastern State U	✓													
Northeastern U			✓		✓		✓		✓	✓				✓
Northeast Louisiana U			✓				✓			✓	✓		✓	
Northeast Missouri State U	✓													✓
Northern Arizona U			✓		✓	✓	✓	✓	✓	✓	✓		✓	✓
Northern Illinois U			✓		✓	✓	✓				✓			✓
Northern Kentucky U		✓								✓	✓	✓		✓
Northern Montana Coll			✓		✓	✓	✓	✓	✓	✓	✓	✓		
Northern State Coll	✓													
North Georgia Coll	✓													✓
Northland Coll			✓		✓	✓	✓	✓		✓	✓	✓		✓
North Park Coll	✓													✓
Northrop U			✓				✓	✓			✓			✓
Northwest Christian Coll	✓													
Northwestern Coll	✓													
Northwestern Coll	✓													✓
Northwestern U			✓		✓	✓			✓	✓		✓		✓
Northwest Missouri State U	✓													
Northwood Inst			✓		✓	✓	✓	✓	✓	✓	✓	✓	✓	✓
Northwood Inst, Florida Cmps	✓													
Norwich U	✓													✓
Nova U			✓		✓	✓		✓		✓	✓	✓		

A "dry" rush is required for social organizations.	The sponsoring of events by alcoholic beverage companies is prohibited.	Alcoholic beverage advertising is prohibited.	The group selling of alcohol for profit is prohibited.	Comments
✓	✓		✓	
			✓	
			✓	
			✓	
✓			✓	
✓	✓	✓	✓	
✓			✓	
✓				
✓			✓	
✓				
	✓	✓	✓	
			✓	
✓		✓	✓	
✓	✓	✓	✓	
			✓	

Comparative Table of Alcohol Regulations

Institution	Alcohol is not permitted on campus.	Social events with alcohol are prohibited.	Social events with alcohol must be registered with the college.	All social events with alcohol must be BYOB.	Nonalcoholic alternatives must be provided where alcohol is served.	Food must be provided where alcohol is served.	Students must show proof of legal drinking age to attend a function with alcohol.	A responsible person of age must chaperone at social events with alcohol.	A limit on the quantity of alcohol per person at social events is specified.	Alcohol cannot be served at sporting events.	Drinking is restricted to designated areas.	Drinking games are prohibited.	Social organizations may not have alcohol at social events.	Social organizations are held responsible for infractions of alcohol regulations at their social events.
Oak Hills Bible Coll	✓													
Oakland U			✓		✓	✓		✓	✓	✓	✓	✓	✓	✓
Oakwood Coll	✓													
Oberlin Coll			✓		✓	✓	✓							
Oglethorpe U			✓		✓	✓	✓	✓			✓			✓
Ohio State University–Marion Cmps			✓				✓	✓			✓	✓	✓	
Ohio Valley Coll	✓													
Oklahoma Baptist U	✓													✓
Oklahoma State U	✓													✓
Old Dominion U			✓		✓	✓	✓			✓	✓	✓		✓
Olivet Coll			✓		✓	✓				✓	✓			✓
Oregon Inst of Tech			✓		✓	✓	✓	✓	✓	✓		✓		✓
Oregon State U			✓		✓	✓	✓				✓			✓
Orlando Coll	✓													
Otis Art Inst of Parsons Sch of Des, New Sch for Soc Res	✓													
Ouachita Baptist U	✓													
Our Lady of Holy Cross Coll			✓		✓	✓	✓	✓						✓
Our Lady of the Lake U of San Antonio			✓		✓	✓	✓	✓			✓	✓		✓
Pace U, White Plains Cmps			✓		✓	✓	✓	✓	✓	✓	✓	✓		✓
Pacific Christian Coll	✓													
Pacific Coast Baptist Bible Coll	✓													
Pacific NW Coll of Art, Oregon Art Inst	✓													
Pacific Oaks Coll					✓									
Paier Coll of Art, Inc			✓		✓	✓		✓						
Palm Beach Atlantic Coll	✓													
Pan American U			✓		✓	✓	✓	✓			✓	✓		✓
Park Coll	✓													✓
Patten Coll	✓													

A "dry" rush is required for social organizations.	The sponsoring of events by alcoholic beverage companies is prohibited.	Alcoholic beverage advertising is prohibited.	The group selling of alcohol for profit is prohibited.	Comments
✓	✓		✓	
✓	✓	✓	✓	
	✓		✓	
✓		✓		
		✓	✓	
			✓	
✓	✓	✓	✓	
			✓	
	✓			Severe restrictions on drinking when it is permitted.
✓	✓	✓	✓	
			✓	
		✓	✓	

Comparative Table of Alcohol Regulations

	Alcohol is not permitted on campus.	Social events with alcohol are prohibited.	Social events with alcohol must be registered with the college.	All social events with alcohol must be BYOB.	Nonalcoholic alternatives must be provided where alcohol is served.	Food must be provided where alcohol is served.	Students must show proof of legal drinking age to attend a function with alcohol.	A responsible person of age must chaperone at social events with alcohol.	A limit on the quantity of alcohol per person at social events is specified.	Alcohol cannot be served at sporting events.	Drinking is restricted to designated areas.	Drinking games are prohibited.	Social organizations may not have alcohol at social events.	Social organizations are held responsible for infractions of alcohol regulations at their social events.
Peabody Conservatory of Music		✓												
Pembroke State U							✓	✓	✓	✓	✓			✓
PA State U at Erie, The Behrend Coll							✓			✓		✓		✓
Pepperdine U	✓													✓
Peru State Coll	✓													
Pfeiffer Coll			✓	✓	✓	✓	✓	✓		✓	✓			✓
Phila Coll of Pharmacy & Science	✓													✓
Pine Manor Coll			✓		✓	✓	✓	✓		✓	✓	✓		✓
Pittsburg State U	✓													
Pitzer Coll			✓		✓	✓						✓		✓
Plymouth State Coll of the U Sys of NH			✓		✓	✓	✓	✓		✓	✓			✓
Point Loma Nazarene Coll	✓													
Point Park Coll		✓					✓			✓	✓	✓		✓
Polytechnic U, Brooklyn Cmps		✓								✓				
Polytechnic U, Farmingdale Cmps		✓								✓				
Pomona Coll			✓		✓	✓				✓	✓	✓		✓
Portland State U			✓		✓	✓	✓	✓		✓	✓	✓		✓
Post Coll			✓		✓	✓	✓	✓	✓	✓		✓	✓	
Prairie View A&M U	✓													✓
Presbyterian Coll			✓	✓						✓	✓	✓		✓
Princeton U			✓		✓	✓	✓	✓		✓	✓	✓		✓
Providence Coll			✓		✓	✓	✓	✓	✓		✓	✓		✓
Purdue U	✓													✓
Quincy Coll			✓		✓	✓		✓	✓	✓				✓
Quinnipiac Coll			✓		✓	✓	✓	✓	✓	✓	✓			✓
Radford U			✓		✓	✓			✓		✓	✓		✓
Ramapo Coll of New Jersey			✓		✓	✓	✓		✓	✓	✓	✓		✓
Randolph-Macon Woman's Coll			✓		✓	✓					✓			✓
Ray Coll of Design	✓													

A "dry" rush is required for social organizations.	The sponsoring of events by alcoholic beverage companies is prohibited.	Alcoholic beverage advertising is prohibited.	The group selling of alcohol for profit is prohibited.	Comments
✓	✓	✓	✓	
			✓	
	✓	✓	✓	
	✓	✓	✓	
	✓	✓	✓	
✓				
	✓	✓	✓	
	✓	✓	✓	
			✓	
	✓	✓	✓	
✓	✓	✓	✓	Beer and wine only are allowed for students of legal age.
		✓	✓	
	✓	✓	✓	
		✓	✓	No kegs; no alcohol in underclass halls.
✓			✓	
✓		✓		
			✓	
	✓	✓	✓	

Comparative Table of Alcohol Regulations

	Alcohol is not permitted on campus.	Social events with alcohol are prohibited.	Social events with alcohol must be registered with the college.	All social events with alcohol must be BYOB.	Nonalcoholic alternatives must be provided where alcohol is served.	Food must be provided where alcohol is served.	Students must show proof of legal drinking age to attend a function with alcohol.	A responsible person of age must chaperone at social events with alcohol.	A limit on the quantity of alcohol per person at social events is specified.	Alcohol cannot be served at sporting events.	Drinking is restricted to designated areas.	Drinking games are prohibited.	Social organizations may not have alcohol at social events.	Social organizations are held responsible for infractions of alcohol regulations at their social events.
Reed Coll					✓			✓						
Regis Coll					✓	✓	✓			✓	✓	✓		
Reno Business Coll	✓													
Rensselaer Polytechnic Inst			✓		✓	✓		✓	✓	✓	✓			✓
Research Coll of Nursing			✓		✓	✓		✓						
Rhode Island Coll	✓													
Rhodes Coll			✓		✓	✓		✓		✓	✓			✓
Rice U			✓		✓	✓								✓
Rider Coll			✓		✓	✓	✓	✓		✓	✓		✓	✓
Ringling Sch of Art and Design	✓													✓
Rio Grande Coll/Comm Coll			✓		✓	✓	✓	✓	✓	✓	✓	✓		✓
Ripon Coll		✓								✓	✓			✓
Roanoke Coll			✓		✓	✓				✓	✓			✓
Robert Morris Coll	✓													
Roberts Wesleyan Coll	✓													
Rochester Inst of Tech			✓		✓	✓	✓	✓	✓	✓	✓	✓	✓	✓
Rockhurst Coll					✓	✓	✓				✓			✓
Rollins Coll			✓		✓	✓	✓		✓		✓			✓
Rosary Coll			✓		✓	✓	✓	✓		✓	✓			
Rose-Hulman Inst of Tech					✓					✓	✓			
Rosemont Coll			✓	✓	✓	✓	✓	✓	✓		✓	✓		
Rutgers, State U of NJ, Coll of Eng			✓		✓	✓	✓		✓			✓		✓
Rutgers, State U of NJ, Cook Coll			✓		✓	✓	✓	✓	✓	✓				✓
Rutgers, State U of NJ, Rutgers Coll			✓		✓	✓	✓	✓	✓	✓	✓	✓		✓
Rutgers, State U of NJ, U Coll–Newark			✓		✓	✓	✓							
Saginaw Valley State U			✓		✓	✓	✓	✓			✓	✓		✓
Saint Anselm Coll			✓		✓		✓	✓		✓	✓	✓	✓	
Saint Augustine's Coll	✓													
St Charles Borromeo Sem	✓													

A "dry" rush is required for social organizations.	The sponsoring of events by alcoholic beverage companies is prohibited.	Alcoholic beverage advertising is prohibited.	The group selling of alcohol for profit is prohibited.	Comments
		✓	✓	
✓		✓		
	✓		✓	
				Alcohol at events must be served by trained servers.
✓			✓	
✓	✓	✓		
✓		✓		
✓	✓	✓		
✓	✓	✓	✓	
		✓	✓	
✓			✓	
✓		✓	✓	
	✓	✓	✓	
	✓		✓	
✓	✓		✓	
			✓	
		✓	✓	
	✓	✓	✓	

Comparative Table of Alcohol Regulations

	Alcohol is not permitted on campus.	Social events prohibited.	Social events with alcohol are registered with the college.	All social events with alcohol must be BYOB.	Nonalcoholic alternatives must be provided where alcohol is served.	Food must be provided where alcohol is served.	Students must show proof of legal drinking age to attend a function with alcohol.	A responsible person of age must chaperone at social events with alcohol.	A limit on the quantity of alcohol per person at social events is specified.	Alcohol cannot be served at sporting events.	Drinking is restricted to designated areas.	Drinking games are prohibited.	Social organizations may not have alcohol at social events.	Social organizations are held responsible for infractions of alcohol regulations at their social events.
St Francis Coll			✓		✓	✓	✓	✓	✓	✓	✓	✓		✓
St Hyacinth Coll and Sem														
St John Fisher Coll			✓				✓	✓		✓	✓		✓	✓
St John's Coll (MD)			✓		✓	✓	✓							✓
St John's Coll (NM)			✓		✓	✓					✓			
St John's Sem Coll										✓	✓	✓		
Saint John's U			✓		✓	✓	✓	✓	✓	✓	✓	✓		✓
Saint Joseph's Coll (IN)	✓													
Saint Joseph's Coll (ME)			✓		✓	✓	✓	✓			✓	✓		✓
Saint Joseph Sem Coll			✓		✓						✓	✓		
Saint Joseph's U			✓		✓	✓		✓	✓	✓	✓			✓
St Lawrence U			✓		✓	✓	✓	✓	✓	✓	✓	✓		✓
St Louis Coll of Pharmacy			✓		✓	✓	✓	✓			✓			✓
Saint Louis U			✓		✓	✓		✓			✓	✓		✓
Saint Martin's Coll			✓		✓	✓	✓	✓	✓		✓	✓		✓
Saint Mary Coll			✓		✓	✓	✓	✓	✓		✓	✓		✓
Saint Mary-of-the-Woods Coll	✓													
Saint Mary's Coll (IN)			✓		✓	✓	✓	✓	✓		✓	✓		✓
Saint Mary's Coll (MI)	✓													✓
Saint Mary's Coll of Minnesota			✓		✓	✓	✓			✓	✓	✓		✓
St Mary's U of San Antonio			✓		✓	✓	✓	✓	✓		✓			✓
Saint Meinrad Coll					✓			✓				✓		
Saint Michael's Coll			✓		✓	✓	✓	✓		✓	✓	✓		✓
St Norbert Coll			✓		✓	✓	✓		✓	✓	✓	✓		✓
St Olaf Coll	✓													
St Paul Bible Coll	✓													
St Thomas U			✓		✓	✓	✓	✓	✓					✓
Salem Coll (NC)			✓		✓		✓	✓						
Salem Coll (WV)			✓		✓	✓	✓	✓	✓	✓	✓		✓	✓

A "dry" rush is required for social organizations.	The sponsoring of events by alcoholic beverage companies is prohibited.	Alcoholic beverage advertising is prohibited.	The group selling of alcohol for profit is prohibited.	Comments
				Alcohol may not be used as prizes for raffles, etc.
				Alcohol available at religious community social functions.
✓				
	✓	✓		College funds may not be used to purchase alcohol.
	✓	✓	✓	
	✓	✓	✓	
✓	✓	✓	✓	
				Alcohol is available for students over 21 in the state-licensed pub.
		✓	✓	
	✓	✓		
✓			✓	
✓			✓	
	✓	✓	✓	
			✓	Applicants for jobs involving driving are asked for driving history.
			✓	
	✓	✓	✓	
				Alcohol permitted at only two campus events.
			✓	
	✓	✓		
✓	✓			
	✓	✓	✓	
	✓	✓	✓	
✓			✓	
			✓	
✓		✓	✓	

Comparative Table of Alcohol Regulations

	Alcohol is not permitted on campus.	Social events with alcohol are prohibited.	Social events with alcohol must be registered with the college.	All social events with alcohol must be BYOB.	Nonalcoholic alternatives must be provided where alcohol is served.	Food must be provided where alcohol is served.	Students must show proof of legal drinking age to attend a function with alcohol.	A responsible person of age must chaperone at social events with alcohol.	A limit on the quantity of alcohol per person at social events is specified.	Alcohol cannot be served at sporting events.	Drinking is restricted to designated areas.	Drinking games are prohibited.	Social organizations may not have alcohol at social events.	Social organizations are held responsible for infractions of alcohol regulations at their social events.
Salem State Coll			✓		✓	✓	✓	✓	✓	✓	✓	✓		✓
Salve Regina Coll	✓													
Samford U	✓													
Sam Houston State U					✓		✓			✓	✓	✓		✓
Samuel Merritt Coll of Nursing			✓		✓		✓	✓	✓		✓			
San Francisco Art Inst			✓		✓	✓	✓	✓						✓
Sangamon State U			✓		✓	✓		✓		✓	✓	✓		✓
Santa Clara U			✓		✓	✓	✓			✓	✓	✓		✓
Savannah State Coll	✓													✓
Sch of the Associated Arts	✓													
Sch of the Museum of Fine Arts					✓	✓	✓	✓						
Sch of the Ozarks	✓													
Scripps Coll			✓		✓	✓		✓		✓				
Seattle Pacific U	✓													
Seton Hill Coll			✓		✓	✓				✓		✓	✓	✓
Shawnee State U			✓				✓	✓		✓	✓	✓	✓	✓
Sheldon Jackson Coll	✓													
Shenandoah Coll and Conservatory			✓		✓	✓	✓	✓	✓	✓	✓	✓		✓
Shepherd Coll					✓	✓				✓	✓	✓		
Shimer Coll			✓		✓						✓			
Shippensburg U of Pennsylvania	✓													✓
Siena Heights Coll		✓					✓			✓	✓	✓		
Sierra Nevada Coll			✓											✓
Simpson Coll		✓								✓	✓		✓	
Sioux Falls Coll	✓													
Slippery Rock U of Pennsylvania	✓													
Smith Coll			✓		✓	✓	✓							
Sonoma State U			✓		✓	✓	✓				✓			
South Carolina State Coll	✓													✓

A "dry" rush is required for social organizations.	The sponsoring of events by alcoholic beverage companies is prohibited.	Alcoholic beverage advertising is prohibited.	The group selling of alcohol for profit is prohibited.	Comments
✓			✓	
				Very limited use at events involving parents, alumni, students.
✓				Possession/consumption of alcohol on campus prohibited.
				Alcohol in Health Education Center under controlled conditions.
			✓	
			✓	
✓	✓		✓	
	✓	✓	✓	Student/college funds may not be used for alcohol.
				Social policy of abstinence.
	✓	✓	✓	Alcohol prohibited in residence halls.
	✓	✓	✓	
	✓	✓	✓	
	✓		✓	Alcohol permitted in dorm rooms and Pub for those of legal age.
			✓	
✓	✓	✓	✓	Only students over 21 may possess/consume alcohol in residence halls.
✓				
				Only faculty and staff may serve alcohol on campus.
	✓	✓	✓	

Comparative Table of Alcohol Regulations

	Alcohol is not permitted on campus.	Social events with alcohol are prohibited.	Social events with alcohol must be registered with the college.	All social events must be BYOB.	Nonalcoholic alternatives must be provided where alcohol is served.	Food must be provided where alcohol is served.	Students must show proof of legal drinking age to attend a function with alcohol.	A responsible person of age must chaperone at social events with alcohol.	A limit on the quantity of alcohol per person at social events is specified.	Alcohol cannot be served at sporting events.	Drinking is restricted to designated areas.	Drinking games are prohibited.	Social organizations may not have alcohol at social events.	Social organizations are held responsible for infractions of alcohol regulations at their social events.
South Dakota Sch of Mines and Tech	✓													
South Dakota State U	✓													
SE Coll of the Assemblies of God	✓													
Southeastern Louisiana U			✓		✓	✓	✓	✓		✓	✓	✓		✓
Southeastern Massachusetts U			✓		✓	✓	✓		✓	✓	✓	✓		
Southeastern Oklahoma State U	✓													✓
Southeast Missouri State U	✓													✓
Southern Arkansas U	✓													
Southern California Inst of Architecture			✓		✓	✓	✓	✓	✓			✓		
Southern Illinois U at Carbondale			✓		✓	✓			✓			✓		✓
Southern Illinois U at Edwardsville			✓		✓	✓	✓	✓		✓	✓	✓	✓	✓
Southern Methodist U					✓						✓			
Southern Oregon State Coll			✓		✓	✓	✓	✓		✓	✓	✓	✓	✓
Southern Vermont Coll			✓		✓	✓	✓				✓			
Southwestern Assemblies of God Coll	✓													
Southwestern Coll	✓													
Southwestern Coll	✓													
Southwestern U			✓		✓		✓			✓	✓		✓	
Southwest Missouri State U	✓													✓
Southwest Texas State U			✓		✓	✓	✓			✓	✓	✓		✓
Spalding U			✓	✓	✓	✓	✓	✓	✓		✓	✓		✓
Spelman Coll	✓													✓
Springfield Coll	✓													
Spring Garden Coll	✓													
Spring Hill Coll			✓		✓	✓	✓	✓		✓	✓	✓		✓
State U of NY at Albany			✓		✓	✓			✓	✓	✓	✓		✓
State U of NY at Buffalo			✓		✓	✓	✓		✓	✓	✓	✓		✓
State U of NY at Stony Brook			✓		✓	✓	✓	✓	✓	✓	✓	✓		✓
State U of NY Coll at Brockport			✓		✓	✓	✓	✓	✓	✓	✓	✓		✓

A "dry" rush is required for social organizations.	The sponsoring of events by alcoholic beverage companies is prohibited.	Alcoholic beverage advertising is prohibited.	The group selling of alcohol for profit is prohibited.	Comments
✓			✓	Alcohol available at specific areas on campus with prior permission.
	✓		✓	
		✓		
	✓			
✓			✓	
✓	✓			
	✓	✓	✓	
				College activity money may not be used to purchase alcohol.
				College is located in a dry city.
				Winfield is a dry town.
✓	✓	✓	✓	
			✓	
	✓	✓	✓	Only persons over 21 may have alcohol at social events.
✓	✓	✓	✓	
✓			✓	Alcohol may not be focus of sponsored activities.
✓			✓	
✓			✓	

Comparative Table of Alcohol Regulations

	Alcohol is not permitted on campus.	Social events with alcohol are prohibited.	Social events with alcohol must be registered with the college.	All social events must be BYOB.	Nonalcoholic alternatives must be provided where alcohol is served.	Food must be provided where alcohol is served.	Students must show proof of legal drinking age to attend a function with alcohol.	A responsible person of age must chaperone at social events with alcohol.	A limit on the quantity of alcohol per person at social events is specified.	Alcohol cannot be served at sporting events.	Drinking is restricted to designated areas.	Drinking games are prohibited.	Social organizations may not have alcohol at social events.	Social organizations are held responsible for infractions of alcohol regulations at their social events.
State U of NY Coll at Fredonia			✓		✓	✓	✓	✓	✓		✓			✓
State U of NY Coll at Geneseo			✓		✓	✓	✓			✓		✓	✓	✓
State U of NY Coll at New Paltz			✓		✓	✓	✓	✓	✓	✓	✓	✓		✓
State U of NY Coll at Old Westbury	✓													
State U of NY Coll at Potsdam			✓		✓	✓			✓		✓			✓
State U of NY Coll at Purchase			✓		✓	✓	✓	✓			✓			✓
State U of NY Coll of Env Sci & For			✓		✓	✓	✓	✓			✓	✓		✓
State U of NY Coll of Tech at Utica/Rome			✓		✓	✓	✓	✓	✓	✓	✓	✓		✓
State U of NY Health Science Ctr at Syracuse			✓		✓	✓		✓	✓		✓			✓
Stephen F Austin State U	✓													
Stetson U	✓													✓
Stevens Inst of Tech			✓		✓	✓	✓	✓		✓	✓	✓		✓
Stillman Coll	✓													✓
Stockton State Coll			✓		✓	✓	✓		✓	✓	✓	✓	✓	✓
Sul Ross State U			✓					✓		✓	✓			✓
Susquehanna U			✓		✓	✓			✓	✓	✓	✓		✓
Sweet Briar Coll			✓		✓	✓	✓	✓	✓	✓	✓	✓		✓
Syracuse U			✓		✓	✓	✓		✓					✓
Tabor Coll	✓													
Tarkio Coll	✓													✓
Temple U			✓				✓	✓			✓			
Temple U, Ambler Cmps	✓													
Tennessee Tech U	✓													✓
Texas A&M U	✓													✓
Texas A&M U at Galveston														✓
Texas Christian U		✓								✓	✓			✓
Texas Coll	✓													

A "dry" rush is required for social organizations.	The sponsoring of events by alcoholic beverage companies is prohibited.	Alcoholic beverage advertising is prohibited.	The group selling of alcohol for profit is prohibited.	Comments
		✓		
✓	✓	✓	✓	
✓	✓	✓	✓	
				Old Westbury is a dry campus.
✓		✓	✓	
		✓	✓	
			✓	
	✓	✓	✓	
✓				
✓			✓	
			✓	
✓	✓		✓	
	✓	✓	✓	
✓		✓	✓	
			✓	
				No alcohol allowed on campus except in private areas.
				Alcohol served at selected functions; all present must be over 21.
✓	✓	✓	✓	

Comparative Table of Alcohol Regulations

	Alcohol is not permitted on campus.	Social events with alcohol are prohibited.	Social events with alcohol must be registered with the college.	All social events with alcohol must be BYOB.	Nonalcoholic alternatives must be provided where alcohol is served.	Food must be provided where alcohol is served.	Students must show proof of legal drinking age to attend a function with alcohol.	A responsible person of age must chaperone at social events with alcohol.	A limit on the quantity of alcohol per person at social events is specified.	Alcohol cannot be served at sporting events.	Drinking is restricted to designated areas.	Drinking games are prohibited.	Social organizations may not have alcohol at social events.	Social organizations are held responsible for infractions of alcohol regulations at their social events.
Texas Lutheran Coll			✓		✓	✓	✓	✓		✓	✓	✓		✓
Texas Tech U	✓													
Texas Woman's U			✓		✓	✓		✓		✓	✓	✓		✓
Thomas Coll			✓		✓	✓		✓	✓	✓	✓			✓
Thomas More Coll			✓		✓	✓	✓	✓			✓			✓
Tiffin U			✓		✓	✓	✓	✓		✓		✓		✓
Toccoa Falls Coll	✓													
Towson State U			✓				✓				✓			
Trevecca Nazarene Coll	✓													
Trinity Christian Coll	✓													✓
Tri-State U			✓		✓	✓	✓	✓		✓	✓	✓		✓
Troy State U at Dothan	✓													
Tusculum Coll	✓													
Tuskegee U	✓													✓
Union Coll (KY)	✓													
Union Coll (NY)			✓				✓			✓	✓	✓		✓
United States International U	✓													✓
United States Merchant Marine Acad						✓	✓	✓	✓	✓	✓	✓	✓	✓
U of Akron			✓		✓			✓		✓	✓		✓	✓
U of Alabama at Birmingham			✓		✓	✓		✓		✓	✓	✓		✓
U of Alabama in Huntsville	✓													✓
U of Alaska Anchorage			✓		✓	✓	✓	✓			✓	✓		✓
U of Alaska Fairbanks			✓				✓	✓		✓	✓	✓		
U of Alaska Southeast					✓	✓	✓		✓	✓	✓	✓		✓
U of Arizona			✓		✓	✓	✓			✓	✓	✓		✓
U of Arkansas			✓		✓	✓		✓			✓			✓
U of Arkansas at Little Rock			✓		✓	✓	✓	✓		✓		✓		✓
U of Arkansas at Monticello	✓													✓
U of Bridgeport			✓	✓	✓	✓	✓	✓	✓	✓	✓			✓

A "dry" rush is required for social organizations.	The sponsoring of events by alcoholic beverage companies is prohibited.	Alcoholic beverage advertising is prohibited.	The group selling of alcohol for profit is prohibited.	Comments
			✓	
✓			✓	
		✓		
		✓	✓	
✓			✓	
	✓	✓	✓	
✓	✓	✓	✓	Alcohol available at small, invitation-only events to those of age.
	✓	✓	✓	
✓				
✓		✓	✓	
		✓	✓	
			✓	Alcohol allowed in rooms of students 21 and over.
			✓	Alcohol permitted on campus for students over 21 in residence halls.
✓			✓	
✓	✓		✓	
✓	✓	✓	✓	
				The University is in a dry township.
✓			✓	Strict guidelines on alcohol advertising.

Comparative Table of Alcohol Regulations

	Alcohol is not permitted on campus.	Social events with alcohol are prohibited.	Social events with alcohol must be registered with the college.	All social events with alcohol must be BYOB.	Nonalcoholic alternatives must be provided where alcohol is served.	Food must be provided where alcohol is served.	Students must show proof of legal drinking age to attend a function with alcohol.	A responsible person of age must chaperone at social events with alcohol.	A limit on the quantity of alcohol per person at social events is specified.	Alcohol cannot be served at sporting events.	Drinking is restricted to designated areas.	Drinking games are prohibited.	Social organizations may not have alcohol at social events.	Social organizations are held responsible for infractions of alcohol regulations at their social events.
U of California, Davis			✓		✓	✓		✓		✓	✓			✓
U of California, Los Angeles					✓	✓								
U of California, Santa Cruz			✓		✓	✓	✓			✓	✓	✓		✓
U of Central Arkansas	✓													
U of Central Florida			✓				✓		✓		✓	✓		✓
U of Central Texas	✓													
U of Charleston			✓		✓	✓	✓	✓			✓	✓		✓
U of Cincinnati			✓		✓	✓	✓	✓			✓	✓		✓
U of Colorado at Denver			✓		✓	✓	✓	✓			✓			
U of Connecticut at Waterbury	✓													
U of Dallas			✓		✓	✓	✓	✓		✓	✓	✓		✓
U of Dayton			✓		✓	✓	✓				✓	✓		✓
U of Delaware					✓	✓	✓				✓			✓
U of Detroit			✓		✓	✓					✓	✓		✓
U of Dubuque	✓													
U of Florida			✓		✓	✓	✓		✓	✓	✓	✓		✓
U of Georgia			✓	✓	✓	✓		✓		✓	✓		✓	✓
U of Guam			✓		✓	✓	✓	✓	✓	✓	✓	✓		
U of Hartford			✓		✓	✓	✓	✓	✓	✓	✓	✓		✓
U of Hawaii at Hilo			✓		✓	✓	✓	✓		✓	✓	✓		✓
U of Hawaii–West Oahu Coll			✓		✓						✓			
U of Houston								✓						
U of Houston–Clear Lake			✓		✓	✓		✓	✓					✓
U of Houston–Downtown			✓		✓	✓	✓	✓			✓	✓		
U of Idaho					✓	✓	✓		✓	✓	✓	✓		✓
U of Illinois at Chicago			✓		✓	✓	✓	✓	✓	✓	✓	✓		✓
U of Iowa			✓		✓	✓				✓	✓			✓
U of Kentucky			✓		✓	✓	✓	✓			✓			✓
U of Lowell			✓		✓	✓	✓		✓	✓	✓	✓	✓	✓

A "dry" rush is required for social organizations.	The sponsoring of events by alcoholic beverage companies is prohibited.	Alcoholic beverage advertising is prohibited.	The group selling of alcohol for profit is prohibited.	Comments
✓	✓		✓	Proof of age is required at events serving alcohol.
✓	✓		✓	
	✓	✓	✓	
✓			✓	
✓			✓	
			✓	
				Eighteen is legal age for 3.2 beer.
	✓	✓	✓	
✓	✓	✓	✓	Banding system used to identify those of age at events.
✓	✓		✓	
✓	✓		✓	
✓	✓			Strict regulations on social events with alcohol.
✓				
	✓			
			✓	Alcohol served at social events under certain restrictions.
✓			✓	
	✓	✓	✓	
✓			✓	
	✓		✓	
			✓	License is required if alcohol is served.

Comparative Table of Alcohol Regulations

	Alcohol is not permitted on campus.	Social events with alcohol are prohibited.	All social events with alcohol must be registered with the college.	All social events must be BYOB.	Nonalcoholic alternatives must be provided where alcohol is served.	Food must be provided where alcohol is served.	Students must show proof of legal drinking age to attend a function with alcohol.	A responsible person of age must chaperone at social events with alcohol.	A limit on the quantity of alcohol per person at social events is specified.	Alcohol cannot be served at sporting events.	Drinking is restricted to designated areas.	Drinking games are prohibited.	Social organizations may not have alcohol at social events.	Social organizations are held responsible for infractions of alcohol regulations at their social events.
U of Maine			✓		✓	✓	✓	✓		✓	✓	✓		✓
U of Maine at Augusta	✓													✓
U of Maine at Farmington			✓		✓	✓	✓			✓	✓	✓		✓
U of Maine at Fort Kent			✓		✓	✓	✓	✓		✓	✓	✓		✓
U of Maine at Machias			✓		✓	✓	✓	✓		✓	✓	✓		✓
U of Mary	✓													
U of Mary Hardin-Baylor	✓													
U of Maryland at Baltimore			✓			✓	✓	✓				✓		
U of Maryland Baltimore County			✓		✓	✓	✓	✓			✓			✓
U of Maryland Eastern Shore			✓		✓	✓	✓	✓	✓	✓	✓	✓		✓
U of Michigan										✓				
U of Michigan–Dearborn	✓													
U of Michigan–Flint					✓	✓			✓		✓	✓		✓
U of Minnesota, Duluth		✓												
U of Minnesota, Morris			✓		✓	✓		✓		✓	✓			✓
U of Minnesota, Twin Cities Cmps			✓		✓	✓	✓	✓	✓	✓	✓	✓		✓
U of Missouri–Columbia	✓													✓
U of Missouri–Kansas City		✓			✓	✓				✓				✓
U of Missouri–Rolla			✓							✓	✓	✓		✓
U of Montana					✓	✓	✓			✓	✓	✓		✓
U of Nebraska at Omaha			✓		✓	✓				✓	✓			
U of Nebraska Medical Ctr			✓			✓								
U of Nevada–Reno			✓		✓	✓	✓	✓	✓		✓	✓		✓
U of New England			✓		✓	✓	✓	✓	✓	✓	✓			✓
U of New Hampshire			✓		✓	✓	✓	✓			✓			✓
U of New Haven			✓		✓	✓	✓	✓	✓	✓	✓	✓		✓
U of New Mexico	✓													✓
U of North Carolina at Chapel Hill					✓	✓	✓				✓			
U of North Carolina at Charlotte			✓	✓	✓	✓		✓	✓	✓	✓	✓		✓

A "dry" rush is required for social organizations.	The sponsoring of events by alcoholic beverage companies is prohibited.	Alcoholic beverage advertising is prohibited.	The group selling of alcohol for profit is prohibited.	Comments
✓	✓	✓	✓	
		✓	✓	
		✓	✓	
✓	✓	✓		
		✓	✓	
	✓			
	✓	✓	✓	
	✓		✓	
				University Center staff tend bar when alcohol is served.
				Alcohol not permitted in campus housing.
			✓	
			✓	
				Alcohol not permitted in campus facilities without special permission.
✓			✓	Alcohol cannot be bought with University or student activity funds.
	✓	✓	✓	Social events serving alcoholic beverages are prohibited for students.
✓				Time limit on the serving of alcohol. Only licensed vendors may sell.
✓	✓	✓		
✓				
	✓	✓	✓	
✓			✓	
✓	✓	✓		
	✓	✓	✓	
✓			✓	

Comparative Table of Alcohol Regulations

	Alcohol is not permitted on campus.	Social events with alcohol are prohibited.	Social events with alcohol must be registered with the college.	All social events with alcohol must be BYOB.	Nonalcoholic alternatives must be provided where alcohol is served.	Food must be provided where alcohol is served.	Students must show proof of legal drinking age to attend a function with alcohol.	A responsible person of age must chaperone at social events with alcohol.	A limit on the quantity of alcohol per person at social events is specified.	Alcohol cannot be served at sporting events.	Drinking is restricted to designated areas.	Drinking games are prohibited.	Social organizations may not have alcohol at social events.	Social organizations are held responsible for infractions of alcohol regulations at their social events.
U of North Carolina at Greensboro			✓		✓	✓	✓	✓	✓	✓	✓	✓		✓
U of North Carolina at Wilmington			✓		✓	✓	✓	✓		✓	✓	✓		
U of North Texas		✓			✓		✓			✓	✓	✓		
U of Notre Dame			✓		✓	✓	✓	✓		✓	✓	✓	✓	✓
U of Oklahoma		✓												
U of Oregon			✓		✓	✓	✓				✓			✓
U of Osteopathic Med & Health Sci			✓		✓					✓	✓			✓
U of Pittsburgh		✓								✓	✓	✓		✓
U of Pittsburgh at Bradford		✓								✓	✓			✓
U of Pittsburgh at Greensburg	✓													✓
U of Portland			✓		✓	✓	✓		✓		✓	✓		✓
U of Puerto Rico, Humacao U Coll	✓													
U of Puerto Rico, Mayagüez Cmps			✓							✓		✓	✓	✓
U of Puget Sound			✓		✓	✓	✓	✓		✓	✓	✓		✓
U of Redlands			✓		✓	✓	✓	✓		✓	✓	✓		✓
U of Rhode Island			✓		✓	✓	✓	✓		✓	✓	✓		✓
U of Richmond			✓		✓		✓			✓	✓			✓
U of Rochester			✓		✓	✓	✓				✓	✓		✓
U of San Diego			✓		✓	✓		✓	✓	✓	✓	✓		✓
U of Science and Arts of Oklahoma		✓								✓	✓			
U of South Carolina			✓		✓	✓	✓	✓	✓	✓	✓			✓
U of South Carolina at Aiken	✓													
U of Southern California			✓		✓									✓
U of Southern Colorado			✓		✓	✓	✓	✓	✓		✓	✓		✓
U of Southern Indiana	✓													
U of Southern Mississippi	✓													✓
U of South Florida			✓		✓	✓			✓	✓	✓			
U of Southwestern Louisiana			✓		✓	✓	✓	✓			✓			✓
U of Tennessee at Chattanooga	✓													✓

A "dry" rush is required for social organizations.	The sponsoring of events by alcoholic beverage companies is prohibited.	Alcoholic beverage advertising is prohibited.	The group selling of alcohol for profit is prohibited.	Comments
✓	✓		✓	
✓			✓	
✓				
	✓	✓	✓	
✓			✓	
✓		✓	✓	
✓	✓	✓	✓	
✓			✓	
		✓	✓	
✓	✓	✓		
	✓	✓	✓	
✓		✓		
✓		✓		
✓			✓	
✓			✓	
	✓	✓	✓	Students 21 or older allowed 3.2 beer in their rooms.
✓			✓	
✓		✓	✓	
				Events with alcohol must be sponsored by Food Services and registered.
✓				
✓			✓	
				Alcoholic beverage advertising allowed in campus newspaper.

Comparative Table of Alcohol Regulations

Institution	Alcohol is not permitted on campus.	Social events with alcohol are prohibited.	Social events with alcohol must be registered with the college.	All social events with alcohol must be BYOB.	Nonalcoholic alternatives must be provided where alcohol is served.	Food must be provided where alcohol is served.	Students must show proof of legal drinking age to attend a function with alcohol.	A responsible person of age must chaperone at social events with alcohol.	A limit on the quantity of alcohol per person at social events is specified.	Alcohol cannot be served at sporting events.	Drinking is restricted to designated areas.	Drinking games are prohibited.	Social organizations may not have alcohol at social events.	Social organizations are held responsible for infractions of alcohol regulations at their social events.
U of Tennessee, Knoxville	✓													✓
U of Tennessee, Memphis	✓													✓
U of Texas at Arlington			✓		✓	✓		✓		✓	✓	✓		✓
U of Texas at Austin							✓			✓	✓			
U of TX Health Sci Ctr at San Antonio														✓
U of Texas Medical Branch at Galveston											✓			
U of Texas of the Permian Basin			✓		✓	✓		✓			✓	✓		
U of the Arts			✓		✓	✓	✓	✓	✓					✓
U of the South			✓		✓	✓		✓	✓	✓	✓	✓		✓
U of Tulsa			✓		✓	✓				✓		✓		✓
U of Virginia			✓		✓	✓	✓	✓			✓			✓
U of Washington			✓		✓	✓	✓	✓		✓	✓		✓	✓
U of West Florida			✓		✓	✓			✓		✓	✓		✓
U of Wisconsin–Madison			✓		✓	✓	✓	✓		✓	✓	✓		✓
U of Wisconsin–Milwaukee			✓		✓	✓	✓			✓	✓	✓		✓
U of Wisconsin–Platteville					✓	✓	✓			✓	✓	✓		✓
U of Wisconsin–River Falls			✓		✓		✓	✓		✓	✓	✓		✓
U of Wisconsin–Whitewater			✓		✓	✓	✓	✓	✓	✓	✓	✓		✓
Utah State U	✓													✓
Valley City State U	✓													
Valley Forge Christian Coll	✓													✓
Valparaiso U	✓													✓
Vanderbilt U			✓	✓	✓	✓				✓	✓	✓		✓
Villa Maria Coll										✓		✓	✓	✓
Villanova U		✓			✓	✓	✓			✓	✓	✓		✓
Virginia Commonwealth U			✓		✓	✓	✓		✓		✓			✓
Virginia Military Inst	✓													
Virginia Polytechnic Inst and State U			✓		✓	✓	✓	✓	✓	✓	✓	✓		✓
Virginia State U	✓													✓

A "dry" rush is required for social organizations.	The sponsoring of events by alcoholic beverage companies is prohibited.	Alcoholic beverage advertising is prohibited.	The group selling of alcohol for profit is prohibited.	Comments
✓			✓	
				Alcohol policy currently being written.
			✓	
	✓	✓	✓	
✓	✓	✓	✓	
✓		✓	✓	
		✓	✓	
	✓	✓	✓	Alcohol permitted in living quarters of students 21 or older.
✓		✓	✓	
	✓	✓	✓	
	✓	✓		
✓	✓	✓	✓	
			✓	
				Off-campus social groups permitted to serve alcohol to those of age.
✓	✓	✓	✓	
	✓	✓	✓	
✓	✓	✓	✓	
	✓			
✓				

Comparative Table of Alcohol Regulations

	Alcohol is not permitted on campus.	Social events with alcohol are prohibited.	Social events with alcohol must be registered with the college.	All social events must be BYOB.	Nonalcoholic alternatives must be provided where alcohol is served.	Food must be provided where alcohol is served.	Students must show proof of legal drinking age to attend a function with alcohol.	A responsible person of age must chaperone at social events with alcohol.	A limit on the quantity of alcohol per person at social events is specified.	Alcohol cannot be served at sporting events.	Drinking is restricted to designated areas.	Drinking games are prohibited.	Social organizations may not have alcohol at social events.	Social organizations are held responsible for infractions of alcohol regulations at their social events.
Virginia Wesleyan Coll			✓		✓	✓	✓	✓	✓	✓	✓	✓		✓
Viterbo Coll			✓		✓	✓	✓		✓		✓	✓		
Wagner Coll			✓		✓	✓	✓	✓		✓	✓	✓		✓
Wake Forest U			✓		✓	✓	✓				✓			✓
Walla Walla Coll	✓													
Walsh Coll			✓		✓	✓	✓	✓	✓	✓	✓	✓	✓	
Warner Pacific Coll	✓													
Warner Southern Coll	✓													
Warren Wilson Coll			✓	✓	✓	✓	✓	✓		✓	✓			
Washington and Jefferson Coll			✓		✓	✓				✓	✓	✓		✓
Washington and Lee U			✓	✓	✓	✓	✓			✓	✓	✓		✓
Washington Coll			✓		✓	✓	✓			✓	✓			✓
Washington State U			✓	✓	✓	✓	✓				✓	✓		✓
Waynesburg Coll	✓													
Wayne State Coll	✓													
Wayne State U	✓													✓
Weber State Coll	✓													✓
Webster U			✓					✓			✓			✓
Wellesley Coll			✓		✓	✓	✓			✓	✓			
Wells Coll			✓		✓	✓		✓		✓	✓			✓
Wentworth Inst of Tech	✓													✓
Wesleyan Coll	✓													✓
Wesleyan U			✓											
Wesley Coll		✓								✓				
West Chester U of Pennsylvania	✓													
Western Carolina U										✓	✓			
Western Connecticut State U			✓		✓	✓	✓	✓		✓				✓
Western Illinois U			✓		✓	✓				✓	✓	✓		✓
Western International U	✓													✓

A "dry" rush is required for social organizations.	The sponsoring of events by alcoholic beverage companies is prohibited.	Alcoholic beverage advertising is prohibited.	The group selling of alcohol for profit is prohibited.	Comments
		✓	✓	Alcohol is not sold on campus.
		✓		
✓			✓	
✓		✓	✓	
	✓	✓	✓	
✓	✓	✓	✓	
✓			✓	
	✓	✓	✓	
✓	✓	✓	✓	
				The WSU Conference Center has an alcohol license.
	✓	✓	✓	
			✓	
✓	✓	✓	✓	
✓	✓	✓	✓	Alcohol is allowed only in residence hall rooms.

Comparative Table of Alcohol Regulations

	Alcohol is not permitted on campus.	Social events with alcohol are prohibited.	Social events with alcohol must be registered with the college.	All social events must be BYOB.	Nonalcoholic alternatives must be provided where alcohol is served.	Food must be provided where alcohol is served.	Students must show proof of legal drinking age to attend a function with alcohol.	A responsible person of age must chaperone at social events with alcohol.	A limit on the quantity of alcohol per person at social events is specified.	Alcohol cannot be served at sporting events.	Drinking is restricted to designated areas.	Drinking games are prohibited.	Social organizations may not have alcohol at social events.	Social organizations are held responsible for infractions of alcohol regulations at their social events.
Western New Mexico U	✓													
Western Oregon State Coll	✓													✓
Western Washington U			✓		✓	✓	✓			✓	✓			
Westfield State Coll			✓		✓	✓	✓	✓	✓	✓	✓	✓		✓
West Liberty State Coll	✓													
Westminster Choir Coll			✓		✓	✓	✓				✓	✓		✓
Westminster Coll of Salt Lake City			✓		✓	✓	✓			✓	✓	✓		✓
West Suburban Coll of Nursing	✓													
West Texas State U	✓													
West Virginia U			✓		✓	✓	✓	✓		✓	✓	✓		✓
West Virginia Wesleyan Coll		✓			✓	✓	✓			✓	✓			✓
Wheeling Jesuit Coll			✓		✓	✓		✓			✓	✓		✓
Wheelock Coll		✓										✓		✓
Whitman Coll			✓		✓	✓				✓	✓			✓
Wichita State U							✓			✓	✓			
Willamette U			✓		✓	✓					✓	✓		✓
William Jennings Bryan Coll	✓													
William Paterson Coll of New Jersey		✓			✓	✓	✓			✓	✓	✓		
William Penn Coll	✓													✓
William Smith Coll			✓		✓	✓				✓	✓	✓		✓
Wilmington Coll	✓													
Wingate Coll	✓													
Winston-Salem State U	✓													
Winthrop Coll			✓		✓	✓	✓	✓	✓		✓			✓
Wittenberg U			✓		✓	✓	✓		✓	✓	✓	✓	✓	✓
Wofford Coll		✓				✓	✓			✓	✓	✓		✓
Woodbury U			✓		✓	✓	✓	✓			✓			
Worcester Polytechnic Inst		✓			✓	✓				✓	✓			✓
Worcester State Coll			✓		✓	✓	✓			✓	✓		✓	✓

A "dry" rush is required for social organizations.	The sponsoring of events by alcoholic beverage companies is prohibited.	Alcoholic beverage advertising is prohibited.	The group selling of alcohol for profit is prohibited.	Comments
				Alcohol prohibited in community.
	✓		✓	
✓			✓	Alcoholic beverage advertising and sponsorship of events monitored.
			✓	Students may drink in dorm rooms; all present must be over 21.
		✓	✓	Special permit required by community for activity involving alcohol.
				Campus located in a dry county.
	✓	✓	✓	
	✓	✓	✓	
	✓	✓	✓	
				Sale and consumption of alcohol limited to specific areas on campus.
✓		✓	✓	
✓	✓			Alcohol permitted in rooms (where residents are legal age), in Pub.
✓	✓	✓	✓	
			✓	
✓	✓	✓	✓	
✓	✓	✓	✓	
✓		✓	✓	Student organizations cannot serve alcohol.
				Campus pub serves beer and wine.

Comparative Table of Alcohol Regulations

	Alcohol is not permitted on campus.	Social events with alcohol are prohibited.	Social events with alcohol must be registered with the college.	All social events with alcohol must be BYOB.	Nonalcoholic alternatives must be provided where alcohol is served.	Food must be provided where alcohol is served.	Students must show proof of legal drinking age to attend a function with alcohol.	A responsible person of age must chaperone at social events with alcohol.	A limit on the quantity of alcohol per person at social events is specified.	Alcohol cannot be served at sporting events.	Drinking is restricted to designated areas.	Drinking games are prohibited.	Social organizations may not have alcohol at social events.	Social organizations are held responsible for infractions of alcohol regulations at their social events.
Wright State U			✓		✓	✓	✓				✓	✓		✓
Yale U			✓		✓	✓	✓							
York Coll of Pennsylvania	✓													✓
York Coll of the City U of New York	✓													
Youngstown State U			✓		✓	✓	✓	✓		✓	✓	✓		✓

A "dry" rush is required for social organizations.	The sponsoring of events by alcoholic beverage companies is prohibited.	Alcoholic beverage advertising is prohibited.	The group selling of alcohol for profit is prohibited.	Comments
✓	✓			
	✓		✓	
✓			✓	

Appendix 1:

Standards of the Network of Colleges and Universities Committed to the Elimination of Drug and Alcohol Abuse

These Standards define criteria for institutional membership in the Network. The Standards are organized within the four areas of Policy, Education, Enforcement, and Assessment.

A. Policy

Network members shall . . .

- Promulgate policy, consistent with applicable federal, state, and local laws, using such means as the student and faculty handbooks, orientation programs, letters to students and parents, residence hall meetings, and faculty and employee meetings.
- Develop policy which addresses both individual behavior and group activities.
- Define the jurisdiction of the policy carefully to guarantee the inclusion of all campus property. Apply campus based standards to other events controlled by the institution.
- Stipulate guidelines on marketing and hosting for events involving students, faculty, staff, and alumni at which alcoholic beverages are present.
- State institutional commitment to the education and development of students, faculty, and staff regarding alcohol and other drug use.

B. Education Programs

Network members shall . . .

- Provide a system of accurate, current information exchange on the health risks and symptoms of alcohol and other drug use for students, faculty, and staff.
- Promote and support alcohol-free institutional activity programming.
- Provide, with peer involvement, a system of intervention and referral services for students, faculty, and staff.
- Establish collaborative relationships between community groups and agencies and the institution for alcohol and drug related education, treatment, and referral.
- Provide training programs for students, faculty, and staff to enable them to detect problems of alcohol abuse and drug use and to refer persons with these problems to appropriate assistance.
- Include alcohol and other drug information for students and their family members in student orientation programs. The abuse of prescription and over-the-counter drugs should also be addressed.
- Support and encourage faculty in incorporating alcohol and other drug education into the curriculum, where appropriate.
- Develop a coordinated effort across campus for alcohol and other drug related education, treatment, and referral.

C. Enforcement

Network members shall . . .

- Publicize all alcohol and other drug policies.
- Consistently enforce alcohol and other drug policies.
- Exercise appropriate disciplinary actions for alcohol and/or other drug policy violations.
- Establish disciplinary sanctions for the illegal sale or distribution of drugs; minimum sanctions normally would include separation from the institution and referral for prosecution.

D. Assessment

Network members shall . . .

- Assess the institutional environment as an underlying cause of drug abuse.
- Assess campus awareness, attitudes, and behaviors regarding the abuse of alcohol and other drugs and employ results in program development.
- Collect and use alcohol and drug related information from police or security reports to guide program development.
- Collect and use summary data regarding health and counseling client information to guide program development.
- Collect summary data regarding alcohol and drug related disciplinary actions and use it to guide program development.

Appendix 2:
FIPSE Grant Recipients

The Fund for Improvement of Postsecondary Education (FIPSE) awards grants to colleges based on proposals for drug prevention programs. Listed below are those four-year institutions that received grants in 1987 and 1988.

1988 RECIPIENTS

Appalachian State University, NC
Benedict College, SC
Bowling Green State University, OH
California State University, Chico, CA
California State University, Fresno, CA
California University of Pennsylvania, PA
Carnegie Mellon University, PA
Central Michigan University, MI
Central Washington University, WA
Dickinson College, PA
East Carolina University, NC
Eastern Michigan University, MI
Florida State University, FL
Framingham State College, MA
George Mason University, VA
Indiana University East, IN
Indiana University of Pennsylvania, PA
Jackson State University, MS
La Salle University, PA
Marshall University, WV
Medical University of South Carolina, SC
Midwestern State University, TX
Nicholls State University, LA
North Adams State College, MA
North Carolina Central University, NC
Northwest Missouri State University, MO
Portland State University, OR
Rochester Institute of Technology, NY
Saint Joseph's University, PA
San Jose State University, CA
Santa Clara University, CA
Seton Hall University, NJ
Sinte Gleska College, SD
Southern Illinois University at Edwardsville, IL
Southwest Missouri State University, MO
Southwest State University, MN
Southwest Texas State University, TX
Stanford University, CA
Texas Southern University, TX
Texas Tech University, TX
United States International University, CA
University of California, Irvine, CA
University of Denver, CO
University of Florida, FL
University of Iowa, IA
University of Maryland College Park, MD
University of Massachusetts at Boston, MA
University of Minnesota, Twin Cities Campus, MN
University of Montana, MT
University of Nebraska at Omaha, NE
University of North Dakota, ND
University of Northern Colorado, CO
University of North Texas, TX
University of Oregon, OR
University of Pennsylvania, PA
University of Rhode Island, RI
University of Rochester, NY
University of South Carolina, SC
University of South Carolina–Coastal Carolina College, SC
University of Texas at El Paso, TX
University of Texas at San Antonio, TX
University of Utah, UT
Western Kentucky University, KY
Western Washington University, WA
West Virginia Wesleyan College, WV
Wilmington College, DE
Worcester Consortium for Higher Education, MA

1987 RECIPIENTS

Austin College, TX
Bemidji State University, MN
Bethany College, WV
Briar Cliff College, IA
Bryn Mawr College, PA
California State University, Dominguez Hills, CA
California State University, Los Angeles, CA
Central Connecticut State University, CT
Converse College, SC
Cornell University, NY
Dartmouth College, NH
Duke University, NC
Emporia State University, KS
Georgia State University, GA
Grambling State University, LA
Howard University, DC
Indiana University Bloomington, IN
Johns Hopkins University, MD
Kansas State University, KS
Marquette University, WI
Missouri Valley College, MO
Northeastern Illinois University, IL
Northern Arizona University, AZ
Northern Illinois University, IL
Northern Michigan University, MI
Northern Montana College, MT
Nova University, FL
Oglala Lakota College, SD

Pennsylvania State University at Erie, The Behrend College, PA
Pennsylvania State University University Park Campus, PA
Piedmont Independent Colleges Association of North Carolina, NC
Saginaw Valley State University, MI
Saint John's University, MN
Sonoma State University, CA
Southern Illinois University at Carbondale, IL
Southern Methodist University, TX
Southern Vermont College, VT
State University of New York College at Old Westbury, NY
Temple University, PA
Texas A&M University, TX
Texas Christian University, TX
University of Arkansas, AR
University of California at Berkeley, CA
University of California, Los Angeles, CA
University of Delaware, DE
University of Georgia, GA
University of Guam, GU
University of Kentucky, KY
University of Mississippi, MS
University of New Mexico, NM
University of North Carolina at Chapel Hill, NC
University of North Carolina at Wilmington, NC
University of Notre Dame, IN
University of Puerto Rico, Humacao University College, PR
University of Puget Sound, WA
University of Southern Maine, ME
University of Southern Mississippi, MS
University of Texas at Arlington, TX
University of Texas at Austin, TX
University of Texas Medical Branch at Galveston, TX
University of Vermont, VT
University of Virginia, VA
University of Wisconsin–La Crosse, WI
University of Wisconsin–Oshkosh, WI
University of Wisconsin–Stout, WI
Villanova University, PA
Weber State College, UT
Wellesley College, MA
Whittier College, CA
Wichita State University, KS
Youngstown State University, OH

Appendix 3:

Organizations Concerned with Drugs and Alcohol on Campus

Addiction Research Foundation

Organized in 1945, the foundation provides treatment, conducts research, and disseminates information about alcohol and drug addiction. It developed CAPE (Campus Alcohol Policies and Education programs), which has been implemented in a number of Canadian universities. A free catalog and a CAPE kit, which includes samples of educational materials and an implementation guide with a model alcohol policy and guidelines for establishing a program, can be obtained from:

Addiction Research Foundation
33 Russell Street
Toronto, Ontario, M5S2S1, Canada
416-595-6000 or 595-6144 (library)

Al-Anon

Based on the belief that alcoholism is a family illness and that changed attitudes can aid recovery, Al-Anon is a fellowship of family and friends affected by close contact with a problem drinker. Groups meet to share experiences, strength, and hope. Al-Anon family groups include Alateen, for younger family members.

Al-Anon Family Group Headquarters, Inc.
P.O. Box 862, Midtown Station
New York, New York 10018-0862
212-302-7240 (or see "Alcohol" in the yellow pages for a local number)

American College Health Association Task Force on Alcohol and Substance Abuse

Organized in 1985, the task force prepared standards on substance abuse, misuse, and dependency. With the American College Health Association, the task force fosters professional development opportunities for those in the college health field.

American College Health Association Task Force
15879 Crabbs Branch Way
Rockville, Maryland 20855
301-963-1100

American Council for Drug Education (ACDE)

An independent nonprofit membership organization, the council educates about the health hazards of tobacco, alcohol, marijuana, cocaine, crack, and other psychoactive drugs. While efforts encompass the public at large, ACDE pays close attention to the especially urgent educational needs of children, adolescents and young adults, codependents and coworkers of drug abusers, expectant mothers, disadvantaged minorities, and other high-risk groups.

American Council for Drug Education
Mr. Lee Dogoloff, Executive Director
204 Monroe Street
Rockville, Maryland 20850
301-294-0600

American Council on Education (ACE)

ACE has recently published a set of guidelines to help colleges deal with drug abuse on campus. The guidelines, entitled "Alcohol and Other Substance Abuse: Resources for Institutional Action," can be purchased from:

American Council on Education
1 Dupont Circle, Suite 800
Washington, D.C. 20036
202-939-9300

BACCHUS of the U.S., Inc.

BACCHUS, which stands for Boost Alcohol Consciousness Concerning the Health of University Students, is a national association for peer education programs stressing alcohol education and healthier campus life-styles. Currently, over 325 colleges have active BACCHUS chapters, which work to promote environments on campus that support responsible decision making, including respect for abstinence, and all applicable campus policies and state laws regarding alcohol. BACCHUS provides an array of educational materials, videos, and training opportunities to support chapter activities. BACCHUS actively promotes campus/community partnerships through a variety of projects, including National Collegiate Alcohol Awareness Week, the BACCHUS Designated Driver Program, and Project GAMMA (Greeks Advocating Mature Management of Alcohol).

BACCHUS of the U.S., Inc.
Drew Hunter, Executive Director
David Leschke, Director of Chapter Services
P.O. Box 10430
Denver, Colorado 80210
303-871-3068

Brown University Center for Alcohol and Addiction Studies

The Brown Center was established in 1982 to enhance interdisciplinary research and teaching. Public policy development and research are ongoing. Brown has become a model for networking services from all parts of the campus community.

Brown University Center for Alcohol and Addiction Studies
David Lewis, M.D., Director
Brown University
Butler Hospital Box G
Providence, Rhode Island 02912
401-863-1109

Campuses Without Drugs

A nonprofit drug-prevention organization, Campuses Without Drugs works to combat the use, influence, and trafficking of drugs on college campuses and in society. It provides drug education and prevention resources to colleges and students, local schools and programs, parents, communities, and businesses and specializes in developing materials for the young adult.

Campuses Without Drugs
Arlene Seal, Ph.D.
2530 Holly Drive
Pittsburgh, Pennsylvania 15235
412-731-8019

College Challenge

A component of National Parents' Resource Institute for Drug Education, Inc. (PRIDE), College Challenge is a newly formed organization. Its aim is to provide resources on drug-prevention programs for campuses. A team of trainers will travel to a campus to assist campus leaders in setting up effective programming policies and leadership.

College Challenge
50 Hurt Plaza, Suite 210
Atlanta, Georgia 30303
404-577-4500

College Consortium on Drugs and Alcohol (CCDA)

CCDA includes over sixty Pennsylvania colleges and is based on the theory that attitudes and behaviors can be most effectively influenced through policies and activities involving institutions throughout the state.

College Consortium on Drugs and Alcohol
Thomas Knadig, Executive Director
Widener University
412 East Thirteenth Street
Chester, Pennsylvania 19013
215-499-4281 or 875-0165

Community Intervention, Inc.

Community Intervention provides training and consultation to help reduce alcohol and other drug use among young people, their families, and communities.

Community Intervention, Inc.
529 S. 7th Street, Suite 570
Minneapolis, Minnesota 55415
800-328-0417 or 612-332-6537 (in Minnesota)

Fraternity Executives Association, Inc.

The organization is dedicated to helping college fraternities develop a responsible attitude toward alcohol.

Fraternity Executives Association, Inc.
Charles N. White Jr.
Sigma Phi Epsilon Fraternity
P.O. Box 1901
Richmond, Virginia 23215
804-353-1901 or 784-4349 (24-hour phone)

Fund for the Improvement of Postsecondary Education (FIPSE)

As a result of the "Anti-Drug Abuse Act of 1986," the Department of Education became responsible for administering new programs, including "Grants for Institutions of Higher Education," implemented jointly by FIPSE and the Secretary's Discretionary Fund. FIPSE has made grants to over 130 four-year colleges to develop, operate, implement, and improve drug education and prevention programs.

Fund for the Improvement of Postsecondary Education
Ronald B. Buckman, Ph.D.
7th and D Streets, SW
Washington, D.C. 20202-5175
202-732-5750

Hazelden Foundation

Hazelden is a national leader in the treatment of chemical dependency. It publishes literature on chemical dependency and conducts training programs, both on and off campus. The Hazelden-Cork Sports Education Program brings together professionals in health education, exercise physiology, and student assistance to plan programs and develop materials to teach athletes about responsible decision making regarding the use of alcohol and other drugs.

Hazelden Foundation
Box 11
Center City, Minnesota 55012
800-822-0080 (training and education) or
800-328-9000 (educational materials)

Integrated Substance Abuse Consultations

Integrated Substance Abuse Consultations provides a variety of services for colleges, including risk-assessment guides, training, evaluation, and consultation.

Integrated Substance Abuse Consultations
Dr. David Anderson
P.O. Box 65557
Washington, D.C. 20035
703-237-3840

Inter-Association Task Force on Campus Alcohol and Other Substance Abuse Issues

The task force is dedicated to promoting education, prevention, research, networking, and national initiatives to help eliminate problems caused by substance abuse on campuses. Membership is open to any higher education association.

Inter-Association Task Force
c/o Drew Hunter, Executive Director, BACCHUS
P.O. Box 10430
Denver, Colorado 80210
303-871-3068

Johnson Institute

Founded in 1966, the institute introduced and has become widely known for its work in elaborating the concept and practice of intervention, a technique to move alcoholic persons into treatment. The institute conducts education and training programs and produces films and printed materials.

Johnson Institute
7151 Metro Boulevard
Minneapolis, Minnesota 55435
800-231-5156

National Association of Alcoholism and Drug Abuse Counselors (NAADAC)

NAADAC represents more than 22,000 alcoholism and drug-abuse counselors. It promotes alcoholism and drug-abuse counseling as a profession and serves as a local and national advocate for counselors on issues that affect the profession.

National Association of Alcoholism and Drug Abuse Counselors
3717 Columbia Pike, Suite 300
Arlington, Virginia 22204
703-920-4644

National Association of Children of Alcoholics (NACOA)

NACOA was founded in 1983 and runs an information clearinghouse, develops training opportunities for professionals and the public, publishes a quarterly newsletter, and holds an annual convention.

National Association of Children of Alcoholics
Gerald Myers, Executive Director
31582 Coast Highway, Suite B
South Laguna, California 92677-3044
714-499-3889

National Association of State Alcohol and Drug Abuse Directors, Inc. (NASADAD)

NASADAD is a not-for-profit organization composed of all the directors of state alcoholism agencies and of single state agencies for drug-abuse prevention. NASADAD's purpose is to foster and support the development of programs throughout all states.

National Association of State Alcohol and Drug Abuse Directors
Bill Butynski, Director
Hall of the State
444 N. Capitol Street, NW
Washington, D.C. 20001
202-783-6868

National Association of Student Personnel Administrators (NASPA)

NASPA helps administrators become effective educators on their own campuses and in association with their colleagues in order to foster students' personal development.

National Association of Student Personnel Administrators
1700 18th Street, NW, Suite 301
Washington, D.C. 20009-2508
202-265-7500

National Clearinghouse for Alcohol and Drug Information (NCADI)

Created in 1987 through a merger of the former National Clearinghouse for Alcohol Information and the National Clearinghouse for Drug Abuse Information, NCADI develops and distributes pamphlets, booklets, reports, and posters on alcohol and other drugs, with special focus on high-risk groups, including college students.

National Clearinghouse for Alcohol and Drug Information
Vipani Owtrakul, Outreach Specialist
P.O. Box 2345
Rockville, Maryland 20852
301-468-2600 Ext. 227

National Collegiate Athletic Association (NCAA)

The NCAA has developed guidelines for drug testing as well as brochures, posters, and other educational materials for use by its 1,100 member institutions. Funds to bring speakers to member campuses and to assist NCAA Conferences to develop drug education programs have also been allocated.

National Collegiate Athletic Association
Frank Uryasz
P.O. Box 1906
Mission, Kansas 66201
913-384-3220

National Council on Alcoholism, Inc. (NCA)

NCA is a national nonprofit organization combating alcoholism, other drug addictions, and related problems. Major programs include prevention and education, public information, medical/scientific information, public policy advocacy, conferences, and publications. NCA's network of about 200 state and local affiliates conduct similar activities in their areas and provide information and referral services to families and individuals seeking help.

National Council on Alcoholism
12 W. 21st Street
New York, New York 10010
212-206-6770

National Prevention Network

The National Prevention Network is an organization of state alcohol abuse prevention representatives that, with NASADAD, provides a national advocacy and communication system for prevention. Its mission is to provide support and enhance national, state, and local alcohol and drug-abuse prevention efforts.

National Prevention Network
Katharine H. Ross
NASADAD, Suite 520
Hall of the State
444 N. Capitol Street, NW
Washington, D.C. 20001
202-783-6868

Network of Colleges and Universities Committed to the Elimination of Drug and Alcohol Abuse

The network was created to collect and disseminate research and practice-based knowledge about successful programs, to provide a forum and mechanism for continuing communication and collaboration among institutions of higher education, and to identify areas and problems for further research and development.

Network of Colleges and Universities Committed to the Elimination of Drug and Alcohol Abuse
Vonnie Veltri, Senior Associate
U.S. Department of Education
555 New Jersey Avenue, NW
Washington, D.C. 20208-5644
202-357-6116

New England College Alcohol Network (NECAN)

NECAN is concerned with substance use and abuse in collegiate settings. Its Steering Committee collects and disseminates a variety of information on issues concerning substance abuse among students.

New England College Alcohol Network
Steve Nelson, Dean of Students
Bard College
Annandale-on-Hudson, New York 12504
914-758-7458

Project Cork Institute and Resource Center

The Project Cork Institute serves as a national resource in medical and health education on alcoholism. The institute has produced educational materials and provides demonstration projects. The resource center has a bibliographic database of alcohol information, offers information services, and provides copies of materials.

Project Cork Institute and Resource Center
Jean Kinney, Executive Director
Dartmouth Medical School
Hanover, New Hampshire 03756
603-646-5809

Rutgers University Center of Alcohol Studies

The Center of Alcohol Studies is involved in research on alcohol use and misuse, the training of professionals to deal with alcohol-related problems, and the publication and documentation of alcohol literature.

Rutgers University Center of Alcohol Studies
Penny Page, Librarian
Smithers Hall, Busch Campus
Rutgers University
Piscataway, New Jersey 08854
201-932-4442

Rutgers University Student Services

Rutgers University Student Services has been in the forefront of developing and implementing a comprehensive campus alcohol policy as well as prevention and treatment programs. In 1980, the Committee on the Use of Alcohol issued a report, which has subsequently been used as a model for policy development and prevention programs by other campuses.

Rutgers University Student Services
Hurtado Health Center
11 Bishop Place
Rutgers University
New Brunswick, New Jersey 08903
201-932-7976

Students Against Driving Drunk (SADD)

The purpose of this organization is to raise awareness about alcohol and drugs on campus and to specifically curb the problem of drinking and driving. SADD is student run with the assistance of college administrators and often serves as a mediating organization between students and administration—helping facilitate discussion and form campus policy.

Students Against Driving Drunk
Robert Anastas, Founder and Executive Director
P.O. Box 800
Marlboro, Massachusetts 01752
508-481-3568

WellWay

WellWay is a facilitating organization that works with health, religious, educational, and business organizations to provide substance abuse prevention and intervention services. Campus Enrichment is a WellWay service that supports college activities that promote healthy decision making about the use of alcohol and other drugs and that offers counseling and assistance for substance abusers.

WellWay
2204 Forest Park Boulevard
Fort Worth, Texas 76110
817-926-2600

Additional Resources: The National Drug Information and Treatment Hotline number is 800-662-HELP (toll-free). Its purpose is to provide drug-related information to the general public, facilitate the placement of drug users in treatment programs, and acquaint those affected by the drug use of a friend or family member with support groups and services. The hotline provides confidential discussion and/or referrals.

MORE OUTSTANDING TITLES FROM PETERSON'S

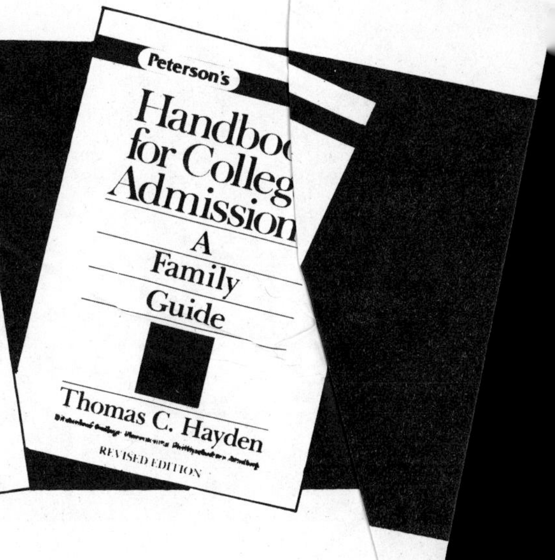

Now Includes College Quest®

PETERSON'S GUIDE TO FOUR-YEAR COLLEGES 1990

New in *Peterson's Guide to Four-Year Colleges 1990* are:

- Peterson's College Quest®, the computerized college and financial aid search programs that have helped thousands of families
- Peterson's College Video Library
- Information on campus computer facilities
- Articles and essays on today's college trends
- A redesigned profile section that makes it easier to use

Profiling 1,950 accredited institutions that grant baccalaureate degrees in the United States and Canada, the guide includes the highest-quality and most accurate data on everything from admissions requirements to campus life.

In-Depth Descriptions of the Colleges—not found in any other college guide—go beyond the data profiles to provide a full, personal look at each college. Nearly 800 of these full descriptions, written by the colleges themselves, are included in the 1990 edition.

Also included are college directories—on over 450 majors as well as cost, entrance difficulty, and geographic area.

". . . a staple of the reference shelf"
— *American Reference Books Annual*

". . . the most current of guides . . ."
—*The Washington Post*

$15.95 pb
$30.95 hc

HANDBOOK FOR COLLEGE ADMISSIONS

A Family Guide

Thomas C. Hayden

Applying to college is a critical family event. This book, written expressly for students and their families, is the ultimate guide to the complex journey called college admissions.

Ten years of working with college-bound students have given the author a wealth of experience to share. He addresses the issues that most commonly cause concern for families, offers a list of dos and don'ts, and gives specific advice on how to gain the critical edge in the eyes of college admissions officers.

New in this third edition are:

- Recent financial aid changes, including the 1986 tax law
- A behind-the-scenes look at how folders are reviewed
- How to get the most out of college at both large and small institutions

The author: Thomas C. Hayden is the Director of Admissions at Oberlin College.

"This readable and information-packed handbook approaches the college admissions process . . . as a family endeavor that offers a rich opportunity for students and their parents to examine their values, goals, and strengths."
—*The Advising Quarterly*

$11.95 pb

New! Peterson's College Quest®, the computerized college search and financial aid service available through student questionnaires included in select Peterson's titles.

Look for these and other Peterson's titles in your local bookstore

MORE OUTSTANDING TITLES FROM PETERSON'S

PETERSON'S GUIDE TO COLLEGES WITH PROGRAMS FOR LEARNING-DISABLED STUDENTS
Editors: Charles T. Mangrum II, Ed.D., and Stephen S. Strichart, Ph.D.

For learning-disabled students and their families, this is the most complete and accurate guide to colleges with learning disabilities programs.

Peterson's Guide to Colleges with Programs for Learning-Disabled Students profiles institutions in two sections so that counselors, parents, and students can distinguish between colleges with full-fledged LD programs and those that offer support services.

This second edition covers two-year colleges as well as four-year colleges. In addition, it offers extensive advice and information on:

- How LD students are admitted
- An overview of college services
- How to select the right college

The editors: Dr. Mangrum and Dr. Strichart are learning disabilities experts.

"The first really comprehensive guide to the . . . colleges and universities that offer full-service programs for students having learning disabilities. . . . Outstanding and useful."

—*Choice*

$19.95 pb

COLLEGE 101
Ronald T. Farrar

College-bound students will find this book indispensable in helping to make the most of their freshman year.

This revised edition has been updated to treat what's happening on campuses *now,* including AIDS, anorexia, drugs and alcohol, roommates, homosexuality, cheating, and minority student concerns.

College 101 poses typical questions and then provides insightful answers with a mild-mannered sense of humor. The questions and answers cover several major areas:

- Adjusting to college life
- Academic concerns
- Getting along with faculty members
- Common problems and where to seek help
- Extracurricular activities
- Financial concerns
- Choosing a major

The author: Ronald T. Farrar is a journalism professor at the University of South Carolina. He has spent many years counseling students and their families about college life.

". . . this book will help relieve some of those pre-September jitters."

—*Seventeen* magazine

"Everything you need to know day by day in the life of a freshman."

—Bill Bresnan
WABC-AM radio
New York City

$9.95 pb

Look for these and other Peterson's titles in your local bookstore